Iron Mining and Manufacturing

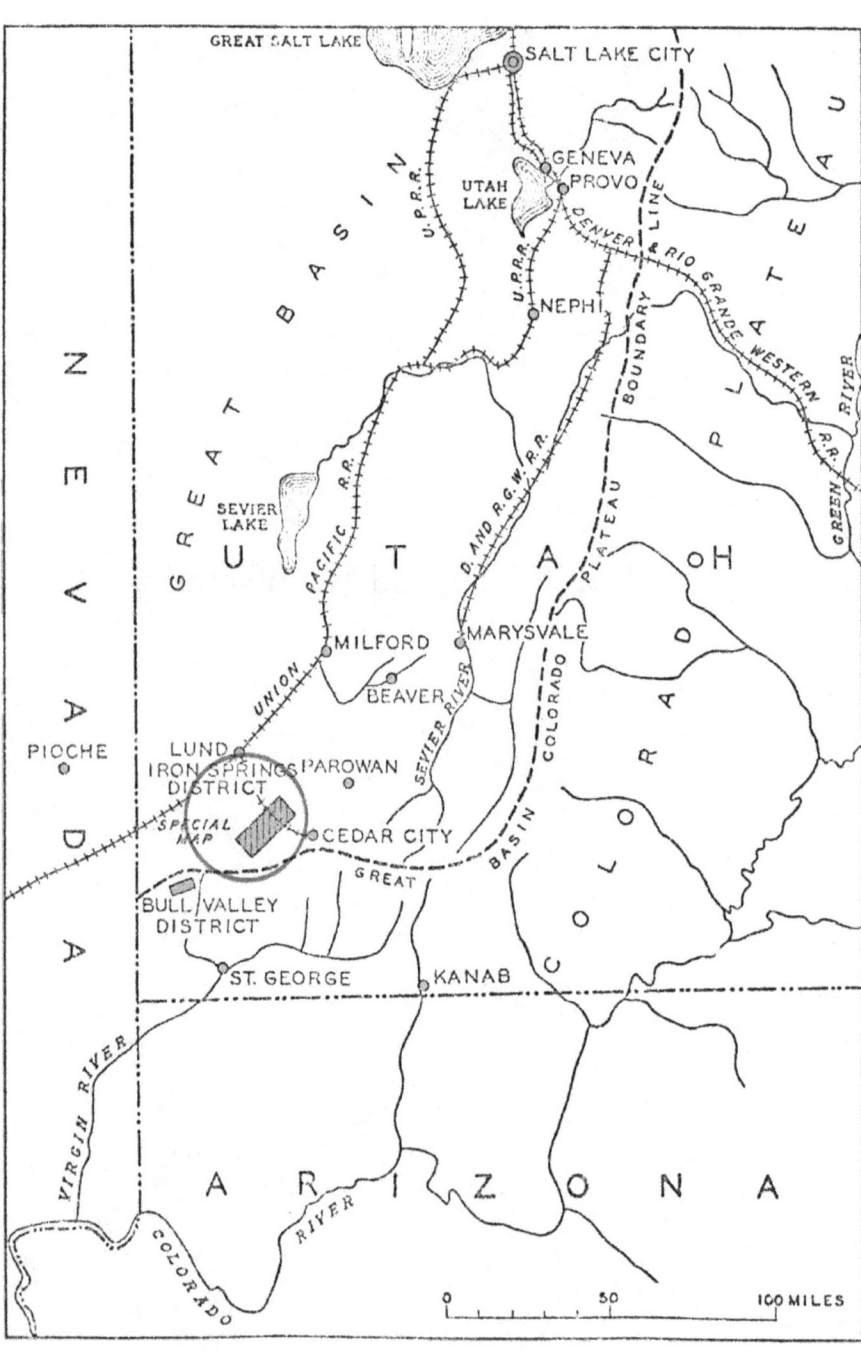

Iron Mining *and* Manufacturing *in* Utah

A History

~~~~~~~~~~~~~~~

Evan Y. Jones
York F. Jones

Southern Utah University Press ▫ *2019*

First published in 2019

© 2019 Evan Y. Jones.

ISBN 13: 978-0-935615-54-7
Library of Congress Control Number: 2018962866

Layout and design by Richard L. Saunders
Cover layout and design by Alyssa Brunson and Jeremiah Dutson

Cover image: The "Thew" steam shovel in the CF&I Pit at Desert Mound in the 1930s. Despite its primitive appearance, it was a considerable improvement over earlier mining methods.

Published by Southern Utah University Press

All rights reserved. No part of this publication may be reproduced, stored in a retrieval system, or transmitted in any form or by means, electronic, mechanical, photocopying, recording, or otherwise, without the prior permission from the publisher. This book is sold subject to the condition that it shall not, by way of trade or otherwise, be lent, re-sold, hired out, or otherwise circulated without the publisher's prior consent, in any form of binding or cover other than that is which it is published and without a similar condition including this condition being imposed on the subsequent purchaser.

Contents

Illustrations	vii
Acknowledgments	xi
Introduction	xiii
Chapter 1 Geology & Exploration	1
Chapter 2 The Iron Mission and Cedar City Iron Works: A First Attempt, 1850–1861	11
Chapter 3 Iron City Iron Works: The Second Attempt, 1868–1885	67
Chapter 4 Hopes, Dreams and Speculation, 1869–1923	117
Chapter 5 The Right Combination: Smelter, Railroad and Mines, 1921–1926	157
Chapter 6 Desert Mound and the Utah Iron Ore Corporation, 1924–1936	199
Chapter 7 Iron Mountain and the Columbia Iron Mining Company, 1935–1943	228
Chapter 8 The Second World War Effort, 1941–1946	246
Chapter 9 The Post-War Boom Years, 1945–1960	276
Chapter 10 A Slow Decline, 1960–1980	330
Chapter 11 The Closures, 1980–1987	373
Chapter 12 After the Closures, 1987–2015	388
Chapter 13 In the End	417
Appendices	423
1 Satellite Views of the Iron Springs Mining Areas	425
2 Mining and Smelting Companies	431
3 Analyses of Cedar City Iron Samples	433
Glossary	436
Notes	441
Works Cited	469
Index	475

Illustrations

	Pinto-Iron Springs Mining District	frontis
	Satellite photomontage of the Iron Springs Mining District	xvi
1.1	Geologic strata visible in Cedar Mountain	2
1.2	Geologic column of Iron Springs district stratigraphy	4
1.3	Ideal cross section through Iron Mountain laccolith	5
1.4	Jefferson Hunt, Parley P. Pratt	9
2.1	Brigham Young, George A. Smith	12
2.2	John D. Lee, Henry Lunt	15
2.3	A salamander or bear	21
2.4	Isaac C. Haight	38
2.5	Model of Deseret Iron Works	42
2.6	The Community Bell	46
2.7	Painting of the Deseret Iron Works	50
2.8	Cross-section of a typical blast furnace	66
3.1	Iron City charcoal kiln	94
3.2	Iron City adobe walls	114
3.3	Iron City stone walls	114
3.4	Iron City foundry stack	115
3.5	Iron City blast furnace foundation	115
4.1	Lund, Utah railroad in the early 1900s	132
4.2	Plat of the Blowout Mining Claim dated April 29, 1879	138
4.3	A typical exploration shaft	140
4.4	Jones ore deposit exploration tunnel	140
4.5	Woodcut illustration of the Blowout deposit made for the 1893 Chicago World's Fair	155
5.1	Ironton Plant located between Provo and Springville, Utah	164
5.2	Aerial view of Cedar City rail loop	168
5.3	First train to Cedar City, June 14, 1923	172
5.4	President Harding's two locomotives parked in Cedar City	174
5.5	President Harding in Zion National Park	175
5.6	Cedar City Train Depot	177
5.7	Iron Springs shearing corral and first train, May 28, 1923	183
5.8	El Escalante Hotel	184
5.9	Iron Springs accommodations	185
5.10	Iron Springs ore processing plant	186
5.11	Mine cars at the Iron Springs ore processing plant	187

5.12	Iron Springs Glory Hole No. 9	188
5.13	Junction at the end of the main tunnel	189
5.14	A blast at Iron Springs near a glory hole	190
5.15	Working at Glory Hole No. 8	191
5.16	Iron Springs mine workings and structures, 1924	194
5.17	Aerial view of the Iron Springs workings and glory holes, 1950	196
6.1	Steam shovel loading mine cars with ore at Desert Mound	206
6.2	The Thew steam shovel loading overburden at Desert Mound	207
6.3	Steam Shovel in the CF&I Pit at Desert Mound	208
6.4	Steam shovel and locomotive in Milner Pit at Desert Mound	209
6.5	Marion electric shovel and crew	212
6.6	Loaded mine cars being pulled out of the pit at Desert Mound	214
6.7	Steam locomotive used to pull mine cars out of the pit	215
6.8	Electric shovel loading mine cars at Desert Mound	216
6.9	Desert Mound operation around 1928	217
6.10	Desert Mound churn drills	218
6.11	The Thew steam shovel, 1929–1930	219
6.12	Aerial photo of Milner and CF&I pits	220
7.1	The Ironton plant	229
7.2	Aerial photo of Pacific States Cast Iron Pipe Company	230
7.3	Start of the new Black Hawk open pit	240
7.4	Aerial photo, Black Hawk operation	241
8.1	The Ironton Plant	248
8.2	Footings in the Geneva Steel Plant construction	250
8.3	Geneva construction in 1942	251
8.4	Aerial photo of the Geneva plant	252
8.5	Kaiser Steel Plant at Fontana, California	260
8.6	Blowout Pit, 1946	267
8.7	Lindsay Pit, 1945	270
8.8	The complicated Lindsay Hill claim map	271
8.9	Lindsay Hill cross section	272
8.10	Iron Springs claim map	274
9.1	World's largest haul trucks at the Burke Pit	299
9.2	Pinto and Burke pits at Iron Mountain	301
9.3	World's largest electric shovel at the Burke Pit	302
9.4	A blast at the Burke Pit in 1953	303
9.5	Ore cars being loaded at Iron Mountain	304
9.6	A Northwest shovel and Euclid truck at Desert Mound, 1950	308
9.7	Desert Mound Plant site and facilities, 1951	310
9.8	Desert Mound as mining begins again, 1951	311
9.9	Desert Mound as the pit deepens, 1956	312
9.10	Texas City, Texas disaster, 1947	313
9.11	Blowout Pit, 1950	314
9.12	Wagon Drills working in the Blowout Pit	317
9.13	Iron Mountain facilities	318

9.14	Comstock Pit and ore processing facility in the late 1950s	319
9.15	The Lindsay Hill Pit, late 1940s	321
9.16	Lindsay Pit, July 28, 1959	322
10.1	Tax check presentation: new shovel at Comstock Pit, 1975	339
10.2	Aerial view of Desert Mound Pit, 1970	348
10.3	Shovel move from Iron Mountain to Iron Springs in a snowstorm	350
10.4	Blowout Pit, October 28, 1966	351
10.5	P&H 1900 shovel and R-75 Euclid truck at Comstock Pit	352
10.6	Blowout Pit, 2017	353
10.7	Beneficiation Plant at Iron Springs	361
10.8	Alluvium Plant at the Comstock Mining Area	363
10.9	Kenworth truck, ore hauler from Comstock to Iron Springs	365
11.1	Desert Mound Pit, 2018	381
11.2	Comstock-Mountain Lion Pit, 2016	383
11.3	Atlantic City, Wyoming Pit, 2015	387
12.1	Loader-truck operation in the Comstock-Mountain Lion Pit	402
12.2	Gilbert Development operation at the Comstock-Mountain Lion Pit	403
12.3	Utah Southern test train from Comstock to Iron Springs, 2008	407
12.4	An engine of the short-lived CML railroad line, 2011	408
12.5	Ore processing facility	409
12.6	Gilbert ore stockpile; Gilbert ore processing facility at Comstock-Mountain Lion mining area	410
12.7	Gilbert Development operation at Comstock in 2018	415
A.1	Index view of iron-mining areas	425
A.2	Three Peaks mining area	426
A.3	Iron Springs mining area	427
A.4	Desert Mound mining area	428
A.5	Comstock mining area	429
A.6	Iron Mountain mining area	430
A.7	Photomicrograph of Sample 193: Cast iron	433
A.8	Photomicrograph of Sample 194: Wrought iron	434
A.9	Photomicrograph of Sample 195: Chill casting	435

Acknowledgments

I would like to thank my father, who unfortunately isn't here to thank in person. Nevertheless, he deserves the credit for starting this book many years ago and collecting much of the information on which the book is based. He worked almost 40 years for Utah Construction Company in the iron mines in Iron County and wanted to tell the story in his book. He took and collected many photographs over time of the mines and equipment. He and his wife Evelyn had written three books previously and this was to be their fourth. However, the effort lost energy somewhere along the line and the manuscript was never completed. Before this book appeared in print, several authors even quoted from the unpublished draft manuscript.

I also thank my dear wife, Carol, who is my inspiration, for being my editor and advisor and for her willingness to wield the red pencil. She has patiently put up with my obsession with the book and my long hours and late nights over the past year and a half. I am also grateful for my family and friends who have encouraged me to take on and continue this daunting task and have patiently listened to my never-ending talk about the book, many of whom have read, commented on and helped me improve this book.

I want to also thank SUU for polishing and publishing the book, particularly Richard Saunders, Abigail Lochtefeld, and reviewers Ryan Paul and John Sillito.

Introduction

THE SUBJECT OF THIS BOOK is the iron mining and manufacturing industry in Utah, specifically the mining of iron ore and the smelters that converted it into pig iron. It is not exhaustive, focusing on the major iron mines of Iron County and the smelters at Ironton and Geneva, with some discussion of the Kaiser and CF&I smelters. There were other iron mines in Utah; some iron ore was even mined by the precious metals' mines. There were coal mines and limestone quarries whose products were used in the steel-making process. There were foundries and other down-stream businesses that converted the pig iron into useful products. These other enterprises were all important but there was neither time nor space to cover all of these in the book.

Utah's story of iron centers by an act of geologic fate on the southwest corner of the state, and on a site at the closest conjunction of ore, water, coal and limestone. There is a strip of land west of Cedar City, Utah, about 21 miles long and 3 miles wide, that contains some of the most extensive and spectacular iron ore deposits in the western United States. This strip of land has over 160 years of history in iron mining, and in its heyday was the West's largest iron ore-producing district. The deposits of ore in the area gave the area its name: Iron County.

Many millions of years ago, a large number of bodies of iron were deposited deep in the earth in the broken rock adjacent to three large magma intrusions. Millions of years of erosion gradually uncovered these volcanic masses, along with many of the nearby bodies of iron ore, creating hills. We now call those hills of rock: Iron Mountain, Granite Mountain and Three Peaks.

In 1849, pioneers of the Church of Jesus Christ of Latter-day Saints discovered a number of these deposits of iron ore, and Brigham Young, the leader of the Church at the time, almost immediately formed the Iron County Mission and sent a group of colonists to Southern Utah with the charge to settle the area and manufacture iron from the ore.

Smelting iron from ore was not a straightforward process, especially for a group of settlers who had little but the clothes on their backs, living in an unforgiving desert. Nevertheless, through great sacrifice and effort, the hard-working pioneers constructed several blast furnaces in Cedar City and produced several dozen tons of "pig iron." This was far less than what they had hoped for and certainly far less than what they had worked and sacrificed for. However, it was a good start from which others could build.

The need for iron in the territory persisted and a few years later in 1868, another group of individuals formed a company to manufacture iron, this time at a location twenty-three miles southwest of Cedar City near the ore deposits at Iron Mountain. They constructed a blast furnace and coking ovens and built the community of Iron City. They rebuilt their facilities in 1874, including a new blast furnace. By the mid-

1870s, the little group was producing pig iron on a regular basis, and also making and selling many useful items in Utah and Nevada. However, in 1876 the operation closed down when it ran into financial problems. Five years later, an effort was made to resurrect the project on a larger scale, but it never got off the ground and the endeavor was abandoned in 1885. The Iron City location was renamed years later and we now know it as "Old Iron Town."

The mining of precious metals boomed during the last half of the 1800s in places not far from Cedar City like Frisco, Silver Reef, Marysvale and Pioche. But iron ore had neither the glamour nor the value of silver or gold and very little ore was mined from the district in the years following the early operations at Cedar City and Iron City. However, there were many parties, including local residents, outside speculators, interested companies and even several of the wealthy Frisco tycoons, who staked and patented claims, conducted exploration, developed their claims and bought and sold properties by the hundreds. Many were convinced that because of the quality and quantity of the iron deposits rapid development was just around the corner and they spent their lives and their fortunes waiting and hoping, but sadly it was not to be.

In the early 1920s a breakthrough occurred. A group of industry leaders developed a multimillion dollar plan to manufacture iron in Utah by building a blast furnace, railroad lines and iron, coal and limestone mines. In December 1922 they formed the Columbia Steel Corporation in Wilmington Delaware. In 1923, Columbia built the Ironton smelter and coke plant near Provo, Utah, expanded the steel plants in California and Oregon to utilize the pig iron that would be produced in Utah and organized the building of railroad lines to the iron ore deposits in Iron County, the coal deposits in Carbon County and the limestone quarry near Salt Lake.

Columbia opened and operated an iron mine at Iron Springs, only a mile or so from the newly constructed branch railroad line to Cedar City. In 1924, the Utah Iron Ore Corporation constructed a railroad spur, opened a mine a few miles to the southwest of Iron Springs at Desert Mound and started selling ore to the precious metal smelters in the Salt Lake area. In 1926, the Columbia mine at Iron Springs shut down after operating only three years and Utah Iron Ore was awarded the contract to supply ore to the Ironton furnace. The Desert Mound mine operated for ten years until 1936 when the Columbia Iron Mining Company, now a subsidiary of the United States Steel Corporation, had the railroad from Desert Mound extended to Iron Mountain and opened a new mine there. The Ironton smelter continued to be the primary customer for the iron ore.

In 1943, during World War II, the federal government took control, added a second blast furnace at Ironton and built the massive Geneva Plant not far from the Ironton location. Expansions were made to steel plants in California and Colorado. At Iron Mountain, Columbia opened an additional pit and Utah Construction Company opened two pits for Colorado Fuel & Iron. Utah Construction also began mining for itself and opened a pit at Iron Springs. Production in the area jumped to over 4,000,000 tons per year.

After the war, the late 1940s and the 1950s were boom years for the iron and steel industries in Utah. In 1949, Columbia opened another pit at Iron Mountain and reopened the Desert Mound mining area. In 1954, Utah Construction opened another pit for CF&I, this time at the Comstock mining area northeast of the Iron Mountain pits. Utah Construction expanded its operations at Iron Springs. In 1953, ore production from the district rose to a high of over 5,300,000 tons.

The picture began to change in 1962 when U.S. Steel moved much of its iron ore production from Southern Utah to Wyoming. In 1966, U.S. Steel shut down the Ironton Plant, dropping the total output from the area to under 2,000,000 tons per year. In the 1970s, foreign corporations, primarily from Japan, began flooding the West Coast market with large amounts of imported steel.

In the early 1980s, a severe steel crisis led to the closure of the smelters in Colorado and California and subsequently the iron mines in Iron County. U.S. Steel's mine in Wyoming closed in 1983. Geneva continued operation until it was shut down by U.S. Steel in 1986. During that time, Geneva's ore was supplied in part by Gilbert Construction from the Comstock mining area.

In 1987, a group in Northern Utah called Basic Manufacturing and Technologies of Utah (BMT) purchased and reopened the Geneva Plant, operating it at a much-reduced level. Gilbert continued to supply Geneva with ore until 1995. In January 2002, Geneva declared bankruptcy and closed for good.

In 2005, Palladon Ventures Ltd purchased BMT's iron properties and made plans to reopen the mines and possibly build a local smelter. They shipped ore to various locations, including China, but the operation was ultimately shuttered in 2014 due to the falling price of iron ore on the world market.

Over many years of mining, a number of different companies mined and shipped over 100 million tons of iron ore from within Iron County's borders. The ore came from several dozen pits and was delivered mostly to plants in Utah, Colorado and California, but also to other locations as far east as Illinois and Indiana and as far west as Japan and China. The mining district still contains somewhere between 200 million and 300 million tons of iron ore that could be mined by open pit or underground methods. Several of the largest deposits in the area remain untouched.

Unfortunately, many of the younger generation and those who have moved to the area from elsewhere are not familiar with this impressive heritage. This legacy of hard work and sacrifice is one that deserves to be remembered. Much of what we have in Iron County and Utah is the result of the hard work and dedication of those in the past who were willing to stick it out through thick and thin.

Iron County has a rich history of iron mining, beginning with the Iron County Mission in 1850 and the pioneers who settled Southern Utah. This book is about the people, companies, smelters, railroads and mines that created that 160-year history, their successes and failures, the mines that were worked, when, where, how, why and by whom. It was written in an attempt to help keep the memories of that remarkable heritage from slowly fading away.

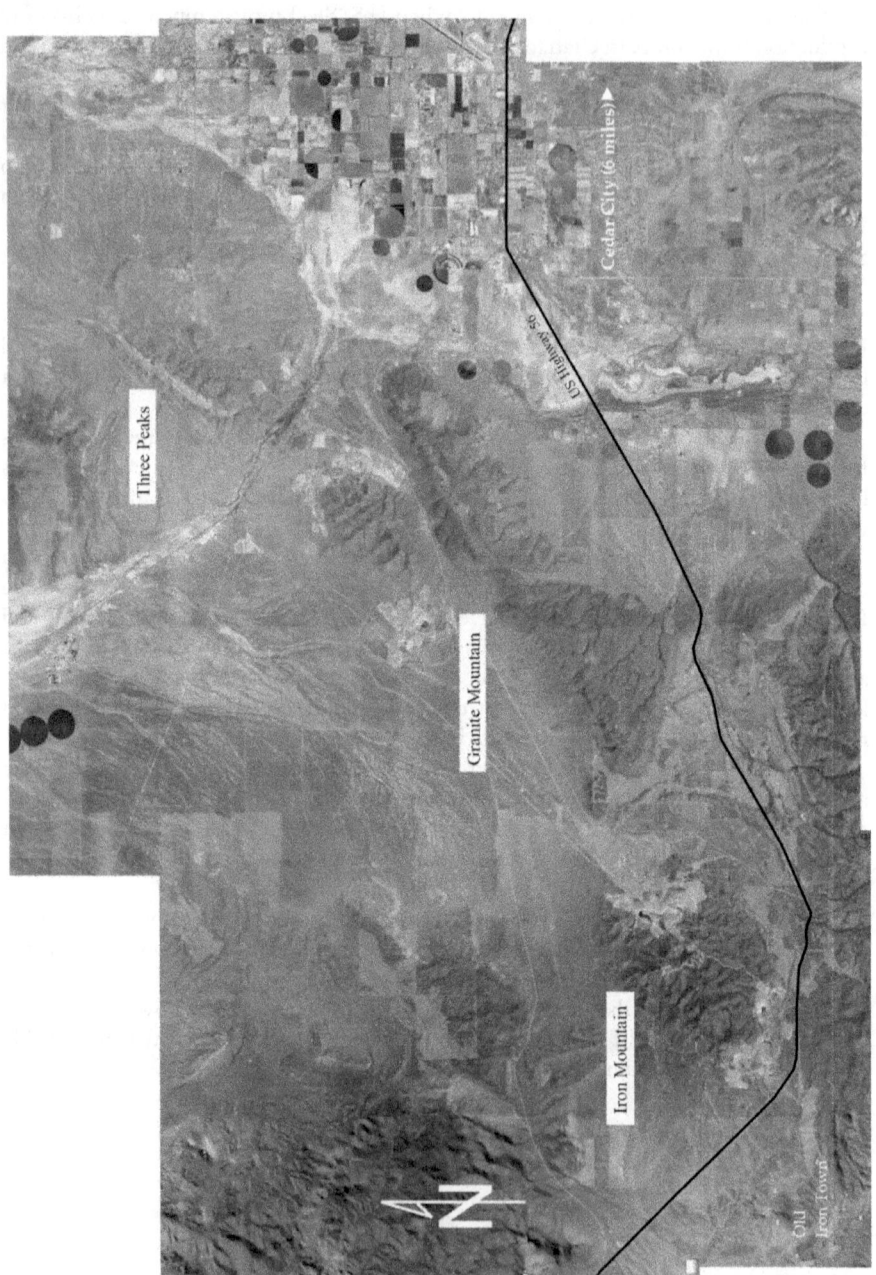

Satellite photomontage of the mountainous region dividing Escalante Valley on the west (out of image) from Cedar Valley on the east, and comprising the Pinto-Three Peaks Mining District.

CHAPTER ONE

Geology & Exploration

To TELL THE story of iron mining in Iron County in a chronological sequence, one must start at the beginning. In this case, the beginning was about 200 million years ago in the late Triassic and early Jurassic periods. The land was relatively flat, and over time became layered with accumulations of wind- and water-borne sediments.

The Navajo Sandstone Formation was formed by wind-blown sand of a sand dune desert like today's Sahara. In places throughout Southern Utah and northern Arizona the formation measures 2,300 feet thick. The sandstone ranges in color from a deep red to bright white, depending upon the amount of iron oxide filling the pore space between the quartz sand particles. It is particularly prominent in Southern Utah where it is the main attraction in many national parks and monuments including Zion Canyon, Glen Canyon, and Canyonlands. It makes up a large portion of the Red Hill east of Cedar City.

Over the next 150 million years, wind and water deposited five additional sedimentary formations, adding a total thickness of about 5,000 feet of material over the Navajo Sandstone.

The Carmel Formation consists of two members. (1) The Basal Siltstone member, which varies in thickness up to 100 feet, with an average thickness of approximately fifty feet. Its color varies from light to dark greenish gray or grayish tan. Maroon banding and mottling are common. (2) The Homestake Limestone member, which varies in thickness from 210 to 300 feet, averaging approximately 250 feet. Its color is primarily gray but can be blue-gray, black, or even white in places.

The Entrada Formation is sandstone that is up to 250 feet thick in the district. Unaltered Entrada sandstone is readily recognizable by its maroon color; however, in some places it has been modified to various shades of gray. The formation also has inter-bedded layers of shale and siltstone.

The Marshall Creek Breccia Formation was formed by disruptions after the Entrada deposition. Several local blocks were uplifted, cracking the Homestake Limestone and the Entrada Sandstone. The material on top of these blocks was eroded off and deposited on the sections that were not uplifted. This deposited material, consisting largely of angular blocks of Homestake Limestone and smaller fragments of Entrada Sandstone, formed a conglomerate called the Marshall Creek Breccia. Breccia is a rock composed of broken fragments of minerals or rock, cemented together by a fine-grained matrix. The Marshall Creek Breccia is very irregular over the top of the Entrada, varying in thickness from zero to 100 feet within short distances.

The Iron Springs Formation varies in thickness. In some places it is more than 3,000 feet thick, composed of beds of sandstone, siltstone, shale and conglomerate with local

Illustration 1.1. The layers of rock important to the formation of the iron ore deposits in the hills west of Cedar City can be seen in the exposed upthrust of the Hurricane Fault, forming the west face of Cedar Mountain: the reddish Navajo Sandstone cliffs, the white Homestake Limestone above it, and the maroon Entrada Sandstone above that. The magma intrusions so crucial to ore forming process are missing in Cedar Mountain, but one can visualize them being forced between the Navajo Sandstone and basal siltstone layers, fracturing all the rock above it and pushing heated gasses and water into and the nearby Homestake Limestone, replacing the stone with iron ore. (Photo by Evan Jones)

beds of limestone and coal. The beds are so irregularly distributed throughout the section that the formation is difficult to subdivide. The conglomerate and sandstone are predominantly brown in color; the shales and siltstones are variegated, ranging from red through gray to green; and the limestones vary from gray to reddish colors. Most of Cedar Canyon between the Red Hill and Cedar Breaks is situated in the Iron Springs formation.

The Claron Formation was formed between thirty and fifty million years ago by the deposition of water-borne sediments and ranges in thickness from 1,000 to 1,500 feet. This stratum primarily rests on the Iron Springs Formation. In some places the pre-Claron erosion surface truncates the Iron Springs Formation and the Entrada sandstone such that the Claron rests directly upon Homestake Limestone. The Claron consists of two principal members: the lower red Claron, made up chiefly of conglomerate, sandstone and fresh-water limestone and characterized by its red color; and the upper gray Claron, composed chiefly of light gray sandstone and conglomerate with some interbedded layers of pink and white limestone. The Claron Formation is brilliantly displayed in Cedar Breaks National Monument and Bryce Canyon National Park.

Igneous Deposition

About thirty million years ago at the end of the Claron Formation deposition igneous formations began to develop, creating three depositions totaling over 2,000 feet.

The Needles Range Formation overlies the Claron Formation and measures up to 1,000 feet in thickness. Its colors are pink to dark red-brown, ranging in intensity from black near the base to light gray near the top.

The Isom Formation is a volcanic deposit that rests on the Needles Range Formation in some places and in other places rests directly on the Claron Formation. The Isom has a total thickness of about 200 feet and is colored dark brown, black, and purplish gray.

The Quichapa Formation is a volcanic deposit overlaying the Isom Formation with a thickness of nearly 1,100 feet. The Quichapa is seen as outcropping in the Pine Valley Mountains, and the visible rock has a variety of colors including black, red, light and dark gray, pink and brown. With the addition of the Quichapa deposition there was nearly 7,000 feet of material over the top of the Navajo Sandstone.

Magma Intrusions: The Iron Ore Is Formed

At or near the end of the time of the Quichapa Formation deposition in the Tertiary Age, changes began to happen deeper in the earth. Three bodies of intrusive magma, fed from stocks deep within the earth, pushed upward through the layers of surrounding rock with tremendous pressure. On their journey upward, they found a zone of weakness between the top of the Navajo Sandstone Formation and the bottom of the Carmel Formation. Instead of continuing upward, the magma forcibly injected itself into this zone of weakness and began lifting the layers of rock above.

The sedimentary and volcanic formations above this expanding layer arched over the top of these massive, mushroom-like incursions, producing steep-sided structural features within the strata and on the surface above. The intrusive forces were so intense that sharp folding, overturning and thrust faulting occurred on the flanks of the advancing magmas along with substantial fracturing and breakage around their boundary contacts. The intrusions were roughly oval, each three to five miles long, with their long axis on a northeast-southwest alignment.

Numerous cracks were formed in the surrounding sedimentary rocks. The intrusions cycled between cooling and surging, causing cracks to form in their outer margins. These cracks allowed superheated liquid and gas containing a variety of dissolved minerals to escape from the magma into the surrounding rock. Early magmatic emanations were likely gaseous in nature, but over time liquid emanations probably dominated. In addition to the dissolved minerals already in this solution, the hot gases and liquids passing through the surrounding rock bleached out minerals which were also added to the mix.

When the proper temperature, pressure and concentration were attained, these dissolved minerals, including a preponderance of the iron minerals magnetite and hematite, came out of solution and were deposited in the nearby rock. Some material was deposited in open joints, giving rise to fissure veins. Other material was deposited in the nearby fractured and broken rock. In addition, significant deposition took place in the relatively soft Homestake Limestone Formation adjacent to the volcanic intrusions.

The 250–300-foot-thick Homestake Limestone Member of the Carmel Formation was separated from the magma intrusions by only the fifty-foot-thick Basal Siltstone Member. The superheated mineral-bearing solutions found their way through numerous cracks into the Homestake Limestone. They readily dissolved the calcium-rich carbonate rocks and preferentially replaced first the calcite, then the silicate minerals, forming large bodies of replacement magnetite and hematite ore. Most of the larger deposits in the Iron Springs District occurred as replacements in the Homestake Limestone Formation.

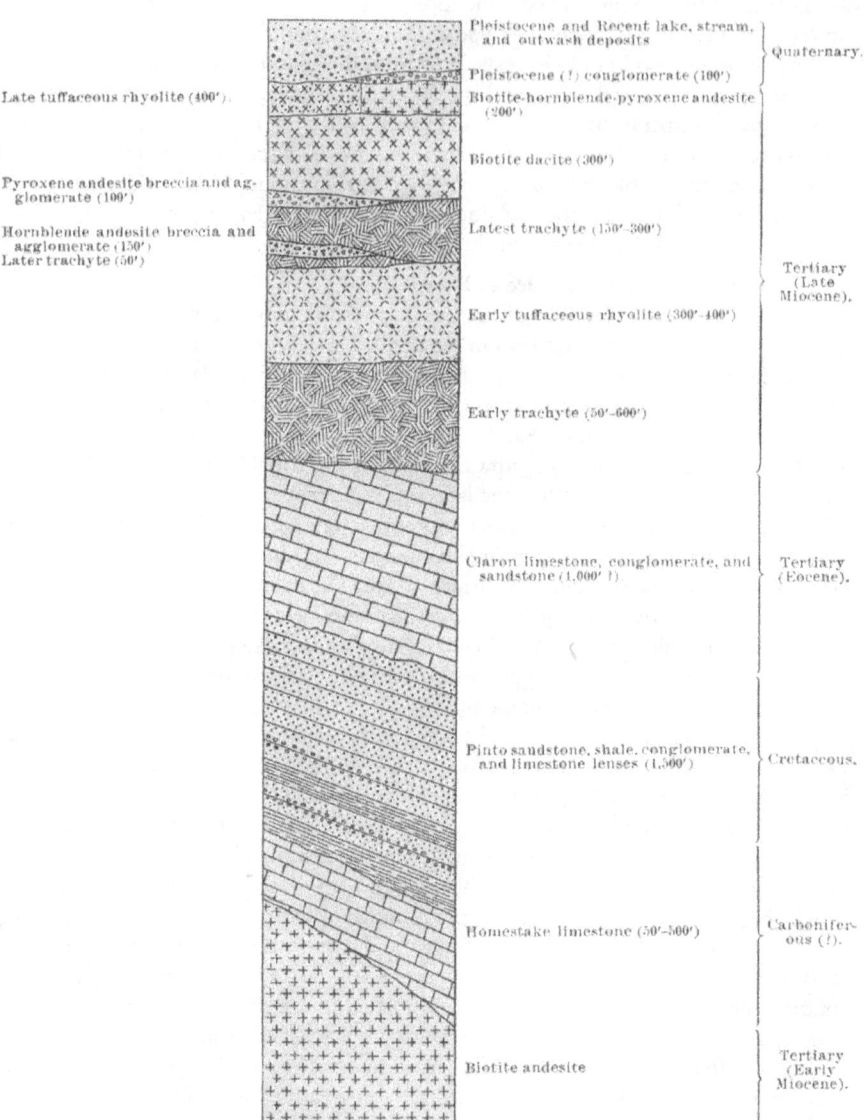

Illustration. 1.2. Geologic column of Iron Springs district stratigraphy. (Leith and Harder)

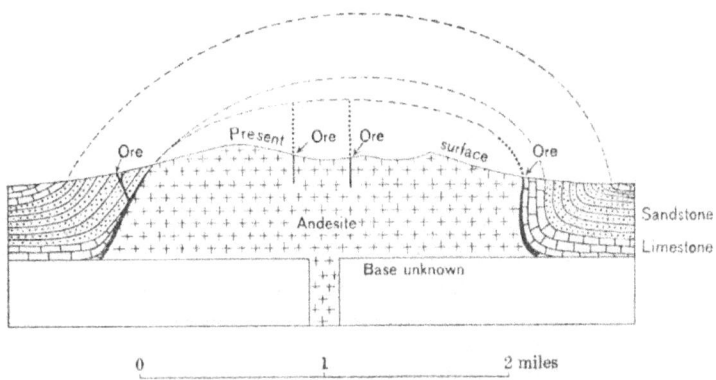

Illustration 1.3. Ideal cross section through Iron Mountain laccolith, showing structural relations of ores. (Leith and Harder)

In some, the entire 250–300-foot thickness was replaced, while in others only the bottom portion was replaced leaving the top portion untouched. Some of the ore bodies were relatively isolated and independent while others extended thousands of feet into the earth.

Throughout the Iron Springs District replacement ore bodies formed, but there were also many ore bodies formed in veins and in broken material. The iron deposition clearly took place after the magma had cooled into a solid state, because the iron ore is not only found in the surrounding sedimentary rocks but is also regularly found in the cracks and fissures in the cooled magma itself. The magma that slowly cooled and solidified while buried in the earth is called quartz monzonite porphyry.

To this day, geologists debate whether these magma intrusions were laccolith "blisters," or more substantial "stocks" that were part of a larger batholith. They also argue about the exact origin of the iron. Was it leached, by diffusion, from the outer edge of the magma, or did it come from solutions originating much deeper within the magma? However, one thing is clear, by some process, dissolved iron came out of the cooling magma and was deposited in massive bodies in the surrounding strata.

Uplift and Erosion

Over the next twenty-five million years, the entire Colorado Plateau, of which Iron County is a part, was elevated. The deposition that formed the previous layers slowed to a stop and was replaced by erosion. Gradually, erosive forces wore away the 3,000 to 6,000 feet of material over the volcanic intrusions, exposing the three granitic humps, which were harder than the surrounding rock. These three intrusive bodies are what we now call Iron Mountain, Granite Mountain and Three Peaks.

Eventually the bodies of iron ore that had been formed around the flanks of the magma intrusions were also reached by erosion. Some of the deposits were totally eroded away, leaving their broken remains scattered on the surface and in the surrounding alluvium. Others remained buried beneath the surface, only to be discovered later using modern magnetometer technologies. Yet others, much like the solidified magma intrusions only on a much smaller scale, were partially uncovered with their upper portions protruding from the ground, sometimes hundreds of feet. A few of the ore bodies were likely partially exposed at one point in time and then reburied with sediment later. The exposed and eroded ore bodies above the surface of the ground were slowly broken into smaller pieces, ranging in size from tiny sand-like particles to massive boulders. The ground near some of the outcropping deposits was literally covered with iron ore both on the surface and in the alluvium, which was composed of up to 20 percent iron. Fine iron particles have been found in washes as far as fifty miles away.

Mineralogy

The most important iron ore minerals in the Iron Springs district are hematite (Fe_2O_3) and magnetite (Fe_3O_4). These minerals are mixed in proportions that vary within a given area or deposit. Ores range from hard pure magnetite to soft friable varieties of hematite. In addition to magnetite and hematite, some specular, or mirror-like, hematite and martite (a variety of hematite) occur in a few ore deposits, and goethite ($FeO(OH)$), limonite ($FeO(OH) \cdot nH_2O$) and turgite (a mixture of goethite and hematite) can be found in relatively small amounts. Gangue minerals, worthless materials that surrounds or are mixed with the ores, are numerous and varied and include calcite ($CaCO_3$), phlogopite (mica), fluorapatite (a phosphate mineral), quartz and chalcedony (both forms of silicon oxide, SiO_2), pyrite and marcasite (fool's gold, FeS_2), diopside ($MgCaSi2O_6$), azurite (a deep blue copper mineral), malachite (a green copper mineral), chrysocolla (a copper mineral similar to turquoise), chalcopyrite (similar to fool's gold, $CuFeS_2$), bornite (a copper mineral known as peacock ore, Cu_5FeS_4), galena (lead sulfide, PbS), magnesite (magnesium carbonate, $MgCO_3$), gypsum ($CaSO_4 \cdot 2H_2O$), barite (barium sulfate, $BaSO_4$), epidote (a calcium-aluminum-iron silicate mineral), garnet (a red silicate mineral), vesuvianite (a complex silicate mineral normally green, but also brown, yellow, blue and/or purple), scapolite (a complex calcium-rich silicate mineral), tourmaline (a complex boron silicate mineral), and chlorite, tremolite, actinolite and wollastonite, all silicate minerals.

Mining Districts

The Iron Springs Mining District lies on the eastern edge of the Basin-and-Range province in Southwest Utah, about twenty miles west of the Markagunt Plateau and the Hurricane fault scarp which form the western boundary of the Colorado Plateau. Originally, the Iron Springs Mining District included only the Granite Mountain and Three Peaks deposits and the Pinto Mining District included Iron Mountain. The Iron Springs Mining District now includes all three iron-producing areas, covering a region about three miles wide and twenty-three miles long.

Utah's iron belt starts at the north edge of the Three Peaks area and extends southwesterly to the southwest side of Iron Mountain. Other traces of iron deposits can be found northeast of the town of Paragonah toward the head of Little Creek Canyon and southwest in a separate mining district, the Bull Valley-Cove Mountain district, ten miles south of Enterprise in Washington, County, Utah.[1]

Exploration Parties

The native peoples who lived in Southern Utah probably did not recognize the dark, heavy rocks for what they were. They certainly did not use the iron ore that lay buried beneath the scattered pinon that graced the desert landscape. The ore bodies remained quiet and patient for newcomers to discover and to perceive its industrial value.

Dominguez & Escalante, 1776–1777

On July 29, 1776, an expedition led by two Franciscan priests, Atanasio Dominguez and Silvestre Vélez de Escalante, and including their cartographer, Bernardo de Miera y Pacheco, and eight other men, set out to find an overland route from Santa Fe, New Mexico to their Roman Catholic mission in Monterey, on the coast of Northern California. They traveled from Santa Fe through many unexplored portions of Western America, including present-day Northern New Mexico, Western Colorado, Utah, and Northern Arizona.

They journeyed from New Mexico into Colorado and on September 12, 1776, crossed what would later become the Utah border near present-day Dinosaur National Monument and camped near modern-day Jensen, Utah. They headed west to Utah Valley and then south, generally following the current-day path of Interstate 15. On October 5, 1776, just north of present-day Milford, a heavy snowstorm hit and made travel very difficult for the group. Several members of the party balked and the group decided, with the early onset of winter, that they would abandon their goal of reaching California and return to their home in New Mexico. They continuing south, traveling near present-day Cedar City, Kanarraville, Ash Creek, Pintura, Toquerville and Hurricane. Heading back toward New Mexico, they then turned east, crossing back and forth along the border between what would become the states of Arizona and Utah.

Guided by local Native Americans, the expedition proceeded to the site of present-day Lees Ferry but found the Colorado River too difficult to cross. They were led to a second location farther north on the River just north of the present-day Arizona-Utah border which is now submerged beneath Lake Powell. It was called Ute Ford by the Indians but was later re-named to Crossing of the Fathers. The travelers carved steps into the canyon walls to get to the river. On November 7, 1776, they forded the Colorado River. The party continued their journey through northern Arizona into New Mexico, finally arriving in Santa Fe on January 2, 1777.[2]

It is rumored and even claimed by some, that Escalante reported that in his travels through what would become Iron County, he had found "rocks with 70 percent iron content and large ore deposits close to the trail," however his diary contains no such language. From his travel descriptions, it appears that the group stuck to the easterly side of the Beaver-Parowan-Cedar valley. On October 8, 1776, they camped near Beaver, on October 9 they camped near Milford, on October 10 they camped some 12 miles south of Minersville and on October 11 they camped about 10 miles north of Cedar City at a location near Enoch now called Rush Lake. On October 12, they started out from Rush Lake, traveled about twenty-four miles during the day and slept that night in the vicinity of Kanarraville on one of the tributaries of Ash Creek. They left the next morning on October 13, traveling down Ash Creek towards Pintura. This would hardly allow enough time for a fifteen- to twenty-mile round trip detour to Iron Springs to see any iron ore. The tired party had already determined that they were headed home to New Mexico and wasted little time heading that direction. No mention was made in their journal of anything identifiable as iron ore.[3]

The Old Spanish Trail, 1829–1848

The route of the Old Spanish Trail was similar in many places to Father Escalante's course; however, it was very different in other places. In Iron County, rather than proceeding south along the present path of I-15 to St. George, it turned at Enoch and headed west around the north end of Three Peaks, then south, passing west of Iron

Springs and Desert Mound and east of Iron Mountain, then turning west to New Castle, then south joining up with the Santa Clara River at Central, on to Veyo, Gunlock, and California.

The Old Spanish Trail was a trade route that developed over time. It connected Santa Fe, New Mexico and Los Angeles, California using various paths through Colorado, Utah, Arizona and Nevada. It had its beginnings in 1765 when Juan Maria de Rivera explored parts of what are now southwestern Colorado and southeastern Utah. In 1776 Dominguez and Escalante traveled similarly through parts of Colorado, into central and southern Utah then prematurely returned to New Mexico by way of the Arizona Strip. Rafael Rivera discovered a shortcut to California in 1828. Antonio Armijo, a merchant from Santa Fe, used the information from these, and other explorers to plot another path to California that connected the routes of the Rivera and Domínguez-Escalante expeditions and the Jedediah Smith explorations. In 1829 Armijo headed a trade party of 60 men and 100 mules to California. His route went northwest to the Colorado River to Escalante's "Crossing of the Fathers," west along the Utah-Arizona border, on through the Mojave Desert along the Mojave River to the San Gabriel Mission.

In 1830, portions of the Armijo route became too dangerous due to hostilities with the Navajo Tribe and a new route had to be found that skirted to the north. A practical route was developed through Ute country that utilized trails of fur traders and trappers. The route went from Santa Fe northwest, passing south of the San Juan Mountains in Colorado, entering Utah near present day Monticello. It then led north, crossing the Colorado River near Moab, the Green River near Green River, Utah then continuing westerly, crossing over to the Sevier River. It followed the Sevier then crossed the mountains coming into the valley somewhere near Parowan, Utah. The route continued in a southwesterly direction to Pinto, then Central, then followed the Santa Clara, Virgin and Colorado Rivers, and connected with Armijo's route on to California[4]

From 1829 to the mid-1850s, hundreds or even thousands of people traveled back and forth on the well-worn Old Spanish Trail, especially the southern portion of the trail called the California Road. A number were explorers like John C. Fremont who kept careful journals of their travels. However, even though there were prominent iron ore outcrops and float rock in the vicinity of Three Peaks, Iron Springs, Desert Mound and Iron Mountain, no one seemed to have made note of them in their journals.

Jefferson Hunt Parties, 1846, 1849

The Mormon Battalion, the only religiously based unit in United States military history, served from July 1846 to July 1847 during the Mexican–American War of 1846–1848. The Battalion was a volunteer unit of about 550 men of the Church of Jesus Christ of Latter-day Saints, led by Church company officers and commanded by regular U.S. Army officers. During its service, the Battalion made an arduous march of nearly 2,000 miles from Council Bluffs, Iowa, to San Diego, California. The Battalion members were released from their duties on July 16, 1847 in San Diego. Jefferson Hunt, the Battalion's highest-ranking Church officer, along with almost half of the group, traveled north to Sacramento. Hunt, along with several others of the Battalion, joined a group of Church members led by Samuel Brannan that was headed east along the Humboldt River to Salt Lake City. The party reached the valley in October 1847.

After arriving, Hunt reported his travels to Church authorities; they were excited enough to send him back to California for more seed grain and supplies. He complied, only this time he traveled south on the California Road. He, along with nineteen others, none of whom had been on the trail before, departed on November 18, 1847. They

Illustration 1.4. (left) Jefferson Hunt (1803–1879), (right) Parley P. Pratt (1807–1857)

arrived in San Bernardino on December 25, 1847. In February they began their return trip to Salt Lake City and arrived in May.

A year and a half later, in October 1849, Jefferson Hunt was called upon again, with an offer of $1,000 and Brigham Young's blessing, to guide another company to California and look for a suitable place for an outpost of the Church of Jesus Christ of Latter-day Saints. Included in the company were Charles C. Rich, an apostle of the church, three missionaries headed for the Society Islands (French Polynesia) and 500 other members of the church. Later they were joined by a party of twenty to thirty prospectors at Beaver Creek, led by a non-church member guide by the name of Captain O. K. Smith.

Smith had a map purportedly describing "Walker's cut-off" which he claimed would reduce the journey to California by some 500 miles. He convinced some of the party to follow him off into the desert, passing through Death Valley, where some of the party lost their lives. In late October or early November, during their journey, the Hunt party camped near what is now known as Iron Springs. Both Charles C. Rich and Addison Pratt, one of the missionaries headed for the Society Islands, noted in their diaries that there were deposits of iron ore in the vicinity. Hunt, reportedly did not keep a journal. The Hunt party arrived safely in San Bernardino on December 27, 1849.[5]

Parley P. Pratt Party, 1849–1850

In November 1849, before Hunt's party even reached California, another exploration party departed from Salt Lake City for Southern Utah, organized by Apostle Parley P. Pratt under the direction of Brigham Young and the provisional state legislature. The company included almost 50 men and was led by Pratt himself. The object of the expedition was to explore the country southward from Salt Lake, looking for prospective town sites and noting streams, potential farming locations, etc.

The party traversed Utah, Juab, Sanpete and the Sevier valleys before emerging through Fremont Pass into Little Salt Lake Valley on December 21. The company camped at Red Creek (present Paragonah) where the historian recorded: "This was judged a suitable place for a settlement of from fifty to one hundred families."

The wagon teams were exhausted, and it was therefore decided to leave the main part of the company in Little Salt Lake Valley to explore the surroundings while Pratt, with twenty horsemen, continued the exploration southward. They paused on Center Creek (present Parowan) and commented favorably on its natural resources. They came into Cedar Valley on December 28.

> [On] Friday, December 28, Pratt's division of the exploring company started at 9 a.m. and passed over Muddy Creek, where it runs in two swift streams, each about 10 feet wide and 10 inches deep. A little way lower, the creek spread out into apparently 40 or 50 streams, overflowing all around, and bringing down flood-wood and a red deposit. On the southwestern borders of this valley are thousands of acres of cedar, constituting an inexhaustible supply of fuel, which makes excellent coal. In the center of these forests rises a hill of the richest iron ore. The water, soil, fuel, timber and mineral wealth of this and Little Salt Lake valleys, it is judged, were capable of sustaining and employing from 50,000 to 100,000 inhabitants, all of which would have these resources more conveniently situated than any other settlements the company had seen west of the States.[6]

The quotation states that wood "makes excellent coal;" however since coal is not made from wood, it is possible that what was meant was charcoal rather than coal.

The explorers continued down Ash Creek to the Virgin River, down the Virgin to the Santa Clara, and up the Santa Clara to Mountain Meadows. When they returned to Little Salt Lake Valley they found the main company had moved to Center Creek. They were welcomed by a flag flying atop a high pole and a salute from a small brass fieldpiece. A celebration followed at which Pratt proposed: "May this, the 8th of January, be kept as the anniversary of the founding of the city of the Little Salt Lake which will hereafter be built."[7]

The main part of Pratt's company returned to Salt Lake City on February 2, 1850. Reports of the Southern Exploring Company encouraged early occupation of the streams and valleys mentioned in them. Several factors influenced a decision for immediate occupation of the Little Salt Lake and Cedar valleys: to plant a colony of the Church of Jesus Christ of Latter-day Saints on the southern route to California in the interest of imports and immigration from the West Coast, to utilize the agricultural resources of the valleys, and to produce iron to meet the needs of the kingdom.[8]

CHAPTER TWO

The Iron Mission and Cedar City Iron Works
The First Attempt, 1850–1861

THE MEAGER SUPPLY of iron brought to the Great Basin by the members of the Church of Jesus Christ of Latter-day Saints was quickly exhausted and developing industry increased the demand for the metal almost daily. Brigham Young, along with many of the early Church leaders, regularly expressed the importance of iron in building the kingdom. "Iron we need, and iron we must have. We cannot well do without it and have it we must."[1]

So, while Parley P. Pratt sponsored the creation of Iron County in the legislature of the Provisional State of Deseret, Brigham Young undertook the organization of the Iron County Mission. The First Presidency of the Church issued a call for volunteer colonists to Iron County in the July 27, 1850 issue of the *Deseret News*.

> Brethren of Great Salt Lake City and vicinity who are full of faith and good works; who have been blessed with means; who want more means and are willing to labor and toil to obtain those means, are informed by the Presidency of the Church, that a colony is wanted at Little Salt Lake this fall; that 50 or more good effective men with teams and wagons, provisions, and clothing, are wanted for one year. Seed, grain in abundance and tools in all their variety for a new colony are wanted to start from this place immediately after the fall conference, to repair to the valley of the Little Salt Lake without delay. There to sow, build, and fence; erect a saw and grist mill, establish an iron foundry as speedily as possible and do all other acts and things necessary for the preservation & safety of an infant settlement among Indians; -for the furnishing of provisions and lumber the coming year for a large number of emigrants, with their own families, and castings of all kinds for all the mountain settlements the coming spring.- Farmers, Blacksmiths, Carpenters, Joiners, Mill Wrights, Bloomers, Moulders, Smelters, &c, Stone Cutters, Brick Layers, Stone Masons, one Shoemaker, one Tailor, &c. &c., in variety of occupations, who have the means, and are willing to sacrifice the society of wives and children for one year; believing that he who forsakes wife and children for the Kingdom of Heaven's sake shall receive an hundred fold, are requested to give their names, in writing, together with their occupation, residence, strength of team, wagons, grain, tools etc. for an outfit, without delay and without further notice to Br. Thomas Bullock.[2]

Brigham Young appointed George A. Smith to head the Iron County Mission. He subsequently issued a call through the *Deseret News* on October 27, for one hundred men to accompany him, and three weeks later on November 16, 1850, the newspaper pub-

Illustration 2.1. (left) Brigham Young (1801–1877), president of the church; (right) George A. Smith (1817–1875), an apostle and first leader of the Iron County Mission.

lished the names of 120 individuals who had been chosen to go and called for fifty additional volunteers.[3]

> Volunteers. - Brother Geo. A. Smith, the president of the mission to L. S. Lake calls for 50 volunteers, and it is right that brethren who can, should respond to the call, and not press him, in the multitude of his cares, to run about the country to pick them up. Some of the brethren may have a delicacy in volunteering their services, and would say "I am ready to go if I have a call, but I don't like to volunteer; if the president wants me he will lay his hand on me and I am ready to go." Just right, brethren, exactly right; fifty of you not advertised in this paper, who can go (and you could all go if a mob were at your heels,) come forward and volunteer, for you not only have a call but the president's hand is on you, and you are wanted. The mission is an important one, as thousands of the saints will be ready to testify when they have spent a few years in the mountains without a stove to cook by or keep themselves warm; a kettle to boil soap in; or a mill to grind their wheat, because there were no castings or iron by which it might be constructed. No mob is wanting to fill such a glorious mission, warm hearts will stimulate the whole. Come brethren, volunteer, and get ready.[4]

On November 20, 1850, Brigham Young wrote a letter to Dr. J. M. Bernhisel, the delegate of the new Territory of Utah in Washington D.C., telling of the Iron County Mission group that was being organized to travel to Southern Utah in two weeks. Young spoke of the change in the name of the county. Parley P. Pratt had named the location the Little Salt Lake Valley, however, Brigham Young did not particularly like the name and stated as much in the letter. Less than two weeks later, Iron County was officially organized.

Our brethren Geo. A. Smith and Ezra T. Benson expect to start in about two weeks for what has usually been termed Little Salt Lake with about 100 men, principally without families, to make a settlement there. They will build a fort, fence in ground and put in seed, then a portion return for their families. The Little Salt Lake is a misnomer; it is nothing but a little saleratus pond [sodium bicarbonate or baking soda], about half the size of the Hot Spring lake in this valley. We have therefore altered the name of the county, and owing to its immense stores of iron ore, have named it Iron County: as soon as the settlement can raise enough to subsist upon, they will devote their energies to the manufacture of iron."[5]

Governor Young, in his message to the Legislative Assembly on December 2, 1850, told of the discovery of iron ore by Parley P. Pratt's exploration party and the mission being organized, and encouraged the legislature to give it whatever support it could.

In the neighborhood of what has usually been termed 'Little Salt Lake' (now Iron County,) our exploring party of last winter discovered inexhaustible beds of the very best of iron ore. A settlement is now being made at that point.... From this city, [Salt Lake] a railroad will most probably be constructed to Iron County, and also continuously to Southern California, terminating at San Diego. Whatever encouragement you find it in your power to extend to an object so full of interest to our citizens, I shall most readily acquiesce therein, being within the range of my constitutional duties.[6]

The General Assembly of the State of Deseret met the next day and passed an organic act to protect the valuable new discovery:

An Ordinance, to provide for the organization of Iron County,
passed, Dec. 3, 1850.

Sec. 1. Be it ordained by the General Assembly of the State of Deseret, that all that portion of country, lying in the southeast corner of the Great Basin; and being south of the divide between Beaver Creek and the Sevier River, and east of the Deseret Range, extending south to the rim of the Basin, and east to the Wasatch Range of mountains; be and the same is hereby known and designated "Iron County."[7]

The Journey to Iron County

Each of the missionaries of the Iron County Mission who had either volunteered, were "called," or were otherwise selected, made their way to Utah Valley, collecting in groups until they finally united at Fort Utah on Sunday, December 15, 1850. In the evening George A. Smith had everyone gather around the camp fire, a hymn was sung and a prayer offered. While standing on the running gears of a nearby wagon, "Smith addressed the camp & gave it the name of the Iron County Mission." He said "that we were as much on a mission as though we were sent to Preach the Gospel." He also promised the group that if they would cease "swearing gambling or using the name of the Lord in vain,... that they shall go & perform their mission in peace, return in safety & not one of them should fall."[8] They broke camp the next morning and continued their mid-winter journey towards Iron County.

After three and a half weeks of travel, dealing with the difficult winter conditions and the "breaking in" of such a large group of men, equipment and animals, the party reached the valley of the Little Salt Lake.

January 10, 1851 The company descended into the area of Buckhorn Flat. The slope was steep and rocky and dangerous for wagons to travel and the cattle were entirely worn out from the journey through the mountains so they camped on the edge of the valley; they had but little water. A portion of the party continued on ahead.

January 11, 1851 The company moved onward 6 miles and found a spring with plenty of water for the thirsty animals, however, several of the teams were so exhausted that they decided to camp and spent the afternoon shoeing lame cattle and hunting rabbits.

January 12, 1851 The camp traveled about 10 miles to Red Creek (Paragonah) and caught up with the rest of the party.

January 13, 1851 The whole of the camp moved on to Center Creek (Parowan) and camped near the mouth of the canyon. There was a very fine rapid stream of water flowing from the canyon. The camp consisted of 120 men, 30 women, 18 children and 101 wagons.

January 14, 1851 President Smith, with an exploring company of about 20 men, left Center Creek headed for Little Muddy Creek (Cedar City). When they reached summit creek (Summit) they met 8 brethren with pack animals traveling from California to Salt Lake City, headed by Captain Jefferson Hunt. Hunt reported that most of the brethren who had gone to California to make their fortunes were now broke. The small group accepted the invitation to join them and stay for a few days to rest and to carry mail to Salt Lake for them. The combined group then traveled the fourteen miles to Little Muddy.

January 15, 1851 The Group explored the canyon and the surrounding area, examining the soil and facilities for farming. They then traveled about eight miles west to the head of a spring with a strong stream of water near a small ridge of mountains on the west side of the valley (Iron Springs). A portion of the group then ascended one of the hills or small mountains of iron ore on foot. Specimens of the ore were collected to be tested. In addition to the hills of iron, there were large amounts of free stone, suitable for buildings, and cedar trees in great abundance. Around noon, seven Indians rode up on horses, led by "old Peteetneet," and talked to the men through an interpreter. They were quite friendly and rode along with them several miles as they were returning to Little Muddy. That evening it was decided that a caucus was needed to organize Iron County. At 28 minutes to 6 the Pres. G. A. Smith, moved that this company be resolved into caucus meeting and that Capt. L. Fulmer take the chair and J. D. Lee act as clerk for the evening, which was carried by vote. Major G. A. Smith addressed the meeting, said it was necessary to organize Iron County and report the same by Capt. Hunt, who will carry our returns to headquarters, and in order to do this we must take into consideration the men to fill the different county offices, and that he should like to hold a regular election, get up a ticket and vote by ballot. On motion, Major G. A. Smith, Capt. Anson Call, adjt. J. D. Lee, Lieut. Thos. Smith and Joseph Horn, Pilot was appointed a committee to nominate by selection and bring before the public such men as they in their wisdom, might think best qualified to fill the necessary offices of the Iron County. The committee retired for a short time and made the following selection; for Representative to the Legislature, Capt. Jefferson Hunt; Edson Whipple and Elisha H. Groves Associate Justices, Anson Call and Tarlton Lewis Justices of the Peace; James Little, Sherriff; W. H. Dame, Surveyor; J. D. Lee, County Recorder; James Lewis, Clerk of the County Court; Philip E. Lewis, sealer of weights and measures; Zacariah B. Decker and Charles Hall, Constables.

Illustration 2.2. John D. Lee (1812–1877), one of the prominent Iron County Mission leaders; (right) Henry Lunt (1824–1902), leader of the first company to settle Cedar City. He played an important part in the Iron County Mission as a church and community leader.

John D. Lee, Chairman of the committee, reported the above-named persons to the convention. On motion the report was accepted and committee discharged by unanimous vote. The Supreme Judge then appointed Lieut. Thos, S. Smith, Capt. Simon Baker and Capt. J. F. Branard, Judges of election, which election he ordered to be held at Center Creek.[9]

The Founding of Parowan

The party arrived in the Little Salt Lake Valley on January 16, 1851. They shortly visited Center Creek (Parowan), Little Muddy (Cedar City) and the iron ore deposits eight miles west near a spring which ran west with a strong stream of water (Iron Springs). Following the visits to the various locations, a lively debate ensued as to where to build the permanent settlement and where to locate the iron smelter. Ultimately, they decided to establish the town at Parowan and construct the Iron Works at Iron Springs in close proximity to some of the iron ore deposits. This decision appears to have been based on the fact that, although that the Cedar City location was closer to the iron deposits and was deemed to have better land for farming, the Parowan location was thought to have a more reliable water supply, better access to timber and would be easier to protect.[10]

"The locale to which this settlement or mission was assigned is on the edge of the bleak and forbidding Escalante desert," observed historian Leonard Arrington, about 250 miles south of the territorial capital at Salt Lake City. "With the exception of the ... Paiute Indians, no group had made an important settlement in that region or on any part of the thousand-mile Spanish Trail between Santa Fe and Los Angeles until the Mormons broke the desert solitude with the Iron Mission."[11]

The first order of business was to build a fort. After that, the settlers began building the community with a sawmill, a bowery, houses, ditches, roads, farms, etc. They surveyed and laid out the lots for houses and located fields for farms. Plowing and setting up the fields, out of previously untilled ground without sophisticated tools, was a difficult endeavor and the settlers needed to take advantage of all available natural resources.

On May 7 George A. Smith led a party to investigate a story that pieces of coal had been found in the Little Muddy Creek. Eventually, the Little Muddy Creek was renamed Coal Creek. It appears that the discovery of first coal particles and later sizable coal seams prompted the decision to build a settlement in Cedar City and construct the Iron Works there rather than at Iron Springs where it had been previously proposed. Availability of adequate water at Iron Springs to power a water wheel for the furnace may also have been a consideration.

On May 9 Brigham Young arrived in the valley with mail from loved ones and a host of visitors, including a number of wives and family members. A census was taken which showed the population in May 1851 was 360, more than double what it was in January.[12] The city was also renamed *Parowan* from the name the Indians had for the Little Salt Lake and its people.[13]

John M. Bourne's study of the Iron County Mission adds detail about location choices. Apostle George A. Smith made the journey northward to participate in the October 6, 1851 General Conference of the Church of Jesus Christ of Latter-day Saints in Salt Lake City. "At the meeting," Bourne notes, "several items of business concerning Southern Utah were discussed. It was proposed that two locations, in addition to Parowan, be settled and populated, one that became Cedar City and the other that became St. George."[14]

Upon returning from the conference, on November 4, 1851 George A. Smith and a small group of men traveled twenty miles south of Parowan to the site that became Cedar City. On the trip they dedicated and surveyed an area for a fort and a stock corral. The event was later documented by John Urie, a local historian.

> On Nov. 3rd, E. A. Groves [E. H. Groves], Wm. H. Dame, James A. Little, Henry Lunt with George A. Smith and others arrived from Parowan on the spot marked out by Parley P. Pratt two years before for settlement. Next day Nov. 4th 1851, Cedar City was surveyed by Wm. H. Dame. It is a distance about a mile due north from the present location. The name Cedar City was given because of the abundance of Cedar trees that abounded all over the country. Geo. A. Smith in humility before God, together with the rest of his fellow Pioneers dedicated the ground just surveyed, the surrounding lands, the minerals in the water, the timber, the grass, to the service of God, in the manufacturing of Iron, machinery and that our necessities might be supplied and the territory built up.[15]

From Urie's reference, it appears that Cedar City was officially named at that time, however, as everyone now knows, the cedar trees were in fact, juniper trees. Cedar City's other names continued to be used for some months. George A. Smith sent a letter to the editor of the *Deseret News* that was published later in November concerning the event.

> Parowan, Iron County, Nov. 5, 1851.
> Yesterday a site was surveyed for a fort and stock caral [*sic*] on Coal Creek, 30 miles from Parowan. Today a company has been organized to commence operations

immediately in the construction of this new post. They are mostly composed of English, Scotch and Welsh miners and iron manufacturers. They have also been organized into two companies of militia, one a horse, and the other foot; and form the 2d Battalion of Iron County. Matthew Caruthers is the Major. The company are all in fine spirits. They will commence on Monday to put up their caral; after which they will move their families which are remaining here and encamp in their caral until their fort is completed. They have a beautiful situation.[16]

On November 11, 1851, the two companies of men arrived at Cedar City, having traveled from Parowan. One was led by Henry Lunt, consisting of 11 wagons and about thirty-five men, among who were Elisha H. Groves, William H. Dame, and James A. Little. Lunt's group arrived at Coal Creek after traveling two days in a snowstorm and camped by the "Knoll" about a mile due north from the present location of Cedar City. On November 18, another train of 16 wagons arrived in Cedar City. These companies were to establish the settlement of Cedar City and, eventually, the Iron Works.[17]

Settling in at Cedar City

The Cedar City encampment was established during the winter of 1851 in the cove on the north side of the north Knoll. This "Wagon-Box Camp" consisted of wagon boxes that were lifted off the wagons and placed on the ground in a straight line facing south and spaced equal distances apart. In front of each wagon box, a circle-shaped wall of sage brush was built, weighted with earth. All were of uniform shape and size and were constructed to form a straight line on the south. These walls were higher than a man's head and thick enough that an arrow would not pierce them. They served as a wind break and as shelter and defense. They also provided a measure of privacy for each family. Inside of the circle, the camp fires were built, and the cooking done. The walls were practically fire proof.

At the wagon on each end of the line, the circle was built solid on the outer side. On all others there were communicating openings through which people could pass along the entire line of wagons and be under cover from attack at all times. When new settlers arrived, their wagons were placed on either end of the line and the same shelters of brush built around them.

In the center of the line of wagons, an enclosure was built of brush and earth, into which the colony gathered morning and evening for prayers, and in which all meetings were held. Logs served as seats. This yard extended to the camp lines, both front and back and the front and rear lines were made straight so that sentries walking the paths in times of danger could see clearly the entire length of the camp.

On the north of the camp a large stockade for the livestock was built by standing drift logs on end in a trench. They were placed close enough together that arrows could not be shot between them. If attacked, the people could pass through the gates into the log stockade.

Across the sentry path on the south and in the center of the line, a Liberty Pole was raised which was dedicated "to Liberty, to Justice, and to God." They had no flag to fly on it but the pole itself had a significance and meaning. Laws and regulations were voted on by the people and were then proclaimed before the Liberty Pole. Those convicted of offenses against the laws were brought before the Liberty Pole to receive sentence.

Port holes were so arranged in all the brush walls that the camp could be defended from every angle of attack. This ingenious encampment cost nothing but labor to build yet it afforded shelter, safety, privacy, and conveniences.[18]

In the spring and summer of 1852, the settlers abandoned this camp and moved to the "Little Fort" to the west, where they were not exposed to potentially hostile Indians shooting from the top of the Knoll. The two stockades were left to serve the community as public corrals, and friendly Indians often made their camps in the brush circles.

The "Little Fort" was 300 feet square and the outside walls were the backs of the houses. Spaces not occupied by houses were filled in with posts and logs set close together vertically. It was a place where men could assemble their house logs and build their homes as they found time and the houses could later be moved. The corner rooms and the bastions were used for meeting and class rooms and for storage of arms and public properties.[19]

Iron Manufacturing

Iron manufacturing of the mid-19th century had changed little from the processes used centuries before. The basic form of the blast furnace and air blast machinery was much the same as the furnace operations of Elizabethan England. The furnace master was like a chef and the old-style blast furnace was his kitchen. He had a mental file of iron recipes, but he improvised as he worked, adding a dash of one ingredient or another, until his taste and sense of propriety were satisfied. Without the aid of modern sophisticated analytical instruments, the early iron master's primary tool was trial and error. The operation at Cedar City was characterized by this experimental approach, as were most other iron operations of the era. In most cases, the resulting product was pig iron conforming to a moderately wide range of standards and mostly usable.

The purpose of the smelting process was to strip the oxygen atoms and any impurities from the iron ore, leaving the pure metallic iron behind. The oxygen was separated from the iron during the smelting process by the process known as *reduction*. The separation was usually achieved by causing the oxygen to react with carbon, hydrogen, or carbon monoxide, leaving pure iron.

The smelting process required stable resources and specialized construction, each of which had to be located and created from scratch by the members of the Iron County Mission.

Iron Ore Metallic iron and steel are made from iron ores which are iron oxides, chemical compounds of iron (Fe) and oxygen (O). Common forms of iron ore are hematite (Fe_2O_3) and magnetite (Fe_3O_4) which are found in a natural state. Rust is an oxide of iron. Pure hematite is 68.4 percent iron and pure magnetite is 70.9 percent iron. Magnetite is attracted to magnets and can sometimes be magnetized itself to become a permanent magnet. It is the most magnetic of all the naturally-occurring minerals on Earth. Magnetite is black or brownish-black, sometimes with a metallic luster, has a Mohs hardness of 5.0–6.5 and leaves a black streak. Hematite is colored black to steel or silver-gray, brown to reddish brown, or red, has a Mohs hardness of 5.5-6.5 and is the most common form of iron ore. While the forms of hematite vary, they all have a rust-red streak. Hematite is harder than pure iron, but much more brittle. The bulk of the ore found in Iron County is magnetite, but hematite is also common, and some ore bodies contain a high percentage of hematite. Iron ore has an average specific gravity value of

5.0, compared to most rocks which have values between 2.2 and 3.0 and water, which has a value of 1.0.

Fuel The heat to smelt iron ore was provided by fuel. Common fuels used were wood, charcoal, coal and coke, all of which contain carbon. Wood and coal are found in nature and contain volatiles, impurities and moisture. Wood is transformed into charcoal and coal into coke by being heated in a limited oxygen atmosphere, where most of the volatiles, moisture and many of the impurities are driven off, leaving just the carbon. Charcoal and coke were generally preferred for blast furnace fuel because they were more chemically pure and therefore burned cleaner than raw wood and coal; they also tended to burn longer and hotter. In addition, they retained their structure better when heated. It is important that the fuel hold its shape and not collapse when stacked and heated in the furnace so as not to be crushed under the weight of the iron ore and limestone, causing the air flow to be blocked off.

Charcoal and coke were made using one of two relatively simple methods. The first was burning the fuel in heaps, where a dome shaped pile of wood or coal was built in a shallow circular depression, with a vertical air channel in the center. The pile was then covered with a layer of dirt and set on fire. With proper handling, the pile would burn slowly down to charcoal or coke in a day or so and then was allowed to cool. The second and most preferred method was using kilns to transform the fuel. The fuel would be stacked tightly in the kiln, the main entrance would be sealed up, and the kiln fired. Using this method there was less contamination and waste involved in the burning. This latter approach was common in Utah and throughout the West in the last century. The old "beehive" charcoal oven at Old Iron Town is an excellent example of this type of kiln.

The 1840s and 1850s marked the beginning of changes in operational techniques which eventually resulted in the development of the modern iron and steel industry. Many of the entrepreneurs were starting to pay more attention to what the chemist and the metallurgist had to teach them and were also experimenting with new fuels and methods. Fuels such as coke and coal were coming into greater acceptance and new processes for making steel were being tried. The use of coke as fuel for iron smelting was relatively uncommon in the United States before 1850. Even though coke made from soft coal had been successfully used as early as 1839 in western Maryland, the practice was not widespread due to tradition and the relative abundance of wood for charcoal. In England, on the other hand, the availability of wood was limited, and the use of coke had been adopted at a much earlier stage. As many of the members of the Iron County Mission were trained in the British methods, however, these men considered coke an acceptable and even desirable fuel.

The debate concerning which of the fuels to use in the blast furnaces built at Cedar City continued throughout the entire life of the operation of the Iron Works. There were proponents of all four types of fuel and all four were used at one point or another. Raw wood and coal were slowly phased out in favor of charcoal and coke, but there was no consensus as to which fuel was the best or least expensive. What was clear, however, was that the iron workers believed that coke would be by far the best fuel, as evidenced by their almost endless efforts to find and mine coal. Unfortunately, the use of coke produced from the unsuitable local coal turned out to be one of the primary causes of less than satisfactory results at the Iron Works.

Good coking coal requires a high level of fixed carbon to avoid being crushed by the weight of the charge as it is heated. It also must have low levels of impurities such as silica and sulfur. As it turned out, none of the coal found in the Cedar City area was very good for iron manufacturing.

Limestone Another important ingredient in the iron making process is limestone ($CaCO_3$). Limestone is basically calcium carbonate and is used as a flux. A flux is a material that renders the slag more liquid at the smelting temperature and acts as a purifying agent to purge the iron of contaminant materials such as silica (SiO_2), alumina (Al_2O_3), sulfur (S) and phosphorus (P), material which are collectively called *gangue*. Removal of these impurities is done by combining the calcium compounds of the limestone with the gangue materials to form slag. The slag has a lower density than iron and floats to the top where it is removed separately from the iron. Limestone is a common material in the Cedar City area and was mined at several locations. Dolomite ($CaMg(CO_3)_2$) was also used as a flux.

These three basic ingredients provided the charge for the specially constructed smelting chamber, only one element of several needed for a functional operation.

Blast Furnace In most conventional steel making processes, the ore was smelted in a blast furnace, yielding pig iron. The basic blast furnace was simple in design. The outside shape of a furnace could be either a traditional round shape, or a rectangular shape, similar to the furnace at Old Iron Town. The furnace was charged, or filled with ore, fuel, and limestone through a small door in the top. The ratio of input materials varied depending on the type of material used. The furnace, once constructed, would gradually be heated over a period of days to avoid damage to the structure. When operating, alternating layers of ingredients would be dumped in measured lots and be consumed or melted when flames broke through the previous charge.

The blast was compressed air, pumped into the base of the furnace below the bosh and above the hearth. The bosh is the section of the blast furnace just above the hearth and below the stack where it is the largest in diameter and the fire is hottest. The air was injected into the furnace by means of *tuyeres* (tubes, nozzles or pipes), placed on either side or at the back of the furnace. The increased air flow was used to make the furnace burn hotter by supplying extra oxygen to the fire.

The air was typically compressed by cylinders powered by water wheel or steam engine. The cylinders were commonly made of wood and were usually very large. The air passing into the furnace could be injected cold or heated, but heated air was preferred. The air was typically heated by passing it through a series of pipes similar to a steam radiator located in the top of a separate furnace. The cold blast was used in the early years and hot blasts were used later. When a furnace was running properly, it was operated continually. "Blowing-out" or letting the furnace cool could crack or disintegrate the lining and it was difficult to remove the solidified mass remaining in the furnace, sometimes called a *salamander* or *bear*. In addition, it would cost a considerable amount of time and fuel to reheat the furnace.

The slag was allowed to drain off the top of the molten iron continually. The iron was drained at intervals, when the furnace operators would break through a clay plug at the base of the hearth and allow the molten iron to drain into a sand mold, forming iron "pigs" or bars.

Foundry A foundry was a factory, including a furnace, designed to melt metallic iron and produce castings. A foundry is not to be confused with a smelter. The smelter, in this case, was the blast furnace, which converted iron ore into metallic iron while the foundry melted this metallic iron so that it could be cast into useful shapes. The foundry

Illustration 2.3. These rock-like objects were called salamanders *or* bears. *They are composed of all the elements in the blast furnace charge: iron ore, charcoal and limestone. Salamanders form at the bottom of a furnace when the smelting process was incomplete. (Photo by Evan Jones)*

process was also used to further reduce the level of impurities in the iron and to adjust its carbon and alloy content.

Cupola The cupola was a miniature furnace, sometimes used like a blast furnace and other times like a foundry. The cupola was lined with fire clay or fire stone refractories. As no water cooling was utilized in the melting zone, the lining had to be repaired with plastic fire clay patching between periods of operations. The charging door was located on the side of the cupola near the top. The cupola was supported by legs, permitting the use of a drop bottom which facilitated the removal of the remaining burden after the last charge was tapped. Intermittent operation was the general rule, but continuous operation was possible.

An iron foundry of this period produced three types of usable iron. Technical descriptions of each type are found in the Appendix.

Pig Iron The product of the blast furnace was pig iron, which has a high carbon content, typically 3.5–4.5 percent, along with silica and other unreduced elements. It is an intermediate product in the overall steel-making process because it is very brittle and not very useful without further refinement. Steel mills typically used open-hearth furnaces to further purify and refine the pig iron, after which it was transformed into more useful forms of iron and steel. The traditional shape of the molds used for pig iron ingots was a branching structure formed in sand, with many individual ingots at right angles to a central channel or runner, resembling a litter of piglets being suckled by a sow.

Cast Iron Cast iron is made in a foundry by re-melting pig iron, often along with quantities of limestone and carbon and taking various steps to remove undesirable contaminants. Phosphorus and sulfur may be burnt out of the molten iron, but this also burns out the carbon, which may need to be replaced. Carbon and silicon content are adjusted to the desired levels, which may be anywhere from two to three and a half percent and one to three percent, respectively, depending on the application of the final product. Other elements are then added to the melt before the liquid is poured into a mold, which contains a hollow cavity of the desired shape. The liquid metal is then allowed to cool and solidify. Cast iron was sometimes melted in a *cupola*, but in modern applications it is more often melted in electric induction furnaces or electric arc furnaces.[20]

Wrought Iron One of the early ways to convert pig iron was to reheat it in a refinery forge and mechanically work it by brute force into wrought iron by extruding, rolling, and hammering. Working the iron would partially remove excess slag and align the fibers within the metal, making it more pliable. Wrought iron is tough, malleable, ductile, corrosion-resistant and easily welded. Before the development of effective methods of steelmaking, wrought iron was the most common form of malleable iron. Many items were produced from wrought iron, including rivets, nails, wire, chains, rails, railway couplings, water and steam pipes, nuts, bolts, horseshoes, handrails, wagon tires, straps for timber roof trusses, and ornamental ironwork, among many other things. Worked-iron products are seldom produced today, as other cheaper, superior products are used instead. Puddling furnaces, Bessemer furnaces and open-hearth furnaces replaced the wrought iron process to make steel. Today steel is made using an electric arc furnace, induction furnace or basic oxygen furnace to burn off the excess carbon and unwanted components and to control the alloy composition.

Work Begins at the Iron Works

In January 1852, barely two and a half months after moving to Cedar City, tests were conducted on the local iron ore and it was judged to be high in iron content. It was also determined that using wood to fuel the furnace produced unsatisfactory results, which only served to intensify the search for good "stone coal." A letter from M. Carruthers to George A. Smith explained the problem.

> The real state of the matter will be more fully understood when the stone coal can be used for fuel instead of the wood, as the wooden fuel is too light and cannot bear up the iron ore in the furnace until the blast acts sufficiently upon it to become perfectly fluxed, but the lightness of the wooden coal allows it to fall down to the bottom of the furnace in an imperfect smelted condition and consequently has to be drawn off from the furnace in the above condition; hence the great necessity of obtaining stone coal.[21]

What Carruthers said about wood being too light was true. The problem with wood, stated in a slightly different way, was that when burned, it quickly turned to ash and collapsed under the weight of the iron ore and limestone placed on top of it. Coke and charcoal maintained their structure longer when burning and did not collapse quite so rapidly. Wood was regularly used, however, when the fire in the furnace was first being started to help get the fire going in the coke or charcoal. Sometimes wood was used as part of the charge, along with charcoal and or coke.

Brigham Young made regular visits to the southern settlements, usually once a year. His visits were greatly anticipated and appreciated. He generally cheered the Saints on and typically had a few suggestions and even directives for the groups. His first visit was in May 1851, his second visit was made in May 1852. Henry Lunt's diary gave the following account:

> Monday, May 10th, 1852. Fine day, Brigham Young and Company arrived at Cedar City about 3 o'clock p.m., some 30 wagons. Our little city was all in excitement through so great a number of visitors; I had the following brethren and sisters who I invited, come to our house, George A. Smith, John L. Smith, Wilford Woodruff, Elisha H. Groves, W. A. Morse, P. Meeks, Seth M. Blair, Bro. Farr, and sisters Groves and Banks. We enjoyed ourselves together. I called a meeting of all the brethren and sisters together in Bro. Carruther's yard. We had a large meeting and were addressed by Brigham Young and G. A. Smith. The principle subject was, to make Iron. Spent a very pleasant evening with our visitors. The delightful notes of the Brass Band cheered our hearts with its music.[22]

On May 11, 1852, while President Young was in Iron County, Burr Frost, a blacksmith in Parowan, conducted a demonstration. Frost successfully smelted a small amount of Iron Mountain ore in a blacksmith's forge and with that iron produced a few nails.[23]

Brigham Young and his entourage appear to have motivated and encouraged the brethren at Parowan and Cedar City. Brigham Young organized the Iron Manufacturing Company with Richard Harrison as superintendent, Henry Lunt, clerk, Thomas Bladen, engineer, and David B. Adams, furnace operator. Although some work had been done previously at the Iron Works, work at the site commenced in earnest.[24]

Understandably however, there continued to be an underlying tug-o-war that never completely disappeared between working at the Iron Works and working on necessities of life like growing food and building houses.

> Here were a few determined men, buffeting the storms of winter, with no shelter but their wagons for themselves and families, dependent upon the stores of a weak settlement for supplies of bread, with no capital but their labor, and no resources but the crude elements of nature. The iron ore was there in rich abundance, but its very richness seemed an objection to many experienced workmen. There were indications of coal in the mountains in almost inaccessible places, but no vein of it had yet been discovered that would pay for working. Materials for building furnaces appeared to exist but everything remained to be tried by the slow process of experiment, in order to establish a basis for permanent operations. After struggling through the winter of 1851-2, in which all possible preparations were made for the labors of the coming season, the summer of 1852 was spent in raising a little grain for the future sustenance of the settlement, making a temporary road into Coal Creek canyon, hunting up, selecting, and experimenting upon the materials which surrounded the settlement, and constructing such works as the means of the settlers permitted, or circumstances seemed to warrant.[25]

The following account of life and work in the Iron County Mission comes from Henry Lunt's diary.

> **Thursday, May 27th, 1852** Very hot day. Thunder and rain on the mountains, creek still raising. I was putting up fence round the big field assisted by two young men. My own fence in the big field has been up more than a month ago. Some 13 men out of about 30 commenced in the iron business, some preparing for the furnace, and some exploring for coal. Some men and the brethren that came with Brigham went to examine the coal and reported that it was of no account.

June 7, 1852 A certain number of men who felt like spending all their time in the Iron Works should be free from the field, and also those men who were farmers and would like to spend all their time in farming, for them to be united and take care of the field. I also counseled those brethren who would engage in the Iron Works to let out their crops to those who would take charge of the field, for one half of their grain, and that would pay them well. I also counseled the brethren to send all their loose calves to Johnson's herd, and also to put all their stock that they needed here into the herd. And if there were men here that would not comply with these requisitions, they had better gather up and leave this place. Sixteen men turned out for the Iron business. Some went to digging out a place for the wheel to blow the blast furnace, and some for timber from the canyon. I was engaged in digging. Very hot day. Bro. Steel and J. L. Smith returned to Parowan, in the morning. Father Bateman came from Parowan to assist in making fire brick for the furnace. Creek falling rapidly.

Tuesday, June 8th, 1852 A very warm day. I spent the morning in writing for the Iron Works. Labored on the Iron Works in the afternoon. I met together with the iron men in the evening, agreed to sound the horn at 1/2 past six in the morning for the men to start to work.

Tuesday, June 22nd, 1852 I labored at working the road up the canyon. About 30 hands were at work. A horse of Alex Easton's was shot with an arrow.[26]

Lunt sent a letter to the *Deseret News* that was published on June 25, 1852 which described the progress (and sacrifices) made at the mission.

We have been very busily engaged in preparing to make iron for the last month. Considerable work has been done. The fire brick for the furnace are ready for laying up and prove to be of the very best quality. The timber which we needed for the framing of the machinery, we hauled from a canyon, 5 miles south of Coal Creek, where there is abundance of beautiful pine timber, and any quantity of poles for fencing. A few hands went with teams and worked the road one day and hauled loads back to the Iron Works the following day. There is a good, extensive blacksmith's shop erected, and the iron work for the machinery is progressing rapidly. It requires a deal of iron for the works, which we principally obtain off our wagons; take the tire off and lay the wood work [to] one side until we can replace the iron from the Works. Our faith is, that in a very few weeks we shall see iron of our own manufacture.

A number of the brethren from Parowan and this place have been working out their taxes in making a road up Coal Creek Canyon, during the past week. Henry Lunt.[27]

Lunt's diary continues:

Saturday, June 26th, 1852. Met at the Blacksmith's shop at seven a.m. I spoke to the brethren respecting their several duties and exhorted them to be diligent and faithful in their mission, and be humble, and united. I told them that every man that was placed at the head of a branch of business should fill his place, and that it was not the place of anyone to find fault with another man's work. After about 1/2 hour's deliberation things were settled and the brethren seemed united. Labored on the Iron Works. Warm day.

Tuesday, June 29th, 1852. Warm day, windy. Labored at blacksmithing for the Iron Works. Made a very heavy gudgeon for the water wheel. Worked all the iron up that we had on hand by noon. Myself and Bro. Harrison visited Bro. Carruthers who lay on his bed with a lame foot, and asked him for some iron for the Iron Works, he has two wagons and a lot of old iron, and he promised one of his wagons and all his old iron, for the Iron Works, at a council meeting held a short time since; but he now said that he had no iron to spare and he thought he should go to the Great Salt Lake Valley. I took the tire off my wagon and appropriated it to the Iron Works. It was a new wagon and the only one I had. May the Lord grant that I may at all times be willing to part with anything that he has placed in my possession, for the building up of his Kingdom. Amen.

Wednesday, July 14, 1852. Myself and Bro. Carruthers and James Williamson sent exploring for iron ore to see if we could find any better than what had been found. We searched about considerable in the mountains west of the Ford [Iron Springs Gap area] and found several different places of iron ore but considered it all to be near the same. We took an ox team with us and brought specimens from each place. A heavy thunder shower fell on the mountains. I shot a hare on my way home.[28]

A sample of iron ore was excavated in 1976 from the blast furnace site in the northeast section of Cedar City, where the old furnace site was located. A chemical analysis confirmed that the sample had high iron and phosphorus content. This information appears to confirm that ore being used at the Iron Works came from the Three Peaks area where appreciable apatite is still found today. Apatite is a mineral made up of phosphorus, calcium and oxygen.[29]

The First Iron is Produced

Lunt's diary continues, reporting progress despite flooding, and finally in late September 1852, the successful production of its first iron.

Friday July 16th 1852 I went up the canyon with nine men to finish working the road up to the coal. Tremendous thunder and lightning and heavy rain up the canyon. Rained down in the valley tremendous for about two hours, commenced about 11 o'clock. The water was 12 inches deep in some of the houses and cellars in the Fort during the storm. Thanks be to God for such a delightful shower, on this dry and thirsty land. Slept all night up in the canyon under some brush. The ground being very wet I did not have a very comfortable night lodging.

Saturday, July 17th, 1852 Labored at working the road in the canyon. Brought a load of stone coal to the blacksmith's shop. Had a meeting of the iron brethren at 1/2 past 4 in the evening, in the Blacksmith's shop. Some business pertaining to the rolling forth of the iron business was transacted.

Tuesday, July 20th 1852 Very close and warm during the morning. About 2 o'clock it thundered tremendously and rained for about 1/2 an hour. There was tremendous storms on the mountains. A cloud bursted on a mountain up the canyon and rose the creek 3 feet all at once, bringing down with a tremendous rush a great quantity of logs, and rubbish and mud; for about one hour the mud kept roiling down the creek as thick as mush. The two dams that were in the creek for the water to the field and Fort were both entirely swept away, and an immense quantity of wood drifted up the mouth of the ditches. I labored on the Iron Works. I am this day 28 years of age.

Friday, July 30th 1852 Very hot day. Labored on the Iron Works. The Bishop called the brethren together in the morning for the purpose of fixing the dams in the creek again, but because the iron men did not go to help them, they would not go, and we have now to pack our water from the Big Creek.

Friday, Aug 13th, 1852 Labored for the Iron Works, worked very hard, hauled loads of adobes to the works, one of fire clay and one of red clay. Had two Indians working for me, one stayed with me all the day, and a better workman I never did see as an

Indian. He returned home with me in the evening, I gave him his supper, he washed his face clean and combed his hair. I invited him to come on the morrow and work for me. He said he would. Very hot day. Thunder and rain on the mountains east. Some of the brethren returned from the canyon yesterday reported that they had found a fresh coal mine 1-1/2 miles nearer than the other, and a thicker and better coal.

Tuesday, Sept. 7, 1852 Binding wheat for Father Whittaker on my own lot.

Wednesday Sept. 8, 1852 Labored on the Iron Works, at digging out the mill race. The brethren seemed to be much dissatisfied with Bro. Harrison. It seems with great difficulty that Harrison can get any of the men to work under him. Bro. Harrison has almost entirely lost the confidence of the Saints.

Wednesday, Sept. 22, 1852 Labored for some 3 hours on working the road up the mountain, then packed (on pack horses) 5 bags of coal down the mountain and drove a load to the Iron Works. Felt very much tired and fatigued in the evening.

Tuesday Sept. 28, 1852 Myself and all hands labored on the Iron Works. I labored until about 12 o'clock at night with several others.

Wednesday, Sept. 29, 1852 Labored on the Iron Works. Commenced charging the furnace and put on the blast about noon. Labored most of the night. The machinery worked most excellent.

Thursday, Sept. 30, 1852 Tapped the furnace about six o'clock a.m. The metal ran out and we all gave three hearty cheers. When the metal was cold, on examination it was not found to be so good as might be wished and also of a very peculiar appearance. This was attributed to so much sulphur being in the stone coal. President J. C. L. Smith visited me in the evening, took supper with me; walked with him up to the Iron Works.[30]

Although the last entry was brief, it contained the clear message that despite almost a year of hard work and great personal sacrifice by the weary group, the quality and quantity of iron produced was not what it had been hoped to be. Nevertheless, it was indeed iron, and it warranted celebration and a trip to Salt Lake to share the news with Brigham Young. The following is an excerpt from a paper written by William R. Palmer, a well-known local historian, given at the dedication of the Utah Trails and Landmarks Association marker at the Cedar City Park in 1933. It told of the September 1852 event.

In February 1852, the Cedar colony began the erection of a blast furnace and by that act an industry was definitely launched. The 35 men in Cedar that summer were divided into two groups, one half to develop the farming possibilities and the other half to build up the Iron Works.

The Record Book of the Iron Company reads as follows: "May 11th 1852, President Brigham Young called a meeting at the home of Brother Ross in Cedar Fort for the purpose of organizing the brethren into a company for the manufacture of iron. Richard Harrison was chosen by vote of the brethren as Superintendent of the Iron Works and Henry Lunt clerk.

"During the Summer a great deal of work was performed consisting principally in building machinery for the Blowing Apparatus, erecting Blast Furnaces, digging stone coal, and building a road to the same.

"On the 29th of September the blast was put on the furnace and charged with iron ore that had been calcined. The fuel used was stone coal coked and dry pitch pine wood in the raw state.

"On the morning of the 30th, the furnace was tapped and a small quantity of iron run out, which caused the hearts of all to rejoice."

These few terse words recorded the happenings of the most dramatic hour in all Southern Utah history. "To be or not to be" was the momentous question that hung on the outcome of the tapping of that furnace. The whole summer had been spent in building and hauling and preparing for this first try out. For several days strong men had swung their sledges and the valley had echoed with the ring of steel as the boulders of ore were being reduced to the proper size for the furnace charge. On that memorable September 29, 1852, the men had spent the day in carefully preparing the furnace for its first run. A thousand times the question had been asked, "What if it fails?" Toward sunset the entire population gathered at the Iron Works to see the torch applied. Amid prayers and speech making the blast was turned on, and all through the chilly night men, women and children huddled around camp fires to watch every development.

At day break came the zero hour when the superintendent said, "Brother Adams, it ought to be ready now, get your rod and try it." In breathless eagerness, the whole populace crowded to the face of the furnace to read their fate in the prod of that stoker's pole. A hard year's work was in that experiment, and if it failed, it meant for most of them, another move. Robert Adams tapped the furnace and a molten stream of iron came pouring out. [Most likely someone else, since no one named Robert Adams appears to have existed at the mission at that time.[31]] Instantly, their pent-up anxiety broke loose in one great spontaneous outcry. With one accord, every throat opened in a wild shout, not of cheers or hurrahs, for cheers could not express their religious emotions, but in shouts of "hosannah, hosannah, hosannah, to God and the Lamb." Men and women wept for joy and thanked their God for His goodness to them. On the spot, a committee of five was selected to carry samples of the iron to Brigham Young, and before nightfall Richard Harrison, Thomas Bladen, Thomas Cartwright, George Wood and P. K. Smith were on their way to Salt Lake City.[32]

A Call for Recruits

With the first smelting finally successful, Henry Lunt's diary records a remarkable reality facing those who labored to produce a product that was only available. "Stormy day. Snow fell about 2 inches, was obliged to stay in the house most of the day on account of my having no shoes or boots to wade in the snow and mud. I would here remark that I have suffered much for the last two years for the want of shoes and every day clothing."[33]

Lunt wrote a letter to the *Deseret News* from Cedar City dated October 5, 1852. It was printed as follows:

President Richards:

Sir: The weather has been very cold lately. October 1st, snowed nearly all day; left about two inches on the ground; very sharp frosts since. Our peaceful little settlement has been a little annoyed of late through California emigrants that have been passing. I was informed on Sunday evening that a small company of three men and two wagons had drove off a two-year-old colt belonging to Bro. George Wood. I immediately called the brethren together, after a few seconds consultation; six horsemen were soon on the track of the thieves. They returned the day following, after pursuing them for 30 miles, brought back the colt, and recovered 30 dollars for expenses, very mercifully allowing them to wend their way to their Golden God.

The prospects for manufacturing that all important article, "Iron" is excellent. I would that we had 500 good men at this time to develop the rich resources of this beautiful vale, and I am satisfied that Iron to almost any amount could soon be manufactured. The machinery is of the best kind, and works well, and would do for a much larger furnace than what is up.

In haste, I am yours, Henry Lunt.[34]

The samples of pig iron that had been produced and delivered to Brigham Young were well received. The Eighth General Epistle of the First Presidency, dated October 13, 1852, declared that iron had been produced in Cedar City.

> A specimen of pig iron, from the furnace in Iron County, was presented at the October Conference, as good as could be expected for the first; and from this time the founders will be relieved from farming to sustain themselves; and have other assistance which they need to prosecute their business; and soon we expect a good supply of iron ware, of home manufacture.[35]

George A. Smith's conference talk, published in the October 16, 1852 edition of the *Deseret News* outlined the urgency of the Iron Works.

> We are almost a world by ourselves; we are a thousand miles from any other place, living amid snow-capped mountains, and surrounded by vast deserts, and whatever is brought here, is imported at a vast expense.
>
> There exists in the mountains round Iron County, a sufficiency of iron, to supply this mountain world with articles of iron; it is the most valuable metal, and with it, power can be carried to an unlimited extent. Parowan is a very pleasant settlement and has rather got the preference of any other settlement; the Indians there are generally inclined to be industrious, and the brethren there are first rate men. At Coal Creek they have raised the best crops, they cannot be beat for quantity, or extent; the best iron mechanics are now engaged in farming, etc., which ought to be done by others, and they suffered to go to work at their own trade. The plows wanting at this present moment, if brought from the States, would cost us $90,000, yet, the iron, the coal, the timber, the fire clay, are there, and you can do it if you have a mind to. You have to buy your soap, because you have not kettles to make soap in, and I fear not to say, that 3,000 kettles are wanted this day; then go to work, patronize the iron company and make your own soap; and at least 3,000 sets of cooking utensils are wanted by this community.
>
> Iron is the sinew of power; of it, your guns, and your wagons are made; all the utensils in husbandry are made of iron; every saw-mill crank that has been made, has cost from $1 to $5 per pound. Elder Benson paid some $500 to make his crank; and the one at Iron County cost $1 a pound for manufacturing it. I invite all to go to Iron County, to increase the number, and strengthen the settlements there. I do know that the fences can be made cheaper of iron, than they are now made of poles. Again, look at the tons of nails, door trimmings, etc., that are annually brought here, at an immense expense—. Now if we will lay hold of this branch of industry, we lay the foundations for our independence, and wealth; and in five years we shall be richer than we ever were. Now brethren, pass on to Iron County, and the blessing of God will go with you.[36]

In response to Lunt's letter and George A. Smith's promptings, among others, a call of one hundred families was made in Salt Lake City at the October Conference of 1852, to strengthen the Cedar City colony. This company was composed of recent converts from Wales, Scotland, and England, who were skilled iron workers, coal miners, blacksmiths, and farmers. These new recruits began to arrive in Cedar City during November and December and proved to be a welcome addition to the enterprise.[37]

During the months of November and December, testing continued on various types of ore in several smaller-sized furnaces; they even tested some lower quality ores from the canyons east of Parowan, with mixed success. The ore from the deposits west of Cedar City proved to be very high grade, some workers thought that it was so pure that it could be worked like pig iron. The relentless search for coal continued, but when a new seam was found, it seemed to always require considerable labor to build a road and develop the mine. Unfortunately, all the coal in the area was part of the same formation and was of similar quality to that which the settlers had already found. Further, the coal outcropped only at higher elevations in the canyons or the mountains, making it difficult to access.

George A. Smith wrote a letter to the *Deseret News* in December 1852 which is quoted here in part:

> Cedar City ... contains over 60 families, mostly settled in a Fort, although a City plat has been surveyed by W. H. Dame, and the new comers of this season have mostly settled upon it. It is a beautiful site. The crops there have exceeded any that I know of in the Territory. A temporary road has been worked to the coal veins about 6 miles up the creek. There have been a number of new veins of coal recently discovered by Mr. Gregory late from the Collieries in England; it will require a heavy amount of labor to complete the road and open the coal veins so as to be made available. Mr. James James, a chemist from Wales, has tested the quality of ores from the different mountains; that from the Iron Springs is 80 percent compared with the Welch Iron; at Little Creek it is richer, and he thinks he can smelt it same as pig iron, and the furnace building at Parowan is for that purpose.
>
> The iron ore at Parowan is 25 percent. An iron mountain about 17 miles from Cedar newly discovered by Mr. Shirts is a mixture of iron and black lead. There is a good furnace built at Cedar City where 40 hands are wanted immediately constantly to run it, and for the lack of which, it lies under the necessity of standing idle....
> George A. Smith[38]

Henry Lunt's diary gives a good idea of the day to day routine of the iron workers.

> **Friday, Dec. 10, 1852** Fine day, spent most of the day in looking out a place in the creek for getting water out to the wheel for blowing the blast furnace.
> **Friday, Dec. 17** Fine day. Very sharp frost. Made a trial yesterday of the ore in a small Cubelo [Cupola]—but did not succeed in making any iron. The wheel was left running all night, but this morning the wheel was froze up. Bro. Calvin returned this morning to Parowan. Spent most of the day about the Iron Works.
> **Thursday, Dec. 30, 1852** Very fine warm day, no frost, remarkably muddy. Made another trial of the iron ore at the Iron Works in the cubelo. After a good trial for about 15 hours, there was no iron and it is the judgment of all that there is something in it that eats the iron away. Attended prayer meeting in the evening, had a first-rate good meeting.[39]

The Deseret Iron Company

Among the numerous and almost insurmountable problems of the Iron County Mission was that of bringing together the necessary capital in a sufficient amount for the development of the new industry. Much consideration and forethought were manifested by the leaders of the Church of Jesus Christ of Latter-day Saints during the early months of 1852. A letter called the "Sixth General Epistle of the First Presidency" was sent to the president of the European Mission. This letter contained a full report of conditions in Utah Territory and also a recommendation to organize a company for the manufacture of iron in the Utah Territory and to sell stock to the wealthy members of the Church, quoted here in part.

> The valley is well supplied with a general assortment of merchandize at the present time; but the exportation of cash having been far greater than the importation the past year, it is to be feared that many articles will remain unsold, which might be used to advantage, were the circulating medium suited to foreign markets in the possession of those who would like to purchase. Shingles are now extensively manufactured and would be very extensively used could nails be procured, but it is not supposed that one-half, and probably not one-fourth enough of shingle nails will be brought this season to supply the market; and the present prospect is, that many buildings will have to be delayed, before another market season, for lack of assorted nails. If a company of brethren could be formed in England, Wales, Sweden, or any other country, to come and make Iron from ore (magnetic ore of the best quality) and machinery for rolling, slitting, and cutting nails, and drawing off wire, it would be one of the greatest auxiliaries for advancement in building up the valleys of the mountains; and the presiding elders in those countries are instructed to examine this subject and forward such a company with the least possible delay.[40]

Complying with the recommendations contained in the letter, Erastus Snow and Franklin D. Richards, who were soon to return to the United States from their missions in London, commenced April 8, 1852, by obtaining from the presiding Elders the addresses of the wealthier members of the church in different parts of the British Empire. They spent most of the month calling on those members and also visiting various iron works in England, Wales, Ireland, and Scotland, obtaining all the general information on the subject of making iron from magnetic and other ores.

On the 28th and 29th of April 1852, at 15 Wilton Street, Liverpool, the Deseret Iron Company was organized, with a subscription of four thousand pounds stock, to be paid on or before the 1st of January, 1853. At this meeting Erastus Snow and Franklin D. Richards were appointed as Agents and Managers of the Company, agreeable to the constitution then and there adopted. On the 8th of May, Snow and Richards left England. On their arrival in Utah the following August, they reported the organization of the Company to the Presidency of the Church, who approved of what had been done and advised the Managers to establish works in Iron County as early as means would permit.[41]

Erastus Snow and Franklin D. Richards left Salt Lake City on November 11, 1852 and arrived in Iron County later that month.

> There being no funds in the Company's Treasury, and as subscriptions of stock could not be made available under about one year and being anxious to set the business of the Company in operation without delay, we proceeded on our own credit to loan money, and with money and credit to purchase the goods with which we commenced the business of the Company in this county.

On our arrival in Iron County, in November following, it seemed to us advisable, in order to promote the best interests of the community, to associate with us the interests and labours of those brethren who were already endeavoring to lay a foundation for the development of the mineral resources of this county; and finding them inclined to unite with us, we negotiated, on behalf of the Company, the purchase of a small Blast Furnace, with the apparatus attached, which they had erected on Coal Creek, for the purpose of experimenting on the ores, together with their right and interest in the Coal Mine of Coal Creek canyon, for the sum of two thousand eight hundred and sixty-five dollars and sixty-four cents.

We next secured to the Company a tract of land extending from Cedar City to the mountains eastward, embracing the numerous water privileges on Coal Creek.

We also endeavored to concentrate the efforts of all the brethren in any wise acquainted with the manufacture of Iron, and appointed John C. L. Smith to superintend their exertions in experimenting on the ores.[42]

To assist in the development of the supply of coal for the company, "Erastus Snow offered one hundred dollars to anyone who would find a good coal mine, for the first ton of coal delivered at the furnace." To prevent inflationary speculation, the company fixed wages and prices. Wages were posted as follows: common labor $1.25/day (raised later to $2.00); carpenters, millwrights, woodworkers $2–2.50/day ($3.00); masons $2.50/day ($4.00); blacksmiths $2.50/day ($3.50); and furnace keepers $2.50/day.[43]

A letter written by Erastus Snow was published in the *Deseret News* on Christmas day of 1852 describing his visit to Iron County. He reported that the group, although not successful in supplying the Territory with iron wares, deserved much credit for their time, labor, diligence and perseverance. He told of some dissention among the ranks between the various factions that had to be settled. He noted that the Iron Works had been purchased by the Deseret Iron Company and that a tract of land had been surveyed east of Cedar City for the proposed erection of furnaces, foundries, a forge with wire-drawing works, and a nail factory. He also made some interesting comments about the quality of the coke made from the local coal.

> In Iron County there are continually new discoveries made in the resources of the mountains. Several rich new beds of iron ore have been found; and besides the coal mines already opened on the south side of Coal Creek Canyon, others have recently been discovered on the north side that, it is believed, will prove superior. As to the iron men on Coal Creek, much credit is due them for their diligence and perseverance. True, they have not supplied us with wares from the Iron Works, but they have devoted much time and labor in the undertaking.
>
> A reason for their not progressing more rapidly or succeeding better in the manufacture of iron, may be found in their lack of experience in its elementary processes, and of union in their organization.
>
> Considerable excitement prevailed through the County, on the subject of iron at the time of our arrival, much heightened by the arrival of those whom we had recently sent there who had been operators in the iron business in Wales and in Pennsylvania, and we found a Scotch party, a Welch party, an English party, and an American party, and we turned Iron Masters and undertook to put all these parties through the furnace, and run out a party of Saints for building up the Kingdom of God. That the cinder is entirely separated from the iron we hardly dare hope, but a sensible improvement in quality of the material we fully anticipate, for the Lord was with us,

and all the people as well as ourselves seemed greatly to rejoice in the improved state of things before we left.

As a final closing up of matters, we purchased their works on Coal Creek for "the Deseret Iron Company," and opened the books of the company for subscription of stock, and there and then received subscriptions from those who felt the greatest interest in the business, to the amount of several thousands, after which, we employed such other desirable workmen as did not take stock, and placed the little furnace now built, under the management of Brother Adams who has had many years' experience as Furnace Keeper in Pennsylvania and in Great Britain. We also employed Brother James from the Victoria Iron Works Wales, to construct a small air furnace in which to try the experiment of fluxing the richer ore without the blast; and further directed that operations be carried forward with charcoal and dry pitch pine wood (which abounds in that vicinity) until a better quality of coke could be produced from the stone coal. This alteration seemed to be warranted by the experiment already made in the furnace which was heat up with pitch pine wood; the first iron that came into the hearth was far superior to that smelted after the furnace was charged with their miserable coke. We committed the superintendence of the business to Brother J. C. L. Smith, President of the stake, whom we regarded as a judicious and persevering man, and from past experiments we feel warranted in indulging the hope of soon furnishing an excellent quality of iron.

We surveyed a tract of land for "the Deseret Iron Company" east of Cedar City to the mountains embracing several sites on the Creek for furnaces, foundries, a forge, with wire drawing works, and a nail factory, all of which works it is the purpose of the Company to erect, and already a commencement is made with a capital of near forty thousand dollars.

On the 4th Dec. we left Iron County and sometimes rolling in deep snow and at others in mud, we reached home (preaching by the way) on the twelfth. May God add his blessings to our mission. Amen.[44]

In January 1853 the Territorial Assembly granted the Deseret Iron Company's petition to form a corporation. Section 1 of 17 Sections is as follows:

To incorporate the Deseret Iron Company.

Section 1. Be it enacted by the Governor and Legislative Assembly of the Territory of Utah, that Erastus Snow, Franklin D. Richards, Thomas Tennant, Geo. A. Smith, Mathew Carruthers, John C. L. Smith, and Joseph Chatterley, their associates and successors, be, and they are hereby created a body corporate, to be known by the name and style of Deseret Iron Company, for the purpose of erecting Furnaces, Mills, Machinery, etc. , for the manufacture of Iron and Steel, and all such articles made of Iron and Steel, as the wants of the community, and the wisdom of the company may determine.[45]

The company's new charter was approved by the Legislative Assembly of Utah Territory on January 17, 1853. The document designated a capitalization of $20,000 and a public appropriation of $7,000 to aid in the opening of the coal mines. Two shares of stock were purchased by the Territorial Legislature and two shares by the Trustee-in-Trust of the Church of Jesus Christ of Latter-day Saints. The two shares purchased by the church were paid chiefly in provisions, clothing, groceries, boots, shoes and a general assortment of goods to outfit the laborers, drawn on several tithing offices.[46]

1 card hooks and eyes	$0.10	1 bonnet	$3.50
1/4 lb. starch	0.13	1 oz. indigo	0.25
1 grammar	1.25	1 straw hat	0.50
1 first reader	0.30	1 geography	1.75
1 lb. sugar	0.50	1 yard de laine	0.40
1 plug of tobacco	1.25	1 yard linen	1.25
1 pr. of shoes	2.00	3 yards edging @ 15¢	0.45
1 pr. of boots	4.50	1 doz. buttons	0.10
1 lb. tea	4.25	1 second reader	0.85
1 lb. of coffee	0.50	1 yard insertion	0.10
1 bar soap	0.55	1 cravat	1.50
1 yard silk	2.20	1 pair slippers	2.00
5 yards cambric	1.25	1 yard corded muslin	1.00
2 yards draper @ 30¢	0.50	1 pair stockings	0.30
3 yards ribbon	1.50	1 shawl	5.00
3/4 yard velvet	4.50	1 yard of alpaca	1.28

Table 1. *Price List of Goods in Cedar City, taken from One Sheet of the Company's Books*[47]

Henry Lunt sent a letter to the *Deseret News* which follows in part. It is interesting to note that it appears to have been the intention of the company to construct not just one, but four blast furnaces.

Local Correspondence

Cedar, Iron County, February 26, 1853

All is peace, prosperity and best of health in this colony, and praised be the name of the Lord for his goodness unto us. We have had very sharp frosts at nights for the last month but delightful fine days. The ground this morning is white with a slight fall of snow the past night.

We have taken up the fence from round the Big Field and made another small field on the south side of Coal Creek, below the new city, will be completed by the 1st of March with an excellent fence all round it 6 poles high, and 2 good strong lumber gates to enter. A dam and water course are in operation to water the city and field. The new city plat has already on it 9 log houses, 2 adobie and 10 good cellars, all inhabited.

We number in the colony, Fort and City together 70 men, about half of which are regularly employed by the Deseret Iron Company. The blast is put on to the furnace this morning. There is a variety of ores on the ground, calcined, ready for experiment. We fully expect this time to become acquainted with the knowledge of manufacturing iron from the ores which so richly abound in this country. An excellent air furnace is nearly finished, built of adobies and rock, with a funnel 300 feet long to convey the smoke to a chimney stack 40 feet high, which are in progress of building. The stack is so constructed as to answer for 4 furnaces when completed. An extensive frame building is erected for a casting house.

Yours etc. Henry Lunt

P.S. It will be well for the saints who come here this spring to provide themselves with garden seeds. Walker the Indian Chief and a small band have been camped here for the last 3 weeks and are very peaceable.[48]

February and March were busy times at the Iron Works. The following chronology, quoted from the diary, summarizes the activities by date.

Saturday, February 26, 1853 Charged the small furnace with 100 pounds of charcoal, 36 pounds iron ore, 26 pounds bog ore and 15 pounds of limestone.

February 27 Discovered the iron had chilled and formed a large piece. Took off the blast and spent the day removing the iron.

March 1 Made another charge, 100 pounds charcoal, 300 pounds iron ore, 200 pounds bog ore and 200 pounds Limestone. Commenced the blast about 2:00 pm.

March 2 The charge produced 250 pounds of iron after blowing 18 hours.

March 4 Ran out of charcoal and had to stop the furnace. Collectively, during these trials about 2500 pounds of iron ran out, mostly white and very hard, this required about 600 bushels of charcoal.

March 15 The men were determined to make castings and constructed a small cupola furnace to melt some of the pig iron that had been produced.

March 16 Finished building the cupola and molded two skillets and a pair of hand irons for the fireplace.

March 17 Heated up the cupola and melted about 400 pounds of iron. Cast a pair of hand irons [andirons] or fire dogs. A number of persons were present to see the sight. The group cried Hosanna to God and the Lamb for ever and ever. Amen. And three cheers were given for Iron County.

March 18 The day was spent altering the inside of the cupola and repairing it for casting.

March 19 Molded up two hand irons, a kettle, two spiders, a skillet, two tweers and plates. The metal was very hard and thick.

March 21 Repaired the furnace and prepared the sand for molding.

March 22 Wood was used to melt the iron in the cupola and it appeared to have done well. Two wheels and two pedestals were molded and looked splendid. A spider and tweers for furnace were also made.

April 1 A charge was made consisting of 100 pounds of pitch pine, 50 pounds of charcoal, 25 pounds of West Mountain ore, 30 pounds of bog ore and 10 pounds of limestone. The resulting iron produced was said to be the best quality so far. Mr. Bladen made a fly wheel for water wheel and attached circular saw for cutting wood and constructed a lathe.[49]

Henry Lunt took the andirons to Salt Lake City, where President Young had them polished and put them on the stand in the Tabernacle during the Church General Conference, as the first cast iron made by the Saints. "The Saints appeared quite excited and well pleased at the sample of cast iron made in the mountains by the Saints."[50]

That same spring John Spiers, a settler in Cedar City in 1853, stated privately that Peter Shirts and Thomas Jones built a smelting furnace, having found a kind of ore which could be worked. The furnace was built outside of the fort wall. John D. Lee opposed this because of the protection the furnace afforded Indians in shooting at the fort. The owners refused to pull down the furnace, with the result that J. D. Lee and his men pulled it down themselves. The ruins made a fine protection for the Indians to hide behind, for where only ten could hide before, fifty could now find protection.[51]

The "Daily Journal of the Deseret Iron Company" contained the following names, together with the number of days worked from January to April 1853, inclusive:

Cedar City Iron Works

Name	Days Worked	Name	Days Worked
Arthur Parks	7	Samuel Lee	13
Benjamin Hulse	70	William Davies	3
Philip K. Smith	18	John Nelson	1
David Adams	105	George Perry	27
Thomas Cartwright	103	David Cook	15
Joseph Walker	100	John Easton	5
Thomas Bladen	106	Thomas Rowland	18
James James	41	Richard Harrison	38
Robert Wiley Mason	81	William Evans	6
George Wood	13	John Griffiths	13
Erastus Curtis	10	William Beddo	3
William C. Mitchell	3	Elias Morris	4
James Williamson	89	Edward Prothero	6
Joseph Hunter	35	William Greenwood	57
John Groves	77	George Hunter	38
William Adshead	20	John Smith	42
James Bosnell	31	Robert Kershaw	30
Alexander Campbell	22	Samuel Kershaw	20
James Thorp	34	William Shelton	71
Job Rowland	11	William Cousins	5
Joseph Chatterley	85	Robert Letham	3
Jonathan Pugmire	105	Richard Varley	42
William Stones	4	Robert Chapman	5
John Ashworth	10	Joseph Clews	45
John White	6	Thomas Muir	4
J. Muir	7	William Lewis	8
William Hewett	5	John Stoddard	2
James Whittaker	49	Thomas Machen	6
William Stack	15	John Kay	8
David Stoddard	75	John Gregory	17
John Yardley	19	James Mitchell	3
Andrew Paterson	70	Alexander Keir	10
William Daken	77	James Bullock	7
Charles P. Smith	25	John Woodhouse	3

2,106 days Total[52]

The following excerpt from the *Millennial Star* gives a good idea of the work that took place during the winter months of 1852–53, in particular the continued search for good coking coal and the beginning of the Walker Indian War.

During the winter of 1852–53, great quantities of charcoal and pitch pine wood were prepared with a view to put the furnace into operation in the spring. This was done during a second visit of Messrs. Snow and Richards, in the latter part of April. The result proved most conclusively that that kind of fuel would not answer the desired purpose, as only small quantities of iron were produced at comparatively great expense, although generally of good quality.

The expenditures of the Territorial appropriations for the benefit of the Iron Interest were placed at the disposal of Governor Brigham Young. Erastus Snow was the bearer of instructions from him to appoint persons to expend the appropriations as ordered. James A. Little and Philip K. Smith were designated as the persons to carry out this object. They commenced operations immediately, and in the course of ten days, several veins of coal were discovered. Their attention was ultimately directed to one which was traced for several miles on the precipitous side of a mountain, at a great elevation above the valley. This vein proves to be of excellent quality, with seven feet of pure coal, and about two feet more separated from the main body by thin strata of rock and fire clay.

This coal bank is within about seven miles of the Iron Works. After its discovery there seemed to be nothing needed but a suitable furnace and a proper combination of material to produce iron in any desirable quantity. In about two months after the discovery of this coal bank, it was opened, a quantity of coal was dug, and a good wagon road made to it, at an expense of some 6,000 dollars, which, in this country, appears extremely trifling for the attainment of so great an object.

Immediately after the completion of this work, news reached the southern settlements, that an Indian war had commenced; and all the energies of the settlements were necessarily directed to making every possible preparation for self-defense, such as moving in the small settlements fortifying the larger ones, securing the grain and hay for winter, with many other important items.[53]

Henry Lunt's Diary adds to the descriptive account:

Thursday, May 19, 1853. Very warm day. Myself and wife planted a few garden seeds in the afternoon. About 1/2 past 4 p.m. it began to thunder and lightning over Shirts Canyon, and in a few minutes the whole Heavens were black with clouds, and the lightning and thunder began to approach very near and was tremendously loud. The wind began to blow in a most terrific manner and large drops of rain descended. I and Ellen then went into the house. She sat down near the fire place, and I went to the wood pile for some wood for the fire. As I came through the door, I pushed it wide open, and just as I was in the attitude of laying the wood down by the side of the fire place, the electric fluid struck the chimney of the house accompanied with the loudest burst of thunder I ever before heard. Knocked a part of the chimney down, rent the house from top to bottom, blew the mantle piece to pieces, took a piece out of the floor, knocked the bottom out of a cooler which was full of water, a hole into a box, knocked the plaster off a wall, tore one of the shoes to pieces on my wife's foot, and a large hole into the other, took the use out of both her legs for some time. I had to carry her out of the house and at the same time my own legs were burning with heat as though I had been in a fire. The house at the moment of the tremendous shock was filled with a blaze of fire. We were both of us sensible at the time, and are now, that had it not been for an over-ruling providence which had shielded us from the danger, we most certainly should have both of us been instantly killed. It was the most awful scene I ever witnessed, and certainly will never be forgotten. Praised the

Lord for his goodness unto us. Attended meeting in the evening. Bro. Cook's boy was knocked down about 100 yards from my house. Bro. J. C. L. Smith and Carruthers came to my house a few minutes after the scene, brought a sample of coal, which was of an excellent quality, that the brethren had dug out of the old mine.

Monday, July 18, 1853. The night much cooler. Fine warm day. Writing all day and settling up accounts with the men in the Iron Works. Another trial was made in the air furnace, the furnace became exceedingly hot, and about 2 o'clock the arch over the grate burned through, and a small quantity fell in. Consequently, nothing much was done. The arch over the fireplace was built of dobies. It was of the opinion of Bro. James that the stack wanted to be taken higher, and the arch to be built of fire brick, and he seemed confident that the furnace would make iron from the raw ore, if they had stone coal for to burn. The Pahvant Chief and the Pihede Chief, with the two Indians that stole a yoke of cattle about a month since, which we got back, and several other Indians, came and wanted to get the Gun back, and gave themselves up to us to punish them as we thought fit.[54]

The Walker Indian War

Brigham Young had always been an advocate of building fortifications at the settlements so that people and animals would be protected in the case of an Indian uprising. The forts also acted as a deterrent. For the most part, relations with the Indians had been quite peaceful in Southern Utah. However, in 1853, it seems that things began to change in that relationship. Perhaps the settlers had worn out their welcome or were becoming too numerous or were somehow impacting the Indians' annual subsistence cycles. As early as April it was noticed that encounters seemed a bit more hostile and things came to a head in mid-July. The *Deseret News* published the following account.

> On the 17th [of July], hostilities commenced by a menace on Springville, in Utah County, but the inhabitants receiving timely notice, and being numerous and watchful, no damage was done. On the 18th, Walker and his two brothers Arrapin and Ammon with many of the tribe were camped on the Peteetneet, just above Payson, in Utah County, and as Arrapin was riding from town to his camp he passed close by Alexander Keele, who was on guard, and though another Indian was nearby, as near as the spectators could judge, it was Arrapin who shot Keele dead on the spot, and this too, after having partaken of a hospitable meal in the fort with apparent friendliness. The Indians then moved up Peteetneet Canyon, the rear firing heavily as they passed, upon some half dozen families in the Canyon, but injuring nothing but their clothing, and leaving quite a quantity of balls in the buildings.[55]

Six days later, on July 23rd, after several encounters with the Indians had ended with shots being fired, a scouting party of settlers, sent out from Manti, came across a company of twenty or thirty Indians. The Indians, through an interpreter, told the settlers that they were their enemies, at which point they commenced firing their weapons. None of the company were injured, however, six Indians were killed.[56]

On July 21 and 25, Brigham Young issued General Orders, outlining military measures and many of the settlers in outlying areas were moved into town with all of their belongings, sometimes including their log homes. Paragonah residents were moved to Parowan, New Harmony residents moved to Cedar City.[57]

Illustration 2.4. Isaac C. Haight (1813–1886), community leader and general manager of the Deseret Iron Company.

In a newspaper article published in the *Deseret News* on July 30, 1853, the citizens of the Territory were strongly advised to build the forts that they had been advised to build years before, and to stop trading guns, weapons and ammunition with the Indians. They were also advised to conserve their resources, watch over their children's safety, make their houses safe from intruders and to be on alert at all times.[58]

On August 19th, Brigham Young, Governor and Ex-Officio Superintendent of Indian Affairs of the Utah Territory published another order which covered similar points.[59] The Walker War, as it was called, officially ended in May 1854, when Brigham Young and Chief Wakara personally negotiated an understanding.[60]

As far as the Iron Works was concerned, the Walker War was a major disruption. Virtually all work stopped while fortifications were built and houses were being moved or built. The local food stores were also permanently affected by the war. During the fighting, the Territorial government passed an edict ordering that all of the local cattle be sent to Northern Utah for protection, and these were, for the most part, not returned after the war.

Just as the routine smelting efforts began again, the young industry suffered a terrific setback. On September 3, 1853 a flood caused by a cloudburst in the mountains, swept away the bridges and the dams on the stream, carrying in its torrent huge boulders, some of them weighing from twenty to thirty tons each.[61] "A tremendous flood came down Coal Creek on Saturday Sept. 3rd," reported Henry Lunt, "carrying away bridges, dams and everything before it; brought an immense quantity of logs and rocks of immense size; and did some considerable damage to the Iron Works.[62]

In addition to carrying off several hundred bushels of charcoal, lumber, etc., the flood inundated the site of the Iron Works to the depth of three feet and made clear the fact that the present site was too close to Coal Creek. Optimistically, however, Erastus Snow and Franklin D. Richards made the following observation:

This freshet brought down an immense quantity of well ground material and deposited the same in various depths from four to ten inches, which when dried, proved to be a very superior for building walls and houses, and has been extensively used for that purpose.

Should the weather continue mild and pleasant as hitherto, the newcomers can spend the winter in erecting to themselves good habitations of these ready-made adobies and close up their lines of fortifications.[63]

During the autumn the dam was rebuilt, and other breaches were repaired so as to allow the Iron Works to be put back in operation.

The First General Meeting of the Deseret Iron Company

The first general meeting of the Deseret Iron Company was held in Cedar City in November, 1853. Erastus Snow and Franklin D. Richards presented the report. The report contained a few extracts from the records of the Deseret Iron Company, calling attention to the business conducted during the year, the financial situation of the company and the amounts expended in Iron County. It was noted that Vincent Shurtleff, an agent of the company, had purchased a stock of goods for the use of the Company which would soon be displayed for sale in Cedar City.

In the course of the first general meeting, the Secretary read the charter entitled "An Act to Incorporate the Deseret Iron Company", which had been approved by the Territorial Assembly the previous January. It provided for a president, a secretary, a treasurer, and four trustees to be elected by the majority votes of the stockholders. After the votes of the shareholders had been cast, the following persons were declared elected: Erastus Snow, President; Franklin D. Richards, Secretary; Thomas Tennant, Treasurer; and Isaac C. Haight, Vincent Shurtleff, Christopher Arthur, and Jonathan Pugmire, Trustees. The officers then filed bonds with the Clerk of the County Court with good and sufficient securities for the faithful performance of their duties. The President and Secretary were required to give bonds in the sum of $10,000 each, and the Treasurer in the sum of $40,000, and the Trustees $2,000 each. The meeting was then adjourned until the first Monday in November, 1854. On November 26, 1853, the Board of Directors and the other members of the Iron Company met and appointed Isaac C. Haight to be General Manager of the Company's affairs. He was required to file bonds with approved security in the sum of $10,000 in addition to the $2,000 he had filed as a Trustee.[64]

During this time, it became apparent that the "Little Fort" was becoming a bit overcrowded, was in the path of the floods of Coal Creek and was difficult to defend in case of Indian attack. A new townsite was planned by the Deseret Iron Company by the name of Cedar City "Plat A," commonly called the Cedar Fort, referring to both the townsite and the fort that was soon to be erected. The new fort was 100 rods square and was used from 1853 to 1858 after the Little Fort was abandoned. The fort was located in the northeast section of Plat A, northwest of the present-day Cedar City. Interstate 15 currently runs right through the center of the Plat A townsite near Industrial Road.

The Cedar Fort walls were three feet thick and nine feet high, built of adobe bricks. The streets were six rods wide, and alleys were two rods wide (one rod equals 16.5 feet; a 40 × 40-rod plot is exactly ten acres). There were sixty-four lots, each sized 4 × 20 rods or 66 × 330 feet. The ten acres in the southwest corner of the Fort were fenced into a 40 × 40-rod public square, called Temple Block, into which the livestock could be gathered. The Liberty Pole stood in the center of this square.[65]

In the summer of 1853 the Walker Indian War broke out. On July 26, Brigham Young, as governor, proclaimed a state of war and called upon the people "to fortify, build forts, arm themselves, move about in armed groups, protect livestock, abandon small settlements, and move to larger centers, post strong guards at night and use every precaution to avoid surprise attacks." Arrington notes that a nine-foot adobe wall three feet thick was built around the town. At that point the city was one hundred rods square and the wall enclosed sixty-three acres. This fort, the largest in Utah, was completed by the 114 men and boys of Cedar City on December 31, 1853—an effort of a little over six months work.[66]

The Noble Furnace

The early trial runs of 1854 continued to be disappointing. The creek was not cooperating, the quality of iron produced was poor and the furnace lining continued to fail on a regular basis. Tests continued through May. About that time the pioneers made the decision to raze the old furnace and build a new, larger furnace, they expected it to be a "noble building" and it became known as the "Noble Furnace." The following account from the official minute book of the Deseret Iron Works describes the activities of the first half of 1854. Elias Morris, the furnace architect, was also the supervising mason of the Salt Lake Temple.

> Furnace and works repaired and on Jan. 9, 1854 new trial was made using coke. Water froze and air blast stopped and iron chilled and labor was suspended. I. C. Haight, manager, wrote to Pres. Snow requesting that a steam engine be purchased to furnish power for blast as creek was unreliable.
>
> Many trials were made with indifferent success. May 30, preparations were made to erect new furnace with a larger water wheel and air cylinder.
>
> Foundation 3 ft. deep 21 ft. square was cut and rock of some hundreds weight put for foundation and corner stone. E. Morris architect. Erected on site of old furnace. Sept. 23, 1854. The Noble furnace is completed of Stone masonry. Size. Foundation 21 ft. square 3 ft. high. Pillars 6 ft. high, front arch 10 ft. span 4 ft. deep in center Arch stone 16" deep, up to square 12' 6" level at top of arch which is worked flush on outside, also height of the boshes inside, 18 ft. above the square is worked to a batter of 2-1/4" to the foot on the outside and 1" to the foot on the inside lining. On the 18 ft. batter are corbels 9" thick projecting over 4". The coping, 6" thick projecting over the corbels 2", on the level of the coping is the Tunnel head, 7'4" square 7'6" high under the cornice. The moulding 9" projecting over 3". The string stone 5" thick over moulding 2". The top block 10" set in 3". The Hearth 22" square, 22" deep. Boshes 6 ft. 6". Top of lining 3 ft. 6" in diameter at the charging place. The Torine arch on the N. and S. 8 ft. span. This lining is worked in courses neatly dressed. Thickness from 6" to 12" the outside worked in rockwork style well bedded and the corner drafted.[67]

The *Millennial Star* quoted a portion of a letter from Isaac C. Haight to Franklin D. Richards, dated September 24, 1854, that gave further details about the new furnace.

> The foundation of a new furnace was laid about the 25th of May, twenty-one feet square, of red sandstone, carried up perpendicularly twelve feet above the ground,

then tapered eighteen feet to the top. The tunnel head is eight feet, making the furnace thirty-eight feet to top of tunnel head. It is six and a half feet in the boshes, three and a half feet at tunnel head inside, and thirteen feet square outside. The lining is of porous sandstone, that will stand the fire well. The cause of lining with rock is that we can get no fire brick that will stand. The hearth is of grey sandstone. It took some six hundred and fifty tons of rock, and cost $3782,45. The particulars of the furnace, brother Elias Morris, who was the Architect, will give you.

We have also enlarged the water wheel four feet and made circular cylinders three and a-half feet in diameter, which also are completed. They work admirably and will give a blast of two and a- half pounds to the square inch.

The furnace is also completed, and is said, by those who have seen it, to be as good a furnace as they ever saw in England, or any other country. The blast pipes are not yet finished but will be by the time the furnace will be heated ready for the blast.

We are also building six coke ovens, of the same kind of rock as the furnace; and after they are finished, I intend to add six more, with which I am in hopes to supply the furnace with good coke and make good iron.[68]

An article written in the *Deseret News*, based on an interview with Isaac Haight, described the newly completed furnace.

I had an interview with brother Isaac Haight, superintendent of the Iron Works, who gave me the following information in relation to the Iron Works of Cedar City, eighteen miles south of Parowan. They have just completed a new furnace, 21 feet square at the base, and 30 feet to the tunnel head, and 6 feet 6 inches in the boshes. It is built of a purple sandstone, the lower part lined with porous grey sandstone, and the upper part with red sandstone. The charge is delivered by water power, which propels the blast.

They have made a new blowing apparatus consisting of two double action cylinders, 3 ½ feet in diameter. They have also completed four large coke ovens, and have two more in progress, made of the same materials as the furnace. They have some three or four tons of fuel on hand, consisting of coal, coke and charcoal, and several hundred tons of magnetic and clay iron ores. They labored under many disadvantages in obtaining their coal, having to haul it one mile and a half down a steep mountain, and then six miles down a canyon to the works…[69]

The ironworkers called the clay iron ore *bog ore* or *lean ore*. The furnace also had an interesting device, powered by the water wheel, which hoisted the charge up a 20° incline to the top of the furnace. The size of this water wheel was increased to assist the new furnace.[70]

Despite the success in building the new furnace, more workers were needed at the Iron Works as described in the following letter to the editor by George A. Smith, published in the *Deseret News* in response to a letter received from Isaac Haight.

Iron County Iron Works

G.S.L. City, Dec 9, 1854.

Mr. Editor, by a recent letter from Mr. Isaac C. Haight, superintendent of the Iron Company's operations in Cedar City, we learn that one of the principal drawbacks to the Iron Works in that place, is the want of mechanics who are properly skilled in the different departments of iron manufacture. Two good furnace keepers, two blacksmiths

Illustration 2.5 Model of the blast furnace and water-powered blower. (Matheson Special Collections)

well skilled in engine work, and two good cokers, are very much needed, and we feel, through your columns, to invite such mechanics as are acquainted with the manufacture of iron, to locate themselves in Cedar City, and apply their skill and ingenuity in unfolding to this territory the rich treasures of the mountains. A good furnace is completed. Seven coke ovens are also prepared, and four hundred tons of fuel on hand. The blowing apparatus is of the best quality, and the spell which has so long hung over the iron operations will soon be broken. George A. Smith.[71]

While the furnace was being heated for use, the company held its third annual meeting, and once again, despite improvements, there were a number of men who withdrew from the concern, including Jonathan Pugmire, a puddling furnace operator; George Wood, a blast furnaceman, and more significantly, George A. Smith.[72]

An interesting article appeared in the *Deseret News* in December 1854. Apparently, the activities in the West and the numerous travelers going to California had been noticed by Washington D. C. and it was decided to appropriate $25,000 for a "Military Road" between Salt Lake City and the California border in the direction of Cajon Pass. The military solicited proposals from responsible parties for the construction of a wagon road that followed a similar path to the one taken by Old Highway 91 many years later. "In short, the object being to improve the southern route as much as possible—to make the very best road that can be made for the sum appropriated." When completed, the road was to be inspected by an officer to be designated by the Secretary of War.[73]

As the new year began, the ironworkers were anxious to try their new furnace. A letter from Elder James Lewis to Elder George A. Smith, written on December 26th and published in part in the *Deseret News*, states it this way: "Great exertions are being made to give the iron ore a trial in a few days, and things in that quarter appear far more prosperous, preparations having been made upon more scientific principles." Charging of the furnace began on New Year's Day. Unfortunately, a variety of startup related issues cropped up during the first run. The two-week long process was recorded in the minute book of the Deseret Iron Works.

Monday, January 1, 1855 [Commenced] charging new furnace at 9 a.m. put on cold, blast, 4 o'clock p.m.

Tues. 2nd cinders up at 9 o'clock p.m. same day. Continued to blow till 4 o'clock a.m.

Wed. 3rd when the wheel froze up. We closed up the furnace and made all air tight to prevent chilling, in this state it remained till 2 o'clock p.m. Same day when water coming down the wheel and blast were put in operation and we continued to blow till Thursday 4th at noon when we tapped and got a casting of iron, hard brittle and white. This morning the pitman or conrod of the cylinder broke and we continued blowing with one cylinder till noon when we put some more metal and cleaned out, then the rod being mended we again put on the blast at 5 o'clock and continued it till 6 a.m.

Friday 5th. When we cast another portion of metal, hard brittle and white. We continued the blast till 11 p.m. when we again cast a portion of similar metal. On the 5th we changed our burden putting 10# more of the magnetic ore and 10# less of the limestone as shown in the table. We continued our blast till 6 p.m. of the **6th Sat**. After this change in our charge the cynder was of a darker color, at this time we had another cast and cleaned out. We stopped about 4 hr. each cast. Early this morning at about 3:00 we had a heavy snow fell which retarded our movements on the inclined plane.

On Sunday the 7th we cast at noon when another pitman broke, stopping till this was fixed and again put on the blast till 6 a.m. **Tues, 9th** before which we had discovered the furnace colder. When we found the metal chilled, commenced shoveling out the whole burden at 9 a.m. This took 9 men 9 hours labor on the **10th**. We took out the bear or salamander of chilled metal. On the **11th** we cleaned out and prepared for repair. The **12th** and **13th** following days occupied cutting rock for hearth walls, etc. and now waiting to get charcoal.[74]

The following table copied from Thomas D. Brown's minutes, lists the charges required for the 720 pounds of iron made in the new furnace between January 2 and January 8.[75]

	No. of Charges	Coke	Char-coal	Utah coke	Utah charcoal	Mag. Ore	Bog Ore	Lime-stone
Jan 2	33	3		99		60	30	20
Jan 3	15	3		45		60	30	20
Jan 4	24	3		72		60	30	20
Jan 5	23	3		69		30	60	20
Jan 6	25	3		75		30	60	20
Jan 7	22	3		66		60	20	30
Jan 8	21	2	80	46–20	16–80	60	20	30

Table 2. Thomas D. Brown's record of furnace charges

While the Noble Furnace was being repaired after the first run, some of the ironworkers decided to make some trial runs in a much smaller furnace. They were still battling with the fuel issue, coke *v.* charcoal, and of course, problems with the lining. The week-long trial went as follows.

Trial Furnace Jan. 19, 1855

Having burdened our trial furnace on the 19th we put on the hot blast. The tuyeries were soon burnt out and this caused the blast to fall back and operate on the lining of the furnace which melted this out also, to the height of the boshes, this lining was composed of fire clay dried sand rick—ground and lean sand all mixed together, which when melted with the burden produced a mixed cynder giving a dark color and feeling much heavier than the cynder usually is. This mixture stood well above the boshes inside the furnace where the hot blast affects were not felt. This casement surrounding the well of the furnace we repaired, lining it with the same materials as above for the cold blast. The produce of the first 8 charges was eaten up. Surely this could not be the sulphur as none was used.

On the **20th** with the cold blast we produced good grey iron but it came in lumps and did not run in a fluid state as usual and was mixed with slag. This cast was about 15 lb. We took this to the smith's fire and worked it into wrought iron rod and nails made from it, on the **21st**.

This trial furnace was then repaired and instead of the sand and clay mixture we made the lining, hearth and boshes of grey sandstone same as in the large furnace, this sandstone much resembles granite but agate and other hard substances are not so abundant in it, it resembles white granite but is softer. We again commenced on the **25th** using the cold blast, result grey iron but much eaten by the sulphur contained in the coke perhaps. On this day we also charged in our burden the charcoal and coke giving more of the former and less of the latter, the result was iron too grey and soft. The product of that on this day when the coke was in greater quantity was eaten up supposed by sulphur.

On the **26 Jan**. 1855 we put equal portions of the charcoal and coke the result on both charges "eaten up" perhaps by sulphur. The last burden as in the preceding table we tried contained a less portion of charcoal and unburnt pine wood in greater portion.

Jan. 27th the heat produced by the latter was so intense that the "cynder" (or slag) was as liquid as the iron should have been from the tapping hole and this intense heat so entirely melted the masses in the burden, the hearth and lining rock that the cynder contained a portion of all these materials and resembled in appearance a ball furnace "cynder" and was composed of iron melted rock etc. In all the burdens there was no "gaubbing up" in cooling of metal in the pots no need to use bars to break out the bears or salamanders. The furnace worked well all the time and the experiments on the trial furnace were carried on by Thos. Bladen, subject to the constant superv. and approval of the mgr. I. C. Haight.

T. D. Brown clk. Pro. Tern.[76]

	Iron Works March 1, 1853		Iron Works April 1, 1853		Iron Works January 1, 1855		Modern Furnace	
	Lbs.	% of Load	Lbs.	% of Load	Lbs.	% of Load	Lbs.	% of Load
Pitch Pine			100	46.5%				
Charcoal	100	12.5%	50	23.3%				
Coke					69	38.5%	2000	28.6%
Bog Ore	200	25.0%	30	14.0%	60	33.5%		
Mag Ore	300	37.5%	25	11.6%	30	16.8%	4000	57.1%
Limestone	200	25.0%	10	4.7%	20	11.2%	1000	14.3%
Total	800	100.0%	215	100.0%	179	100.0%	7000	100.0%

Table 3. Comparison of Furnace Charges

Understanding the Charge

To partially understand the dilemma expressed by T. D. Brown regarding the furnace output, it is helpful to understand an analysis of the furnace charge.

In 1976, York Jones obtained and tested samples of iron ore, slag, sand mold and iron ingot found at the old furnace site in Cedar City and samples of "bog ore" and limestone from old diggings east of the Iron Works site near the base of the Red Hill east of Cedar City.[77] The sample of iron ore assayed at 58.5% iron, 0.016% sulfur, 1.02% phosphorus and 0.014% copper. Furnace specifications of today limit phosphorus to a maximum value of about 0.3%, this sample was more than three times that value. Phosphorus is the only element entering the blast furnace over which the skill of the furnace man has essentially no control. Its compounds are completely reduced, so that all of it remains in the metal. Phosphorus causes brittleness in pig iron and has the effect of reducing the total carbon. The "hard, brittle and white" pig iron produced at the Iron Works was probably a result of high phosphorus and silica in the ore, along with high ash and sulfur in the coke.

The bog ore or limonite ore had the appearance of having high iron content, but its analysis indicated that it contained only 15% Fe_2O_3 with a very high SiO_2 content of 59.7%. The cut-off for iron to be used in a blast furnace today is a minimum of 40% Fe and a maximum of 10% SiO_2. A high lime burden is needed to flux the SiO_2. The very low Fe content in the "clay iron ore" or "bog iron" simply did not produce much metal and the SiO_2 all went to make a high slag volume. The limestone tested was of fair quality having 2.3% SiO_2 and a 50.5% CaO. The slag was found to have 0.4% Fe, 0.07% phosphorus, 0.004% sulfur and 57.5% SiO_2. Normal slag has only about 11% SiO_2 and 16% Fe_3O_4. The sample of the sand mold iron was found to be very good iron, having a carbon content of 0.12%. The furnace pour or ingot sample had a carbon content of 3.73% which is in the range for good carbon steel.

The coke that was used probably produced from coal of the Leyson mine in Right Hand Canyon, in the mountains above Cedar City. Near the mine are some old coke ovens. As the Iron Mission discovered, the coal was unsuitable for the production of good metallurgical coke. A sample taken from the nearby Webster-Nelson mine in 1926 was tested by the U.S. Bureau of Mines. The following chart compares that local coal sample with typical coking coal data from S&P Global Platts.[78]

Iron Mining & Manufacturing

Illustration 2.6. The Community Bell, cast in Salt Lake City by the Public Works Department in 1855 from Iron County iron. The Bell displays the initials "DIC" and date "1855" in the casting on both front and back. The bell is currently on display at the Frontier Homestead State Park in Cedar City. (Photo by Evan Jones)

	Webster Mine	Platts Data
Moisture	6.40%	10%
Volatile Matter	40.70%	20%
Fixed Carbon	41.70%	70%
Sulfur	6.50%	0.5%

The local coal was found to have high volatiles, low fixed carbon and very high sulfur, clearly unsuitable for the production of good metallurgical coke. It is instructive to compare the composition analysis of several Iron Mission test runs made in the 1850s with modern blast furnace charge ratios.[79] Despite the rocky start in January, by springtime of 1855, the prospects began to look up. An April 19, 1855 letter to George A. Smith from J.C.L. Smith told of some success with the new large furnace. The iron works, Smith reported, "are doing a good business. Bro. Haight has started the large furnace; it works well; so say the brethren that have come from there since I came home. They are making as high as seventeen hundred pounds of good iron in twenty-four hours, and prospects are good."[80] The prospects looked brighter and it was time for the Iron Mission to produce something publicly useful. Historian, Leonard J. Arrington described the spring 1855 event.

> In anticipation of Brigham Young's visit to Cedar City in the spring of 1855, every effort was made to institute a successful run at the furnace. In order to keep the furnace burning, a large quantity of sagebrush was piled before the flue. On the first twenty-four-hour run, seventeen hundred pounds of "good iron" were produced. By constant effort, another ten tons were manufactured in April. It was from some of the iron made in this run that the company made the only casting which survives—a bell cast by the church public works department in Salt Lake City. The ringing of this bell called the colonists to church.[81]

Until 1880, the bell was in constant use in Cedar City. Henry Lunt rang it on many occasions: funerals, weddings, dances, theaters, business and church meetings, danger signals, fires, floods and celebrations. The bell was as much a part of the public affairs as the people. The broken and cracked bell was loaned to U.S. Steel in Provo, Utah where it rang the announcement and opening of the Utah Steel Day, June 3, 1924. It was also on display at the State Capitol for some time. Sherman Frazier, carefully mended the crack in the bell in the 1940s.

Eight years after the bell had been made, in May of 1863, Brigham Young and his party made their annual trek through Southern Utah. They stayed in Parowan the night of May 1st and left the next morning and arrived in Cedar City at noon. A meeting was held in the social hall with the residents, who were addressed by Presidents Young and Kimball and Elders Orson Hyde, George A. Smith and Lorenzo Snow. The bell was rung to gather everyone and Lyman O. Littlefield, the scribe, wrote the following description.

> That bell, that bell—that real bell of home manufacture; that bell produced from the ore of these mountains and cast in struggling Cedar City [*sic*]; that bell which was a "real bell," and not a "cracked skillet," did ring; and though its tone was not so loud, shrill, clear and melodious as we have heard; yet it called us to church and we went.[82]

The party traveled on to Kanarraville, Washington and St. George. On the morning of May 11, they left St. George, traveling north past the cinder cones near Veyo and on to Pine Valley where they stayed the night. At sunrise they headed northwest through Grass Valley to Pinto, where they had lunch and had a meeting with the local residents. Their journey continued towards Cedar City.

> Refreshed and delighted with Pinto Valley, we passed rapidly on over the divide into Coal Creek valley, and at three o'clock, p.m., entered Cedar City again, making about forty miles' travel that day. We came in, once more covered with dust, which had been extremely liberal in its deposits.
>
> Here we found all the arrangements complete. Again, THAT bell rang; and, as it is rather a celebrated bell, and its character is bandied about considerably by critics, I thought to examine and enquire for myself. On its outer surface I traced "D. I. C., 1855," which, fully rendered, reads, Deseret Iron Company, cast 1855. I learned that such a company had expended a large amount of labor and means in this place, endeavoring to produce iron from the ore with which exists here in great abundance; that they had toiled years to mature and bring this much-needed material into use; but in consequence of some properties being incorporated with the ore with which they were unacquainted, they finally became discouraged and abandoned the project for the time being, after, however, producing a few castings among which was this bell. There seems to be a little flaw in it which deadens the sound and prevents that clear ringing tone which it would otherwise produce. Still, I am told it has been heard three or four miles. Again, it sounded, and I said, "Ring on; for it bears testimony that iron in great abundance will yet be produced here."[83]

As these accounts reveal, the settlers found it very difficult to find and maintain the factors of production in the proper proportion to make a success of the business. A shortage of help at the Iron Works caused the following announcement to be sent to Salt Lake City:

Parowan, May 14, 1855

One hundred and fifty men are wanted at the Iron Works immediately, in this County, to carry on the Iron Works successfully; those most needed are wagoners, miners, colliers, Laborers, lime burners, joiners, machinists, charcoal burners, and furnace men. Fifty additional teams are necessary to keep the furnace supplied with fuel and ore. The people are in high spirits on the iron subject; the furnace having been kept successfully in operation two weeks satisfied the most skeptical that nothing was wanting, but to continue the charge as the furnace was 'blown out' simply for want of fuel.[84]

On May 27, 1855, President Brigham Young, delivered an address in the Tabernacle, Great Salt Lake City concerning the Iron Works in Iron County. He gave a good description of the hardships and trials of the people, but also of their successes.

Coal and Iron Works

We have visited the Ironworks in Cedar City, Iron County, and as far as I am capable of judging, I will say, that the brethren have done as well as men could possibly do, considering their impoverished circumstances, and the inconveniences they have had to labor under. They have probably progressed better than any other people would upon the face of the earth. They are without sufficient capital to rapidly accomplish so great a work, and many are without suitable clothing, and almost destitute of bedding, and other things necessary to supply the common comforts of life for themselves and families. Although they have been thus destitute, yet in the midst of all that, they have progressed almost equal to men of capital in the older states.

I am not familiarly acquainted with the fluxing or separating the metal from the ore, but those who understand building furnaces and their operations are aware that it is very injurious for a large and expensive furnace to blow out, as they call it, hence policy requires the blast to be continued as long as possible. I have learned, of late, from men of experience in these matters, why it is desirable to continue the heat — it is because no furnace can be heated up for two or three weeks, and then blow out, or stop, without risk of spoiling the furnace, or destroying its lining; and it frequently so injures the furnace that it has to be rebuilt, or at least a portion of it. Hence, when it costs from one to five thousand dollars to prepare a furnace to bear a long blast, it is a great loss to any company to have it blow out in a short time.

Our brethren who have been operating in Iron County, have a very fine furnace, but they are so weak handed as not to be able to continue the blast over fourteen days, and I have learned that they want help. This is the main object of my speaking upon this subject, and my mind inclines in favor of their having it, and I want to see whether the brethren will turn out with their teams and help them. The Church has done much for them, and we are still intending to aid. Our last winter's operations have helped them; the Territory took two shares, and the Trustee in Trust, two; still they are not able to carry on the business profitably. Iron we need, and iron we must have. We cannot well do without it, and have it we must, if we have to send to England for it. We have an abundance of the best quality of iron ore. A trial furnace was made, and kept hot for sixteen days, and produced as good pig metal as can be found in the world; this they puddled and brought forth excellent iron. I believe the castings made from the pigs will be superior to any in the world. I repeat that iron we must have, and we are right on the threshold of obtaining it; we have our feet on the step, and our hand holds the latch of the door that leads to the possession of this invaluable material.

From the time I first went to Iron County until now, I had thought that perhaps the brethren were dilatory—my feelings were tried; I would not say, however, that I had suspicions pertaining to the doings of the Iron Company there; but let that be as it may, it is all right with me now, the iron we must have. From the time I went to Sanpete, and saw the beautiful coal bed, averaging eight feet thick, with its stony strata of nine, five, and three inches, which probably will give out, and learned that iron ore was close by the coal bed, I took into consideration the distance from Cedar City to this place, and the distance from here to Sanpete. When I had weighed all the circumstances, my mind balanced in favor of the works at Cedar City for the present; and if I can get brethren to join me, I will send one or two teams myself, with teamsters. We want fifteen good teams, with men with them who are willing to take hold and quarry out the ore and the coal, and get wood and lime, or anything else that is wanted. Twenty or twenty-five men besides these teamsters are wanted and we wish to send them now, in the fore part of the season. If we will do this, and we can if we have a mind to, I suppose that in two or three weeks after they arrive there, the blast furnace can be kept running for several months, or until they are obliged to stop in consequence of the deficiency of water. There is a large stream of water there, but it is a singular stream, sometimes it will sweep across the flat, carrying down rocks that would weight perhaps twenty or thirty tons, and appear as though it would sweep everything before it; and when the cold weather comes, and you would naturally think that you were going to have water to turn a mill wheel, or to create the blast for the furnace, and every use for which it might be needed, in one freezing night it will perfectly close up, insomuch that there will not be enough to water a horse.

That is a singular feature, but it is the way it operates. The brethren are now making an engine, so that they can continue their blast through the winter. If any are disposed to forward this work I call upon them to lend their aid, to send the men and teams, and we can have the iron.

The distance from here to the Iron Works is about 290 miles. This should not deter us from bringing iron from there, though it could be quicker come at if Iron Works were established at Sanpete, which is not much over 100 miles from here. I have this to say, if any of the brethren feel disposed (as the grasshoppers have taken their crops, and they have not much to do) to go there, I think it would be a good course to pursue.[85]

As Young noted in his address, if the settlers' problems weren't enough, drought and grasshoppers took their toll during the summer of 1855.

The grasshoppers have destroyed all the grain at Paragoonah, nine-tenths at Parowan; all the wheat at Fort Johnson, and about one-tenth of the grain at Cedar City; the grain at Harmony is uninjured.... The fields look like a desert and every separate bench appears to be hatching out fresh crops of grasshoppers. Several companies have started to the Panguitch Lake, on fishing excursions. The water is lower than has ever been known before and but a small portion of the land resown can possibly be watered.... The public square at Parowan city (10 acres) has been planted with potatoes in the hopes that the united efforts of men, women, and children, chickens, ducks, turkeys etc. etc., [to control the grasshoppers] may save a sufficiency to have occasionally a little potato soup next winter.[86]

Illustration 2.7 Painting by R. David Adams in the early 1900s. According to his wife, Adams took his grandfather, David Barclay Adams, a former official of the Iron Works, to this spot in northeast Cedar City and painted this from the description and the ruins that still stood on the bank of Coal Creek at the time. (Matheson Special Collections)

More Work, More Problems

During the remainder of 1855 and into 1856, the problems of the company grew greater and failure threatened the operation. Once again, severe winter conditions cut them off from their coal and stopped the water wheel. However, the casting plant was still able to operate and in February of 1856, and the workers began casting machinery for a steam-powered air blast. When the weather became more moderate, a crop shortage threatened the inhabitants with starvation and left their teams too weak to haul coal. The company persevered and started up their furnace again, but the tuyeres burned out. In July, the labor shortage led Thomas Bladen, the chief machinist, to go to England, "to convert and recruit skilled Iron Workers."[87]

In February 1856, a group of thirty men were diverted from their work at the Iron Works to a deposit of lead ore that missionaries of the Church of Jesus Christ of Latter-day Saints had discovered some thirty miles southwest of Las Vegas, Nevada. Using equipment hauled from Salt Lake City, the men were able to produce about 9,000 pounds of lead, which they made into bullets. Lack of water and feed for their animals and impurities in the ore made production difficult and the effort was abandoned in March 1857. Ironically, the impurity in the ore that plagued the refining process turned out to be silver and several years later, prospectors discovered the silver and developed very rich mines near the location.[88]

By August 1856, the furnace was repaired, but then a drought stopped the water wheel, and in addition there were numerous mechanical breakdowns. Isaac C. Haight, the manager of the works, felt compelled to write Heber C. Kimball that "many have got discouraged in this place and for fear of starving to death, are going to Beaver." He continued, "I am sure that if the people would see their best interests they would unite in this great interest but as yet they think they must spend the summer in raising grain." He stated that he needed more men and about fifty were planning to leave Cedar City in the fall. "I have counseled them continually not to go but to stay here and be united in the great course of building up this place and making iron and not be uneasy and running about."[89]

The following is a letter written by Elder Thomas Bladen July 1856 to President John Taylor from New York City, while on his way to England on the mission to convert and recruit skilled iron workers to come to Utah.

> Pres. John Taylor.
>
> Dear Sir; In passing thru this city on my mission to Europe, I deem it not amiss to give you a few items of information relating to the present and future prospect of the Deseret Iron Works of Cedar City, Iron County, Utah, where I labored in connection with my brethren on a blast furnace, 33 ft. inside measurement 6 ft. 6 in. It has two splendid blowing cylinders 41-1/2 inside diameter and 43-inch stroke working at right angles with each other. This is driven by a master driving wheel. The furnace can be driven by hot or cold blast as the manager may desire. There is an inclining plane and car conveying the ore and fuel from the mine to the tunnel head of the furnace. This car is drawn up by gearing attached to the water wheel and has a self-acting motion. The ore that the iron is produced from, is very rich, yielding about 75% from the blast and is easily procured, being found in large masses on the surface of the earth. Coal is also found on the side of the mountain, which saves labor, and the health of the men. The coal is strong and suitable for all kinds of smith work. It makes a strong coke which carries a heavy burden on the blast furnace and is likewise suitable for the cubalo for the melting of the pit iron. From this it will be seen that the faculty for producing the material are equal to any other place in the world. Many tons of iron have been manufactured into machinery, such as heavy lathes, cranks, wheels, gudgeons, pedestals, and etc. for the use of the companies work to replace the old wooden machinery.
>
> There is an extensive range of building for the work shops where a great number of mechanics are employed in almost every branch of the Iron trade. Other mechanics will shortly be wanted to assist in carrying out the work. The company is fast preparing to supply the rising State of Deseret with everything in the Iron trade she will require from a nail to a steam engine. Brethren who feel an interest in the great work, will do well to arise and assist in rolling on the same, that the Deseret may be independent of the nation for the most valuable of all materials — iron. The bees of the hive of Deseret are at work.
>
> Thomas Bladen – Monday July 12th 1856, Engineer, Deseret Ironworks
> Arrived in Liverpool Aug. 7th, 1856, with the missionaries.[90]

Despite Bladen's optimism, 1856 continued to be a difficult year for the manufacture of iron at the Iron Works. The furnace was tried in June but was met with failure. Under the command of an inexperienced keeper, the blast pipes accidentally burned out. Another run was attempted in July but the iron chilled and the furnace had to be stopped. David B. Adams, the furnace keeper, quit and moved to Beaver County, probably due to the terrible drought.[91] During August, the Iron Works was basically shut down due to lack of water for the water wheel.[92] The Works remained down over the winter of 1856–57.

Finally, a Steam Engine

In March, 1857 Isaac Haight noted in his diary in that he had "Received a letter from Pres. Young that we might have his engine for the Iron Works, for me to send up a company of faithful saints with tithing wheat and get their endowments and bring the engine home. The Directors of the Iron Works thought I had better go up myself and see to bringing it down."[93]

Activity in all areas of the Iron Works continued to slow down, but in April 1857, the steam engine arrived from the abandoned attempt at a sugar-mill outside Salt Lake City and the men worked to set it up. It took several months to install the newly received steam engine but the problem of the creek freezing in the winter or running dry in the summer would be solved. They would no longer need to depend on Coal Creek or the water wheel to supply the power to drive the air blower. In spite of this, the work force continued to drop, and the company struggled along, primarily working on repairs to broken machinery and improvements to the plant.[94]

By July, the engine was working. However, as noted in the following journal entries, getting it going was not without problems. It took two months to erect a building to house the engine works and another month to get the flue working properly. Sand in the feed water coming from the creek caused the engine cylinders to bind up and they had to construct a small reservoir to act as a settling pond to allow the water to clear before being used in the boiler and steam engine. The action can be followed from Isaac C. Haight's 1857 diary.

> **April 6** The engine sent down by Pres. Young arrived in this city 4 P.M. and on the morning of the 9th was taken to the Iron Works, examined and found correct according to invoice, except cold water pump.
> **April 13** Commenced clearing for foundation of engine house, size 32 foot by 18 clear. Two stories high.
> **April 21** Hauling rock.
> **April 27** Laying foundation and pit of engine house, and for the wheel to work in. Engineers busily laying down the timbers for the cylinders to rest upon, and for the wheels to work
> **May 28** Commenced on the adobie work of the engine house, completed it on the 3rd of June.
> **July 8** Started the engine for trial, worked very well and free there not being sufficient draft for the boiler fire, concluded to line the stack.
> **July 13** Preparing furnace, lining and boshes, putting in timp stone [the crown or arch of the opening in front of the hearth] ready for starting.
> **July 18** Tried the engine, after lining the stack, making it less. 20 inches in diameter inside, not sufficient draft yet. Engineer wanted the stack raised 20 feet higher, worked at raising stack to 23 July.
> **July 27** Run a flue inclining about 6 feet from the fire box to the stack, shutting off old flue underground, tried engine again, the draft was great deal increased, and concluded to try the furnace with what blast it would make. Commenced filling with

wood and coke. Charged with 152 lbs. coke, 50 lbs. charcoal, 30 lbs. magnetic ore, 60 lbs. lean ore, and 30 lbs. limestone.

July 28 Put blast on the furnace 11 A.M. worked very well until 11 P.M. when end of the flue in boiler sprung a leak, which caused a stoppage at the same time forged a new [feed] pump, the other being too small to supply the boiler.

July 30 About 6 P.M. put on the blast again, the water being muddy, owing to rain up the canyon. About 5 A.M. of 1st the engine was stopped by the quantity of sand worked in the steam cylinders. It was then thought necessary to build a reservoir for the supply of good clear water for boiler. Made a call upon the brethren and men and teams turned out. It was completed 1st August 8 P.M. with a good puddled bottom of fire clay and gravel. The reservoir is 75 feet long average 25 feet wide. The boiler was filled from the tank, and about 12 A.M. the blast was put to the furnace, about 4 P.M. one of the valves in the blast cylinder broke and was driven down to the bottom of the receiving pipe. Manager Haight first noticed the accident and caused the engine to be stopped to make a new valve. Started again 6 P.M. Break of day next morning tapped and run a little iron. The keepers report it to be better than they ever noticed from so short a run in any country. Furnace worked pretty free all day, towards evening appeared cool and stiffer. Evening 7 P.M. tapped, cinder and iron, very little ran out.

August 3 Furnace in the same state, altered burthen to 200 lbs. coke, 50 magnetic, 50 lean, 50 limestone.

August 4 Furnace working very stiff, tweers dug out several times during the day, very black above tweers, same during the night.

August 13 Furnace works about the same, altered limestone charge to 90 lbs. Tapped 10 A.M. bogus and iron, very little. The furnace not being large enough inside for the amount of blast, the burthen pressed too heavily and came down too quick, concluded to blow out, and take down the lining. 1 P.M. tapped and 4 P.M. during the night turn tapped, 10 P.M. and 5 A.M. A little iron

August 14 Tapped again 10 A.M. and 2 P.M.

August 15 Taking out the bears, some little iron in the bear.

August 17 Commenced taking down the artificial lining.

August 18 Finished taking down lining 2 P.M. and commenced putting in the hearth and lining up to boshes.

August 20 Put fire in to warm up.

August 21 About 6 P.M. commenced filling with wood and coke. Kept doing so all night.

August 22 Charged with the following: 400 lbs. coke, 60 magnetic, 120 lean, 70 limestone.

August 23 1/2 past 9 A.M. put on the blast, during the day worked very hot, cinder fluid and hot from tapping hole, twice during the night the same.

August 24 Altered charges to 400 coke, 80 magnetic, 60 lean, 35 limestone. Tapped 1/2 after and very little iron. Cinder hot and black. Furnace working tolerable free. Afternoon working better. Tapped 3 P.M. little more iron. Altered charge to 400 coke, 60 magnetic, 120 lean, 70 limestone. During the night tapped twice, 9 P.M. and ½ after 3 A.M.

August 25 Very little cinder and bogus. Furnace not working very well; tapped again 1/2 past 9A.M. no difference, tapped again 1/2 after 3 P.M. same kind of stuff. Furnace working very bad 6 P.M. altered charge to 400 coke, 100 magnetic, 60 lean, 90 limestone.

September 5 Furnace working very middling, cinder stiff, tapped several times during the day, little bogus ran out, during the night time about the same quantity of cinder run from the tapping hole, a small quantity of iron of a good quality towards morning. Furnace works more free, and the keepers report will keep improving. All hands labor very hard. About 12 concluded to dig out the congealed stuff in the bottom of the hearth, found it very hard and tough, afterwards concluded to dig out the stuff and start afresh: by 7 P.M. the furnace was clear except the bear in the bottom.

September 6 Got the bear out and put in new hearth and timp rocks, at 7 P.M. put fire in and 20 bank charges of new coke and pine wood. Afterwards charged with the following, 400 lbs. coke, 50 magnetic, 100 lean, and 50 limestone.

September 7 Put on the blast at 3 P.M. Furnace worked very well through the night, and about ½ past 5 A.M. of the 8th tapped ran out cinder and iron about 75 pounds. Altered the limestone charge to 55 lbs. Tapped 11 A.M. more iron and less cinder: no cinder yet run over the plate. 5 P.M. tapped again, same success. 1 A.M. of the 9th same success, little iron clear from cinder. Altered limestone to Creek limestone 60 lbs. charge. Middle day cinder run over dam plate, tapped about 10 A.M. (Bogus). Tapped 7 P.M. same success. Furnace worked during the night as usual. 10 A.M. tapped. Iron very little better. Altered coke charge 450 lbs. 4 P.M. tapped, keepers think improving a little. During the night took the tweers out. Tapped 9 P.M. and 4 A.M. a little iron. Altered limestone to 70 lbs. Casted 11 A.M. more iron than usual. Cinder cold and stiff. Tapped 1/2 after 5 P.M. considerable bogus, reduced the blast 6 P.M. During the night the furnace worked rather cool, tapped, very little iron. 12 P.M. put on full blast. 6 A.M. cinder run more free and worked easier. Tapped 1/2 past 12 not much iron, considerable bogus. 5 o'clock P.M. tapped again, same. Tapped 2 P.M. same. During night furnace worked poorly. Tapped 1 A.M. and 6 A.M. cinder bogus, little iron.

September 26 Altered burthen 400 coke, 100 magnetic, 90 limestone, and 1 box clear cinder. Work cool and stiff at bottom. Tapped 12 A.M. bogus and cinder. Furnace improving. Tapped 9 P.M. and 4 A.M. of 27th very little iron. Tapped again at 11 A.M. cinder and bogus; afternoon furnace is better than has been since commencement; working very well. Tapped 4 P.M. little iron, bogus and cinder, cool iron taken from back of timp.

September 28 Furnace about the same, Tapped at [ ] & 3 p.m. Cinder and bogus with a little Iron. Iron thrown from under Timp. Changed the burthen to 400 lbs. coke, 100 lbs. magnetic ore, 100 lbs. Limestone, 50 lbs. lean ore. Tapped once during the night burn 9 P.M. and 5 A.M. of the 29th. Some very poor iron thrown under the timp. This morning manager I. C. Haight with others started exploring for a different ore for flux. Furnace warm working free. Congested stuff in the Hearth. Keepers obliged to tap pretty high. Result bogus and cinder. 5 P.M. the same. 8 P.M. manager Haight stopped filling (reports from the north warranting us for stopping, troops on our border &c. All hands required to gather up grain & secure it). Tapped twice during the night turn. Iron ran from the tapping hole. 30th Tapped at 11 A.M. Considerable Iron. Also tapped at after 4 P.M. and 11 A.M. Stopped the blast. All out except the bear.[95]

With the new engine, the iron workers were able to work through the summer and winter when low water levels in the creek had previously hampered or stopped the operations. However, as evidenced by the above diary entries, despite their hard work, they were not able to produce much iron, and what iron that was produced was of questionable quality. It appears that they had all but abandoned the use of charcoal in the furnace, instead, using exclusively coke, with the exception of fifty pounds of charcoal being used on July 27. Raw pine wood was used to get the fire going in the coke when starting the furnace. It is also noteworthy that the furnace supervisors continued to use "lean ore" in equal or greater quantities than the high-grade "magnetic ore."

Paradoxically, in his diary and in the Deseret Iron Company minutes of November, Isaac C. Haight clearly stated his misgivings about the materials they were using in the furnace. He said that that he was looking for different ore for flux, meaning the lean ore that they had been using and that the materials that they were using, namely the coal and the lean ore, had a "great portion" of sulfur and it was a "great evil." To their credit, after that time they began using more charcoal, less coke and less lean ore, however, they did not ever completely stop using either material.

In September 1857 the iron workers received a shut-down order for the smelter. "Had received word to suspend all business and take care of the grain as the United States were sending troops into the Territory to oppress the Saints, and force officers upon us contrary to our wishes and the Constitution."[96] Arrington made the following comments concerning the unfortunate incident.

> Partly as the result of the hysteria created by the approach of the army, the Cedar City and Parowan colonists became involved in the Mountain Meadows Massacre, in which more than a hundred men, women, and children from Arkansas were slaughtered. The revulsion and fear of justice or reprisal that followed this despicable atrocity may account for the fact that some of the colonists moved from the county in 1857–1858. It may also explain the spirit of disunity that seems to have prevailed among settlers after the massacre took place. The general manager of the iron company, Isaac Haight, was the person who reputedly gave the order that resulted in the killing.[97]

The Deseret Iron Company held a stockholders meeting on November 16, 1857. Isaac C. Haight presiding and Joshua Arthur secretary, both pro-tem. The secretary read the audit and balance sheet. The president then observed that "those present were pretty well acquainted with what I have done the past season. There have considerable means expended in putting up an engine house and gearing, and our operation is making iron, although with not much success. There has been a little iron made and we have found out one great evil, that has been a deterrent to us all the time, that is the sulfur in the minerals, the lean ore containing a great portion." The members voted to replace Thomas Tennant, the former treasurer, who had died. Isaac C. Haight agreed to accept the position if they wanted him. They thought he would have enough time to do the job, although he also held the position of manager. They voted as follows:

Henry Lunt	1 vote
Christopher Arthur Sr.	4 votes
George Coray	1 vote
James Walker	1 vote
Jonathan Pugmire	2 votes
James Whittaker, administrator for Joseph Chatterley	1 vote
Richard Harrison, administrator for Catherine Chatterley	1 vote
Isaac C. Haight	2 votes

Christopher Arthur was re-elected for another 4-year term as director of the company, and Isaac C. Haight as manager. An expression of confidence in Haight was expressed. Richard Harrison and Henry S. Cook asked to be released as shareholders, which was granted. Haight also asked that George A. Smith be released as a shareholder as he had not paid his assessment and only a part of the interest. This was granted. They did not think it prudent to do anything at the works and the meeting was adjourned until the next annual meeting in 1858.[98]

A New, Smaller Furnace

In March, Brigham Young gave the word to resume operations at the Iron Works. However, it appears that the workers may have been frustrated and tired of working with the larger furnace, the time it took to repair it and the volume of material that it took to operate it, especially as they were dealing with reduced manpower levels. The new furnace was much smaller than the Noble Furnace, as evidenced by the fact that it took less than a month to build and the size of the charge was about 20 percent of that used by the big furnace. The workers also built a casting house and a calcinating kiln. The minutes mention a furnace #2 and a #4, but the #4 appears to have been a mistake in typing or copying somewhere along the line since there were only two furnaces. The workers used more charcoal during the runs but continued to use both coke and lean ore, and for some reason started to add sand as a flux in addition to limestone. Unfortunately, the iron that was produced continued to be rather disappointing in both quality and quantity.

The Isaac C. Haight diary for 1858 reports that work on iron production continued despite the upheavals.

> **March 10** Received a letter from Pres. Young to send a company to explore white mountains to find a place for the Saints to hide from the gentiles.
>
> **March 12** Received a letter from Pres. Young to go ahead with the Iron Works.
>
> **April 14** Mr. [William H.] Dame arrived having orders from Pres. Young to raise another company to go west to explore for a place to hide up from the face of our enemies. Called upon me to raise fifteen men from the expedition. I called a meeting for the purpose and raised the "requisite" number of men and animals. We are building a new furnace.[99]

During the same period, the minutes of the Deseret Iron Company show that work continued on new buildings:

> **March 30, 1858**. Commenced digging for a foundation for a new blast furnace of small dimensions.
>
> **April 12**. Completed laying the foundation.
>
> **April 24**. Furnace #4 completed.
>
> **April 28**. Began a calcinating kiln on one of the old lime kilns for calcinating ore. Completed May 4.
>
> **June 1**. Built a casting house, 13 x 20 feet by sinking posts and nailing boards on them. Filled the furnace in the afternoon with 45 bushels of charcoal and brands.
>
> **June 2**. 11 A.M. Put the first charge as follows: 80 lbs. Charcoal, 25 lbs. Magnetic ore, 25 lbs. grey sandstone for flux.
>
> **June 3**. Put on the blast. After 1/2 of 10 A.M. to work two tweers. It was afterward thought advisable to take out one tweer as they blowed opposite each other and the bottom of the Bosh so narrow. 2 P.M. took out 1 tweer. Furnace working cool. Took

off 5 lbs. mine and 5 lbs. sand to a charge and put on 4 blank charges. Toward evening working warmer which continued during the night.

June 4th. 1 A.M. altered the charge of sand back to 25 lbs. which it is supposed caused the furnace to work stiff and cool above the tweers, also black. Put on 4 blank charges and changed the burthen to 20 lbs. ore and 10 lbs. of sand. Tapped at 11 A.M. No Iron ran. 1/2 after 4 P.M. put on 5 lbs. sand and added 10 lbs. limestone. At 6 P.M. put on 60 lbs. coke and 75 lbs. charcoal. Worked free during the night. Cinder ran over the notch of a dark color. Tapped twice during the night. A little Iron both times.

June 5th. Altered the fuel charge to: 1 basket of wood, 50 lbs. coke, 50 lbs. of charcoal. Worked stiff during the day. At 4 P.M. softened the blast. Working about the same during the night.

June 6th 6 A.M. altered the mine charge to 20 lbs. Mag., 25 limestone and took off the sand, (the tweers has kept bright from the second day). Tapped twice during the day. No iron ran, but considerable in the crucible (or hearth) which is very stiff and cool. No cinder ran today and working very stiff during the night, and at 6 A.M. put on 13 lbs. lean ore and took off 25 lbs of charcoal.

June 7th. Working free. Put on 2 tarers [?] with 2 inch Naurrles [?] before blowing through 1 ½ inch) to soften the blast & put on Mag ore without being calcined, it being Bro. Turley's opinion that the Mag ore (volcanic) was lifeless enough without calcining & that the calcining was to put in the carbon and should be calcined in an air tight charcoal pit. Tapped at 7 A.M. No Iron. A little cinder of a black color running over the notch, very brittle. Changed the burthen to 3 baskets of wood & 1 of coke, all the charcoal used up. At 1/2 after A.M. Tapped again during the night which brought forth Iron of a greyish color. At day break of the 8th commenced blowing out for want of fuel. . .

From the June 8 to September 15 the time was spent building and sinking Fire (or charcoal fire) a flue with adobie pipes to melt down scrap into slugs, building adobie blast pipes for blast furnace and gathering fuel &c. Together for another trial on Blast furnace #2.

September 15th. Commenced filling the furnace (No 2) with 8 baskets of pine wood and 56 baskets of coke.

September 16th. Filling up the furnace as she burns down with blank charges. At 1/2 6 P.M. put on the following charge: 60 lbs. charcoal, 2 baskets pine wood, 20 lbs. raw lean ore, 20 lbs. of 1imestone.

September 17th. The timpstone being cracked, it was thought prudent to put in a new Timp. which was done and at 2 P.M. charged with 10 lbs. raw Mag ore in addition to the lean ore and limestone. Blast regular and smooth passing through the new adobie pipes. Tapped at 12 P.M. of the 17th and 5 A.M. the 18th. Nothing but cinder run out & that of a dark color. Put on 5 lbs. more Mag and tapped at 12 A.M. Since the charge of burthen has come down the furnace works cold & cinder is very stiff. 2 P.M. altered the charge back to 10 lbs. Mag and put on 5 lbs. more lean. Tapped at 4 P.M. All cinder comes out conglomerated. Seems to be no separation working inside. Worked cool and stiff & scaffaled above the tweers during the night turn.

September 19th. Altered the burden to 20 lbs. lean ore, 20 lbs. limestone & 10 lbs. mag the lean ore calcined also Mag. Furnace working much easier. At 12 A.M. Tapped. A small streak of Iron with cinder ran out. Put on 3 lbs. more limestone at 6 P.M. During the night turn the furnace worked free. Tapped twice. A little white

Iron came out both times. Furnace cool at the back and bottom & filling up on the hearth with a mixture of Iron, Cinder & c.

September 20th. Furnace working free. Put on 5 lbs. more lime. Tapped at 5 P.M. White Iron and cinder. The blast comes from the cylinders through a wood pipe to the ground then passes through a serf of 13 inches square to the furnace & is regulated on the top of the Iron elbow pipe by a large wooden tap at each tweer. In the night turn of the 20th the hearth filled with a hard, cool mixture of iron under and setting under the tweers.

September 21st. 8 A.M. Tapped. A little Iron ran out. Put on a softer blast and took off 1 basket of wood and put on 66 lbs. of stone coal. Also took off 5 lbs. of limestone. Charges are at the present: 2 baskets of charcoal, 1 basket of wood, 66 lbs. of stone coal, 20 lbs. of lean ore, 20 lbs. of 1imestone, 10 lbs. of magnetic ore. During the forenoon worked very well & seemed good. Tapped in the evening. A little Iron ran & dig out a piece of cool, stiff Iron from under the Timp. Put on 5 lbs more limestone.

September 22nd. Worked about the same as yesterday and dug Iron from under the Timp.

September 23rd. Put on two blank charges & afterward the charge as follows: 2 baskets of wood, 2 of charcoal, 16 lbs. limestone, 16 lbs. lean and 8 lbs. mag. No change. 10 P.M. tapped. No iron ran out but dug several pieces from under the Timp.

September 24th. Altered the charge to: 20 lbs. limestone, 15 lbs. lean ore, 5 lbs. mag ore. Afterwards took off 5 lbs. limestone. Tapped three times today and also at night. Nothing but cinders ran out. The hearth full up to the tweers of cool stiff of Iron & cinders. Lining above and about tweers burnt out. 10 A.M. commenced to blow out & by day break of the 25th all was still. From the 25th of September to the 6th of October we have been busily engaged taking out the bear out of the hearth, repairing furnace, building up the opening at the filling place of tunnel head making the furnace 6 feet deeper & built a new tunnel head.

October 6. Commenced to fill the furnace with coke and charcoal.

October 7th. Put on 15 lbs. limestone for 5 charges and put on 11 charges with 15 of limestone and 15 of lean ore.

October 9th. 1/2 after 8 A.M. put on blast & charged with 2 baskets or 50 lbs. of charcoal, 1 basket of wood, 50 lbs. of stone coke, 15 lbs. lime, 25 lean ore, & 5 lbs. mag ore. Furnace loose all day.

October 10th. Tapped. Nothing but cinder. Altered the burthen to 20 lbs. lean ore and 5 lbs. mag ore. The furnace is not working so free. Cinder stiff. Tapped three times. A very small piece of Iron ran out. 6 P.M. Altered the charge to 10 Mag, 10 limestone, 20 lean ore. Changed the limestone from mountain limestone to creek. What iron has run is white and hard. Altogether about 5 lbs. this trial.

October 11th. Furnace working cool. Commencing to settle on the bottom of Hearth. Engine working slow, making a very poor blast. 4 P.M. put on 5 lbs more limestone. Blast better. Furnace warmer & looser on the bottom. 10 P.M. Tapped. A little Iron ran Fluid.

October12th. 6 A.M. Furnace cool. Cinder stiff. Hearth filling up in the bottom. Needs sledging. Much better towards noon. Tapped at 12 A.M. and 6 P.M. Very little Iron ran out. 10 P.M. Furnace loose and warm & clear at the bottom of the hearth. Tapped. Cinder more fluid & a little iron ran out.

October 13th. Tapped at 2 A.M. & 6 A.M. A small portion of iron each time. 6 A.M. Altered the charge of fuel to 100 lbs. charcoal and 45 lbs. wood. Tapped at 1 P.M. and 6 P.M. Iron fluid at 1 P.M. Not much Iron at 6 P.M. Cinder raising and warm. Furnace free and loose. Tapped at 10 P.M. 45 lbs. of light grey Iron ran out. Tapped at 2 A.M. No iron. Again at 6 A.M. About 10 lbs. of Iron ran out. Put on 2 new clay tweers at 7 A.M. & sledged out some pieces weighing 102 lbs. Also tapped at 1 P.M., 6 and 9 P.M. Iron each time ran out. Furnace is now working pretty well. A flame is perceived issuing out between the joints in the back of the furnace. Supposed that the lining has given way. Tapped several times during the night. Considerable Iron ran out.

October 15th. Tapped often. Iron each time. 7 P.M. A heavy slip came down. Was obliged to dig out both tweers & make a passage there from tweer to tweer. Looks black. Stopped 1-1/2 hours & put on the blast 1/2 after 8 P.M. & after seeing that the lining had given way & the furnace getting cold, it was thought advisable to blow off, which was accordingly done.[100]

The Iron Works Shuts Down

On October 8, 1858 Brigham Young once again ordered Isaac Haight to close down the Iron Works, this time permanently. Brigham Young's letter follows:

> We think it would be well to abandon the idea of making Iron for the present and let all the brethren; pursue those avocations which they please. Put everything in as good a condition for preservation as possible, and let it rest. Such fruitless exertions to make Iron seems to be exhausting not only the patience, but the vital energies, and power of the settlement. Hence, we consider it best for the present, at least to suspend further operations, in such useless endeavors to produce that important article.
>
> If, however you succeed in your present attempt, which I understand you are now making in producing iron from the ore (which I must confess is hardly a supposable case) of course it would materially alter the case, and I should be very agreeably disappointed and wish you to go ahead with the works. Brigham Young.[101]

Young's letter expressed a realistic assessment of the status of the Iron Works and was a substantial departure from his previous determination and optimism. The happenings of 1857 and 1858 had to have influenced this disheartening decision: the government troops in the area, the mountain meadow massacre, the departure of many of the County residents, not to mention the repeatedly disappointing results of the Iron Works.

The annual meeting of Deseret Iron Company shareholders was held in the Company storehouse. Erastus Snow and Franklin D. Richards were reelected as President and Secretary of the company. Isaac C. Haight's term was up. Elias Morris was elected to the position for a 4-year term. The voting results were as follows:

Elias Morris	1 vote	George Wood	1 vote
Henry Lunt	1 vote	Joseph Walker	1 vote
Chris. Arthur Sr	4 votes	Isaac C. Haight	2 votes
Chris. Jones Arthur	1 vote	George Coray	1 vote

The auditor's report and balance sheet were read. Haight then remarked: "I believe the brethren here were mostly acquainted with our operations on the Ironworks this year.

The great difficulty was in getting material to stand the fire heat and our last trial was pretty successful until the lining gave way and the iron of a fair quality." The meeting was then opened to the brethren. Commodore Perry Listen said he and a few others had taken shares in the Deseret Iron Company expecting to pay from the sale of property which did not materialize and asked to be released from the obligation. This request was approved, providing the interest was paid. An inventory was to be made of all the pattern & tools etc. of the company and gathered up. The buildings were to be closed and placed under the supervision of the Trustees. The books of the company were to remain open for one month to make individual settlements and the Deseret Iron Company was closed until the next annual meeting of the Stockholders in November 1859.[102] Arrington notes that "When the books were closed on October 31, 1858, the company still owed more than $37,000 in accounts payable, not counting the thousands of days of unreimbursed labor."[103] In the final analysis, around $150,000 had been invested in the Iron Works, producing only about 25 tons of pig iron.

> Within five months of the closure, the population of Cedar City dropped by two-thirds. Those with means left. Those who had given their wagon wheels to the Iron Works remained behind. Iron workers had little to show for their labor. What little pay they received had been in goods from the company store.[104]

The following year of 1859 was turbulent, and, for many settlers, frightening. Reports such as this entry in the Isaac C. Haight diary show the panic which spread through the saints:

> **April 29, 1859** A messenger came to us and said Judge Cardlebough and 200 U.S. Troops were at Beaver coming south with the intention of taking me and some of the brethren and hanging us without a trial for a supposed crime. Taking the law into their own hands in violation of the Constitution of the U.S.[105]

The minutes of the Deseret Iron Company report that "A few of the shareholders appeared." Because there were so few stockholders present, Haight suggested that they adjourn until November 28.[106] There were no other minutes entered in the book.

Aftermath

After the blast furnace at the Iron Works was shut down, a few individuals stepped in with small foundries which melted scrap iron that was then cast or forged into various shapes. Charles Simkins and Jonathan Walker were two such individuals. These men operated a small foundry on or near the site of the old Iron Works and made castings for several threshing machines and sugar mills, plus a number of other useful articles such as skillets, flat-irons, etc.[107]

In 1861, seven wagon loads of cannon balls, left behind by federal troops, were hauled to Cedar City, melted down by Walker and John P. Jones and made into needed items.[108]

Erastus Snow took much of the Deseret Iron Company's removable assets, including machinery, to the new colony at St. George, however many of the smaller items were auctioned off to local citizens on December 19, 1861. Transactions continued through May 16, 1867 when the Deseret Iron Company journal was closed.[109]

> Almost ten years of labor had resulted in nothing more than a few andirons, kitchen utensils, flatirons, wagon wheels, molasses rolls, and machine castings. These were

presumably given to officers and workers of the iron company or to church officials in Salt Lake City. The only reward of the great majority of the iron missionaries was that they had served an honorable mission, at the request of leaders of the church, to help build the Kingdom. "I was constantly busy for the people both night and day and worked for nothing," wrote one colonist, "I never received one cent, neither from tithing, donation, or gift." In terms of [what] they could have earned in areas of better opportunity, the iron missionaries must have sacrificed more than the equivalent of a million dollars. At any rate, the Deseret Iron Company expended an estimated $150,000 without producing a commercial supply of good malleable iron.[110]

Many were called, but few went, throwing the burden on the shoulders of a few who stayed as long as they could. An account published in the *Deseret News* described the remains of the Iron County Mission as they appeared in October 1865.

This morning we visited the locality where some years ago much labor and means were expended toward making iron. The Iron Works were located a little north of the present city, and around them are scattered the debris of the furnace, and scores of tons of iron ore, with portions of patterns, massive castings, pieces of framework, cast and wrought iron bolts, pieces of machinery, the remnants of a steam engine, a massive grind stone (possibly a flywheel) hurled from its former position, parts of a large cast iron lathe, etc., etc. The engine house has been overflowed and we did not learn what articles lie covered with mud and wash. There is much property which is exposed to the wasting influence of the elements which seemingly might be applied to some useful purpose.[111]

Summary

Several factors hampered the Iron County Mission and caused it to be less successful than it otherwise might have been. Some of the causes were obvious at the time, others surfaced only with the insight gained by the passing of time and in some cases, with the use of modern technology.

Location Colonizing a remote location with a group of people with very limited resources in an isolated wilderness, 250 miles from civilization and then expecting them to accomplish a major task was a daunting challenge. The Iron Missionaries were sent to Southern Utah with not much more than the things that they could carry. There were accounts of individuals not having adequate resources to even buy a pair of shoes or boots to wear. Virtually everything that was constructed had to be made on site, usually by hand. Just getting to a point where the community was more or less self-supporting was a substantial undertaking. Homes needed to be built, fields cleared, plowed and planted, ditches dug, roads built, timber cut, rock quarried, all by people struggling to find or create food and shelter for themselves and their livestock. The desert was unforgiving and erratic, with floods, drought, grasshoppers, freezing in the winter and heat in the summer. In the summers of 1855 and 1856, drought and grasshopper infestations were so dire that the little community found it a struggle just to survive.

Iron technology Iron smelting was a complex process requiring individuals with knowledge and experience. For the most part the leaders of the Saints were able to find those types of individuals, but because these men received their training in the British Isles and elsewhere, they were unfamiliar with the ores and other raw materials available in Southern Utah. Without the benefit of modern chemical analysis, the ironworkers faced challenges of which they were not even aware. When the results of their work were not what they expected, they could only guess at the reasons behind the unexpected results. The Three Peaks ore deposit from which they chose to procure their iron ore, although it was the closest to the Iron Works and had a high iron content, had three times the amount of phosphorus needed to make good pig iron. The "bog ore" that they continually used in their furnace was only 15% iron and 60% silica, not much better than ordinary dirt, especially compared with the high-grade magnetite that approached 70% iron in some samples. The coal that they mined in Cedar Canyon had five to ten times the amount of sulfur, twice the amount of ash, twice the amount of moisture and a fixed carbon value that was half of what was required to be to make good coking coal. By modern standards, the very best coking coal in the State of Utah is considered only marginal for making metallurgical grade coke. Using that criterion, Iron County coal would be off the charts, in the wrong direction. Not only was local coal not suitable for iron-making, huge amounts of time, effort and expense had to be spent finding, building roads and developing mines to procure coal. These efforts diverted valuable resources from the Iron Works that could have been better utilized elsewhere to aid in the success of the project.

Substandard components kept the ironworkers continually guessing at the proper mix to make good quality pig iron, making trial after trial in hopes that things would somehow turn out right. Unfortunately for the dedicated workers, there was little chance of obtaining the perfect mix with the materials they were using. They went back and forth between using coal, coke, wood and charcoal. They kept thinking that their bog ore was helpful when its composition suggests that it probably wasn't. The ratio of the input materials remained a mystery to the very end. They did come close at times when they used charcoal instead of coal. A few years later, when settlers endeavored once again to manufacture iron at the Little Pinto Creek site, they used iron ore from a different deposit that had lower phosphorus, charcoal instead of coal and no "bog ore" and were able to regularly produce a superior product.

Construction materials   There were problems with the construction materials used to make and line the furnace. Next to the issues of the chemical composition of the raw materials, the poor quality of the fire brick and stone was probably the second biggest issue the iron workers faced in producing good iron. The entire interior of the furnace had to be lined with special refractory materials that needed to withstand the high temperatures required to melt the ore and limestone. Most of the material available in the local area did not make durable fire brick. The workers experimented with a number of substances, but none would fully withstand the heat needed to melt the iron ore. The bricks would bubble, melt, crack, spall, collapse, or even explode as the temperature rose. Even if the lining was of adequate quality to withstand the heat at first, when subjected to continuous operation over a few days or weeks, the lining would fail. When the brick or stone of the lining failed and collapsed, the furnace would have to be allowed to cool, the debris would have to be removed, many times including a solidified mass of iron and cinder at the bottom that needed to be broken up and removed. The lining would then have to be rebuilt. Other times, since manpower was limited, there would be only enough supplies to run the furnace for a few days or weeks and then the furnace operation had to be shut down and the lining would crack and fail as it cooled. Even in modern days, whenever a furnace cools off, extreme care must be taken to prevent the lining from cracking and deteriorating. This was a continual problem. The ironworkers spent countless hours and days making bricks or hewing blocks of stone to replace the failed lining. Other components of the furnace were also subject to failure because of poor quality or repeated heating and cooling. Cracks in the lining or structure would allow heat, gases and even slag to escape, compromising the efficiency of the operation. In addition, it has also been suggested that soil in the area may not have been able to support the 640-ton weight of the Noble Furnace. If the furnace was subject to settling, this would have caused additional cracking in the structure.[112]

Coal Creek As a water source, Coal Creek was both a blessing and a curse. The Iron Works needed to be located close enough to the creek so that it could be used to turn the water wheel to power the blower for the blast furnace. However, when the creek flooded each summer as it was wont to do, it would do tremendous damage, washing out structures, carrying off supplies, depositing mud and debris and inundating the area. In July 1852, the dams that were in the creek were entirely swept away and an immense quantity of wood drifted up the mouth of the ditches. In September of 1853 a flood swept away the bridges and the dams and carried huge boulders downstream. The site of the Iron Works was inundated with three feet of water, causing great damage and carrying off valuable supplies. The Iron Works would not have been the only thing impacted by the creek flooding. The ditches and fields would have been covered with debris, rocks, sand and red clay, fouling the irrigation system and smothering the crops.

The creek was very undependable. The low flows in the summer after the spring runoff reduced the capacity of the waterwheel. This impacted the smelting operation and also the crops. In the harsh desert environment, the only real source of water for the fields was the creek. Rain falling directly on the ground was good but was even less dependable than the creek. Many times, when the plants needed the water the most, it was the scarcest. In these times water, if it was available, had to be diverted from the smelter for use in the fields. In the winter the creek would freeze, and the flow would be reduced to a trickle or stop completely. Other times it would freeze and lock up the water wheel in ice. The situation in Parowan was not much better as Coal Creek and Center Creek had similar problems. The steam engine that was added in 1857 alleviated some of the problems caused by the fluctuating creek flow but its arrival was almost too late.

External Forces One would think that being so far from civilization that the Iron colony would have been fairly immune to external forces and political issues, but this was not the case. The first issue was with local Indians. Most of the time the relationship was a peaceful one but at times it escalated and, in any event, there was enough unrest in the rest of the Territory that it was deemed necessary to spend substantial time and energy building fortifications. They built a fort in Parowan and several forts in Cedar City. Many times, they were forced to post armed guards around the clock to ensure the safety of the inhabitants and livestock. Outright attacks were rare, but the Indians saw the settlers' cattle as a communal source of food. The Walker Indian War in 1853 caused a considerable disruption to the operation of the Iron Works when the operation was shut down and resources were diverted to building forts instead of making iron. The settlers were even ordered to relocate all of their cattle to Salt Lake in order to protect them from the Indians.

The Indians were not the only disruptors. In 1857-58, the United States government sent an army into the Territory which threatened the entire State. Brigham Young declared martial law throughout the Territory. The Iron County militia was placed on special alert to guard the southern flank of the region. The work of making iron was shut down for a period of time until the perceived threat was over. Men were sent out to look for refuge areas and even alternative living locations. In September 1857, in the midst of the conflict with the U.S. government, many of the local militiamen were involved in the infamous Mountain Meadows Massacre. It was a horrible event and it negatively impacted the entire settlement. Many ironworkers moved away; others withdrew emotionally. Trust and confidence in the leadership was fractured and tarnished.

Organization Another vexing problem was organization. To be successful everyone needed to work together and this is not an easy thing to accomplish in any organization, let alone one with such minimal resources. Almost from the beginning, there were two communities instead of one, Parowan and Cedar City. The settlers also labored under two separate and often conflicting objectives: 1) building up the community, including growing food and building houses and 2) manufacturing iron. There were times when the farmers had food and the ironworkers did not. Many times, in part due to the overwhelming circumstances, there was a shortage of manpower. It was difficult to get new recruits and not easy to convince them to stay once they got there. Many left the area to settle in places where the environment appeared more hospitable. There were a number of individuals and families who became disenchanted with the numerous personal sacrifices and challenges associated with conquering the wilderness and making iron from scratch. Often, they left contrary to the advice given by their leaders. Some returned to Salt Lake, others went to other settlements or moved on to California where the grass was perceived to be greener.

There were a fair number of disputes among members of the community and even between leaders, which took time and effort away from the Iron Works and had to be addressed by the local leaders. Thankfully, things worked out most of the time, but some problems had the habit of reoccurring, and it was a disruption to the business every time they happened. Some of the members of the group, particularly the leaders, had multiple demanding roles in the community. Isaac C. Haight, for example, was simultaneously general manager of the of the Deseret Iron Company, Cedar City Stake President of the Church of Jesus Christ of Latter-day Saints, mayor of Cedar City, major of the militia, local postmaster, and representative to the Territorial Legislature. Apostle George A. Smith was the first leader of the Iron County Mission when it traveled to Iron County. The Iron Works operation was deprived of his leadership when he was called elsewhere on a proselyting mission. Not counting the move from Parowan, the town was also relocated to three different sites, requiring substantial effort each time.

Lack of capital Lack of direct investment and downright poverty was always an issue. Building something as sizable and demanding as an iron manufacturing enterprise and associated facilities from scratch with limited funds and minimal resources was a herculean task for the little community, especially considering the fact that they had to build the community and grow their own food at the same time. The Deseret Iron Company was formed specifically to provide financing for the project, however, it was not enough, and stock subscriptions were never completely paid. Cash flow was always a problem. Community members were allowed to pay their taxes by working at or on projects related to the Iron Works, which turned out to be very helpful. Church tithing donations were often collected in the form of farm produce and were sometimes used to help iron workers. In the end, the iron workers sacrificed a great deal to keep working on the project. Some of the time, the workers were paid for the time that they worked at the Iron Works but much of the time, because of lack of financing, they were paid nothing, and yet they kept working.

The question has been asked many times over and continues to be asked, was the Iron Mission a success or was it a failure? There is no debate as to the commitment and sacrifice of those involved in the endeavor, but with respect to the objective of being able to supply the Territory with enough iron to meet its needs, it was a failure. However, despite the surcharge of challenges, problems and repeated failures, the community managed to build several respectable blast furnaces in the middle of a wilderness, smelted and produced a noteworthy amount of good iron and made a number of useful implements. With regard to its other, but no less important purposes, it was clearly a success. Permanent settlements were established in Southern Utah to guard the southern border of the Territory. Many of the descendants of the early settlers still live in the Parowan-Cedar City area. The successes and failures of the first iron manufacturing effort prepared the way for the next endeavor to manufacture iron. And finally, on a more personal level, the integrity and religious commitment of the men and women involved in this undertaking and the trials and sacrifices that they faced and overcame is a testament to the type of people they were, putting aside their personal interests in favor of the common good. The generations that followed were able to build upon the foundation established by this stalwart group of pioneers, allowing them to make strides and improvements that otherwise would have been impossible.

On October 19, 1950, Benjamin Fairless of the United States Steel Corporation made the following comments before the annual meeting of the California Manufacturers Association, San Francisco.

> The Mormons had courage, and vision and muscle and brains, but it took more than that to make steel for the West. It took modern tools, huge machines, giant furnaces and millions of dollars.... And it took seventy years to create on the Pacific Coast, a company that was big enough to bring the iron ore of Utah and the steel mills of California together into one integrated operation.[113]

Iron Mining & Manufacturing

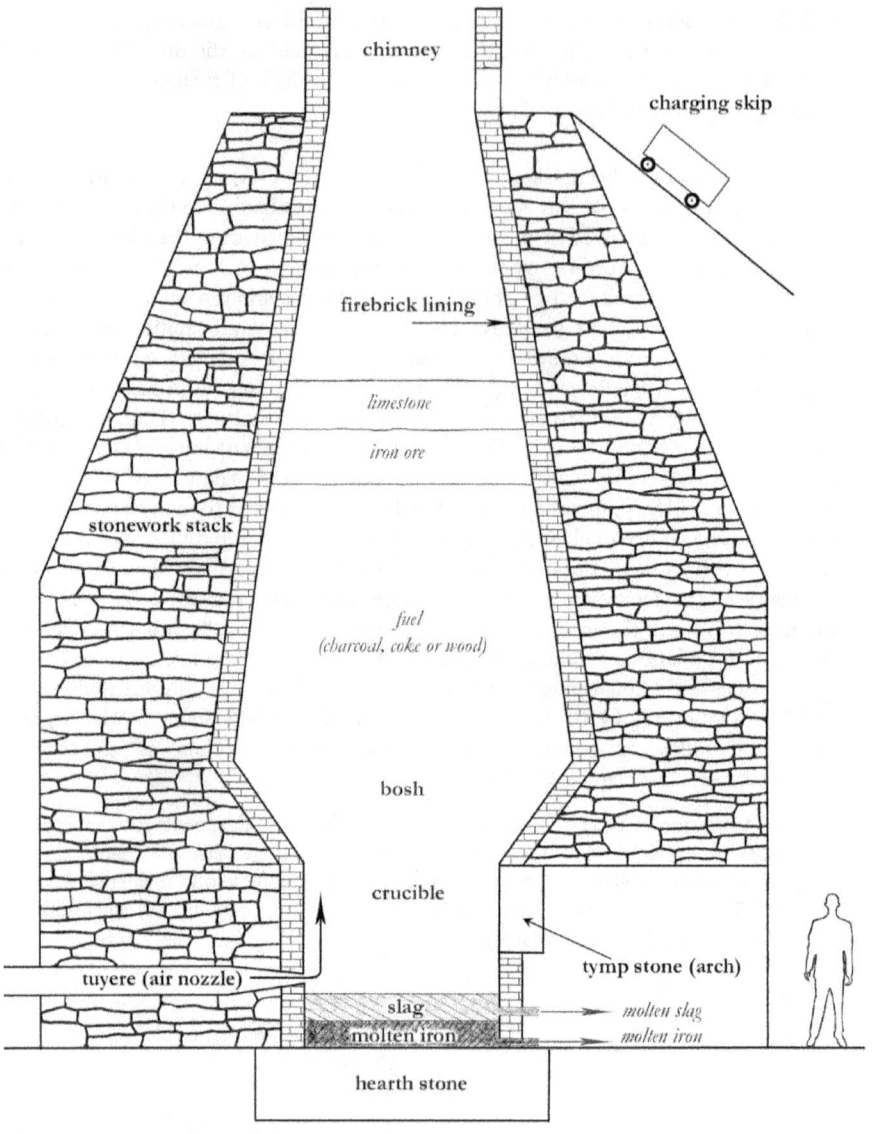

Illustration 2.8. Cross-section of a typical blast furnace something like the structure the Iron Mission would have constructed and operated. With the charge loaded in layers, as shown near the top, the furnace would have been lit and the temperature raised by air blown in through the tuyere. As heat consumed the fuel, the molten metal settled to pool at the bottom, as shown. (Evan Jones and Richard Saunders)

CHAPTER THREE

Iron City Iron Works
The Second Attempt, 1868–1885

THE LAST IRON associated with the Iron County Mission smelted in Cedar City was created in the small trial blast furnace on October 15, 1858, when the fire was allowed to go out after the lining gave way and collapsed. For the next ten years iron smelting activity in the area took a rest. There were small foundries and forges that utilized scrap iron to make useful implements, like melting down the cannon balls left by federal troops, but no one had the furnaces or the facilities to convert raw iron ore into metal in any appreciable quantity.

In 1868, a group of individuals formed a new company to make another attempt at manufacturing iron. Over the next nine years, the company organized four different times under four different names, but it retained many of its founders. It was eventually successful in making a substantial quantity of high quality pig iron. The concern later added a foundry, machine shop, pattern shop, blacksmith shop and several other facilities which enabled it to convert the pig iron produced by the blast furnace into useful products. It regularly shipped its products to locations in Utah and Nevada. The company built a workable blast furnace, tore it down and built a second one in its place and was seriously contemplating replacing it and building a third. Unfortunately, despite its success, it had difficulties remaining solvent. There were several reasons for the company's financial difficulties, including the high cost of operation and transportation, the small size of the furnace, the widespread money panic of 1974 and changes in management and related issues. In 1877, the operation shut down.

The company's failure disappointed the leadership of the Church of Jesus Christ of Latter-day Saints, which was very interested in supporting home industry both to aid in the economic independence of the Territory and to provide meaningful jobs for its residents and immigrants. Four years later, in 1881, with the encouragement of the church-established Trade Committee, a new company was formed, the fifth to be organized to manufacture iron at the Iron City location. For several reasons, it had difficulties getting off the ground and the company reorganized two years later in July 1883 with George Q. Cannon, an apostle of the church, as its president. Its founders were determined to learn from their predecessors and manage the problems that had compromised their success. The company planned to have several furnaces, appreciably larger in size than any of the previous furnaces. The company even planned to have a railroad to haul raw materials. Unfortunately, the endeavor was beset by a number of problems both internal and external, and it seems that their plans were bigger than they had the ability to implement. Even the first furnace was never completed and only its foundation was constructed. The railroad was purchased, but not all of its parts made it to Iron City. The company had difficulties raising cash and dissolved in April 1885. The external issues worsened with time and iron ore was not to be smelted again in Utah for forty-five years.

The Union Iron Company

On June 12, 1868, a group of prominent local citizens formed a company for the purpose of manufacturing iron from the extensive iron ore deposits found in Iron County. The company was named the Union Iron Company. Ebenezer Hanks was President and Peter Shirts, Robert Richie and Seth M. Blair were Directors, with Chapman Duncan as Agent.[1]

This time, unlike their forerunners who built their manufacturing facilities right in the town of Cedar City, adjacent to Coal Creek, the company selected a location close to the iron deposits on Little Pinto Creek, twenty-five miles southwest of Cedar City. It was at the extreme southwestern boundary of the mining district, on the southern edge of Iron Mountain about three miles southwest of what later became known as the Duncan ore body. The Cedar City operation utilized a water wheel to power its furnace air blower for most of its life and only replaced it with a steam engine near the end of the operation. In the beginning the new company owners planned to use a creek-powered water wheel. However, by the time they were ready to go into full operation some two and a half years later, a steam engine had been purchased so that they were not constrained to depend on the creek. Compared to the ore used at Cedar City, the operation had access to several nearby ore bodies with improved ore quality.[2]

As time went on, the Company laid out a town site and a town grew up in the area by the name of "Iron City." By 1870, Iron City had a population of ninety-one people. Years after the works had shut down the location was renamed and became known as "Old Iron Town."

By August 1868, the Company was busily collecting materials and starting on the construction of the various facilities that would be required to manufacture iron. It was "hauling lumber and rock, making bricks, and attending to other necessary preparations." After working for a month or more, trying to find refractory material to line the furnace that would withstand the heat, they were finally successful and began to move forward with the task of erecting the blast furnace. The location was close to several outcropping ore bodies and there was an abundance of good wood, limestone and other necessary materials in the area. The company regularly communicated with leaders of the Church of Jesus Christ of Latter-day Saints. In July 1868, a letter was sent by Chapman Duncan to Elder George A. Smith that was summarized in an August article in the *Deseret News*. Smith at the time was first counselor to President Brigham Young of the Church, an important figure and ideally placed to give the company help if the Church opted to do so.[3]

The company was also anxious to get help from the Territorial government and it appears that they enjoyed some success. On February 13, 1869, Ebenezer Hanks presented a petition to the Territorial Legislature requesting exemption from taxation.[4] Four days later, a resolution was approved by the Legislature exempting the furnaces and other machinery of the Union Iron Company from Territorial and County taxes.

Resolution Exempting Certain Iron Works from Taxation.

Be it resolved by the Governor and Legislative Assembly of the Territory of Utah: That in consideration of the commendable efforts of the Union Iron Company to manufacture iron near the southern boundary of Iron County, in this Territory, that the furnaces and other machinery of said Company (used for said purposes) be, and the same are, hereby exempted from Territorial and County taxes until otherwise provided by law.[5]

Just over a year later, on April 30, 1870, another letter was written to George A. Smith, this time by Seth M. Blair, Director of the Union Iron Works at Iron City. It was published in the *Deseret News* on May 18, 1870. The letter was basically a status report on the progress of the Iron Works, but it was also a not-so-subtle request for funding from "capitalists," directed at the Territorial government and the Church.

The letter also asked others in the Territory to build foundries to convert the pig iron into useful end products. Company finances were stretched, this letter claimed, and they had more than enough to do just building a blast furnace to convert the iron ore to pig iron. It was apparent that the Company was tired of being the only ones financing and building facilities to convert Iron County's iron ore.

Iron City, Iron County
April 30, 1870
President George A. Smith:

    Dear Brother -- As our superintendent of iron works purposes to visit your city and desires to see you, to whom I have given him a letter of introduction, it appears time for us to report progress, as you will learn from him that which, up to this time, we have been careful not to report, to wit -- the certainty of success in producing a good article of grey cast iron.

    We commenced here a year ago last July, ignorant of the process of reducing our iron ores into merchantable iron, or of the material from which a fire proof brick could be made, both of which obstacles we have overcome and have now sent for engine crusher, and other machinery to New York, and anticipate that before the fourth day of July next we shall be producing daily from three to five tons of as good grey cast iron as can be made in the United States. From the fact of our iron ores being the richest known (assaying seventy two percent) which we reduce with charcoal, we shall be able to offer the best of cast iron, highly charged with carbon and silicon, from which the finest steel, by the Bessemer process, can be made, also wrought iron unsurpassed in any country.

    The great query, "can iron be made in Utah?" being now solved, another arises "can it be produced at figures to compete with the eastern market?" Yes. We will contract, obligate and bind ourselves to furnish as good an article of grey cast iron, (or other) delivered at our works, for the price charged for the freight for the like amount from Chicago to Salt Lake, with the addition of one cent per pound. The only query with us is, having made the iron, can we sell it? Or shall we be forced, with our limited means, to erect foundries and cast our iron into stoves, grates and sad irons, or manipulate it into wrought iron, before we can dispose of it? Or shall we be encouraged in the hope that those having capital will see the greatest enterprise of the day opened up for them to bless their labors and prove themselves benefactors to the citizens of Utah by erecting a foundry to cast our pig iron into stoves, &c., and also work it up into wrought iron, furnishing nails, horse shoes and the thousand other demands on iron daily required for home consumption, thereby saving to the people the tens of thousands of dollars annually sent east and west for the very article that our mountains are filled with, which can be produced and obtained for the product of the farm, the orchard, the vineyard, the cotton mill, the woolen manufactory, the tan yard, dairy and work shop?

We invite capitalists to visit us, or other friends to bring or send their experts and examine for themselves our works, with our advantages to perform what we propose; and should none be found to aid this enterprise, the present stock holders: E. Hanks, Homer Duncan, Chapman Duncan, Peter Shirts, Dr. Scheuner, (our Superintendent) and your humble servant, with a small subsidy from the legislature or aid through the Deseret Agricultural Society or otherwise, will accomplish our object, viz: furnish Utah, Eastern Nevada, the settlements on our borders in New Mexico, and Arizona, their iron. The demand for mining machinery protected by the (tariff) freight, is alone an item that demands an expenditure of tens of thousands annually, which must and will be purchased of us, provided we can furnish it.

Having said so much on our prospects, hopes, desires and purposes, I will add that we have laid out a town site, known as Iron City, and have a Post Office established here. Our location is in the midst of an inexhaustible forest of cedar, good water, good range for cattle, and other stock. Our lands are good, though limited for agricultural purposes. Our iron ores are close by our works. Our place is twenty-three miles west of Cedar City, sixty miles from Pioche, and forty-five north of St. George. The climate is about the same as your city.

We anticipated and hoped we should have had the honor of President Young and party giving us a passing call, but we will not be disappointed. He will come by next time he visits our Dixie.

You will please accept the best wishes of the members of the company for the encouragement given to the iron business by yourself, the President, and others in bygones, with a hope that you may kindly remember that the "lost cause" is revived; and we feel an assurance that our appeal will not be in vain for that encouragement that we all appreciate, -- your blessing on our labors. A word from you, Brother Woodruff, or any friend of home manufactures will be much appreciated by us.

Truly yours in the new covenant,
SETH M. BLAIR
Director Union Iron Works, Iron City, Utah.[6]

It appears that, despite the company's public request, none in the community was willing to spend the time and money to build a foundry. A year and a half later, the Company succeeded in acquiring the resources to construct a foundry of their own at Iron City so that castings and other products could be fabricated and sold. The additional facilities which the company was forced to create, however necessary, would have increased the company's debt load significantly.

In 1870, "Iron City" was included in the federal census. The Company founders, Hanks, the Duncans, Shirts, Scheuner and Blair, were living there with their families along with a dozen other families and individuals. Ebenezer Hanks was apparently absent at the time of the census.

Iron City Iron Works

Iron City Census—July 1, 1870

Dwellings, 24
Families, 19
Individuals, 91

	Surname	First Name	Age	Occupation
1	Richie,	Robert	64	Farmer
		Elisabeth	62	
		Sarah A.	42	
		Anna	23	
		Rachel	5	
		Anna	4	
2	Scheuner,	T.L.	45	Metalurgist
3	Blair	Seth M.	51	Lawyer
		Sarah	51	
		Texana	30	
		Jedediah	16	
		Martha	13	
		?	10	
		Wilmirth	7	
		Lenora	8	
		George E.	6	
		Vilate	2	
4	Duncan,	Chapman	58	Herdsman
		Rosanna	39	
		Taylor C.	5	
		Rosetta	2	
5	Edwards,	Evan	55	Blacksmith
		Elizabeth G.	54	
		Elizabeth A.	26	
		Josiah E.	7	
		David V.	4	
		Lawson H.	1	
6	Woolsey,	William A.	28	Laborer
		Danah	23	
		George W.	4	
		Elizabeth A.	3	
		James A.	8/12	
7	Shirts,	Peter	60	Farming
		Matilda	50	
		Elsie	17	
		Peter	14	
		Thomas	14	
8	Pinney,	Charles	27	Laborer
		Susan	50	
		Archibald	5	
		Mariana	3	
		Infant	3/12	
		Matilda	24	
9	Duncan,	Homer	55	Ranchman

		Asenath	48	
		John C.	22	Herdsman
		Mary	11	
		Emma	5	
		Don. D.	2	
10	Miller,	George	29	Cabinetmaker
11	Gilbert,	James	57	Farmer
		Armenta	85	
12	Hanks,	Sarah	24	Homework
		Almira A.	8	
		Jane A.	6	
		Ebenezer	4	
		Nancy L.	3	
13	Duncan,	John	90	Farmer
	Lewis,	Fisher	19	Farmer
14	Hamilton,	John	68	
		Mary	63	
	Chamberlain,	Lawrence	57	
15	Fife,	Peter M.	64	Farmer
		Mary H.	46	
		Peter B.	19	Farmhand
		Alice	16	
		Jane	10	
		Joseph M.	7	
		Jeanette	5	
	Andrews,	Jens	17	Laborer
16	Middleton,	John	30	Farmer
		Jane	29	
		Amy D.	7	
		George	4	
		Anna E.	1	
17	Alexander,	Gennmith	34	Teamster
		Anna	35	
18	Hamilton,	John J.	35	Farmer
		Mary	32	
		John C.	13	
		William	11	
		James	8	
		Samuel	7	
		Robert	5	
		Mary S.J.	3	
		Sarah E.	7/12	
		Anna	11	
19	Ahlstrom,	Charles	23	
		Sarah	22	
		Eugene Benson	23	
		Charles	3	
		David	6/12	

The Utah Iron Mining Company

For reasons not obvious to the casual observer, just two years later, on August 16, 1870, a new company was formed out of the old Union Iron Company, named the Utah Iron Mining Company. The most likely reason for the new company was to raise more capital to aid in the financing of the operation. The courthouse record included a list of property that was transferred into the new company.

Utah Iron Mining Company

Date of Incorporation: August 16, 1870.

Duration: Twenty-five years.

Incorporators: Ebenezer Hanks, Parowan – President, Seth M. Blair, Iron City, Utah, Homer Duncan, Cedar City, Utah, Edmund Ellsworth Jr., Weber Co., Preston A. Blair, Weber Co.

Purpose: To manufacture iron, copper, zinc, and other materials at Iron City, Iron County, Utah.

Incorporated under: Act of the Governor and Legislature of Utah.

Approved February 18, 1870.

Incorporated for: $100,000.00 in shares of $26.00 each. [The capitalization was raised February 13, 1873 to $250,000]

Schedule of property on stock belonging to and paid into the Utah Iron Mining Company by the members of the association at the time of their incorporation. Townsite 320 acres. Improvements: One air furnace, one blast furnace, one assay furnace, one office, one dwelling house, chemicals, and fixtures for assaying, one Deastero flume ditch water wheel, franchise from the County Court for the control of the water of Little Pinto Creek for machinery and irrigating purposes, one corral for hay, six lots fenced. Land claim: One meadow fenced 40 acres, one pasture fenced five hundred acres. Iron mines - 160 acres Burokn [*sic*] or No. 3160 Duncan, 80 fire clay and fire stone loads or lodes, silver zinc and copper loads or lodes. Mountaineer 2400 feet, Mammoth 2300 feet, Gen. Putman 3000 feet. Mules, wagon and harness. One Roots ten horse power engine and boiler with fixtures complete, one Roots rotary blower, belting etc., 1200 pounds iron to bind furnace, 100 lbs. nuts, crucibles and instruments to test heat in furnace (California Bill), 2000 bushels coal, 75 cords of wool cut, 10,000 brick, 2000 fire brick, 3 axes, 2 scythes, 1 fork, 1 hoe, 4 crowbars, 4 drills, 1 sledge, 2 hammers, 2 spoons, 1 temp, iron, 2 augers, powder and fuse, 1 press for keeping fire brick, one boiler, lumber, timber, stage pools together with all material used in making brick. Water tweers, gearing, patterns, cast iron at Cedar and flanges, patterns, shovels, picks, gads, claim and labor done on stone coal bed, 1-1/2 inch rope.

The above described property is valued and received by the members of the company at ($25,000) twenty-five thousand dollars.

List of stock subscribed for this 16th August 1870.

Ebenezer Hanks	10,000
Homer Duncan	10,000
Chapman Duncan	6,000
Seth M. Blair	6,000[7]

On September 7, 1870, Chapman Duncan, Esq. visited the offices of the *Salt Lake Herald* and gave an update on the Iron Works in Southern Utah and the newly created "Utah Iron Mining Company." He stated that $32,000 of the $100,000 capital stock had already been taken. He announced that the Root's engine, purchased in New York and the Root's patent blower, purchased in Sacramento, had arrived and would soon be installed at the Iron Works. He said that the company had only been testing so far but that as soon as the equipment was installed "the company would be prepared to manufacture iron on quite a liberal scale."[8]

Six months later, on March 1, 1871, Elder George A. Smith of the First Presidency received a telegraphed dispatch from Erastus Snow. The message was subsequently communicated to and published by the *Deseret News*.

> Pres. Geo. A. Smith: -- I received last night, a specimen of soft gray iron from the Pinto Iron Works, suitable for foundry use. Success to the enterprise! The last of the muddy settlers are here on their way to Long Valley. I am bedfast with rheumatism.[9]

The announcement that iron production had begun came four months earlier than Seth M. Blair had predicted in April 1870. On April 17, 1871, Richard S. Robinson, bishop of the Pinto Ward of the Church of Jesus Christ of Latter-day Saints, sent a letter to the *Deseret News* with a more complete description of the activities at the Iron Works.

> Pinto, April 17, 1871
>
> Editor Deseret News: -- Dear Brother: -- On Friday, the 14th, I visited the Iron Works in our Ward, and saw the brethren actually making iron. After some three years hard struggling, success has crowned their efforts. I saw several tons stacked by the works, and they were tapping the furnace at regular intervals, and running out some eight hundred pounds every eight hours. No interruptions or stoppages by non-fluxing or chilling or uncontrollable obstructions occur, as perplexed the brethren at Cedar City years ago; but everything seems to work very satisfactorily. Brother Richard Harrison of this place was present, a man long experienced in molding iron in England, and he pronounced the iron "No. 1." Bro. Adams, Bishop of Adamsville, who is their furnace manager, and has had a long experience in the business in England, calls it the very best of iron. Their blast is blown by a small steam engine, imported from the East at considerable cost. The members of the company, few in number, have labored hard and long to bring about the present result. There are some dozen or fifteen hands at work, running night and day, and when the material on the ground is used up they will be compelled to stop and blow out the furnace, not having hands or capital enough to keep it running and supply it at the same time. The company is making arrangements to cast the iron into useful articles, such as hand irons, sad irons, hollow ware, and stoves, and show to the people in Utah and the world that the manufacture of iron in Utah is a fact.
>
> As I said, the few that stuck to the enterprise have labored hard, and have become somewhat reduced in circumstances, but as success has attended their efforts, they are quite elated in their feelings at the prospects of the future. The company is organized on the co-operative principle, with Brother Ebenezer Hanks as President, who is quite a businessman. Brother Homer Duncan is Vice President, with good men for Directors. Brother Seth M. Blair is Secretary.

This enterprise is worthy of being pushed forward, as we need cast and wrought iron and steel; and if it is manufactured in the Territory it will enable us to keep the means at home that we now send abroad, and thus take another step to live within ourselves. Here, then is good opportunity for some of our capitalists to invest their wealth, enrich themselves and build up the country. The production of iron here is no phantom, but is a fact, and I am told the ore is rich and inexhaustible, giving at least 75 percent, and the fluxing material is nearby. Stone coal is found nearby, a little of which was shown me, and there are thousands of acres of cedars, good wood to make into coke nearby, so you will perceive that all the material wanted to carry on iron making on a large scale is here. I hope to see the time when all the iron that is needed for railroads, quartz mills, and domestic use will be produced in our midst. I understand a specimen of this iron is to be sent to President Brigham Young's office and you will have the pleasure of seeing it yourself.

A few words with regard to other matters and I will close. Grasshoppers are hatching out thick, rendering the prospects for farmers rather poor. We shall soon have our co-operative dairy in operation and be able to produce a large quantity of butter and cheese of good quality.

Hoping you and yours are well, I remain, yours in the gospel,
Richard S. Robinson
Bishop of Pinto[10]

Later in the year, on July 27, 1871, Seth M. Blair sent an update letter to Wilford Woodruff an apostle of the Church of Jesus Christ of Latter-day Saints and president of the Deseret Agricultural and Manufacturing Society. Information from the letter on the iron concern was published in the *Deseret News*.

Iron City

Hon. Wilford Woodruff, President of the Deseret Agricultural and Manufacturing Society, received a letter a few days since, dated Iron City, Iron Co., July 27th, containing considerable information about the progress of iron manufacture in that locality. Many of our readers are aware that a few men for the past year or two, have been endeavoring to make iron from the ore which, it is well known, is abundant and of fine quality in some sections of Southern Utah. The letter received by Mr. Woodruff from the secretary of the company, S. M. Blair, Esq., says that their labors have been successful, and the problem of manufacturing iron from the native ores has been most satisfactorily solved.

The company was incorporated on the 17th of March, 1870; and since that date the company has erected furnaces, imported machinery and are now successfully smelting the ores, and producing a quality of gray cast iron equal to the best. As early as 1868, the gentlemen composing this company commenced their labors; but it was not until about two years had passed that they found material to manufacture fire brick for lining for their furnaces; and when this task was accomplished they were at a loss for a competent smelterer. He was finally found in the person of Mr. David B. Adams, of Beaver Co., and now their most sanguine hopes are so far realized that iron of the finest quality is being produced in limited quantity and can be to any amount as soon as the means can be obtained to erect buildings, etc. to prosecute the requisite appliances. The capacity of their present furnace is twenty-five hundred pounds per day. The company have now nearly completed a good brick building for a foundry; they have secured the service of a competent moulder, and, at the date of writing, the foundry was expected to be in operation in a few days. It is the intention to erect during the present year, a large smelting furnace, also one for steel, and a forge for wrought iron.

The president of the company, Ebenezer Hanks, Esq.; the directors Chapman Duncan and Seth M. Blair, Esqs.

The importance of the preceding information cannot be overestimated for the inauguration of iron manufacture in Utah is of far more importance, and more pregnant with prosperity to her citizens than a thousand mines of gold and silver were each of them of fabulous wealth. But in no branch of business is capital more needed, than in this; and as the time is not far distant when the Utah Southern railroad will extend and probably pass through or near to the iron districts, the worth of the iron mines and their wealth creating powers will be appreciated, and men of capital will be ready to invest; and there is no doubt that a big iron trade will grow up in Utah, and a great amount of prosperity be enjoyed by the people engaged therein.[11]

The census report of 1872 for Iron County (including Panguitch) was 3,328. This was outlined in a report to Robert L. Campbell, Assessor, in Salt Lake City, from Jesse N. Smith, County Clerk, and dated March 26, 1872.

Dear Sir: The following shows the returns of the census of this County so far as received:

Location	Count
Paragonah	220
Parowan	876
Summit	162
Johnson	56
Cedar City	500
Iron Springs	34
Hamilton's Fort	57
Kanarra	242
Pinto (probably)	250
Iron City (probably)	60
Hebron (probably)	100
Antelope Springs (probably)	60
Desert Springs (probably)	16
Sulphur Springs (probably)	15
Panguitch (probably)	620
Johnson's Mill (probably)	15
Sherwood's Mill (probably)	20
	3,328

This certifies that the above Census of Iron County is correct according to the best of my knowledge.

Jesse N. Smith - County Clerk[12]

An appeal was made to "capitalists" in a *Salt Lake Herald* article published on June 22, 1872. It stated that the Iron City operation was "languishing for want of a little capital." It reported that the iron works were successful in every respect, producing 3,000 pounds of castings daily, but were too small. A fifty-horse-power engine was needed to replace the ten-horse-power engine so the local demand for iron could be met. Unfortunately, financial issues seemed to be a recurring theme for the Iron City iron works.[13]

The Great Western Iron Mining and Manufacturing Company

On September 4, 1873, just three years after the formation of the second company, the company was again reorganized into a third company, again, apparently for the purpose of raising additional investment capital. This time the name changed from the Utah Iron Mining Company to the "Great Western Iron Mining and Manufacturing Company," with capital stock of two million dollars.

> The intention of said company being to enter immediately upon the manufacture of iron for railroad and other purposes at Iron City, situated twenty-two miles southwest of Cedar City. The company will forthwith commence the erection of furnaces and other appliances and conveniences for the manufacture of iron, and there is no doubt whatever that the long talked of and often advised development of the rich mineral deposits of that region will now be prosecuted with vigor.[14]

At first it may have appeared strange that the newspaper article stated that "the company will forthwith commence the erection of furnaces and other appliances and conveniences for the manufacture of iron," since a blast furnace, foundry and other appliances were already in existence. However, from future news articles it became clear that, indeed, much of the complex was being replaced or rebuilt.

In addition to forming a new iron manufacturing company, Ebenezer Hanks and associates organized a railroad company on September 15, 1873, to be named the "Iron Mountain and Utah Valley Railroad," with capital of eight million dollars. The line was to be about 270 miles long and would run from Iron City north, to connect with the Utah Southern Railroad somewhere in Utah Valley, near Provo, Utah. A preliminary survey of the road had been commenced and the grading of the road was scheduled to begin shortly. The rails were to be manufactured at Iron City, and the laying of them was to commence as early as practicable.

Articles in the papers assured readers that many of the leading citizens of Iron and the surrounding counties were shareholders in both the preceding companies, that a large amount of capital had already been subscribed and that "hundreds" would soon be employed.[15] The Company was even planning to build a second furnace at Iron City[16] and a rolling mill in Provo, Utah.[17]

Despite all of the good news, there were substantial difficulties getting the new company going. A newspaper article published in October 1875, two years after the founding of the new company, revealed some of the proceedings of Great Western after its incorporation in September 1873. With the infusion of capital, the old Utah Iron Mining Company had been completely overhauled with new machinery, buildings and blast furnace. The article went on to explain that there were many obstacles in the way and that the company had appeared to be in danger for a time, but that the company had been working hard, had started well, and was well on its way to production.

The great extent of country to be looked after, the varied character of the interests involved, the crude nature of the project were all obstacles in the way, but gradually order came forth and the routine of work was entered into by all parties interested with an earnestness that betokened success. Engines were secured, material and machinery for moulding and casting iron, a blast furnace, an air furnace, a pattern shop, and offices for the transaction of business were erected, and matters were assuming an appearance that augured well for the future, when the great money panic of 1874 came upon the business world and a tip of the famous tidal wave struck the Great Western Iron Company, so that they, in common with the business interest of even the great commercial centres of the world, were necessitated to draw in their purse strings and husband their means to enable them to pass safely over the shoals where on many a richly laden bark had gone down. Retrenchment became the order of the day, and such men as Nicholas Groesbeck, Homer Duncan and Umpstead Rencher, worked with a will to carry out the designs of the stockholders. An assessment was levied and accumulated debts are being paid, confidence is being restored, and the company today starts on their new year with the most brilliant prospects for the future.[18]

The Great Western Iron Company

One year later, on September 4, 1874, the company organized a fourth time named the "Great Western Iron Company." This time, the company planned to begin with capital stock of $2,000,000, "to carry on, operate and conduct a general business of mining for iron, coal and other minerals; and to manufacture iron, copper and zinc, and all articles made therefrom."[19]

It is not known how much the money panic and retrenchment affected the time it took to build the new blast furnace and accompanying facilities. Although the new facilities had been begun in 1873, with the previous iteration of the company, the construction of the new blast furnace was not completed for another year. The furnace was put into operation in October 1874, a little over one year and one month after the third company was formed. On October 9, 1874, the following short message was sent from Iron City to the *Salt Lake Herald*.

Fired Up –

A dispatch from Iron City, says the Great Western Iron Company's furnace at that place was put in operation yesterday. Everything about it worked satisfactorily, and the prospect was that it would have a long and successful run.[20]

One week later, on October 17, 1874, Henry Lunt, one of the original Iron County Mission members, wrote the following statement to the *Deseret News*, confirming the successful operation of the blast furnace.

The Iron Works in Successful Operation

Cedar City, Oct. 17, 1874

I have just received information from Ebenezer Hanks Esq., superintendent of the Great Western Iron Co., Iron City, per William Holyoak and John Eyre, who have just returned from that place, that the blast furnace is doing splendid business. The furnace is tapped every ten hours. The last run was twenty-five hundred pounds. They expect next week to make five tons of pig iron per day. They shipped two tons for Provo yesterday. Everybody here is rejoicing at the prospect of the development of the immense deposits of iron stone in this region.[21]

The two tons of iron indeed made it to Salt Lake, was inspected by someone from the *Deseret News* and was found to be of excellent quality. The newspaper also reported that the Company intended to establish rolling mills to make railroad iron at the earliest practicable day.[22]

On January 28, 1875, W. B. Pace was in Salt Lake City and gave the following report to the *Salt Lake Herald*.

The Iron Company

General W. B. Pace, vice-president of the Great Western Iron Company, is in town and gives a flattering report of the corporation. The smelters are running constantly, and turning out large amounts of iron, some of which is being brought to this city, but the most of the product is being piled up at Iron City, for shipment when the roads shall be in better condition. The Salt Lake City Iron Company has contracted to build ten flat cars for the Utah Western road, the iron for which will be furnished by the Great Western.

Another enterprise is on foot that will add greatly to the wealth of southern Utah, by opening and developing that country, and bringing its immense resources into use. We refer to the recent organization of a company for the purpose of building a narrow-gauge railroad from Iron City to the head of navigation on the Colorado River. The length of the road will be about 125 miles, the southern terminus being somewhere in northern Arizona. Work is to be commenced early next season, and we understand the company is sufficiently able to crowd the line to an early completion.

And so, the work of developing the territory goes bravely and energetically forward. Ere another decade shall have gone by Utah will have more miles of railroad, more valuable coal, iron, lead, copper and silver mines than will be owned by what are now the other territories combined. "So must it be!"[23]

The people of Southern Utah were anxious for a railroad to be built to connect the area with the outside. Another company was organized to build a second railroad. This road was planned to head south to the Colorado River in Northern Arizona and would have hauled cargo to the river from which it could be sent by barge up and down the river from Northern Arizona to the Pacific Ocean. Much like the railroad that was supposed to have been built to Utah Valley in 1873, construction on the project was to start immediately, if not sooner. Another glowing report was published in the *Salt Lake Herald* on April 13, 1875.

Great Western Iron Co.

By private advices from Iron City, we learn that the above company is running its furnace to the extent of its capacity and is turning out large quantities of soft iron, much of which is being shipped to Pioche. The Great Western is steadily increasing in importance, and from appearances, is destined to become a gigantic iron manufacturing concern. Eighteen months ago, its monthly payroll aggregated only $500; now the company pays the employees every month $4,000, and the demand for iron made by it continues to increase.[24]

On September 29, 1875, a lengthy article was written about the Great Western Iron Works and Iron City, Utah. It was published two weeks later in the *Deseret News* on

October 13th. It spoke of the great quantities of high-grade iron ore readily available in Iron County and recounted the history of iron manufacturing in Southern Utah dating back to 1852. It mentioned that Iron City had grown and that a number of substantial buildings had been erected. Portions of the article are quoted below.

> Within a radius of ten miles from where I write, there probably exists a greater quantity of iron than can be found in any locality of one hundred times its dimensions. The quantity cannot be estimated because of its unlimited extent, any more than you can estimate the given number of pounds in one of the loftiest peaks of the Wasatch Range, or the aggregate weight of one of its broadest canyons; for here we find valleys of iron, hills of iron, mountains of iron. The float rock of the country is simply iron in an almost unadulterated condition. Think for one moment that millions of tons of iron are in sight, that will assay 76 percent, when by tunneling and drifting we succeed in our eastern mines in securing ore that will assay only 34 percent; that, in addition to the richness of the ore, within easy distance of the furnace can be found everything needful for fluxing or tempering the metal to any desired degree; that there is no single article needed by the furnace man but what can be found in any desired quantity; that the galena ores are declared to be equally rich with the richest of the ores of Star and Lincoln Districts; that here can be found rich zinc and copper mines; that timber for any amount of charcoal can be obtained within a very few miles of the furnace.
>
> Iron City itself has become quite a little town within the past year or two. Several substantial buildings, both brick and frame, have been erected. A commodious brick schoolhouse has been built upon a sightly eminence, neatly finished and substantially constructed. A day school is in session, under the supervision of Miss Deseret Page, whose quiet lady-like influence in the schoolroom, coupled with her ability as a teacher, is doing much to control the actions of the youths who are growing to man's and woman's sphere and stature here. Homer Duncan, Esq., has almost finished a two-story framed residence that would do credit to the suburbs of the metropolis of the Territory. The machine shop, engine house, pattern shop, and store are substantial brick buildings, and of a character to denote the earnest intention of the projectors of this great enterprise.
>
> At the recent election of Directors, John W. Young, Nicholas Groesbeck, Homer Duncan, Umpstead Rencher, Richard Bentley, Ira N. Hinckley, and W. N. Dusenberry were elected Directors, who in turn chose John W. Young for President, Ira N. Hinckley, Vice President, Umpstead Rencher Treasurer.[25]

On November 28, 1875, Judge Dusenberry sent another short, but glowing report to the *Salt Lake Herald*. Although for the most part this report is positive, it is interesting to consider why he chose to say that they would "soon" be doing an extensive business when they were supposedly already doing so.

Great Western Iron Company.

A telegram received yesterday by Judge Dusenberry, managing director of the Great Western iron company, brings the pleasing news that the company's furnaces at Iron city are in successful operation, and turning out an excellent quality of iron. Adams and Smith are managing the works and give fair promise of soon doing an extensive business in the way of supplying iron for this region.[26]

The largest project of the Great Western Iron Company was the Church of Jesus Christ of Latter-day Saints' St. George Temple baptismal font. Pig iron was shipped to Salt

Lake City, where it was cast into twelve oxen and the basin of the font. They were shipped by rail as far as the Juab station, then hauled by wagons pulled by oxen on to St. George.

> Iron oxen were cast in Salt Lake City to support the baptismal font. C. L. Christensen (age twenty) and several companions, traveled to the rail station in Juab County to pick up the font and freight its parts to the temple. He recalled that his load, which was the bottom of the font, weighed 2,900 pounds, along with two cast oxen, each weighing 600 pounds. Much of the travel back to St. George was done at night when it was cooler for both men and oxen. On the return trip, Christensen and other freighters frequently were forced to search for oxen that had broken away in search of water. But as Christensen relates: "The teamsters had plenty of good Dixie wine to keep them cool and we certainly enjoyed it."[27]

The Source of Iron Ore

When describing the Iron City location, the reporter of the previous *Deseret News* article, published on October 13, stated that "millions of tons of iron are in sight, that will assay 76 percent." Other reporters even stated that the ore was as high as 90 percent iron. Although the description of the quantity of iron ore in the area was no exaggeration, the estimation of the ore's quality was too high, since pure magnetite ore assays at 70.9% iron, and it can be stated with substantial certainty that there was no elemental iron to be found in the ore bodies of Iron County.

It is unclear exactly where the operators of the Iron City Works procured the iron ore for their blast furnace. Iron City was located relatively close to five different ore deposits that outcropped on the southern flank of Iron Mountain. The 1874 incorporation papers indicated that the Company owned both the Blowout and the Duncan claims, along with several dozen other claims. It is most likely that the majority, and perhaps the entirety, of the ore was mined from these two claims. The Duncan was closest to Iron City and may have been named after either Homer or Chapman Duncan. The Blowout ore body was farther to the east but its ore was readily available where a mountain of high-grade ore literally protruded out of the ground.

In May 1978, York Jones obtained several iron ore samples from the Iron City feed stockpile and had them assayed using modern qualitative analysis. York was intimately familiar with the types of ore from both pits, since he worked for Utah Construction when it was mining in the Duncan and Blowout pits in the 1950s and 60s. He concluded from the results of the tests that the Iron City operation used ore from both locations. The assay results are summarized in Table 1 at the top of the following page.

Component	Sample No. 1 (Bright Fe_3O_4) Looked like Blowout Ore			Sample No. 2 (Dull Fe_3O_4) Looked like Duncan Ore		
	Value (%)	Rank	Assessment	Value (%)	Rank	Assessment
Fe	66.100	High	Very Good	65.800	High	Very Good
SiO_2	1.500	Very Low	Good	2.900	Very Low	Good
S	0.003	Very Low	Good	0.004	Very Low	Good
P	0.090	Very Low	Good	0.050	Very Low	Good
Cu	0.010	Low	Good	0.140	High	Bad
Ni	0.020	Low	Good	0.010	Low	Good

Table 1. *Assay report of ores from the Old Iron Town furnace feed stockpile.*[28]

Financial Crisis

Despite the very favorable reports that had been coming out of Iron City since 1871 and which had increased since October of 1874, on January 9, 1876 a telling article was published in the *Salt Lake Herald* concerning the Great Western Iron Company. On the surface, things seemed to be going well, and certainly all of the updates given by the Company were optimistic, but there were several indications that were worrisome and hinted at underlying problems.

News from the Iron Region—Iron County

January 2, 1876 - Messrs. Adams & Smith having leased the furnace and property of the Great Western Iron company, they have put the furnace and machinery in good repair, are running the furnace to its full capacity, and are running out an average quantity of No. 1 iron, considering the small capacity of the furnace. But it is impossible for them to make it pay, as it is not the right kind of furnace for the ores and is entirely too small. The citizens being satisfied that the right kind of men have got hold of the property, met last evening and proposed to Adams & Smith to furnish the necessary labor to build a new furnace, without pay, providing they furnish them with supplies while erecting it and getting it in successful operation. They could sell in Pioche quite an amount of iron, if they only had the facilities for manufacturing it. The citizens are in earnest, knowing as they do that the manufacture of iron and castings will be a great source of wealth to southern Utah, and especially to Iron City. Home manufacture is the motto of the citizens of this place.[29]

It appears that Adams and Smith were hired by the Company as experts to operate the Iron City Iron Works. They put everything in order but they also had quite a bit to say about the operation. The comment that the furnace was entirely too small and of the wrong design for the ore, leading to the conclusion that it was impossible for it to pay, must have been quite a revelation and would have been very discouraging to the long-time owners and operators of the Iron City works. The furnace was the second one to be built at the site, had been operating only a little over a year and had taken over a year to build, costing substantial money and effort. The settlement's optimism, and their powerful support of the company, is visible in the locals' willingness to sacrifice their time and effort to support the company in this trying time. While Adams and Smith's declaration that they needed to build a new furnace must have been depressing, the company would have been amazed and probably touched that the citizens were willing to pitch in and build it, even without pay! Another article published a month later gives more insight into the situation.

The Iron Interest

Iron City, Jan 23, 1876.

    Times are dull here at present owing to Messrs. Adams & Smith shutting down the furnace. They made a successful run and are now shipping their iron to the Raymond & Ely Company, Pioche. They have contracted with them for twenty tons monthly. The furnace will start up again in two weeks. There is strong talk of erecting a new furnace here or at Iron Springs at once. Messrs. Adams & Smith own and control a large amount of property at Iron Springs, and they have propositions from Nevada capitalists to furnish them the necessary machinery and supplies for the purpose of putting up works at that place. They are only waiting to hear from the Great Western Iron Company's agent to see what they intend to do in regard to the proposition they have made them to erect a new furnace here. The G. W. I. Co. have expended a great deal of money here in erecting works and developing their mines, and it looks like bad policy on their part to stop just when they might, with a very little more outlay of capital, get their works in a paying condition and control the iron trade in Utah and Nevada. I am glad to see the railroad question agitated, as the greatest need we have is cheap transportation. We defy the world as to copper, iron and coal, both in quality and quantity. I hope you will give the iron and coal in southern Utah your attention, as the wealth of the country is in our iron and coal.[30]

It seems that Adams and Smith not only wanted to build a whole new furnace but also desired to move the entire operation to Iron Springs for reasons not completely understood. It may have been because of the mining claims that Adams and Smith supposedly owned or something totally unrelated, but it appears that the company owners and investors were becoming somewhat skeptical of the plans of Adams and Smith. Apparently, the offers of machinery and supplies from the Nevada capitalists never materialized. And even though it was stated that the greatest need of the company was to have cheaper transportation, nothing ever happened in that regard. It is unclear, if the furnace was too small and was having trouble keeping up, why it would be shutting down for two weeks at a time.

    The situation of whether and where to build a new furnace was eclipsed in April by money issues, as it had been two years earlier in 1874. The company was not able to meet its financial obligations. They may have been looking to the future to be able to finance the new furnace that Adams and Smith had recommended. Whatever the case, the company levied an assessment on its shareholders of one dollar per share. It is unclear when the furnace made its last run but it appears to have been sometime in 1876.

The Great Western Iron Company

We observe by published notice that the Great Western Iron Company has levied an assessment of one dollar on the share of its capital stock. This we learn is necessitated by the embarrassed condition of the company in meeting its liabilities, and also to place it in a condition to withstand a longer siege of the "hard times."

We have never heard a doubt expressed by anyone as to the magnitude of this company's property; and a similar view entertained by the stockholders can but prompt them to respond to this call, thereby permanently securing to them that which in the near distant future will prove to be of great value.[31]

Of course, the assessment was not well received by the shareholders, and the situation became ugly. Two months later, the Company took their first shareholder to court for non-payment of the levied assessment and won.

The First.

Some time ago the Great Western Iron Company levied an assessment on its capital stock, which it has had considerable difficulty in collecting. Many of the shareholders promptly paid the sums due from them, but others refused to do so, thus compelling the company to institute suits against the delinquents, in order to protect and deal fairly with those who had paid. Yesterday the first of these suits was tried before Justice Pyper, judgment being given for the plaintiff against the defendant for the assessment and costs of suit.

We understand the company proposes to prosecute suits against all delinquents. The result of the action yesterday will have a tendency to hasten others in the matter of paying their assessments, for the benefit of the company and the prompt shareholders. There is no question that with proper management the Great Western Iron Company will yet become one of the most successful industrial institutions in the country, but it will require money to get it in operation and place it upon a paying basis.[32]

During the last half of 1876 and the first half of 1877, things were fairly quiet concerning the business except for several court cases where the Great Western Iron Company was either being sued or suing someone else in court. Thomas Taylor attempted to sell his 282 shares of stock in the company on the 21st of August, apparently without any takers.[33] There was an annual stockholders meeting announced for September 12, 1876, to be held in Iron City.[34]

A notice appeared in the *Deseret Evening News* on November 13, 1876 informing the stockholders of the Company of a meeting to be held on December 4th, in Salt Lake City, "for the purpose of voting upon the question of issuing mortgage bonds of said company, and executing a mortgage of all the property of said company to secure the payment thereof."[35] Apparently adequate funds were not raised and on May 11, 1877 the following announcement was published in the *Salt Lake Herald*.

Auction Sale!

One Steam Engine and Boiler, complete, One No. 4 Blower, Six Buildings, also
All the Mining Properly of the Great Western Iron Company, to be sold May 19th,
2 p.m., at the Court House, Parowan, Iron County.[36]

The announcement came without much explanation or forewarning. Looking closely at the company's operations, however, it becomes evident that even with shareholder assessment, the financial woes continued. It is uncertain how much the furnace was operated between January 1876 and May 1877, and it is possible that it was not operated at all. When the Great Western Iron Company failed in 1877, it did its best to dispose of its assets in order to pay its creditors, but there were not many buyers. An article published on February 2, 1881 in the *Deseret News* explained the situation concerning the valuable mining claims that were held by the company:

In 1874, however, the Great Western Iron Company, formed for the purpose of working the ores in Iron County, bought up the claims which had been held by various parties back to 1866, when the mining district was organized there. But this company, not making the progress expected, the enterprise began to dwindle, and in January 1878, Bishop Thomas Taylor became the chief owner of these various claims, by purchase from the Great Western Company. That gentleman finished his assessments and went on with the work of development, fulfilling the law, and made formal application for a patent.[37]

The news article above stated that the mining claims came into the possession of Thomas Taylor by purchase from the Great Western Company. A news article published in 1899 in the *Salt Lake Tribune* almost twenty years later, told a more complete story about the claims and included a good summary of the Great Western Iron Company's activities.

Great Western Iron Company

After a suspense of some four years it was again decided to erect a plant for the manufacture of iron, and accordingly about 1870 the Great Western Iron Company was organized. By this time the superiority of the Iron City iron had been discovered and a new plant was erected at the place. Among the heavier contributors to the latter enterprise were John W. Young, Nicholas Groosby [Groesbeck], James Williamson, Umstead Rencher, and Thomas Taylor. The expense of building up the town, erecting smelters, shops, etc., and supplying the needed machinery consumed about $200,000. In the previous attempts to smelt iron, a mixture of coke and charcoal had been used, but this time charcoal was exclusively employed. Substantial charcoal pits were erected, which are still standing, as also are a number of the other buildings.

The company made many hundreds of tons of excellent iron, much of which is still on the ground, property of Thomas Taylor, the present owner. Castings were made for the quartz mills at Pioche, Bristol and Bloomville, and quantities of pig were shipped all the way to Salt Lake City by team, where it was used by Davies, Howe & Co., the Salt Lake foundry, under the management of Thomas Pierpont and by William J. Silver, all of whom pronounced the product first class. Silver manufactured the finest kinds of castings, plates with filigree work, etc., which require the best of iron. It was in fact, declared to be better than the Pittsburg product.

But with all the success attained by the latter company in the merit of their output, the project proved a financial failure on account of being so far removed from the railroad, the nearest terminus then being Salt Lake City. The company became heavily involved, Thomas Taylor of Salt Lake City, who had credited them to the amount of $10,000 worth of merchandise front from his store, being the heaviest creditor. The company confessed judgment to Mr. Taylor who thus came into possession of the entire property, which at this time consisted of a patented quarter section of land with the buildings upon it, the title to the small stream of water and some thirty iron claims with no government title to any of them. The property was a white elephant upon his hands and he offered to sell at one half the cost to him, but was unable to do so, and was consequently obliged to make the best of the bargain.

By careful analysis of the various ores he was enabled to select the best of the claims, which he proceeded to patent. He also acquired coal lands in the canyon east of Cedar City. At the time Mr. Taylor came into possession of his iron properties he was financially able to have carried on the manufacture of iron on quite an extensive scale but he was so constantly harassed by people who were trying to force his acquisitions from him that he was compelled to waste the bulk of his fortune in litigation. Mr. Taylor came into possession of the property in 1877.[30]

Claim Jumpers

In January 1879, Allen G. Campbell, Matthew Cullen and others endeavored to "jump" Thomas Taylor's mining claims. Both men had made fortunes at Frisco and apparently wanted to add to their wealth in Iron County, even if they did it illegally.

Iron and Justice Gain the Victory

In January 1879, one Allen G. Campbell—now commonly called "M. C." or minority Campbell—attempted in true mining freebooter style, to "jump" these claims, assisted by another mining adventurer named Matthew Cullen, and others. This was done by putting up location notices on the claims owned by Bishop Taylor, the "jumpers" swearing in emphatic, if inelegant terms, that they were not going to see him taking up such valuable country. However, Mr. Taylor continued with his work of development, and they commenced suit by protest against the issuance of the patent, so that they might gain possession, thinking that the Bishop, who had met with some financial reverses, would not be able to defend.

They had reckoned without their host. Mr. Taylor obtained the legal services of Sutherland & McBride, A. Bruce Taylor, and Warren N. Dusenberry. The case was tried at Beaver, before Judge Emerson, from the 8th to the 12th of December last, and arguments were heard in this city before the same judge on the 28th and 29th of December, Judge Sutherland speaking for Mr. Taylor and Presley, Denney and P. Van Zile for Campbell & Co. Judge Emerson has now given a decision to the effect that the location of plaintiffs was not in accordance with law, and that Mr. Taylor's claims were not open to relocation...[39]

The Campbell group's strategy to outlast Taylor in court in an attempt to run him out of funds failed. Taylor won the case, but it did cost him dearly. The case was appealed to the Territory Supreme Court where the ruling of the lower court was affirmed.

Important Suit Settled

The judgment of the Second District Court in the suits of Allen G. Campbell et al. against Thomas Taylor was, a few days ago, affirmed by the Supreme Court of the Territory. The property in dispute consisted of a number of valuable iron mines, situated in Iron County. The affirmation of the decision of the lower court is just what might have been expected, Mr. Taylor being the bone fide owner beyond question, while the claim made by Campbell et al. was nothing short of a jumping transaction.

Mr. Taylor, on account of being put about for means, has had a hard struggle in the courts, but his persistent determination is now rewarded by the defeat of the parties who sought to wrest his property from him. We congratulate him on the successful termination of the suits and hope his valuable mines will prove to him a prolific source of pecuniary benefit.[40]

That was not the end of it, however. Campbell and Taylor were in the courtroom again in October 1882 debating the first of 25 additional cases. The court cases continued for at least the next six months with Thomas Taylor winning most, but not all, of the cases.[41]

There were other similar cases in the area instigated by the bunch from Frisco, including a conflict at Iron Springs between James R. Lindsay of Frisco and the Walker Brothers of Salt Lake City. Apparently both parties ended up with property as evidenced by the various iron claims in the Iron Springs vicinity.[42]

Home Industry and Zion's Board of Trade

When the pioneers first came to Utah, they were isolated from the rest of the nation. Transportation and communication were, at best, primitive. The settlers and their families grew their own food and made many of their own items. What could not be made within the family was usually found elsewhere in the community. They were independent and self-sufficient; they had no other choice. It was an era of "home industry."

In 1869, the transcontinental railroad was completed through Northern Utah and at long last it transported essential supplies into the area and opened the market for goods to be shipped and sold elsewhere. The railroad brought items into the area, sometimes at a lower cost, sometimes at a higher quality and almost always with less effort on the part of the pioneers. One of the downsides of the opening up of commerce with the outside world was the effect that it had on the production of goods within the Territory. There was a marked decline in the amount of home manufacturing compared to what had occurred in the past.

Coupled with the decline in home industry, and even more devastating in its effect on iron mining in Utah, was the fact that employment was being created outside the communities and often outside the Territory. This was especially true of the smaller outlying communities that didn't have adequate population to support manufacturing on a larger scale. The Church of Jesus Christ of Latter-day Saints had established colonies in remote areas, such as the Iron Mission in Iron County, that were far from the population centers and had a difficult time retaining people, especially their young men and women who left the areas in search of employment elsewhere.

As members of the Church gathered together in Utah, there was a continual flow of immigrants into the cities. The railroad made it much easier for settlers to cross the plains and people came to Utah in droves. This influx, combined with the lack of industry, compounded the problem of unemployment. In addition, many of the immigrants were trained industrial workers but there were few industrial jobs. In 1877, it became evident to John Taylor, Brigham Young's successor as President of the Church, that stimulation of "home industry" was an attractive solution to the growing unemployment problem. The Church and President Taylor devoted considerable time and effort to create local manufacturing. New home industries received extensive organizational and financial support in the late 1870s and early 1880s. Tullidge summarized the situation as follows:

> This movement of the Board of Trade promises to be the greatest industrial event that has occurred in the settling and growth of our Territory. The Mormons are eminently a manufacturing community and Utah is a mineral country with a great mining and manufacturing destiny before her. Hitherto, the community has not been engaged in their proper and special work. Natively they are a manufacturing people rather than an agricultural, and our Territory very much resembles Great Britain in its resources of iron and coal and the class of industries which properly belongs to her. The majority of the British Mormons are from the manufacturing and mining districts of England, Scotland, and Wales. Thousands of them were workers in the old country... And yet the British people in Utah have not been engaged in scarcely any of their native industries...[43]

The Zion's Central Board of Trade was established by the Church on April 8, 1879. President Taylor was president and took a personal interest in its success. A number of Stake Boards of Trade had already been organized, holding meetings and placing prominent leaders in positions to carry out ambitious plans. With the creation of the Central Board of trade, financial aid was sometimes offered to Stake Boards in critical areas in order to encourage growth. The following is an excerpt from the Articles of Association of Zion's Central Board of Trade.

Preamble

The objects of association are: To maintain a Commercial Exchange; to promote uniformity in the customs and usages of producers, manufacturers, and merchants; to inculcate principles of justice and equity in trade; to facilitate speedy adjustment of business disputes; to arrange for transportation; to seek remunerative markets for home products; to foster capital and protect labor, uniting them as friends rather than dividing them as enemies; to encourage manufacturing; to aid in placing imported articles in the hands of consumers as cheaply as possible; to acquire and disseminate valuable agricultural, manufacturing, commercial and economic information, and generally to secure to its members the benefits of co-operation in the furtherance of their legitimate pursuits, and to unite and harmonize the business relations of the Stake Boards of Trade, now and hereafter to be organized throughout the Territory, with those of the Central Association....

Article 1

The name of this Association shall be Zion's Central Board of Trade, and the period of its existence shall be twenty-five years, from and including this eighth day of April, 1879, and shall consist of not to exceed fifty members, representing the several stakes of Zion as follows: 17 from Salt Lake; 2 from St. George; 1 from Kanab; 1 from Parowan; 1 from Beaver; 1 from Panguitch; 1 from Millard; 1 from Sevier; 3 from San Pete; 1 from Juab; 1 from Wasatch; 5 from Utah; 1 from Tooele; 2 from Davis; 1 from Morgan; 3 from Weber; 1 from Summit; 2 from Box Elder; 4 from Cache, and 1 from Bear Lake.[44]

In November 1880, almost two years after the Central Board was organized, two renowned mining experts, Professor John S. Newberry of the Columbia University School of Mines in New York, and E. D. Wassell of Pittsburg gave very favorable reports concerning the iron and coal fields in Southern Utah.[45]

The reports once again brought Iron County iron ore and coal into the limelight, especially with the increased focus on home manufacturing. In January, 1881, an article was published in the *Deseret News* that linked the need for good employment opportunities in Utah with building the iron manufacturing industry in Southern Utah. With regards to Zion's Board and Home Industry it could not have been more timely. It was no wonder that the manufacturing of iron and coke ended up on the top of the list. The article emphasized the importance of iron to both employment and commerce.

Iron

It has been truly said that a person who can teach people how to help themselves is their truest friend.

I met a man on the street today, who said can you tell me where I can get employment? And the question is often asked, "what shall we do with our boys?" There seems to a real necessity for someone to originate something for people to do, and if we are going to do anything, let us commence with the industry most needed, one that would lay the foundation for the prosperity, wealth and self-sustenance of the Territory of Utah, and open up an avenue of commerce with the surrounding State and Territories.

That industry, in the writer's opinion, is the manufacture of iron. We have a country abounding with it. So much so that we have called one of the counties of our Territory, Iron County, and the quantity and variety of ores are such that any kind of iron or steel might be made therefrom. It is not now a question as to whether iron could be made or not; it has been made, pronounced to be of as good a quality as is made anywhere. This is attested by Messrs. Amos Howe and T. Pierpont of Salt Lake City who have both used it.

Let us see what others say. Mr. E. D. Wassell, of Pittsburg, says (from an article published in the DESERET NEWS.)

"I was surprised beyond what I am able to express at the great mineral wealth of Iron Co., abounding as it does with iron ores and coal. The iron ores, so far as I am able to judge, surpass anything of the kind I have ever seen, both in regard to quantity and quality," etc., etc.

I quote also from the Baldwin expedition (as published in the S. L. Herald:)

"Utah's great wealth lies not in its hundreds of valuable gold and silver ledges, but in its iron and coal fields. The seemingly fabulous stories of the immense iron deposits in Southern Utah but told part of the truth. Pinto Iron Mining District, in which are the famous iron mountains, is one vast extent of rich magnetic and hematite iron ores; the ledges crop out of the earth in places hundreds of feet high and appear on the surface for eight hundred and a thousand feet, inviting capitalists to double and treble their fortunes, with scarcely a possible risk of losing a cent.

A few weeks ago, professor J. S. Newberry, read before the National Aca-demy of Sciences, a lengthy account of the enormously extensive mines of iron and coal veins in Southern Utah. He said:

"Its iron ore is without a rival, and the Territory possesses not far from these ferruginous beds, four thousand square miles of coal veins that are equal to any in Illinois."

Now how does it not appear that nature had placed within our reach the resources of skilled labor of immense amount that we might thus find our people employment, and give our sons trades at mechanism and manufacture, and not have them do the drudgery now necessary for many, making ourselves the poorly paid farmer, the railroad grader, the hewers of wood and drawers of water, but perform the skilled labor for making things we now import?

The manufacture of iron would naturally open up a very extensive use of it. The manufacture of castings could be entered into at once, and without much cash outlay, such as water mains and pipes, gas mains, beams, pillars, castings for smelters, stamps for crushing mills, stoves, etc. The manufacture of various kinds of malleable ware would furnish employment for miners, smelters, designers, pattern makers, finishers, and a number of other skilled laborers who command good wages. Commencing with these first branches, we could in a little while make all the castings for rolling mills, puddling furnaces, etc., and this would gradually pave the way for every branch of the iron trade and give employment to thousands of people and be the very resort that our youth require.

To commence a bank, we need money. To commence a mercantile institution of any kind, we, of course, need money. To commence manufactures generally in our present condition, in order to import machinery and material, we need money. But to commence this, the foundation, the greatest and best of all institutions, we do not necessarily need a large amount of money, but intelligent and well directed labor, which is the best of all capital.

At some future time, I will try to show how this can be accomplished. ONE WHO IS INTERESTED.[46]

A month and a half later, on April 15, 1881 the following notice was published in the *Salt Lake Herald* concerning a meeting to be held by the Zion's Central Board of Trade. At that time a list of nineteen areas of initial concern was generated for the boards to discuss and work on. The first item on the list was the manufacture of iron and coke:

Board of Trade

April 15, 1881

To the Stake Boards of Trade:

There will be a meeting of Zion's Central Board of Trade on Tuesday, May 17, 1881, at the Council House, Salt Lake City, for the purpose of arriving at a better understanding of what is needed to more thoroughly develop and assist our home industries; to establish them on a better and firmer footing, and to utilize the natural resources of the Territory.

You will therefore please instruct the members who represent you in Zion's Central Board of Trade to meet with us on the above date, prepared not only with all the information possible on such subjects as may interest and benefit your section, but to discuss the following subjects, and suggest such plans for carrying them out as shall tend to the best interests of the Territory.

The following subjects will be taken up in the order mentioned:

First.—Manufacture of iron and coke. Our iron foundries. The deposits of iron ore in Utah, are said to be the largest in the world, and the manufacture of the ore into iron would be the means of giving employment to hundreds of our people who, though skilled in its manipulation, are today engaged in less profitable and congenial employments. Fuel being required in large quantities, the manufacture of coke would come under this heading, being necessity for making finer grades of iron.

In connection with the iron ore beds of the Territory red and yellow ochres abound. Samples of lead, iron and chrome pigments; venetian red, chrome red, yellow and green; and white and red lead are to be seen in our Deseret Museum in this city, yet none of these have been produced in quantity sufficient to even supply the home demand.

Second.—Manufacture of white lead, lead pipe, and sheet lead for roofing purposes, etc. Pure lead is now being shipped to California, and there manufactured into white lead and reshipped to Utah, thus costing the people freight both ways, and the labor and profit incident thereto are entirely lost to us.

Third.—Manufacture of glass.

Fourth.—Wool and woolen manufactures.

Fifth.—Manufacture of clothing.

Sixth.—Silk and silk manufactures.

Seventh.—Manufacture and importation of wagons, carriages and agricultural machinery.

Eighth.—Hides; manufacture of leather and boots and shoes.

Ninth.—Manufacture of paper.

Tenth.—Butter and cheese.

Eleventh—Flour, corn meal, starch etc.

Twelfth.—Soap

Thirteenth.—Cultivation of sugar-cane and beets for manufacturing sugar. The importance of our making an effort in this direction will readily be seen, when it is remembered that the people of Utah consume annually of over half a million dollars' worth sugar.

Fourteenth.—Manufacture of matches.

Fifteenth.—Salt.

Sixteenth.—Glue.

Seventeenth.—Hats and caps.

Eighteenth.—To encourage planting and raising forest, fruit and shade trees, shrubbery, flowers and bulbs suitable to our climate, and thus prevent thousands of dollars being annually sent out of the territory.

Nineteenth.—To encourage the breeding and raising of fine stock and discourage the people from sending their means out of the territory for such stock, when it can be obtained here at as reasonable rates.

By counseling together, we hope to be able to see the way clearer for establishing some of the industries referred to; of devising methods for assisting those already started, and utilizing for the benefit of all, some, at least, of the many natural resources of our rich and growing territory.

In behalf of Zion's Central Board of Trade

T G Webber, Secretary.   John Taylor, President[47]

The fact that iron and coke were first on Zion's Central Board of Trade list of commodities did not go unnoticed. The next week after the notice was published; the following article appeared in the *Deseret News*.

Practical Measures for Zion's Progress

We notice that iron and coke occupy the first place in the list of subjects to be discussed. This is gratifying to all who know anything of the vast resources of Utah in this particular line, the amount of suitable labor, skilled and otherwise, ready to hand for embarking in the business of manufacture, and the great market which is open for these necessary products. Iron, no doubt, can be made in Utah to supply all this rapidly opening region with the most precious of metals, and the railroad facilities and prospects are such as to warrant not only large consumption of the invaluable article, but cheap and speedy transportation to the points of demand. Utah is bound at some time to be a great iron-producing and iron-consuming country.[48]

As announced, on May 17, 1881, the Zion's Central Board of Trade along with eighteen of the twenty Stake Boards of Trade, met in Salt Lake City. A discussion was held and a separate committee was appointed to investigate and report upon each of the nineteen items listed on the agenda. More time was spent on some subjects than others and it was reported that the first topic of iron and coke took up by far the most time. A full report of the meeting was published in the *Deseret News* on June 1, 1881. For the sake of space, only the section on the manufacture of iron and coke is included.

Zion's Central Board of Trade

The board met in the Council House at 11 o'clock, on Tuesday, May the 17th, President John Taylor presiding. Eighteen out of the twenty stakes were represented, and when it is considered the long distance some of the delegates had to travel, the representation, especially at this season of the year, was good, and conclusively shows the interest taken in the important subjects which were to come under discussion. Below we give a full list of the committees appointed to investigate and report upon the several subjects detailed in the circular of April 15th last, viz:

Iron

First. -- Manufacture of iron and coke. Our iron foundries. Upon this important subject a committee of seven were appointed and instructed to take all necessary steps to organize a company for the manufacture of iron and coke. Those necessary steps will be the preparing of articles of incorporation, opening books and soliciting subscriptions of stock thereto, the capital to be fixed at a nominal sum, with powers to enlarge the same, as circumstances may require, to the extent of a million dollars. It is understood the company when formed, will proceed to thoroughly test the different qualities of iron ore and coal in the Territory, so as to arrive at as thorough a knowledge as practicable, how best to make these minerals subserve the end in view. The committee are as follows: Wm. Jennings (chairman) and W. H. Hooper, Salt Lake City; A. O. Smoot, Provo; W. B. Preston, Logan; Henry Lunt, Cedar; John Sharp and Thomas Taylor, Salt Lake City.[49]

All of the men on the "iron" committee were well-known business leaders as well as prominent members of the Church of Jesus Christ of Latter-day Saints in leadership positions. Several members, such as Thomas Taylor and Henry Lunt, were intimately familiar with previous iron manufacturing endeavors in Southern Utah. The committee was to gather information and write a comprehensive report for the October 1881 meeting of Zion's Central Board of Trade.

On August 24, 1881, an article was published in the *Deseret News* written by Thomas Taylor. At that point in time, Mr. Taylor wore several hats. He was a Bishop in the Church and a Salt Lake City store owner, he was a member of the new committee formed by Zion's Central Board of Trade to investigate and organize a company for the manufacture of iron and coke, he was a heavy investor in the previous mining company, and, last but not least, he was the owner of some of the richest mining claims in Southern Utah. In the article Mr. Taylor states that his mining claims, of which he had somewhere between 15 and 30, were offered to the committee appointed by the Board of Trade to commence operations at very reasonable terms.

Mr. Taylor took exception to two of the statements made by a *Deseret News* correspondent in a previously published article. The correspondent intimated that there was "no place in the immediate vicinity of the southern iron mines suitable for extensive iron manufacture etc." He also, according to Mr. Taylor, claimed that the Blowout Mountain was in the Iron Springs Mining District, which it was not at that time. It was in the Pinto Mining District. Mr. Taylor extolled the virtues of the Iron City location, the iron deposits situated nearby and the general importance of iron manufacturing in the territory.

More about Iron

The manufacture of iron in Utah as an extensive enterprise engaging much capital and a vast amount of labor, skilled and ordinary, is in our opinion one of the things that are sure to be, as anything not actually accomplished. We have published several articles on this subject, some theoretical, others practical, and now give place to a communication from the proprietor of large claims in Iron County who ought to know whereof he speaks. We expect to present other suggestions and arguments, and statements of fact bearing on this question, that it may be kept before the attention of our wise men and those who are able to engage in a business that requires considerable money, but promises a rich return for the investment:

It does appear to your correspondent that the manufacture of iron is of such vast importance to our Territory that those who wish to encourage it should aim at the most speedy and practical way of going to work, not only on paper, but by the building of blast furnaces, making pig iron, and supplying our home market with that article.

Your correspondent of the 2d inst. intimates that there is no place in the immediate vicinity of the southern iron mines suitable for extensive iron manufacture etc.

Now let me state what there is there, for I have spent a great deal of time and observation upon the subject during the last four years. Iron City is beautifully situated in a most healthy location, being north of the rim of the basin and consequently is not excessively hot or dry and has an abundance of land well suited for the establishment of the largest iron works there are at least a dozen flowing springs of water within half a mile of Iron City. Mr. E. Hanks, one of the former owners, tells me that the old company had grants of water above the works, but by digging g wells from 10 to 20 feet, they struck such an abundance of excellent water, sufficient for every purpose that they never troubled themselves about getting water from above; and of late, in opening a body of coal two miles above the works (which bears evidence of being as good quality of coal as any yet found in Utah) at a depth of 30 feet, we struck so much water that we had to stop work until we could put in a pump.

In the next place, I will show that iron ought to be made here. In the first place, it has been made here, and came very near being a great success, although it was 200 miles from a railroad; and if iron could be made at $32 per ton, and

Illustration 3.1. A charcoal kiln, reconstructed with original materials, as it presently exists at the Iron City site. A second kiln was located just to the left of this oven. (Photo by Evan Jones)

freight the ore and charcoal from 30 to 168 miles, it could be made for $25 per ton at Iron City, where every prerequisite is found in close proximity and the charcoal can be obtained for 10 cents per bushel, there being tens of thousands of acres of timber right around Iron City. So, then I have shown that we have a beautiful, healthy location sufficient for a city of 5,000 and large iron works, plenty of good, pure spring and well water, coal and charcoal. We have also plenty of building rock and clay for brick, on the ground, out of which there is now ready for use, a foundry, machine shop, pattern shop, black smith shop, dwelling houses and a school house built of brick, besides other buildings of rock, adobies and lumber, consisting of engine house (with a 20 horse power steam engine) butcher shop, store, offices and dwelling house, charcoal house, two charcoal kilns, with the land on which the buildings stand with government title secured. A large quantity of material, such as cut rock for a large blast furnace, the present one being too small. There is also a great many tons of pig iron reserved for castings for the new furnace; there is also an air furnace built of brick, 30 feet high, there are fire rock, fire clay, molding sand, lime rock of the best quality, and the be best of iron fluxes all within two and a half miles of Iron City. Within a quarter of a mile of the town commence the iron mines, a group of nine claims of hematite, assaying from 60 to 70 percent metallic iron, containing millions of tons of ore on the top of the ground adjoining each other for two miles.

Next comes the Blowout Mountain which is 1,100 feet long by 500 feet wide, over 100 feet high, five miles from Iron City and not in Iron Springs mining district, as stated in the article of the 2nd inst. The ore is a magnetite, continuing in five other claims, assaying from 70 to 75 percent, containing millions of tons of ore on the surface, culminating on the top of what is termed the Great Western Iron Mountain, with a large body of black magnetic ore on the summit that can be seen in all directions for 50 miles. There are some 15 other claims of different kinds of ore, all of it good enough to ship if necessary. The foregoing property was offered to the committee appointed by the Board of Trade to commence operations with at very reasonable terms, and would it not be the very place for the commencement at least? I am satisfied for one that if it was taken hold of with intelligence and economy that it is the very thing needed for this community in the right place, and "there is millions in it."

Thomas Taylor[50]

The Utah Iron Manufacturing Company

On August 24, 1881, as a direct result of the assignment made by the Zion's Central Board of Trade for the Iron and Coke committee to organize a company for the manufacture of iron and coke, a group of men met in Salt Lake City to consider the advisability of organizing such a company. The meeting was called to order by William Jennings who was the chairman of the committee and who became its president when it was formally organized a week later on August 30, 1881. Jennings was a successful businessman in Salt Lake City and was involved in a butchery and tannery business and later a mercantile business. He was part of ZCMI, was in the leadership of two different railroad companies, was the director of the Deseret National Bank and was elected mayor of Salt Lake City in 1882.[51]

The following article published in the *Salt Lake Herald* on August 26, 1881, documents the meeting and the articles of incorporation of the newly formed "Utah Iron Manufacturing Company."

Iron - A Company Organized for the Manufacture of Iron

At 11 o'clock on Thursday a number of gentlemen prominently identified with the material wealth of the territory, met at the Deseret National Bank, for the purpose [of] taking into consideration the advisability of organizing a company for the manufacture of iron. The meeting was called to order by Hon. Wm. Jennings, upon whose nomination Hon. John Sharp was chosen chairman and Col. J. R. Winder secretary and temporary treasurer. The object of the meeting was explained, and the draft of articles of incorporation, which were to serve as a basis for deliberation, was read. After due consideration the draft was approved, a copy of which is given below, the name being the "Utah Iron Manufacturing Company." Five hundred shares of the stock were then subscribed for, and in accordance with the law regulating the incorporation of such companies, 10 percent of the amount of stock subscribed for was paid into the hands of the treasurer -- the sum amounting to the neat little nest egg of 500 hard good dollars. This done, the election of officers for the ensuing twelve months was commenced, resulting as follows: President, William Jennings; vice president, Amos Howe; directors, John Sharp, F. Little, John Taylor, W. H. Hooper, H. S. Eldredge, the president and vice president being members of the board, who together with the secretary and the treasurer -- to be hereafter elected by the board—will make the nine members necessary to constitute the board of directors as provided for in the articles of incorporation.

The stockholders meeting then adjourned sine die, and the board of directors met. Their business being the election of a secretary and a treasurer, Col. J. R. Winder was chosen secretary and L. S. Hills treasurer. The company has not yet decided what active steps will be taken or where the iron works will be located.[52]

Utah Iron Manufacturing Company

Following are the Articles of Agreement and Incorporation of the Utah Iron Manufacturing Company organized yesterday:

Articles of Agreement and Incorporation of the Utah Iron Manufacturing Company:

We, the undersigned, residents of the Territory of Utah, being desirous of associating ourselves together for the purpose of establishing and conducting the business hereinafter specified, and to incorporate for that purpose, do hereby mutually enter into and adopt the following articles of agreement that is to say:

Article 1. – The name of this association shall be the Utah Iron Manufacturing Company. Its principle place of business shall be at Salt Lake City, Utah Territory, and the time of its duration shall be 50 years next succeeding the first day of June, A.D. 1881.

ART. 2 – The pursuit or business of this association shall be that of mining and production of coal and manufacturing of coke; also mining and production of iron ores and the manufacture of iron in all its branches, qualities and departments.

ART 3 – The amount of the capital stock of the association shall be fifty thousand dollars and shall be divided into shares each of or the par value of one hundred dollars, and the limit of the capital stock of said association shall be one million dollars.

ART 4 – [This article contains the names of the subscribers and the amounts subscribed.]

ART 5 – There shall be nine officers of this association namely a president, vice-president and five directors, who, together shall constitute the board of directors of said association and shall be annually elected by the stockholders of the association, at a regular meeting thereof, to be held on the fourth Thursday in August of each year; also a secretary and treasurer to be annually appointed by the board of directors, at the first regular meeting of such board after the election as aforesaid.

ART 6 – No person shall be eligible to election or appointment as an officer of this association unless he is a stockholder thereof. The term of office of each officer of the association shall be one year and until his successor is elected or appointed and qualified.

ART 7 – Any officer appointed by the board of directors may be removed from his office for cause, by a two-thirds vote of said board, and any elective officer of the association may for cause, by a like vote of the board of directors, be suspended from office until the next regular or called meeting of the stockholders of the association. And the board of directors shall have power to fill a vacancy occurring in any office until the time of regular election. Any officer of this association may resign by giving thirty days' notice in writing to the board of directors.

ART – 8 Stockholders of the association, by a two thirds vote at any regular or called meeting, may remove any officer thereof for cause after reasonable notice thereof.

ART 9 – The board of directors shall have the control, management and supervision of all the business and affairs pertaining to the association, to establish by-laws and all other proper rules and regulations for the good government and welfare of the same, to provide for the appointment of such subordinate officers and agents and employees as may be necessary, and to prescribe the duties and powers of all officers, agents or employees of the association.

ART 10 – The private property of the stockholders of the association shall not be liable for the obligations thereof.

The officers of the organization are as follows: President, Wm. Jennings, Vice President, Amos Howe; Directors, John Sharp, F. Little, John Taylor, W. H. Hooper and H. S. Eldredge; who are elected for one year. John R. Winder was chosen Secretary and L. S. Hills Treasurer.[53]

Early in 1882, the Edmunds Act was passed in Washington D.C. by the federal government. Technically, the Edmunds Act had nothing to do with iron manufacturing in the Utah Territory; however, it affected the people and organizations supporting the work. The bill, among other things, outlawed the practice of polygamy in the United States. A number of high-ranking members of the Church of Jesus Christ of Latter-day Saints and many prominent Utah businessmen were polygamists. Members of both groups were involved in the Central Board of Trade, the newly formed Utah Iron Manufacturing Company and subsequent companies organized for the purpose of manufacturing iron in Utah. As the federal government became more and more engaged in tracking down and prosecuting those persons involved in polygamy, it became a huge distraction and, eventually, many individuals went into hiding, including the President of the Church.[54]

Despite the enthusiasm for iron manufacturing that was generated in 1881 by Zion's Central Board of Trade and the Iron and Coke Committee appointed by it, and even by the company that was organized as a result, very little was accomplished in the next two years. As discussed earlier in the chapter, Thomas Taylor was forced into litigation to prove many of his best mining claims and the Utah Iron Manufacturing Company was largely dependent upon those claims. Most likely the Company was not able to move forward until the claim titles were cleared. The court battles between A. G. Campbell and Thomas Taylor continued for several years and were not all settled until the first half of 1883. Once all the cases were settled, interest rekindled in iron manufacturing plans and a new company was organized.

On July 26, 1883, almost two years after the Utah Iron Manufacturing Company was organized, Elder Abraham H. Cannon, the son of George Q. Cannon, spoke to a group of businessmen concerning the manufacture of iron.

Yesterday afternoon a meeting of Salt Lake business men was held to take into consideration the manufacture of iron. It is the intention to stock the rich mines of iron formerly owned by Bishop Thomas Taylor, situated in Southern Utah. Our leaders realize that some industry must be established in the south, or that country will gradually become depopulated, as there is not sufficient land and water to sustain even those who are now there, and some of the best families are beginning to leave. Consequently, it is thought advisable to commence this new industry, which, if successful, will be a blessing which is very much needed in these mountainous regions, and there is no reason, that I can perceive, why it should not be manufactured as cheaply here as in our neighbor state, Colorado. I, at least, have great faith in the enterprise.[55]

The Iron Manufacturing Company of Utah

In July 1883, a new company was organized, or to put it more correctly, the old company was reorganized and renamed with a new president and new directors. The name of the company was changed from the Utah Iron Manufacturing Company to the "Iron Manufacturing Company of Utah." George Q. Cannon was President, Thomas Taylor, Vice President and General Business Agent, and John C. Cutler, Secretary. The new company owned all the property that was previously owned by Thomas Taylor and before that, the Great Western Iron Company. At the time of its incorporation 175,450 shares were subscribed for, of which 106,500 shares went to Thomas Taylor in return for his properties, and 62,500 shares went to the Church, represented by John Taylor and George Q. Cannon.[56]

The following two articles, one from the *Deseret News* and the other from the *Southern Utonian*, tell of the new company.

Manufacture of Iron

A new company organized for the establishment of the industry

In another part of the paper appears an advertisement of the Iron Manufacturing Company of Utah, of which Hon. Geo. Q. Cannon is President. The organization has been incorporated and perfected under the Territorial laws and proposes proceeding forthwith in the accomplishment of its object. The plant of the Great Western has been purchased, a number of very extensive and rich iron claims (in Iron County, Utah), for seven of which U.S. Patents have been obtained, are in possession of the new company, besides a number of coal claims, the product of which is admirably adapted for the manufacture of iron. The first practical operations of the company will be the erection of furnaces for the production of pig iron, and from that branch will spring those numerous, valuable and lucrative industries that are its natural outflow.

The capital stock of the enterprise has been placed at $250,000, and the shares at one dollar each, to be paid up in full and unassessable. The placing of the shares at an exceedingly low figure is a judicious provision, as it places the possession of an actual interest in the enterprise within the reach of all classes of the community. There is no industry that should be more popular than this, as it enters into almost every existing avenue of business and will contribute more extensively than any other to the prosperity and material development of the Territory.

Entertaining this positive view, we unhesitatingly recommend the people to step forward and take stock in one of the most important and promising enterprises ever established in Utah. We are all the more confident in making this recommendation on account of an unqualified conviction regarding the progress and success of the company.

All who wish to take stock in the company can do so by calling upon the Secretary Mr. John C. Cutler, constitution buildings.[57]

Iron Works.

We acknowledge with much satisfaction the receipt of a prospectus and bylaws of the "Iron Manufacturing Company" referred to in our issue of the 10th inst. The following from the prospectus will show we were correct in stating that the organization meant business:

"The Iron Manufacturing Company of Utah has in its possession in Southern Utah exhaustless fields of iron ore of every variety necessary to make the best article of iron and steel in the market. The iron claims comprise the Great Western, Iron, and Blowout Mountains. United States patents have been obtained for seven of these claims, which comprise pure magnetic, specular and hematite iron ores. There is sufficient ore in sight to furnish a number of blast furnaces for fifty years. All the labor necessary to prepare this ore for use is to break it into smaller pieces and haul it to the furnace. The Blowout itself has a body of ore on the surface 1100 feet long, 500 feet wide and 300 feet high, consisting of millions of tons which assays seventy percent pure metallic iron magnetic and specular. The Duncan claim is a hematite ore with a vein over 400 feet wide exposed nearly the whole 1500 feet of the length of the claim, and assays over sixty percent pure iron. The other claims are also large and rich in ore.

In proximity to these iron mines are beds of coal, of which the Company is a large owner, that possesses all the qualities necessary to furnish suitable fuel for the manufacture of iron and steel in all their stages. Besides coal there is an abundance of limestone, fire rock, fire clay and sand, also in the immediate neighborhood.

The Iron Manufacturing Company owns the old iron works at Iron City, Iron County, with considerable adjacent land. This property consists of foundry buildings, machine shop, blacksmith shop, pattern shop, store and offices, three dwelling houses, a number 4 Root blower, and a steam engine and engine house. In addition to these buildings and other property, there is a large quantity of rock of suitable quality which has been prepared for the erection of a blast furnace." We shall have more to say on this subject hereafter.[58]

In September 1883, Richard S. Robertson was employed by the Iron Manufacturing Company of Utah to superintend the building of furnaces at Iron City.[59] When first starting, he made a visit to Southern Utah and was interviewed by the *Deseret News* as he returned to Salt Lake City.

Local and Other Matters

Fine Prospect – Yesterday we had some conversation with Brother Richard S. Robertson, who has returned from a visit to the mines of the Iron Manufacturing

Company of Utah. He says he never saw such iron deposits in his life. There is in one place an entire mountain of ore, nearly eighty per cent of pure iron. The other facilities are also of the same extraordinarily favorable character. Brother Robertson, who understands the whole process, from the making of the brick, building and arranging of the furnaces to the making of the pig iron, considers the prospects of the company excellent. All that is requisite is the means to set it a going. In his view, which is a correct one, it is bound to be an industry of remarkable profit.[60]

Robertson and his family moved to Iron City the next month.

Southern Interest

The Record learns that Mr. R. S. Robertson the Scotch iron furnace expert engaged by the Utah Iron Manufacturing company moved with his family last week to the site of his forthcoming labors at Iron City. In conversation with a gentleman on the road he said that it would take an expenditure of fully $100,000 and a period of one year before the works which he contemplates erecting are in successful operation. This large expenditure or time and money he says, is not only rendered necessary by the magnitude of the works as designed, but also by the peculiarly refractory nature of the ore which has to be treated. Of its ultimate success, however, Mr. Robertson says he has not the least doubt.[61]

On October 16, 1883, Thomas Taylor made a progress report to the *Southern Utonian* in Beaver, which was picked up by the *Salt Lake Herald*.

The Iron Interest

The public are pretty well advised of the progress so far made in relation to the organization of a company and the creation of works for the purpose of making iron in Southern Utah. We have further information from Mr. Taylor, one of the principals in the enterprise, who informs the *Utonian* that the company's new blast furnace is about ten rods east of the old one which was torn down. It is about ten feet in the bosh and forty-five feet high. Twenty men are already employed and will be increased as needed. The castings for the hot air furnace will be made this winter. They will use the cupelo and machinery already on hand. The pig iron for castings referred to is mostly on hand amounting to 100 tons. Capital stock sells readily. The works will be in full blast next summer, and probably a railroad to ship the wares. Mr. Taylor says he has, independent of contested claims, ore enough to run any reasonable number of furnaces, for the space of 1,000 years.[62]

The Zion's Central Board of Trade held a regular meeting on October 9, 1883 and again iron was a major concern.

> The following was presented by T. G. Webber:
> I move that, as a board of trade, we lend our influence and support to the Iron Manufacturing Company of Utah, an organization incorporated for the purpose of developing the iron mines of Southern Utah and manufacturing iron; and that, as individuals, we subscribe for stock in said company and use our influence to induce others to become subscribers." Carried unanimously...[63]

Henry Lunt attended the Central Board meeting as the representative from Iron County and before he returned to Southern Utah he stopped to talk to the *Deseret News*. The following article was published in the *Deseret News* on October 24, 1883, concerning his visit.

Local and Other Matters

The Iron Industry. – Brother Henry Lunt, who recently returned to his home in Cedar City, called in at this office the day before leaving. He took occasion to speak of the iron industry in Utah, and of the great future before the people in which this important enterprise of iron manufacture is destined to play a prominent part. The subject, it appears, was mooted at an early day in our history. Brother Lunt, himself, one of the oldest settlers in Southern Utah, was sent down there thirty-two years ago, when Parowan and its adjacent towns were settled with a direct view to the manufacture of iron. He assisted to make the first iron ever produced in the Territory, and as early as 1853 brought up to this city a pair of home-made hand irons. Brother Lunt, though well advanced in years, feels that he will yet live to see the iron industry flourish in southern Utah and become a paying business. He looks upon the formation of the Iron Manufacturing Company of Utah as a prophetic movement in that direction. Great credit, he thinks, is due to Bishop Thos. Taylor for his spirited and successful opposition to the adverse claims and law suits of those parties who desired to gain possession of the valuable mining property which is at last secured to its rightful owners. The mines referred to are in Iron County, about twenty miles from Cedar, and contain more iron ore, he says, than it would be possible to work up in a thousand years. The patents for seven mines are held by the officers of the Iron Manufacturing Company of Utah.[64]

In an initial installment on August 1883 and continuing on a regular basis through September, 1885, a running article was published in the *Southern Utonian, Deseret Evening News* and *Salt Lake Herald*. It was very clear that the Company wanted investors, and at one dollar per share, suggested everyone could buy a share or two. The company must have paid in advance for a full two years of publicity, because the advertisements continued for over three months after the Iron Manufacturing Company of Utah was declared dissolved.

The Iron Manufacturing Company of Utah.

For the purpose of promoting the manufacture of iron this company has been incorporated according to law and has purchased the plant of the late Great Western Iron Company at Iron City, Iron County, Utah, together with the immense rich iron claims, for seven of which United States patents have been obtained. The company also owns interest in some of the best coal claims in Iron County, for which Government title has also been obtained, the product of which is of excellent quality for the manufacture of iron and steel.

The intension is first to erect furnaces for the manufacture of pig iron. When success is obtained to that, to gradually extend to other branches.

The time has come when the manufacture of iron and steel can be made profitable, and their manufacture will prepare the way for other industries. All who have the welfare of our Territory at heart are invited to subscribe for stock. The books are now open.

Capital stock, $250,000 shares one dollar each, certificates of which can be had by paying in full to the Secretary, John C. Cutler, Old Constitution Building, Salt Lake City.

Geo. Q. Cannon, President
Thomas Taylor, General Business Agent[65]

A couple of weeks after the Central Board meeting, Thomas Taylor returned to Salt Lake City from his stay in Southern Utah and gave the *Deseret News* an update on the construction activities at Iron City. The following article appeared in the *Deseret News* on November 7, 1883.

Local and other Matters

The Iron Industry – Bishop Thomas Taylor of this city, returned yesterday from a business visit to southern Utah, in the interests of the Utah Iron Manufacturing Company. At Iron City, which is in Iron County and situated about 22 miles west of Cedar, the work of erecting the company's new blast and hot air furnace is progressing steadily. The foundations of the blast furnace are laid, the jambs erected and all is ready for springing the arches upon which the furnace proper is to rest. It will be built of rock and lined with fire brick, the latter material manufactured by the Company. The hot-air furnace will require, in its construction, one hundred tons of castings, the iron for which is already procured and will be worked up into the material needed at Iron City during the coming winter. The productive capacity of the furnace now in course of erection, will be from fifteen to twenty tons of pig iron per day but the proposed addition of two more hot air furnaces will increase this to fifty tons per day.

Iron City was founded seven or eight years since and has been built up entirely by the iron industry. Works were erected there early in the settlement of the place, and hundreds of tons of pig iron produced, but during later years the business declined. The buildings formerly used have all been purchased by the new company, some of them pulled down to make room for the erection of furnaces, and others left standing to be used for various purposes in the present undertaking. The Company's iron mines, the ore from which has been proved to be of the best quality, are situated from two and a half to six miles distant from Iron City, to which place (pending the arrival of the railroad in that vicinity and the construction of branch lines between the furnaces and the mines) the crude material will be hauled by teams. Iron City is fifty miles distant from the present southern terminus of the Utah Central Railway, a future extension of which over the route now contemplated, will pass within five miles of the settlement. A branch line to Iron City and to Cedar, at the latter of which vast deposits of excellent coal are to be found, will doubtless be among the early things thought of subsequently. The coal at Cedar is said to be superior for furnace purposes, to even the popular Pleasant Valley product. Ovens will be constructed for the manufacture of coke. In regard to the iron works now going up, the officers of the company feel confident of disposing of enough capital stock to raise means for pushing the work forward to its proposed completion next summer. The iron industry is a very important one for Utah Territory and the present undertaking will in due time undoubtedly create employment for many people and develop into a first class paying enterprise.[66]

It should be noted that the earlier blast furnace was used by the Great Western Iron Company in the mid-1870s and that had just been torn down, could produce five tons of pig iron per day. The proposed new furnace was being designed to produce twenty tons per day, a fourfold increase over the old furnace. With the possible erection of a total of three furnaces as suggested, a massive twelve-fold increase in capacity would be achieved.

The above article mentioned the pending arrival of a railroad. The Company decided to speed up the process a bit. They found a bargain on a used narrow-gauge railroad setup in Nevada and bought the Pioche and Bullionville Railroad also called the Nevada Central Railroad. Thomas Taylor was in charge of getting the newly purchased equipment moved from Pioche, Nevada to Iron City. The following article published in the *Salt Lake Herald* on January 17, 1884 told the story.

Iron Manufacture

Bishop Thomas Taylor, of the Iron Manufacturing Company of Utah, has just returned from Southern Utah and Nevada, whither he has been on business concerning the removal to Iron City, of the Pioche & Bullionville railroad, recently purchased by the company. The Iron Company got a bargain in the little road, all of which was bought, including over twenty miles of track, two locomotives, more than twenty cars, besides the necessary turn tables, scales, tools, machinery, water tanks, and apparatus of a well-equipped line. Much of the property has already been removed to Iron City, and the removal of the track, locomotives and cars will be undertaken as soon as spring opens. As before stated in The Herald, an effort will be made to have the road transport itself, by pulling up the rails at the furthest end of the track and relaying them at the nearest, and so on repeating the operation until Iron City is reached. Should this plan prove unsuccessful another will be tried. Mr. Robertson is now on the ground superintending the transportation of the road. The road will be run from Iron City to the coal mines, about thirty miles distant and also connect the iron ledges with the furnaces. Bishop Taylor is well pleased with the purchase and is confident that with cheap coal and the small cost for transporting ore that will be secured, the company will be able to produce iron cheaper than it can be imported. The company is preparing for quite extensive operations in the spring.[67]

The intended use of the railroad was to haul coal from east of Cedar and iron ore from the mines to the furnace by rail rather than by team-drawn wagons. In preparation for the arrival of the railroad, nearly $1,000 was spent in grading a roadbed in Cedar Canyon in order to lay the track and transport coal from the canyon to Iron City.[68] It was reported that the price paid for the railroad equipment was $15,000.[69]

It is very curious that the people continued to be convinced that the local coal was of a "superior" quality and could be used to make coke for use in the blast furnaces. Granted, using charcoal in the furnace was an arduous and expensive proposition, but none of the coal found in Southern Utah ever proved to be suitable for producing good pig iron in a blast furnace. On February 1, 1884, a mere fifteen days later, Thomas Taylor was back in Beaver but had decided to use teams to haul the railroad equipment from Pioche rather than laying track down in front of the locomotives and taking it up behind them.

Iron, Iron, Iron

Bp. Thomas Taylor, agent for the Iron Manufacturing Company of Utah, arrived in town yesterday and held a meeting in the LDS Meeting House last evening in the iron interest. Mr. Taylor informed our citizens that the company had decided to haul the locomotive and railroad material from the vicinity of Pioche to the Iron City furnace, with teams instead of taking up and continuously laying down the rails. He desired one hundred teams from this place to be loaded with hay and grain from here. When the engine and other material was delivered at the Iron Works, the teams could go to work on the Utah Central railroad, which was expected to reach Iron City by early summer, to freight iron which would be manufactured by that time. He desired as far as possible to pay for the team work in shares in the iron works. Those who could not take all in that way, to take all they could – one half or more. This will give a most excellent opportunity for an investment in one of the best interests of the Territory. This bonanza being far ahead of all others.[70]

The method used to get the railroad equipment to Utah, of laying track down in front and taking it up in back turned out to be expensive and problematic. It was reported that a difficult hill was encountered near Jack Rabbit, Nevada and the decision was made to transport the material the remainder of the distance, about eighty miles, by ox-cart and wagon.[71]

It was also reported that some of the items were left scattered over the desert.[72] Apparently, one of the locomotives made it to Milford where it sat for several years until it was hauled to Cedar City in August 1888.[73] Historian Leonard J. Arrington tells the story.

> The little road was not destined to be used for its projected purpose. Other factors, as we shall see, were to interfere even while it was being transported to its intended destination. At first thought, it appears that company officials demonstrated bad judgment in purchasing the Pioche and Bullionville Railroad before testing operations gave clear indication that the Cedar Canyon coal was technically usable for reducing the Iron Mountain ore. Although there is no obligation to assume that Church business (and ecclesiastical) leaders were omniscient, it seems probable that the "premature" purchase of the little twenty-two-mile railroad seemed wise from two standpoints: (a) the price seemed, at the time to be a "bargain"; and (b) the impending possibility of new railroad construction in southern Utah would facilitate the sale of the railroad to other interests if the iron enterprise proved to be unprofitable. As to the wisdom of making the other expenditures—on the scale indicated—before adequate experimentation had been carried out on a small scale, favorable judgment is on weaker grounds.
>
> According to William R. Palmer, Cedar City, Utah, in a letter written to the writer, [Leonard J. Arrington] dated October 16, 1950, the engines, cars, rails, and other effects of the short Nevada railroad were stacked up on a vacant lot belonging to Thomas Taylor. Most of the rails were used in the coal mines around Cedar City, and for other similar purposes, but the remainder of the equipment was sold as scrap iron to a junk dealer during World War I and went to the smelters in Salt Lake County.[74]

From the previous experience of the Great Western Iron Company, the officials of the new company knew that they had to solve the transportation and furnace size issues to be successful and were determined to do so. One thing was very clear, however: they vastly underestimated the difficulty of transporting the two small locomotives and associated equipment from Nevada to Southern Utah.

In April 1884, General Conference of the Church of Jesus Christ of Latter-day Saints was held in Salt Lake City. During the conference, both President John Taylor and his counselor, George Q. Cannon spoke on the subject of home industries. President Cannon appealed to the members of the church "to practically support home manufactures by confining their consumption to such as was produced at home, wherever possible, and thereby dispense with the importation of those things." His remarks forcibly illustrated the desire of the community of Saints of the Church to become more self-supporting. President Taylor "asked the consent of the Conference, by vote, to permit him as Trustee-in-Trust, to extend aid to the iron manufacturing company now being formed in Iron County of this Territory." A unanimous approval and consent were given by the large congregation.[75]

In the conference, Church Apostle Erastus Snow spoke as well as President John Taylor. Both individuals discussed home industry and the commodities sponsored by the Central Board. Iron was specifically mentioned. President Taylor asked the congregation, in addition to the Church assisting the Iron Works, for individual members to personally assist the effort. The following article published on April 9, 1884 in the *Deseret News* summarized the two talks.

Fifty-Fourth Annual Conference

Apostle Erastus Snow said that all persons who reflected upon it must feel that the subject of home production was one of paramount importance. In the early settlement of this territory there was plenty of work in cultivating the earth and developing the natural resources of the country. In those times goods were high and money scarce and people resorted to the spinning wheel and handloom. Tanneries were common, and many articles were manufactured at home which are now imported. We had abundance of iron, coal and precious metals, but while we were consuming vast amounts of iron, glass, leather and other articles that could be procured here, we manufactured scarcely anything. We were getting to be a commercial rather than a manufacturing people, having large mercantile establishments, and depending principally upon our silver mines. Where agriculture was properly conducted, it was the foundation of self-sustenance. Next to this, home industry should be cultivated. The same capital invested in manufacture employed ten persons where one would be employed if invested in commerce. Those who took a comprehensive view of this question would seek the welfare of their fellows, for any other course must sooner or later result in their own ruin. This was an opportune moment to establish home industries in view of the scarcity of money and abundance of labor and provisions. Efforts were being made to develop our iron, glass and fine crockery ware. There were some who were sanguine of success, but their efforts were not seconded as they should be by men who had means. The development of iron and steel in view of the immense consumption was infinitely more important than that of the precious metals. Our agricultural resources and cultivatable lands were not by any means exhausted, though much had been done, there was yet much that might be done. There were many places that would support a much larger population if the natural facilities were properly developed, and the people should avail themselves of these advantages. Capitalists should seek to employ the surplus labor in manufacturing, and on the other hand, laborers should be ready to work for fair wages, so that they might obtain more steady employment and be better off. It was a mistaken idea that a man could do as well to earn large wages for six months, and remain idle the rest of the year, there was nothing more demoralizing than idleness.

President Taylor: "I have been very much interested in the remarks which have been made on this subject -- the subject of home industries. And I would ask this congregation if I may have the privilege of aiding them as Trustee in Trust. We have some iron works started in the south, and I want to know if this congregation will authorize me to assist those iron works? If you do make it manifest by raising the right hand [a forest of hands went up]. I believed that you would feel just so, and I have already assisted them. (laughter.) There is another thing I want to ask associated with this affair. You have given me the privilege of assisting this industry, now I want to ask if you yourselves, will assist in this matter; and all who are in favor of doing so, hold up the right hand [all hands went up.] Now we will say Yankee Doodle do it."[76]

In response to the comments made in General Conference, a meeting was held in short order by Zion's Central Board of Trade. President Taylor had authorized assisting the Iron Works but before any Church funds were to be expended, a due diligence review was apparently requisite. A review committee was formed within days of the conference and Central Board meeting.

The Board of Trade

The meeting of this board was held as arranged at the City Hall, yesterday morning at 10 o'clock, and after due consideration of the subject it was determined to appoint a committee of inquiry to investigate the iron interests of Iron County, and to make a report on the general condition and prospects of the affair. Following are the names of the committee, who are to report to the Board of Trade: Wm. Jennings, Moses Thatcher, Erastus Snow, J. R. Murdock, F. M. Lyman, J. R. Winder and Elias Morris.[77]

The committee appointed by the Central Board did not wait long to get started on their investigation and scheduled a trip to Southern Utah the following week.

From Wednesday's Daily, April 16 [1884]

Going South – Presidents John Taylor and George Q. Cannon accompanied by Presiding Bishop William B. Preston, Counselor R. T. Burton, President A. M. [A. H.?] Cannon, President L. J. Nuttall, Bishop John Sharp and Elder John Irvine, will go south by the 3 o'clock train tomorrow afternoon. One of the objects of the journey is to visit the Utah Iron Works at Iron City, but most of the party will continue on as far as St. George and visit some of the intervening settlements on the way home. They will be absent three or four weeks.

The party will be accompanied by the committee of Zion's Central Board of Trade, who will examine into the prospects of the iron manufacturing industry in that locality, with a view to reporting their findings hereafter for the benefit of the public. The committee is composed of the following named gentlemen: William Jennings, Moses Thatcher, Erastus Snow, John R. Winder, F. M. Lyman, John R. Murdock and Elias Morris. Most of these will return to the city as soon as they have finished their business in Iron County, the others will go on with President Taylor's party to St. George.[78]

Two of the members of the party who went to Southern Utah to examine the site where the iron manufacturing facility was to be built were John Sharp and William Jennings. Both men were top executives of the Utah Central Railroad, a subsidiary of the Union Pacific and owner of the Utah Southern Railroad. At the suggestion of President John Taylor these men located a route for a fifty-mile extension of the Utah Southern railway to run almost due south from Milford along the western base of the range of mountains to Iron City. The lack of water in the area was to be supplied by boring artesian wells. It was hoped that the building of the railroad would soon be commenced.[79]

Sharp and Jennings were separately interviewed by the *Salt Lake Herald* when they returned separately to Salt Lake City. Each of them disclosed a few items about the investigation as well as giving their own thoughts.

From these interviews it was clear that neither Sharp nor Jennings were in a position to communicate any finalized findings of the committee; however, it was obvious that they each had their opinions and readily shared them. The following insights were gained from the interviews.

> 1. Iron ore was not an issue; there was plenty of ore to make any kind of iron.
> 2. The coal, however, had not yet been examined to ascertain whether it would be usable for making iron. Sharp clearly stated that the committee's report would depend in large measure on the testing of the coal. Jennings, however, was of the opinion that the coal was very suitable for coking and even went so far as to say the local coal could be used, even without being coked.
> 3. There seemed to be a strong feeling that the manufacturing facility should be located at Iron Springs rather than at Iron City and that the work at Iron City should be halted at once.
> 4. There was consensus that railroad would not be built beyond Milford during the year, and maybe not for some time.
> 5. Jennings stated that he thought some $500,000 of capital would be required to develop the business and hoped to raise this money by extensive local subscription.
> 6. At first, the enterprise would be costly, but the stimulus to home industry would nevertheless make it worthwhile.

Apostle Moses Thatcher, another committee member, stayed behind at Iron City to visit the mines and observe the coal testing to be done by Mr. Robertson, the master ironmonger.[80] Leonard J. Arrington commented:

> Moses Thatcher, brilliant and energetic young Apostle of the Church, who was active in the direction of many of the Church's business interests, remained at Iron City for almost a month making a careful and thorough examination of the iron mines and coal beds. His report, important as it must have been, cannot be uncovered, and the newspapers of the times are silent about it. Undoubtedly, however, the report was pessimistic. The probabilities are that Thatcher stayed at Iron City long enough for Robertson to test the fluxing powers of the coal. As in all preceding and succeeding experiments with the Cedar Canyon coal, Thatcher and Robertson undoubtedly found the sulfur content of the coal deposits too high to produce good coke.[81]

The conclusion that the coal was not suitable and that the Iron Works should be relocated to Iron Springs from Iron City would have been devastating news to those who had been working on the project. For most of a year, work had been progressing at Iron City, old buildings razed, a blast furnace started, a railroad purchased to haul coal and iron ore, not to mention all of the old buildings and machinery that still existed. Thomas Taylor's mining claims were also nearby and it would have been a long haul to transport the ore to Iron Springs.

The report on the interview with William Jennings mentioned an article written by a *Salt Lake Herald* correspondent named "Wallace," apparently from Beaver, Utah. The article was very sobering, and yet seemed to be mostly true. He was optimistic that the best quality of iron and steel could be made in Iron County and that the county would become one of the richest and most populous in Utah. However, he had grave concerns about whether the conditions at the time would support the establishment and operation of iron works in the area. He had three fundamental questions, each critical to the success of the business: (1) could iron be manufactured at a sufficiently low cost to be competitive, (2) was there a market for the iron and (3) could that market be obtained once the iron was produced.

Wallace had strong opinions about the third question. He said that the railroads, both the Union Pacific and the Denver & Rio Grande, would absolutely not support shipping commodities out of the Territory, and would give little support to shipping material on short hauls within the Territory. He stated in his article that:

> The policy of the Union Pacific from first, to date has been to oppose home industries, as is evidenced in our inability to ship salt out of this Territory, where it can be secured for a song... Railroad policy in the west is to secure a long pull, and home manufactures, when successful, prevent that; and unless the policy has been changed, I do not believe that one ounce of Utah made iron can ever be shipped out of Utah over the U.P., unless the U.P. owns the mines and furnaces. Over the D&RG the case is even more hopeless, for in addition to those things, just as applicable to it as the other, is the fact that the D&RG at Pueblo Colorado, owns mines and furnaces of its own which are in operation, and when we hope they will help an industry where it could compete against their own, we hope for that which none but the insane could expect. As for instance: The Utah Central hauled D&RG iron over its road for points where the latter was to compete with former. When Utah Central asked the D&RG to return the compliment the latter declined, but said: We will furnish you our iron, our rails laid down at any point on our road, but we will not haul the rails of others.

Wallace's conclusion therefore, was since products could not be sold externally, the internal market would have to be the sole justification of the business, leading to the question: "Is there a home market sufficient to justify the expenditure of the money necessary to establish iron works that will be creditable and sufficient? If so, go ahead, and get the market outside as fast as possible; if not, it would be best to wait, for every failure discourages and only success begets success." He stated that if the endeavor failed, it would hurt more than it helped by making people dependent on the outside cash flow. It would bring in additional men, families and support facilities by creating a temporary market and then, if it collapsed and went away, it would impose hardships that would be worse than if it hadn't come at all. Lastly, Wallace stated that he and the people of Southern Utah firmly supported building the iron works at Iron Springs in preference to Iron City. He said that Iron Springs had more water, more space for building, was closer to the coal and would have favorable railroad grades to both the iron ore and coal deposits.[82]

In contrast to the article written by Wallace, Thomas Taylor wrote a very optimistic letter that was published in the *Salt Lake Herald* on October 26, 1884. At the time, Taylor was the vice president and general business agent of Iron Manufacturing Company of Utah, which may explain his determination to support the production of iron. Taylor explained that there were vast bodies of the best quality of iron ore in the area, very near the surface and hundreds of tons of excellent iron had been made from the ore with charcoal as fuel. He said that there was plenty of the best of limestone for fluxing and vast deposits of coal within six miles of Cedar City. He said that the company had a railroad that could haul the coal much cheaper than was the current practice. He went to great lengths explaining that even if the coal had been assayed with a sulfur content of seven percent, that there were several different methods that could be used to lower the sulfur content, including building a facility to wash the coal. He stated that a number of operations in Europe had been successful by washing their coal and that it could be done for no more than 2 dollars per ton. Mr. Taylor was convinced that a successful and profitable iron works could be built in Iron County, specifically at that time and at the Iron City location.

> I believe that Iron County, Utah, is not excelled anywhere for the vastness and excellence of its raw material for the making of iron and steel successfully and profitably; and if the people of Utah could see the necessity of creating these home industries, for out of the iron, numbers of others would flow, people might have employment, the farmers a home market for their produce, and everybody be benefited. It takes a large amount of means, and that is really the obstacle to its speedy accomplishment. Men who should be interested in the welfare of the Territory have sought excuses, for fear, if they invested, they would not get immediate returns. The iron trade being dull east, is a good reason why we should make our own iron in Utah and keep the millions that go east for iron and ironware at home, to circulate as a medium to prevent dull times here.... I can see no reason why the business could not be made profitable in this Territory, with so many States and Territories around us manufacturing no iron; at least we could make what we require ourselves.[83]

Many of the early individuals were firmly convinced that Iron County coal would make good coking coal. Thomas Taylor was one of those individuals. He stated that the coal could be washed at $2.00 per ton, if need be, to remove the sulfur. It is true that in the modern world, most of the metallurgical coal used to make coke for steel making is washed before it is coked to remove sulfur, ash and other impurities. A coal washing facility was even built for Carbon County coal when it was used at the Geneva Plant, which was much higher quality than Iron County coal. However, almost nowhere do they start with coal that has 7% sulfur and washing the coal would have done nothing to raise the low fixed carbon value of the Iron County coals. Furthermore, the early settlers had their hands full building blast furnaces, coking ovens and foundries, let alone taking on the task of building a wash plant, and maintaining an adequate water supply to keep it running.

Stopped in Its Tracks

Less than five months later and with little or no forewarning, on March 21, 1885, the following notification was published in the *Deseret Evening News*.

Stockholders' Meeting.

Notice is hereby given that a meeting of the Stockholders of the Iron Manufacturing Company of Utah, will be held at the office of the company, in Salt Lake City, Salt Lake County, Utah Territory, on Saturday, the fourth day of April, 1885, at 11 o'clock a. m., for the purpose of considering the question of a voluntary dissolution

of the corporation, and, if a dissolution is considered advisable, passing resolutions authorizing it, and transacting such other business as may come before the meeting.
John C. Cutler
   Secretary.
Dated Salt Lake City, March 20th, 1885.[84]

Apparently, the decision of the stockholders of the Company was to proceed with the Company's dissolution and the following notice appeared in the *Deseret News* a few weeks later on April 22, 1885.

Notice

Pursuant to an order of said Probate Judge in said matter, entered herein on the 20th day of April A. D., 1885, notice is hereby given, that Wednesday, the 27th day May A. D. 1885, at 10 a. m. of said day at the office of the Hon. Elias A. Smith, Probate Judge of Salt Lake County, at the County Court House in Salt Lake City, has been appointed the time and place for the hearing of the application of John C. Cutler as Secretary of "Iron Manufacturing Company of Utah," Salt Lake County, praying, among other things for an order declaring said company dissolved as provided for by law.[85]

Evidently, the hearing was delayed, postponed or required more time or information, as evidenced by the following notice published in the *Deseret Evening News* on September 23, 1885.

Notice

In the District Court for the Third Judicial District of Utah Territory, Salt Lake County. In the matter of "The Iron Manufacturing Company of Utah," to dissolve and disincorporate.

Upon the petition filed in said Court on the 21st day of September, 1885, praying for a decree of dissolution of said corporation, and the statutory notice may be given of the time and place for the hearing of said petition, and in pursuance of the order made by said Court in said matter, notice is hereby given, that on Wednesday, the 28th day of October, A. D. 1885, at the opening of Court on that day, or as soon thereafter as counsel can be heard, at the Court Room of said Court in the Wasatch Building in the City and County of Salt Lake, Territory of Utah, is fixed as the time and place for the hearing of said petition.[86]

A year later, on October 6, 1886, the following article was published in the *Salt Lake Herald*, almost as an epitaph to the once bustling works at Iron City.

The Iron District

October 2, 1886

    Cedar City was in days gone by frequently referred to in the columns of The Herald, in connection with her vast coal fields and immense deposits of iron ore; but of late we seem to have been forgotten at least as far as the columns of The Salt Lake Herald are concerned. However, we are still here and so are the iron and coal fields; the former in undisturbed state, the latter would be, only for the little obtained for local use. Thousands of dollars, Mr. Editor, have been spent with a view to developing these vast resources, but up to the present the efforts of those who have taken interest in these matters seem to have the word failure written on every move. An effort was made some four years ago by an enterprising citizen from the northern part of this Territory who seemed to take up the business with a determination to put it through. Money and labor were subscribed by quite a number of the citizens of Southern and middle Utah; some eight or ten miles of a railroad purchased, known in the flourishing days of Pioche as the Nevada Central; nearly $1,000 spent in grading up our rugged canyon in view of connecting the vast coal fields of this county by rail, with this and Iron City, which lies about twenty-two miles west of us, and in close proximity to the iron ore. But today, as far as the iron industry is concerned we are as quiet as a church yard and nothing left to remind us of our past hopes and great anticipations but the roadbed above referred to, a few pair of railroad car wheels, a portion of a locomotive and tender, and a few hundred feet of rails, all of which seems to be quietly laid away, at least until times brighten up, and a little more enterprise is manifested for home industry amongst us.

We are in one of the best manufacturing districts in the Territory of Utah, and with the exception of a few thousand pounds of wool per annum, the converting of a few cow, sheep and calf skins into leather, we are doing nothing by way of exporting, and today the citizens of this place are not as well prepared in the matter of home industry as they were several years ago.[87]

Reasons for Failure

There is never a single reason for any failure. Failure is a combination of circumstances. In the case of iron smelting, the challenges piled atop each other.

The Great Western Iron Company

The Great Western Iron Company, including its three predecessor companies, made hundreds of tons of excellent iron. Castings were made for the quartz mills at Pioche, Bristol and Bloomville, and quantities of pig iron were shipped all the way to the Salt Lake foundries. The finest kinds of castings and plates with filigree work, etc. were manufactured using Iron City iron, which was declared to be better than that produced in Pittsburg. However, despite the company's success, several issues eroded its viability and ultimately led to its downfall.

Furnaces may have played a role. Adams and Smith claimed that the furnace was too small to be economically viable and that it was of the wrong design for the local ore. It is unclear what design changes they had in mind but eight years later, when the next effort was made to build a blast furnace, it was to be four times bigger than the Great Western furnace. From the outside it appears that the companies spent too much time and money building furnaces and not enough time running them. It took almost three years for the first company to produce iron with the first blast furnace. The furnace ran for barely two and half years and was torn down. The second furnace took 13 months to build, during which time no iron was being produced. It operated just fourteen months before Adams and Smith wanted to build a third furnace.

Transportation costs were high. All raw material inputs and all the finished product outputs were hauled by ox cart or wagon. Iron ore is heavy and metallic iron is even heavier. Wood for making charcoal had to be cut with hand saws and axes and gathered from miles around. It was a substantial distance to the markets and the nearest railroad terminus was in Northern Utah. Several news articles stated that pig iron was being stockpiled at the site because of bad road conditions. The transcontinental railroad was completed through northern Utah in 1869. Although it didn't happen all at once, as time went on, manufactured goods from the east and west became more and more available. This not only increased the competition and drove down the cost of iron products, but it also caused investors to think twice before putting a lot of money into the local business.

Adams and Smith wanted to move the entire operation to Iron Springs. They may have been motivated by self-interest since they supposedly owned iron ore claims there. It seems that Adams and Smith had mostly given up on the Iron Works and were partly to blame for its failure. It would be hard to run a thriving business if the operators were not dedicated to make it happen. However, in the end, financial issues caused the shutdown of the operation. Cash flow was inadequate, it couldn't pay its bills or its workers and everything ground to a halt. The money panic of 1874 almost sunk the enterprise; the financial crisis in early 1876 finally did. The Company attempted on three separate occasions to get more money from the stockholders, and even went to court to try and force the issue, but it was case of too little too late. The Company also spent much time, money and effort on trying to finance and build railroads, none of which ever came to fruition.

The Iron Manufacturing Company of Utah

A number of causes factored into the failure of the Iron Manufacturing Company of Utah. The Thatcher report, a less-than-stellar report by Moses Thatcher given to the Central Board of Trade and to the leaders of the Church did nothing to gain moral and financial support. Low-quality coal became another concern as the coal in the area once again proved unfit for making coke, a huge negative factor. No matter how much the company wanted the coal to work, geology proved that its usefulness was severely limited. Charcoal had been proven to produce quality iron, but the company was doggedly determined to use coal. Location, particularly the declaration by the board members and others that the works should be moved from Iron City to Iron Springs, created a substantial setback, with almost a year's work wasted and substantial cost added.

The problems associated with moving the Pioche and Bullionville Railroad to Iron City were costly, diverted critical resources and did nothing to help the credibility of the company and market and transportation continued to be a big question. Maybe, if the facilities had been successfully completed, the railroad would have been extended to the area. But even then, it was doubtful if the company would have been able to competitively sell product beyond the Utah area. The railroad companies were not at all supportive.

The imports coming to Utah by way of the transcontinental railroad continued to erode the urgency of building an iron manufacturing complex in Southern Utah.

Anti-polygamy laws were another factor, probably the biggest and most important, that was discussed earlier in the chapter. The United States government had attempted since 1862, in one way or another, to stop the practice of polygamy in Utah and to weaken the Church of Jesus Christ of Latter-day Saints. In 1882, the Edmunds Act was approved, which provided heavy fines and penalties for those found guilty of polygamy and/or cohabitation. In October 1884, the first trial case went to Territorial Court and was eventually upheld in the United States Supreme Court in the spring of 1885. The outcome of the trial case sent Federal Deputies rushing throughout the Territory, hunting for offenders. Almost all of the Church leaders and many of the industrial leaders went into "hiding." President John Taylor's last public appearance was February 1, 1885, in the Salt Lake Tabernacle. He died while still "underground" in July 1887.[88]

When this frontal assault on both individuals and the Church was launched by the federal government, Church leaders and members lost focus on almost everything except self-preservation. After late summer of 1884, the Iron Company expended no more money and held no further meetings except in April 1885 to decide to dissolve the company. Church leaders terminated their plans to establish an iron industry and, for that matter, they discontinued virtually everything on which the Central Board had been working.

Overall, the Iron Manufacturing Company faced an issue of having "bitten off more than one can chew." The first efforts at Iron City had been small, but manageable and successful. A blast furnace, coke ovens and a foundry were built, and a substantial amount of good quality iron was produced. End use products were fashioned and sold. However, the new owners and operators remembered that the reason for financial failure was the high cost of transportation and that the furnace was too small and was of the wrong design for the iron ore being used. The new company was determined to solve those problems. They designed a furnace that would have been four times bigger than the first furnace and wanted a total of three furnaces. They weren't satisfied with wagons and teams to haul ore and coal; they wanted a railroad. In the end it was just too big of a jump, requiring too much up-front work and capital.

When the company failed, ownership of the mining claims that Thomas Taylor had contributed, went back to him. He continued to promote the industry and tried to sell his claims, but the forces of opposition, both internal and external were too strong. He was an advocate of establishing the iron manufacturing industry in Southern Utah almost until the day he died. Ultimately, his heirs sold his claims to CF&I of Pueblo, Colorado in 1903, fifteen years after the company had failed.

The failure of the Iron Manufacturing Company of Utah was a huge disappointment to those who had fought to make it work. It resulted in substantial losses to its many investors, both large and small, and it was a loss to the church, which had spent both time and money in its behalf hoping for growth in industry and employment. It was a setback to the citizens of Southern Utah who had to wait nearly another forty years before iron ore was successfully mined and a railroad built. Unfortunately, although the iron ore reserves were eventually mined, a locally controlled, financially successful iron manufacturing business was never built in southern Utah.

The last iron was produced at Iron City in 1876. When the operation shut down there were a number of facilities in existence including a foundry and foundry buildings, a machine shop, a pattern shop, a blacksmith shop, three dwelling houses, a brick school house, a blower, a steam engine and engine house, a butcher shop, stores and offices, a dwelling house, a charcoal house, a blast furnace and two charcoal kilns.

The buildings and iron works sat idle until sometime in 1883, at which time the new owners of the works, the Iron Manufacturing Company of Utah, took over the property. The old blast furnace and some of the buildings were torn down to make room for three new furnaces which were to be built. Other buildings were left standing to be used in the new undertaking. The first new furnace was located about ten rods (165 feet) from where the old furnace stood and was to be about ten feet in the bosh and forty-five feet high. By October 1883, "the foundation of the furnace had been laid, the jambs

Iron Mining & Manufacturing

Illustration 3.2. Photo taken April 25, 1950. The adobe walls can be seen on top of the lower stone walls. (Photo by R.D. Adams, Matheson Special Collections)

Illustration 3.3. The Iron City ruins as they looked in the 1950s. Unfortunately, most of the construction visible here was removed by people appropriating the historic building stone for private use. Very little remains today. (Matheson Special Collections)

Iron City Iron Works

Illustration 3.4. The foundry stack and building as they existed in 1950. (Matheson Special Collections)

Illustration 3.5. The foundation of the third blast furnace that was started in 1883 but never completed. The business was dissolved in early 1885. (Photo by Evan Jones)

erected and all was ready for springing the arches upon which the furnace proper was to rest."[89] However, that is as far as they got when everything came to a grinding halt.

Over time, nature took its course and many of the adobe buildings began to crumble. Those built of stone fared better, but much of the stone, so nicely cut into squared blocks, was hauled off by local residents to be used in their homes and buildings. Even between 1950, when some of the photographs reproduced here were taken, and the time the State Park was established and the site fenced off and protected, many of the structures were destroyed by nature or vandals and were in ruin. Historic or not, the crumbling walls became a hazard to visitors and were subsequently demolished.

CHAPTER FOUR

Hopes, Dreams, and Speculation
1869–1923

THE EARLY ATTEMPTS to locally manufacture the much-needed iron and steel products in Utah were successful in a number of aspects but the businesses failed to develop into viable, ongoing commercial enterprises. As a result, relatively little actual iron ore was mined by these operations. The deposits of iron ore were still there in the ground, waiting, lying dormant. The residents of Southern Utah, as well as any others, were aware of this abundant and precious resource and many were anxious to see it developed so that the ore could bring growth and prosperity. Some individuals were obsessed by the iron ore fields and worked almost continuously to claim, develop and advertise them to the world. Many spent a good portion of their lives and much of their wealth working on their claims, thinking that good fortune was just around the corner. In most cases it took more than a generation or even two before any return was made on their investment.

Even before the last Iron City endeavor was shut down, many things were happening in the world outside of Iron County involving mining, railroads, and smelters that would have a long-term effect on the local iron industry. Within the County, even though the smelters and foundries had been shut down, this time period was one of the most active for staking, developing, buying and selling mining claims. There were winners and losers in these activities and the results often determined who would become the future claim owners and miners in the area. The owners of these claims often joined with other owners and packaged their claims in groups. The larger and more valuable groups attracted the attention of investors from near and far. Several Eastern syndicates became interested in Utah iron ore and purchased a number of valuable claims. The precious metal tycoons secured a number of claims. Colorado Fuel & Iron Corporation (CF&I) focused its efforts on Southern Utah and accumulated dozens of claims. Many thought that CF&I was going to build a large facility in Utah, like the one it had built in Colorado. If not that, it was thought the company would at least help build a railroad to transport Utah ore to its Pueblo smelter. However, in retrospect, the securing these valuable reserves by CF&I and other outside companies had the effect of delaying rather than accelerating the building of an iron industry in Utah. Outsiders were more interested in the plans and timetables in their own state than in what was happening in Southern Utah.

The last half of the nineteenth century was a time when precious-metal mining boomed all over the western United States. Some locations were very close to Cedar City: Silver Reef, Frisco, Marysvale, Eureka, Pioche, and many more. Some of the boom towns were many times larger than Cedar City in population, even when Cedar City was counted with nearby towns. Some of these wealthy boom-town entrepreneurs were attracted to the iron deposits of Iron County.

With mining being such big business in the area and all the prospectors and investors circulating nearby, it may appear strange that Iron County was left undeveloped. But, despite its importance, iron was not nearly as valuable as silver and gold, nor was it as easy to refine. It became clear that a blast furnace and a railroad were needed before the County's iron ore was going to be mined. Everyone hoped that these would come quickly.

In that environment, speculation was rampant. Rumors were everywhere about developments that were "certain" to occur in the "very near" future. There were many news articles written with the specific purpose of attracting interest to Southern Utah and its mineral wealth. Many times, these were nothing but pure conjecture, but other times, company officials made actual statements that plans were being made for immediate development of smelters or railroads. Unfortunately, despite all the talk, nothing came to fruition. After the blast furnace fires went in Iron City in 1876, no producing mines operated in the area for over forty-five years.

Hopes and Speculation

An article was published in the *Salt Lake Tribune* in August 1881 which was representative of the speculation and excitement that existed even before the last smelting attempt at Iron City was put to rest. The author of the article seemed to be imagining the future possibilities for Southern Utah. In his mind, there was no doubt that one or more railroads would be at Iron Springs within two years, that Iron County contained "the most wonderful iron ore deposits in the world," and that "Iron Springs and Iron City would be the sites of the greatest cities in Utah after Salt Lake." The article is quoted in part.

Our Iron and Coal: The Greatest Iron Deposits to be Found in the World
It is understood that the Texas Pacific is to be run northwestward from El Paso through Arizona, crossing the Rio Colorado at the most eligible point between Prescott, Arizona and Iron Springs, meeting the California Central (Col Lyman Bridges) at Iron Springs or at Crystal Springs, 100 miles west (to be governed by the nature of the approaches to the Colorado River.)

The California Central is projected to run from San Francisco via Yosemite and Big Tree, Silver Peak, Nevada, and Crystal Springs to Iron Springs, Iron City, or thereabouts. (After looking over the ground we should say to Iron Springs.)

The Utah Central will have extended its main line from Milford to Iron Springs within less than one year, doubtless within six months.

The Denver and Rio Grande is making rapidly for Utah, and for whatever there is in sight in Utah, and two years will doubtless see its engines watering at Iron Springs....

... Practical iron workers have also visited the ground and had the ores tested and have invariably pronounced them the most wonderful iron ore deposits in the world, whether considered with respect to quantity or quality.

It is no exaggeration to say that the supply is inexhaustible. The blowout is a solid mass of iron ore rising 100 feet above the surface of the country, perhaps twice that and standing, on an average, 200 feet thick for 300 or 400 feet in length, representing in itself perhaps a million tons of ore "in sight," and this taking account only of pure ore.

The hill top on the Adams patent, in part, is five acres in extent, not all solid ore in place, but apparently nearly so. Some of the ledges are fifty yards wide, in place, and 300 to 600 feet long. A ledge on the Blair Patent, in part, is a comb standing forty feet high for 100 yards, twenty feet thick and 900 feet long altogether, visible ten miles away. Thousands of tons have fallen and cover the hill sides—blocks twenty feet long and six or eight feet square, like those [ ] partly hewn in the quarries of [Syria] and Palmyra.

There are probably 50,000,000 tons of iron ore embraced in these claims, above and within easy reach below the surface of the ground. Not all good quality, not all available for any purpose, but including, nevertheless, many ledges of a quality unsurpassed in the world. Themselves practically inexhaustible and sufficient, without intermixture save with each other, for the production of Bessemer iron and steel.[1]

The failure of the Iron Manufacturing Company of Utah's smelter attempt at Iron City in early 1885 did little to dampen hopes and speculation. If anything, it seemed to fuel the fire. The Blowout deposit alone seemed to inspire all who saw it and led them to believe that someone would be rushing in to put its ore to use. An article published in February 1888, raved about an "unlimited supply" of iron ore of a superior quality that had "no equal in the world."

Utah's Metallic Wealth

The metallic wealth of Utah, especially in iron, has never received the attention it rightfully deserves, for if these resources were developed to a proper extent it would become clearly evident that this Territory would be a successful rival of the famous Lake Superior mines in the output of iron ore. The very best quality of this metal can be found all over Utah in every conceivable variety. The most important beds are located in Iron County, some 308 miles from Salt Lake City.

The belt in this section is two miles wide by sixteen miles long. The ores are magnetite and hematite, and assays carefully made by Prof Newberry, the well-known scientist of Columbia college, New York, show that they contain an unlimited supply of Bessemer ore of a superior quality. It is estimated that over 3,000,000 tons can be seen above the surrounding ground on Blowout Mound alone in Iron County. There are upwards of fifty claims around the Iron Spring and Iron City groups, which at the lowest calculation, hold in their rocky embrace, over 500,000,000 tons of iron, the intrinsic value of which, for the number of tons, has no equal in the world.[2]

Thomas Taylor, who ended up owning a large number of prominent and valuable iron ore claims from the last Iron City endeavor, continued to promote the mineral wealth of Southern Utah for many years. His attempts were naturally focused on attracting someone to buy or utilize ore from one or more of his own properties, but he appeared to be genuinely interested in the growth of the iron manufacturing industry in the area and certainly kept it in the public eye. The following article, written by Thomas Taylor himself, was published on Christmas day, 1889.

The Inexhaustible Mountains of Wealth in Southern Utah.
By Thomas Taylor

There is no iron or steel being made from ore in the territory, and that which has been the foundation of the real prosperity of the richest nations, including our own, has not yet been developed. If the opinion of the Baldwin exploring expedition is correct, which I quote, "Utah's great wealth lies not in its hundreds of valuable gold and silver ledges, but in its iron and coal fields. The seeming fabulous stories of the immense iron deposits in Southern Utah but told part of the truth.

On reaching the iron fields, we found them covered with thousands of acres of the finest pine and cedar timber (suitable for making charcoal) sufficient for the requirements of the country for years to come. Pinto iron mining district, in which are the famous Iron and Blowout mountains, is one vast extant of rich magnetic, specular and hematite ores. The ledges crop out of the earth in places hundreds of feet high and appear on the surface for eight hundred and a thousand feet, inviting capitalists to double and treble their fortunes with scarcely a possible risk of losing a cent. But a few miles distant are immense beds of coal with which to melt out this huge body of material wealth."

This county has been visited by the most eminent professors of mineralogy—Newberry, Hewitt, and others of New York; E. D. Wassell, of Pittsburg, Penn.; Blake of New Haven, Conn.; L. E. Holden of Cleveland, Ohio, and others, who have written and spoken in the highest terms of the richness and immensity of the iron and coal of Iron County. Iron ore of general good quality is found all over the territory.

A very elaborate blast furnace was built at Ogden some years ago. A Mr. Jones of Pittsburg, started it up, and made a few tons of the best quality of pig iron, but he told the writer that Iron County was the place to make the pig iron. A rolling mill might be built at Ogden, but it was too far away from the coal, for coal is the principal factor in the manufacture of iron and steel. It requires, for all purposes connected with the manufacture of one ton of iron or steel, an average of five tons of coal, and all iron companies erect their works as near the fuel as possible.

A semi-anthracite coal has been found in Iron County, and there is no doubt but a pure anthracite exists there and will be found as the coal fields are developed. There are a number of first-class foundries in Salt Lake City, where they turn out the best of workmanship. There are also foundries in Provo, Ogden, Logan and other places, and there is no question but what their business would be much increased if they could obtain pig iron at the price that it can be made for in our own territory, and surely it could be made as cheap here as in any part of the United States.

The coal of Utah would, any of it, make coke if it were put through a practical process of crushing and washing, such as is adopted in England and other countries. The crushing and washing are done there at a cost of about four pence per ton. It is believed that some of the coal of Iron County would do for the blast furnace without coking, as pieces have been picked and analyzed giving less than one percent sulphur. Then, with iron ore of the purest kind in inexhaustible quantities already mined, lead ore and limestone for fluxing, equally accessible; with charcoal, fire rock, fire clay, and every other ingredient within a few miles of the plant, why not be able to make pig iron cheap in Utah?

From inquiry made five years ago, it was found that Utah was importing yearly over five million dollars' worth of iron and steel, and manufactured articles whose principal material was iron and steel. From statistical reports we find that in the year 1888, there was made and manufactured at the several ironworks in the United States over twelve million tons of iron and steel, being something like four hundred pounds for every man, woman and child in the country, for we use more of these materials than any other nation of the earth. Utah's proportion would be about forty thousand tons per year.

Look at the vast amount of money that would be kept in our territory, and the amount of skilled labor that would be employed in its manipulation into some of the different useful articles that we import every year, such as heavy castings for machinery, stamp mills, grist mills, furnaces, smelters, water jackets, water pipes, gas pipes, pillars, columns, and for fireproof buildings, stoves, light castings, malleable iron, etc., wrought iron, and steel for railroad locomotives, car wheels, bridges, cars, turntables, scales, etc.; tools, implements of husbandry, plows, harrows, reapers, mowers, threshing machines, steam engines, steel and iron rails, edge tools and cutlery nails, bolts, screws, etc., too numerous to detail, all of which have their representative skilled workmen, and could be made in Utah, adding to the wealth of the territory, its profitable returns. We are now about to be connected by rail with every part of our country and with the Pacific Ocean, creating a market for the numbers of large iron works which will undoubtedly be established in Utah in the near future.

The establishment of extensive iron works in Utah with cheaper pig and merchant iron than can be brought from the east, will make it possible to build and operate foundries and machine shops in our neighboring states and territories, where they make no iron at the present time. There is none made in Wyoming, Idaho, Montana, Nevada, California, Arizona, New Mexico, nor in Old Mexico, of any consequence.

Capitalists are already looking this way and it may not be long before all the railroads we have now will be wanted to distribute our vast production to the adjoining country.

Our various kinds, and rich quality, and immense deposits of iron ore, with low railway freights, will ere long, find their way to other localities than Utah. For making special articles of iron and steel, special kinds of iron ore are required. Sometimes an ore not found in a certain country is found in a foreign land and required to mix with native ore; thus, in the year 1888, there were imported into the United States from foreign countries, reported by the American Iron & Steel Association 1,337,017 tons of iron ore. It may be that in Utah's varied store of iron deposits is the very kind required.

When the railways connect us with the ocean by a little span of 450 miles we shall be able to furnish Pittsburg, New York and Chicago with our pure iron ore at reasonable rates. The prospect for the establishment of iron and steel works is very good, and in the opinion of the writer, Utah has a splendid future, growing out of her great iron industries.[3]

In late 1890, an interesting exchange took place in the *Iron County News*. The first article stated that Andrew Corry, a local resident, had shown a man from Salt Lake City around Iron City. The man stated that he was making a report for potential investors regarding Iron City". The article was picked up by several newspapers, including the *Salt Lake Tribune* and the *Utah Enquirer*[4]. Thomas Taylor wrote a biting letter to the editor of the *Iron County News* which was included in the following week's publication. Taylor stated that neither Corry nor the speculator from Salt Lake had any business exploring Iron

City or the nearby iron deposits. He stated that "I am the owner of Iron City, Iron Co. Utah, and of everything in it and I own the only mines that are worth working in that neighborhood both for quantity and quality of ore; ... hundreds of thousands of dollars have been expended to get my property in the shape that it is in, and to obtain title thereto; ... what would these parties say of me if I were to engage for the sake of making a few dollars to take speculators around, and show them bands of horses, herds of stock, flocks of sheep, ranches or farms, and tell said strangers how I thought they could get possession without purchase as contrary to the wishes of the owners; I have bought and paid for all I claim in Iron Co. and I am not desirous of any one's aid in disposing of it."[5] Thomas Taylor was obviously tired of claim jumpers and others thinking they could acquire his property, legally or illegally, without even talking to him!

The following article gave a quite detailed account, not only concerning the various areas of Southern Utah and in particular, the iron ore deposits, but also much of the rest of the State and the modes of travel at that point in time. The reporter started out in Northern Utah traveling on the railroad heading south until he reached the Milford terminus, and from there, he traveled by stagecoach to Cedar City, then on to St. George. He concluded, among other things, that there were many locations in Southern Utah that were in desperate need of a railroad. The article was published in October of 1891.

Neglected Wealth

ST GEORGE, Oct. 14 – We left Salt Lake Tuesday on a four weeks tour of the south and southwest via the Union Pacific. The run through Salt Lake and Utah counties, past the great factory of the Utah Sugar company and through the heavily laden orchards and fields of ripening grain, was unaccompanied by any incident until the vicinity of American Fork was reached, when the train was overtaken by a thunderstorm and the rain came down in sheets, literally blotting out the landscape. The storm soon spent its fury and, although a slight sprinkle continued all through the night, the progress of the train was undisturbed.

At Juab we changed cars and took possession of one of the Union Pacific's "palace cars," which that road still imposes upon the unsuspecting public. For the slight consideration of $1 each we were allowed the great privilege of occupying a bunk, made by turning three seats down and covered by two blankets, which from their appearance might have done yeoman service in the late unpleasantness. It is perhaps just as well for the traveler that the country between Juab and Milford is covered with a veil of darkness, as the scenery through that section is, without exception, the most dreary in Utah.

Upon reaching Milford, the southern terminus of the Union Pacific, those bound still farther south, are enabled to take in the surrounding country and stretch their weary limbs before starting on their two days and nights' ride across country. The railroad at this point seems most busily engaged tearing up the work done last summer. From Milford to Pioche, a distance of 145 miles, the road has been graded, and about twelve miles of track laid out from Milford. Several months ago, word was received from headquarters at Omaha to tear up the track and ship the material north and east to be used in repairing the roadbed. Since that time a work train has gone out each morning, and about three carloads of rails and ties have left Milford on all regular northbound trains. The end of the track is now about three quarters of a mile out from the road running up to Frisco, and the next two weeks will see it all loaded on board cars. As one railroad man said, about all the Union Pacific has to do now in the south is to tear up what it has already done. The sulphur mines at Clear Creek furnish about two carloads of sulphur daily, which is loaded at Blackrock. The mines at Frisco are also daily shippers, although the output of ore has materially diminished within the last year.

The real estate boom at Milford is a thing of the past and the eastern company which rumor said had bought in and platted all land in the vicinity is likewise a thing of the past and lives only in the minds of those who got taken in, to their profound sorrow.

The stage leaves Milford about 7 o'clock and reaches Beaver in time for a late dinner. When the last government contract was let, the route which used to run over the mountain from Minersville to Cedar was changed so as to pass through Beaver, Buckhorn Springs, Red Creek and Parowan to Cedar, thus adding about thirty miles to the already long and tiresome journey and necessitating an all-night-ride. Only those who have taken the trip in day-time and under the most favorable circumstances can appreciate the "goodness" of the government in this move. To sit on the outside seat of an old-time covered stagecoach and keep from falling off when it strikes rocks and ruts, requires the dexterity of a circus rider and can only be likened to the antics of a bucking bronco.

The people of Beaver are anxiously awaiting the next move of the Rio Grande Western southwards. They have long since given up all hopes of the Union Pacific ever reaching them, but the chances of getting the Rio Grande are now brighter than ever. Surveyors for this road have run a line south from Salina, following up the Sevier, running through Richfield and over the mountains through Clear Creek canyon to Beaver. From the latter city it crosses the fertile valley and runs out across a low pass in the mountains, entering Parowan valley at the north end near Buckhorn Springs, and continuing south through all the settlements. The only difficulty they experienced with the grade was through Clear Creek canyon, north of Beaver. In several places the pass was so narrow as barely to furnish room for the track and river, and in order to hold this valuable outlet, a large force of men was put to work and a good grade established for twenty miles.

The proposed road runs near the famous sulphur beds of Clear and Cove creeks, and these mines alone, when a market thus guaranteed, will furnish an immense amount of freight. The supply of sulphur, which when taken out is nearly pure and needs little refining, seems inexhaustible, and the owners feel confident that they have a fortune in their prospect. The mines have been worked for years but as transportation is so limited they were never thoroughly developed and their extent is still almost unknown. A considerable force was out on some time ago and considerable sulphur has been taken out. From what could be learned it is the intention of the Rio Grande to run a branch line to Marysvale, the great mining camp situated under the shadow of Old Baldy. The mines of this place are among the richest in the country, and when brought into closer communication with the north and east, will startle the world with the value of their output. Gold in considerable quantities has been discovered and half of the camps resources has never been told.

The southern country has been thoroughly soaked during the last two weeks, the storm extending south as far as Arizona. We were rained on during the entire trip from Milford to Paragoonah and when the coach reached Beaver the washed-out condition of the road necessitated putting on a double team and we crossed the mountain behind four large horses driven by ex-Sheriff William Hutchings, who amused his passengers by tales of early time experiences during the term of his rather hazardous office. The country never looked better and the land fairly groans with its load of grain and fruits. Harvesting is now going on in the northern counties and the yield is tremendous. As we passed farther south the air became more balmy and the country took on a different aspect. The coach rolled into Cedar about 6 o'clock a. m. and a short stop was made for breakfast. At Cedar are located the large coal beds which furnish fuel for the people of that vicinity. They have never been thoroughly developed, however, and are almost idle, awaiting a railroad. The coal is of a superior quality and makes the best of coke. The mines are very accessible and can be worked cheaply, thus insuring plenty of fuel for the railroad.

Lying about twenty miles almost directly west of Cedar are the famous iron deposits of Iron City. Some time ago it was stated that an eastern and English syndicate had been formed to erect smelters at that point and manufacture steel rails. The project included the building of a branch road from the Union Pacific's Pioche extension, but as that has been given up for an indefinite period, it was stated the plans had been changed and a line would be built west from Cedar and the freight sent west via the Rio Grande, or the first line to tap the vast resources of Dixie. In regard to the ore deposits Iron County, Prof. J. S. Newberry of the Columbia school of mines of New York City says: "These ore beds have been long known and were to some extent utilized by the Mormons in their first advent. They constitute perhaps, the most remarkable deposit of iron ore yet discovered on this continent.

The iron region lies nearly 200 miles directly south from Salt Lake City and is situated in what is really the southern prolongation of the Wasatch Mountains. The iron ores occur in the northern portion of a subordinate range, which attains its greatest height in Pine Valley Mountain, near Silver Reef. The ore beds form a series of protruding crests and masses set over an area about fifteen miles long in a northeast and southwest direction and have a width of three to five miles. Within this belt, the iron outcrops are very numerous and striking, and many claims have been located upon them. The most impressive outcrops are in the vicinity of Iron City, Oak Springs and Iron Springs. Near Iron City the "Big Blowout" as it is called, is a projecting mass of magnetic ore, which shows a length of perhaps 1,000 feet by a width of 500 feet and rises in castellated crags 100 feet or more above its base. There is considerable diversity in the character of the ore, although it is about equally divided in quantity between hematite and magnetic. Some of the beds of both are exceedingly dense and compact, while others, though rich in iron, are soft and can be mined with a pick. Most of the ore is very pure, containing a small amount of earthy matter and no foreign minerals.

Those beds of ore have attracted the attention of capitalists and several attempts have been made to start work at Iron City. Furnaces were erected and considerable ore smelted but the project was given up, awaiting the advent of the iron horse. It is impossible to estimate the output of this region alone, but it would when in full blast, furnish one road with sufficient freight to pay for the building of the line.

Leaving Cedar, the stage route follows the old line, and the stakes of two railroad surveying parties are always in sight. One of these is the Utah, Nevada & California, which for some time past has had headquarters at Provo and whose proposed terminus is in the southern part of California. The statement made in a late issue of The Herald that dirt would fly within forty days on this road, has created much interest in this section, as a railroad means Dixie's salvation. No country offers the same inducements for a railroad as this, and the company first to build, will reap a harvest of blessings and ducats. The grade from Beaver to St. George is almost self-established and the expense of preparing a roadbed would be merely nominal. From this place the surveyor found easy outlet to the coast with few cuts and fills.

At Bellevue where we stopped for dinner on the second day out from Milford, Thomas Judd, James Andrus and your correspondent were shown through the orchards and vineyards of Mr. Gregorson. The yield, the latter gentleman states, has been greater than any previous year, and the fruit is of a splendid quality. The ground under the trees was covered with luscious peaches, pears, apples and plums, wasting and rotting for want of a market. The trees were loaded to such an extent that the boughs almost touched the ground. To see such a vast amount of fruit going to waste seems wrong but nothing can be done with it. If the peaches could be placed in the Salt Lake market they would easily bring $2.50 a bushel, and here they are almost worthless. Thus, are thousands of dollars thrown away for want of transportation. The Gregorson orchards are only one among thousands of other cases of this kind all through Washington County. The yield has been enormous with no market whatever.

When we reached Silver Reef, the smoke from the smokestack of the Christy mill made known the fact that another run was being made. The mines are now being worked exclusively by chlorides and the mills only make occasional runs. The mill men expect to get out about $6,000 this time. Silver Reef is another example of want of railroad facilities. When the mines were yielding phenomenally rich ore these stamp mills were kept busy all the time and the camp was one of the best in the territory, but as soon as the high-grade ore became practically exhausted, the tremendous expenses caused the shutting down of the mills, and the camp gradually went to pieces, until today it only supports two stores and a saloon. The mines are none of them worked out, however, but need heavier mining machinery to raise the water, which has caused the cessation of work on a great many prospects. Mining experts state that when that is done, just as much rich ore will be taken out as formerly, and the camp will resume its old-time activity. Lack of cheap fuel has also been a great detriment to the camp, and this difficulty can only be remedied by a railroad. The great white sandstone reef, which yet contains so many millions of dollars, can be traced in a southwesterly direction as far as St. George, and numerous good prospects have been located along its line.

The stage now reaches St George about 7.30 p. m. The first thing seen on entering the valley in which the town is situated, is the great white temple, at present receiving its semiannual coat of calcimine. The building boom seems to have struck this place and no fewer than fifteen new houses are now under way. Carpenters and brick-layers are in great demand and the material market "is not in it." The young men have all received renewed confidence in Dixie and evidently intend to stay and grow up with the best country on earth. Work on Woolley, Lund & Judd's smelter is being pushed vigorously and they expect to make a trial run within the next few days. The ore comes from the firm's group of mines which lie about eighteen miles west of here and goes high in copper and lead. These mines are bound to be a bonanza to the owners and the ore seems inexhaustible. The intention now is to ship the high-grade rock east and reduce that which assays lower.

More anon. E. G. Jr.[6]

The Smelters

Despite a relatively quiet time in Utah as far as an iron ore smelting industry, the steel industry was growing on both the east and west coasts. The population was growing rapidly on the West Coast, starting with the gold rush of 1849 and the arrival of those looking for their fortunes in gold and continuing with a substantial influx of immigrants. With an expanding population came an increasing need for all varieties of iron and steel implements. Forges and foundries were built to reprocess scrap iron into useful items including a number of small smelters to make pig iron.

In 1868, pig iron was being manufactured with iron ore from Clipper Gap near Auburn, California. Total production was reported as 14,635 tons. A blast furnace built by the Oregon Iron Company at Oswego, Oregon made cast iron off and on from August 1867 until 1894 with a total production of 93,404 tons. The Puget Sound Iron Company operated a blast furnace at Irondale, Washington, spasmodically on a small scale until 1919, producing some 66,000 tons of pig iron. During the latter part of this pig iron phase in California, steel production began in open-hearth furnaces built near San Francisco in 1910, 1915, and 1917; at Pittsburg, California in 1910; and at Torrance, California in 1916.[7]

Rapid western expansion of the early railroads resulted in the organization of the Colorado Coal & Iron Company, later to become Colorado Fuel & Iron Corporation, located in Pueblo, Colorado. CF&I constructed a facility at Pueblo to manufacture iron and steel, which was the first integrated iron and steel mill west of St. Louis. On September 7, 1881, the first pig iron was cast at the plant. The complex manufactured products that included rails, pig iron, iron and steel bars and plates, and cut nails and spikes. Colorado and Wyoming iron mines supplied the iron ore to the Pueblo plant for many years.[8]

In 1889, CF&I came into Southern Utah seeking to lock up raw materials for the future operation of its Colorado plant. From that time forward, until a few years after the turn of the century, they were very active in staking, developing and buying claims in Iron County. They purchased a substantial number of large mining claims in the Pinto-Iron Springs Mining District, including claims in each of the future mining areas at Iron Mountain, Comstock, Desert Mound and Iron Springs. By 1903, CF&I owned one-third of the iron ore claims in the district.[9]

Locals were optimistic about the prospect of CF&I beginning Ore production in Utah. However, as it turned out, CF&I's accumulation of claims was not for the purpose of short term or even intermediate term mine development. The company wanted the rights to Utah iron in order to assure long-term reserves for its Pueblo smelter for use far in the future.

The following article was published in the *Leadville Democrat* on February 5, 1881 concerning the smelter that was being constructed in Pueblo.

Colorado Coal and Iron Company

The magnificent steel works now being erected will surpass anything of the kind in the west. It is probable that that there are not more complete works in the United States. No money is being spared in their construction, and the entire cost of the works, when completed, will fall very little short of five million dollars. The works are being erected by a consolidation known as the Colorado Coal and Iron Company, a corporation comprised of many of the wealthiest men of the Denver and Rio Grande railroad and other prominent capitalists. The capital stock of the company is ten million dollars.

The steel is to be manufactured by the Bessemer process, the iron ore to be procured near Canon City. Steel rails will be the principal manufacture. It is expected that the works will be in operation very early in the summer, and a thousand men will then be employed. Several hundred are now busily employed at the works, but their progress has been somewhat retarded by the very severe winter that will soon close.

The value of these works to the state and particularly to Pueblo cannot be estimated. They are situated about two miles from South Pueblo on the Denver and Rio Grande road. The full extent of the enterprise can only be realized by a visit to the works. It is generally thought that this is only one of many manufacturing establishments that will be established in the vicinity of Pueblo during the next few years.[10]

In November 1913 a rumor about southern Utah's ore resources, captured first by the *Salt Lake Tribune* and subsequently by the *Iron County Record*. Southern Utah was anxious for good news, so many were inclined to believe the story, and in fact parts of it could have been true. As the story went, eighteen capitalists from different parts of the United States and Canada representing half a billion dollars' capital, met at the Hotel Utah to perfect plans for the development of the vast iron and coal deposits of Utah, and the establishment of a mammoth steel plant in San Diego.[11] It was said that a gigantic corporation was to be formed that would not only build and operate a smelter in California but also build and operate iron ore and coal mines in Utah. As part of the plan, the corporation to be formed would extend the railroad to the mines in order to transport the raw materials to the San Diego plant. It appears from the list of people who attended the meeting, that this was the beginning of what was to become one of the two conglomerates that were involved in building the smelter at Ironton ten years later.[12]

Mr. F. U. Nelson of CF&I just happened to be in the Cedar City area arranging for the annual assessment work on the Hillman Fractions, contiguous to the Desert Mound that were owned by his company. He was asked what he thought of the meeting that was held in Salt Lake that was reported earlier in the newspapers. He stated that he knew nothing of the formation of the billion-dollar company and that no one had taken any options on any of the iron ore owned by his company or by any of the companies that he knew of in the area. He said that a company of the magnitude spoke of could not justify proceeding without any of these properties. He was also struck unfavorably by the notion that an aggregation of big capitalists should give out so much about their plans before they had acquired the properties that they would need, or at least secured options upon them. He therefore, was forced to the conclusion that the stories did not seem probable.

When asked if there would be any conflict between the interests of the proposed company and those of CF&I, Mr. Nelson said that there would be none whatever. He said the new company would supply the West Coast and CF&I would supply the country's midsection and that if anything happened, it would necessitate the building of a railroad to the area, which would be very convenient in case his company should wish to ship any of its Utah iron to Pueblo.[13]

A year later, Rolia E. Clapp, a consulting engineer hired by the Southwestern Pacific Railroad Company to look specifically into smelter building in Utah and California, was also pessimistic about the building of a smelter in Utah or even in California, at least in the very near future. His report was printed in the *Iron County Record* in December 1914 He stated that a year previous, the conditions conducive to the construction of a possible steel plant for Southern Utah were very encouraging, but that the outlook had changed dramatically "owing to the greatest calamity that has ever presented itself during modern times—the European War." He said that the steel companies were neither willing nor able to finance such an endeavor at that time.

Mr. Clapp further stated that since the Panama Canal had become operative, freight rates were lower on all steel products. This caused the competition to increase even under the best of conditions and was prohibitive given the war. He also mentioned that there were iron ore deposits in Lower California that had been offered up for use in California, and although they were inferior to those in Southern Utah, they were closer and less expensive to transport. The consultant's conclusion was that it was not the time to be building a smelter, but that a smelter might be a good proposition in the future if the conditions were to change.[14]

In 1915, anticipating the needs for steel incident to World War I, the Utah Iron Ore and Steel Corporation, later the Utah Steel Corporation, was formed to build a small steel plant in Midvale, Utah, a short distance south of Salt Lake City. By this time the Los Angeles Branch of the Union Pacific Railroad had been completed which made the iron ore in Iron County easily accessible if needed. The steel plant survived solely on Government contracts, so when the war ended, the contracts ended as did the steel plant.[15]

A number of smelters were built during that time in the Midvale area to process copper, lead, silver and gold. However, except for the short period in 1915, iron ore wasn't on their list of metals. A few years later, the Milner operation at Desert Mound obtained contracts with some of the Salt Lake smelters to supply iron ore to be used as a flux for smelting of some of those other ores.

Most of the smelting efforts were on a very small scale, not too much different from the efforts of the early settlers of Iron County. The residents of Iron County were very anxious for a large scale western steel industry to come to the area, especially those individuals who had invested heavily in mining claims.

The Railroads

Several milestones were achieved during the 75 years before the railroad came to Cedar City. Many of these events took place right in Utah, not too far from Iron County. They served to add fuel to the already burning fire of the hopes and dreams of the Southern Utah residents, but they seemed to move in slow motion, many times with dozens of years lapsing before the next step occurred. In 1869, the Transcontinental Railroad was completed through Northern Utah. This was a great leap for the whole nation, but it was particularly important to the State of Utah and Southern Utah. It brought the world's markets to within 250 miles of Cedar City and had the potential to connect Iron County to the steel markets of both the East and West coasts. The following is a small portion of a newspaper article published in the *Deseret News* on May 19, 1869, just a few days after the completion of the Transcontinental Railroad at Promontory Point, Utah. The author of the article was very impressed the magnitude of the achievement and believed that it reflected well on the nation and mankind in general.

The Completion of the Pacific Railroad

The 10th day of May 1869, will form an epoch in the history of this country and in that of the whole civilized world, as the day on which the connecting tie of the Union and Central Pacific Railroad was laid, completing the great Transcontinental Highway and connecting the shores of the Atlantic and Pacific Oceans. The vast importance of this wonderful work, when viewed in its ultimate consequences, cannot be apprehended by the most far-seeing of minds. It is undoubtedly fraught with more momentous interests and destined to accomplish greater purposes than any work ever yet accomplished, in any age, by uninspired man. As a mere work of science and art, it far surpasses those boasted monuments of Pharoahic ages—the pyramids, or any other memento of ancient engineering skill that now excites the wonder and admiration of the human mind; and when viewed from a utilitarian point of view, the latter sink into complete insignificance. The great Pacific Railroad is at once an imperishable monument of the genius, enterprise and wonderful vitality of this great nation.[16]

Iron County residents were further tantalized when the railroad was completed as far south as Milford, Utah in May 1880.[17] Milford became the bustling terminus of the Utah Southern Railroad for nineteen years. Interestingly, the railroad company didn't seem to blink an eye at completing a fourteen-mile spur from Milford to Frisco in less than six weeks after the rails reached Milford.[18] This, of course, was due to the amazing wealth that was being generated by the Frisco mines at that time with the precious metals boom. It also didn't hurt that the Horn Silver Mining Company of Frisco contributed 25 percent of the cost of the construction of the 137 miles of road from Juab to Frisco.[19]

By road, Milford, Utah is only fifty-three miles from Cedar City, and yet it was a very long forty-three years after the railroad was brought to Milford before it was extended to Cedar City.

Once the railroad made it to Milford it was presumed by Iron County residents that it would be continued on to Cedar City within the year. The Union Pacific line was not the only railroad about which there was supposition. Just a little over a year after the railroad to Milford was completed, an article was published in the *Salt Lake Tribune*, quoted at the beginning of this chapter, which discussed four different possible routes by which the railroad could come to Cedar City, Iron Springs and Iron City. Some of the options were quite imaginative when you consider the details, especially compared to the simplicity of running a line down the desert from Milford. It would have been an expensive and difficult proposition indeed to cross the Grand Canyon from the south, the Sierras from the west or even the mountains between the Sevier valley and Cedar City from the east. Nevertheless, residents had great hopes for any one of the four major railroads to arrive.

The Utah Central Railroad Coming from Milford to Iron Springs and then on to Cedar City, the Utah Central Railroad would have been the simplest of the hoped-for connects. The line was predicted to extend to the Iron City location at the south end of Iron Mountain. It was forecast that these lines would be built within the year.

The Texas Pacific Railroad If the article's suggestions had been taken, the Texas Pacific Railroad would have run northwestward from El Paso through Arizona, crossing the Colorado River somewhere between Prescott, Arizona and Cedar City and ending at either Iron Springs or Iron City.

The California Central Railroad The California Central Railroad was projected to run from San Francisco via Yosemite and Big Tree, Silver Peak, Nevada, and Crystal Springs to Iron Springs, Iron City, or thereabouts.

The Denver Rio Grande Having passed the Sevier, people suggested, the road could proceed to Marysvale, then across the mountains to Beaver or Parowan, then on to Cedar City, Iron Springs and Iron City. "Two years will doubtless see Denver and Rio Grande engines watering at Iron Springs," claimed the *Salt Lake Tribune*.[20]

In 1898, efforts were made to extend the railroad towards Los Angeles. David Eccles of Ogden and R. C. Lund of St. George along with several associates, negotiated with the Oregon Short Line for right of way for an eighty-mile line from Milford to the Stateline mining district in Iron County, due west of Cedar City, extending into Nevada. The line was to run partially on the old Pioche grade. They were negotiating for the purchase of rails in addition to the use of the grade. Eventually this was the route taken by the railroad when it was extended a few years later to Los Angeles.[21]

Railroad Completed to Lund

In January 1899, the railroad was extended to Lund, Utah. Once completed, the railroad line ran only thirty-five miles west of Cedar City. The Union Pacific specifically promised the local residents that a branch would be built shortly to Cedar City. In fact, they were told that surveys for that branch "will be started very soon." The Union Pacific was true to their word as far as building the branch, because they did eventually build a line to Cedar City; but as far as being "very soon," unfortunately it wouldn't be built for another twenty-four years.[22]

Lund was originally named "Sulphur," but when the railroad was completed to that point, the station was quickly renamed to something more appropriate, and it officially became "Cedar City Junction." However, it was re-named once again, this time to "Lund," shortly after the railroad arrived, after Robert C. Lund of St. George, who was a Utah state legislator, local mine owner, a director of the Union Pacific Railroad and was involved in negotiating for the construction of the project.[23]

Lund remained the terminus for only a brief time on the line that would eventually be connected to Los Angeles; however, it was the closest station to Cedar City for the next twenty-three years. During that period Lund did a booming business with hotels, stores, stables, saloons and quite a number of houses and shanties. Even after the branch line was completed to Cedar City, Lund remained functional for quite some time. Little by little, however, the trains no longer stopped there, and the once vibrant little town fell into disrepair. The following article printed in January 1899 described the coming of the railroad to Lund.

Cedar City Junction – Made Permanent Station

Chief Engineer Joseph West of the Utah & Pacific is in the city. He received a telegram from the front yesterday which stated that the road was completed to the terminus which will be used for the next two months. It is exactly thirty-seven miles from Milford and trains will run today.

To avoid confusion, and at the same time make it more appropriate, this place will not be named Sulphur as it first intended. It is christened "Cedar City Junction," for here the branch to Iron County will be started, surveys for which will be started very soon. It is thirty-five miles from Cedar and the same distance from Parowan.

Mr. West has already surveyed the townsite and fifteen lots have already been sold. A hotel, stable and three saloons have arisen besides many shanties and sheds. The company is putting up a neat rustic station house, engine shed and tank. All the buildings are being built much more elaborate than would be required for a two-month's terminal station, which proves that the place will have permanency and that the branch to Cedar will be built from that point. No attempt will be made to change the terminus this winter, but work on construction will be pushed on with no decrease in the force. Deseret Springs will be reached by the time spring opens, and that point will be the next terminus and a permanent station for St George, fifty-five miles distant from Deseret.

Mr. West would not talk of the Los Angeles terminal or of the line beyond the State line. He said that all work now being done is confined to Utah, and what is to come in the future only the head officials of the company could state.[24]

Over the next five years the line was extended, one increment at a time, until it had made it all the way to Los Angeles. Once completed, there was a marked increase in the traffic over the line. The following short statement in the *Iron County Record* marked the event: "The first through train from Salt Lake City over the San Pedro, Los Angeles & Salt Lake railroad arrived in Los Angeles on the 3rd at 7:40 a.m."[25]

The route lay through the Escalante Desert settlement of Lund. Lund was a hub of activity for travelers and freight after the railroad arrived in 1899. After the branch line was built to Cedar City, the railroad built a stately new depot in Lund, designed by the well-known architect, Gilbert Stanley Underwood. Union Pacific Railroad commissioned Underwood to design depots and lodges, including the lodges for Yellowstone, Yosemite, Cedar Breaks, Zion, Bryce and the Grand Canyon North Rim. Sadly, the architecturally significant depot at Lund was demolished in 1970 after passenger trains ceased stopping there.[26]

Marysvale, Utah is a small town on highway 89 between Richfield and Panguitch and is situated about 25 miles northeast of Beaver as the crow flies. Between Marysvale and Beaver lie the Beaver Baldies in the Tushar Mountain range. In the late 1860s the discovery of high-grade ore containing gold, silver, lead and copper, brought prospectors and miners by the thousands to Marysvale and the surrounding area. The town was actually an outgrowth of Bullion City, a nearby mining camp, and flourished until the mines closed in 1907. Between 1868 and 1959, Piute County produced approximately 240,000 ounces of gold.[27]

In 1890, a rail line was built by the Denver and Rio Grande Railroad to Manti, Utah. In 1896, the line was extended to Belknap and in 1900, it was again lengthened to reach Marysvale. After 1907, the line survived on agricultural, coal, and wallboard traffic until 1983, at which time a major mudslide filled the narrow valley and covered the track with rock, dirt and mud. Subsequently, water backed up and formed a lake. The cost of rebuilding miles of track to reconnect the branch to the mainline was deemed to be too expensive, the line was officially abandoned and the rails were pulled in 1989.[28]

Illustration 4.1. Lund, Utah in the early 1900s. (Photo, Sherratt Library)

For the fifty-four years following the completion of the transcontinental railroad in 1869, stories abounded about the railroad coming to Cedar City. Various theories were volunteered, each claiming to be based in some reliable source, about when and where it would be built and by whom. Of course, a branch line from Lund would be the most straightforward and simplest solution. However, when the railroad stalled out at Lund, with no end in sight, people lost faith in Union Pacific and its plans. This gave more credence to the rumor that the D&RG was planning to extend its line from Marysvale to Cedar City. It was one of the more prevalent rumors that persisted for quite some time, from 1899 to at least 1916. The well published reports of the exploration and development activities of CF&I, obviously a Colorado company, seemed to add more credibility to the claims. The following four short news articles give a flavor of the Marysvale rail-extension rumor.

Branch Railroad Road [1899]

To afford an outlet for the ore the Rio Grande Western is pushing its work with all possible energy, and while a big troop of graders are now in Marysvale canyon, a corps of surveyors is blazing the way from Marysvale to Cedar City. The extension of the railway to the iron region is all that is needed to make it one of the most popular and productive camps in the State.[29]

Marysvale Extension [1903]

A prominent Iron County iron deposit owner in this city, and syndicate representative, stated today, as a matter of opinion, that the management of the Colorado Fuel & Iron Company, Rockefeller and Gould, would without delay, extend the D&RG from Marysville, direct into Iron County, and thence south to St. George also that the great deposits in Iron County, would be opened, and the ore shipped to the furnaces at Pueblo. However, in time, furnaces might be erected at Cedar, or other location convenient, and the pig iron shipped out instead of the crude ore. It was claimed that the outlook now for the development of Iron County and the southern iron fields is better than ever before.[30]

Local News [1904]
The work with the diamond drill on the claims of the Colorado Fuel & Iron Company is completed, and Superintendent Nelson was in town Thursday for the purpose of superintending the shipping of the machinery to some other part of the company's holdings. Mr. Nelson informs us that the contract for the building of the railroad from Marysvale to the iron fields has not been let yet, so far as he knows, and that although the contracts are ready, the company is probably in no particular hurry, as they do not intend to begin work until next spring.[31]

Cedar City Happenings [1916]
Encouraging reports continue to leak out of the intended extension into this County of the Denver and Rio Grande line. The Colorado Fuel & Iron company has extensive iron holdings here, for which the heavy consumption caused by the war is creating a demand. It is only about 100 miles from Marysvale into the iron district, and the engineering problems are said to be quite easy of solution.[32]

Local Attempts to Get the Railroad Built

Lack of action on a rail line to Cedar City didn't lessen the need for a railroad. Several issues became more apparent as the Southern Utah communities expanded. The road between Lund and Cedar City had become one of the most used roads in the county but was basically undeveloped and was in serious need of improvement. No one wanted to spend large sums of money to upgrade the road if a railroad was going to be built in the near future, virtually eliminating the need for the road. Washington and Kane Counties were also in need of railroad access and plans were being made to possibly build a line from Modena to St. George that would bypass Cedar City. There was a developing need to access the Kaibab Plateau and its vast lumber resources. Public interest was also growing in the National Parks including Zion Canyon, Bryce Canyon and the north rim of the Grand Canyon and access to those destinations was very limited, especially by rail.

In October of 1915, the citizens of Iron County, in conjunction with the State Engineer and the Salt Lake Route Railroad, with support from Washington and Kane Counties, proposed a plan to finally get the long-awaited branch railroad constructed to Cedar City. The following news article gave details of that plan.

Good Prospects for a Railroad
An important meeting of the citizens and members of the Cedar City Commercial Club is called to meet this evening at 7:30, in the auditorium of the Lyceum building for the purpose of considering what appears to be a very feasible proposition for the securing of the long cherished but never realized railroad into this section of Iron County. The proposition as brought home by Pres. U. T. Jones on his return from conference and the state fair, is about as follows:

The State Engineer and officials of the Salt Lake Route have been holding conferences and discussing ways and means for securing the building of a branch railroad from Lund to Cedar City which will accomplish the double purpose of giving the Salt Lake Route a feeder line into this section, and supply transportation to the settlements of this section of Iron County, and shorten the distance from Washington and Kane County points to the railroad, without the building and maintaining by the state of so much expensive and not altogether satisfactory wagon road; and the conclusion arrived at by these conferences is that the state engineer will grade the road bed with the state convict labor, and the Salt Lake Route will supply the rails and rolling stock if the people will furnish the necessary ties.

These determinations were communicated to Mr. Jones by State Engineer Beers, J. H. Manderfield being out of the city at the time, and the object of the meeting tonight is to present the matter to the people and the commercial club for their consideration.

Believes Project Feasible.

In the opinion of Pres. Jones as expressed to a representative of this paper, the project is entirely feasible, and the most practical and tangible proposition ever submitted looking to the securing of railroad facilities for this section. Mr. Jones has roughly estimated that if the local sawmills can be induced to saw the ties practically for cost, and the government will permit the cutting of the timber free of charge from the forest reserve, the actual cost of the ties at the mills will not exceed $20,000. The hauling of the ties for stock in the proposed company should be easy of attainment. If the people are fully alive to the importance of this attainment there should be no difficulty in getting the ties furnished for the road.

What Road Will Mean.

If this branch road is built it will mean a great boon to all this section of country. It will solve the problem of transportation completely for this immediate section of country; it will shorten by several miles the haul between Parowan, Paragonah, Summit and Enoch and their railroad depot; it will cut over 30 miles from the distance that separates all the towns of eastern and central Washington County from the railroad, and will do the same service for several of the towns of Kane County; it will give a nearer, better and less expensive route to the Grand Canyon, and will practically benefit every resident of Iron, Washington and Kane counties. It may be the incentive and means to the opening of our iron and coal deposits on a commercial basis, and possibly result of the establishment in this county of great reduction works for the handling of the immense iron mines through which the road would pass.

It might prove the signal for the ushering in of the great industrial activity for which the people of this locality have waited so long and patiently.

Would Organize Local Company.

According to the plan worked out, it is proposed to incorporate an independent company with sufficient capitalization to build and equip the road, and issue stock for the value of the rails, rolling stock and ties, as well as the other labor required in the building of the road, after the grading is completed. It would be stipulated, in consideration of the state convicts building the grade that the general public should have the privilege of using the grade for vehicles, etc. This, it is believed, can be arranged in such a way that the people desiring to do so may operate automobiles or auto-trucks upon the rails, or the grade may be made wide enough to permit of being used as a wagon road as well as a railroad track. These are details that can be satisfactorily worked out in the future.

It is Now Up to the People.

The State Engineer and the Salt Lake Route have expressed their willingness and ability to perform their part of the compact, if the people will do theirs and furnish the ties—not as a gift, but for stock in the proposed company. Bear in mind that the matter will not be decided until you have agreed to contribute your part, so that it is important that as many as possible attend the meeting at the Library auditorium tonight.

At this meeting further details will be furnished and the matter considered from every angle. The notices for the meeting are issued under the auspices of the Commercial club, but it is the purpose to have all the public-spirited citizens in attendance.[33]

By December the people of Cedar City and Southern Utah were on board with the endeavor and were awaiting meetings with the State Engineer and representatives of the Salt Lake Route.

Local News

It is a matter of congratulation to the people of Cedar City in particular and all southern Utah in general, that everything seems exceedingly favorable for the early building of the proposed branch railroad from Lund to Cedar City. The leading people of this city are taking hold of the matter with a spirit that brooks no such thing as failure or undue delay. A railroad is the thing that is needed now for the development of this section of the country, and apparently, a railroad is what we are going to have, even if we have to do the lion's share of it ourselves. In the past Cedar City has shown that it is capable of arising to an emergency, and it is going to give another manifestation of this kind in the near future. Besides this, we have the promise of a lot of splendid help from the other settlements of the district, as well as from the Salt Lake Route and other powerful and potent interests in the north. Representatives of some of these interests will shortly visit us and go more into details in the undertaking in hand. Watch for the announcement of a meeting with them in the near future.[34]

For some reason, the undertaking never came to pass. It is unsure what exactly derailed the endeavor; it could have been that one of the parties backed out or maybe it was the onset of World War I. It also could have been that, somehow, credence was given to the reoccurring rumor that a big consortium was going to build a railroad in the near future.

In 1918, another story surfaced about a huge conglomerate company being assembled. This story was very similar to the report published in 1913 and quoted earlier and may even have been a repetition of the same rumor. Sometimes it was hard to determine how much was fact and how much was fiction, in this case it appears that the account was mostly fiction.

The story went that, in spite of efforts to keep the plans secret, they became known when sufficient backing had been guaranteed to make the project a success. It was claimed that a company named the Southern Utah Development Company had been organized in Salt Lake for the purpose of building a railroad from Lund to Cedar City and erecting a steel mill at Lund, for a total cost of 100 million dollars. The fact that CF&I engineers were spotted in the vicinity by a prominent railroad official seemed to lend credence to the report since CF&I was said to be a branch of the United States Steel Corporation, and everyone knew that USSC built the steel city of Gary, Indiana. The story also claimed that the Church of Jesus Christ of Latter-day Saints had decided to finance the enterprise. The account went on to state that the iron ore deposit was eight miles wide and 150 miles long and was 95 percent pure and was only a short distance from a huge coal deposit.

By 1918, work could have been begun on assembling a large company to manufacture iron and steel. However, the likelihood of Lund, of all places, becoming the Pittsburg of the West was extremely low. Rumors that CF&I was a branch of U.S. Steel and that the Church would finance such a large endeavor were pure fiction. Additionally, the writers claim that the iron ore deposit was 150 miles long and was 95 percent pure and that the coal in the vicinity was good enough to make steel, makes it apparent that the author didn't know what he was talking about.[35]

The General Mining Law of 1872

In 1866, Congress passed the Lode Law, which permitted private lode development on public lands. In 1870, this law was extended to include the development of placers. These two laws were later combined into one law in 1872.

A new mining bill was approved by the Congress of the United States and was signed into law on May 10, 1872 by President Ulysses S. Grant. It was officially called the General Mining Law of 1872 and formalized the process by which companies and individuals could stake claims on mineral discoveries made on public lands. Early western prospectors, such as those of the 1849 California gold rush, staked claims on public lands without the express consent of the federal government.

Prior to the enactment of the 1872 law, even though the practices for open mining on public land were more-or-less universal in the West, and supported by state and territorial legislation, they were still illegal under existing federal law. Some Eastern congressmen regarded Western miners as squatters who were robbing the public, and proposed seizure of the Western mines to pay for the Civil War. A bill was even introduced for the government to seize the Western mines from their discoverers and sell them at public auction. A Representative proposed that the government send an army to California, Colorado, and Arizona to expel the miners "by armed force if necessary to protect the rights of the Government in the mineral lands." He advocated that the federal government itself work the mines for the benefit of the treasury.

The primary purposes of the 1872 law were (1) to promote mineral exploration and development on federal lands in the Western United States, (2) to offer an opportunity to obtain a clear title to mines already being worked, and (3) to help settle the West.

All claim locations were required to be registered by the applicable mining district recorder and tied to the applicable Section, Township and Range of the Federal Land Survey. In this same time frame, United States Land Surveyors were surveying in Southern Utah so most of the claims that were staked were referenced to the Salt Lake Base and Meridian.

Under the General Mining Law, any individual United States citizen or corporation could explore federal public domain lands in search of valuable minerals. In the event that the prospector discovered an area that he or she believed to contain valuable minerals, subject to the law, he or she could stake a claim on that land. There was no limit to the number of claims an individual or corporation could stake, and it was not required that production of the claim ever begin.[36]

Lode and Placer Claims There are two types of mining claims, a lode claim and a placer claim. The most common claim was and still is the lode claim. A lode is defined as a mineral deposit occurring in solid rock. Usually these deposits occur as *veins*, that is, as fissures, faults, or cracks in a rock filled by minerals that have traveled upwards from some deep source, or as ore bodies. A placer is a deposit of alluvial material such as sand or gravel, containing valuable minerals such as gold, silver, tin, copper, iron or even diamonds. The lode claim was designed to cover vein deposits. In iron ore, it is allowable to locate claims end to end and side by side in order to cover the entire ore body. A lode claim is specified to have maximum dimensions of 600 feet by 1500 feet, however, there is no requirement for it to be rectangular, and many were not. Lode claims may exceed twenty acres, but placer claims cannot exceed twenty acres. A provision was made for a lode claim to include a larger area, for example, eight persons could file on one hundred sixty acres or a quarter of a section. Companies could also file claims but were to be treated as individuals.

Staking a mining claim was easy but not free. The claimant was required to pay fees to register and maintain the claim. Claims had to be surveyed and a prescribed amount of improvement work was required each year to hold a claim. For a lode claim, the cost per acre was $5. For a placer claim, the cost per acre was $2.50. The law typically required that one hundred dollars' worth of assessment work be performed per claim per year. Early assessment work on iron ore claims usually consisted of one or more vertical shafts sunk into the ground, and possibly a drift or two. This type of effort was required to prove that an ore body was commercially viable, especially if the claimant wanted to have his claim patented.

Patented Claims If a claimant desired to get his or her claim "patented," a substantial amount of additional work and proof was required. The claimant had to prove that the deposit to which he had staked a claim, was "economically recoverable" and that he had performed development work on the claim equaling at least $500. He could file for a patent to obtain title to both the surface and mineral rights of the land.

After a claimant filed for a patent on his claim, a Federal Mineral Inspector had to be inspect and certify that the claim met legal requirements. At that point, the claim would be officially surveyed and in due time the claimant would receive actual title to the land. Similar procedures were required to patent a placer claim. Filing for a patent required the payment of a one-time $250 application fee. Provided that the application was approved, the claimant could purchase title to the land's surface and mineral rights. Once the patent was received, annual assessment work was no longer required. Under the claim and patent system, claimants were not required to pay royalties to the federal government on minerals recovered from public-domain lands. Starting in fiscal year 1995, Congress implemented a moratorium on the patent program, effectively barring new claimants from filing for a patent and the moratorium is still in place.

It was not necessary that a claimant file for a patent in order to develop minerals on his or her claim, but unpatented claims went back to the government if the annual payments and requirements were not met. Patents to early homesteads included mineral as well as surface rights to the ground without filing mineral claims. Years later, mineral rights were deleted from homestead patents.

In the early days, before the advent of more modern surveying technology, coupled with the limited availability of qualified surveyors, many claims were not located correctly. Overlaps and gaps were the least of their problems. Some areas had multiple claims located on top of each other, and others were erroneously described or improperly laid out in the field. There were disputes between lode claim owners and placer claim owners. There were even a few claim jumpers whose intentions were not strictly above board. Fights, feuds and even murders resulted from disputes over valuable claims. Many of these problems had to be settled in the courts since the property could not be mined legally until a clear title was established. All too often, the original claimant would lose all or part of his rights through these legal maneuvers.[37]

Iron Mining & Manufacturing

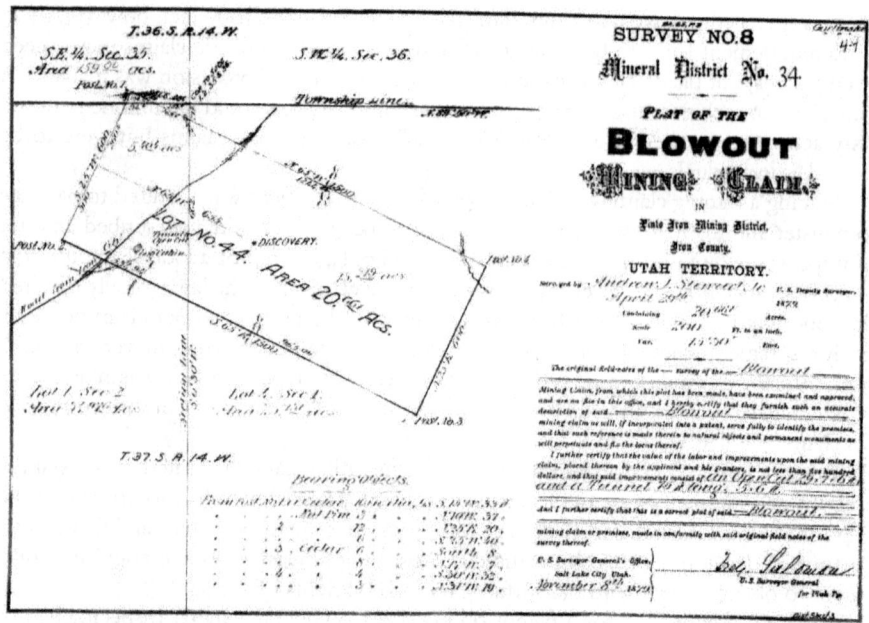

Illustration 4.2 Plat of the Blowout Mining Claim dated April 29, 1879. (Photo from York Jones)

In the late 1800s and early 1900s, a great many man-hours and substantial sums of money were spent prospecting and developing lode and placer claims around Cedar City. A good example was S. B. Milner of Salt Lake City, who was convinced that development was near. He patented a large number of claims in the district. After Milner died in 1906, his sons C. E. Milner, A. C. Milner, and J. S. Milner, carried on his legacy. Additionally, the companies in the iron and steel business like Colorado Fuel & Iron, staked, patented, or purchased major claims at Iron Mountain, Comstock, Desert Mound, and Iron Springs. Utah State Archives summarized the history and a description of mining district records in an agency history worth citing.

The Pinto Iron Mining District

The Pinto Iron Mining District was organized in 1868 to facilitate iron mining in the mountains southwest of Cedar City. In accordance with established practice, which Congress enacted into law in 1872, mineral deposits in the public domain were free and open to exploration, and locators of the same, had exclusive right of possession. Local mining districts managed mining operations and recorded claims. The Pinto Iron Mining District record books primarily contain notices of location for mining claims. For each notice the mining district recorder reported the names of locators, the name of the mining claim, and a description of the claim, including both a legal description and a description of the way the claim had been marked. The recorder reported dates for location and recording. In addition to location notices, these record books contain some of the following documents: minutes for miners' meetings, notices of location for mill sites, notices of relocation or amended location, intentions to hold and work a claim, deeds selling mines or mining interests, and notices about water rights.[38]

The Iron Springs Mining District

In March 1879, the Iron Springs Mining District was officially organized, located on and around both Granite Mountain and the Three Peaks area, it encompassed many of the iron ore deposits of Iron County. Its organizational document provides a good example of how a mining district was structured and met the needs of prospectors and mine developers.

Iron Springs Mining District
Organized March 27, 1879

A Miners meeting was called at Iron Springs on the date above mentioned for the purpose of forming a district and electing a Recorder on motion Nat Stoddard was elected chairman, J.R. Lindsay Secretary.

Article 1st The boundaries of this District are as follows: Commencing at Shirts Creek or Hamilton's Fort, and thence running West 12 miles, thence North 12 miles, thence East 12 miles, thence South 12 miles to place of beginning.

Article 2nd The District shall be called the Iron Springs District.

Article 3rd The election of Recorder shall be held annually on the 27th day of March. John V. Easley being duly elected Recorder shall continue in office until March 27, 1880.

Article 4th The fees for recording shall be three ($3.00) dollars for each mining claim of 1500 feet or less in length. The Recorder or his Deputy shall be obliged to visit a claim and note its boundaries before recording. The same fees shall apply for recording a mill site or other location.

Article 5th The Recorder or Deputy, after surveying a claim shall be authority sufficient to issue a certificate of the assessment labor performed thereon; his fee shall be two ($2.00) dollars for each certificate.

Article 6th The laws of this District in regard to the length and width of a mining claim shall be the same and conform to the United States Mining Law approved May 1872 with one hundred ($100) dollars' worth of labor performed each year.

Article 7th A notice of location with description of locality or near what claims if any shall be recorded in the records of said District within thirty (30) days from the day of location.

Article 8th The records of this District shall be free and open—always in the presence of the Recorder—for the inspection of interested parties during business hours.

Article 9th It shall be the duty of the Recorder on receiving a written request from three (3) or more miners of the District to call a public meeting to post notices on his office door and other conspicuous places specifying therein the nature of the business to be transacted ten (10) days prior to the date of the meeting.

Nat Stoddard   Chairman

J.R. Lindsay   Secretary[39]

At some point in time after 1977, the Pinto Iron and Iron Springs mining districts were merged into one, under the name of Iron Springs. However, many documents still refer to the districts separately or collectively as the Pinto-Iron Springs Mining District.

One month after the Iron Springs Mining District was organized, in April 1879, the first mineral survey was made on the "Blowout" claim. It was the first lode claim in the Pinto Iron Mining District to be patented. The Blowout ore body was located at the south end of Iron Mountain. It was one of the more spectacular and noteworthy deposits in the region and appeared in many news articles.

Iron Mining & Manufacturing

Illustration 4.3. A typical vertical shaft sunk for development and exploration.

Illustration 4.4. A horizontal exploration tunnel near the Jones ore deposit in the Three Peaks Mining Area. The area was later mined using surface mining techniques. (Photos by Evan Jones)

By 1880 there were twenty-three mining claims on record in the Pinto and Iron Springs Mining Districts. By 1900 there were over one hundred claims, and by 1922, fifty years after the 1872 mining law was enacted, there were over a thousand patented and unpatented mining claims all over the district.

To stake that many claims, there were hundreds of prospectors, often on foot, going over every inch of the 100 square mile mineral belt with a fine-tooth comb. They located claims of all kinds, all over the country, very often without the help of any kind of surveying instrument. A large majority of the claims had no ore on them and were totally worthless. Many of the claims that were lucky enough to have ore on them were never mined. The surnames of some of the early and seemingly more dedicated prospectors include: Duncan, Milner, Cullen, Page, Campbell and Younger. Locals on the record include Smith, Jones, Murie, McGarry, Webster, Hunter and Nelson.

Pig iron producers gradually added steel finishing processes to blast furnaces, which appeared to be the trend in future expansion. During the 1870s and 1880s, the national steel industry was primarily located east of Chicago near the continent's iron, coal, limestone deposits. The bulk of the iron ore for the industry came from huge, high-grade "iron range" deposits around Lake Superior in Michigan and Minnesota. The owners of the ore properties rapidly became wealthy from ore sales royalties. Some of these people sent agents to Southern Utah to invest in its iron ore reserves. They located and patented some claims, bought others and also purchased a number of old homesteads. Their purchases involved large acreages in both the Pinto and Iron Springs Mining Districts. The surnames of some of these investors were: McCahill, Savage, Sundean, Chute, and Thompson, all of which still appear on maps and in claim records of the region. They didn't realize much from their investments but some of their property contained fair-sized ore bodies at depth.[40]

Exploration and Assessment Work

Once a claim was staked and officially registered, annual assessment work was required to be able to keep the claim. Additionally, to get a claim patented, substantial work had to be done in order to "prove" the claim. These two requirements provided substantial incentive for claimants to do assessment work on their claims. There was a third reason for some claimants and some ore bodies; the claimants wanted or needed to understand the extent of the deposit either to be able to mine it or to sell it. If a claimant was prudent, assessment work and exploration work usually complemented each other.

In the early years, since exploration drills were generally unavailable or very expensive, exploration was limited to hand-dug shafts and drifts. As a result, on large deposits, claim owners had very little idea of the extent of their holdings and were limited to only what they could see on the surface. To better understand the size and shape of their deposits, claim owners would sink *shafts* (vertical tunnels) or drive *adits* (horizontal tunnels) into the side of the hills and then drive drifts or cross-cuts (horizontal tunnels) further into the ore bodies. As one can imagine, it was very difficult to dig more than a couple of hundred feet in the hard, abrasive ore. The work required drilling and blasting, accomplished exclusively by manual labor. Ventilation also became an issue. In reality, a number of the ore deposits were quite wide and virtually bottomless, reaching literally thousands of feet into the earth. Because of the limitations of their hand-dug endeavors, the owners were left with an incomplete understanding of the depth and breadth of their deposits.

With the passage of time, drills capable of drilling into and sampling deposits became more available and proved to be valuable tools for assessment work and exploration. They were also capable of reaching much deeper depths than achievable with the old hand-dug shafts and drifts and thus they were able to gather data on the whole deposit, not just its upper portions. However, even today, because of cost and need, the total depth of some of the iron deposits remains unknown.

Buying and Selling Claims

As time went on, several major players with deep pockets became interested and involved in procuring claims. Claims were regularly bought and sold and, in many cases, they traded hands several times. They were consolidated, as many owners joined together to share the costs of buying and developing their claims. Speculation fueled the staking of thousands of claims, many of which were not even close to an ore deposit. The people of Iron County waited for many years before the hoped-for development occurred and even then, it did not happen all at once. Tens of thousands of people did not rush to Iron County like they did to the silver and gold fields. The iron mining industry developed at a slow and steady pace, but its presence was nevertheless felt and over time it became the largest single employer and tax payer in the county.

All of this activity and all of the local workers employed in exploration tended to further whet the appetites of those who anxiously awaited the building of a railroad so that the iron ore could get to market. The following two newspaper articles, the first from November 1899 and the second from December 1902, discussed some of the claims that were on the market at the time and the people or organizations who owned them.

A Push for Utah Iron

The eagerness with which the big iron deposits of Iron County are now being sought and the rivalry with which representatives of a half dozen steel manufacturing concerns are pressing their overtures has not been half told, said S. B. Milner, who came in from the south yesterday, and while those who have so long slumbered over opportunities down there find it hard to realize what is going on, the scene is just now one of the most exciting in the State. The Colorado Fuel & Iron Company of Pueblo has two active representatives on the ground in Messrs. Ladd and Hills, who have left Zion last week and who were going in while Mr. Milner was coming out. Then there are parties from Denver with another energetic aggregation from Cripple Creek, all of whom are scouring the locality for ground that may have been overlooked and scores of locations have poured into the offices of the Recorder. The Woods Investment Company, a big Cripple Creek concern, also has a representative on the ground, while the big British syndicate has its forces in the field and has already tied up what it conceives to be the cream of the country.

The Groups

The impression prevails at Cedar City, which is just now experiencing more life than at any time in its career, that the Thomas Taylor group of six claims is as good as gone at $1,000,000. At all events, the purchasing syndicate is paying the owner a given amount each day that negotiations continue. It is estimated that in this group alone are as much as 15,000,000 tons of ore that will average no less than 60 percent. Mr. Milner himself, bringing in samples that show as much as 70 percent. Walker Bros. of this city, it is said, have put their holdings in on the British purchase at $400,000, these consisting of 160 acres near Iron Springs, for which a patent was secured a long time ago.

Another interesting proposition is that owned by Matt Cullen and Allan G. Campbell, and that consists of five locations containing nearly as many tons as are to be found in the Taylor group.

In the Milner group there are no less than twenty-one claims that constitute a veritable empire of iron ore. In the vast holdings he is associated with Messrs. Dear and Lerch, the iron kings of Duluth, Minn. and while the owners have been requested to name the figure at which they were willing to part with the group, they have thus far refrained from it. It is their intention to operate it under a system of royalties, retaining the title themselves. At present they are engaged upon the work necessary to a patent and are working a small army of men and engineers that it may be put through with all possible dispatch.[41]

Marvelous Promise of Utah's Iron Fields

"Within a few years, Utah should be producing more iron than any other state in the Union. The deposits in the southwestern part of the state are the greatest I have ever seen, and I have examined all the principal iron deposits in the United States, Cuba and Venezuela.

The close proximity of the iron to an ample supply of fuel and lime flux makes it possible to produce iron in Utah cheaper than anywhere else in the United States. Iron works can be erected in this state which will produce iron so cheaply that, with fair railroad rates, the finished product can be laid down in Chicago on at least equal terms with the product of the United States Steel Corporation or any other producer. The low cost of production would make it possible for the Utah iron and steel work to control absolutely the trade of the western part of North and South America and the Orient. It will take a little time to get the Utah iron and steel works into shape for steady production but when they are completed they must become an important factor in the industry in the United States. John T Jones"

The above statement was made to the Herald by John T. Jones of Iron Mountain, Mich., one of the most celebrated iron experts in the United States. It was on his recommendation that P. L. Kimberly and F. W. Buhl, experienced and wealthy iron operators of Sharon, Pa., headed a syndicate a few months ago to purchase a large area of iron-bearing ground in Iron County, to open up the mines and build a manufacturing plant, with railroads and other accessories, at a cost approaching $30,000,000. Besides Mr. Jones, other famous experts have examined the iron and coal of Utah and they have all reached the same conclusion, most of them being far more enthusiastic in their expressions than Mr. Jones.

Within a short time, it is expected that formal announcement will be made of the syndicate's plans for the development of the iron resources of Utah. For months experts have been working out the details, and complete reports have been made on the different phases of the undertaking. An enterprise of this kind requires years to complete, but the wealthy men back of the project have practically completed in outline, their plans.

Iron Mining & Manufacturing

Immense Plants

Somewhere within the borders of Utah will be erected blast furnaces, steel rail mills, wire nail mills and plants for the manufacture of sheet steel, structural steel, iron bars, armor plate and every other variety of manufactured iron and steel. The iron mines will be opened up, new coal mines will be developed, coke ovens will be constructed, railroads will be built, lime quarries opened and deposits of manganese will be worked. Cities and towns will spring up close to the manufacturing plants and the mines and railroads will be built to bring the materials together and to ship the finished product in all directions. Thousands of people will be added to the population of Utah and millions of dollars to the wealth of the state.

This is not an idle dream. It represents the plans of men worth scores of millions of dollars which they have made in iron and steel; clear-headed, practical men of wide experience in this line, who have reduced everything to a scientific basis. They are ready to put their millions into the enterprise, confident that that they will receive returns many times the size of their investment.

A slight idea of the advantage which will be enjoyed by the Utah manufacturers may be gained from the following table, showing the estimated cost per ton of Bessemer pig:

Utah	$5.50
Utah, crediting by-products	$4.78
United States Steel Corporation	$7.20
Birmingham Ala.	$9.00
Shenango and Mahoning valleys	$12.53

Can Produce Cheaply

Thus, it is seen that it will cost the Utah manufacturers $2.48 a ton less to make Bessemer pig than it does the United States Steel Corporation, and 62 percent less than some other manufacturers. It costs the big trust even more where the iron ore is not transported in its own vessels, the cost per ton in this instance being run up $10 a ton. The figures on the Utah cost of production are based as on the supposition that the iron from Iron Mountain and the coal and coke from Emery and Carbon counties are transported to a manufacturing city at Virgin Falls, on the Virgin river, and there made into the finished product.

The value of the Utah iron deposits is so enormous as to be almost beyond conception. Charles M. Schwab, president of the United States Steel Corporation places valuation of $2 a ton in the ground on iron ore. The lowest estimate ever made on the amount of iron ore sight on the ground controlled by the Kimberly-Buhl syndicate is 500,000,000 tons. This would make the value of the iron as it stands $1,000,000,000. And this does not include it all.

More than this, it costs the steel trust 50 cents to $1.50 a ton to mine its ore. The estimated cost for mining the Utah ore is 15 cents a ton, or even less with the use of steam shovels.

Fine coking coal, with a percentage of 55 and upwards of fixed carbon, is found within easy reach of the iron, while the state contains plenty of lime and manganese for flux. It is the fact that all the materials are so close to each other that makes it possible to produce the finished product so cheaply in this state.

Where the Deposits Are

The principal deposits of iron in Utah are found in Iron County, twenty miles east of Lund station, on the Oregon Short Line, and twelve miles west of Cedar City. There rising out of the level desert plain, tower aloft three isolated mountains. The highest is Iron Mountain rising 1,500 feet above the plain and 7,400 feet above the level of the sea. Seven miles away is Iron Springs mountain, and between the two is Desert Mound, a solid mass of iron a mile square.

For eight miles around Iron Mountain, in a semi-circle, runs an enormous ledge of iron, 400 to 1,100 feet across, and averaging 65 percent and upward of the best grade of iron. The deposits of iron on Iron Springs Mountain are three miles long and 400 to 700 feet across, while Desert Mound, as stated, is solid iron.

Bishop Thomas Taylor was the first to realize the value of these vast deposits. Many years ago, he located and patented several claims on Iron Mountain, leaving them to his heirs when he died. The Walker brothers, senior, also took up and patented some claims years ago, and so did Matthew Cullen, Allen G. Campbell and James McGarry. A few years year ago Colonel S. B. Milner of Salt Lake began mining for copper in that region and became interested in the wonderful iron deposits. He located a large number of claims, until he controlled the major part of the iron.

Capital at Last Interested

Efforts were made for years to get capital interested in the development of these deposits, but only failure resulted until a little over a year ago, when the owners mentioned, pooled their holdings and gave Witcher Jones of Salt Lake an option on all. After many months of negotiations with different groups of capitalists, Mr. Jones finally closed a deal last summer with Messrs. Kimberly and Buhl to purchase the entire block of ground for $2,500,000, and the initial payment was made. These two men and their associates promptly began to work out their plans for the opening up of the mines, the building of manufacturing plants and the securing of transportation facilities and this work is now in progress.

The Colorado Fuel & Iron Company has also acquired a heavy interest in Utah iron. This company has purchased the holdings of Daniel and Robert Page and others on Iron Mountain and in the vicinity and is taking steps to patent the ground. The management has not yet stated whether it intended to put up a separate plant in Utah or to ship the ore to its Pueblo plant.

The development of the iron resources of the state means necessarily the building of many miles of railroad. It is expected that both the San Pedro and the Rio Grande will build branches to the coal and iron fields, and the iron syndicate may build a road of its own to haul its fuel and ore to the site of the manufacturing plants. The details of these arrangements have not yet been worked out, but the word of some of the strongest capitalists and iron manufacturers in the United States is given that they propose to build up another great industry in Utah and erect within its borders a city which can with justice lay claim to the title of "Pittsburg of the west."[42]

The Seven Lode Claims of the Taylor Estate

In the 1880s, Bishop Thomas Taylor of Salt Lake City was the General Business agent and Vice President of the Iron Manufacturing Company of Utah and was its largest investor. Early on he had credited the business with $10,000 worth of merchandise from his store. When the business failed in 1877 he, as the heaviest creditor, came into possession of the entire property. In addition to the patented quarter section of land containing the buildings, and the title to the small stream of water, he became the owner of some thirty of the best iron ore claims in the area, including the Blowout, Desert Mound and Duncan claims.

Mr. Taylor proceeded to get most of his claims patented and acquired coal lands in the canyon east of Cedar City. He tried to get investors interested in buying his property for over twenty-five years but he died before his claims were sold and his property was passed on to his heirs.[43]

John C. Cutler Jr., Taylor's son-in-law, became the agent for the heirs of Thomas Taylor. Mr. Cutler was involved with the buying and selling of many of the claims in the area and actively worked to sell the Taylor claims. He was closely associated with first Thomas Taylor and then his heirs, his wife being an heir. He was the secretary of the Iron Manufacturing Company of Utah when Thomas Taylor was General Business Agent. As a matter of interest, Cutler was elected the second Governor of Utah in 1905.[44]

The mining claims ultimately were split apart and were sold in several groups. One group of notable claims that made the newspapers on a number of occasions was pursued by several groups of investors. Eventually, all the claims were sold, but in the meantime, it was a roller coaster ride for both the buyers and the sellers of the properties.

Starting in 1901 through 1903, at least six attempts were made to secure the titles of the seven large iron ore claims that were held by the Taylor estate; five of these attempts failed, and in each case, thousands of dollars of option money was non-refundable and was credited to the Taylor Estate's account.

The first offer to buy the Thomas Taylor group of claims was made in May 1901 by an Eastern U.S. party to whom the Thomas Taylor heirs reluctantly gave an option of $250,000. Their agent, John C. Cutler Jr., traveled to New York to meet the principals in the proposed purchase.[45]

An article published a couple of years later in 1903, stated that "A few years ago John W. Gates, the Chicago steel magnate, had an option on the Taylor iron claims, but he relinquished it after having paid over $10,000 to hold them." The unnamed "Eastern Parties" mentioned in the above article were likely connected with John W. Gates, a board member of CF&I who attempted a takeover of the company which ultimately failed.[46]

The second offer for the group of claims was made in April 1902 by the syndicate of Col. S. B. Milner, S. V. Schelp, M. H. Walker, J. R. Walker, Matthew Cullen and Allen G. Campbell. An option for the property was purchased from the sixteen heirs of the estate of Thomas Taylor for $175,000 and included the seven patented claims covering some 140 acres. Some considered the claims "to be the most valuable iron land on the earth's surface." One of the claims purchased, most likely the Blowout deposit, was estimated at over 3,000,000 tons of ore in sight; with a solid body of ore extending 300 feet above the surface of the hillside and said to contain 70 percent iron. The new owners said that they would go to work at once to put the claims on the market.[47]

Colonel Milner and J. R. Walker of the purchasing syndicate stated that one of the primary reasons that they jumped in and consummated a deal was to thwart the plans of CF&I to buy the claims.[48] However, three months later when the syndicate was required to pay $45,000 to keep the option, they failed to come up with the money and the claims went back to the Taylor heirs.[49]

The third offer came in September 1902, the *Deseret Evening News* published an article about John C. Cutler Jr. visiting Iron County. He had had a vested interest in the Blowout claim and he had just sold it to the Kimberly syndicate of Sharon, Pennsylvania. They paid $50,000 of $250,000 for the option on the claims but Kimberly forfeited their money and surrendered their option a few months later when they failed to make the next payment. The claims were turned back to the Taylors for Mr. Cutler to try and sell again.[50]

The fourth offer was made by CF&I in April 1903. It was presumed that the total price for the option was around $200,000. Neither John C. Cutler nor the Taylor estate would confirm the deal, but the newspaper maintained that it was "a positive fact."[51]

Colonel Milner was also convinced that CF&I was going to end up being the owner of the seven claims. He was interested in the potential owner of these claims because one of them was the Desert Mound claim, which was adjacent to claims that he owned in that area.[52]

In June 1903, John C. Cutler Jr. received official notification that CF&I would not meet its payment of $175,000 that was due on June 24. The reason given for the forfeiture was "the stringency in the eastern money market."[53]

Promptly after the CF&I option expired, the fifth offer was made by Utah Senator Reed Smoot. He was given a sixty days' call on the property for an undisclosed amount. His option expired around August 25, 1903.[54]

On the morning of August 26, 1903, after over 2 years of deal making and at least five failed offers, CF&I paid $90,000 cash to purchase the now-famous "Seven Properties" from the Thomas Taylor Estate. News broke wildly, but John C. Cutler Jr., confirmed the validity of the report.

"During the day, Mr. Cutler drew from McCormick & Co.'s bank the sum of $90,000, delivered the deeds to the seven iron claims involved in the deal and before night had distributed the sum named among the thirteen heirs of the estate, share and share alike, and the business was closed up." Cutler later commented that he believed the purchase was able to occur because of the change in the ownership and management of CF&I from the Osgood to the Rockefeller faction.

Cutler identified the seven claims as the Duncan No. 1, Desert Mound, Blowout, Chesapeake, Excelsior, Pot Metal and Black Magnetic. The claims were counted among the most valuable in the district and they helped to round out the possessions of CF&I to seventy-four patented lode claims and many other claims not yet patented. Cutler also commented on what he thought CF&I's intentions were concerning the claims that they had just purchased.

> He understands that the Rio Grande will now build without delay from Marysvale straight through to Cedar City and tap the newly acquired properties. As far as is known now, the policy of fuel company is to ship all the ores to Pueblo for reduction instead of treating them in Iron County, though it is possible that before long the company may erect blast furnaces for production of pig iron destined for the Pacific Coast.[55]

CF&I wasn't the only entity that owned a large number of valuable claims.

> The balance of the wonderful deposits is held largely by the Milner-Dear-Lerch syndicate, which has no less than 123 claims in the same district. Of that number, seventy-two are patented and forty-one are now in process of patenting. Colonel S. B. Milner owns seventy-four claims individually, while Dear and Lerch are interested with him in the others. The remaining heavy holdings in the district are the eleven claims which the Cullen-Campbell syndicate recently bonded to A. B. Lewis for a term of two years and six of which are said to contain solid masses of iron.[56]

The Desert Mound Pit was eventually opened on several claims including the Desert Mound claim by Utah Iron Ore Corporation in 1924 and again by U.S. Steel in 1949. Commercial mining on the Duncan and Blowout ore bodies did not commence until 1942, during World War II when CF&I contracted Utah Construction Company to open the two pits on the property. The Black Magnetic was mined in the 1960s by Utah Construction. The Chesapeake and Excelsior were mined between 2010 and 2014 by Gilbert Development, and the Pot Metal deposit was never mined.

The two following articles are about actual rather than rumored or hoped sales of claims. Twenty-four McGarry and a dozen Campbell claims sold in 1908, plus some coal claims sold in 1921.

Big Iron Mine Deal Is Closed [1908]
Chicago Millionaire Operator Pays Final $50,000 for the McGarry Mines

One of the most important and significant mining deals that has been consummated in many a long day was finally closed up in this city Wednesday afternoon, when Thomas F. Keeley, the millionaire Chicago operator, made final payment in the sum of $50,000 for the McGarry group of twenty-four lode and one placer iron claims in the Iron Springs district, Iron County. It is now eighteen months since Mr. Keeley acquired an option on these properties from James C. McGarry and Ernest C. McGarry of Beaver City. During that time, a great deal of development work has been done, and the various payments under the option have been regularly made as they became due.

What the total sum paid for the property was could not be learned, but it is believed to approximate $225,000. Edward McGurrin represented Mr. Keeley, and the firm of Dickson, Ellis & Ellis represented the vendors in the transaction.[57]

Coal and Iron Claims Sold. [1921]

Monday afternoon the administrator of the estate of Allen G. Campbell, deceased, sold at public auction in front of the public library in Cedar, valuable coal and iron claims belonging to said estate. The property was disposed of for a consideration of $50,000, the purchasers being Thos. F. Keeley of Chicago, Nellie T. Cullen and the Campbell heirs, Allen G., Byron C. and Caroline Neil Campbell.

The Iron claims sold were the Little Alley, Vermillion, Great Western, Pioche, Wanderer, Lindsay and Little Mormon in the Iron Springs mining district, and the Burke Nos. 2, 3 and 5, Tip Top and Red Cloud in the Pinto mining district. The coal property consists of 160 acres in township 36 south, range 10 west, and sold for $5,000 to the same parties.

This sale was to have been held at an earlier date but owing to some law which had not been fully complied with; it was postponed and held last Monday.[58]

Colorado Fuel & Iron Company in Iron County

As discussed previously, CF&I built an integrated steel plant near Pueblo, Colorado in 1881. In 1899, agents for CF&I came into Southern Utah looking to supplement their iron ore reserves. They located, patented and purchased a large number of claims in most of the major mining areas, on the south and east sides of Iron Mountain and on the southwest and northeast sides of Granite Mountain. They even prospected iron ore showings northeast of Paragonah. This level of activity, particularly from a reputable iron and steel producer, sparked interest in the Southern Utah ore deposits.

The comings and goings of their representative were carefully observed Since the railroad terminal had been recently completed at Lund, nearly all travelers went through Lund. This allowed interested observers to closely follow the movements of major players, so that when CF&I was in town, it seemed that everyone knew about it. On October 4, 1902, the following observation was made by someone from the *Salt Lake Tribune* that happened to be in Lund when the CF&I men came through.

Activity in Iron District

Lund, Oct. 2. – Mr. W. E. Ladd and R. E. Fossdill, representing the Colorado Fuel & Iron Company passed through today en route to Iron City. The Colorado company seems to be making efforts to capture as many claims as possible; between them and the Kimberly company, there are very few more to capture. Even possible placer properties, hitherto considered worthless, are being located and every foot of ground near the iron deposits is being staked off.[59]

A similar article appeared in the *Deseret Evening News* a few months later, on January 30, 1903, again tracking the movements of the CF&I representative and trying to get a statement for the press.

From the Iron Fields

W. E. Ladd, representing the Colorado Fuel & Iron Company, who has been looking after that corporation's interests in the iron fields of Iron County, has returned from the diggings and taken his departure to Denver. It is said that this Colorado Company will expend $45,000 this year in securing patents for its holdings in the Pinto iron district.[60]

Some were excited to see a large concern with substantial capital in the area. They believed in its potential to bring new business into the area. Others were not so sure, especially those who were in competition with it. At that time, CF&I was one of the largest companies in the area and it not only owned iron and coal reserves but also railroads and telegraph lines. During this time, there was an extended fight over the control of the company and, despite being an iron and steel manufacturing company, CF&I got in the middle of a fight between the owners of the Rio Grande railroad and the owners of the Oregon Short Line. Each of the companies had different plans and goals for their activities in the West. The following article was published in the *Salt Lake Tribune* on November 27, 1902.

An Immense Concern

Facts about the Colorado Fuel & Iron Co., Gould Makes an Alliance with the New Stilwell Road to the Great Surprise of the Railroad World.

With the two greatest railroad magnates fighting for control of the Colorado Fuel & Iron Company, magnates who control the local railroads and the greater part of the fuel in the intermountain region, the interest in the company and its affairs, shown by local people, is intense. The Colorado Fuel & Iron Company is one of the largest concerns of its kind in the United States. It operates its own railroads with 36 locomotives and 450 cars. It runs a weekly magazine of its own to set forth the growth and changing conditions of the company. It operates in the three states and one Territory—Colorado, Utah, Wyoming and New Mexico. For the fiscal year ending June 30th last, it employed 15,087 men, with an average monthly payroll of $731,700.

Its output last year, or rather for the year ending June 30th, was 1,029,124,800 pounds in the iron department and 11,357,681,400 pounds in the fuel department. The capital stock is $40,000,000. The gross earnings for 1901 were $12,246,546. After paying all expenses and taxes, dividends and fixed charges, there was a surplus of $651,921 for the year.

It even owns and operates 2000 miles of telegraph wires and its hospital is far and away superior to that of any railroad company with 5000 miles of track.

Aside from the fact that the Rio Grande and Oregon Short Line owners are fighting for the control, there is another reason why there is a decided local interest in the company. It owns some of the coal and iron lands in Iron County, this State, and the promise has been made that it will eventually develop that section.[61]

As discussed previously, in 1903, after a lengthy battle with competitors, CF&I purchased seven large lode claims that were held by the Taylor estate. The purchase brought the total number of patented lode claims owned by CF&I to seventy-four. In addition, it owned numerous other claims which had not yet been patented, and if it won a court case involving the Walker brothers, to be discussed later, it would add another twenty-two claims to its holdings. At that time, CF&I controlled over one-third of all the iron ore deposits in the district.[62]

In its claim-buying spree, CF&I's holdings included the Blowout and Duncan claims at Iron Mountain, the Comstock and Homestake claims at Comstock, the Desert Mound and Tarantula claims at Desert Mound, and the Adams and Armstrong claims at Iron Springs along with many others. These claims were some of the largest deposits in the Pinto-Iron Springs Mining District.

In 1903, CF&I began exploration work on its claims in earnest, employing over one hundred men for a lengthy period of time, doing assessment and exploration work, sinking shafts, driving drifts, etc. They even paid to bring in a diamond drill to ascertain the depth of some of their deposits. The purpose of the work was not only to determine the extent of the deposits that they had claimed or purchased but also to establish their right to procure patents on the claims that were not yet patented. It seems they even stockpiled some narrow-gauge rails at Lund for some unknown reason. Needless to say, all of this activity caused no small stir with the locals.

Not to be outdone, Col. Milner also employed a considerable force of men to work on his properties at Desert Mound which were right alongside some of those owned by CF&I. He also stated in a newspaper article that he was in a position to know that CF&I was making arrangements to supply its plant in Pueblo, Colorado with iron from the mines it had purchased in Iron County. It seems that any excuse would do to start a good rumor. At times CF&I even made statements about helping to bring in the railroad, either from Marysvale or from Lund. Despite these statements, CF&I didn't start mining on the Duncan and Blowout claims for another forty years, long after the railroad was completed to the area.

The following newspaper articles from 1903 and 1904 discuss some of the activities of CF&I in the area.

Homestake and Comstock

The Colorado Fuel & Iron Company is again at work in the iron district, and work is to be commenced immediately on the Homestake and Comstock properties. The shaft on the Homestake which is now 200 feet deep, and in which the water has risen to a depth of sixty feet, is to have the water hoisted out of it and drifting will then be vigorously prosecuted under the supervision of the company's agent, Mr. F. U. Nelson. This property contains both copper and iron, but iron is what the company is after this time.

The Comstock, upon which there is at present a tunnel, 300 feet long, and which is said to run in the best body of Bessemer iron in Southern Utah, will be developed by sinking and drifting in the tunnel, and also by sinking three shafts at different places in the claim and cross-cutting from the bottom of each shaft to determine the extent of the ore body. Contracts for the work on the Comstock have been let to Magnus Ahlstrom, Sam Pollock and others, and the work is to begin immediately. It is also reported that the company intends to begin work soon on the Blowout.[63]

Colorado Fuel & Iron Co. Put 100 men to Work near Cedar.

That Utah is on the eve of a decided boom in iron mining becomes more apparent as the days go by. This is brought to mind in a forcible manner by advices which were received by Col. Milner this morning from Cedar City, Iron County. In the communication received by the Colonel, it is stated that the Colorado Fuel & Iron company has recently increased its force of men at its iron county mines to fully 100. Work is being projected all along the iron zone on the company's holdings, a distance of over 11 miles. This work consists in sinking shafts to determine the extent of the iron deposits.

Between six and eight of these shafts are being driven at the present time. As the ore is taken out, tests are made of its quality and character, and a record carefully kept. All the shafts so far made, while experimental in their character, are be driven that they can be used when the actual work of taking out ore in quantity is reached.

In speaking of the iron mines around Cedar City, Col. Milner said that he also had a considerable force of men at work on his properties which lie directly alongside that of the Colorado company. He intends to keep increasing this force as the time goes by. At present he is busy securing patents upon the ground and yesterday paid in to the receiver of the land office $1,720 in final proof on a tract.[64]

Utah Iron for Pueblo Plant—Rails Stacked Up at Lund.

Another significant thing at the present time is the fact that the big Colorado company [CF&I] has been industriously piling up a large quantity of steel rails at Lund on the line of the San Pedro railroad. These rails though are lighter than those used on main lines of railroads, and it is thought that the material will be used in track building around the mines. Col. Milner says that he is in a position to know that the company is making arrangements to supply its plant in Pueblo, Colo., with iron from the mines it has purchased in Iron County.[65]

Local News

The work with the diamond drill on the claims of the Colorado Fuel & Iron Company is completed, and Superintendent Nelson was in town Thursday for the purpose of superintending the shipping of the machinery to some other part of the company's holdings.

Mr. Nelson informs us that the contract for the building of the railroad from Marysvale to the iron fields has not been let yet do far as he knows, and that although the contracts are ready, the company are probably in no particular hurry, as they do not intend to begin work until next spring.[66]

Utah Iron Mines Enormously Rich—Colorado Fuel & Iron Company's Holdings More Valuable than At First Thought.

That the mines of Iron County are enormously rich in the class of ore contained in them, is evident from the following which appeared in this morning's issue of the Chicago Inter-Ocean and was sent to James A. Pollock & Co. their private wire by Logan & Bryan, their Chicago correspondents.

"Investigation of new ore property recently purchased by the Colorado Fuel & Iron company, in Utah, shows that it has enormously increased its holdings of raw material. Since the acquisition of control by the Rockefeller-Gould combination the company has purchased six additional iron claims in Iron County. Investigation since made by the company develops the fact that the Blowout claim has at least 2,000,000 tons of ore on the surface. It is expected to develop into one of the best ore bodies in the west. Eventually the company will build a railway to these mines."[67]

The Claim Battle between the Walker Brothers and CF&I

In 1903, a dispute and resulting legal battle began over a group of claims just west of Iron Springs Gap. The Lindsay ore body was by far the largest deposit in the Iron Springs-Three Peaks area. The deposit and subsequent pit encompassed numerous load claims including the Cora, the Utes, the Lees, Wanderer, Lindsay, Armstrong, Little Allie, Adams and parts of several others. Several placer claims were also overlying or near the ore body including the Wilson Iron, Walker Iron, Armstrong, Adams and Excelsior. The pit contained about twenty million tons of iron ore and was Utah Construction Company's mainstay for much of the time it was in operation. Iron County is presently using the Lindsay Pit for waste disposal.

As outlined earlier, lode claims are primarily intended for veins and deposits of ore in undisturbed rock that are underground or extending under the ground. Placer claims are generally intended for ore on or near the surface found in alluvial material not directly connected to a lode or ore body. In outcropping deposits, like many of the early discoveries of ore in Southern Utah, where the upper portion of the ore body is at or above the surface of the ground, it was difficult for claimants to distinguish what was a lode and what was a placer. In these cases, the ore from the top of the lode deposit had been disconnected from the core and was spread all over the surface intermixed with the alluvium material surrounding the deposit. To fully cover all of the ore associated with a deposit, both lode and placer claims were needed.

In the early 1880s, the Walker family staked at least two placer claims, the Walker Iron placer and the Excelsior placer. Convinced that these claims could be lucrative, the Walkers did the required work to get the claims patented. Some twenty years later, in the late 1800s and early 1900s, CF&I came to the area and staked and purchased many mining claims. During this time, they staked the Adams lode claim and the Armstrong lode claim over the top of the Walker's placer claims. CF&I's reasoning was simple and turned out to be correct; the Walkers staked out the alluvium but CF&I staked out the ore body (the lode). Because of the difference in definitions of lode and placer claims, CF&I technically was not a claim jumper.

In August 1903, the Walker Brothers took the matter to court to be officially resolved. It was a pivotal case because there were many other situations in the area that were very similar, and the legal decision would set precedent. The Walker's lawyers maintained that the action of granting the patents on their placer claims was final and couldn't be superseded. The CF&I lawyers maintained that even though patents were issued on the placer claims, the Walkers failed to file claims on the underlying mineral lodes. Their application didn't even indicate that the lodes were present, even though they were known to exist at that time.[68]

In June 1904, the district court sustained the contention of the lode claimants and stated that CF&I owned the lode and the Walkers owned everything within their placer lines outside of the lode lines.[69] The matter did not end there but was appealed, taken to federal court and tried before Judge John A. Marshall.

The result was that CF&I's contention was upheld in federal court with the modification that the surface area of CF&I claims had to be confined to the lode plus fifty feet on either side of the lode. CF&I would be entitled to all the lode extending into the earth after it left the vertical side lines of the narrow claims. The lode at the location was about 500 feet wide on the surface and more than half a mile long. The court's decision, therefore, left the lode claimants in possession of the heart of the lode down to the side limits of the narrow claims and all the lode from there on down. Under such conditions, the ground was of little value to anyone but CF&I.[70]

While CF&I won their court case, it is ultimately unclear which of the two parties succeeded in attaining ownership of more land. From later transactions it appears that the Walkers may have gained control of some of the claims by purchasing CF&I's portion. Moreover, the placer claims involved in the court case were not the only claims that the Walker family owned.

Twenty years later, in 1944, when mining was resumed at Iron Springs, Senter F. Walker of Salt Lake City, was the one who dealt with Kaiser Steel Company. Apparently, the Walker family still owned iron ore properties in the Lindsay Hill area at that time.[71]

In 1921, when things were beginning to heat up again regarding smelter and railroad rumors, the Walker Brothers had optioned some of their holdings to an unnamed eastern firm for $4,000,000. The properties originally belonged to the late Bishop Thomas Taylor and were bought from the Taylor estate some 21 years prior. A little later, CF&I also secured some very valuable claims from the Taylor estate. From newspaper reports, it appears that the claims secured by the Walker Brothers through the Excelsior Iron Company from the same estate rivaled the value of the CF&I claims. Unfortunately, the names or even general locations of the claims involved in the purchase were not disclosed.[72]

At first glance, the following article that was published in the *Salt Lake Telegram* on July 1, 1923, appears to be just one more rumor about eastern capitalists looking to spend money in Iron County to build a smelter. However, the article specifically concerned ten bankers from the Walker family and the Walker Bank in Salt Lake City taking a trip to Iron County to visit their iron ore claims, possibly with an eye to sell them to an interested party. The group took the very first passenger train to Cedar City to inspect iron ore claims that had been in the family for 43 years. From the description, the claims to which the article referred were near the railroad line at Iron Springs, possibly the ones that were involved in the legal dispute with CF&I. Again, however, the article does not give the names of the claims visited.

Another Steel Plant in Utah Seems Likely
Entrance of Eastern Capital Forecast as Salt Lake Capitalists Leave for Great Iron Deposits.

Entrance of Eastern steel capitalists into the iron fields of Utah and the construction of another large steel works in this state is forecasted with the departure last night for Southern Utah of a party of ten Salt Lake bankers and capitalists. No definite information could be obtained from any members of the party before departure Saturday afternoon, the statements being that none was at liberty to divulge the names of the Eastern interests or the possible nature of the deal which, it was reported, will be Utah's second big step into the steel industry of the country.

The party consisting of J. R. Walker, C. A. Walker, D. F. Walker, E. O. Howard, president of Walker Brothers Bankers; Walker Cheeseman; Ogden, W. R. Walker, S. F. Walker, Walter Lewis left early last evening over Union Pacific for Iron Springs, Iron county, where the Walker estate owns the largest single deposit of iron ore in the United States, and one of the largest deposits known to exist in the world, it is stated.

Railroad Near

This deposit of iron ore is known as Iron Hill and has been owned by the Walkers for forty-three years. When the Union Pacific constructed its new branch line from Lund to Cedar City the commercial possibilities of this great mountain of iron was realized, as previous to that time it was too far removed from transportation facilities to be of any great value for industrial purposes. This new branch of the Union Pacific passes within 1000 feet of Iron Hill, tapping the deposit for commercial purposes.

Mr. Lewis, one of the party who left last night, said that at the present time Eastern capital was reported interested in this deposit, but would not state definitely that the present trip had something to do with a possible new steel industry for this state. He said that he was not at liberty to commit himself further on the matter and could not state whether any Eastern capitalists interested would be represented at the inspection.

Mr. Lewis stated that there was much activity in Utah's new iron fields now that railroad facilities were at hand. He stated that the California steel interests, who are putting up the blast furnaces and steel works near Provo, were not in any way interested in the Walker iron deposit, but that they were entirely different and [were] Eastern steel interests.

First Train Today

The first regular train to be run over the new Lund-to-Cedar City road will be operated on schedule today on which train the Walker party will travel. The party will return to Salt Lake the first part of this week.

J. R. Walker stated before leaving that the present trip to Iron Hill was more of an inspection trip for members of the party as many of them had never seen the deposit of ore.

Illustration 4.5. Woodcut illustration of the Blowout deposit made for the 1893 Chicago World's Fair. (Salt Lake Tribune)

The report has been current in banking and financial circles of Salt Lake for some time, that Eastern capitalists were interested in iron ore deposits in Southern Utah and that the construction of the branch line from Lund to Cedar City was invigorated by the interest of these capitalists in ore deposits to be opened by the new railroad. While members of the Walker party were noncommittal, they admitted that there was considerable activity and no denial of the report of new steel interests for Utah was made.[73]

General Interest
Utah Iron at the Chicago World's Fair

In 1893, at the Chicago World's Fair, an exhibit was set up and was awarded first prize, displaying photos and samples of ore from the famous Blowout deposit.

> The cut shown on this page [*see above*] gives the apex of the Blowout mine deposit owned by Thomas Taylor, which holds undisputed title to being the best iron deposit in the country. It is 1000 feet in length by 500 feet in width and rises 150 feet at the apex, a solid mass of iron, almost pure. On the top of the ore may be seen Mr. Taylor and Don Maguire, while on the side is shown William Taylor, son of the proprietor. The pine tree in the left of the cut is growing in the solid iron ore. The photo was taken for the World's Columbian exposition, where it was exhibited with samples of ore from the same mine, which were awarded first prize. Specimens of the ore from the Blowout have assayed as high as 70 percent metallic iron.
>
> Besides the wonderful Blowout, Mr. Taylor has a considerable number of other very valuable iron properties, embracing the best and richest propositions that the district affords. Within them are included magnetite, hematite and all the other varieties known to the world.[74]

In 1904, the State of Utah and a group of local individuals went so far as to ship ten tons of Iron County's finest iron ore to be displayed at the St. Louis Exposition with the hope of raising interest in the world-class deposits that no one else seemed to be noticing. The article that appeared in the February 17, 1904 edition of the *Iron County Record* tells of the exhibit at the St. Louis Exposition Iron County Iron Exhibit.

Iron County Iron Exhibit.

Iron County will be represented at the St. Louis Exposition by a very fine display of iron ore. The gentlemen who have charge of the Utah exhibit realize that the iron deposits of this county are likely to become the most valuable resource in the state and are therefore giving it the most prominent place in our state mineral exhibit.

The Colorado Fuel & Iron Co. were asked to contribute some of their iron ore for the exhibit, but they refused all aid in the matter. So far as can be learned from reliable sources it seems to be their policy to depreciate the value of the deposits here, and to keep other investors out.

When Col. S. B. Milner was approached in regard to the same matter he gladly consented to do all in his power to make such a collection of iron ore as would do justice to the county and to the state.

To Mr. B. A. Perkins, who is making the collection, he gave a letter of introduction to his foreman, Mr. Fred Croton, expressing the desire that we furnish him with whatever ore he wanted, and that we also aid him in securing representative samples from other properties. Five tons of hematite were secured, partly from the Milner property on Desert Mound, and partly from McGarry property on Iron Springs Mountain; and five tons of magnetite ore from the Great Western property by Mr. Joseph F[ ].[75]

Developing New Coal Supply

Dr. E. F. Green has a force of men running a tunnel into a 10-foot ledge of fine appearing coal on his property on what is known as Lone Tree Mountain north of the Lake Flat [now Green's Lake]. Henry Pretsch, an experienced miner is in charge of the work, and at the present time the tunnel is about 45 feet long. The coal in the face of the work is beginning to assume a merchantable grade and it is believed that as great depth is obtained the quality will naturally improve. The thing that makes the development of this coal deposit important to Cedar City is the fact that by an air line the coal is within two miles of the doctor's town property in the southern part of the city, and by some means of economical transportation, such as the aerial tram, chute, or something of this kind it can be laid down here at a very low price, and at a good profit to the owner.

Northern capitalists are already figuring on the proposition, and it is likely that the property will be equipped with some such device in the near future, and used to supply at least the local demand, thus saving a wagon haul of seven or eight miles down the rough canyon road.[76]

CHAPTER FIVE

The Right Combination
Smelter, Railroad and Mines, 1921–1926

EVER SINCE THE discovery of the extensive deposits of iron ore in Southern Utah by the pioneers in 1849, dreams had been dreamed, plans had been drawn and multiple attempts had been made to build a thriving business using Iron County iron. Many spent their fortunes attempting to develop the resource; many lost much of their wealth on unfounded speculation. Unlike precious metals like gold and silver, or even other metals like copper or lead, iron ore is a bulky, unwieldy mineral that is difficult to convert into a useful metallic form. In addition, its value per unit weight, in a monetary sense, is far less than its precious siblings. Despite being tremendously more important to society than its relatives, its worth is not measured by the caret, ounce or even the pound. Its value is measured by the ton, hundreds of tons or even tens of thousands of tons.

For materials like iron ore and many other commodities used in bulk, because of the high cost of transportation in relation to their value, proximity to the market is all-important. And of course, like all commodities, iron ore has to have a market before any of its worth can be realized. No matter how valuable we may think an item is, it is only worth what someone is willing to pay for it, assuming there is someone who wants to buy it at all.

In the case of the spectacular deposits of iron ore in Southern Utah, to have any value, all of the following elements had to be in place.

Materials The raw materials had to be available as well as a means to mine them at a reasonable price. In this case, the raw material included not only iron ore but also metallurgical grade coal and good limestone.

Transport There had to be a way to economically transport both the raw materials and the finished products to and from the Iron Works. Because of their bulk and weight, the only economical method of transporting iron ore, coal, limestone, metallic iron and steel is the railroad. This was critical in the early days when the only viable alternative was the ox-cart, and it also continues to be true in modern times.

Facilities There had to be both a smelter to convert the raw iron ore into usable metal and a foundry or factory to turn that metal into usable end products. Raw iron ore, in and of itself is not very useful except maybe as a doorstop, paper weight or counter weight. However, some types of hematite and magnetite are used in jewelry. The only ones who need and are willing to pay for raw ore are those who a have facility to convert the ore into metal and make functional end use items. There are a few who use iron ore in their furnaces as a flux to help extract precious metals or as a cement additive, but this use also requires specialized facilities.

Market For all commodities and manufactured products, there has to be a market for a business to be successful and the items that are produced must also be competitive in the marketplace in both quality and price.

In the early days in Iron County, much of the first element was clearly available. High-grade ore was just lying on the surface such that it didn't even require appreciable mining. The pioneers just had to break it loose, load it into the back of their wagons and haul it to the blast furnace. The coal, however, was and continues to be problematic. There is plenty of coal in Southern Utah, but as discussed at length in previous chapters, it was good for heating ovens and other thermal applications, but it did not make good metallurgical coke. There was, however, a substantial amount of limestone in the area that was easily accessible and suitable for use in iron making.

Economic transportation, the second element, was a problem for the early operations. Even when a good product was manufactured with reasonable consistency, getting the raw materials to the furnace and transporting the finished products, once manufactured, the long distance to market was difficult and costly. The roads were almost nonexistent, and the vehicles were wagons, pulled by teams of horses or oxen. The elements seriously affected the roads, especially in the winter when they could be blocked by drifting snow or be turned into ice or mud. A railroad, including locomotives, cars and tracks was even bought for the Iron City operation, just to haul coal from Cedar Canyon across the valley to the Iron Works. There were times when good quality pig iron, produced at Iron City, was stockpiled at the site because of poor road conditions. Although some men used ox transport for small quantities of material, there were and are no substitutes for a railroad when it comes to hauling, iron, coal and limestone.

The third element, namely building and operating a blast furnace to convert raw ore into pig iron was no easy matter, especially in the middle of the wilderness. Today, furnace components come from locations all over the globe, but in the early days, transportation was not available to ship heavy components, even if doing so had been affordable. The builders of the first furnaces in Iron County struggled to find suitable materials to construct and sustain the operation of a blast furnace, let alone finance it.

The fourth element, having a market and being able to compete in it, was critical even in the early days. The Iron City works were successful in producing a quality product but could not control the cost of operation. There was a continual concern about how much pig iron the local market could support at the price. Being able to sell to out-of-state markets was critical for a manufacturing operation to be feasible.

The bottom line was that iron manufacturing could not be successful on an ongoing basis until there were mines, railroads, smelters and a market.

For a long time, the situation was irresolvable. The railroad companies would not build a new line to the ore deposits without a smelter in place, and no one would build a smelter without a railroad in place. There was not a source of good metallurgical coal within Iron County, and markets outside of Utah were needed to utilize the products that would be made. This combination did not come together until 1923, almost seventy-five years after the ore deposits were discovered by the pioneers of the Church of Jesus Christ of Latter-day Saints. It took a huge coordinated effort by a half a dozen companies, with a large amount of capital, to bring all the resources together, the iron, coal, limestone, railroad, smelter, market and water.

A Grand Plan

In 1921 and 1922, two new companies or "industrial projects," were organized by two separate groups of resource and steel-making companies. The steel companies were located on the West Coast but were almost completely dependent upon the resources of the Eastern United States for their supply of both pig iron and coke. These conglomerate project companies planned to bring together the raw materials, the transportation, the smelter and the market to build a viable iron manufacturing business in the Western United States, much of which was to be in Utah.

The first company, by the name of Columbia Steel Corporation, contained an amalgamation of the resources of the Utah Coal & Coke Company of Sunnyside, Utah; the Columbia Iron & Steel company, which had plants at Pittsburg, California and Portland, Oregon, the Southern California Steel Company of Los Angeles and several rich iron properties in the Iron Springs Mining District in Iron County, Utah. The announcement made in San Francisco by the company stated that the merger was valued at $25,000,000.[1] The location and ownership specifics of the iron ore properties were not revealed but apparently the claims were located at Iron Springs.

The second company, named the Pacific Steel Corporation, combined the plants of the Pacific Coast Steel Company in San Francisco, Seattle and Portland and the Southern California Iron and Steel Company in Los Angeles and San Diego, and added the "vast" coal and iron ore properties of the Milner Corporation of Salt Lake City, headed by A. T. Milner. The merger involved $40,000,000.[2]

In November 1922, these two conglomerated companies announced that they would merge and be consolidated into one mammoth enterprise which was to be incorporated under the laws of Delaware, adopting the name of the first company, the "Columbia Steel Corporation." This huge industrial venture listed the following projects required for the enterprise to be successful. Each item, in its own right, was a large and expensive undertaking:

1) Development of the coal mines in Carbon County, Utah.
2) Erection of a byproduct coke-plant to produce the fuel to smelt iron ore.
3) Building a railroad to connect the coal properties with the Denver & Rio Grande lines, and building tipple and mine entries.
4) Opening the iron ore deposits in Iron County, Utah.
5) Building a 25-mile branch railroad to connect the iron mines with the main line of the Los Angeles & Salt Lake railroad at Lund.
6) Acquisition and enlargement of large limestone quarries near Salt Lake.
7) Construction of a 500-ton per day blast-furnace on a tract of land between Provo and Springville near Utah Lake.
8) Expansion of the existing steel plants in California and Oregon to use the pig iron that would be produced by the new Utah smelter.

As it turned out, construction work for Columbia Steel Corporation had been under way for some time. Work had begun at the coal property, including the building of a railroad to connect the property with the D&RG lines and building of tipple and mine entries to bring the property into production. The company had acquired and taken options on a tract of land between Provo and Springville on which its blast furnace was to be built. The company had even been granted the right to have a railroad line constructed from the Salt Lake Route at Lund to its iron ore deposits at Iron Springs.

Each of the participating parties had something to gain and accomplished something together that none of them could do individually. An increased pig iron supply was brought to California to permit successful competition with iron and steel produced by the Eastern U.S. plants, a blast furnace and a coke plant were established in northern Utah, a railroad was created connecting the coal beds and the iron ore deposits and last but not least, new iron, coal and limestone mines were established.

One of the casualties of the merger was the blast furnace in Southern Utah for which many of the local residents had hoped. The plans of the Pacific Steel Corporation called for a blast furnace to be built in Iron County, near the iron ore deposits. The company had chosen a place near one of the Milner owned ore bodies. Ultimately these plans were scrapped in favor of Columbia Steel Corporation's plans, which had already progressed to the point of purchasing land for the plant. The Columbia location was also more central to the coal mines and the limestone quarries and had a more than adequate supply of water, which was an issue for any Iron County location.[3] Had the smelter been constructed in Iron County instead of Utah County, Cedar City would have been the boom town rather than Provo and Springville.

After waiting nearly seventy-five years, construction started almost overnight on the smelter, the railroads and the mines. Iron County and its iron reserves had not been developed because it had never been able to achieve critical mass, but now, with a stroke of fate or luck and many millions of dollars, the stars were aligned, or more correctly, the resources were aligned, and it was happening. Several locations in Utah, including Iron County, were to become the beneficiary of the very elaborate, coordinated and expensive investment.

The Smelter

In 1922, even before the final merger with the Pacific Steel Corporation, the newly formed Columbia Steel Corporation had decided on a location for the new smelter and had begun purchasing land. It didn't take long to get things rolling. Unlike building the railroad or even the mines, to build a smelter, thousands of tons of machinery would have to be detailed, manufactured, purchased, transported and erected, requiring a great deal of logistics, many hundreds of men and substantial time.

The Columbia Steel Corporation commenced work on the proposed steel plant near Provo on Monday, March 12, 1923.[4] The following news article, published less than three weeks later in the *Salt Lake Telegram*, gave a good indication of the progress of the smelter.

Ironton Chosen Official Title of Steel Town

Ironton Utah is the officially selected title for the new industrial community between Springville and Provo, which will center on the pig iron plant of the Columbia Steel Corporation according to an announcement today by L. F. Rains, vice president of the corporation. The name Ironton will appear on the station of the Salt Lake & Utah railroad to be erected at the entrance to the pig iron plant. Firms making freight shipments to the plant will be notified at once of the terminal name.

Thousands of tons in machinery and equipment needed in erection of the blast furnace and byproduct coke oven units, that will have a daily capacity of 500 tons of pig iron, are now en-route to the plant site, according to Mr. Rains. Immediately upon transfer of deeds to the plant site, firms with which purchase contracts had been made were notified to start shipment. These should begin to arrive early next week, when it is expected the laying of spur tracks will have been completed and actual erection of the furnace and ovens may commence.

Meanwhile, excavation for the blast furnace foundation is under way. Pouring of concrete for its base is planned to start as soon as trains can pass over the spur tracks. A representative of John Mohr & Sons of Chicago, blast furnace contractors, is expected to arrive within the next few days to consult with resident engineers of the steel corporation over details of furnace construction.[5]

Another article published in the *Salt Lake Telegram*, some five weeks later, in May, gave an idea of the immensity of the undertaking. People came from all over to apply for and fill the hundreds of job openings.

150 Men Work on Steel Mill—Pouring of Concrete to Start Friday

Construction of the blast furnace and by-product coke oven units of the Columbia Steel Corporation at Ironton, near Springville, will commence in earnest Friday, when it is understood the Lynch-Cannon company of this city will commence pouring concrete for the foundation base of the blast furnace. Within a few days, the Koppers Company of Pittsburg, Pa., will begin similar work on the foundations for the coke ovens, which they are to erect. Grading and excavation work has been in progress for several days. A network of sidetracks has been laid over the plant site and switch engines have been leased for the purpose of shunting the trainloads of material which are due to begin pouring in, not later than next week.

More than 150 men are already employed on the ground. This number will increase to exceed 400 by June 1, and by July 15, when it is expected work on the blast furnace section will be in full swing, between 600 and 800 men will be employed. Freight shipments of material already ordered and in transit exceed 100,000 tons according to L. F. Rains, vice president of the corporation. This tonnage will require more than 2500 freight cars for transportation to the building site. Heavy equipment orders have also been placed and shipments so timed, that the various materials will arrive daily, as needed.

Every effort is being made to speed up construction so as to overcome the delay experienced at the outset several weeks ago and complete the plant so that pig iron may commence in March of next year, according to Mr. Rains.[6]

In October, an Ironton Plant update was printed in the *Salt Lake Mining Review*.

Making Rapid Progress at Steel Plant

Iron ore from the Columbia Steel Company properties in Iron County will begin arriving at Ironton, the new steel city, the latter part of this month or the first of November, according to J. D. Watson, engineer in charge of construction at the steel plant.

In the meantime, work is thirty days ahead of schedule, much substantial progress having been made the past few weeks. The immense smokestacks have reached their proper height and the work of lining them is being rapidly completed.

The steel work, steel trestles, wooden trestles and cleaning system, according to engineer Watson, are about 95 percent completed.

Brick work in the stoves, under course of construction, will probably be completed by February 1 and are now 20 percent finished. The entire steel work also is about 20 percent completed.

Brick work at the by-products plant and coke ovens is about 25 percent completed. In fact, the plant is assuming proportions that it lacked some few weeks ago.[7]

Another update on the Ironton Plant was printed in January 1924. The target date for completion was estimated to be between April 1 and April 15. The coal and iron mines were nearly ready to start shipping their products.

Columbia Steel Plants at Ironton Are Rapidly Nearing Completion

Work on the Columbia Steel Corporation pig iron plant at Ironton, is progressing rapidly, according to L. F. Rains, vice-president of the company, who returned from a regular inspection trip to Ironton a few days ago. The boilers and boiler house are fully completed and ready for operation and the power house is within sight of completion within a short time.

The large stoves for pre-heating the air for the blast furnace and the furnace itself are complete and have been under heat for about three weeks. The heating follows the completion of the brick work inside the furnace and stoves and requires some time to dry them out completely.

The brick work of the coke and by-product ovens—the largest and most intricate job of brick work—will be finished by February 1 and will be under heat shortly after that time. The plant will be in full operation between April 1 and 15.

The coal and iron properties are ready at present to start shipments in amounts required to keep the blast furnace in operation, but development work is still being carried on at both places. Construction work, buildings and machinery, at both Columbia [the coal property] and Iron Springs is complete.[8]

The facilities were completed in April as predicted and on Tuesday, April 29, 1924, the charging of the blast furnace with iron ore, limestone and coke began and continued through Wednesday morning. The following article in the *Springville Herald* marked the event.

Utah's Iron Industry Begins with the Flowing of Pig Iron at Ironton Plant Wednesday

The first iron ore in Utah County fused with lime and coke was ready to be formed into pig iron early Wednesday afternoon at the Columbia Steel Corporation plant at Ironton. The flowing of the iron from the blast furnace marks the real beginning of the iron and steel industry in the state of Utah.

Officials of the steel corporation together with Provo citizens invited especially for the occasion were at the steel plant Wednesday afternoon to watch the first operations of the blast furnace. D. H. Botchford of San Francisco and L. F. Rains of Salt Lake City, vice presidents of the corporation, were among the officials at the plant.

The charging of the blast furnace with strata of iron ore, lime and coke was begun Tuesday, and continued Wednesday morning.

From now on, the operations of the steel corporation will be in full swing and the making of pig iron to be sent from Utah County to the steel mills of the Columbia Steel Corporation at Pittsburg or Torrance, California, will be shipped before the end of this week.

"The plant is now going," said W. R. Phibbs, superintendent of the plant, this morning. "Thirty or forty hours will be necessary to turn out the first castings, but thereafter castings will be made every six hours. Everything is progressing nicely."[9]

A grand day of celebration was held in June for "Utah Steel Day." The Ironton plant was a big deal, Utah had been trying to get the iron industry going in the State for almost seventy-five years, and it was finally happening.

It meant significant new jobs in the area of the smelter and also in the area of the mines. It also meant that there would be many auxiliary jobs needed to supply the business with the products and services that would be required to keep them running. Thousands of people attended the event. The event's proceedings appeared in the following article in the *Iron County Record*.

Big Steel Day Celebration

Our special reporter was on the ground at Ironton, Utah, the home of the Columbia Steel Works, Saturday, June 7, 1924, to attend the celebration of Utah Steel Day, which marked the dawn of a great industry in the richest of natural resources in the world, and was agreeably delighted to note that there were thousands of people in attendance from all parts of Utah and adjoining states, and a number from several middle west and eastern states, who had come to the new steel plant to hear about the wonderful development made in the iron industry in the past year, and to see the great works erected by the Columbia Steel Company, one of the richest steel corporations in the United States.

The opening of this plant marks the first great development of the coal deposits in Carbon County and the unlimited iron deposits of Iron County, brought together at the junction of Utah County.

After allowing the thousands of visitors to view the plant from a roped safety zone, giving them a good conception of the workings, a meeting was held on the side hill east of the plant. To the inspiring music of the hum of machinery of Utah's first steel plant, the visitors heard prominent State and Nationally known industrial men give the history of the development of the iron industry in Utah and forecast its growing into one of the greatest industries in the United States.

Exhibited on the stand was an old iron bell, the first product of the iron industry in Iron County, made in 1855, by the pioneers sent to Cedar by Brigham Young to develop the iron resources.

Mr. Hinckley, Secretary of the Provo Chamber of Commerce and chairman of the meeting, gave a brief outline of the history of the development of the industry in Utah from the time of the first plant at Cedar City in 1855, up to the present stage.

Thomas E. McKay, president of the State Utilities Commission, representing Governor Charles R. Mabey, congratulated the leaders in this development and the people for supporting them in such a way as to make this development possible. Mr. McKay dwelt upon the history of the industry and upon the foresight of Brigham Young and the pioneers.

One third of the industries of the world are either directly or indirectly dependent upon the iron industry, and Utah with every natural resource for the development of this great industry, the coal and iron ore, and all raw materials, and industrial leaders prophesying that the steel industry will be centered here,

Illustration 5.1. The new Ironton plant was located on the shores of Utah Lake between Provo and Springville, Utah. (Photo used by permission, Utah State Historical Society)

and that the great plants will be located on our lake shores, Utah bids fair to become one of the leading industrial states of the nation.

In the words of Wigginton E. Creed, President of the Columbia Steel Co., "we will not have a hot house growth, but it will be a steady development that nothing can tear down."

"Capital follows character as readily as it does resources", says Mr. Creed, "and as the character built up in Utah by the pioneers is really greater than our unlimited natural resources, we need have no fear that Utah's industries will grow to immensity and capital will flow freely."

In speaking of bringing capital to Utah, Mr. Creed said "that the Columbia Steel Corporation had not come to Utah just to show appreciation of the invitation, but that we had laid before them the natural resources and ended a long search for the combination of materials to continue their great development work."

Mr. Creed says "that it will not be just a Utah industry, but one of the whole West. That with the development of the Pacific slope and the outlet through the Pacific harbors our resources will be developed to such an extent as to make the West economically independent, meaning that we'll have everything to make this an independent industrial empire."

"We must develop a spirit of cooperation", said Mr. Creed. "With the splendid cooperation that has already been manifested by Utah people, we have but to continue as we have in the past to make this the leading steel producing state in the United States."

Mr. Creed congratulated the pioneers and early leaders on laying the foundation for a great industrial empire, by first rooting the population solidly and developing the state agriculturally.

The music for the meeting was furnished by the Murray and Payson bands and by Mrs. Thora Thornbird, soloist of Springville.

Mayor C. C. Neslen of Salt Lake City, as did all the other speakers, lauded L. F. Rains, for his part in the development of Utah's Steel Industry. Mr. Neslen stated that "to Mr. Rains should go the credit more than to any other person, as it was his untiring efforts that brought capital to Utah to develop our natural resources."

Mr. Neslen said, in speaking of Mr. Rains, "I don't know what the L. F. of his name is for; I used to think it meant "Long Foresight", but later I concluded it meant "Legitimate Finance", but at last I have decided that it means, 'Loyal Friend."

"With this development, Utah will become the leader in two distinct lines, scenic and industrial," said Mr. Neslen. Utah's spirit of cooperation could be expressed in the phrase, "Let me live in a house by the side of the road and be a friend to man."

Pres. Heber J. Grant, of the Church of Jesus Christ of Latter-day Saints, spoke a few words of congratulation to the Columbia Steel Corporation officials and to the people of Utah, and also thanked the speakers for the tributes paid to the pioneers and character builders of our state.

In the afternoon there were sports in both Springville and Provo, consisting of a Wild West show, ball games, boxing and wrestling bouts, etc.

Springville held its annual Strawberry Festival on that day, and a free barbecue was given by the Columbia Steel Corporation at both Provo and Springville.[10]

An interesting article appeared in the *Provo Herald* on June 6, 1924, the day before the Steel Day Celebration. The article was re-published in the *Iron County Record*. Based on a rumor from supposedly reliable sources, it stated that Wigginton E. Creed, president of the Columbia Steel Corporation, was going to make an important announcement in his speech at the Steel Day Celebration.

> From fairly authoritative sources it is learned that the next step of progress at Ironton will be the building of open-hearth furnaces for the conversion of pig iron into raw steel. This step is held to be necessary for the conservation of fuel, millions of cubic feet of gas now being wasted daily. Another blast furnace and additional ovens are believed to be included in the program of development.[11]

Apparently, the rumors were not true because the announcement was never made; open-hearth furnaces were never built at Ironton and a second blast furnace was not constructed at Ironton at that time. Not until some twenty years later, during World War II, was a second blast furnace relocated and erected at the Ironton location.

The Market

The original capacity of the Columbia Steel plant at Ironton, Utah, with Blast Furnace No. 1 in operation, was 500 tons of iron per day. In 1924, virtually all of Ironton's production went to California. The iron was split between Pittsburg California and Torrance California (formerly owned by Llewellyn Steel Corporation, merged with Columbia Steel in April 1923). There was no other source for pig for the open-hearth furnaces at Pittsburg or Torrance, unless Columbia wanted to purchase it on the open market from the East and strand its investment in its own blast furnace.[12]

The Ironton plant was vitally important to the West Coast iron and steel industry as the following *Salt Lake Telegram* article pointed out.

California Is Prime Market for Steel Produced in Utah

William Lacy, in an article on "Steel" in the *Southern California Business Magazine*, recently issued, says of the importance of the steel industry in Utah:

"The foundation of this basic industry [in Southern California] is pig iron, which, previous to May, 1924 when the Columbia Steel corporation's blast furnace at Provo, Utah, was blown in, was not produced west of the Rocky Mountains. This was one of the only three new blast furnaces s built in the United States within the past four years. The operation of this furnace has been continuous, and today it is turning out about 400 gross tons of pig iron for basic open hearth and foundry purposes every 24 hours, 365 days in the year.

"There is a splendid and growing demand for the product of this furnace as, demonstrated by the fact that during the first six months of 1924 some 80 per cent of the pig iron used by foundries and steel mills in the Los Angeles area was imported from foreign countries and eastern United States, whereas at the present time over 80 per cent comes from the Utah furnace.

"That a great market for pig iron in Pacific coast territory exists is found in the fact that there are 500 iron foundries and 19 open hearth furnaces west of the Rocky Mountains."[13]

In 1926, the Pacific States Cast Iron Pipe Company opened a casting operation adjacent to the Ironton plant and began taking some of its output.[14]

It is a bit ironic that in the beginning, all the pig iron produced by the Ironton blast furnace using Utah raw materials, went to California, not Utah. But that was where the open-hearth furnaces, mills, foundries and most of the markets were located.

The Railroad

Once all the work had been done to create the massive industrial project, it didn't take long for the ball to get rolling; this was also true of the railroads. Even before the final merger, the Columbia Steel Corporation filed a request with the public utilities commission for a certificate of convenience and necessity for construction of a railroad from the Salt Lake Route to its iron ore deposits at Iron Springs. The Union Pacific Railroad Company subsequently filed a request with the Interstate Commerce Commission for the right to build this road, which was granted.[15]

After waiting for almost seventy-five years for a railroad to be built, Cedar City was to become the beneficiary of a branch of the Union Pacific Railroad built for access to the new iron mine, and fortuitously extended into the city center for its use. It is interesting to note that both the Columbia Steel Corporation and the Pacific Steel

Corporation specifically listed as one of their objectives the construction of only a twenty-five-mile branch railroad line from Lund to the iron ore deposits at Iron Springs. Somewhere along the line, probably after consultation with the Union Pacific Railroad and the Interstate Commerce Commission, the project scope was changed to a thirty-three-mile railroad line that would extend the extra eight miles into Cedar City.[16]

Early in March 1923, things got moving on the construction of the railroad. It is interesting to note that the Utah Construction Company, which did a large part of the work on the railroad line from Lund to Cedar City, was the same company that later became one of the major mining companies in Iron County. The following newspaper article documented the event.

> The Union Pacific has ordered the Utah Construction company to move all its railroad construction equipment from Ogden and Delta, to Lund and be ready to commence the building of the branch line from Lund to Cedar, which so far as we can learn, will commence next week or the week following.
>
> Bids are called for the erection of the steel bridge over Coal Creek in the northern part of Cedar and the bids will be opened March 12, next Monday. Utah Construction Company engineers have been here this week looking over the site for the bridge, the abutments and approaches so that an intelligent bid may be submitted. Work on this structure is to commence within two weeks after the opening of the bids, should any of them be accepted by the government and state.[17]

Even though the announcement concerning the erection of the steel bridge over Coal Creek appeared in the same news article as the information about the new branch railroad line, and the Utah Construction Company was involved in both ventures, the bridge was an independent project just north of the rail loop into Cedar City. It was completed in late September or early October 1923.[18] The two-lane steel bridge was replaced in October 1952 by new four-lane structure with pedestrian walks on each side. Replacing the original bridge "eliminated one of the worst hazards on U.S. Highway 91 in this part of the state."[19] The new bridge is still in existence today.

It appears that Union Pacific had to assemble background information for some sort of a justification or explanation for building a new rail line. In March, a letter was sent to all traffic representatives and local agents of the Union Pacific Railroad concerning the new line. The letter mentions the reasons for the line as farming, livestock and scenic features in the area, in addition to its primary purpose of providing access to the iron deposits to supply iron ore to the new blast furnace at Springville, Utah.

> **To: All Traffic Representatives and Local Agents.**
> **SUBJECT: Railroad's New Branch Line from Lund to Cedar City, Utah.**
> The required certificate of convenience and necessity for construction of a branch line of railroad from Lund to Cedar City, Utah, approximately 33 miles, has been granted to the Union Pacific System by the Interstate Commerce Commission. Construction of the line has been authorized and will begin soon. Its location is illustrated by the map on reverse side hereof.
>
> Cedar City is already a thriving town of 2500 population, and in its immediate vicinity there are large deposits of iron ore, development of which is assured by the operation of blast furnaces at Springville, Utah, by the Columbia Steel Corporation, who will erect furnaces at that point for the transformation of the iron ore into pigs.

Illustration 5.2. Aerial view of the Cedar City railroad loop (east at the top) as it existed before sections began to be removed in late 1977. The white line traces the track, including side tracks for access to local businesses and to switch out and park freight cars at various locations. (Evan Jones)

While the livestock industry in the southern Utah territory has been predominant because of ability to drive stock to rail shipping points, climatic and soil conditions are such as to make diversified farming profitable. The land, in large part, is irrigable and the soil productive. These two factors, in combination with intelligent and aggressive farming and horticulture, should be productive of a substantially increased traffic, of development of the territory, and of profit to the individual.

Also, this branch line will be exceedingly important from a passenger traffic viewpoint, as Cedar City is the gateway to the wonderful scenic features in Southern Utah, among which are Cedar Breaks, Zion National Park, and Bryce Canyon, and in Arizona, the Kaibab Forest and the North Rim of the Grand Canyon of the Colorado River.

In the development of these scenic attractions, a program of good roads, hotel and camp construction, and adequate automobile transportation, is being given the necessary attention.[20]

By mid-April, only a short while after approval of the new line, construction began on the branch railroad and over two miles of track had been completed. The new rail line would come right into the center of Cedar City and included a large teardrop-shaped loop within the city. The loop allowed passenger stops at the depot and freight stops at other locations before the train headed out of town with the steam locomotive heading the proper direction of travel. The trains of today generally have diesel-electric locomotives that can move equally well in either direction, and many trains have a locomotive at each end. There were downsides to the plan: because of the location of the railroad line and the loop, there were quite a number of houses and buildings in town that had to be moved or torn down in a relatively short amount of time.

The following article from the *Iron County Record* tracked the railroad's progress.

R. R. Work Progressing [April 1923]

Work on the branch railroad from Lund to Cedar is progressing at fair rate and some two miles of steel has been laid.

Three gangs of graders are at work on the route and within the course of four weeks, grading will have been done, and steel laid for several miles, while it is confidently expected that all the steel from Lund to the city proper will have been laid by the 15th of June.

Work has commenced on the vacating of property in town, purchased from the people for the right of way, and the cutting of trees and tearing down and moving of buildings is now going on. The people from whom the property was purchased received word on the first of this month to move within 30 days, and to do so within this time means that active work must be carried on steadily, every day. So far, fair progress has been made and the vacators have no fear but that they can live up to the demands made upon them.

We have received word that the railroad officials believe that before the 1st of July, trains will be running on the new line, and that transportation of tourists will be an everyday occurrence, after that date.

Skeptics that have scouted the idea that there would ever be a railroad to Cedar City are now lying rather low and making but very few remarks. Indeed, some of the people who were the most skeptical a few weeks ago, are now the ones that are doing the most talking and telling the people "I told you so! I knew that the U.P. would build to this city this year."[21]

Iron Mining & Manufacturing

On June 15, 1923, another letter was sent to all traffic representatives and local agents of the Union Pacific Railroad, in addition to being an update of the construction, it contained various information about the area.

To: All Traffic Representatives and Local Agents.

Concerning the Lund-Cedar City, Utah, branch we are glad to be able now to supplement our previous advice with the announcement that the construction work has been progressing very satisfactorily, and at the present writing, our engineers estimate the line will be completed to Cedar City about June 25. You will duly receive schedules fixing the exact date and character of the service, but pending receipt of these schedules, as well as the freight and passenger tariffs, it is desired that you have before you, certain facts, for the information of the public and yourself, concerning the line and this important territory for the development of which the Union Pacific System is spending approximately $2,000,000.

STATIONS: The stations with distances from Lund, Salt Lake City, and Los Angeles, are as follows:

Station	Miles from Lund	Miles from Salt Lake City	Miles from Los Angeles
Lund		242.6	541.4
(Siding)	9.5	252.1	550.9
Iron Springs	20.1	262.7	561.5
(Siding)	25.2	267.8	566.6
(Stock Yards)	29.9	272.5	571.3
Cedar City	32.5	275.1	573.9

ELEVATION: The elevation at Lund is 5091 feet, the contour slightly rolling, with very gradual ascent to approximately 5800 feet at Cedar City. East of Cedar City there are high, forested tablelands ranging from 7,000 to 10,500 feet altitude.

SOIL: The country traversed by the branch line is the western portion of what is known to geologists as having been the bed of an ancient lake [Lake Bonneville], which at some prehistoric period covered a large part of the valleys of Utah, with an outlet to the Columbia River via the Snake River. The erosion of the mountains filled these lakes with layers of gravel and sand, overlaid with clays and silt, which form the very rich alluvial soil of today.

LANDS AVAILABLE: The United States Government is now engaged in research work to determine the acreage of land which is susceptible to irrigation. Much of it is privately owned and can be purchased at reasonable prices, in some instances as low as $5 per acre. A small portion of the land is open for homestead under the United States land laws and information on that subject may be obtained from the U.S. Land Office in Salt Lake City.

WATER SUPPLY: The water supply of this territory is obtained from the snow, the mountain streams, and from wells which, in some places, furnish a supply of flowing water at a depth of 100 feet or less, while in others it is necessary to pump from 8 to 50 feet to raise the water to the surface. Gasoline engines are used at present for pumping power but electricity generated in the mountain streams; will be available.

PRODUCTS: The following list of some of the commodities shipped from Lund is indicative of the diversity of the products of this country:

Cattle	Wool
Hogs	Alfalfa Seed
Bucks	Honey
Sheep	Fruits

There is an extensive and very fertile valley commencing about 30 miles south of Cedar City, familiarly known as "Dixie," and watered by the Virgin River, which is highly productive of fruits, vegetables, melons, and even of some products which we usually associate with distinctly southern climes, such as figs and pomegranates; in fact, the early Mormon settlers there grew some cotton for their own needs.

IRON DEPOSITS: The new branch line will tap the very valuable iron deposits in the Iron Mountains, said to be among the largest in the United States. The ores will be shipped to the blast furnaces of the Columbia Steel Corporation near Provo, Utah, which are now under construction.

TOWNS POPULATION: The terminus, Cedar City, is the metropolis of this section and the gateway to Southern Utah. It has a population approximating 3,000, and is a thriving commercial center with excellent schools, a branch of the state agricultural college, churches, and a modern attractive hotel, now nearing completion, which is owned and will be operated by the Union Pacific. To the north of Cedar City is Parowan, population 1700, the county seat of Iron County; and to the south, St. George, population 2,300, the county seat of Washington County, in the heart of the "Dixie" country; also, other important towns with populations as follows: Hurricane 1021, Toquerville 331, Springdale 230, Rockville 200, Virgin 181, LaVerkin 156. The combined population of these towns, not including other small communities and the ranchers, is approximately 10,000.

SCENIC FEATURES: The Union Pacific, by the extension of its line to Cedar City, renders easy of access many scenic features which, in grandeur and marvel, are comparable to, and different from, anything found in our other great National Parks. These attractions, Zion National Park, Cedar Breaks, Bryce Canyon, Kaibab Forest, and the North Rim of the Grand Canyon of the Colorado, have been visited by thousands of tourists in the past seasons, and you are already more or less familiar with them.

The Union Pacific is making a number of substantial improvements in tourist facilities in Southern Utah, and the highway development, Federal, State, and County, is well under way. However, it is not likely that we will be in position this season to take care of more than the tourist travel which may be attracted by the publicity already given to this wonderful section, although because of its importance, not only to the Union Pacific, but in the general development of Southern Utah, we are giving it brief mention in this Circular Letter.

You will await advertising literature and circulars for details concerning these tourist attractions, transportation, etc., which will duly reach you when our

Iron Mining & Manufacturing

Illustration 5.3. The first engine to Cedar City June 14, 1923, which arrived before the track was officially completed. David Bulloch at age 78 can be seen riding on the front. (Matheson Special Collections)

Passenger Traffic Department is ready for its active tourist campaign. In order to take care of this season's travel you are already in receipt of Passenger Department Circular of May 12, 1923, covering fares, routes, etc., including, also, a special map showing the highways and mileage.

    W. S. Basinger,   F. W. Robinson,
    Passenger Traffic Manager.   Freight Traffic Manager.[22]

Branch Railroad Line Completed

About halfway through the railroad construction effort, word was received that Warren G. Harding, the President of the United States, his wife and their entourage wanted to stop in Cedar City and travel to Zion National Park while on their whistle-stop tour of the western United States and its national parks. The message that "the track must be ready," reverberated throughout the Union Pacific organization from the president of the company right down to the workers on site. The company now had a deadline that was cast in concrete, so to speak, and the work had to be right. The president's train would be heavy, and everything had to be in order and sparkling clean. In addition, the construction of the depot building, including all the approaches, light poles etc., had to be completed to first-rate standards.

The railroad from Lund to Cedar City was indeed officially completed on June 25, 1923, as predicted by Union Pacific. The first locomotive, however, had traveled to Cedar City ten days earlier on June 14 with much fanfare by the local citizens. David Bulloch, a 78-year-old resident, was given the honor of riding on the front, near the "cow catcher." At age seven, on November 11, 1851, he rode in the first wagon to settle Cedar City.

The two trains arrived at the Cedar City depot at 8:00 a. m. after traveling throughout the night. The people of Southern Utah had been preparing for weeks for the visit. The train was met by an estimated 3,000 to 6,000 citizens, depending on the account, who were jammed around the depot grounds and lined Main Street for a quarter of a mile.

President and Mrs. Harding greeted and spoke to the crowd and shook many hands. The President took particular notice of the thirty-six local Native Americans who had assembled to shake hands with him.

The entourage was then directed to a line of between twenty-four and thirty-two highly polished automobiles, the number again depending on the account. The cars were owned, furnished and driven by Cedar City residents who volunteered their cars and services.

> [Thus] began the journey from the depot grounds past the new hotel and on south on Main street, the line of travel having been roped off and the people lining each side.
>
> Fifty special policemen kept the street clear of people and guarded the street from top to bottom. The special policemen were all ex-service men, many of them in uniform and were stationed about 50 feet apart on each side of the thoroughfare through which the party passed.
>
> As the guests were conveyed past the throngs of people, children with smiling faces, threw roses in front of the President's car, making a literal drive way of roses. As the President and Mrs. Harding were being driven along, they constantly waved greetings to the people which were heartily returned, and all seemed to radiate a feeling of welcome that appealed to the visitors. The President was heard to remark that the welcome extended by the people was generous and full of warm cordiality, and that the appearance of so many lovely children was an inspiration to him.
>
> After the party had driven through the principal thoroughfare of the city, it proceeded on the way to Zion Canyon, the cars traveling about one hundred yards apart.[23]

The cavalcade, containing close to 100 celebrities and newsmen, headed south to Zion Canyon, traveling through each town along the way, through Hamilton's Fort, Kanarra and down through the Black Ridge canyon. The residents of each town had gathered to line the streets, dressed in their Sunday best, waving and cheering at the passing convoy. At Echo Farm they stopped for fresh fruit of several kinds and a drink of "ice cold water." The Party traveled to Toquerville where the town was "beautifully decorated with the national colors," and "practically the entire population of Toquerville, Hurricane and LaVerkin" were lined up to meet them."

> Upon request, the President addressed the people for five minutes and among his remarks he said that "I am more than pleased to greet such a representative body of people, citizens of this great country, the United States. Great honor is a due the rugged pioneers who came and settled this country, and proud should the descendants be, to have for parents such noble and loyal men, whose foresight was providential. And let me say, that nowhere in all this land have I seen finer American citizens, fitting descendants of those pioneers gone before."
>
> Mrs. Harding also spoke a few moments and expressed her pleasure in being in this part of the world and meeting with such warm hearted and industrious people. As the party left the town, sixty beautiful girls, 30 from Toquerville, 20 from Hur-

Illustration 5.4. The locomotives of the President's train and the pilot train, side by side at the Cedar City Depot. The pilot locomotive, No. 7863 on the right, and the President's locomotive, No. 7864, was on the left. The President's trains were the first passenger trains to come to Cedar City, arriving on the morning of June 27, 1923. (Matheson Special Collections)

ricane, and 10 from LaVerkin, placed in each car, a basket of choice fruits, and a large bouquet of beautiful roses and other flowers. The fruits, bouquets and baskets had been prepared by the good ladies of the three towns mentioned, and each basket was nicely decorated with the national colors...

At Springdale the President was given a unique reception, in front of the welcoming party stood a fife and drum corps, the drummers being the same corps that used to greet Brigham Young in the early days. These drummers, each more than 70, shoot a lively pair of sticks.[24]

The Party then proceeded on through Rockville, to the Zion Park entrance and to the Wylie camp in Zion Canyon, not far from the base of the Great White Throne.

The Party arrived at the entrance in good order without the least vestige of trouble. Here they were greeted with patriotic music by the Dixie College silver band. After registering, the party continued to the Union Pacific Zion Park camp where everyone alighted, having enjoyed a remarkable ride, pleasant in every way.

The guests were escorted to the hotel where hundreds of Washington County people were gathered to do honor to the President of the United States. While the party was dining, a program of songs and musical numbers was rendered by St. George talent which was appreciated, not only by the President and party, but by the people assembled as well. The program was under the direction of Prof. McAllister of the Dixie Normal, and carried out with enthusiasm.

"America" and Mormon hymns were sung with such gusto that the music was echoed back and forth from one great rock mountain to another...[25]

After dining and being entertained by the program, President Harding and the group drove further up into the canyon.

The Right Combination

Illustration 5.5. President Harding in Zion National Park, posing in chaps, bandanna, boots and gloves. (Photo courtesy National Archives, No. 79-G-17-F-4))

Mrs. Harding stood the trip well but she balked at the trip on horseback.

When the party came to the end of the road and proceeded to mount saddle horses, Mrs. Harding demurred "I'll stay in the car and you can tell me about it," she told the president....

If the president had had any dignity on the trip he shed it with his coat as he climbed into a pair of chaps and wrapped a bandana around his neck. A ranger tried to put 10-gallon hat on the president's head, but it fit only where it touched and that was not often....

After the introductions, President Harding and about forty of the party were taken up the canyon to view the magnificent scenery, riding horses which had been secured specially for the occasion.

Two hours were consumed in viewing the grandeur of the Park. And each and every one was thunderstruck and gazed with awe and reverence on the gigantic cliffs that reared their majestic heads, three and four thousand feet in the air. Exclamations of wonder from all visitors were numerous and many expressed the wish that their stay might have been extended so that they could feast their eyes to the full on Southern Utah's wonderland of which they had heard much but had never dreamed of its immensity....

Motion picture cameras stripped for action, filmed the cavalcade as it returned to camp. Small cameras clicked as the dignitaries rode up.

A secret service man, not much at home in the saddle, attempted to dismount in a hurry when his horse stopped to drink in the creek.

Rabelaisian guffaws from the army officers greeted this incident and Admiral Rodman, more accustomed to the main deck of a dreadnaught than the poop deck of a mountain bronco, paused to remark that the army had better not laugh at the navy if anything happened at the ford.[26]

With very little fanfare, after the group returned, they gathered back into the waiting automobiles with their local drivers and headed back to Cedar City.

The trip back to Cedar commenced at shortly after 4 p.m. and was made in scheduled time. At every hamlet and town, the people were again assembled to wave goodbye to the nation's chief and first lady of the land.

The party arrived in Cedar at 8:30 p. m., where a larger crowd of people was gathered to greet the President than had assembled in the morning. The President made a twenty-minute speech from the rear of his private car and among his remarks he said the following:

"I am acquainted with pioneer stock. It has made the United States. By the difference between the arid and cultivated sections, I can read the story of your work. To you men and women who came with your families in covered wagons into this country when the water still flowed through its natural gorges, the nation owes a debt of gratitude. I am the first President of the United States to come and express that gratitude, but I feel sure that when I tell of this trip to my successors, all future Presidents will come to visit this country of wonders."[27]

Following his speech, several others spoke and upon their conclusion the President's Special pulled out of the depot grounds amid the cheering of the multitude and the call from hundreds of "Good Luck Mr. President." The train made its return trip to Salt Lake City where the President was joined the next day by more celebrities including President and Mrs. Heber J. Grant of the Church of Jesus Christ of Latter-day Saints.

President Harding's group then proceeded north through Idaho, Montana, Oregon and Washington, then departing from Tacoma, Washington, traveling by ship to Ketchikan, Alaska. On July 27, the navy transport carrying president and his party rammed the destroyer *Zeilin* in Puget Sound. The transport was not seriously damaged, and the presidential party landed in Seattle the next day on July 28. The president suffered an attack of ptomaine poisoning and in order to recover he cancelled his proposed trip to Yosemite Valley and traveled on to San Francisco in his train, arriving on the morning of July 29, 1923. He was rushed to the Palace Hotel where doctors found that he had pneumonia and was having heart problems. By August 2, 1923, he appeared to be doing better, even sitting up in bed. That evening, while he was listening to his wife read him a flattering article about himself, he collapsed and died, apparently from a heart attack.[28]

Ten days after the President's visit, the following tribute was printed in the *Iron County Record*. It was written by Lafayette Hanchett to the railroad men who completed the branch line between Lund and Cedar City in record time.

Pressure Exerted Building Road

This is the story of eighty-seven days' work—a story of a record in accomplishment in railroad construction. If you were to sign a note at your bank,

Illustration 5.6. The Cedar City Train Depot as constructed in 1923, viewed from the rear showing the railroad tracks. In March 1929, Union Pacific spent $100,000 on improvements to the depot, including more than doubling the shelter area for passengers and buses on the south, paving driveways and sidewalks, additional lighting and construction of a new commissary building.[30] *(Matheson Special Collections)*

payable in ninety days, you would realize how very short a period of time it is to the due date of the note.

On last April 2, the right-of-way men, acting for the Union Pacific railroad, secured possession of the needed ground for the construction of the railway from Lund to Cedar City, and on that date the first scraperful of earth was turned on the railway grade. The contractor strung his men out in sections and as fast as a section was completed on the western end, the track laying crew took possession and the rails and ties were set in place. Crowding upon their heels was the ballast crew, and so the work was pushed toward Cedar City.

At the end of seventy days, Superintendent Williams drove an engine pulling his private car into Cedar City. The graders were still working in the yards, ballast trains were dumping gravel six miles to the west. The track Superintendent Williams put his engine over was but a lot of ties, lying upon a dirt grade without ballast and with no trimming or alignment of rails.

In the middle of the campaign of this track building, word had been received that the President of the United States would visit Zion National park, provided the track was in shape for use by his train on his arrival in the West. From the president of the Union Pacific down through the ranking officers, the engineers, the construction foremen to the humblest graders and track layers went the inspiration that the track must be ready. Men worked like devils. Then came the Tribune's announcement that the trip to Southern Utah had been cancelled. This was followed by a telephone message from the governor's [office] confirming the report. There was a feeling of discouragement and a disposition among the men to let up on the pressure. But their superintendent said to them: "None of our people have squawked yet. You fellows keep going." And they did.

Then came the word that the President would come. This brought about a high-pressure finish to the job. Only forty-eight hours before the arrival of the President's train, the depot site at Cedar City was strewn with the foundations and debris left from the removal of houses that had been carted away or torn down. There were old outbuildings, remnants of old barnyards, weeds, broken-down shrubbery. A crew of bridge carpenters arrived on the scene. They climbed into the old trees, cut out the dead branches, shaped up the live ones, trimmed out the growing sprouts and shrubbery at the base. A dozen teams were brought in from a grading outfit. The old foundations were cleaned up, the yards were smoothed down, barnyards disappeared, ballast trains brought in clean white gravel, covered up the dirt, giving it all a neat surface. An approach, twenty feet wide for automobile travel, was graded and surfaced with gravel and grounds were roped off. Twelve hours before the president's train came, the electricians were erecting the poles and stringing the lights along the railway track in the station yard. Every bit of unsightly new material for use in the depot construction was removed and the foundation work put in a very neat and shipshape appearance.

Superintendent Strong rode into Cedar City on the pilot train ahead of the presidential train and met his yard foreman who was just finishing his second twenty-four-hour continuous shift that week. He was all grime and dirt; a half inch of rough beard covered his face. The superintendent said to him, "You better hurry up and get shaved." "I am too damned tired and I have too much respect for the President of the United States to appear before him in an unshaved condition. I am going to my car. I will see him when he comes back tonight." This man dragged himself up into the car within five hundred feet of where the presidential train stood that day, and he slept so soundly that he never saw the president.

Seventeen days after the first engine pulled into the Cedar City yard; the heaviest train on the Union Pacific system brought in the presidential party in ten Pullmans. It came over a track from Lund to Cedar City that had been fully ballasted, that had been raised twice through this ballast and lined up, trimmed and put in shape in every way equal to the main line standard of the road through the Wyoming Mountains.

At Modena last night, Superintendent Strong admitted that he had been resting a good portion of the day and that he was going north on the evening train from Milford for the sole purpose of enjoying a hot bath. The wind had been blowing a gale for the five days preceding the arrival of the presidential party and he and his force of men had had all kinds of dust literally drilled into them. And he fully deserved at least one hot bath as a fitting close to a tremendous campaign of eighty-seven days.

Ballast was brought from Black Rock. Nine ballast trains were operated. The first ballast unloaded about seventy miles distant from the steam shovel and the last ballast unloaded one hundred and ten miles from the shovel. There were moved one hundred carloads a day. The biggest day's output was 119 cars. This meant 5000 tons of ballast gravel were dug up each twenty-four hours, hauled an average of 100 miles, spread along the track and put in place under the ties, for a total of nearly one half million of tons in eighty-seven days.

In the district traversed by these gravel trains they had the right of way over every other train on the road. Upon this piece of track there had been spent in eighty-seven days, $140,000. Surely the spirit of E. H. Harriman hovered over the scene.[29]

The first ticketed passengers traveled over the new branch line to Cedar City on July 1, 1923. The first person to buy a ticket over the new branch railroad from Lund to Cedar City was William Lunt of Salt Lake City who traveled to Cedar City to attend the funeral services of his sister, Eva Jones.[31] Also on the train were the Walker brothers and their party of ten, owners of the iron ore deposit known as Iron Hill (later Lindsay Hill). As discussed in the previous chapter, they traveled on the first train to inspect their property at Iron Springs that was relatively close to the new branch railroad line. The Iron Hill deposit had been owned by the Walkers for forty-three years. The departure for Southern Utah of a party of ten Salt Lake bankers and capitalists caused quite a stir and triggered rumors of the construction of another large steel works in the state. The rumor was widespread enough that it was even captured by the newspaper.[32]

On September 12, 1923, a momentous celebration took place in Cedar City. The following article in the *Union Pacific Magazine* detailed the event.

Golden Rail Laying, Cedar City, Utah

The celebration at Cedar City, Utah, on September 12, was noteworthy for several reasons. It signalized the completion of the 33-mile extension of the Union Pacific System from Lund to Cedar City. It commemorated the visit of the late President and Mrs. Harding on June 27; the President's train having been the first regular passenger train to use the line. It brought together a notable company of distinguished men, many of whom made addresses.

The event could not be called a "gala day", for while there was no lack of enthusiasm and merry-making, a note of intense seriousness pervaded the speeches and other features of the day, which culminated in the laying of the golden rail. Gratitude that Cedar City and Southern Utah had been permitted to entertain the Nation's Chief Executive, sorrow over his untimely death, a quiet determination to keep his memory green, and to preserve unsullied the spirit and traditions of the pioneers to whom President Harding had paid such a highly deserved tribute, were emphasized quite as much as the joy and gratification which the people felt over the coming of the railroad. The railroad will bring material blessings, it was said; tourists by the thousands; it will stimulate the development of Southern Utah's resources of soil, minerals and scenery; it will make business for the merchant, banker, lawyer, doctor, and tradesman; but it must not be at the expense of the spiritual life and wholesome hospitality of the people.

It is those two things, the speakers pointed, out, which will make Southern Utah, with its Zion National Park, Bryce's Canyon, Cedar Breaks, and North Rim of the Grand Canyon, a different recreational area from any of the other national parks. The others are resorts where the care of the parks and the tourists is the chief concern, while here the development of the people and the building of a stalwart citizenry will be the binding force around which the industrial enterprises and recreational activities will revolve. "Prove all things but hold fast to that which is good" was quoted by Congressman Don B. Colton, as a text for his message, and it might be called the keynote of the morning addresses.

In the afternoon came the principal address of the day by United States Senator Reed Smoot, a memorial address in memory of President Harding. Senator Smoot was a close friend of the late President and was primarily responsible for his visit to Southern Utah in June. He told of the great joy which the visit brought to President and Mrs. Harding, and of their expressed wish to return again. "Harding was human through and through", said the Senator, "and his heart was always attuned to the heart of the American people. He lived for America, he died for America, and so long as time shall last, he will be loved by America."

Vice-President Harry M. Adams of the Union Pacific System followed Senator Smoot. He brought the regrets of President C. R. Gray at his inability to attend the celebration. He spoke of the gratification which the officers of the Union Pacific felt over the successful completion of the project. He paid a tribute to the loyalty of the people of Cedar City and Southern Utah, and of their feeling of neighborliness toward the railroad which, he said, would do its utmost to prove itself a good neighbor in return. Southern Utah, Mr. Adams declared, was on the threshold of a marvelous development, being rich in those things which make for greatness, such as its iron and other minerals, fertile soil, vast ranges for cattle and sheep, unparalleled scenic beauties, but above all, the high quality of its citizens who had inherited from the pioneers a precious legacy of virtue, industry, and integrity. He reminded the people that scenery was unlike anything else, in that it could be sold and resold without diminishing in value or needing to be replaced. "It enriches all," he said, "and impoverishes none." He pledged the aid of the railroad in meeting, in every practicable way, the wishes of the good people of Cedar City and the country tributary to it.

All of the speeches were informative, instructive, and inspiring. Space will permit of only a brief mention of the others.

Stephen Mather, U.S. Director of National Parks: "The attractions of Southern Utah are becoming more widely known all the time. I join with you in thanking the Union Pacific for what it is doing in this vicinity. There was a fifty percent increase in travel to Zion Park this year over last. We shall try to popularize a route via the Santa Fe from Los Angeles, to Grand Canyon, thence across to the North Rim, then taking in Zion, Bryce and Cedar Breaks, connecting at Cedar City with the Union Pacific."

Harry Chandler, proprietor of the Los Angeles Times: "If Cedar City obtains the same results from the building of the Union Pacific that Los Angeles secured, they will be great indeed. The population of Los Angeles has increased 800 percent since the advent of the Union Pacific. Los Angeles has a large leisure class, and the attractions of Southern Utah will make it a Mecca for thousands of that class."

M. de Brabant, Assistant Traffic Manager, Union Pacific System: "We are here, not merely as railroad men, but as citizens of this great western country. Transportation is yours for the asking. It is up to you to develop your natural resources so that markets which are available will be reached with your commodities. The population of Southern California will have to be fed. If the power of the Colorado River can be carried 350 miles to supply the industries of Los Angeles, the same power can be brought to Cedar City, provided you have the vision of the commerce and overseas trade which, through the great harbor of Los Angeles, is right at your very door. The Union Pacific has agricultural and research departments at your disposal. I suggest you appoint a traffic committee to work with our traffic department to study your traffic needs."

President Heber J. Grant of the Mormon Church recalled feelingly the visit of President and Mrs. Harding. He read an article by Lafayette Hanchett of Salt Lake City, describing the departure of the Presidential party from Cedar City, when the multitude spontaneously broke out with "God be with you till we meet again". Mr. Hanchett's article was telegraphed by President Grant to President Harding, on the high seas. The article appears elsewhere in this issue.

Other speakers were Senators Hirschi and Seegmiller, Matthew Hale of Washington, Mayor C. C. Neslen of Salt Lake City, Charles P. Bayer, of the Los Angeles Chamber of Commerce, Mayor Parley Dalley, of Cedar City, W. H. Comstock, General Manager of the Los Angeles and Salt Lake unit of the Union Pacific System, Hon. James W. Good of Chicago, Randall L. Jones who acted as chairman at the morning meeting, and H. W. Lunt, who presided at the afternoon session.

Owing to a heavy shower during Vice-President Adams' address, the crowd was forced to disperse, and on that account, the address of Governor Charles R. Mabey could not be given.

Laying of the Rail

The golden rail was fastened in place with four iron spikes made at Old Iron Town in Iron County about sixty years ago. The spikes were driven by Governor Charles R. Mabey, D. S. Spencer, R. H. Rutledge and David Bulloch, representing, respectively, the State of Utah, the Union Pacific System, the Forest Service, and Iron County. The rail was conveyed to the point of insertion by a fairy queen, drawn in a chariot.[33]

The "fairy queen" was "little Miss Mary Farnsworth," who presented the memorial rail, carried on a miniature float drawn by four small boys dressed in white.[34]

The following extract reprints the above-mentioned tribute letter, written by Mr. Hanchett to Heber J. Grant, President of the Church of Jesus Christ of Latter-day Saints. It is a tribute to the sincerity, dedication and patriotism of the people of Cedar City and Southern Utah.

Two Prayers

For five days prior to the visit of the Presidential party to Zion National Park, it seemed as if the elements had conspired with the Evil One to make the visit impossible. The Wind Gods drove their chariots through the air with forty-mile gales; the dirt and dust rose in vast clouds.

The good "Mormon" people of Iron and Washington counties raised their voices in prayer, asking that the President of the United States be permitted to see the world wonders within their borders in both comfort and safety.

When the presidential train was leaving Salt Lake City, the wind was still raging across the southern desert; but it suddenly stilled—the morning dawned, bright, beautiful and quiet. The President came, journeyed safely to the great canyon, and returned to his train. As he climbed the steps of his private car, a silent prayer of thanks went up from the gathered throng -- the prayer of the day before had been answered.

The President had ended his speech to the group hovering about the train— he entered his car; the door closed and the curtains were tightly drawn, and then the great day seemed over, when the silence was broken by a women's voice in song—first one or two, then ten, then twenty, then a hundred or more joined. There was no officious conductor; no paid chorus; no orchestra accompaniments; just these honest country people singing. It grew upon me that this was not a song; it was a prayer welling up from the hearts of these good women, when the words "God be with you till we meet again" came timidly, sweetly and tremulously from a thousand throats.

I have heard the great music of Wagner rendered by the artists of Munich and have been enraptured by the masters of song in Grand Opera at Paris, and have thrilled when the voice of Caruso, lifted in majestic grandeur above a singing congregation of twenty thousand, in Madison Square Garden, as he sang "America." But never have I been so deeply touched as I was by the voices of those good people that night as they sang "God be with you till we meet again," for it seemed as though He who sets the Great Stage of Life, had set this scene, and had turned streams of moonlight down through the foliage of the great old trees, and here and there, had so shot a moonbeam, that it touched a bowed and grizzled old head, from which a quavering cracked voice joined devoutly in the refrain.

It was not a song, it was a prayer.

The article was sent by Mr. Hanchett to President Heber J. Grant with the request: "Do me the favor to read this." President Grant was so impressed with the beauty of Mr. Hanchett's tribute that he wired it in full to President Harding, then at Tacoma on his way to Alaska.[35]

Iron Springs Spur Completed and First Iron Ore Shipped

Even before the branch railroad to Cedar City was completed, Columbia Steel began work on the railroad spur running from the branch line going through Iron Springs Gap to the new mine under construction, just west of the line.

> Columbia Steel engineers and surveyors are now in this locality and surveying railroad spurs, loading sites, and camp sites, besides lining up on the boundaries of the property owned by the company.[36]

The spur was completed, and the first carload of ore was shipped on Monday, October 8, 1923 from the Columbia Steel Company's mines to Los Angeles where tests were made to ascertain the iron content of the ore. Soon thereafter, ore was shipped to the Ironton Plant and stockpiled to be ready for the smelter's completion and operation.[37]

After forty-three long years since the railroad had been completed to Milford and twenty-four years since it had been completed to Lund, the railroad from Lund to Cedar City was constructed from start to finish in just under three months. An earlier quoted internal letter by the Union Pacific Railroad listed a number of reasons for building the new railroad branch, but there was one that really made the difference:

The Right Combination

Illustration 5.7. The Iron Springs sheep shearing corral is shown with the first train to Iron Springs in the background. This occurred on May 28, 1923 and assuming the date was correct, it was about a month before the President's train arrived. The corral was built about 1895 and had an average annual clip of about forty thousand head of sheep. Prior to the railroad, all the wool had to be carted across the valley to Lund. The corral was located only a mile or so from the Pioche Pit. Note the wool sacks, the horse drawn wagon and an early model farm tractor under the shed. (Photo by R. D. Adams, Matheson Special Collections)

Cedar City is already a thriving town of 2,500 population, and in its immediate vicinity there are large deposits of iron ore, development of which is assured by the operation of blast furnaces at Springville, Utah, by the Columbia Steel Corporation, who will erect furnaces at that point for the transformation of the iron ore into pigs.[38]

El Escalante Hotel

In 1919 the United States Congress established Zion Canyon and Grand Canyon as a National Parks.[40] Bryce Canyon became a National Monument in 1923 and a National Park in 1928 and Cedar Breaks was made a National Monument in 1933. As these scenic destinations became popular, the number of tourists visiting Southern Utah increased dramatically. In August 1919, the "progressive citizens" of Cedar City decided that they would construct a hotel to accommodate the increasing numbers of visitors and tourists coming to town by automobile.[41] In November, Randall Jones, a local architect, had drawn up preliminary plans for the hotel.[42] By January 1920, $50,000 worth of stock had been raised and by February, excavation had started on the hotel.[43]

However, despite the commitment and enthusiasm of members of the community, due to problems including financing difficulties, construction on the project lagged and the project was still not complete by 1923 when the President visited.[44] In early 1923, in conjunction with building facilities at Zion, Bryce, Grand Canyon and Cedar Breaks, Union Pacific decided to purchase and complete the partially erected Cedar City hotel.[45]

Iron Mining & Manufacturing

Illustration 5.8. *Above appears the El Escalante Hotel, built across the street from the train depot on the Southwest corner of 200 North and Main Street in Cedar City. It cost $265,000, began operation in 1924 and was demolished in 1970. It was owned and operated by the Utah Parks Company, a subsidiary of the Union Pacific Railroad, until it was purchased in 1958 for $110,000, by Cedar City.[39] (Matheson Special Collections)*

On March 29, 1924, a large banquet, with about 300 celebrities and guests attending from all over the state, was held at the 100-room hotel to celebrate its completion.[46] The first person to register at the hotel was James Younger of Iron Springs, Utah, who requested the Union Pacific to grant him the privilege of registering at the hotel.[47]

The Mine

The Pinto-Iron Springs Mining District contained literally dozens of potential mining sites, many of which were at or near the surface. Several factors came into play in choosing the location for the first commercial iron mine to be excavated in Iron County. (1) The deposit needed to be relatively near to the new branch railroad since there was neither time nor money to spend on building a lengthy railroad spur from the branch line to access the mine. (2) The deposit needed to be on or very near the surface so that minimal overburden removal was required. (3) The deposit needed to have iron ore of adequate quality and quantity to meet the specifications of the new Ironton smelter being constructed. (4) The ore deposit needed to be either owned by Columbia Steel Corporation or be easily purchased or leased by them.

The only location that met these requirements was the Iron Springs mining area since the branch rail line ran right through the Iron Springs Gap on its way to Cedar City. There were several ore bodies in that area that outcropped on the surface that were within a mile or so of the railroad. The Great Western and Smith ore bodies were located to the northeast and the Pioche, Vermillion, Eclipse, Twitchell, Little Mormon and Lindsay Hill ore bodies were located to the southwest. The Great Western claim was one of the sources of ore for the pioneer smelters in Cedar City.

Ultimately two ore bodies at the north end of Granite Mountain were selected that were within about a mile of the rail line and were virtually connected to each other. They were the Pioche and Vermillion deposits, the Pioche being the largest of the two. In

Illustration 5.9. The Iron Springs accommodations. Bud Morgan, the lab chemist, is pictured in the left photo. The right photo shows the Iron Springs dormitory. Left to right the figures in the right photo are, Sam Heyborne, Claude Edwards and Ken Urkhart. (Photos courtesy of Hal Christensen).

addition to the deposits being close to the railroad, their elevation was slightly above that of the branch line, whereby the spur could be straightforwardly constructed to access the mine and the rail cars could almost coast to the main line. The deposits were owned by Columbia Steel. The quality and certainly the quantity of the ore did not appear to be a problem.

These two ore bodies essentially ran in an east-west direction and dipped to the north at about 40 degrees. Both were replacement deposits in the Homestake Limestone and could be traced on the surface for almost 2,000 feet. It is estimated that between the two deposits there was approximately eight million tons of iron ore available. This was more than enough to supply the Ironton plant, as it was first constructed, for thirty to forty years, assuming that most of the ore could be extracted. The ore bodies were said to contain "what would seem to be, an unlimited lode of approximately sixty percent ore."[48]

By March 1923, work had begun removing the light overburden above the ore at the new mine location at Iron Springs.[49] The Columbia Steel Company prepared only a small portion of its holdings at first, a section reaching from the tunnel portal a half mile to the southeast and a mile and a half to the west.[50]

Before the mine could be developed in earnest, a town site had to be developed. Actually, the Younger town site was already in existence but Columbia needed to construct a larger town in which its employees could live while working at the new mine. The Iron Springs town site had a water system and water was supplied from a well that was drilled and operated by Columbia. The water was pumped a distance of about three quarters of a mile into tanks above the town site and piped to the various workings of the company and to the lots at the town site. The Dixie Power Company extended their power lines to the Columbia Steel property for the use of the company in the mining

Illustration 5.10. The Iron Springs ore processing plant on July 28, 1924, where the ore hauled out of the mine was crushed, screened and separated into various grades to meet the specifications of the smelter. The tracks on the elevated trestle to the left carried the mine cars from the mine tunnel into the facility. Immediately to the left and behind the plant can be seen part of the waste pile that was dumped when the tunnel was first driven through rock. The portal or adit cannot be seen in the photo but was located directly behind the facility. A 500-ton capacity ore bin was installed over the rail spur and used in loading the larger rail cars that carried the ore to the smelter. It appears that the bin was a short distance to the north of this facility. The processing plant and tipple at Iron Springs was built with native lumber furnished by the local saw mills. (Photo by E. F. Burchard, courtesy of U.S. Geological Survey)

operations and the lines were tapped for lighting purposes for those who would be living at the townsite.[51]

Within close range, was the railroad spur from Iron Springs, ending with a wye, or a Y-shaped section of railway track, near the yards, depot, section houses, pump houses, scales and stock and shearing corral. Immediately adjoining the Columbia Steel property and between the mines and the depot was the ranch of Mr. J. F. Younger and the town site by that name. Mr. Younger had secured the deeds for that property twenty-two years prior, and the mine was located on part of his former property.[52]

The Younger Townsite boasted a voting precinct, a well-stocked grocery store, a pool hall, a post office and even a jail. Another town site by the name of Aberdeen was laid out just east of Iron Springs.[53]

A large boarding house was built to accommodate up to seventy-five employees of the company and a number of modern homes were built for the officers within easy access to the offices and shops. A number of small bungalows were erected to be occupied by the married men and their families. Prior to the erection of the boarding house, the workmen were domiciled in tents.

Sleeping quarters for the men and dining rooms for all were on the main avenue and were supplied with steam heat and electric lights. "Ample and in all features, up to date bath houses" were convenient to the works.[54]

The Right Combination

Illustration 5.11. Mine cars at the Iron Springs ore processing plant. Ore was brought from under the glory holes via the underground tunnel system on 5-ton railroad cars. The cars were pulled with an electric engine using power supplied by the overhead line, which can be seen above the mine cars. The ore was dumped, crushed and screened before it was loaded into a holding bin and then into full-sized rail cars that hauled it to the Ironton Plant. The processing facility and crusher are to the right of the photo. (Photo courtesy of Hal Christensen)

Near the processing facility were warehouses, offices, assayers, sample crusher and laboratory, two large compressor buildings and other service buildings. The company also installed its own electric transformers costing several thousands of dollars. Electricity was used to power drills, locomotives, compressors, ventilating fans, lights, etc.[55]

Illustration 5.12. Iron Springs Glory Hole No.9. (left) The mine plan was to scrape the shot ore into windrows so that it could be delivered to one of the glory holes. A scraper can be seen attached to a team in the rear, a regular farm plow was used with the team in front. (right) Hal Christensen is standing on the left and an unidentified surveyor on the right, around 1925 (Photos courtesy of Hal Christensen)

> Since the Columbia Steel company uses compressed air, made by means of electricity, for running its drills and for ventilating the shafts and tunnels, it was necessary for the company to install its own electric transformers costing several thousands of dollars. Besides the electric compressors, the company has gasoline compressors so that nothing need be held up when the power is off.[56]

At first, the crusher did not break the ore adequately; even after crushing, much of the ore came out in large blocks. This was a problem for the workers at the processing plant with the chutes plugging, etc., and also unloading at the smelter in Ironton. A new crusher and grizzly were installed in March 1924.[57]

A 500-ton capacity ore bin costing $5000, was installed above the spur track for use in loading the full-sized train cars which were pulled onto the branch line, then west to Lund and north on the main line to Ironton.[58]

The "mine" railroad ran from the primary tunnel and mine portal to the processing facility. It was constructed with lighter weight, forty-pound rails and was set up to use a narrow-gauge railroad to accommodate the smaller cars and locomotives that would travel into the mine itself. The mine ore cars had a capacity of five tons each and were built sturdy enough to withstand the uncrushed, raw ore being loaded or dropped into them. There were a sufficient number of mine cars to haul a maximum of one thousand tons daily. The locomotives ran on 440-volt, direct current electricity, and required overhead lines to carry the power and connect with the locomotives.[59]

Provisions were made at the processing facility for any waste material that was hauled out of the mine to be discarded. This was especially important during the development

The Right Combination

Illustration 5.13. The junction at the end of the main tunnel section in January 1924, where it divided into the east and west drifts. The 8 × 8-inch timbers and the overhead electric lines for the train as well as other electric lines are clearly visible. (Photo used by permission, Utah State Historical Society)

phase at first, when the primary access tunnel was being driven in solid limestone and no ore was being produced.

The primary access tunnel, or *adit*, was called "Tunnel No. 1." It extended through the portal, 750 feet into the side hill, more or less on the level, mostly in the Homestake Limestone Formation, in which the ore had been deposited millions of years before. The tunnel took over two months to excavate using men working a double shift schedule. The entire tunnel was built with eight-by-eight-foot dimensions inside the timbering.[60]

> The tunnel is studded with bents [uprights] of 8x8 inch timbers and caps set about eight feet apart and with its well-trimmed sides and clean roadway and its banks of incandescent lights resembles the corridors of Hotel Utah or the stately avenues of the Leviathan.[61]

The *SS Leviathan* was one of the largest, fastest and most prestigious luxury ocean liners of the 1920s, a comparison which suggests how highly the tunnel was regarded.

The mine railroad line was laid on the floor of the tunnel to carry the pit cars in and out of the mine. Once in the body of ore, the main access tunnel branched into two lateral tunnels or "drifts," the West Drift and the East Drift. By March 1924, the East Drift extended about 900 feet to the face with four shafts that went from the surface down to the elevation of the drift. The West Drift was also about 900 feet long but had only three shafts at that time.

Illustration 5.14. Holes were drilled into the ore with jackhammers and black powder or dynamite was used as the explosive. A blast is pictured above. The edge of a glory hole is seen on the left of the photo. (Photo courtesy of Hal Christensen)

On the surface, these shafts or *raises* were enlarged to take on the appearance of the bells of large funnels, with the lower end of the funnels ending in the drift below. These funnels were called *glory holes*. Ore slid, dropped or rolled through these openings, down the chutes to the steel mine cars waiting below, then was hauled out of the mine and dumped at the processing plant.[62] According to the numbering system used at the time, there were at least fourteen shafts in existence or being constructed by April 1924.[63]

Additional shafts were likely constructed during the life of the mine. The maps used to aid in the design of the Eclipse Pit by Utah Construction and Mining Company in the early 1970s showed that the West Drift extended very near, if not into, the Eclipse ore body in 1925. The Eclipse ore body was located just west of the Vermillion deposit. The aerial photo taken in 1950, shown later in this chapter, clearly shows the excavations.

The Right Combination

Illustration 5.15. Working at Glory Hole No. 8, with horses pulling fresno scrapers, moving ore into the glory hole, and then into a chute and railroad cars. A powder tamper is visible in the background. (Photo courtesy of Hal Christensen)

None of the excavations ever reached the bottom of the ore deposits. In addition to the shafts that were dug to become glory holes, there were shafts dug for access and ventilation. Those shafts were timbered and had ladders for the men to climb in and out of the workings if necessary.

All of the ore and waste material, including that on the surface and that in the tunnel, drifts and shafts, had to be drilled and blasted. Fourteen hydroelectric drills or water jacks were used against the face and upward raises and twenty borings were made in the solid ore. About two hundred sticks of 40-percent dynamite, set off by cap and fuse, were used with each shot, which usually netted about forty tons.[64] Black powder was also used at the mine as an explosive. In addition to the hydroelectric drills, jackhammers, driven by compressed air, were used to drill holes on the surface. The surface holes were loaded and blasted in similar fashion to those underground but used different drill patterns and more holes drilled per shot since working space was not so limited. Separate magazines were used to store caps, powder and dynamite. These magazines were built in solid rock and conveniently located in safe positions remote from the town and mine buildings.[65]

In addition to the drills employed for blasting, an exploration drill was also used at the mine to obtain information about the ore body in advance of actual mining. The drill appears to have quite impressed the newspaper reporter.

> In the west drift, twelve hundred feet from the pit mouth is located a new Turbo 34 model drill which is worth a trip to any mine. This machine has a boring reach of two hundred and fifty feet. Its bits and shafts may be sent any direction to test deposits, strata and formations which enables the engineer to plan attack several days before advance of actual mining. One gallon of water each minute of motion is consumed by this drill and sections of the solid mass can be read every six feet. This is the most wonderful and latest invention in any kind of mine work. Its patent date is only six months past and its use not only secures safety to the men, but it pays for itself over and over again at every bore. During the half shift ending at noon the day of our visit, the drill had gone through 32 feet of ore to the top outcrop at an angle of forty-five degrees.[66]

On the surface, after the ore was broken up by the drilling and blasting operation, it was graded or carried along the surface and pushed into win-rows into the glory holes by horse-drawn scrapers called *fresnos*. In illustrations 5.12 and 5.15 it appears that regular farm plows were used at times to loosen and move the material. The ore slid down the raises or chutes into the waiting rail cars below.[67]

It has been suggested that a heavy grid or screen was installed over the top of each glory hole, over which the horse-drawn scrapers would cross and empty their loads.[68] Although this practice would have reduced the possibility of men, horses and equipment falling into the glory hole and down the shaft, no such grids were seen in any of the photos or mentioned in the papers. The feasibility of such grids is also suspect. The grid openings would have to have been appreciably smaller than the horses' hooves, thus preventing much of the ore from passing through. In addition, from the pictures taken at the time, a number of the glory holes appear to have been in excess of a hundred feet across and the fabricating of such a structure with that fine of grid and that length of span to support the heavy teams of horses would have been highly impractical.

It appears that at the bottom of at least some of the glory holes were gates that stopped the ore from flowing freely into the drift and covering up the rail cars. The gates would have been opened and closed manually to load the cars with ore as they were positioned, one by one, under the chute. In one incidence, a man was killed when he fell down a chute and his body was recovered from below. A gate at the bottom of the chute was mentioned.

> Immediately the alarm whistle was sounded and the whole camp was out ready to do all in their power to get the unfortunate man out of the chute. The tram cars were put to their fullest capacity in getting out the ore from the gate at the bottom of the

chute as there was no way whatever to get him out from the top. Some twenty cars of ore were taken out before the body was recovered.[69]

Considering this arrangement, it is likely that the chute portion of the glory holes were regularly plugged with ore, resulting in long tedious, dangerous hours of manual labor trying to get them cleared, especially at night. One has to wonder how often men, animals or equipment, having to work so close to the funnel-like openings, slid either partially or all the way in, resulting in serious injury. No less problematic would have been the situation down below when a gate wouldn't close, resulting in a car getting buried. Trying to loosen ore that had hung up above the gate by reaching through the gate opening or using a stick of dynamite would have been equally hazardous. By February, 1924, a mechanical shovel loader was bought to help with the cleanup.[70]

In addition to having to maintain their many mechanical devices, the mine had to have corrals, feed yards, sheds, hay stacks, watering troughs, etc. to accommodate multiple teams of horses. It would have also required a number of men who were well trained in using and caring for livestock.

A newspaper article published on April 3, 1925 in the *Iron County Record* captured the progress of the mine at that time.

> In making a tour over the iron fields of this county one is led to marvel at the immense amount of work that has been accomplished since the advent of the railroad in 1923. Since that date the Columbia Steel Corporation has opened up and has operated continuously the ore body near the Iron Springs. The entry tunnel of 800 feet in length is in iron ore all the way and taps a hill just back of which lies the large body of ore that has been stripped. Glory holes have been made and the work of shooting the ore from these is going on every day, the total tonnage being shipped to Ironton, Utah, reaching to near 700 tons daily.[71]

In late 1925, the Iron King, a precious-metal mine in Eureka, Utah, opened and began shipping a small amount of iron ore, about eight cars a week, to the Ironton Plant. It is uncertain why Columbia Steel would do this, possibly to supplement the production from Iron Springs, or maybe it was less expensive since it was a byproduct of the mine.[72]

Premature Closure

On June 29, 1926, after only three years of mining, the operation at Iron Springs was shut down and abandoned.[73] The total ore mined and shipped for the three years the operation ran was just over 600,000 tons. The grand plan for Iron Springs and nearby townsites to become large population centers with thousands of residences, failed to come to fruition. However, given the mining technology available at the time, it was a huge accomplishment to have been able to supply that much ore using those mining methods.

	Tons Mined
1923	63,527
1924	159,518
1925	260,231
1926	140,251
Total	623,527[74]

Iron Mining & Manufacturing

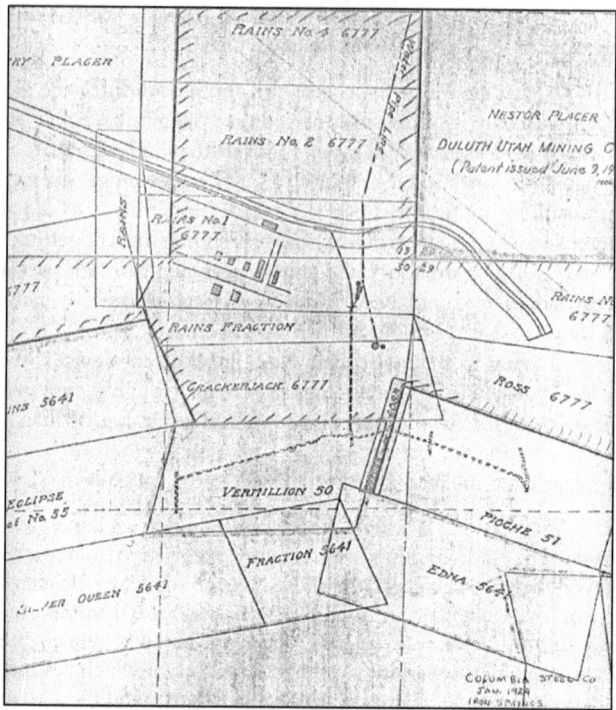

Illustration 5.16. Iron Springs mine workings and structures as they existed in January 1924. The railroad spur can be seen in the upper part of the map, drawn in parallel solid lines, running off to the left. The main tunnel can be seen as a dashed line running north to south. The East Drift and the West Drift can be seen as double dashed lines running into the Pioche and Vermillion claims. Later, the West drift appears to have been extended further west, almost to the Eclipse claim. Some of the other structures were also plotted on the map. The claim numbering suggests that the Vermillion, Pioche and Eclipse claims (Nos. 50, 51 and 55) were early claims and that the surrounding claims, with much higher numbers, were staked quite a bit later on ground that probably did not have any ore but which offered hope of finding it. (From York Jones)

Although the mining methods seem crude by modern day standards, it must be remembered that at the time, there were no large off-road vehicles. Cars and small trucks were just starting to be commonplace. More importantly, excavators that could actually "lift and load" material were almost unknown. The internal combustion engine was just coming into its own, most of the heavy-duty applications like trains, ships and heavy industry, continued to use steam engines for power for quite some time.

The glory hole system of mining was capable of producing upwards of 1,000 tons of ore per day and was a substantial accomplishment for the time. However, it was comparatively slow, labor intensive, expensive and dangerous. It was also subject to interruptions due to problems in the glory holes and in the tunnel and drifts below. Digging tunnels and laying track into hard, abrasive, dense ore was not an easy proposition, neither was driving raises or sinking shafts by hand. The horse-drawn implements on the surface were not much better; the ore was sharp and abrasive and substantial care and maintenance of the equipment and the horses' hooves and legs was required. Drilling and blasting was dangerous and not very effective. Safety was also an issue; several men were killed or seriously injured in the operation's short lifetime.

In addition, it has been suggested that the chemistry of the ore from the Pioche and Vermillion deposits was not exactly right for the Ironton blast furnace.[75] Assuming that this statement is true, without better documentation it is unclear whether the ore itself was inherently problematic, or that the mining method did not lend itself well to delivering a product suitably free of dilution and contamination.

The following epitaph comes from the United States Steel Corporation Handbook-1959.

> The method of mining was a modification of the glory hole system. A tunnel was driven under the ore body and a series of raises were then driven to the surface. Ore fragmentation was achieved by jack-hammers, and then transported by team and scrapers to the raises where it passed down the raises into the ore cars, to be hauled to the crusher. This system was slow, very expensive because of high labor costs, and in iron ore, did not prove to be practical.[76]

General Interest

One Man Killed, One Injured [1923]

Antone Olson was crushed to death and Leland Sullivan badly injured when a large amount of earth and rock caved Sunday morning at 3 o'clock in tunnel No. 1 at the Columbia Steel camp near Iron Springs. Screams for help awakened other company employees and fifty men went to the rescue of Olson and Sullivan. Olson was completely covered by the earth and rock while Sullivan was only partially covered and was able to get out to the mouth of the tunnel before collapsing.

The debris was hastily removed from Olson and it was found that he had been crushed almost to a pulp. Nearly every bone in his body was broken and it was evident that his death was instantaneous. The body was brought to this city and was prepared for burial at the Cedar Lumber Co. undertaking parlors. Monday it was shipped to Leeds, Utah, the home of the dead man, where interment was had that afternoon. Sullivan was brought to the County Hospital where he is now doing as well as could be expected and has every chance of complete recovery from the injuries he received at the cave-in.

The men were engaged in mucking at the time of the cave-in. Two other men, Glen Olson and Evan Sullivan, were working with them but one had gone to the mouth of the tunnel with a car of rock and the other was a short distance from the scene of the accident. The workmen in the tunnel had been on shift for a couple of hours and were removing the muck left by the preceding shift. The tunnel is heavily timbered to within a few feet of the cave-in.

So far as can be learned, no warning of the cave-in was given, the men having no time to step out of reach of falling rock. The slip of rock and earth came like a bolt of lightning from the sky and the men had no chance to escape.[77]

Iron Mining & Manufacturing

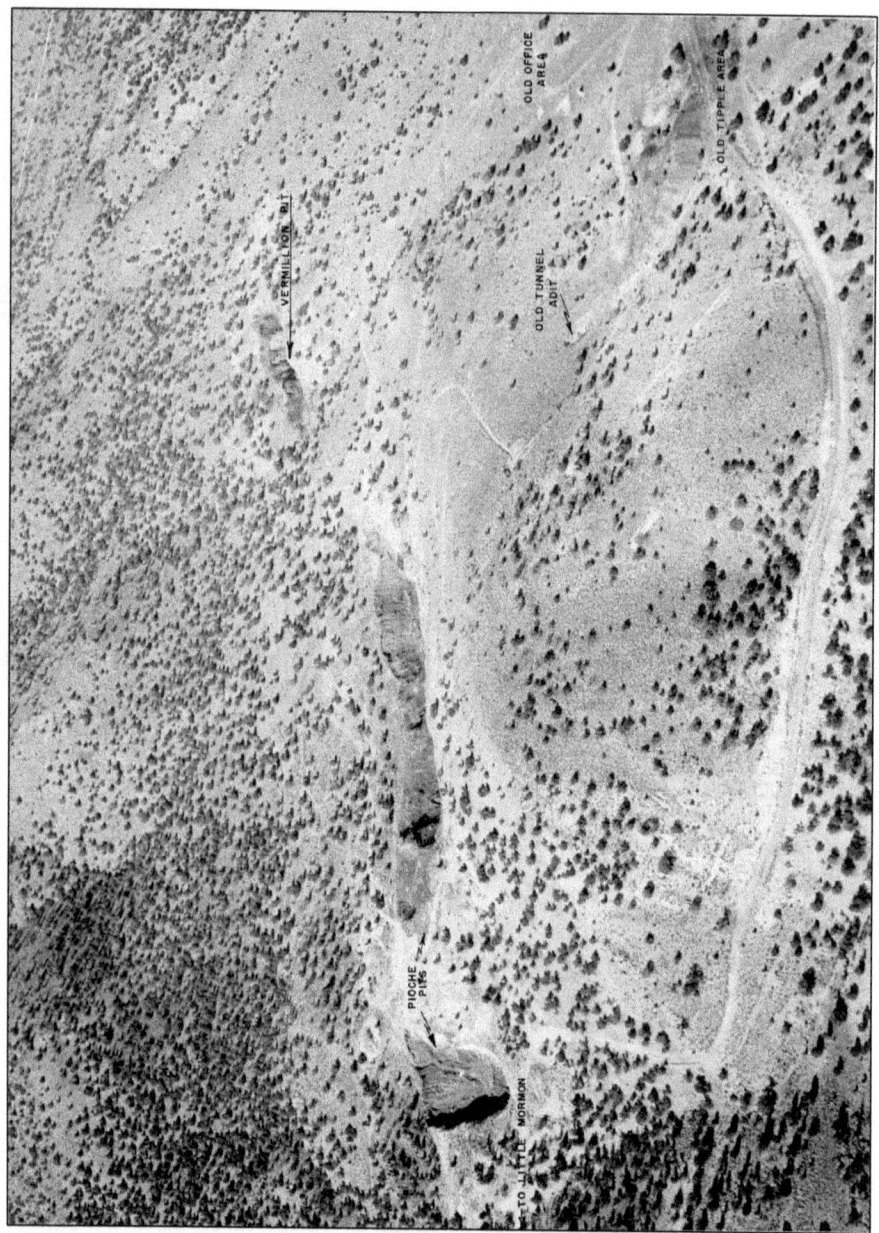

Illustration 5.17. An aerial photo taken in July 1950 shows the old expanded glory hole excavations in the Pioche and Vermillion deposits. It also shows the adit into the underground portion of the mine and the waste pile that was excavated from the mine and dumped next to the tipple when the main underground tunnel was first driven. (Photo from York Jones)

Man Injured [1924]

Mr. Otto Tullis, of Enterprise, who had such a narrow escape last week in the mine has been at home for several days recruiting [sic] up after his experience. It seems that Mr. Tullis was running the new Shoveloder the company recently installed to load the ore from the floor of the tunnel into the tram cars, when in some manner unknown he was caught between the scoop of the machine and the wall of the drift. He had no bones broken, but his right leg was very bruised and he will be lame for some time to come. He will not return to camp till he is able to go to work again, and in the meantime Ray Hoffman has taken his place till his return.[78]

Miner Killed at Iron Springs [1924]

Once more the big mining operation of the country has claimed a victim, this time it being Con McCarty, a miner from the Silver King mine of Park City, who had been here but a few days. Monday he was working on night shift at the No. 14 "Glory Hole" and had gone down in the hole a distance to put in some pop shots to loosen some of the ore which had lodged. He and a companion were standing side by side and had just prepared a small shot or two ready to touch off when the boulders of ore on which the men were standing suddenly and without any warning gave way beneath their feet and McCarty made a desperate effort to grab some hold of the sides. He succeeded for a few seconds in holding on but the nature of the side of the hole was such that he had to let go when more dirt began to give way in his hand, and he went down some seventy feet and the balance of the loose ore around and above him followed him into the hole of blackness. His companion succeeded in scrambling out and giving a shout, ran for help as fast as possible. Wallace Flannigan, of Cedar City, was standing at the edge of the hole and just turned away and hearing the shout of the man coming out, he saw just the hands of McCarty as he went down and could do nothing to save the same. Immediately the alarm whistle was sounded and the whole camp were out ready to do all in their power to get the unfortunate man out of the chute. The tram cars were put to their fullest capacity in getting out the ore from the gate at the bottom of the chute as there was no way whatever to get him out from the top. Some twenty cars of ore were taken out before the body was recovered.

In a very few minutes the camp responded to a man and very heroic work was done in a very few minutes time in getting the mass of that heavy ore out of the chute and the body came down the gate way.

McCarty was a man of 36, single, and was known as a good miner. He knew his business thoroughly and did his work well, what time he has been in the employ of the Columbia Steel Corp. at their camp. Word of the accident was phoned in to Cedar as soon as it was known and Dr. Bergstrom answered immediately and was on-hand when the body was brought out of the mine. After an examination it was found the man had his skull crushed in near the crown of his head, and also one hip broken.

There is no blame whatsoever to be attached to the company. It was unforeseen. The workmen speak in the highest of terms of the manly and efficient way Superintendent Cook and Foreman Spencer conducted themselves in handling the men in the exciting time of the rescue. Their cool judgment and wisdom were such notable things that the men were, and are now, unanimous in their praises for these two men. This is the second tragic event of this kind to be met with in this camp and as a consequence it casts a gloom over the boys when called on to face such things among their comrades.[79]

County Hospital News [1925]

Wm. Pucill had a narrow escape from death Wednesday at Iron Springs being buried in a slide of ore. As a result, he will be in the hospital for some time. His helper, Ernest Barlocker of Enterprise, was partially buried, escaping with painful lacerations about the head.[80]

Hospital Notes [1926]

Oliver Christine of Iron Springs, was brought in to the hospital from the mines the first part of the week suffering from a broken pelvic bone. Since receiving surgical attention, he is recuperating rapidly.[81]

Buried at Iron Springs [1926]

Funeral services over the remains of James Younger, who recently passed from this life were held at the Presbyterian chapel, Tuesday afternoon, Rev. Geiser officiating. After the services the body was taken to Iron Springs and on the ground on which stands the home he occupied while living. Quite a number of friends and acquaintances of the deceased attended the services and accompanied the body to its last resting place. Word was expected from relatives in Oregon as a to the disposition of the body, but as none came, it was decided by county authorities to bury it at Iron Springs, in conformity with requests frequently made by the deceased long before his demise.[82]

Mr. Younger located some iron ore at Iron Springs in 1902, and twenty years later sold it to Columbia Steel Corporation. Tunnel No. 1 was opened on one of the Younger claims in April, 1923, and as a strange coincidence of fate, Tunnel No. 1 was closed indefinitely on the very day of Mr. Younger's death. Ore from other workings will be depended upon to supply the Provo furnaces.

On the purchase of the right-of-way for the Cedar City branch, Mr. Younger presented deed No. 1 to the U.P. System, allowing easement through part of his property. This deed was called "Jim Younger's Valentine," and was framed and occupied a place in the lobby of the Cedar's Hotel until needed for filing. Later Mr. Younger was the first guest to register at the El Escalante Hotel and as Guest No. 1 he was assigned to room No. 1.[83]

Iron Springs Has Fire [1927]

On the 14th day of this month, about midnight, the Iron Springs pool hall and grocery store combined caught fire and was burned to the ground. There being but little water it was impossible to subdue the flames and as a consequence, the building and contents were entirely consumed. At the rear of the hall were living rooms and the household effects, with the pool tables and stock of groceries, together with the frame building, constituted a loss of in the neighborhood of $2,000.00.[84]

CHAPTER SIX

Desert Mound and the Utah Iron Ore Corporation 1924–1936

THE DESERT MOUND mining area is situated approximately three and a half miles southwest of Iron Springs and has one of the larger groups of iron ore deposits in the Pinto-Iron Springs Mining District. Most prominent of these was an outcrop of iron ore located on a hill above the surface of the surrounding desert, hence the name. Some of the ore bodies at Desert Mound were on or near the surface, conducive to open pit mining methods. Other deposits were deeper and were not discovered until later. Early on, Desert Mound's most active owner was the Milner Corporation of Salt Lake City. In the late 1800s, Colonel Stanley B. Milner of Salt Lake City patented many claims in the district. After he died in 1906, his sons, Clarence E. Milner, Archibald C. Milner and Jay S. Milner, carried on his legacy. The Milners were determined to see their iron ore deposits mined. Shortly after the branch railroad was completed between Lund and Cedar City, the Milners paid for a spur to be built to the Desert Mound area and secured contracts with two smelting companies for the sale of their ore. The Milner Corporation created a wholly owned subsidiary to operate the mine, named the Utah Iron Ore Corporation. Shipments of ore were made from Desert Mound as early as August 1924.

The Smelters

In January 1924, the Milner Corporation announced that it had obtained contracts with two smelters in Salt Lake City: one with the United States Smelting & Refining Company and the other with the International Smelting Company. The contracts called for a minimum of 72,000 tons of iron ore to be delivered annually. Unlike the Ironton smelter which manufactured pig iron from raw iron ore and used limestone as a fluxing agent, these smelters used iron ore for fluxing purposes to refine other ores such as gold, silver, copper, lead or zinc.[1]

In July 1926, when Columbia Steel's mining operation shut down at Iron Springs, the Utah Iron Ore Corporation at Desert Mound signed a contract with Columbia Steel and became the sole supplier of iron ore to the Ironton Plant.[2]

In 1927, Columbia Steel Corporation needed additional coke ovens at Ironton to meet both the increased demand for pig iron and the continued use of coke by other Utah smelters to reduce lead, silver and copper ores. A 1927 news article published in the *Salt Lake Telegram*, discussed the need for additional coke ovens and included a number of facts about the Ironton complex. It also mentioned the Pacific States Cast Iron Pipe foundry built in 1926.

Iron Mining & Manufacturing

Columbia Steel Operates Large Plant in Utah—Coke Ovens, Blast Furnaces Are Running at Full Capacity

Utah has for many years been recognized as probably the only state west of the Missouri river with resources from which a great steel industry might be developed. It remained for the great war and subsequent shortage of steel scrap, upon which in the past, steel mills of the west coast have been dependent, to bring to fruition these dormant possibilities.

Although the production of pig iron in Utah had a very modest beginning, the state is so strategically located for economical distribution of iron products that it can look forward with confidence to a tremendous development in this new western industry.

During the past four years, the Columbia Steel Corporation has had in successful operation at Ironton, Utah, a blast furnace and thirty-three byproduct coke ovens. This is the only plant west of the Rocky Mountains producing pig iron. The plant site of about 800 acres is situated between Provo and Springville on the state highway. Buildings and yards now utilize about 200 acres, the rest being held in reserve. The coke ovens and blast furnace are operating at full capacity and increased use of Columbia coke has made it necessary to augment the present battery of three-thirty byproduct coke ovens by the building of an additional unit which will comprise twenty-three byproduct coke ovens. This also calls for additions to the byproduct recovery plant to take care of the increased production of the byproducts of coal. These additional units will be operating before the end of January, 1928.

Many Iron Mines

Iron mines of this company are located in Iron County, Utah, on the Union Pacific railroad, and coal mines in Carbon County, Utah, on the Denver & Rio Grande railroad. These holdings approximate 20,000,000 tons of hematite iron ore, assaying 57 to 58 percent iron content and 80,000,000 tons of high grade coking coal, containing 34 to 38 percent volatile matter, with 55 percent fixed carbon and yielding 64 percent coke.

The heavy freight charges attendant upon shipping from the east, coupled with the growth and development of the western states, will bring about as a natural sequence the manufacture in this state of such articles as enter into the production of electrical, agricultural, mining, automotive, building and railroad equipment, as well as radiators and furnaces. The canning industry of the Pacific slope consumes a very large tonnage of steel, all of which is now produced in east. It is not at all remote that industries kindred to those mentioned will be established in Utah. The markets are near at hand and Utah, besides having the raw material, is the logical center of distribution.

In November, 1926, the Pacific States Cast Iron Pipe foundry, a subsidiary of the Columbia Steel Corporation and the McWane Cast Iron Pipe Company of Birmingham, Ala. started operations at Ironton, Utah. The original capacity of this unit was fifty tons of soil and pressure pipe per day. The demand for this product was much larger than anticipated and during the past year, additions have been made to the foundry, increasing the capacity to eighty tons of cast iron pipe per day, all of which finds a ready market in Utah and other western states.

Without question, this is the forerunner of many iron and steel industries which have heretofore found as a barrier, the lack or uncertainty of raw materials.

Much Ore Required

Upon completion of the units now under construction at Ironton during January, 1928, the blast furnace will require about 700 tons of iron ore per day, which will produce about 400 tons of pig Iron. The two coke oven batteries will require approximately 1300 tons of coal per day, producing about 700 tons of coke. A large portion of this is used in the blast furnace to smelt the iron ore and the balance distributed to Utah smelters for the reduction of lead, silver and copper ores. In addition, the byproducts produced will be about 6,000,000 cubic feet of excess gas, 14,000 gallons of coal tar, 4,000 gallons of light oil and 39,000 pounds of ammonium sulphate per twenty-four hours.

The blast furnace and cast-iron pipe foundry, along with the coal and iron mines employ approximately 900 men.

Besides owning its own coal and iron mines and blast furnace in Utah, the Columbia Steel corporation operates steel mills at Pittsburg and Torrance Cal. and a foundry at Portland, Ore., so that from mine to mill the corporation performs a multitude of steps in producing its finished products of steel castings, sheet steel, billets, rods, bars, light structural shapes, wire, wire nails and allied products.[3]

It is interesting to note that the article mentions that Columbia Steel owned "many iron mines" in Iron County. At the time, Columbia Steel owned many claims but was not operating any mines in the County. An interesting article about the Columbia Steel Corporation and the Ironton Plant was written in 1929 by Alex Rollo, the owner and editor of the *Iron County Record* and makes the increasingly troubled position of Columbia Steel evident.

Does Southern Utah Appreciate the Columbia Steel Corporation?

For some time past we have wondered if the communities of Southern Utah, and especially those of Iron County, appreciate the benefits that accrue from the operations of the Columbia Steel Corporation.

We know in a general way, through the shipping of iron ore from this county to the steel works in Ironton, Utah, there is a payroll connected with it, but to what degree it affects our county, we seem to be oblivious.

When it is taken into consideration that 30,000 tons of iron is mined and shipped by the Iron Ore Corporation to the works at Ironton, and that the monthly payroll for mining this is in the neighborhood of $25,000, it is easily seen that the activities of the Columbia Steel Corporation are of a great benefit to this country, to every man, woman, and child, because this money is actually circulated hereabout. $25,000 per month makes a yearly payroll of $300,000. Yet with all of this money being circulated here, and going into the hands of practically every citizen, and coming in $25,000 lots monthly, there seems to be a tendency to belittle the Columbia Steel, and a failure on the part of many to lend moral support to the enterprise.

And not only here in Iron County is the company mentioned, a big benefit, for at Ironton a large force of men is employed, the payment for their labor necessitating about $600,000 yearly; again, the company through its coal mining operations in Carbon County, has to pay an added payroll of $500,000 annually, to all of which other activities are added, bringing the total payroll for the entire operation of the company in the State of Utah to $3,000,000 per annum.

Certainly, a neat payroll for a Utah concern. Yet with all the money spent in this state by the Columbia Steel, many communities seem to conspire to fight them, and when it comes to buying iron and steel products, favor that from the east.

This seems unjust when it is taken into consideration that the product put out by the company is the equal, if not superior to the product manufactured in the East. The difference in cost, it seems to us, does not warrant securing eastern manufactured stuff.

And remember that which is "Made in Utah Makes Utah." We believe in lending our moral support as well as our purchasing support to home concerns, and we trust that the communities that have in the past secured iron and steel products from eastern and western manufacturers, will from now on use only products manufactured at home, especially when those products are up to the standard as the Columbia Steel products are.[4]

U.S. Steel Buys Columbia Steel

Late in 1929, two events occurred that had significant long-range impacts on iron mining in Southern Utah. The first was the stock market crash and the subsequent depression that ensued. The second, which occurred two days later, was the purchase of the Columbia Steel Corporation by the United States Steel Corporation. The Great Depression affected the whole world by curtailing the demand and production of almost every commodity including pig iron from Ironton and iron ore from Southern Utah. The purchase by U.S. Steel also affected the Ironton Plant and Southern Utah. This purchase affected not only the ownership of the properties but also the operation and direction of the company for years to come.

The stock market crashed on October 29th and the U.S. Steel announcement was made on October 31st. According to the company, the deal had been in the works for some time and the stock market crash didn't materially affect the equity balance between the two companies. The deal involved approximately $46,630,000, payable on February 1, 1930, entirely in the stock of the purchasing company. It included the Ironton plant, the iron mines in Iron County and the coal mines in Carbon County.[5]

In 1930, after purchasing Columbia Steel, U.S. Steel discussed its plan to spend 200 million dollars for a "vast expansion" but it declined to give any detail on where that expansion was to take place. It seems that everyone, particularly the newspaper men, were always looking for a good story. This was especially true during the depression, when the prospect of 200 million dollars pouring into the economy offered hope to the local community. In the end, the Ironton plant and the supporting iron mines in Iron County were not expanded until midway through World War II when the federal government bought a second furnace for Ironton and built the Geneva plant. This article erroneously assumed that because Columbia Steel, now owned by U.S. Steel, opened the first mine at Iron Springs and ran the Ironton smelter it therefore also owned and operated the mine at Desert Mound. In fact, Desert Mound was owned and operated by the Utah Iron Ore Corporation.[6]

Another article was published a few months later that again speculated about future expansion. Despite the hope the article appeared to offer, Desert Mound was not expanding, Boulder Dam was not hiring for quite some time and the General Steam Company was a pipe dream and a borderline scam. The article once again failed to realize that the Desert Mound operation was not owned or operated by the United States Steel Company.

> The United States Steel Company is putting on more men at Desert Mound and increasing their output of ore very materially. With the tariff out of the way, Boulder Dam ready for construction and the General Steam Co. on the verge of commencing work on its plants, it now looks as if this section of country is due for great development in the immediate future.[7]

In August 1931, the blast furnace at Ironton was shut down thirty days for repairs. There had been no repairs since 1927 and the furnace needed to be relined with fire brick. Relining of the furnace was required every three or four years. During the repair, no iron ore was shipped from Desert Mound to Ironton, which reinforced the fact that the iron mining operation at Desert Mound was inextricably tied to the mechanical availability of the Ironton plant. During this relatively short shutdown, however, the workforce at the mine was kept at its normal level because there was substantial work to be done remodeling the processing plant and stripping overburden in the pit. The company used their own trucks to do the stripping rather than contracting the work out as it had been done in the past.[8]

In March 1933, the United States Steel Corporation was the low bidder for the construction of a major portion of the San Francisco-Oakland trans-bay bridge with a bid of $13,732,471. The major portion of the pig iron that would be processed into steel for the bridge was to come from the Ironton plant and of course, the iron ore for the Ironton plant came from Southern Utah. This was good news for everyone concerned, but especially during the depression years. Again, the iron mines were dependent on the marketing of the Ironton plant's finished products.[9]

At least one of the claims at the Desert Mound Area was owned by CF&I, and ore mined from that claim was shipped to CF&I's smelter in Pueblo, Colorado.

The Market

The market for Southern Utah iron ore expanded with the move to the Desert Mound mining area. The mine shipped ore to the United States Smelting & Refining Company and the International Smelting Company, both in Salt Lake City. It also shipped ore to the Ironton plant and the pig iron produced by the plant continued to go to the furnaces in Pittsburg and Torrance California. An increasing amount went to the Pacific States Cast Iron Pipe foundry next to the Ironton plant. Ore from the CF&I claims was shipped to Pueblo, Colorado. From 1924 to 1936, the Utah Iron Ore Company mined 2.4 million tons of iron ore, with 1.5 million tons supplied to Columbia Steel, 778,350 tons sent to the CF&I furnace at Pueblo, and 134,000 tons sold for flux to various foundries and smelters.[10]

The Railroad

In January 1924, less than seven months after the branch railroad to Cedar City was completed, the Milner Corporation of Salt Lake City announced the sale of bonds to the Stephens Company of California. Proceeds of the bond issue were used, in part, for construction of a three and one-half mile long, standard gauge railroad spur from the branch railroad line of the Union Pacific Railroad between Lund and Cedar City to the

Desert Mound iron holdings of the Milner Corporation. These bonds were a direct obligation of the Milner Corporation and were specifically secured by a first mortgage on the Desert Mound properties, conservatively appraised at $1,500,000, or twelve times the amount of outstanding bonds. This was the only funded debt of the Milner Corporation, which had a net worth of about $4,500,000.[11]

Construction of the spur was started soon after the announcement in January. It was completed six months later on July 12, 1924.[12] The track was laid with substantial material to support the largest locomotives and tonnage that could be expected on the line. In addition to the spur, about a mile of side track was laid near the mine load-out tipple for rail car storage and loading purposes. The side track had a storage capacity of 100 railroad cars which, at that time, were each designed to carry sixty tons of ore.[13]

The Mine

In 1924, the Milner Corporation owned 527 acres of patented iron ore lands in the Iron Springs Mining District, with known iron ore reserves estimated at 15,000,000 tons within a depth of 100 feet. Engineering tests showed ore to extend to a depth in excess of 340 feet.[14]

The Desert Mound mining area included a number of ore bodies and a number of claims owned by various entities. Some of the claims involved were the Desert Mound, Short Line, King No. 1, Contact, Little Jim, Tarantula, State Section 2 and Thompson. The Short Line claim was discovered in 1930 by a ground magnetometer survey and better defined later by a number of churn drill holes. The State Section 2 and Thomson claims were discovered by the U.S. Bureau of Mines during its geophysical surveys of the district in 1944 and 1945. The Tarantula claim was purchased by CF&I in 1903 from Thompson and Frue for considerations said to be worth about $10,000.[15] The Desert Mound claim was purchased by CF&I in 1903 from the Thomas Taylor estate.[16]

Towards the west, five additional substantial deposits were discovered in the 1944–45 magnetometer surveys: the Section 2, Section 3, Section 4, Section 9 East and Section 9 West deposits. The total reserves in the immediate vicinity of Desert Mound were estimated to be 30 million tons. The five deposits just to the west contained approx.-imately 60 million tons of iron ore.[17]

The Utah Iron Ore Corporation started mining on the surface outcrops of the Desert Mound and King No. 1 claims. Mining moved from the Desert Mound claim to the Contact claim in 1931. Mining continued on the Contact and King No. 1 claims until 1936, when operations shifted to the Iron Mountain area. The Desert Mound ore body was owned by the CF&I and the Milner Corporation.[18] As mining progressed on the deposit, two pits evolved: the Milner Pit and the CF&I Pit.

The completion of the new railroad spur was critically important to shipping ore to the smelters in Northern Utah but before any ore could be shipped, equipment had to be designed and purchased, a mine needed to be built and a processing plant had to be erected. Even though the Desert Mound operation was initiated shortly after the operations at Iron Springs, substantial improvements had been made in mining methods and technology, and the Milners took advantage of those improvements.

The ore deposits at Iron Springs and Desert Mound were both surface outcroppings. However, the pits at Desert Mound were developed using open pit methods, whereas the Iron Springs operation used a combination of surface and underground methods.

No adits, tunnels, drifts, shafts, raises or glory holes were required at Desert Mound and the use of horse-drawn implements was slowly phased out. However, an in-pit mine railroad, similar to the one used by Columbia at Iron Springs, was used to haul ore out of the pit to the processing plant, except that this time the small ore cars were loaded on the surface with a steam-powered mining shovel instead of being loaded underground by ore falling down chutes from the surface. They were pulled by a small steam-powered locomotive rather than an electric locomotive powered by an overhead electric line. A smoke belching steam locomotive was probably not the best piece of equipment to be working underground from an air quality standpoint.

By July 1924, the overburden covering a section of Desert Mound ore had been stripped away and mining of the ore was expected to begin on August first.

> The Utah Iron Mines Corporation, operating at the Desert Mound, is spending approximately $5,000 monthly for labor. Now that the R. R. spur has been completed to the Mound, the stripping of the ore completed, shipping will soon commence which will necessitate the employment of fifty or more men. This will increase the payroll considerably.[19]

Another article noted that: "The camp takes on an air of encouraging activity, complete in every department. Clarence Milner who has been on the ground day and night for several months with commendable zeal; should be congratulated on the business-like aspects of the surroundings."[20]

In open pit mining, non-ore material called "overburden" or "waste" had to be removed or "stripped" away before the ore could be mined. This material was found above, below, on the sides and sometimes even within the ore deposit, but especially above and around the perimeter of the deposit. Additional material had to be removed to accommodate ramps and the back slopes and benches in the pit walls. The waste material was hauled away, leaving the ore relatively uncontaminated to be mined, processed and shipped to the smelter.

Initially, the overburden and the ore at Desert Mound were both loaded by the single mining shovel, a steam-powered shovel with a one cubic yard capacity bucket, mounted on caterpillar type tracks.

The overburden was hauled away by trucks and dumped in waste dumps in locations beyond the limits of the ore body, unlike the iron ore, which was hauled out of the pit by the small rail cars and taken to the crusher. The Desert Mound operation was one of the first, and possibly the very first, in the United States to use a shovel and truck combination. Later on in the operation trucks were also used to haul the ore.

It appears that the operators at Desert Mound got a little bit ahead of themselves and started to mine and ship ore before an adequate amount of overburden had been removed. The operation started shipping ore in August 1924, but only a couple of months later it found that it was shipping ore that assayed too high in silica and therefore contained a high amount of overburden material. They had to stop mining and shipping ore for a period of time in order to catch up on overburden removal. They reallocated their resources, a stripping campaign was undertaken and the ore was fully uncovered and cleaned. They were able to resume mining and shipping ore a few months later in late December. They had a workforce of fourteen men under the supervision of Gordon McMillan, shipping three sixty-ton carloads of ore to market daily.[21]

Iron Mining & Manufacturing

Illustration 6.1. The steam powered mining shovel at Desert Mound loading iron ore into the small mine cars after the limestone cap above it had been removed. The rails had to be laid up next to the shovel on almost every move. (Photo used by permission, Utah State Historical Society)

In open pit mining it is easy to become overly focused on ore removal and get behind on stripping, after all, there is a daily reminder of the ore that needs to be shipped and overburden removal can usually be allowed to slip a little until one day there is not enough ore uncovered to be able to meet the daily ore shipping requirements. It seems that this was a continual problem at Desert Mound and eventually led to its somewhat premature closure a few years later.

By April 1925, the Desert Mound operation had increased its ore shipments from 180 tons per day to 300 tons per day and was looking to increase to 500 tons per day. To meet the additional demand, the operation added a second shift and hoped that the demand for ore would increase enough that a third shift would be required within a year. A three-shift operation would employ an estimated 100 to 150 workers. The crews were working to remove overburden from an area measuring fifty-five by 100 feet, after which they would remove a fifty-foot-thick lift of ore below it.[22]

In September 1925 a news release described the progress at Desert Mound.

Big Development at Desert Mound

Last week a representative of this paper made a trip of inspection of the development that is being done at the Desert Mound by the Utah Iron Ores Corporation and was surprised at the amount already accomplished and that outlined to be finished before the end of the present year.

What is known as the upper pit is opened up, the lime overburden removed exposing iron ore of high grade for a distance of 125 feet, with a wall of solid ore of a depth of approximately 30 feet. And this is merely the top, as a test shaft

Desert Mound

Illustration 6.2. The "Thew" steam shovel and truck seen in the foreground are removing waste at Desert Mound. The shovel had a one cubic yard bucket. The drill seen in the background was used in the drilling and blasting operation. Note the smoke coming out the top of the shovel from the boiler and the steam being ejected from the end of the boom after powering the crowd function on the dipper. (Photo courtesy of Hal Christensen)

sunk in this neighborhood years ago showed a depth of 150 feet with the bottom of the body of ore not in sight.

In connection with the above, the company is now removing the lime capping from the southern end of the "lower pit," which already shows a body of ore for a distance of 250 feet in length to about 75 feet in width. The removing of the capping from the south end is being done for a distance of several hundred feet and when finally completed, which will be within a short time, ore will be in sight for a half mile in distance with a depth of 50 to 60 feet. The amount of ore now in sight is estimated at 1,000,000 tons and it is estimated that there is at least 25,000,000 tons of ore in the body at Desert Mound.

This ore body is the easiest mined in the known world, and is loaded on the cars by steam shovel, at a very small cost per ton, in fact, it is estimated that the cost is better than three-fourths less than the cost at other mines in the United States.

The Milner interests of Salt Lake City own the controlling stock of the corporation and now have a fair-sized force of men at work, local men at that, which will be considerably increased before the next year rolls around.

At present, the company is shipping, mainly for fluxing purposes, 400 tons per day, and it is expected that when the removing of the lime capping is finished at the "lower pit," the tonnage mined and shipped will be increased to 1,200 to 1,500 tons per day.

Iron Mining & Manufacturing

Illustration. 6.3. The steam shovel in the CF&I Pit at Desert Mound in the 1930s. It used coal for fuel and was quite a sight to behold, belching smoke and steam in the confines of the pit. If the men working around the shovel were lucky, a breeze pushed the constant smoke away and kept the air breathable. Despite its primitive appearance, it was a considerable improvement over the horse-drawn scrapers and glory holes used at the Iron Springs operation. (Photo courtesy of Hal Christensen)

The great majority of our readers will remember several years ago, in fact, nearly a quarter of a century ago, the Milner interests secured the property and the senior Milner always said that the time would come when vast tonnage would be shipped from the property to be used for the making of steel and the fluxing of the precious ores of Utah and Colorado.

That idea was also held by Clarence Milner, son of the first owner, and he is now the directing head of the corporation and has been since the formation of the company and the commencing of the development of the mine. His idea of 25 years ago has been followed out practically to the letter and today he sees that idea nearly consummated.

Clarence Milner also has had it in mind to employ local men as much as possible for this development and has done so right along, and it will be seen that the majority of men working at Desert Mound are local men. He believes in furnishing employment for the "home boys," as he puts it, first, last and all the time.

Illustration 6.4. The Milner Pit at Desert Mound. The steam shovel mined the iron ore and loaded it into the 5-ton capacity mine railroad cars seen parked at the right. The small gasoline powered locomotive seen in the center of the photo was used in the pit to position the cars. A larger locomotive was used to pull the string of loaded cars out of the pit to the crusher. It was a constant job to locate and relocate the tracks in the pit for these small mine cars. The main line railroad with 60-ton capacity cars can be seen in the background. (Photo used by permission, Utah State Historical Society)

Mr. Gordon McMillian of Salt Lake City is the general superintendent of the Desert Mound workings, and under his efficient management there has been more development of a high order done in a little less than a year and a half than is usually accomplished in double that length of time.

Thousands of dollars have been spent for the development of this property, and thousands are yet to be spent for further development. In fact, the work is to be continued until the ore body is opened up so that mining and shipping can be carried on a scale considerably larger than any other like proposition in the United States.[23]

Desert Mound Secures the Ironton Contract

In late 1925, the Utah Iron Ore Corporation signed an agreement with Columbia Steel, the owner and operator of the Ironton Plant, to begin shipping iron ore to its site starting July 1, 1926. At that date, the Columbia Steel operation at Iron Springs was to be shut down and the Desert Mound operation would be responsible for the full ore supply to Ironton. Shipments would also continue to the Salt Lake smelters and to CF&I in Pueblo. This required the mining and shipping rate of Desert Mound to increase substantially.[24]

To be able to meet this sizable increase in demand, the Utah Iron Ore Corporation did indeed gear up. In January 1926, it announced that it would be installing twin ore crushers at its operation at Desert Mound.[25] By the end of May 1926, a portion of the new crushing plant had been installed with the remainder to go into operation within a month. The oscillating crusher weighed 161,000 pounds and was powered by a large electric motor. After going through this primary crusher, the ore was carried by conveyor belt to two rotary secondary crushers that were designed to be able to crush 3000 tons of ore per eight-hour shift. The ore was then transported by conveyor belt to the sorting tipple where it was sorted automatically into three grades ready for dumping into railroad cars.

> The steel framework of the crushing plant, the largest ever erected in the west and second to none in the United States, according to engineers, is made from Utah ore smelted and made into steel in Utah and forged by a Utah concern located in Provo and erected by Utah men. The entire plant is a Utah production and is considered to be the best of its kind in the United States.[26]

In addition to upgrading almost the entire ore processing facility, the company purchased a new electric mining shovel to work in the pits along with the steam-powered shovel already operating on the property. The following article published in July 1926, gave a good description of the mine and the processing plant as they were upgraded to meet the increase in demand.

Iron Ore Production by the Utah Iron Ore Corporation—Description of Plant and Equipment for Handling Ore

Five miles west from Iron Springs station on the Cedar City branch of the U.P. railroad in Iron County, Utah, is located the Desert Mound iron ore property of the Milner Corporation of Salt Lake City. This property comprises some 600 acres of iron-bearing areas which have been leased for development and operation to the Utah Iron Ore Corporation, also controlled by the Milner Corporation. The iron ore bodies are a contact formation occurring as a limestone replacement between limestone and andesite and range from 150 to 300 feet in thickness. A portion of the ores are comparatively free from overburden while other sections of same, carry capping of varying depths, but not so deep as to interfere with economic stripping and mining of the ore. Based upon development in the form of tunnels, shafts and churn drill holes so far accomplished, the engineers and geologists of the company estimate ore reserves in the properties at 15,000,000 tons, of which 2,000,000 tons have been blocked out and analyzed. The ore averages approximately 55 per cent iron, 7.5 silica, 1.8 aluminum oxide and low in phosphorus and sulphur.

Open Pit Methods of Mining

The company has constructed a standard gauge railroad from a connection with the Cedar City branch of the Union Pacific railroad, a distance of 4.6 miles; also, about one mile of side tracks for car storage and loading purposes—capacity for 100 railroad cars. The mine is operated by the open pit method, similar to that employed by the Utah Copper Company, both the stripping and mining being handled by power shovels, one being a Marion, No. 37, 1-3/4-yard capacity electric shovel, full swing, and mounted upon caterpillar tractors, while the other is a "Thew" steam shovel of one-yard capacity, caterpillar type. These two shovels have a capacity of 2000 tons in eight hours. The shovels are served by Koppel two-way five-yard steel lined dump cars, specially designed and constructed to handle heavy material like iron ore and are spotted for loading by a Vulcan seven-ton four-cylinder gasoline locomotive.

After cars are load loaded they are picked up by a Vulcan 20-ton six-cylinder gasoline locomotive which transfers the cars from the pit to the loading bin or hopper which serves the crushing plant. This hopper is of ample dimensions to contain one hundred tons of ore, and is constructed of 3/8" plate, lined with 35-pound railroad rails. It is loaded over a 42" pan feeder, which feeds the material directly into the jaw crusher. This is one of the very few instances of the successful application of a pan feeder to a jaw crusher at the head of a mill.

Lumps coming from the quarry or pit, range in size from fines to 36" material, the average perhaps being from 24" to 30" lumps. The pan feeder is driven directly from the crusher shaft and is provided with a clutch to enable the crusher attendant to regulate the feed at will from the most convenient point on the crusher floor.

The Ore Crushing Plant

The main head crusher consists of an Allis-Chalmers 36" × 48" jaw crusher, which reduces everything to 4" or 6" size. This product is taken on a 24" conveyor belt, and discharges onto a 1-1/4" scalping screen. The oversize from this screen goes to a 10" Traylor gyratory crusher, which is guaranteed to reduce 6" material to 80% minus 1-3/8". The undersize from the screen, together with the crusher product, is conveyed by a 24" belt to the top of the storage bins, where it is divided into three products, ranging from minus 3/4" to 1-3/8" maximum. This screening operation is accomplished by double-deck screens, the oversize from the larger screens going directly to the center bins, and the middlings and fines being conveyed by 18" conveyors to end bins, respectively.

There are three main divisions to the bins, each fourteen feet long, which are subdivided, as it may prove desirable later to effect a magnetic separation in addition to the mechanical separation. The bins are of all-steel construction, and with the type of bunker construction that was adopted it makes a very neat and economical installation of storage capacity. In order to get the proper height for storage above the railroad track, and for the screening operations, it was necessary to elevate the material approximately 50 feet above the discharge from the gyratory crusher, and this was accomplished by elevating the conveyor, using a steel conveyor gallery for the purpose, about 90 feet long.

It was also necessary to elevate the product from the jaw crusher to the gyratory crusher in order to get the necessary head room for the screening operation at the gyratory. This was accomplished by another section of conveyor gallery one-half as long as the part leading from the gyratory crusher to the top of the steel bins.

In other words, three sections of conveyor gallery were built with the idea in mind that at some future date this plant might be moved and rearrangement of the conveyors might be made, and it is possible to utilize a conveyor gallery either 90 feet long or 135 feet long. For this same reason the small amount of framing around gyratory and jaw crushers was made of wood, only sufficient housing being erected to support an I-beam trolley above each crusher to facilitate repairs, and the necessary frame work for corrugated iron sides.

Illustration 6.5. *The Marion electric mining shovel was added in 1926 when Desert Mound got the contract to supply the ore to the Ironton Plant. The shovel had a 1-3/4 cubic yard bucket. Top center is Gordon Matheson with Albert Cane at the controls and Will Macfarlane standing. E. S. O'Conner was the General Superintendent. The identities of the other individuals are unknown. (Photo courtesy of Hal Christensen)*

The topography of the country was admirable for the construction of this plant, as the material had to be conveyed about 200 feet from the end of the industrial to track to the main line of the railroad, and it was necessary to utilize two stages of crushing. This enabled the conveyors to be worked out on a minimum of head room that was necessary for the various screening operations and gravity spouting, and also enabled the conveyors to be worked up the maximum angle of inclination for a minimum of belt length—the crushers being set at ground level with a minimum of excavation and concrete for foundations and footings. The two crusher foundations are of concrete, set on solid granite.

Power Plant, Sampler and Other Features

Power for this project is furnished by the Dixie Power Company at 33,000 volts, being transformed in an outdoor steel substation to 440 volts for the motors. A very unique and compact arrangement of substation was effected in that a rotary 37-KV switch, together with choke coils, fuses, horn gaps, lightning arresters, disconnect switches for power transformers, disconnect fused switches for lightning transformers, secondary bus metering, and all secondary feeder switches, were combined on the steel work in an outdoor installation and less than 3000 pounds of steel was utilized for the mounting of this apparatus. All the wires run from the substation to the crusher building, a distance of approximately 50 feet, in underground conduits. All electric wiring is in rigid iron conduit. Oil switches are provided at the substation to control the various motor feeds, and all the motors are controlled by magnetic line contractors with thermo relays for the motors.

All units in this plant are interlocked successively to prevent piling up of material; for instance, if a certain conveyor stops it will stop all crushers and conveyors behind it so that no material will be loaded onto a dead belt. This was accomplished by using no other than standard apparatus.

An automatic sampler will be installed on the loading spouts underneath the bins, enabling about 50 pounds of sample to be taken with the loading of each car. This will be dumped directly from the small hopper into the laboratory bin, where it will be ground and about 10 pounds of sample taken and the remaining forty pounds returned to the fine bin by small bucket elevator.

The spouting and chutes in the entire plant are lined with chilled cast iron liners, so that these should wear practically indefinitely. The screens used throughout are a vibrating type, originally developed by the Chino Copper Company and redesigned at the Utah Copper plant. They were redesigned to fit the special requirements of this plant. Over two hundred and fifty tons per hour is being screened on a screen surface measuring 3' 4" by 6' 3".

All machinery, other than crushers and motors, was manufactured by the Provo Foundry and Machine Company at their plant in Provo, Utah. Leon T. Petit, chief engineer of the Provo Foundry and Machine Company, was retained as engineer and designed the entire plant and superintended construction of same. On the initial turnover, about 500 tons per eight hours were run through the plant, and this daily schedule has been increased materially since.

Transformers and switches were furnished by the Westinghouse Electric and Manufacturing Company and the motors and starters by the General Electric Company. The Utah Iron Ore Corporation serves the blast furnaces of Columbia

Iron Mining & Manufacturing

Illustration 6.6. Desert Mound about 1930. The railroad cut on the southeast side of the Milner Pit. The locomotive pulled 8 to 10 railroad cars, each of the cars carried about 5 tons of ore. Hal Christensen operated the steam locomotive pulling the mine cars. Tom Mosdell was the brakeman and Dave Reese was the engineer. The Marion shovel can be seen in the background. (Photo courtesy of Hal Christensen)

> Steel Corporation at Ironton, Utah, the Salt Lake Valley smelters with fluxing ore, and also numerous users of iron ore on the Pacific Coast. Present rate of production is approximately 300,000 tons per annum.²⁷

In February 1927, Desert Mound was producing roughly 700 tons of ore per day. A representative of the *Iron County Record* visited the operation and made the following report.

> Men were busily engaged stripping, drilling, operating steam and electric shovels, dumping ore, watching crushers, conveyors, and grading machines, laying track, and

Desert Mound

Illustration 6.7. The railroad "Shay" steam engine, fired with coal from Carbon County. The engine and cars were used early on to haul ore out of the Milner Pit to the crusher. This steam locomotive was later replaced by a gasoline powered locomotive. Later in the operation, ore haulage by railroad was replaced with trucks. Hal Christensen and Roy Lessing are in the engine. (Photo courtesy of Hal Christensen)

loading railroad cars with the crushed raw ore to be shipped to northern Utah points. The stripping of the overburden of the ore is a mammoth job, there being about 35 feet of limestone that must be removed before the mining of the ore can take place.

At present something like 700 tons of raw ore are mined daily, but after the completion of the stripping now in progress, three or four times that number of tons can be mined each day with the force of men now employed. The grade of ore now being produced is very high and there is every indication that the same grade will maintain throughout the vast deposit that lies at Desert Mound.[28]

In March 1929 a disruption occurred at the mine which was uncommon at the time. It was one of the first recorded labor disputes in the district but was not the last.

Short Time Strike at Desert Mound.

Saturday afternoon, according to officials at the Desert Mound Iron Mine, 20 workmen went on strike, having objection to a new foreman that has come on the job from northern Utah. From information we get, the strike only lasted three-quarters of an hour, all the strikers being discharged. Monday morning more men were secured and the work of mining and shipping of ore was on again in regulation fashion.[29]

Charlie Heyborne, who worked at the mine, was a young man at the time and remembered the incident well. The company had brought in a new maintenance foreman

Illustration 6.8. By December 1927, work had begun on the surface of the Desert Mound deposit. The Marion electric shovel is loading material into the mine train. The ore was hauled to the crusher and the overburden was hauled to a waste dump. A drill is in the background. The "mound" of Desert Mound can clearly be seen. (Photo used by permission, Utah State Historical Society)

with "new-fangled ideas" who was quite unreasonable in working with the men. All of the men ended up in the manager's office and gave him an ultimatum—it was either them or the foreman. The manager terminated all of them. However, sometime later the foreman was transferred and eventually most of the men were rehired.

The Great Depression

The stock market crashed of October 29, 1929 and the effects of the Great Depression spread throughout the country affecting all markets, including the smelters using Desert Mound iron ore. Output was reduced from nearly 1,000 tons per day to a mere 300 tons per day.[30]

As mentioned previously, just two days after the stock market crash, the announcement was made that the United States Steel Corporation was taking over Columbia Steel. Nine months later, U.S. Steel announced the formation of a subsidiary company "designed to engage in iron mining operations in Iron County," named the "Columbia Iron Mining Company." It is interesting how the name of the previous company was retained for its mining and smelting operations; however, it was forever a point of confusion to many in the area as to whether to call the mining company "Columbia" or "U.S. Steel" or both. It is also interesting to note that at the time, neither company had any operating mines in Iron County.

The Articles of Incorporation for the Columbia Iron Mining Company were filed on July 5, 1930 in the Third District Court. The organization was capitalized for $1,000,000, divided into 10,000 shares of $100 par value. The company owned and had options on

Desert Mound

Illustration 6.9. *The Desert Mound operation around 1928. In the center are the processing facilities for crushing, screening, sampling and loading the ore. The oil house is on the right, the blacksmith shop on the left, and the bunkhouse and mess hall and office are in the background. Dell Hunter and Roy Clothier ran the blacksmith shop. Claude Edwards was the electrician. The railroad tracks in the center show the small cars which led from the hopper at the crusher to the Milner Pit and the railroad tracks on the right, by the water tank, led to the top of Desert Mound Pit. The large Union Pacific Railroad cars were loaded and moved to the right and onto Lund. (Photo from York Jones)*

87 iron mining claims in the Pinto and Iron Springs districts, which, with property in Cedar City, were estimated to have a value of $750,000.[31]

In February 1933, the Milner Corporation asked for tax relief from Iron County. The company owed some $14,000 but felt like the payment should only be $3,000 since the company did not operate the mine, but merely owned the property. The Desert Mound mine was operated by the Utah iron Ore Corporation which was a subsidiary of the Milner Corporation. Since the tax was assessed by the State Tax Commission, the County Commissioners referred the request to the State.[32]

By March, 1934, the Country was clearly not out of the grips of the Depression but things were looking up for the Desert Mound operation, its ore shipments doubled from five cars a day to ten. The company proved its dedication to the community and its insight, when the workforce was cut back years earlier. The company had the choice of eliminating half the employees or everyone working half time and gave the choice to the workers, who chose to keep everyone working.

Ore Shipments from Desert Mound Doubled [March 1934]

Reflecting a general improvement in conditions in the iron and steel industry, the Utah Iron Ore Corporation has doubled its ore shipments from its holdings at Desert Mound in this county within the fortnight.

For a number of months this company, which is working the Milner holdings under lease and shipping to the U. S. Steel Co. at Provo, has been loading out only

Illustration 6.10. Desert Mound churn drills drilled 4" diameter holes that were loaded with explosives and detonated. Noting the horses in the photo, the mine hadn't yet done away with animal power in mine operations. (Photo courtesy of Hal Christensen)

Desert Mound

Illustration 6.11. The Thew steam shovel, 1929–1930. Roy Clothier is on the left and Cliff or Hal Christensen on the right. (Photo courtesy of Hal Christensen)

five cars of ore daily. Since March 12, however, the number has been doubled and ten cars are being shipped each day. Though this increased activity hasn't provided employment for any more men locally, it has provided more work for those whom the company has held on its payroll during the depression. Instead of one or two days a week, these men are now employed four or five days, with a maximum of forty hours weekly. Local men who are affected by the increased shipments are Bill Heyborne, Granville Warren, Wayne Nostija, Burt Jones and Chester Stubbs. About twice this number from the other end of the county are also affected.

When decreased production became necessary a couple of years ago the company gave employees a choice of drawing cuts to eliminate half the employees or of all working about half time. The group chose the latter alternative and so practically the entire force has been carried on the payroll at one to three or four days a week. Asked about the increased activity at the mine, Superintendent E. S. O'Connor had no comment other than that they were shipping double the amount of ore since the 12th of March.[33]

On August 23, 1934, E. S. O'Conner of the Utah Iron Ore Corporation attended a County Commissioner's meeting in Parowan, Utah. He asked the Commission to construct a road to connect the Iron Mountain mining area with the road between Cedar City and Modena which passes near the Desert Mound operation. He stated that the ore at Desert Mound would soon be exhausted and that equipment would be moving to Iron Mountain and needed a good road. E. S. O'Conner worked for Utah Iron Ore but later became employed by United States Steel.[34]

Illustration 6.12. Aerial photo of the Desert Mound mining area taken around 1950, showing the Milner Pit and the CF&I Pit as they were left when operations were abandoned in 1936. In 1949, mining operations were resumed and the remainder of the huge underlying ore body was uncovered and mined along with the Short Line ore body, the edge of which can barely be seen at the bottom of the photograph. (Photo courtesy of The Magnet*)*

Clearly, plans were being made in 1934 for the inevitable shutdown of the Desert Mound operation. In October, at U.S. Steel's request, the Union Pacific Railroad filed to extend the 4.19-mile-long Desert Mound Spur an additional 11.31 miles to Iron Mountain.[35] The extension was granted in mid-November.[36] Construction of the spur was completed on August 15, 1935.[37]

Desert Mound Mine Abandoned

In 1936, after ten years of operation at Desert Mound, the Utah Iron Ore Corporation had removed all of the easily accessible ore from the deposit and the mine was abandoned. This action marked the end of the Utah Iron Ore Corporation, but the Milner Corporation continued to manage their large ore reserves for many years, deriving considerable income from ore leases.

The Desert Mound operation was quite remarkable. It started with its own secured capital, constructed a railroad spur on its own, built a new mine and processing plant from scratch based upon contracts with smelters and CF&I, took over the contract from Columbia Steel to provide ore to Columbia Steel's Ironton smelter, ramped up production from the mine significantly to meet the added demand and last but not least, produced ore, provided jobs and made a profit during some of the most difficult years of the great depression.

However, during its ten years of operation, only 2.4 million tons of ore were removed from a deposit containing an estimated 20 million tons. As mentioned earlier in this chapter, the removal of overburden was an expensive but necessary task. Proper mine planning and prudent operating practices require the stripping of overburden to be kept in sync with the mining of the ore. When this doesn't happen and the point of focus is primarily on the ore, what miners call "high grading" occurs and after a while a pit becomes unworkable. That appears to be how the Desert Mound operation ran out of ore and was abandoned after only one tenth of the reserve was mined. This was borne out in 1949, when the Desert Mound Pit was completely redesigned and reopened by U.S. Steel using newer mining technology and information obtained by further exploration drilling.

To be fair, the financial and technological limitations of the 1920s and 1930s were considerable and the operators did the best that they could with what they had. It would have been a monumental task to have cleared all of the overburden off of the huge Desert Mound ore body.

When Utah Construction Company reopened the area in 1949, it stripped over 2,000,000 cubic yards of overburden over the top of the Desert Mound ore body just to get the mining started for the Columbia Iron Mining Company. A detailed understanding of the ore body would have been absolutely essential before that level of investment could have been made. Additionally, the demand for the ore would have needed to have been much higher and certainly the equipment would have to have been much larger and more technically advanced.

General Interest

Leslie Morris Died Wednesday [1927]

The passing of Leslie Adams Morris, a young man of St. George, caused a gloom to come to a great many people of Cedar who were acquainted with him.

Last Friday the deceased suffered an accident at Desert Mound by which he received a badly mangled and crushed foot in the crusher. The unfortunate young fellow was brought to the hospital in Cedar City, where a portion of the mangled foot was removed in the hope that the rest of his foot could be saved, but gangrene set in and it became necessary to amputate the entire foot.

The victim withstood the amputation well, but infection set in and could not be stopped, the unfortunate young man passing away as above stated.

The body was embalmed and prepared for shipment to St. George Thursday, funeral services being held in that City today.[38]

Sustains Serious Injury [1927]

Wm. Stephens was brought in from Desert Mound yesterday morning suffering from a very serious injury received while working as switchman on one of the ore trains that operate between the mine and the crusher.

It appears that Mr. Stephens had just switched onto the main line and had jumped to the rear car, having his left leg hanging down from the car, when the second ore train came up unnoticed by him and collided with the train he was working on, catching his left leg, breaking both bones and mangling the flesh terribly just above the knee.

The injured man was rushed to the county hospital where his injuries were given surgical attention by Dr. J. W. Bergstrom.

Reports from the hospital are that Mr. Stephens is resting and doing as well as could possibly be expected considering the nature of his injury.[39]

Loses Life When Crushed Between Two Freight Cars [1928]
Hold last rites for Morris Smyth here Monday

The entire community of Milford was shocked Friday to hear of the death of Morris Smyth, caused by injuries received in a railroad accident. The accident happened at Iron Springs, Utah, about eleven o'clock; he was rushed to the Iron County hospital at Cedar City and died there at one o'clock that afternoon.[40]

Contacts with Electric Wire, Instantly Killed [1930]
Wednesday afternoon, shortly after five o'clock C. Q. Barnson, an employee of the Utah Iron Ores Corporation at Desert Mound, was instantly killed by coming in contact with a high tension electric wire.

It appears that the man, having just purchased a radio, was attempting to put up an aerial, attaching it to a pole carrying the electric current to the Desert Mound works, and while he was on the pole, standing on a cross arm supporting telephone wires, a stiff wind sprang up blowing the aerial wires onto the electric wires, making a circuit through which 3200 volts were shot through his body, killing him instantly, and knocking him to the ground a distance of about 25 feet.

A coroner's inquest was held on the scene, and the findings of the jury were to the effect that the deceased had come to his death accidentally by coming in contact with a high tension electric wire.

The deceased is about 32 years of age, a resident of Junction, Utah. He leaves a wife and one child.

The body was brought to the Southern Utah Mortuary and prepared for shipment to Junction, Utah where interment will be held.[41]

Hands Badly Scalded by Escaping Steam [1930]
This morning Wm. Stephens while working at Desert Mound had the misfortune to have both hands badly scalded by escaping steam.

Mr. Stephens was attending to the boiler to which is attached a hot water tank, and as he was regulating it, a plug blew out, the escaping steam striking him on his hands, very badly scalding them before he could step back out of reach.

Fortunately, he was standing erect and the steam did not strike him in the face. Both hands however, caught the full force and cooked the skin and flesh of his hands and fingers. Mr. Stephens was brought to Cedar immediately and the family physician treated the scalded hands within an hour and a half after the accident.

This is the second accident Mr. Stephens has suffered while at the Mound. Three years ago, he was crushed between ore cars and had his leg badly broken. For months it was feared that he would lose his leg and was taken to the Holy Cross hospital in Salt Lake City where he received treatment for several months. His leg was saved and although slightly lame he has been able to use it and do light work.[42]

Impressive Rites Held for Wm. Stephens [1934]

William Stephens, 53, died early Saturday morning after an illness of four weeks duration from blood poisoning and pneumonia from which he suffered severely until relieved by death. The blood poisoning was caused from infection in a cut on his hand which he received while working on the sewer system. General Septicemia was the direct cause of death.

Seven years ago, this month Mr. Stephens was very seriously injured when he was crushed between two ore cars while working at the iron mines at Desert Mound and complications developing from those injuries had greatly impaired his health and weakened his system to a point when he was unable to resist the ravages of his latest affliction. He had been able to be about during much of the time since he was hurt and although very lame had worked at various jobs but was never really recovered and suffered pain practically every day.[43]

Baseball

Baseball played an important part for the residents of Iron County and for many of the employees at Desert Mound and a number of other businesses in the area.

Iron Ore Succumbs to Agriculture [1930]

In the first baseball game of the season played in Cedar, Coach Linford's B.A.C. team defeated George Ten Eyck's Utah Iron Ore Corporation team Sunday by a score of 13 to 8. The first few innings of the game were played on an even basis, but as the game progressed the school team gradually drew away.

Dell Carpenter did the pitching for B.A.C., going the full game and turning in a very nice performance. The Mine's team used three pitchers, each performing on about an even basis.

The B.A.C. team will meet the Cedar City Athletic Club team next Sunday and are drilling hard to be able to add another victory to their list.[44]

Stacey Scores Home Run [1931]

The Cedar-Desert Mound baseball team added another victory to their list when they defeated Enterprise 8 to 7 in an exciting game on the local grounds last Sunday.

Cedar started the scoring in the first inning when Hal Christensen, the first man up, hit a three bagger and scored shortly after. The local team continued to add a run or two each inning until they had a lead of 8 to 1 at the beginning of the seventh inning, only to have Enterprise stage rallies in the seventh and ninth innings and almost tie the score.

In the seventh, the Enterprise players started to hit and scored four runs before the side could be retired. In the ninth, they scored two more and had the tying and winning runs on third and second bases when the final put-out was made.

Jim Stacey hit a home run in the fifth, driving the ball over the left fielder's head so far that he was on third base before the ball was recovered. Ten Eyck got a three bagger in the sixth that scored two runners.

Both teams played well in the field and the runs, for the most part, were scored on good solid hitting. Carpenter pitching for Cedar, held Enterprise batters well in hand until his team staked him to a good lead when he eased up and the game became much more exciting.[45]

Big baseball game [1931]

...between the champion teams of Iron and Beaver counties—Cedar-Desert Mound vs. Beaver—and a real battle is scheduled to be staged. Both teams are well up in the art of baseball and each is determined to "copper" the game. Fans will do well to see this game. It will commence at 3:00 p. m. at the Rodeo grounds, North Main Street.[46]

Field Trip

B.A.C. Geology, Chemistry Classes Take Field Trip [1927]

On the morning of April 22, the geology and chemistry classes, under the direction of Mr. Fife and Mr. Dalley, took a trip to Iron Springs for the purpose of studying the formation of that section of the country.

The first stop was at the summit of Eight Mile Pass. Here the reading of the altimeter showed the elevation to be 6,000 feet. A short walk of about 100 yards brought the classes to outcroppings of the claron formations, some partly metamorphosed conglomerate, and a bluish colored limestone. A little farther on was found some andesite, the original laccolith, that had been dug out of a test hole.

The party then went down to the iron works at Desert Mound and were shown about the place by one of the officials of the mine. Here could be seen, from the exposed surfaces, how the laccolith had raised the sedimentary formations, how the iron had been precipitated into the fissures caused by the shrinking of the laccolith.

It was noted that next to the ore was the blue limestone called "Homestead Limestone" and on top of that an orange colored sandstone called "Pinto Sandstone." The Homestead being called after an old homestead claim at Iron Mountain, and the Pinto Sandstone after the town of Pinto, where there are outcroppings. Here also was seen examples of faulting and exposures of the andesite formations. It was learned that the ore was about 50-50 hematite and magnetite, that it was from 50 to 55 percent pure, and that the company was shipping about 1,000 tons daily.[47]

Speculation

More Investigation [1927]

Rumors are current that there is to be quite a little investigation into Iron County resources this year.

We hear that there is a group of Los Angeles capitalists coming to look into the coal proposition, principally having to do with what is locally known as the tramway coal field, with a view of purchasing more land containing coal, and to open up the mines to such an extent that a daily output of 2,000 tons can be maintained daily to be shipped to some place in southern California for extraction of by-products.

And we are told that men of wealth interested in oil are coming to look over the prospects for wells in Cedar valley. We are told that hundreds of acres of land

Desert Mound

have been optioned, all of which, according to geologists contain oil at not more than 2500 feet in depth.

In connection with the above it is said that there are Californians coming to open up another iron mine which will be fully as large in an operative sense as the Desert Mound properties.

All of which sounds good, and we certainly hope will come true.[48]

Iron Mine Production May Be Increased in the Near Future [1928]

Capitalists Looking This Way with a View to Opening up Rich Bodies of This Much Needed Metal

Constantly we are receiving word that in the very near future the iron mines of the county will be opened up and made to produce many times more ore than is at present being shipped by the Iron Ore Corporation to the Columbia Steel mills at Ironton, Utah.

We are told that the United States Steel Corporation has longing eyes on large bodies of ore and are contemplating the erection of smelters somewhere in southwestern Utah, which will be fed the raw ore from this county.

We are told also that the General Steam Corporation has acquired large holdings of iron ore and are planning the erection of reduction works, together with a factory to manufacture hot air and hot water heaters; it is also contemplating the erection of electric power plants which will be used in furnishing power to operate the iron mines, the reduction works and factories.

The company has acquired, so we have been informed, a large acreage of coal lands and that the furnace factory and electric light plants are to be located near the right-hand canyon in Coal Creek Canyon; and that the iron reduction works are to be located somewhere in the Cedar Valley.

This means that railroad branches will be necessary, and it need not surprise our readers if there should be railroad lines from the iron district to Cedar Valley, then up Coal Creek Canyon to the right-hand canyon. And they need not be unduly surprised to see the cars on lines driven by electricity rather than steam or oil.

To sum all this up, the development of this section of the state has begun and cannot be stopped, and the day is not far distant when the "south end of Utah will be known as the head."[49]

Corporation Reaps Utah's Wealth [1930]

Utah is a state of marvelous resources. Her diversified vaults of wealth, hidden in the mountainous ranges, covering the greater part of the state's area, are not seen by the ordinary visitor. They are known only in part by the geologist.

The impression of the casual observer is that the state is a limited agricultural region. Soil of extreme fertility covers the floors of its valleys. Irrigation through panoramic networks of canals and ditches, supplies the moisture. Bountiful crops of fruits, vegetables and grains are produced. The streams, however, supply only part of the irrigable land. Utah is an arid state. Without artificial moisture the land is barren and desolate.

Limited by its water supply, agriculture will always be secondary. It is the mineral deposits that are amazing. Utah is the leading producer of silver among the states. She ranks third in the production of lead. Her yield of copper is second only to Arizona. The fame of the Utah Copper Mine is worldwide. It is the greatest open cut mine on the planet. Unlike the gold mines of California, which, from the grass roots, produced millions of dollars, to their owners, the mineral wealth of Utah can, in the main, only be exploited by large capital.

Great as is the wealth produced by the copper mountains of Bingham it will, beyond doubt, be surpassed by the fabulous iron ore reserves of Southern Utah. This region is only four hundred and seventy-five miles from the Pacific Coast. Here there is sufficient ore in the iron range traversing Iron County to supply the ever-growing needs of the Pacific Coast for generations. It is of hematite and magnetite, qualities running as high as 50 to 72 percent iron.

The Columbia Steel Company, that recently began the exploitation of Iron County ores, disclosed by diamond drilling that the numerous blowouts or blossoms frequently seen along this iron range are but fantastic upper thrusts of colossal iron bodies beneath aggregating hundreds of millions of tons—the quality of unparalleled richness.

The courage and judgment of Columbia Steel Company's founders and officials were vindicated against the pessimistic counsels of local bankers and skeptical investors. Its signal success attracted the attention of eastern steel magnates to this great western reserve of the world's most useful metal. The interest of the United States Steel Corporation was aroused. After investigation, Columbia Stockholders received an offer for their stock. It was a munificent one, and so attractive that the Columbia Company became the property of U.S. Steel.

In this age of industrial combinations in magnitude beyond the dreams of other periods, where organized industry is backed by almost unlimited financial resources, the individual of small capital has disheartening difficulties. Leroy A. Wilson, the General Steam Corporation's master mind, has never been appalled by these difficulties.

His inventive genius and ability to organize quickens his determination to succeed. His hobby is steam power. Graduating in 1916 from the Agricultural College of Utah, he began intensive study and research of the principles of heat transfer and combustion. Scientific articles from his pen frequently appeared in magazines devoted to industry. After a few years he patented an invention involving steam power, the Counter Flow Heater. The success of his device was instant. Wilson's reputation as an inventor was established.

Among those attracted by his genius was Thomas J. Yates, a Cornell graduate of engineering. Earlier in life, Yates had lived for years in the iron region of Southern Utah. He was thoroughly familiar with its resources of coal and iron and became aware that it possessed physical advantages found in few places elsewhere.

True, the extensive coal seams that for 80 years had furnished fuel for the settlers, is non-coking and therefore unsuitable for blast furnaces. But reasoned Yates, this coal is highly volatile and will produce steam for electric power. With Wilson's patented Counter Flow boilers located in a power plant beneath the discharge tunnel of the mine, electric power can be made at insignificant cost.

His representations fascinated Wilson. Together they made a thorough examination of those possibilities. The assistance of Dr. Murray O. Hayes, head of the department of geology of the B.Y. University, was obtained and his qualifications as geologist and his knowledge of patent requirements became invaluable.

Immediately Wilson conceived the plan of a holding company, capitalized sufficiently large to enter the field and acquiring from local owners all available iron holdings and in addition the highly valuable patented coal properties adjacently located.

For a period of four years the campaign was waged. Parcel after parcel of iron claims, for which many of their owners refused substantial cash offers, were sold to the General Steam, the holding company, in exchange for shares of their capital stock. Today they are the unencumbered owners of iron ore properties that contain an estimated tonnage exceeding 400,000,000 tons. They also own or control over 5000 acres of patented coal seams containing millions of tons. There is today a great demand for sponge iron made from Iron County ore. It is the equal of the famous Swedish sponge iron for which the steel manufacturers of the United States are paying $60.00 per ton. Through the low temperature method of reducing these ores for sponge iron (which method will be adopted by the General Steam Corporation, using the efficient Counter-flow principal) this company has demonstrated that sponge iron can be produced at a fractional part of the above price.

Today blast furnaces costing hundreds of millions of dollars are producing the major part of our steel. Eminent authorities, however, declare that the days of the blast furnace are numbered. The advent of the electric metallurgical furnace is here. With electric power, the chief item of cost reduced to less than two mills per K.H., no blast furnace can long survive in competition.

The General Steam Corporation has all the essential requisites for success. Efficient retorts for the manufacture of low temperature sponge iron will be employed. The raw material, both coal and iron, will be delivered to their factory at insignificant cost. The latest designs of furnaces for the electrical manufacture of steel will be installed.

The strategic position held by the company is most apparent. The factory sites of 1000 acres in the heart of the valley and within a few miles of its supply of coal and iron is highly adapted for its purpose. Railroad facilities, splendid automobile highways, radiate from this location. Citizens of southern Utah are active in their support of this coming industry. AN INVESTOR[50]

CHAPTER SEVEN

Iron Mountain and the Columbia Iron Mining Company 1935–1943

IN AUGUST 1934, E. S. O'Conner of the Utah Iron Ore Corporation attended a County Commissioner's meeting in Parowan, Utah. He spoke, and his statement to the Commission included two key facts: one, the deposits at Desert Mound would soon be exhausted, and two, work would soon be starting on a new mining operation at the Iron Mountain area to replace the Desert Mound operation.[1]

It was reported that more than half a million dollars would be spent over a ten-month period in 1935 to develop the new mine at Iron Mountain, twenty-five miles southwest of Cedar City. Three organizations were needed in order make this happen: (1) the Southern Utah Power Company of Cedar City had to spend approximately $10,000 to install the necessary power transmission lines, transformers, etc., to power the equipment at the mine, (2) the Union Pacific Railroad needed to spend $300,000 to build the roadbed and lay twelve miles of track for the new line and about two miles of sidetrack, and (3) the Columbia Iron Mining Company, a subsidiary of U.S. Steel Corporation, needed to spend the remaining $200,000, starting earthmoving operations at the mine and building a crushing, screening and loading facility, along with office buildings, bunk houses, maintenance buildings, roads, etc.[2]

The power line was completed in April 1935, the railroad spur from Desert Mound to Iron Mountain was completed in August 1935 and by April 1936 the Columbia Iron Mining Company was ready to mine and ship ore from its new Black Hawk Pit at Iron Mountain. The Iron Mountain location was a little less than three miles from the old Iron City Iron Works location.[3]

The Market

The market for the Iron Mountain mine was different from the Desert Mound mine. Utah Iron Ore Corporation was an independent operator and sold its output to anyone who was willing to purchase it. The new Iron Mountain mine was a captive mine, with both smelter and mine being operated by Columbia. As a result, non-company users like the Salt Lake smelters would not be getting any ore from the new Iron Mountain mine, nor would CF&I since Columbia sold only to the Ironton Plant.

Iron Mountain & Columbia Iron

Illustration 7.1. The Ironton plant. (Photo used by permission, Utah State Historical Society)

The Smelter

The opening of Columbia's mine at the Iron Mountain area changed nothing at the Ironton plant. Desert Mound ore was simply replaced by Iron Mountain ore.

The following *Parowan Times* article discussed the status of the Ironton Plant as it existed in 1938 and its importance to Iron County and the State of Utah.

A Payroll Builder

A comparatively new industry, the manufacturing of iron, has become one of the most important in Utah. The air photo above shows the Columbia Steel plant at Ironton, a subsidiary of United States Steel Corporation.

Operations of the Steel company have increased the payrolls of the state $1,000,000 yearly, have augmented the movement of freight by 976,000 tons annually and brought to the railroads an additional $2,000,000 each twelve-month period. The annual expenditure for supplies approximates $1,000,000.

Besides the pipe manufacturing operations, Ironton now has 56 coke ovens, with a 15-ton coal capacity each. Coal coked per day equals 1,550 tons, producing 840 tons of metallurgical coke, 18,600,000 cubic feet of gas, 18,600 gallons of tar, together with ammonium sulphate and motor fuel.

Fifty per cent of the ammonium sulphate is shipped to Japan and the Hawaiian Islands, and 50 per cent is consumed on the Pacific Coast.

The Blast furnace will average approximately 480 tons of pig iron per day and consumes 820 tons of ore. The ore which yields these materials is drawn from mines in Carbon County and Iron County, which are owned and operated by the company.[4]

Illustration 7.2. Aerial photo of the Pacific States Cast Iron Pipe Company next to Ironton. (Mount Pleasant Pyramid, September 16, 1938)

In September 1938, an article appeared in several Utah newspapers concerning the Pacific States Cast Iron Pipe Company that had begun operation in November 1926 and had grown substantially over the years. Pacific Pipe was one of the few Utah companies that fabricated products from the pig iron produced by the Ironton Plant.

Expands Operation

Starting with a small unit in 1926, the Pacific States Cast Iron Pipe Company has gradually increased its operations into a million-dollar-a-year industry. The accompanying air view shows the company's plant at Ironton, adjoining the plant of the Columbia Steel Corporation, from which it draws the pig iron for manufacture of its products.

Capacity of the plant has been increased 100 percent since 1926 and since 1931 a completely new manufacturing unit has been installed. The company's payroll amounts to a half-million dollars a year and normally approximately 400 men are employed. Products of the company, which include pressure water pipe, plumbing fixtures, gate valves, fire hydrants and circulating heaters are sold in all parts of the west.

While Utah is one of the nation's leading producers of raw materials, few of its metals are fabricated within the state. The state needs and should have more refineries and fabricating plants such as The Pacific States Company at Ironton.[5]

The Railroad

The 12-mile extension of the railroad spur from Utah Iron Ore Company's old processing plant at Desert Mound to the Iron Mountain mining area had to be approved and constructed before any iron ore could be shipped from Columbia Iron Mining Company's new Blackhawk mine. In addition, two miles of sidetracks were required near the mine to store incoming empty cars until they could be loaded and outgoing loaded cars until they could be scheduled for pickup and shipment to the Ironton facility. The sidetracks would also enable the cars to be switched, relocated and loaded.

On September 24, 1934, the Los Angeles & Salt Lake Railroad Company, part of the Union Pacific system, filed an application for a certificate with the Interstate Commerce Commission at Washington D. C. to construct and operate an 11.31-mile-long extension of the railroad from Desert Mound to Iron Mountain. The building of the new section of railroad was contracted by, and under the direction of the Union Pacific Railroad.[6]

The contract for the grading and bridge work for the spur was let on April 16, 1935 to the Morrison-Knudson Construction Company of Idaho. The construction equipment was to be relocated immediately and the work was to be started within a week, starting at the Desert Mound end of the line. The bidders on the job contemplated using mostly local labor. The work to secure the railroad rights-of-way and surveying and cross sectioning of the line had already been initiated but the contract for the laying of the track was let at a later date. It was reported that there had been some issues in obtaining the right-of-way for the line.

> Although it is the plan of the railroad company to have the line completed and in operation by August 1st, the selfishness of a few property holders may cause considerable delay in construction. It is understood that the company has experienced much difficulty obtaining a right-of-way for the road, three claim holders in the section causing all the trouble. It is understood that these three, one from Salt Lake City and the other two from the East, are demanding exorbitant and prohibitive prices for the rights-of-way across these three short sections. All other property holders, the officials report, have given excellent cooperation, some of them giving the right-of-way free and others charging only a nominal figure.
>
> Union Pacific officials are emphatic in the statement, that regardless of this difficulty, the road will be completed, and in the shortest possible time. They state that everything possible will be done to effect a reasonable settlement, but if this fails, condemnation proceedings will be started.[7]

The total cost of the line was projected to be more than $300,000 and it was expected that a number of local residents would be employed, both in construction of the road, and in mining activities of the Columbia Iron Mining Company in preparation for the shipment of ore.[8]

Construction of the railroad spur from Desert Mound to the south side of Iron Mountain was completed on August 15, 1935 for a final cost of approximately $350,000. The new rail line ran right next to the old loadout facility at Desert Mound and opened the way for the Columbia Iron Mining Company to ship iron ore to the Ironton Plant from its new Blackhawk mine at the Iron Mountain mining area.[9]

Exploration and Claim Buying

The Columbia Steel Corporation began making plans for potential future mining opportunities at the Iron Mountain mining area more than a decade before mining physically started at that location. Ten years previously, in 1925, Columbia Steel conducted an extensive exploration project on the several claims that it owned at Iron Mountain with two diamond drills and a number of workers. The following article published in the *Iron County Record* on April 3, 1925 described the event.

> [Columbia Steel Corporation] is now preparing to set up two diamond drills on what is known as the Pinto Claim No. 15, just west of the "Blowout" hill about a half mile. Six cabins to house the workmen are being built and as soon as they are completed, the actual work of drilling will commence, which will be in the neighborhood of four weeks. The drills are now on the way from the factory, and as soon as the they arrive at the Iron Springs station will be shipped by team overland ten or twelve miles to the Iron Mountain.
>
> Much prospecting has been done on the Pinto No 15 and wherever the overburden has been removed, the iron ore shows up strongly. Tests have proven it to be of very high grade. It is the depth that the Columbia Steel Company is now determined to find out, which, if as is anticipated, reaches in the neighborhood of four to six hundred feet, a permanent camp will be erected and the ore mined and shipped to Ironton to supply the second unit mill that is contemplated being built.
>
> There is no doubt whatever but that there is a large body of ore on Pinto No 15, as the outcroppings and the stripping that has been done shows very rich iron ores. And judging from the "Blowout" nearby, the depth will easily reach six hundred feet. Adjoining claims show equally well, and when once stripped, can be handled with steam shovel direct to the railroad cars, thus eliminating haul through tunnels on small mine cars and then reloading on railroad cars. This will mean a great saving in the expense of mining and loading, over the cost of the "Glory Hole" style of mining and loading, teams being necessary to scrape the loosened ore into the holes.
>
> It is understood that if the depth of the ore on the Pinto No 15 is sufficient, a line will be built, and already in anticipation of this, surveyors of Columbia Steel Company at Iron Springs are making tentative surveys for the line.[10]

The next month, in May 1925, Columbia Steel Corporation took out an option on additional unnamed Iron Mountain properties owned by the Milner Corporation of Salt Lake City.[11] Columbia continued its exploration work, probably to prove up the Milner property. From the description, one of the deposits may have been the Black Hawk which was said to contain upwards of ten million tons of ore. In September Columbia Steel formalized the acquisition of the Milner-Dear-Lerch holdings at Iron Mountain, consisting of fifty-one claims covering 921 acres.[12]

With fifty-one claims involved, the locations could have been almost anywhere in the Mining District, however, from the description, the claims were most likely situated in the Iron Mountain mining area on the south end of Iron Mountain and possibly the Comstock mining area on the east side of Iron Mountain. The Dear claim, presumably named after the Dear family, was located in the Comstock mining area and may have been part of the purchase.

In July 1928, Columbia Steel purchased the Iron Mountain mining properties of the Burke Iron Company which almost certainly included the large Burke ore body. The deposits involved in the deal were estimated to contain a total of 15,000,000 tons of iron ore. The company continued its drilling program to determine the extent of the acquired ore bodies. The Burke Iron Company was owned by the heirs of Allen G. Campbell, Dennis Ryan and Matthew Cullen.[13]

It became obvious, from the substantial acquisitions at Iron Mountain, that the Columbia mining group's long-range mining plan was to supply iron ore to Ironton from Iron Mountain after the reserves at the Iron Springs' "Glory Hole" mine were exhausted. The situation must have been fairly certain and time critical for the company to buy two new diamond drills from the factory and begin making plans to survey a new railroad line from Iron Springs. As it turned out, the plans failed to come to timely fruition. The rumored second unit at Ironton mentioned in the news article was not built until World War II and Columbia did not start mining at Iron Mountain when the Iron Springs mine shut down in 1926.

As discussed in chapter five, the early mining methods employed at Columbia's Iron Springs "Glory Hole" mine were less than satisfactory for a number of reasons. Apparently, these had become unsatisfactory to the point that Columbia was willing to prematurely shut the operation down. This would have been a difficult decision for Columbia to make, given the substantial investment that had been made at Iron Springs and the fact that the mine had been in operation for only three years. To make matters worse, preparations at Columbia's Iron Mountain properties were not far enough along to be able to get it running soon enough to meet the need. Columbia made the hard choice to shut down its own operation and contract an outside mining company, the Milner Corporation, to supply its Ironton plant with iron ore from Desert Mound. As a result, Columbia did not operate an active mine in Southern Utah for almost ten years until it started mining at Iron Mountain in 1936. The spur to Iron Mountain that was planned for in 1925, was not built until 1935.

As a side note, the April 3 news article quoted above stated that ore at the new mine could be loaded directly into full-sized railroad cars in the pit and then shipped to the smelter. Although that sounds nice, it didn't happen that way. First, the ramps were far too steep and the pits much too confined to accommodate regular rail haulage, and second, the ore had to be dumped and reloaded in any case because crushing, screening and blending were required before it could be shipped to Ironton. The article was on target, however, when it mentioned the difficulty and high cost of using horse-drawn teams to scrape ore into glory holes.

The Mine

In 1935, there were ten ore bodies of consequence in the Iron Mountain mining area located on the southern perimeter of Iron Mountain. Collectively, the ten deposits had estimated iron ore reserves of 220 million tons. This represented the largest concentration of reserves in the district. Five of these deposits were on or near the surface and were ultimately mined out. They contained an estimated fifty-six million tons. The other five were deeper underground and were left untouched. These are still in the ground with an estimated reserve of over 160 million tons, an approximation that some experts claim is too low.

The Columbia Iron Mining Company owned five of the ten deposits, three of which were eventually mined, the Blackhawk, the Pinto and the Burke. The two unmined Columbia deposits were the Lime Cap and the Rex.

Lime Cap ore body is on the southwest side of Iron Mountain between the Burke and McCahill ore bodies. The ore deposit is a mid-sized, off-dipping replacement in the lower part of the Homestake Limestone. It was judged to be similar to the nearby Duncan ore body and its ore has moderately high sulfur content. It contains an estimated 5 million tons of iron ore.[14]

Rex ore body is located on the west side of Iron Mountain and produced a strong pear-shaped magnetic anomaly about 3,000 feet in diameter. This was the strongest and most extensive observed in the district over the course of the magnetic surveys conducted by the U.S. Bureau of Mines in 1944–45. Drilling operations disclosed this deposit to be the largest replacement and breccia filling ore occurrence in the Pinto-Iron Springs Mining District, containing in excess of 100 million tons of ore. Unfortunately, the top of the main body of ore lays 600 feet beneath the surface. The Rex ore body will be further discussed in a subsequent chapter.[15]

A and B ore body, the sixth deposit, was owned jointly by Columbia and CF&I and was never mined. It is located on the southwest end of Iron Mountain, immediately south of the Black Hawk Pit and west of the Blowout Pit. The ore body was discovered and outlined by magnetometer studies in the 1950s. Exploration drilling was conducted on it by both the Columbia and CF&I organizations. It is thought that the ore body is probably a westward continuation of the Blowout ore body. The top of the deposit lies beneath 300 to 400 feet of cap rock and alluvium along a major fault structure extending along the south side of Iron Mountain. It is a replacement ore body occurring largely in vertical and overturned Homestake Limestone. The mineralization consists of a mixture of magnetite and hematite extending to a depth of more than 2,000 feet. This is the greatest depth that ore has been traced in the district by drilling operations. The ore body has a potential of thirty to forty million tons. Unfortunately however, underground mining would be required to recover the deeper ore.[16]

CF&I owned two of the ten deposits, the Blowout and Duncan, both of which were eventually mined by the Utah Construction Company under contract to CF&I.

Calumet ore body, the ninth deposit, was owned by the Milner Corporation and was never mined. The deposit was discovered by an aerial magnetometer survey conducted by the U.S. Steel Corporation. It is located 400 to 600 feet below the surface and measures about 400 feet long and 200 feet wide and is a replacement type ore deposit that occurred in the lower portion of Homestake Limestone. The limestone strikes north 70° west and dips 30° southwest. The Calumet ore body has an ore potential of nearly three million tons.[17]

McCahill ore body, the tenth deposit, was owned by the Duluth and Utah Iron Mining Company and C. M. Denny and was never mined. The deposit is on the southwest end of Iron Mountain, west of the Lime Cap and Burke ore deposits. The ore body was disclosed by a magnetometer survey conducted by U.S. Steel. The ore body does not outcrop and lies 500 to 800 feet beneath the surface, a tabular replacement ore body that dips to the west. Ore is traceable for about 1,200 feet down-dip; in places the full thickness of the Homestake Limestone was replaced. The ore body is cut by a fault which thins the ore body. The deposit has a mixture of hematite and magnetite and has a fairly high sulfur content due to the presence of pyrite. The ore potential of the property approaches twenty million tons.[18]

The following newspaper article gave details on the new Iron Mountain power line.

The Southern Utah Power Company has started construction of a power line to Iron Mountain to furnish electrical service for the Columbia Iron Mining Company. About two miles of new line is to be constructed and four miles of old line rebuilt, at a cost of between $6,000.00 and $7,000.00. Construction of the line will be completed in about two weeks, after which time electric service will be available to the company. Although no announcement has been made as to the plans of the mining company, it is understood that the power will be put to use within a very short time for drilling and mining preparation, that actual mining of ore can be undertaken as soon as the railroad to the locality is completed.[19]

In preparing for the operation of the new mine at Iron Mountain, there also arose a controversy about where to build the highway to access the mine for workers who would travel to and from Cedar City. The main road up to that point in time went first to the Iron Springs area, then to Desert Mound, then past the Comstock area to the Iron Mountain area and then on to New Castle. Columbia, the workers at the new mine and the Cedar City Chamber of Commerce were in favor of a shorter, more direct route past Woolsey's ranch. Ultimately it was decided to improve the road that went past the Woolsey's ranch and this is the route which the road follows today to New Castle. The other route exists today as an oiled road from Iron Springs to Desert Mound and a good gravel road from Desert Mound to Comstock then to Iron Mountain where it joins the oiled road to Newcastle.[20]

Black Hawk ore body was located on the south end of Iron Mountain at an elevation of about 6,500 feet above sea level. The ore body was a large replacement deposit in a roof pendant of the Homestake Limestone Formation. A roof pendant is a mass of rock, in this case limestone, that was almost entirely surrounded by the igneous intrusion. Near the surface, the ore was extremely hard and dense but with depth, the ore changed to large masses of soft, granular ore containing both magnetite and hematite. These ores had a greater average iron content than either of the nearby Pinto or Burke deposits and contained a smaller amount of impurities. The property had an ore potential of about twenty million tons.[21]

The Columbia Iron Mining Company put its first crew of workers into the field shortly after April 1, 1935. Many of these workers had been engaged in exploration drilling activities which had begun the previous May and had lasted almost a year. This drilling was done to better define the Black Hawk ore body and enabled the engineers in developing mine plans, not only for the work that would occur in the immediate future but also for the life of the mine. Preliminary work on the mine and the crushing plant had been in progress for some time before the work on the mine began in April 1935. The plant construction began on August 1, 1935 and was completed the following April. The crushing, screening and loading plant was constructed a short distance southwest of the pit. The receiving hopper and primary crusher were only 700 feet from the edge of the pit.

In August 1935, mining equipment started to arrive by way of the newly completed railroad spur, including a new 2-1/2 cubic yard electric mining shovel. Although the Black Hawk deposit was close to the surface and partially outcropped, a substantial amount of work was required to remove extraneous material from on top of and along the sides of the ore body before the ore could be mined. By mid-August a 600 foot by 4000-foot area had been stripped of overburden and leveled in preparation for mining of the ore beneath.

The following newspaper article gave a good description of the ongoing events.

Huge Operations at Iron Mountain Will Be Under Way Soon

Preparation for the actual shipping of ore from Iron Mountain by the Columbia Iron Mining Company is moving forward at a rapid pace and the greatest development of the mining industry in the history of Iron County is expected to get underway in the near future.

The new branch line of the Union Pacific railroad, running from Desert Mound to the south side of Iron Mountain, a distance of about 14 miles, is to be completed with the exception of some finishing touches, and will be formally accepted by the company on this August 15th. The line has been built at a cost of approximately $300,000, and the work has been done in record time by the contractors, The Morrison-Knudson Company.

Equipment and materials have already been shipped over the line, and on the first of the week, ten car loads of such had been shipped in. Included in this shipment was a 135-horsepower electric shovel, with 2-1/2-yard capacity, to be used in the open-cut mine and for development purposes.

Although the mining company has not made an official announcement, it is understood that development work and buildings to be erected in preparation for mining activities will cost approximately $150,000. Buildings to be constructed will include a warehouse, office building, laboratory, machine shop, truck garage, compressor house, change room, employees' garage, electric substation, and facilities for storing gas and oil. The water supply for culinary and mining purposes has already been developed at the mine.

It is understood that the plant will be constructed with an eye toward ore handling on a large scale and will have loading bins which will be located over three tipped bins, making possible the loading of three cars simultaneously. The newly crushed ore will be run through a screen and secondary crusher, then conveyed to a screening and loading tower located over the tracks where it will be separated into different specifications and then loaded and shipped to the blast furnaces. The crushing and loading facilities will have the capacity of loading and moving [ ] cars per day. The first property to be developed will be the "Black Hawk." It will be an "open cut" mine, the work being done mostly by electric or steam shovels. The first ore shipments from the plant are expected to be on about November 1st.[22]

Another update was given by a different newspaper two weeks later.

Iron Mountain Rails Are Laid

Cedar City, Aug 15 – Construction of the 12-mile railroad from Desert Mound to the virgin iron ore deposits of Iron Mountain, 25 miles southwest of here, was completed today.

The trackage opens way for operation of the Columbia Steel Corporation of Provo at Iron Mountain. Ore from deposits there is expected to replace that now being obtained by the steel company at Desert Mound.

Shipment of ore from Iron Mountain will be made after expenditure of almost half a million dollars by the steel company, the Union Pacific system and the Southern Utah Power company.

Drilling to Continue

A force of steel company employees has been stationed at Iron Mountain since May. Prospect drilling of ore deposits is expected to continue for another six months.

A huge electric shovel, powered through extension of transmission lines by the utility company for more than three miles, has stripped and leveled an area 600 feet by 4000 feet. The surface dirt has been removed from a huge body of ore which will be mined by the open pit method.

The steel company plans to construct a screening and crushing plant at the pit to handle the ore, which will be shipped to Provo for smelting. Office buildings, shops and garages will be erected.

Equipment Ready

Erection of the buildings is expected to start about August 1. Foundation for the screening and crushing plant has been completed and some permanent equipment is ready for installation. Fabricated steel for the buildings is expected to arrive about September 1 and the working crew of 25 men then will be increased to 75.

The entire project is expected to be completed by January 1. Date on which operations will be transferred from Desert Mound to Iron Mountain is not known.

The final link of the transportation unit is nearing completion. The Utah state highway commission is constructing a road from Stake Well, west of Cedar City, to the boundary of the Dixie national forest. Forest service officials have ordered the road extended from the boundary line to Iron Mountain. Total distance is about 15 miles. Labor is being supplied locally on all units of the projects.[23]

A further update was given in January 1936.

Ore Shipments from Iron Mountain Soon to Start

W. R. Phibbs of San Francisco, general manager in charge of operations for the Columbia Steel company, inspected the new construction and developments at Iron Mountain, Thursday. Although he made no comment as to the future plans of the company, he reported that work was progressing satisfactorily, and indicated that ore shipments would start as soon as the development program is completed.

The first two units of a three-unit crushing mill are complete, with the exception of the installation of the heavy machinery, and work on the third one has been started. Two water storage tanks have been completed, with a combined storage capacity of more than 30,000 gallons, and wells are now in operation to provide the plant with water. Enormous areas have been cleared and considerable ore is blocked out ready for operations to commence as soon as construction is completed.

Approximately fifty men have been employed at Iron Mountain since the completion of the 14-mile branch of the Union Pacific railroad last August. The new railroad was completed at a cost of about $350,000 and reaches Iron Mountain from the Utah Iron Ore company plant at Desert Mound. It is reported that when operations are commenced, nearly a million dollars will have been spent in this section by the two companies.[24]

Iron Mining & Manufacturing

In March 1936, the construction was completed on the ore processing plant at Iron Mountain. The machinery had been thoroughly tested and was ready to go. The mine was developed to a point to where ore was ready to be mined and hauled to the crusher. Ore shipments to the Ironton plant were to start by April 1st.[25]

E. S. O'Conner worked as the superintendent at Desert Mound for the Utah Iron Ore Corporation until about the time that the operation closed. At that time, he was hired by the Columbia Iron Mining Company and began working at Iron Mountain. In September 1936, he was transferred to the company's coal properties in Carbon County. Even after his transfer, he authored several articles about the iron mining operations in Southern Utah.[26]

In December 1936, a news article was written by Mr. O'Conner that summarized the move from Desert Mound to the Black Hawk operation at Iron Mountain.

> Due to depletion of open pit ore of suitable grade at the Desert Mound location of the Utah Iron Ore Corporation operations, the Columbia Steel Company, a subsidiary of the United States Steel Corporation, which, in 1930 purchased the entire properties of Columbia Steel Corporation, decided to develop property at Iron Mountain, 12 miles southwest of Desert Mound. The Columbia Iron Mining Company was organized to do this work. This required the construction of 12 miles of standard gauge railroad.
>
> The survey of this line was started in the fall of 1934 and construction of the railroad was started May 1, 1935. The sub-grade was completed July 3, 1935, and the track was laid to the plant site July 15. The railroad construction was completed August 25. Due to lack of railroad facilities and very poor roads, preliminary work only was undertaken until the completion of the railroad. Construction work on the new plant started August 1, 1935, and the plant was put in operation April 1, 1936.
>
> There are several ore bodies adjacent to the plant site. One of these, the Black Hawk, was selected to be developed first. The elevation of the site is 6500 feet above sea level. The Black Hawk is an open pit operation. The pit was started at a point, 700 feet from the receiving hopper of the primary crusher.
>
> The ore is broken by drilling and blasting six-inch churn drill holes. Due to the rough character of the ore, a large amount of secondary blasting is required. The open pit face is 60 feet high by 160 feet long.
>
> The ore is loaded by a two and one-half yard electric shovel into two trucks, the capacity of each being 28 long tons. There is an 800-foot haul from the pit to the receiving hopper at the primary crusher.
>
> A pan feeder conveys the ore from the receiving hopper to a 60 × 48 inch jaw crusher. A 30-inch belt conveyor conveys the ore to a scalping screen which by-passes the finished product, the oversize passing through either a 20-inch reduction crusher or a 5-1/2 foot cone crusher.
>
> The product from this operation, which is all two inches and under in size, is conveyed by a 30-inch belt to a double deck finishing screen which produces three sizes as follows: First grade under 5/16-inch; second grade 5/16 to 1 inch; third grade 1 inch to 2 inches.
>
> The ore is loaded into railroad cars and shipped 230 miles to the blast furnace at Provo.
>
> Since the Columbia Steel Corporation opened the iron mines at Iron Springs in 1923 there have been continuous [mining] operations in the district.

The development of the iron industry in Utah had a great influence on the construction of the Cedar City branch of the Union Pacific Railroad. Since the construction of this line, the iron mines have been the largest source of revenue for the railroad. They have also been the largest consumers of power in the southern part of the state. The original plant at Iron Springs was built entirely of native lumber furnished by the local saw mills.[27]

In the latter part of 1937, two very insightful articles were published in the *Iron County Record* concerning Columbia's operations at Iron Mountain and the iron industry in Iron County in general. The first one, published in July, was authored once again, by E. S. O'Conner. Ironically, in his reciting of history, he failed to mention Utah Iron Ore Corporation's Desert Mound operation.

The second article was published in September 1937 and was written by Alex H. Rollo who was the editor and owner of the *Iron County Record* at that time.

Iron Pays Utah Bills
By E. S. O'Conner

The one metal whose mining in Utah was not only tolerated but heartily encouraged by the authorities of the Mormon Church in the early days was Iron. The alternative was a long and costly wagon haul from the east. Welcome, therefore, was the discovery that iron ore existed in abundance near the colony of Cedar in Iron County.

In 1851 half the men at Cedar were set apart to develop an iron industry. During 1852 a blast furnace was erected, coal was coked and on September 30, a stream of liquid iron was drawn from the furnace. In November, a company -- the Deseret Iron Company, took over the plant from the colony. Money was raised in Europe and, for seven years, the company continued to operate. Upon the building of a railroad to Utah in the '60s the cost of iron products was cut and the home industry became inactive. An effort to revive it on a cooperative basis was made by Ebenezer Hanks and the Great Western Iron Co. in 1868 at Old Iron Town. The company was absorbed in 1883 by the Iron Manufacturing Co. of Utah. A local market for iron castings is said to have been developed, but the projected railroad on which the company relied did not materialize.

The appropriation of iron land began in 1877 with the survey of a lode claim called the "Blowout." Locating claims was the feature of the iron business for several decades. Those most active in acquiring claims were Matthew Cullen, S. B. Milner and the Colorado Fuel & Iron Co. The ground once patented, a search for capital to develop and exploit it was in order. The clock of time pointed to 1923 before a successor to the Old Iron Town enterprise appeared. In that year the Columbia Steel Corporation went actively to work at Iron Springs using a tunnel and glory hole system. The following year shipments of ore to a blast furnace at Ironton were commenced.

Nineteen-thirty was an eventful period for the Utah iron industry. The United States Steel Corporation came west and purchased all the properties of the Columbia Steel. There was no lack of capital now. Operations were shifted to Iron Mountain, 12 miles southwest of Desert Mound, and a railroad to that point was planned. Surveying for a standard gauge line was started in the fall of 1934. Construction began May 1 1935 and was completed on August 25th.

Illustration 7.3. The start of the new Black Hawk open pit mine at Iron Mountain showing the electric mining shovel loading the haul truck. Many of the large boulders in the photo would have been too large to fit in the shovel bucket and would have required secondary blasting. Some were too large to fit in the truck, even if they could have been loaded. A blast-hole drill can be seen in the background. (Photo, The Magnet*)*

Preliminary work on a mining and crushing plant had been in progress for some time. On August 1, 1935, the building of the plant was actually begun and the following April it was completed....

The iron mines have been the largest source of revenue for the railroad and also the largest consumers of power in the southern part of the state. Their payrolls have always been substantial. From them have been derived most of the $90,000 of taxes paid annually by the railroad to Iron County. Payments by the railway, mines and power company to the county are well over $100,000.

Although it has not been feasible to smelt the ore in Iron County, it is done within the state, so that the coal mines, stone quarries and transportation companies contribute to the employment of labor and the tax revenue of the state, the counties and the municipalities. Farmers and local merchants are secondary beneficiaries of the wealth produced by the Iron industry.

It is a highly competitive industry. The Utah field must compete not only with domestic producers, but also with foreign interests fortified by cheap labor. To do so it needs the same support throughout the state that it receives from the people of Iron County.[28]

Illustration 7.4. Aerial photo of the Black Hawk operation, by itself at the Iron Mountain location when it was opened in 1936. However, that situation lasted only until the 1940s when CF&I contracted Utah Construction to open two pits and Columbia opened two more pits, all in the same general area. This photo, taken in July 1951, shows the Black Hawk pit at the center of the photo. CF&I's Blowout pit is on the right and the processing plants of Columbia and Utah Construction are at the left of the photo, one on the north side of the railroad tracks, the other on the south. The highest point on Iron Mountain, where the Tip Top claim was located, can be seen near the "Iron Mountain" label and arrow at the top of the photo. Nowadays, a number of antennas are located there. (Matheson Special Collections)

Columbia Mining Co. Operations Second Largest in Nation
By Alex H. Rollo

Very few people of Iron County, in fact in southwestern Utah, know or realize the extent of the iron mining that is being done at Iron Mountain, some 20 miles west of Cedar by the Columbia Mining Co. on the United States Steel Company property. Should they be interested enough to make a trip to the property, they would be surprised at the magnitude of the proposition. In the first place, any visitor would be astounded at the vast body of ore that has been opened up on the mountain, the face now opened, showing solid iron ore about 100 feet and a face depth of 90 feet or more, with ore showing back of this for two or three miles, while drill tests that have been made proves that below, the ore of same quality reaches a depth estimated at better than 2000 feet, and the bottom was not tapped by the drills.

But one of the most interesting things about this mammoth property is the mills and machinery installed for the handling of the ore, blasting, crushing and sorting into three grades.

In blasting the ore loose from the mountain, a series of holes are made back twenty feet from the face of the mineral and drilled to a depth of 100 feet at ten feet intervals, which are loaded heavily and fired by means of electricity. And when the blast has loosened a mass of some 40,000 to 50,000 tons of ore, it is ready for the steam [electric] shovel to load it into mammoth trucks of 20 tons capacity, and trucked to the mouth of the crusher, the second largest in the United States.

After going through the first crusher which reduces boulders of a ton weight to fragments of a few pounds, the ore then passes through a second crusher, being reduced to nugget size and carried by an endless belt conveyor to the sorting machines which separates the ore into three grades, and automatically loads it into railroad cars to be taken to Ironton near Provo smelting.

In order to keep all machinery in the best of condition, experienced men are employed in the machine shops which are equipped with the best and latest of machinery for the sharpening of the huge drills, which weigh two or three tons and are of a thickness of 4 to 5 inches.

Compressed air is used in the operation of all machinery, even to the discharging of the blasts for the breaking down of the wall of ore. It is also used to force water from a well whose depth is some 400 feet and blown to tanks on the surface for use of certain machines, and for the culinary use of the camp.

At the present time 75 men are able to blast loose, haul to the crushers and sorters, and load for shipment twelve cars per day, each car of a capacity of 50 tons or better. During the summer and up to a couple of weeks ago, these same men with a few additional, handled 18 cars per day.

Every car mined, crushed, sorted and shipped is assayed for content and quality of ore, and a careful record kept of each car. This department of the company is handled by men who have had years of experience and who are considered to be the best in the assaying field.

With the space at command it is impossible to give in detail all that is to be found at the Iron Mountain in the operation of the second largest iron ore mine on the American continent.[29]

G. D. MacDonald worked for United States Steel for many years and managed its operation at Iron Mountain for a period of time. He shines a different light on the startup of the mining operations at the Black Hawk deposit, from perhaps a closer perspective. These views are reflected in his writing of *The Magnet*.

During 1935 and early 1936 the railroad extension was completed to the south side of Iron Mountain about in the center of some of the largest ore deposits in the district. The U.S. Steel plant site was located just south of the North Quarter Corner of Section 2, T-37-S, R-14-W, S.L.B.&M. near a good ore deposit outcropping on the Black Hawk Mine claim, at an elevation of near 6,500 feet. As the crow flies this would be about twenty-three miles southwest of Cedar City and only three miles from where the earlier miners had built Old Iron town, also known to some as Iron City in the 1870s.

The new mine at Iron Mountain was equipped with the first in the area, electrically powered shovel, an electric powered churn drill equipped to drill 9" blast holes, and two special built Mack trucks rated for a 24-ton load. The trucks were easily and continually overloaded. There was a rash of broken frames and hoists. These were reinforced until the trucks were hauling thirty or more tons per load. This was a big load in 1936.

The shovel was the first piece of equipment to reach the mine by railroad. It served in road building, site preparation and as a crane in the erection of all the mine buildings. When the shovel started loading the iron ore the dipper teeth wore out in about a third the time expected; the dipper sticks kept breaking into two pieces; the electric motors and generators on the shovel were continually overloaded, overheated and shorted out; and the power cable, a large extension cord, was often pulled apart or cut by a tractor running over it. Both the operators and the manufacturers soon found a much more rugged piece of equipment was needed in an iron ore mine than was used in a gravel pit.

As soon as the first ore was processed through the crushing plant it was evident the equipment was not up to the job. The plant was a carbon copy of the plants used in the eastern limestone quarries where they did well in the soft stone. But the iron ore chunks soon wore through the steel chutes, bins and crusher wear plates. The rubber conveyor belts were cut to ribbons by sharp pieces of ore. The belts were too narrow and too slow to match the crushers and as a result spilled more ore over the sides than went up the belt. The screens were much, much too light. Broken frames and drive shafts were commonplace. All in all, the operators learned the 'HARD IRON' way but eventually worked out good specifications for equipment most adaptable to iron ore handling, often at a cost.

The Black Hawk ore was a hard, dense magnetite, higher in iron content than other available ore and was selected purposely to give the best possible material to the struggling blast furnace. As a result, furnace performance improved, and business increased.

Most of the pig iron was shipped to the Columbia Steel Company's steel producing plants on the West Coast. However, there was a small local market developing such as the Pacific States Cast Iron Pipe Company which was built next door to the Ironton blast furnace in 1926, and which plant has been making cast iron pipe from that day to this.

From 1936 to 1942 mining was concentrated in the Black Hawk ore body while the annual requirement at the furnace was gradually increasing from 175,000 tons per year to nearly 300,000 tons. By 1941, the mine was showing the effects of "high grading." The pit was too narrow; the required stripping had not been done; and the ore available was not high grade. There were barren rock contacts on the two outsides of the pit where there was a strata of low grade ore. The mining face might be 150 feet long, and the ore might vary from 60 % iron to less than 40 % in that length. Under such a condition, the mine attempts to mix highs and lows in order to affect a fairly uniform mix. This mix is seldom attained which adversely affects furnace production and approaches a near impossible situation until other sources of ore are made available. In these types of ore bodies, the mine should have two or more shovels operating in different ore bodies in order to more efficiently blend the different types of iron ore. If one takes only the best or high grades, before long the best will be low grade and be unacceptable.

The mining face in front of the shovel was from 50 to 60 feet in height, which was much too high to get good fragmentation in blasting. This resulted in large boulders the shovel couldn't handle, and which had to be drilled and blasted again. This slowed down the operation as well as creating safety hazards to both men and equipment.

The height of the mining face was gradually reduced to 35 feet and much better results were attained. More time was needed in stripping activities to remove the surface and side stripping material in the Black Hawk ore, but more especially, it seemed prudent to open up another mining area. It was obvious more shovel and truck capacity was needed which the parent company claimed could not be afforded at this time. It appeared this was to be the situation all during the life of the Columbia Iron Mining Company, which possibly was the smallest, most remote and the least significant subsidiary of the United States Steel Corporation with the corresponding priority.

Seemingly, the blast furnace had to get into difficulty from lack of good ore, which was there in the ground, but could not be reached due to lack of equipment. The furnace had to justify the expense before relief was forthcoming. Consequently, advance development work was usually a day late and two dollars short.[30]

The statement made in the above referenced material, that the mining shovel that went to work at the Black Hawk Pit in 1935 was the first electric shovel to be used in the area was not quite correct. A Marion, No. 37 electric shovel with a 1-3/4 cubic yard bucket was put into operation at Desert Mound in 1927 by the Utah Iron Ore Corporation.

The Black Hawk mine was the only source of iron ore for the Ironton plant for almost eight years. By 1944, when the Geneva Plant was built, barely three million tons had been mined out of the pit's total reserve potential of twenty million tons. It continued to be a workhorse, supplying ore to Ironton and Geneva plants, until 1957 when it was finally depleted of ore.

The Iron Mountain mining area on the south end of Iron Mountain contained more than 50 percent of the total iron ore reserves in the Pinto-Iron Springs Mining District. There were five large outcropping ore bodies at that site that were mined between 1935 and 1968 and five more even larger ore bodies that did not outcrop and were never mined. Almost 70 percent of the remaining ore reserves in the District are located at the Iron Mountain mining area.

General Interest

Karl Heyborne Has Miraculous Escape from Death [1940]

Karl Heyborne narrowly escaped serious injury or death Wednesday when he was caught in an avalanche of iron ore at the Columbia Steel Company's mine at Iron Mountain.

Heyborne was prying loose a ledge of ore when the slide started, dragging him down the hill with it. Tons of ore and rock gathered in the avalanche, and at times Heyborne's body was completely covered, according to workers who witnessed the accident. However, the victim escaped without serious injury. He was brought to the hospital in Cedar City where it was found that there were no broken bones and it was necessary to treat him only for cuts and bruises.

He was released from the hospital today.[31]

Mine Worker Looses Life in Drill Accident [1943]

Howard H. Leigh, 31, was killed instantly Monday afternoon at the Columbia Iron Mining Company mine west of Cedar City, when through some mishap he fell into a churn drill that was in operation. Although two other workmen were nearby, no one saw Howard fall and consequently it is not definitely known what actually caused the accident.

The unfortunate man evidently fell forward with his head striking the steel frame of the drill just as the huge rocker arm was swinging downward, crushing his head between the frame and the arm, causing instant death.

Leigh was working as a helper on the drill with Pat Williams as driller. Williams, busy with his work, had his back to the drill when the accident happened and Donald Duffin, another worker at the mine, who was climbing up the hillside toward the drill and who saw Leigh standing by the drill a few seconds before, had turned away a few seconds and during that interval the accident occurred.

A Coroner's jury, composed of Lee Forsyth, Sam Heyborne and Blaine Stapley, all workers at the mine, returned a verdict of death by accident. The inquest was held before Precinct Justice Alex H. Rollo, with County Attorney, Durham Morris, questioning the following witnesses: Roice Knight, G. W. Adams, Donald Duffin, L. G. McDonald, and Pat Williams.[32]

CHAPTER EIGHT

The Second World War Effort
1941–1946

WORLD WAR II WAS a global condition that lasted from 1939 to 1945, although there were related conflicts that began even earlier. It involved the vast majority of the world's countries—including all of the great powers—eventually forming two opposing military alliances, the Allies and the Axis. It was the most widespread war in history, and directly involved more than 100 million people from over thirty countries. In a state of total war, the major participants threw their entire economic, industrial, and scientific capabilities behind the war effort, erasing the distinction between civilian and military resources. Marked by mass deaths of civilians, it resulted in an estimated fifty million to eighty-five million fatalities. World War II was perhaps the single deadliest conflict in human history.

Japan aimed to dominate Asia and the Pacific and was already at war with the Republic of China in 1937. However, the Second World War is generally said to have begun on September 1, 1939 with the invasion of Poland by Nazi Germany and subsequent declarations of war on Germany by France and the United Kingdom. The war continued primarily between the European Axis powers and the coalition of the United Kingdom and the British Commonwealth. On June 22, 1941, the European Axis powers launched an invasion of the Soviet Union, opening the largest land theatre of war in history, which trapped the major part of the Axis military forces into a war of attrition. On December 7, 1941, Japan attacked the United States and European colonies in the Pacific Ocean, and quickly conquered much of the Western Pacific. This brought the United States into the war.[1]

The entry of the United States into the war brought changes to the mining industry and specifically to government regulation and oversight. Well before the bombing of Pearl Harbor in December, 1941,

> on August 22, 1940, Congress chartered the Defense Plant Corporation (DPC) in anticipation of war hostilities and assigned it the task of expanding production capabilities for military equipment. Its charter permitted both the building and equipping of new facilities and the expansion of existing structures.
>
> Previously, in 1932, Congress had established the RFC [Reconstruction Finance Corporation] as an independent government agency whose original purpose was to facilitate economic activity by lending during the Great Depression. The RFC would make and collect loans and buy and sell securities. At first it lent money only to financial, industrial, and agricultural institutions, but the scope of its operations widened greatly as a result of revised legislative amendments. These amendments

allowed for the making of loans to foreign governments, providing protection against war and disaster damages, and financing the construction and operation of war plants. Approximately two-thirds or $20 billion of RFC disbursements went toward U.S. national defense, especially during World War II.

The RFC financed much of American industrial expansion during World War II. Various government departments such as the War and Navy Departments, the Office of Production Management, the War Production Board, and the Maritime Commission would request what they needed from the RFC, and in turn the DPC would ensure that the plants (mostly new factories and mills) were constructed, equipped, and operated...

From its inception in 1940 through 1945, the DPC disbursed over $9 billion on 2,300 projects in 46 states and in foreign countries. In general, the government owned the plants and then leased them to private companies to operate. In spending these billions of dollars, the government acquired a dominant position in several industries including aircraft manufacture, nonferrous metals, machine tools, synthetic rubber, and shipping. The materials and supplies produced during the war ranged from bearings to giant guns, tanks, ships, and airplanes. About half of the spending of funds went directly or indirectly for aviation. One of the DPC's largest projects involved a $176 million Dodge-Chicago plant that manufactured aircraft engines for the B-29 and B-32 airplanes. The plant's 19 one-story buildings stretched over 1,545 acres of floor space. It was so large that it had its own steel forge and aluminum foundry and could take in raw materials at one end and turn out finished engines at the other. Congress dissolved the DPC on July 1, 1945.[2]

The DPC also became heavily involved in the iron and steel industry. Its primary focus was building military war ships in California. The Kaiser plant in California and the Geneva Plant in Utah benefitted from the DPC by either expansion or building from scratch. The Geneva Plant was one of the DPC's largest projects with a final cost of close to $200,000,000.

Early in 1941, even with Ironton sending most of its output to California, pig iron was in short supply on the West Coast and adequate supplies were unavailable even for defense projects. On April 22, 1941, a meeting was held at the White House, attended by Henry Kaiser of California and Utah Senator, Abe Murdock. A plea was made to President Roosevelt for the government to help build additional pig iron capacity in Utah utilizing Utah iron ore and expanding the steel-making and ship-building plants in California.

W. A. Hauck, consultant on steel, was sent by the federal Office of Production Management to Utah, Washington and California, to survey steel production facilities in the three states and "to develop any further measures that may be found necessary and appropriate to facilitate and expedite steel deliveries on the Pacific coast."[3]

The Smelters

In May 1941, more than six months before the attack on Pearl Harbor, a news article was published in the *Iron County Record* about a new pig iron plant being proposed in Utah. The Cedar City Chamber of Commerce began working diligently to convince federal government and State officials that Iron County was the logical place for the plant to be located. This was something that residents had wanted for years, almost from the time that iron was discovered in the County. Several conferences were held with

Illustration 8.1. The Ironton Plant. (Library of Congress Prints and Photographs Division)

Herbert B. Maw, then Governor of Utah, and it was felt that Iron County stood a good chance of receiving serious consideration. The Governor seemed to favor the idea and suggested that they send to the government agent who was investigating sites for the plant, all the available data on water, ore, freight rates, power, and other items which must be taken into consideration for such a project. Obviously, Iron County did not get the nod for the new plant, but it eventually did supply most of the iron ore.[4]

Early in 1942, to further bolster the nation's war effort and in anticipation of a shortage of scrap and pig iron in the Pacific Coast area, the federal government (DPC) requested Columbia Steel Company to dismantle an idle blast furnace at Joliet, Illinois and re-erect the unit at Ironton, Utah. The DPC bought the used furnace and paid for its removal and transport from Joliet. The furnace was enlarged and modernized as part of the move. Ironton's first blast furnace was rated at 600 tons per day; the second furnace was rated at approximately 1100 tons per day, so the addition almost tripled the capacity of the Ironton plant, especially after upgrades were made. A 50 percent increase in the number of local people employed at Ironton resulted from the added blast furnace.[5]

When the second blast furnace was on its way to Utah, Columbia Steel made additions and improvements to its steel plants in Pittsburg and Torrance, California. These changes enabled the plants to process more iron and therefore to process the additional product from the Ironton plant. Officials said financing of the Coast plants was to be with corporation funds, but that the new Geneva plant and the Ironton furnace costs were to be paid by the government.[6]

The second Ironton blast furnace, in addition to requiring iron ore, also needed a supply of coke, so 500 beehive coke ovens were installed at Columbia, Utah in Carbon County. The ovens were constructed at an estimated cost of $1,000,000 and were built for and at the expense of the federal government. Each coke oven could convert six tons of coal into three tons of coke per charge. Unlike the coke ovens operating at the Ironton plant at the time, which captured chemical byproducts such as ammonium sulfate, tar, benzol and natural gas, the beehive coke ovens did not salvage any byproducts.[7]

On May 11, 1943, E. N. Barber, vice president of the Columbia Steel Company, Defense Plant Division, announced that Columbia had completed the required construction on the Joliet blast furnace and the Beehive Coke Oven Plant and that the plant was being held in readiness for operation, pending advice from the government that its pig iron was needed by the West Coast steel plants.[8]

> August 1943. The Ironton No. 2 furnace was blown in on July 1, 1943 and is now producing pig. This is the second furnace to be blown in the far West in the previous six months (the other was Kaiser), for a total of three furnaces in the West. Ironton No. 2 is rated at 900 tons daily. The Ironton No. 1, rated at 600 tons, was until 1942 the only blast furnace in the far West. Approximately 75 percent of the pig is shipped to coast plants of Columbia steel in Pittsburg and Los Angeles, with some foundry grade being marketed (locally).[9]

By the time the second Ironton blast furnace and 500 coke ovens were operational, the war was halfway over. Therefore, both the beehive coke ovens and the blast furnace were in operation for only two years. It was reported that the construction of the beehive coke ovens at Columbia, Utah cost $3 million and the relocation and installation of the blast furnace cost $9 million.[10]

In addition to the second Ironton furnace that was to be added, the federal government determined that another, much larger steel plant was needed in Utah for the war effort. In the six months from May to November, 1941, the development scope evolved from a modest Ironton plant expansion costing $20,000,000, to a full-blown steel plant costing close to $200,000,000.

The DPC program in Utah called for the immediate construction of a three-furnace pig iron plant with a capacity of 750,000 tons annually. The Geneva Steel mill was constructed with federal funds from November 1941 to December 1944 by Columbia Steel Company, a subsidiary of United States Steel Corporation. Its location in Utah was chosen because iron ore, coal, limestone, and other resources necessary for primary steel making were located in nearby areas. A second important reason for choosing the Utah location was that Utah Valley was far inland, away from potential future attack by the Japanese on the West Coast. The location also served as a precaution against the closing of the Panama Canal.

Illustration 8.2. Footings in the Geneva Steel plant construction. (Library of Congress Prints and Photographs Division)

The Geneva Steel Plant was located in Vineyard, Utah and began operations in December 1944. Its unique name came from a resort that once operated nearby on the shore of Utah Lake. Iron ore for the plant was supplied from the same Columbia Iron Mining Company mines in Southern Utah that had been supplying the Ironton Plant. Coal for coking was mined near Columbia, Utah in Carbon County.

On March 9, 1942, officials of the DPC began buying the land at Vineyard, Utah for the Geneva works. The farmers were paid approximately $500,000 for the 1500 acres of land including water rights, which averaged a bit more than $300 per acre. Condemnation proceedings were not necessary. The Utah Construction Company of Ogden, the Morrison-Knudsen Company of Boise and the J. H. Pomeroy Company of San Francisco were contracted to do the earthwork, which was scheduled to start on April 4. Farmers were encouraged to remove anything of value from the land before that date,

Second World War Effort

Illustration 8.3. Geneva construction in 1942, partly finished open-hearth furnaces and stacks. (Library of Congress Prints and Photographs Division)

including houses, barns etc., since the government bought only the land, not the improvements. No formal groundbreaking ceremonies were scheduled since all efforts were directed toward a speedy construction. The plant was planned to take two years to complete, cost $126,000,000 and include three blast furnaces, a coke byproduct plant, nine open-hearth furnaces, a slabbing mill and a steel plate mill.

It was projected that 6,000 workers would be employed during construction with about 4,500 needed to run the plant once it was completed. The plant would use mostly Utah labor and would train local personnel for technical jobs.[11]

The building and operating of the Geneva plant was a massive undertaking. The May 28, 1943 edition of the *Salt Lake Telegram* reported that nearly 9,000 men were employed at the Geneva plant and that at the peak of construction, which would be reached in August, between 10,000 and 11,000 men would be employed. Once completed, 4,500 men would be required to operate the plant. That did not include the hundreds of people that would be employed by the coal and iron mines, the limestone quarry and the railroads.[12]

The following newspaper article published in the *Salt Lake Telegram* on June 2, 1943, gave details about the construction of the Geneva plant.

Illustration 8.4. Aerial photo of the Geneva plant. (Used by permission, Utah State Historical Society)

Completion of Geneva Works Predicted by End of Year

Provo – The huge Geneva steel works now being built for the government, near Provo, is rapidly becoming a "bastion of steel," Columbia Steel company officials said Wednesday.

Although completion of the project has been materially retarded by inability to obtain priorities of sufficiently high rank to secure contemplated early deliveries of essential items of equipment, the huge works should be ready for operation by the end of this year, they said.

The plant will be by far the largest integrated steel mill west of the Mississippi, a plant of the most modern design, costing over $150,000,000. It is being erected by Columbia Steel Company, U.S. Steel subsidiary, for the Defense Plant Corporation, a governmental agency. The plant was ordered by the government to provide steel for war shipbuilding needs of the Pacific coast.

Units Ahead of Schedule

While a number of the units comprised in this gigantic plant are ahead of schedule, other phases of construction are behind the original schedule, due primarily to difficulty in obtaining equipment when desired because of stringent priority regulations and the need for similar articles in other government war projects.

This priority situation has been improved recently through the efforts of the war production board. Another factor which has slowed work at Geneva to some extent has been a shortage of labor. Unless further delays, not now foreseen are encountered, the Geneva plant should be completed ready for operation by the end of this year.

In spite of these obstacles, the tremendous size of the Geneva mill with its lofty smokestacks, towering blast furnaces and other structures protruding from the landscape over some 1600 acres, is apparent now that many thousands of tons of structural steel have been erected to form the numerous buildings.

Operation in August

The Geneva plant will have four batteries of by-product coke ovens, each battery containing 63 ovens. These batteries now are at least 70 percent completed. The first of the three blast furnaces at Geneva, each having an approximate capacity of 1200 tons of pig iron daily, is approaching completion and should be ready for operation, if desired, in August.

One building, the continuous plate mill, indicates the immensity of the project. This mill, now under construction, resembles a fortress of steel sentinels -- actually row upon row of hundreds of steel columns stretching across the terrain for more than two-thirds of a mile. When the mill is completed it will be one continuous building 3750 feet long.

Other indications of the size of Geneva can be gained from the fact that some 70 miles of conduit pipe are becoming part of the slabbing and rolling mills. There will be several steel girders in one of the steel furnace buildings which weigh well over 100 tons each. So large are they that over 6000 rivets were used to secure reinforcing plates to them. Huge cranes will ride these girders carrying tons of molten steel from the nine open-hearth furnaces, each with a steel capacity of 225 tons daily.

Concrete Substituted

Shortage of materials has made necessary the use of great quantities of concrete in place of steel. Four hundred thousand cubic yards of concrete have already been poured into the various structures. Before the project is completed this figure will approximate 500,000 cubic yard yards. From one vantage point on the plant site can be seen elevated conveyor ways, coal and ore storage bins and stacks all made of concrete, although ordinarily of steel, thus resulting in a conservation of from 25 to 30 percent of this vital material.

Also winding around the site are miles and miles of railroad tracks which will service the mill facilities. When completed, 65 miles of railroad tracks will have been laid within the plant site. In short, Geneva works, upon completion, will rank among the largest of manufacturing plants west of the Rocky Mountains.[13]

In August 1943, the United States Steel Corporation announced that arrangements had been completed with the Defense Plant Corporation for the operation of the Geneva plant during the war. The plant would be operated for the account of the DPC by the Geneva Steel Company, a newly organized subsidiary of United States Steel Corporation. Under the agreement, no operating fee was to be paid to Geneva Steel Company for their services in directing the wartime operation of the plant. All costs incidental to its management and operation were to be paid by the DPC, and all proceeds on the sale of its products were for the account of the DPC.

No construction fee was paid to U.S. Steel or to any of its subsidiaries for designing and directing the construction of Geneva Works. It only received reimbursements for its out-of-pocket expenses. U.S. Steel made available to the government, without charge, its vast experience and knowledge in the engineering and construction of steel mills of this character. The completed cost was estimated to be $180,000,000, an increase from the June estimate of $150,000,000.[14]

The first blast furnace at the government's new steel plant at Geneva was "blown in" and went into operation on January 3, 1944. The first iron was tapped within 40 hours after the furnace fire was ignited. The project took almost two years to complete. The blast furnace embodied the most modern features of design and was one of three which were erected at Western America's largest integrated steel mill.

Iron ore was shipped to Geneva from Columbia Iron Mining Company's open pit iron mine at Iron Mountain, near Cedar City, Utah. An automatic conveyor-stacker was used to bed down the ore at the plant in neat, elongated piles to assure a uniform iron content when it was fed into the blast furnaces. Coke was produced in the coke byproducts ovens at Geneva, which began operations December 14, using coal from the newly developed Geneva mine in Southeastern Utah. Limestone and dolomite, the other raw materials used in the smelting of iron ore, were obtained from Keigley quarry, a part of the Geneva project located 25 miles from the plant.[15]

On August 7, 1945, the United Nations announced the end of the war in the Pacific, brought about by Japan's unconditional surrender. Emperor Hirohito told his people that Japan had accepted unconditional surrender per the Potsdam Declaration and ordered all Japanese armed forces to lay down their arms. President Truman declared a two-day holiday for federal employees and announced the end of all manpower commission controls and said that 7,000,000 men in the armed forces would be released in 12 months.[16]

Geneva stopped production after only twenty-one months of operation on V-Day, September 3, 1945, which signaled the official end of the war. Everyone was relieved that the war was over, but some four thousand employees connected with the United States Steel Corporation's operations in Utah wondered what their fate would be. The fact that the war had ended so abruptly seems to have caught many off guard. This apparently was the case with the government as well as the DPC.

On October 8, 1945, Geneva Steel officials said that the Geneva plant would continue to operate until sale or lease arrangements could be made. They said that there had been no indication that the RFC would terminate its operating contract with Geneva Steel in the immediate future. They explained that the termination date was fixed for 90 days after the ending of the war, which would be on November 12, but the contract did provide for extension if the RFC asked for it.[17]

Two days later, on October 10, 1945, the story was a bit different. The director of the Reconstruction Finance Corporation sent a wire to the president of Geneva Steel Company stating that they were to discontinue steel production and to terminate rolling mill operations upon completion of the present plate mill order schedule, no later than November 12, 1945. Thereafter, only maintenance operations and production of limited pig iron quantities were permitted. However, the continued operation of one blast furnace and one battery of coke ovens using coke oven gas to keep the remaining three batteries of coke ovens hot was permitted. In addition, the power plant, the coal mines and the Keigley quarry were allowed to continue operations.[18]

As one would expect, this order was not well received by anyone in the area, whether connected with the plant or outside looking in. The newly constructed Geneva plant had been an enormous boon to the area and thousands were employed by the plant and the industries associated with it. The following article published in the *Salt Lake Telegram* on October 11, 1945, just one day after the announcement, expressed some of the frustration felt by much of the population.

Geneva to Quit Producing Steel

The expected order to discontinue steel production and rolling mill operations at the Geneva steel plant has come. As soon as the present plate mill schedule is completed, and no later than November 12, all operations at Geneva other than maintenance and limited pig iron production will be discontinued. Under the order to Walther Mathesius, president of the Geneva Steel company from Sam H. Husbands of the Reconstruction Finance Corporation, only one battery of coke ovens and one blast furnace will be continued in operation. Operations at the Geneva coal mine will be continued, with any excess production disposed of under the direction of the solid fuels administration. The power plant will continue in operation, with disposal of any surplus power to the Utah Power and Light Company. Pig Iron from the one blast furnace will be produced and sold or stockpiled.

This will place Geneva on an operational basis similar to that of the Columbia Steel plant at Ironton. Such a basis of operation, of course, means nothing to Utah other than a small amount of employment. Geneva could not profitably operate on such a basis and it would have no value as the foundation of industrial development in Utah or the west.

What happens to Geneva from now on is anybody's guess. The maneuverings and crackpot statements of politicians and long-haired administration bureaucratic theorists have placed Geneva in a position where it has at the present time, no future. There is no firm offer from any one for its future operation, under lease or purchase. Government red tape, procrastination and throwing of monkey wrenches has brought Geneva to its present pass -- and there does not honestly seem any reason for hope that those who have failed so miserably to keep Geneva going, can be looked to for the miracle of its resurrection.[19]

On December 14, 1945, the RFC announced that it would receive sealed bids for the sale or lease of the Geneva plant until March 1, 1946. The bids were to include the steel plant, the coal mines, the iron ore mines and the limestone quarry. The total cost of the plant was said to be $190,000,000. The RFC said bids could be on a cash or credit basis and that purchase terms would include a down payment and a waiver of interest up to two years. Final maturity for the purchase would not exceed eighteen years.

It seemed that three major players were in a position to buy the Geneva facility: U.S. Steel, Colorado Fuel & Iron and Kaiser Steel. However, all three had vacillated in their desire and commitment to submit a bid for the property. U.S. Steel announced that it was not going to bid at all and Kaiser was negotiating with the RFC over the value of its Fontana California plant.[20]

On January 24, 1946, the President of the United States himself, Harry S. Truman, disclosed that the federal government could become the operator of the Geneva steel plant. This announcement in the middle of the bidding process threw a bit of a wrench into the works. The President explained that Geneva was the only government-owned steel mill that was not integrated into some other privately-operated plant. The entire facility was basically 100 percent owned by the federal government. He said that consideration was being given to federal operation of the government-built Utah plant. Apparently, this proposal was never acted upon, but it showed the high level of visibility that the idled Utah plant had.[21]

On February 2, 1946, in a seemingly unconnected news article in the *Salt Lake Telegram*, the War Assets Corporation announced that Geneva had been able to achieve a 25 percent reduction in gross coke consumption per ton of iron ore during December 1945. The agency stated that "this is the performance, for which Geneva has been striving for the past two years, had this record been attained from the beginning of operations, it alone would have reduced the cost of hot metal approximately $3 a ton." It was explained that the saving was accomplished by an improvement in the coke making, through "a slight increase in oven temperature, a reduction of coking time, and more selectivity in coal charges to the ovens."[22]

On March 1, 1946, the government extended the due date for the sealed bids for the Geneva plant to be opened, from April 1, 1946 to May 1, 1946. Apparently, some of the potential bidders had complained to the government that they did not have adequate time to assemble their bids. W. A. Hauck, chief of the iron-steel division of the War Assets Corp., agreed and said: "Bidding on the plant is a difficult job. Reconversion costs, prices, freight rates and many other operating factors must be figured closely." He also indicated that Colorado Fuel & Iron, which submitted a five-year-lease bid some months ago, would make another offer, but had no information about U.S. Steel or Kaiser Steel's plans.[23]

On May 1, 1946, tendered bids for the Geneva plant were received and opened by the War Assets Administration. The proceedings were observed by Governor Herbert B. Maw of Utah, Senator Murdock (D., Utah), Representative Robinson (D., Utah) and Gus Backman, secretary of the Salt Lake Chamber of Commerce. The bids were as follows:

1. Kaiser Corporation of Oakland, California. The proposal turned out not to be a bid but rather a communication from Henry J. Kaiser requesting an adjustment of RFC finance charges on his steel plant at Fontana, California, to allow it to compete on a fair basis with Geneva.
2. Judson S. Warshaw, industrial consultant, offered to buy the plant at two-thirds of its value, making twenty payments without interest, with an alternate plan of leasing the plant and operating it with the RFC as a partner.
3. United States Steel offered to purchase the plant and its inventories for $47,500,000 and spend $18,600,000 on new facilities. It specified that full payment would not be made for two years, the estimated time for making improvements. It proposed to build a $25,000,000 sheet and tin plate mill at Pittsburg, California and to use the Geneva plant solely to provide semi-finished material for the Pittsburg plant. It said Geneva employment would be about 5000.
4. Colorado Fuel & Iron said that it would rent the plant from the government for fifteen years with the government to make $47,000,000 of improvements. It would retain an option to purchase at a minimum of $80,000,000 with the final price to be based on Geneva's established value.

5. The Riley Steel Company proposed to buy the plant for $222,607,840, payable in eighteen annual installments. The company said it planned to produce 750,000 tons of steel products annually and would require an RFC loan of $28,844,000.
6. Pacific American Steel offered 20 percent of the $202,000,000 cost, payable in forty annual installments and would require a $25,000,000 RFC loan. As an alternative, it proposed to operate Geneva cooperatively with the government, sharing the profits.
7. Assets Reconstruction Corporation offered to buy the plant for $38,750,000, payable on execution of a contract and proposed to spend $37,500,000 on improvements.
8. Blue Star Enterprises submitted a proposal by telegram to buy the plant at $302,000,000, payable in twenty annual installments. Blue Star was a very small mining firm and when contacted, one officer of the company stated that he knew nothing of the bid, another officer said that they were fronting for an Eastern outfit.

At the time, the Geneva plant was regarded as the most modern in the country, perhaps in the world. However, it was built specifically for the production of plate and structural steel. Its peacetime production would be tin plate, seamless tubing, strip and sheet steel. It was estimated that converting the plant would cost from $41,000,000 to $73,000,000. The peacetime value of the plant was figured as low as $38,000,000. The plant made and sold $50,000,000 worth of products during the war, on which the government made a $10,000,000 gross profit.[24]

After the bids were opened on May 1, it took twenty-three days for the War Assets Administration to evaluate the seven bids and choose the future buyer of the Geneva plant. U.S. Steel, the company that constructed and operated the plant during the war, was selected. It is difficult to analyze the government's process for coming to that conclusion without having all the details; however, the size of the company and its track record for being able to operate a giant complex like the Geneva facility were clearly important considerations. Additionally, several of the bidders requested large loans from the government as part of the purchase which apparently was not considered ideal by the selection committee.

On May 23, 1946, the War Assets Administration approved the sale of the Geneva steel plant to the United States Steel Corporation for its bid price of $47,500,000. The agency's action had to be approved by the Justice Department. As a matter of information, it was stated that the Geneva plant was constructed to produce 1,283,400 tons of ingots, 700,000 tons of plates and 250,000 tons of structural shapes annually, all for ship construction.[25]

On the day that U.S. Steel was announced as the winning bidder, Colorado Fuel & Iron officials held a press conference in Denver, Colorado, to gain the support of the Colorado press and government officials, to be able to make a second bid on the Geneva plant. Apparently, CF&I felt that it didn't completely understand the type of bid that the War Assets Administration wanted, and it desired to make a second bid that would be more comparable to the U.S. Steel bid. The situation quickly devolved into a war of words between Colorado and Utah on several levels; company officials, governors, chamber of commerce representatives and even political party chairmen entered the fray.

The following article, published in the *Salt Lake Telegram* on May 23, 1946, detailed the controversy raised by CF&I and the subsequent response by Utah's leaders.

Utah Leaders Open Fire on CF&I Plan

Utah leaders came out in open and official opposition to the Colorado Fuel & Iron Corp. Thursday, following reports that CF&I may try to reopen the Geneva steel plant bidding since the War Assets Administration approved a bid other than that submitted by the Colorado concern.

Acting Gov. E. E. Monson wired Atty. Gen. Tom Clark, warning against a "threat to further delay" the bid considerations through a "propaganda campaign" by Colorado Fuel and urging that the matter not be allowed to deteriorate "into a fight between the people of Colorado and Utah."

In Denver Wednesday, J. D. Sullivan, CF&I president, was quoted as saying, "We will do everything possible to have our bid accepted even if we lose this first round." Colorado's Gov. John Vivian applauded the Colorado offer and said "I heartily indorse this program."

Acting Gov. Monson's retaliation, copies of which were sent to Utah's congressional delegation, read in full:

"Understand propaganda campaign by Colorado Fuel & Iron is being undertaken. In my opinion best interests of the state of Utah and United States government will be served in accepting bid which will relieve government of necessity of further interest in plant. Best assurance of operation of plant, which is real concern to us, will come in our opinion from organizations willing to provide their own finances for purchase, expansion and operation.

"Threat to further delay consideration of bids we believe will probably lose United States Steel bid and imperil possibility of Geneva plant ever operating. We further believe that matter should be considered on the merit of bids only and not deteriorate into fight between people of Colorado and Utah but should be viewed on basis of the best interests of entire west."

Backman Agrees

Gus P. Backman, executive secretary of the Salt Lake City chamber of commerce, said that as a representative of the group interested in the sale and operation of Geneva he was "100% in accord with the statements of the acting governor."

"We believe the situation is becoming critical and are hopeful that an early decision will be reached," he added.

Roscoe Boden, state Democratic chairman, also took a slap at Eugene Cervi, Colorado Democratic chairman, who has expressed an opinion that U.S. Steel acquisition of Geneva would be "monopolistic."

Hits Colorado Rule

"Colorado has been trying to regulate Utah's life too long," said Mr. Boden. "Utah has to all but gain clearance through Denver to get to Washington. U.S. Steel is not a monopoly and I hope they get the bid. They can do the most for Geneva and that is what we want. When you want a doctor, you want the best you can get and the same thing goes when we want someone to run Geneva."

The controversy began Wednesday in a Denver press conference which CF&I officials held to gain the support of the Colorado press in the Geneva bidding.

Uphold Bid

Mr. Sullivan and A.M. Riddle, CF&I director of market research, upheld their bid as best and most beneficial to the government. The offer would entail a 15 to 25 year lease at $2 per ton rental on a "conservatively" estimated total production of 800,000 tons annually. However, the company would have an option on buying the

$200,000,000 plant for not less than $80,000,000 after the government has invested another $48,000,000 conversion loan.

The officials told the Colorado newsmen 2500 to 3000 workers would be on the payroll from the start turning out sheet and structural steel and another 1000 to 1500 would be engaged in construction work during the two-year conversion program.[26]

On May 27, 1946, the bid for the government-owned Geneva steel plant was debated by the House in Washington D.C., Colorado Representative Chenoweth declared that the plant should be sold to CF&I "to preserve the economy of the western states" and that the award of the plant to the U.S. Steel Corporation "violated the spirit, if not the letter" of the surplus property act. He demanded that CF&I be allowed to make a second bid. Representative Granger of Utah chimed in that the date of the sale was changed twice, giving all parties ample opportunity to submit bids. Senator Murdock of Utah stated that the award of Geneva to U.S. Steel "speaks well for the soundness of the board's decision."[27]

It appears that the second bid that CF&I wanted to make was never made, or if it was made, that it was not considered by the War Assets Administration or by Washington, where it was debated.

On June 17, 1946, United States Steel officials received the ruling made by United States Attorney General, Tom C. Clark, on their offer to buy, for $47,500,000, the government's $200,000,000 steel plant at Geneva, Utah. Attorney General Clark stated that he did not view the sale of Geneva, the government's largest single surplus industrial establishment, to United States Steel Corporation as a violation of the antitrust law. His statement virtually assured the sale of the plant. The only thing required after that, was the execution of a sales contract and payment of a check for $5,000,000.[28]

On June 21, 1946, U.S. Steel commented on Attorney General Clark's approval. The company stated that the agreement reached on Thursday gave it technical ownership of the plant until the formal contract was signed and that it would be retroactive to June 19. It said that Geneva would increase its payroll "immediately" with the production of unconverted types of pig iron and steel and that existing facilities would be put to work as soon as possible in producing pig iron, plates, structural slabs, billets and semi-finished steel. He further stated that final conversion plans would be made, and additional workers would be hired to prepare buildings and foundations for new equipment.

WAA and steel company attorneys began working on the formal contract and when it was signed, that the down payment would be handed over to the government and the Geneva Steel Company would become extinct and be replaced by Columbia Steel Company.[29] Apparently, the name change was not made and the Geneva Steel Company name continued, as a subsidiary of the United States Steel Corporation.

On June 28, 1946, C. L. Waggoner, the recently appointed general superintendent of the Geneva plant, made several comments concerning the plant's production. He said that there was considerable demand for steel plate and should Geneva get a portion of it, that would mean production at full capacity for some months. He said that the plate mills' full-rate capacity was 700,000 tons per year and that under present plans, the Geneva steel plant would have two blast furnaces, two batteries of coke ovens, three open-hearths and the slab and plate mill in operation within the next six weeks.[30]

The Geneva Steel mill was designed to take raw materials in one end, and send shaped steel out the other. The plant had the ability to convert raw coal into coke on site and collect and process the by-products of the conversion into saleable products

Iron Mining & Manufacturing

Illustration 8.5. Kaiser Steel Plant at Fontana, California. (Photo courtesy Fontana Historical Society)

such as fertilizer. It had three large blast furnaces that converted the raw iron ore into pig iron. The pig iron was converted into steel by nine open-hearth furnaces. During the war, the plant was structured to produce steel for shipbuilding but after the war, its steel finishing facilities were converted to make peacetime products such as plate, pipe, and various structural shapes. The Geneva plant was the largest plant west of the Mississippi River and by 1993, the only one. It was said that at its peak the mill produced 60 percent of the steel used in the Western United States.[31]

An average of 4600 employees worked at Geneva and brought into the County an annual payroll of more than 70 million dollars.[32] During its operation, besides providing thousands of jobs for its own employees, Geneva Steel attracted many ancillary businesses to the area and provided jobs for those who worked at the mines, the railroad and power companies, along with numerous other service providers throughout Utah and the neighboring states.

The rapid western expansion of the early railroads resulted in the organization of the Colorado Coal & Iron Co., located in Minnequa, Colorado, near Pueblo. On September 7, 1881, the first pig iron was cast at the Pueblo plant and the Colorado Fuel & Iron Corporation became the first large scale iron producer west of the Mississippi river. In 1889, CF&I came into southwestern Utah seeking iron ore to assure plant operation for far into the future. They purchased mining claims all over the District, the most important of which were two large deposits at Iron Mountain. Much to the chagrin of the locals, the ore deposits remained dormant for some 40 years.

That changed in 1942, when CF&I urgently needed more iron ore to supply their Colorado steel plant located a long rail haul away. The combination of the demands of

World War II and the fact that their sources of iron ore in Colorado and Wyoming were being depleted, brought them to their reserves in Southern Utah.

The Kaiser Steel plant was located in Fontana, California, just west of San Bernardino. It was operated by the Kaiser Steel Co. and during the war, sold most of its steel to the west coast shipbuilders. The plant was located 50 miles inland, a condition imposed by the DPC and the U.S. Army to make it more secure from a potential attack by Japanese bombers. It became known as Henry Kaiser's "Inland Empire." However, after the war ended, its location became more of a liability than an asset. The inland location increased the cost of many of the incoming raw materials and the outgoing items produced by the plant, by requiring "double handling," having to be hauled both by rail and by ocean-going ships. The Kaiser plant used Utah coal from a Kaiser-operated mine at Sunnyside, Utah, near Price.[33]

The following news article published in the *Salt Lake Telegram* on December 30, 1942 tracked the plant from the beginning of construction in April 1942 to the first pig iron produced a mere eight months later in December.

'Pig Farm to Pig Iron in 8 Months' Tells Story of Kaiser Mill

FONTANA, Cal., Dec 30 (AP) From pig farm to pig iron in eight months.

That's the story of "Miracle Man" Henry J. Kaiser's iron and steel mill here—the first integrated steel plant west of the Rocky Mountains—where a huge blast furnace was scheduled to be "blown in" during ceremonies Wednesday.

The program called for Mrs. Kaiser to throw a switch igniting coke within the huge milk bottle-shaped furnace, named in her honor. "The Bess," which stands on land that was a hog farm when ground was broken last April.

Iron for Ship Plates

"Within 30 to 36 hours after Mrs. Kaiser ignites the furnace," said a company announcement, "the first molten pig iron will be drawn off, and within a year more than 400,000 tons of pig iron will have been produced, to be made into great ship plates, structural steel and alloy steels." The public was invited to the "blowing in" ceremonies, in which Kaiser was to be principal speaker.

The "blowing in" moved further toward completion the famed shipbuilder's project in steelmaking, undertaken nine months ago when the Reconstruction Finance Corporation authorized a loan now totaling $83,000,000.

Two huge batteries of coke ovens, completed by an army of bricklayers in a little over six months, are producing thousands of pounds of coke a week. Into each of more than 80 ovens goes 15 tons of coal supplied by a Kaiser-operated mine at Sunnyside, Utah. When carbonized, the coke is placed in the 100-foot blast furnace.

Elements Fused

There, at 2700 degrees, coke, limestone, iron ore and air are fused by a hurricane blast into molten pig iron and slag.

The "pigs" will be taken to six open-hearth furnaces in a building expected to be ready for operation soon. There, commercial scrap iron, manganese, dolomite and clays containing aluminum will be added and the mixture heated to 3500 degrees to produce steel. The steel ingots will be conveyed to the rolling mill, also nearing completion, and flattened like baker's dough into great plates.[34]

Apparently, when Kaiser completed the construction of its new blast furnace and associated facilities in Fontana, California, in record time on December 30, 1942, it was believed that it was going to be able to supply all the necessary iron ore for the plant from its own mines. However, in 1945, Utah Construction Company was called upon to mine and ship iron ore from Southern Utah to the Kaiser plant to supplement the ore that was mined from its own mines.[35]

The Railroads

After the announcement of the extra tons to be mined and shipped by Columbia from Iron Mountain, the Union Pacific Railroad found that there were several improvements to its rail lines that would be required as a result of the increased ore shipments to the new Geneva plant. By September 1942, two surveying crews were in the field making surveys for the railroad and highway development. The rail lines leading to the mines would need to be able to handle 200 carloads a day instead of the twenty-seven cars a day that were being shipped at the time.[36]

In addition to the improvements made to the rail line to the Columbia mine at Iron Mountain, a new rail spur was built next to the Columbia line to access the processing plant and load-out tipple that was being constructed by Utah Construction for CF&I's new Iron Mountain mine utilizing the Duncan and Blowout pits.

A new spur was also built at Iron Springs to accommodate Utah Construction's new load-out facility, which needed to ship ore to the Kaiser Steel smelter at Fontana, California. The spur was 2,500 feet long and connected the operations with the Union Pacific branch line from Cedar City to Lund. The new facility was located immediately west of the branch line.[37]

The Mines

In July 1942, in anticipation of the completion of the Geneva Plant and the increased activity at the mines at Iron Mountain, Army engineers visited Cedar City to study the need for the construction of a road from Cedar City to the iron mine, under the Army's Accessibility Road program. Surveys were being made by the State Road Department. The project received favorable consideration by all government officials. The road, if built, would be to Federal Standards, would be oiled and would reach from the Lund highway at the Union Pacific Stock Yards west of Cedar City to the mine, a distance of approximately eighteen miles.[38]

In September the State Road Commission announced that it was going to spend at least $185,000 on the road between Cedar City and the mine at Iron Mountain to bring it up to federal standards.[39]

During World War II, the nation's need for strategic materials increased substantially. This brought on a great deal of exploration work that no one in the past was willing or able to commit financially. The work, which was Government financed, covered a variety of investigation techniques conducted in the field.

Between 1942 and 1945, the Bureau of Mines, in conjunction with the United States Geological Survey, conducted a program under the strategic minerals program. However, the Bureau of Mines did not publish the results of the work until 1947. The exploratory work comprised geological and topographic mapping, geophysical prospecting with a magnetometer, diamond drilling, trenching and test pitting, sampling ore exposures and old workings, and constructing and repairing roads. The document was assembled and edited by Mr. W. E. Young and revealed a great deal of information concerning the mining district. It stated among other things:

> The Pinto and Iron Springs Mining District is the most important known source of iron ore for the steel plants in the West. The future economic status of the Intermountain and Pacific coast regions will depend largely upon the successful development and exploitation of substantial iron ore bodies in this district.[40]

Another program, based on the information gained in the earlier study, was conducted from March 1944 to July 1945 by the Federal Bureau of Mines' Division of Geophysical Exploration. The results of the study were assembled and edited by Kenneth L. Cook and were published in 1950. The detail given in these documents was extremely useful to those who were interested in pursuing and/or developing iron ore properties. The information was directly related to a number of properties, some of which were open claims and others of which were unknown up until that time. Much of the information in these reports was revealed even before publication. Apparently, there were several individuals who seized the opportunity and beat the big mining companies to the punch at staking claims. It is interesting to note some of the names on the claims during this period.

The 1944–1945 study focused on the results of the magnetometer studies and follow-up diamond drilling that were conducted earlier. The purpose of the study was to determine the extent of outcropping ore bodies, to find new ore bodies, to determine locations for diamond drilling, and to obtain a tonnage estimate of the near-surface iron ore reserves of the entire Pinto-Iron Springs Mining District. The magnetic surveys were confined to the geologically favorable zone at the margins of three separate igneous intrusions in the district. About 62,000 magnetometer stations were sampled over a total traversed distance of about 300 miles.

Outcropping ore bodies were surveyed to determine, insofar as was possible from the magnetic data, their probable length, width, depth, extent, strike, dip, and tonnage. Geologically favorable areas where no ore was exposed were explored in an endeavor to find new ore bodies. Favorable locations were determined for exploratory diamond drilling, both in areas of exposed ore bodies and in areas of newly discovered magnetic anomalies.

Forty-five separate magnetic anomalies were observed indicating the possible existence of ore bodies. They fell into the following categories: thirteen anomalies were caused by outcropping ore bodies of proven commercial size. Five anomalies were discovered, in whole or in part, as a result of the geophysical surveys and were caused by non-outcropping ore bodies of proved commercial size. Six anomalies were discovered by the survey and were probably caused by large, unexposed replacement ore bodies. Nine anomalies were discovered by the survey and were possibly caused by large, unexposed replacement ore bodies. Six anomalies were discovered by the survey and were probably caused by unexposed magnetite veins of some small commercial importance. It is unknown how the remaining six anomalies were classified, but most likely they were deemed to be not significant.

The Federal Bureau of Mines tested ten different ore bodies by drilling thirty-six bore holes. These holes gave helpful information to aid in the correlation of geology and geophysics and served to check the qualitative interpretation and prior quantitative estimates of depths and sizes of the ore bodies. As a result of these USBM surveys, the A and B, April Fool, Calumet, McCahill, Clive-Constitution, King, Little Jim, Rex, Section 2, Section 3, Section 4, Section 9, State Section 2 and State Section 16 ore bodies were discovered. The "Milner Anomaly," later simply named the Rex Ore Body, proved to be the largest ore deposit in the district. The Rex ore body will be discussed in a subsequent chapter.

When the geophysical surveys were started, the wartime ship-building program had not yet reached its peak, and steel production in western steel plants was steadily increasing. The Geneva plant had not been entirely completed and was not yet running at full capacity. The Pinto-Iron Springs Mining District was already supplying ore at a rate of 1,500,000 tons a year to all the principal steel plants of the West. Kaiser's Fontana plant was the only exception, and eventually even that facility was also destined to utilize ore from Southern Utah. Although the drain on the district reserves was large, no appreciable exploratory drilling had been done by private companies before 1944; and, except for a few ore bodies in the immediate vicinity of those being exploited, little was known of the potential reserves of the entire district, one that contained some of the richest and most easily accessible ore bodies in the West.[41] This affected more than one firm mining actively in Southern Utah.

In December 1946, the U.S. Bureau of Mines, in an address to the American Institute of Mining and Metallurgical Engineers in Salt Lake City, released the new estimated reserve data that they had calculated. They stated that "assured" iron ore reserves in the Iron Mountain, Granite Mountain and Twin Peaks regions of Iron County were estimated at 350 million tons. They also said that when "assumed ore" was added in, it would bring the "probable" reserve to 500 million tons. They were careful to explain that part of the reserve would have to be recovered with underground mining methods as opposed to the open pit methods that were presently being used.[42]

Columbia Iron Mining Company at Iron Mountain

The Geneva plant, when completed, combined with the addition of the second blast furnace at the Ironton plant, caused a huge increase in the iron ore delivery requirement from Southern Utah by the Columbia Iron Mining Company. The firm's Black Hawk mine at Iron Mountain, which was the only iron mine operating in the area at the start of World War II, was tapped to supply all of the ore to both facilities. The Defense Plant Corporation was aware of the situation and part of the $35,000,000 that was advanced by the DPC for the Geneva steel mill was used to expand Columbia's mining operations.[43]

Surprisingly, as of June 1942, even after all the announcements had been made and construction had started on the Geneva plant, there had been no official announcement about specific plans for development in Iron County. The only thing that had happened as far as the local citizens were concerned was that the Army engineers had recently visited Cedar City to study the need for the construction of the road from Cedar City to the Iron Mountain mine and that the State Road Department was surveying the route.[44] The first ore train from Iron Mountain to the Geneva Plant, consisting of sixty-five cars, was delivered the latter part of December, 1943.[45]

Eventually, with the help of funding from the federal government, the equipment, processing plant and other and facilities were expanded and upgraded to handle the 700% increase in iron ore needed by the time the new plants were ready to operate. New shovels, trucks and drills were bought and put to work on a multiple shift basis. Roads were built, overburden stripped and development drilling done to open the Pinto Pit, the second pit to be located at the Iron Mountain mining area. The number of people working at the mine was increased from twenty-one working in 1940 to over two hundred in 1944. Iron ore shipped from Iron Mountain by Columbia Iron Mining Company was 358,718 tons in 1942, 630,361 tons in 1943, 1,235,552 tons in 1944 and 1,248,200 tons in 1945.[46]

Pinto ore body was located on the southwest side of Iron Mountain between the Burke and Black Hawk ore bodies. Claims covering the deposit were located early in the history of the district, but no large-scale mining was done until it was opened during World War II. Pinto ores were formed by metasomatic replacement of the Homestake Limestone, and the property was bounded by a fault at the south end of the deposit. The iron ore minerals were mixtures of hematite and magnetite. Only a thin mantle of overburden covered the main ore body. The property had the potential to produce more than 10 million tons of good quality ore.[47]

On February 2, 1946, six months before the sale of Geneva was finalized, the WAC announced that a fifteen-year contract had been signed for the supply of iron ore for the plant. The ore, under the provisions of that agreement, would be available to any purchaser of the Geneva plant, whomever that might be. It was no surprise that the agreement was made with the Columbia Iron Mining Co., a subsidiary of U.S. Steel, the same company and mine which the government had paid to be enlarged during the war. Columbia was to supply the ore at cost, f.o.b. the mine, plus a depletion charge of 25¢ a ton. The pact would expire on August 17, 1961.

Interestingly, in the news article announcing the ore contract, the government also announced that the Bureau of Mines had made a new reserve estimate of iron ore in Iron County of 154,775,000 gross tons, of course, to the nearest thousand tons.[48] In December the Bureau raised the value to between 350,000 and 500,000 tons.[49]

On June 20, 1946, the *Iron County Record* published the following article. In this article, the local resident's concerns were finally put to rest concerning the final disposition of the Geneva steel plant and the future role of the iron mines in Iron County as Geneva's supplier. With the continuation of the plant's operation, the mines were virtually guaranteed a very bright future indeed.

Sale of Geneva Steel Mill Assures Continued Activity at County Mines
Of tremendous importance to the future development of Cedar City is the final settlement of the Geneva Steel plant sale to the United States Steel Company. The sale was given final approval this week when the United States Attorney General ruled that the sale would not violate the anti-trust laws.

Completion of the sale assures the peace-time operation of this great war-developed plant and brings to the west its greatest chance of industrial development. Operation of the plant to supply the west with steel products will bring to the area many new industries and assures the industrial future of Utah and other western states.

And since the Geneva plant is dependent upon the ore from Iron County mines to feed its blast furnaces, Cedar City immediately takes its place as an important cog in the industrial development of the West and will benefit tremendously from the continued operation of the Geneva plant.

The iron deposits of Iron County have promised to play an important part in the development of Cedar City ever since Brigham Young sent a party of pioneers to settle this community and manufacture needed equipment from the iron ore found here, but always it has been a promise for the future - not for the present.

With the construction of the Geneva plant as a war time necessity the promise became more real, but many feared that with the coming of peace, the plant would be closed down and activity at the local mines discontinued. But with the final approval of the U.S. Steel Co. bid for the Geneva plant, this threat is past, and iron mining will undoubtedly become one of Cedar City's leading industries for many years to come.[50]

Utah Construction Company for CF&I at Iron Mountain

In 1942, CF&I contracted with the Utah Construction Co. for the construction of a crushing and loading plant, a haulage road, and the initial work required to uncover the ore and open a mine at Iron Mountain. The first pit opened was on the Duncan Claim which CF&I had purchased from the Thomas Taylor estate in August 1903. It was located about a mile west of the crushing plant. The Utah Construction offices and preparation plant were located directly south, across the railroad tracks from the Columbia Iron Mining Company operations at Iron Mountain.

The contract with Utah Construction was to last for only a six-month period. However, as time progressed, CF&I apparently decided that the company was doing a fine job and retained them to mine and ship iron ore from the Duncan Pit. Two years later, in 1944, mining expanded to the spectacular Blowout deposit, another one of Thomas Taylor's claims. Ten years later, in 1954, a pit was opened on the large Comstock ore body located further to the northeast on the east side of Iron Mountain.

The Duncan ore body was located on the southwest side of Iron Mountain and was owned by the CF&I Corporation. The ore body occurred as a massive replacement of Homestake Limestone. The ores were medium soft to medium hard and had a high sulfur content. A fissure traversed the deposit and was bounded by pyrite mineralization. The pyrite gave the ore a sulfur content of 1 percent and higher in some areas.[51]

The deposit was mined from 1942 until 1968 on an intermittent basis. The mining rate was restricted at times because of high sulfur content. The ore potential of the pit was estimated at about 5 million tons. The mining claim next to the Duncan was the "Pirate Prince." This outcropping ore was probably used at the Iron City operation in the early 1870's as it was only about two miles from the old furnace.

H. L. Humpherys, a longtime employee of Utah Construction Company, worked at the Iron Mountain location for years. He recalled some of the mining practices and the associated equipment used at the Duncan Pit, starting in 1943.

> Most of the equipment used to start mining the Duncan came from Davis Dam, which was shut down for the duration of World War II (1942).
>
> The first equipment consisted of one Lima Shovel, two Northwest 80-D shovels, five 6FD 15-yard Euclid trucks, two D-8 Cat 46A tractors, one Adams road grader, and eight air-operated wagon drills. The drills had air to the hammers only, no power to move. They had to be pulled by hand from hole to hole. Three-inch holes were

Illustration 8.6. This image shows the Blowout Pit in 1946, not long after it had been opened. Careful examination of the photo shows an electric mining shovel loading ore into a truck at the left, and three wagon drills drilling blast holes in the center. At the center-rear of the photo, the boom of another shovel can be seen, probably loading overburden being hauled away by the trucks seen on the horizon on the right. At that time, much of the ore formation protruding into the air had been mined, but the prominent hill was still evident. (Photo from York Jones)

drilled on four-foot centers, 30 feet deep to maintain a 25-foot face, one operator per drill with a helper for two drills. Air was piped from a compressor located just outside the pit. Holes were loaded with 60% 2 × 8 stick dynamite. Electric caps were used with about 25 holes wired in series. There was a lot of secondary drilling which was done with jack hammers.

Ore was hauled about one mile and dumped on a grizzly with 10-inch openings between bars. The oversize which would not go through the grizzly was beaten through with a crane having a large drop ball. Ore was fed out of the grizzly with a pan feeder on a 36-inch belt, up an incline to a 16" × 24" jaw crusher, then to a stockpile, then to a loading tipple, and screened to two sizes and loaded into cars.

When the Blowout was started in about 1944, an electric 120-B shovel (SHE-1) came in from Davis Dam. At that time this was considered a big shovel. The five-yard bucket which came on the shovel was replaced with a three-yard as soon as possible because of the heavy iron ore. The 7 LD 30-ton trucks were used sometime later, and also the 2 FFD 40-ton tandem Euclids [came] later.[52]

The Blowout ore body was located at the south end of Iron Mountain immediately east of the Utah Construction railroad loadout facility. The Blowout deposit originally formed a prominent outcrop. The ore potential of the Blowout Pit was estimated at 7.5 million tons. The ore from the Blowout deposit consisted of hard massive magnetite with an average iron content of nearly 60 percent. The original surface outcrop measured about 850 feet long and 400 feet wide with a height of nearly 200 feet. Drilling operations indicated that the ore body extended to a depth of well over 800 feet.

The Blowout ore body was located along the Calumet fault zone that traversed the south side of Iron Mountain. Downslope and south from the ore body overturned Homestake Limestone was essentially unreplaced and was part of the upper plate of the Laramide-Iron Springs Gap thrust. Between the Homestake Limestone belt and porphyry, and extending for about two miles between Blowout and Pot Metal ore bodies, was the Calumet fault zone. Breccia several hundred feet wide in this zone contained fragments of Homestake, Entrada and Iron Springs lithology, which was probably the mashed lower plate of the Laramide thrust. The Blowout ore body was a breccia pipe replacement along this faulted structure and was located mostly in quartz monzonite porphyry.

The Blowout breccia pipe was an excellent example of a previous channel-way that provided a deep plumbing system for iron-rich hydrothermal solutions. The core was high in quartz which occurred mainly in vugs. A *vug* is a small to medium-sized cavity inside rock. Most commonly formed by cracks and fissures opened by folding and faulting, vugs are often partially filled by quartz, calcite, and other secondary minerals.[53] White and drusy quartz was present, and amethyst quartz was common near the surface. The ore also contained galena, chalcopyrite, bornite and pyrite, with the pyrite content increasing with depth. The ore body contained an unusual variety of fibrous magnetite that occurred at every level. The Blowout ore deposit was a good example of an ore body showing a hydrothermal origin.[54]

The elevation of the top crest of the pit was 6,700 ft. The very hard magnetite ore was almost impossible to drill. The ore was mined in twenty-five-foot lifts and the stripping ratio was very low, especially in the early years when much of the deposit was above the surface of the ground surrounding it.

Quartz monzonite porphyry is a type of igneous rock that was formed as magma cooled in the earth. A porphyry is a volcanic rock with visible large-grained crystals. Monzonite contains less than five percent quartz. Quartz monzonite contains between five and twenty percent quartz. Granite contains more than twenty percent quartz. From a purely technical perspective, the Salt Lake Temple of the Church of Jesus Christ of Latter-day Saints, its Administration Building, and the Utah State Capitol Building in Salt Lake City, are actually constructed of quartz monzonite, not granite.[55]

Utah Construction Company at Iron Springs

The Utah Construction Company was a large, well-known construction company in the area that had worked on many major projects in the west including Hoover dam. It was contracted by Union Pacific to help build the railroad from Lund to Cedar City in 1923. It had worked on quite a few mining projects around the world and decided that the mining business looked pretty good. After all, it already had the earth moving expertise and most of the equipment it needed. In the mid 1940s, Utah Construction Company purchased and leased property and mining claims on and around Granite Mountain and Three Peaks on both sides of the branch railroad line running through Iron Springs Gap.

In 1944, Senter F. Walker of Salt Lake City, representing the Walker Company, announced that the company had signed contracts with the Kaiser Steel Plant in Fontana,

California to provide more than 1,000,000 tons of high grade iron ore from the Excelsior deposits in the Iron Springs area that were owned by the Walkers. The ore from Iron Springs was combined with ore from Kaiser Company's mines in other parts of the country and used at the Fontana plant as feed and charge ore for its open-hearth and blast furnaces. The Kaiser mill produced steel plate for the ships of the maritime commission fleet and the U.S. Navy and furnished steel for 155 mm and eight-inch high explosive shells.

The Utah Construction Company was contracted to install and operate the mining, crushing, conveying and loading facilities at Iron Springs that were estimated to cost upwards of $300,000. Utah Construction had been mining ore for some time at the Iron Mountain properties for CF&I, shipping ore to Pueblo Colorado. The Kaiser project had been started at the time of the announcement and the mine related facilities had to be rushed in order to be able to ship ore to the Kaiser facility in the designated time frame. Temporary structures were constructed to expedite the process, and permanent facilities and buildings were built later as time allowed. The crushing and loading facility was constructed on the south side of the railroad tracks in the Iron Springs area. The plant was designed to process a minimum of 1500 tons of ore per day.[56]

The installation allowed Utah to sell ore on the open market. Their first mining location at Iron Springs on the Walker claims was in the Lindsay Hill area, just southwest of Iron Springs Gap and south of the Pioche deposit where Columbia Steel had started mining in 1923.

The following is from an account written by Jim Smith in 1960.

Construction of Iron Springs' plant began in about October 1944. C. A. Mason, Project Superintendent, and C. J. Wasmuth, Office Manager. An 80-D Northwest shovel with C.S. Lewis as operator began working on the road just below present crusher and then proceeded up the hill making cuts and fills to get to the original No. 1 pit (Utes, Dee's and Lee's). At this time drilling on the Excelsior Claims was going on, and in the first slope on top of the hill, both ore and waste was in the first shot. George Bowman was drill and shoot foreman.

In the course of the plant construction, a grizzly (No Crusher) and a shot loading belt extended to the R.R. tracks from the north side of the area where the crusher is now located. When cars were loaded for Kaiser Company, a man stood alongside the belt and raked the lump ore off the belt to load later as open-hearth ore. When the plant was finished it included primary crusher, "A" belt to stockpile, and "B" belt from stockpile to loading tipple. A screen on top of the loading tipple to screen ore for Kaiser open-hearth, 5" to 10" as the crusher made 10" minus.

Al Geiger was the loading plant foreman. Paul Volp was master mechanic. Brown, shop foreman and Tom O'Mara was electrical superintendent, who sent for Lee Spencer to come and work with him. He arrived in January, 1945.

The first Shipments to Kaiser Company were about 26,000 tons of ore per month. Of which, about 1,500 tons were open-hearth ore. The contract for this was from Excelsior Mining Company who had the contract with Kaiser Company.

The lab crew consisted of two men with Karl Boyns as Mine Chemist, employed by Kaiser Company and paid jointly by Kaiser and Excelsior, Senter Walker was in charge for Excelsior, representing mainly Walker Bank in Salt Lake. Ralph Edwards also started in the lab. Later some of the Walker Bank officials came to Iron Springs to check the operation.

Iron Mining & Manufacturing

Illustration 8.7. The Lindsay Pit on May 28, 1945, looking north, not long after it had been opened. A shovel can be seen in the pit and a haul truck is visible on the far left of the photo. (Photo from York Jones)

The B.E. 120 Shovel arrived early 1945 and began the production in the pit. There was about 16 - 5 FD Euclid Trucks to haul the ore. 15-ton loads were about average as the trucks coming down the hill had to use gears to maintain control, as trucks at that time had only air brakes. Normal hauling was about a load an hour. Distance was about 1-1/2 miles. Sometime late in 1945, Kaiser shut off ore and Iron Springs had only four men working.[57]

Ore Bodies

Lindsay Hill is located on the eastern flank of Granite Mountain southwest of Iron Springs Gap. The deposit was the largest in the Iron Springs-Three Peaks area and contained over 20 million tons of iron ore. The ore body was oriented in a north-south direction running along the side hill. It was more or less continuous and was extensive enough that it was covered by multiple claims, both lode and placer.

Each of the various claims had different financial arrangements. Some had been bought outright but many others required a royalty payment of some sort when ore was mined from within claim boundaries. These payments could be an amount per ton or a percentage and often there were minimums. When the pit was in operation, keeping track of which claim was being mined in order to ensure the accurate payment of royalties was a substantial challenge for the surveyors, engineers and accountants.

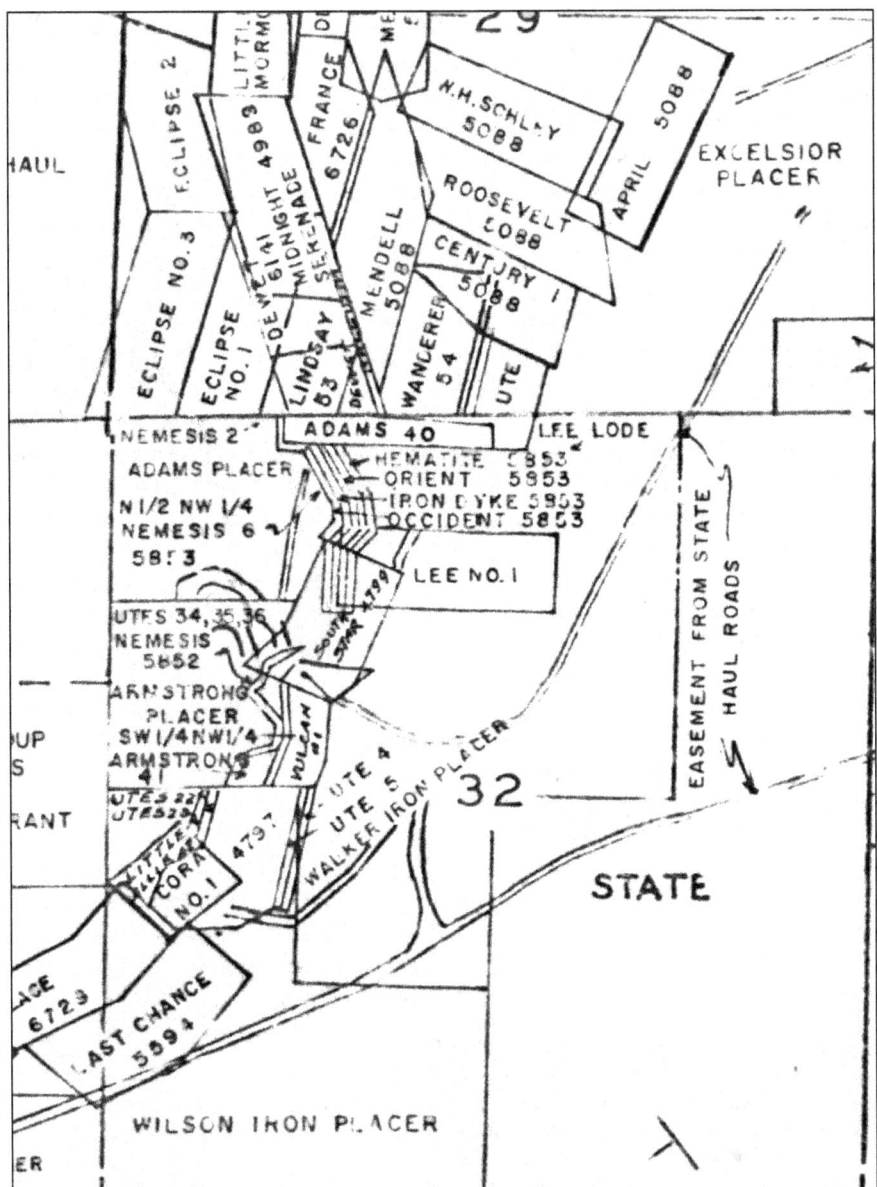

Illustration 8.8. The complicated Lindsay Hill-area claim map. (From York Jones)

Lindsay ore body originally outcropped along its strike for about 1,300 feet; its widest surface exposure was about 300 feet. The deposit extended an additional 700 feet southward beneath bedrock and alluvium and dipped toward the east. The quartz monzonite porphyry and the basal siltstone member of the Carmel Formation were west

Iron Mining & Manufacturing

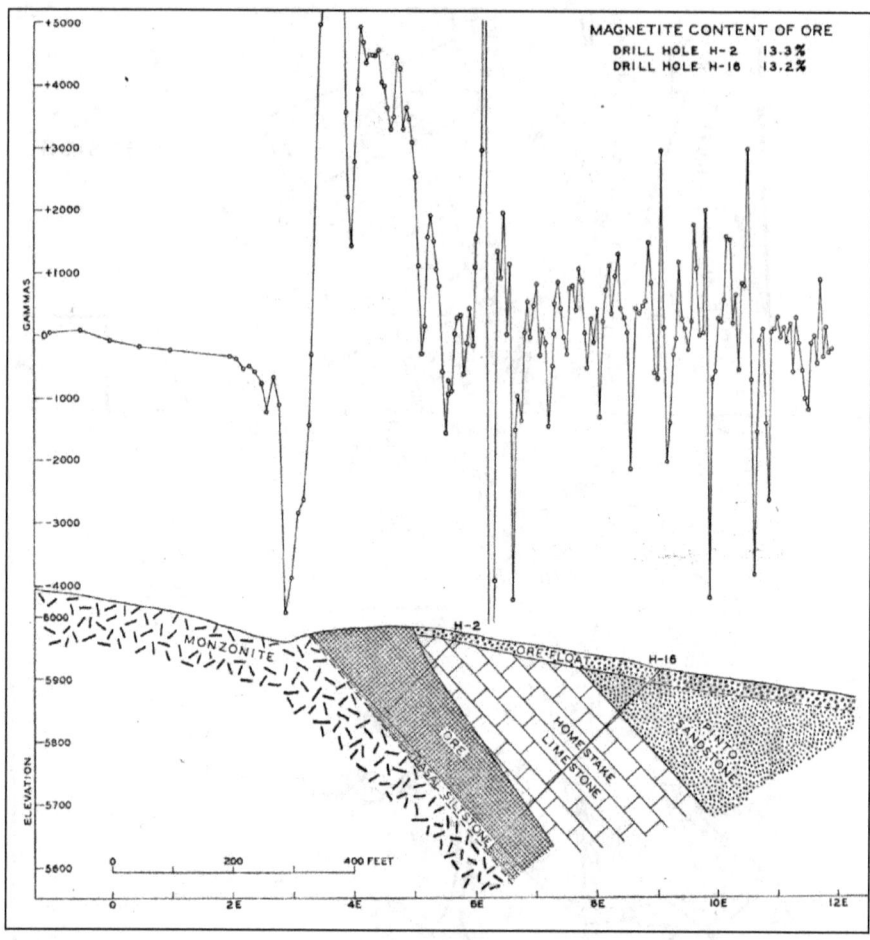

Illustration 8.9. Magnetic profile and geologic cross section of Lindsay Hill by W. E. Young. Notice the steep dip of the ore body. The original bedding in this area was pushed to almost vertical by the magma intrusion on the left (west). The cooled magma intrusion is labeled monzonite, or more correctly quartz monzonite porphyry. Notice in this particular case only the lower portion if the Homestake Limestone was replaced by the iron ore, the upper portion remained intact. Pinto Sandstone and Entrada Sandstone are different names used by geologists for the same formation. This profile of Lindsay Hill is fairly representative of many of the deposits found around the perimeter of Granite Mountain.[60] (US Bureau of Mines)

of the deposit; the upper unreplaced limestone beds of the Homestake Limestone member of the Carmel Formation were to the east.

The formation struck approximately north-south and dipped about 45° east. The dip of the ore body was somewhat steeper, 55° to 60° east. At the northeast end of the Lindsay Pit the ore was nearly vertical.

The deposit originally measured up to 200 feet thick and extended down-dip for at least 1,100 feet. The deposit was essentially a tabular pod with little or no lensing. At depth, however, the deposit apparently merged into a breccia pipe deposit, suggesting that the Lindsay deposit was fed from depth and not from the adjacent porphyry as suggested by Mackin in 1954. The upper eastern contact of the ore with the limestone was sharp. The lower quartz monzonite contact however, was not, and the ore was often lean and poor near the contact. The property was owned by Utah International Inc. and had a reserve of sixteen to eighteen million tons of ore.[58]

Little Allie ore body was located on the east side of Granite Mountain. The ore body was located on the Cory-Armstrong in-dipping thrust fault which had a throw of about 1,300 feet. The Iron Springs Formation was in fault contact with quartz monzonite porphyry. The deposit was pipe-like in form and situated mostly in the quartz monzonite porphyry and was associated with a strongly brecciated zone which likely served as a feeder pipe for iron-bearing hydrothermal solutions. Breccia fillings and replacements extended northward from the main ore body along the Cory-Armstrong fault. Ores consisted of massive and fibrous magnetite and intimate intergrowths of magnetite and quartz, and vugs of quartz and amethyst were common. The property, operated by Utah International, Inc., had potential reserves of over three million tons of ore.[59]

Armstrong ore body was located on the east side of Granite Mountain. The property was about one-third of a mile south of the Lindsay deposit. The ore body wholly replaced a wedge of Homestake Limestone. Monzonite was west of the deposit, and the Iron Springs Formation was in fault contact to the east. The deposit was associated with the Cory-Armstrong fault, a major in-dipping thrust fault that dipped west and brought the quartz monzonite porphyry against steeply dipping beds of the Iron Springs Formation. The throw of this marginal thrust exceeded 1,300 feet. The Armstrong ore body was lens-shaped at the surface, extending about 1,000 feet along the contact zone and measuring about 270 feet at its widest surface outcrop. Below the surface, the ore narrowed and extended downward along the fault zone to an undetermined depth. At about 350 feet the ore averaged forty feet thick and became a breccia filling and replacement along the Cory-Armstrong thrust fault which dipped about 70° west. Angular blocks of quartz monzonite were associated with fault breccia, indicating a late intrusive fault. The fault breccia is impregnated with magnetite and doubtless served as a conduit or feeder for the Armstrong ore body. Little Allie, Armstrong and Lindsay ore bodies form a more or less continuous ore zone with ore bodies of varying vertical and horizontal dimensions, some of them separated by faults. Armstrong ore was somewhat harder, more massive, and higher in magnetite, silica and phosphorous content than other deposits on the east side of Granite Mountain. Mining by Utah Construction, Inc. began on the Armstrong deposit about 1948. The property had an iron ore reserve of five to eight million tons. The deeper ore would have to be recovered by underground mining methods.[61]

General Interest

Iron County Scrap Salvage Reached 1,286,000 Lbs. [October 1942]

A total of 216,000 pounds or 103 tons of scrap metal was hauled into the Salvage Depot in Cedar City, Wednesday in one of the most successful cooperative community efforts yet undertaken here. The day long drive was the result of cooperation between the Junior Chamber of Commerce, the local salvage com-

Iron Mining & Manufacturing

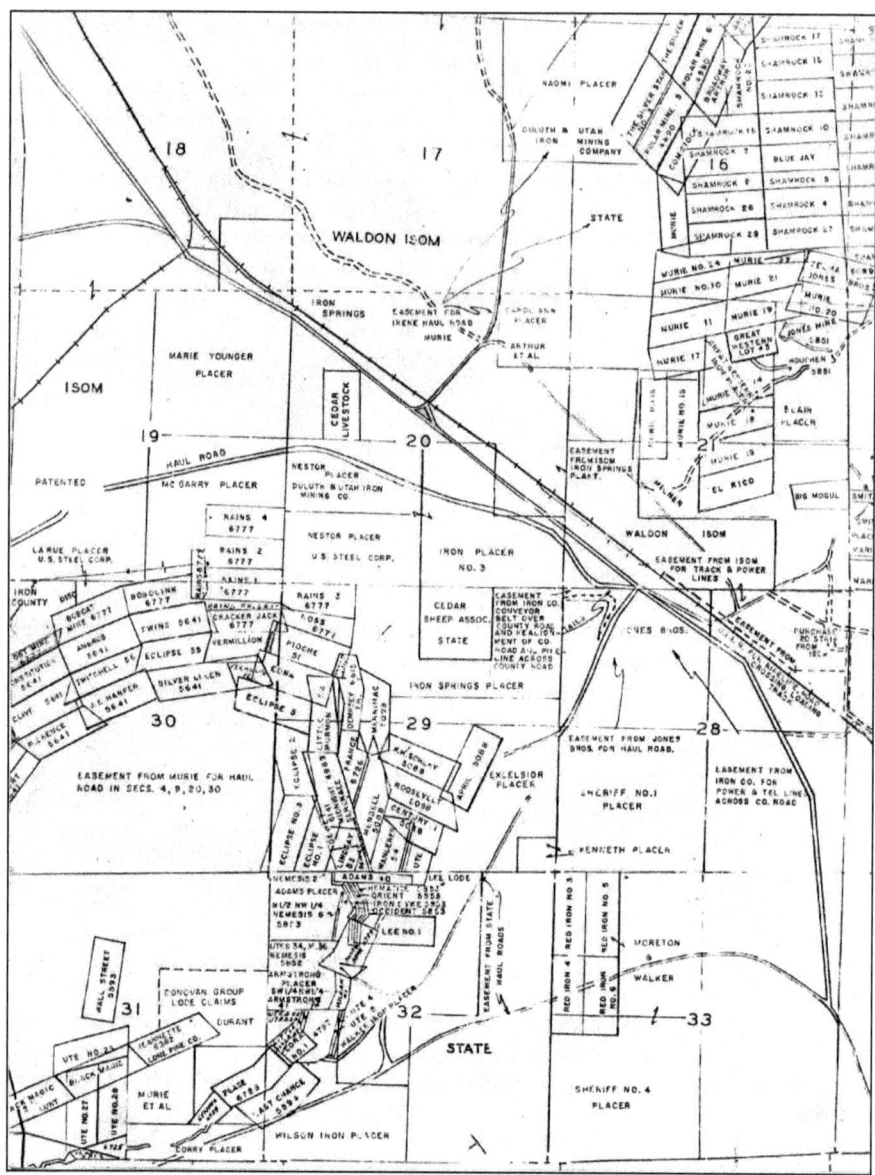

Illustration 8.10. *The claims of the Iron Springs mining area. The string of claims that eventually were mined and became pits can be followed around Granite Mountain starting in the lower center part of the map, Cora, Little Allie, Armstrong, Utes, Lees, Dees, Adams, Lindsay, Wanderer, Little Mormon, Pioche, Vermillion, Eclipse, and Twitchell. On the Three Peaks side on the left can be seen the Smith, Great Western, Jones, and Zelma. The overlapping claims were very confusing, especially since placer claims and lode claims can legally overlap. (From York Jones)*

mittee, and the schools, together with the whole-hearted support of business people and people generally.

The drive brought to a close, a ten-day campaign by the school children of Cedar City in which every corner of the town was covered with children, from six years of age to high school age, carrying into the school depot anything from the smallest bolt to old water tanks, stoves, rails, and old farm machinery.

As a result of this ten-day campaign, the children accumulated approximately 50 tons of scrap, and yesterday the students joined with the Junior Chamber of Commerce to help man the trucks and haul in the 108 tons of scrap. Thus, in addition to accumulating a large scrap pile the students have gained an important lesson in patriotism and community service.

Adding the 108 tons gathered in the Junior Chamber drive, the 50 tons contributed by school children, to the 85 tons the local salvage committee had previously collected, and the 400 tons gathered in the county by W.P.A. workers, give Iron County a total salvage record of 643 tons of metal with outlying schools and towns yet to be heard from.

The scrap drive will not be discontinued now, but instead it will be continued until not one more piece of metal can be found anywhere in the County.

The officers and committee members of the Junior Chamber of Commerce, together with the Salvage Committee and school officials, take this opportunity to express their appreciation for the fine support they received. Government agencies and local individuals furnished trucks for the drive, stores were closed, and children were permitted to leave school, in order that every interested person could lend his assistance. The effort put into the campaign was certainly justified by the success evidenced in the report of totals of scrap collected.[62]

On June 29, 1944, an article was published in the *Iron County Record* telling of a devastating fire that occurred at Iron Mountain at Utah Construction Company's compressor and tool sheds, resulting in several thousand dollars worth of damage.

Fire Destroys Buildings on Iron Mountain [June 1944]

Fire of an undetermined origin destroyed the compressor and tool sheds and shower rooms of the Utah Construction Company at Iron Mountain Monday night, resulting in several thousand dollars damage. The fire occurred sometime between midnight and the time the men went on shift Tuesday morning. Everything was all right when the men left work Monday but the buildings were burned down when they returned to work the next day.

In addition to the buildings destroyed, three air compressors, the companies' tool sharpening equipment, and considerable smaller equipment and supplies were also destroyed. However, work is continuing at the mine with the crew of men split into two shifts in order to utilize the equipment still available, while work has already been started on replacing the buildings and repairing the damage.

The Utah Construction Company mines iron ore for the Colorado Fuel Company, for use at the company's smelters in Colorado.[63]

CHAPTER NINE

The Post-War Boom Years
1945–1960

DURING THE WORLD War II years, Northern Utah went from having one smaller-sized blast furnace at Ironton, Utah, to having a small and a large blast furnace at Ironton and three large blast furnaces at Geneva. Kaiser doubled its capacity in California with a second blast furnace. The iron mining companies in Southern Utah incurred a similar sort of leap in production as they responded to the demand for iron ore by the new furnaces. Columbia Iron Mining Company went from one pit at Iron Mountain to two. Utah Construction entered the mining business at Iron Springs with a new pit. CF&I, using Utah Construction, started mining and shipping iron ore from Southern Utah with two new pits at Iron Mountain to supplement its sources in Colorado and Wyoming. Iron County went from having a single pit to having five pits in a relatively short time. To be able to sustain this high level of production, the mining companies had to scramble, not only to open up new pits, but also to manage their operations to ensure that they had adequate reserves for the future. Local providers also had to work hard to establish the infrastructure to provide the mines with the needed equipment, supplies and services.

The late 1940s and the 1950s was a time of great production for the mines but was also a time of substantial turmoil. The labor unions seemed to have found their feet after the war. During the fourteen years following World War II, the Steel Workers Union struck five times, once in each of the following years: 1946, 1949, 1952, 1956 and 1959. The Steel Workers' strike in 1959 stretched for 116 days and had lasting effects from which the steel industry never recovered. If this wasn't enough, the United Mine Workers union, representing the coal miners supplying coal and coke to the smelters, struck or threatened to strike on alternate years with the Steel Workers. A coal strike would shut down Geneva and Ironton which subsequently shut down the iron mines.

The strikes were very unsettling, not only for the employees involved, but also for their families, the businesses being shut down and the public in general. Confidence in the industry's ability to reliably produce was certainly tarnished. However, that did not slow down the State of Utah and Iron County from dreaming up a variety of schemes to try and get what they thought was their "fair share" of the money being generated by the iron and steel industry. The companies were hit with almost as many taxes as they were strikes. Ultimately, over two thirds of Iron County's taxes came from iron mining and related businesses. Sometimes it was hard to tell if just the golden goose's eggs were being harvested or were some of its feathers and meat also being taken.

In retrospect, despite the issues, the 1950s turned out to be the best decade in history for iron ore production from Iron County. Columbia Iron Mining Company shipped ore to Ironton and Geneva in Northern Utah. Utah Construction Company shipped ore for Colorado Fuel & Iron to the CF&I plant in Pueblo, Colorado and for itself to Kaiser Steel in California and to several other locations around the country.

The combined output of these companies for the ten-year period was 42 million tons—over 600,000 rail car loads. In excess of 4 million tons were shipped per year for six out of the ten years. The decade was a glorious time for State and County governments and citizens, as revenues from taxes paid by the mines were at an all-time high and employees working at the mines averaged over 600, not counting those who worked providing services to the mines and miners.[1]

It is hard to accurately estimate the long-range impact that the smelters, mines and railroads had on the State of Utah with the thousands of jobs and millions of dollars in taxes that were created within the State, but the impact was certainly huge.

The Smelters

On January 21, 1946, not long after the end of World War II, the United Steelworkers of America staged a month-long, nation-wide strike that shut down the Ironton Plant at Provo and Columbia's mine at Iron Mountain. In addition, it shut down a portion of Utah Construction's activities due to the fact that CF&I's Pueblo plant was also shut down by the strike. All of Union Pacific's employees that were involved with shipping ore to the two plants were also put out of work. At that time, Geneva's future was in limbo and it was operating at a level just to keep the furnaces warm. The strike affected about 100 workers in the Cedar City area. Coincidently, the United Mine Workers union went on strike at about the same time, putting most of the coal miners and copper miners out of work.[2]

Ironton Plant

The number two blast furnace at the Ironton Plant and the 500 beehive coke ovens at Sunnyside, Utah were shut down when World War II ended. All were owned by the federal government and had only operated for about two years during the war. For two and a half years after the war ended, the future of the second Ironton furnace was uncertain. United States Steel was operating the number one furnace at Ironton and it was assumed that it would probably buy and operate the number two furnace when it went up for sale. But the company seemed in no hurry to do so. It appeared that U.S. Steel had its hands full getting the massive Geneva plant up and running and wasn't interested in taking on a fifth blast furnace, even if it was in its own backyard.

Finally, in 1947, Kaiser Steel, the outsider from California, stepped in and purchased both the blast furnace and the 500 beehive coke ovens from the War Assets Administration for $1,150,000. Mr. Kaiser was quoted as saying "the purchase is aimed at helping relieve the nation's acute shortage of pig iron by opening the idle plant and producing about 300,000 tons of pig iron a year."[3]

The deal was finalized in December of 1947 and Kaiser made a number of substantial additional investments to get the furnace in shape to begin operations. A formal "blowing in" ceremony was held on May 5, 1948 when the flame was set to the charge in the renovated furnace. The furnace was to run continuously after that, to be interrupted only when the furnace needed to be relined.[4]

About 240 workers were employed at the plant and another 50 at the Carbon County coke ovens. Company officials estimated that the new enterprise would have a monthly payroll of about $40,000 and would spend $500,000 to $740,000 per month for raw materials. Once it was up and running it began supplying pig iron to the Kaiser plant in Fontana, California as well as to the Chicago District mills.[5] During the time that the Ironton number 2 blast furnace was owned and operated by Kaiser-Frazer Parts Company, it used iron ore that was mined at Iron Springs, supplied by Utah Construction Company.[6]

In July 1948, after less than three months of operation, Kaiser determined that several additional improvements were needed. These improvements would be primarily to the coke ovens, but there would also be renovations to some items around the furnace area at a cost of $350,000. The beehive coke oven coal bins were to be covered and heated, the hammer mill building was to be enlarged and dust-proofed, and various pieces of new equipment were to be purchased. At Ironton, new track scales for weighing the pig iron were to be purchased and additional railroad trackage was planned. Purchase of new equipment was also slated, including badly needed slag ladles. Kaiser officials also announced that a 2.7-mile haul road in Carbon County had been completed from the coal tipple to the coke ovens along with 60 new homes at Sunnyside for workers at the coke ovens. The homes were built for Kaiser by the Utah Construction Company.[7]

On May 19, 1949, after only one year of operation and over 4 million dollars of investment, Kaiser-Frazer Parts Company unexpectedly announced that it was shutting down the Ironton number two blast furnace. The closure was said to be a result of market conditions for steel on the West Coast and no date was announced for resumption of operations. Between 200 and 300 employees were laid off when the firm closed down the operation.[8]

Two years later, on May 9, 1951, the United States Steel Corporation announced that it planned to lease the Ironton number two blast furnace from Kaiser. Dr. Walther Mathesius, president of Geneva Steel Company said that preparations to put the furnace into operation would start immediately. The contract had a three-year term with an option to buy or extend the lease at the end date. At end of five years, U.S. Steel could still elect to purchase the property. It would take an estimated 40 days to put the 300,000 ton per year facility back into production.[9]

> Harold B. Makin, general superintendent of the Ironton plant, stated:
> Geneva Steel Co. leased the furnace to add to Ironton's pig iron capacity to alleviate the growing shortage of metallics required to maintain full steel production at the Geneva steel plant. Leasing of the additional blast furnace at Ironton has required employment of 250 more men.[10]

In October 1951, Geneva Steel Company reported that it had completed rebuilding the 23 coke ovens associated with the number one blast furnace at Ironton that had operated continuously since they were built in January 1928. The work of tearing down and relining the coke ovens had taken over a year.[11]

It seems that the old Ironton Plant was destined for a roller coaster ride that closely followed the ups and downs of the national steel industry. In April 1952, the United Steelworkers of America went on strike and put 200 workers out of work for a month.[12] The steel union went on strike again in June for 55 days and the plant was idled once again.[13]

In December 1953, after a two-year run, L. F. Black, general superintendent of the Geneva Works, announced that the Ironton furnaces would be shut down and put on a standby basis beginning January 4.

> [He stated] that operations were partially curtailed in November, due to lack of customers' orders for merchant pig iron. There has been no improvement in the demand for merchant pig iron and our stocks have continued to increase, which makes it necessary to revise our operating program at the Geneva Works, which in turn results in the placement of Ironton on a standby basis for the time being.[14]

He said that about 200 employees would be affected by the shutdown.[15]

Ten months later when the steel market rebounded somewhat, the number one furnace, along with its complement of coke ovens, was put back into service and the 200 workers put back to work. However, the company explained that it was unable to forecast how long the furnaces at Ironton would continue to run.[16]

It was 5-1/2 months later before the number two furnace came back on line, partially due to the fact that the company had taken the opportunity to reline and repair the furnace during the lull in steel demand. An article in the *American Fork Citizen* on March 24, 1955 gave some interesting details about the blast furnace.

Blast Furnace Goes into Operation after Relining

Number two blast furnace at Geneva Steel plant was lit Tuesday afternoon following a shutdown for relining and repairs last month. This furnace, originally put into production on February 24, 1944, was last relined in September, 1951. Since the last relining it has produced 1,500,000 tons of Iron.

At lighting time, the furnace contained a burden of 400 tons of coke, 160 tons of iron ore, 15 tons of manganese, 50 tons of limestone, 25 tons of dolomite, and 25 tons of gravel. Ten hours were required to charge this material into the furnace.

Two-thirds of a million fire bricks (695,000 to be exact) enough to fill 121 railroad cars, were used in relining. Five carloads of mortar were used.

Normally the furnace is cast five times during a 24-hour period; however, the first cast from No. 2 furnace will be 26 to 30 hours after it is lighted. Slag will be flushed in 24 hours. Under normal conditions, 72,000 cubic feet of air per minute is blown into a furnace. Air will be blown into No. 2 furnace at 20,000 cubic feet per minute and gradually increase during the first 24 hours until it reaches the normal blow. The temperature of the air is 800 to 1400 F.

Normal production of each blast furnace at Geneva Works is 1,250 tons of iron per 24-hour period, plus 1,000 pounds of slag for each ton of iron produced. Ironton Works, sister blast furnace plant of Geneva Works located 3-1/2 miles south of Provo, has two blast furnaces.

Each furnace at Geneva produces 155,520,000 cubic feet of blast furnace gas daily. This is cleaned by three separate operations and contains less than 0.002 per cent of dust...

...To make one ton of iron requires 1500 pounds of coke, 3800 pounds of iron ore, and 500 pounds of limestone, dolomite and miscellaneous materials.[17]

Two years later, on June 3, 1957, the number one furnace was taken down for a complete overhaul. After five years of nearly continuous operation, the thirty-five-year-old furnace was scheduled for rebuilding.

A unique feature of the rebuilding job will be the replacement of the bottom third of the furnace while the remainder of the 120-foot high structure is held in place by temporary supports. Geneva engineers say this is similar to removing the bottom four floors of a 12-story building without disturbing the upper floors. The rebuilding job, which will include repairing the furnace's auxiliary equipment, is scheduled for completion in about two months.[18]

In January 1958, the number two blast furnace was taken down again, this time to perform needed repair work. The work required the layoff of about 200 employees and was to take sixty days. However, at about the same time as the furnace was taken down for repairs, the steel market took a nosedive and the number two furnace was not brought back on line until December when the market picked up. The callback put 150 employees back to work. The Geneva Plant was also impacted in January and had reductions at that time.[19]

Geneva Plant

Within ninety days after World War II ended, the Geneva Plant's operations were cut to a bare minimum. It took a year to get the facility auctioned off and the sale completed. Finally, by mid-June 1946, the debates were over and the plant was officially owned by the United States Steel Corporation. It took several more months to get it converted to peacetime applications and recover from being mothballed.

By the end of February 1947, the Geneva Plant was starting to hit its stride. From the standpoint of plant facilities in production, it was very near equal to its average wartime operation. The fourth and last battery of coke ovens and the seventh of nine open-hearth furnaces had just been put into production and the slab and blooming mill had begun a three-shift, around-the-clock operation.[20]

Unfortunately, as was often the case, just as the Geneva Plant was getting on its feet the vultures spied the fresh meat and began to circle. In February 1947, the Utah State Tax Commission levied a 2 percent sales tax on the purchase of the Geneva Steel plant by the United States Steel Corporation from the federal government.[21] U.S. Steel took the matter to the courts and eventually won the case, two and a half years later in August 1949, at the Utah Supreme Court level, when the ruling of the Utah Tax Commission was reversed and the $423,526 sales tax charge was dismissed. The *Salt Lake Telegram* was convinced that the tax was an attempt to gouge the industry and was grossly unfair, unwise, unexpected, unjustified and, as the Supreme Court finally agree, illegal.[22] State and local taxes were always an item of contention. If the rates were higher than those paid in neighboring states, the steel plant was put at an economic disadvantage. The governments, however, were always looking at ways to get into the supposed "deep pockets" of the bigger companies.

Also, in February, a conflict over freight rates arose. Freight charges, primarily from the railroad, were a big part of Geneva's cost structure, affecting both the raw materials coming into the plant and the products leaving the plant. The railroads were, in most cases, not subject to competition like most other businesses. The Interstate Commerce Commission (ICC) was therefore regularly called upon to keep the railroads from charging unreasonable freight haul charges. In this particular case, Geneva felt that the freight rates charged by the railroad were too high and asked the ICC to intervene to establish fair and reasonable rates that were comparable to rates on similar hauls of similar products in Utah and elsewhere in the country.

However, in a somewhat unusual move, the United States Reconstruction Finance Corporation (RFC) intervened and requested that the Interstate Commerce Commission deny the rate reduction requested by Geneva. It became apparent that RFC was concerned about protecting the loan that it had made to Henry Kaiser's Fontana California steel plant. It was seen as a "slap in the face for the entire West to have the RFC take a stand which threatens our whole industrial future in an attempt to salvage a bad loan."[23]

Kaiser, of course, also wanted to have its say, and quickly made a number of statements to the ICC and the press. If the ICC lowered Geneva's freight rates, it also wanted lower rates. This was important to Kaiser because 90 percent of its coal and 55 percent of its iron ore was shipped from Utah. Kaiser made the following assertion:

> If the railroads, in their managerial discretion, have the power by lower freight rates to bring United States Steel's Geneva plant closer to its markets on the Pacific coast, while at the same time leaving the raw materials for the Fontana plant by high freight rates as far away as before, then their managerial discretion gives them the power to destroy the Fontana plant.[24]

A week later, the Interstate Commerce Commission approved a decrease in Geneva's railroad freight rates to the Pacific coast, despite Kaiser's objections. The change was to go into effect on April 1 and would reduce rates by 22 cents per hundred pounds.[25]

In March 1947, Geneva Steel purchased the entire Carbon County town of Dragerton, from the War Assets Board for $1,553,000.

> The town consists of 604 family dwellings of four, five or six rooms each, a shopping center, post office, school building, church, hospital, clinic, recreation areas, water and sewage disposal systems and a fire department. The townsite covers 377 acres of land, located nine miles from the Geneva coal mine in Horse canyon, Carbon County. In submitting its bid, the steel company stated that its policy would be to lease the houses to its employees at fair and reasonable rentals and eventually to offer the homes for sale at fair and reasonable prices.[26]

The Geneva Plant became the hub of industrial activity in Northern Utah. It was predicted that during the next twenty-five years, Utah's agricultural and industrial production would more than double, in large part due to the Geneva Plant.[27] Dozens of downstream industries sprang up using steel from the plant to produce all kinds of end-use products. By September 1948, Geneva was the largest employer in the state of Utah with over 6,000 direct employees and an annual payroll of more than $20 million. The great majority of these employees were residents of Utah and the intermountain region.[28]

Strikes by organized labor unions were a constant threat to Geneva. The plant was totally dependent on its suppliers, and disruptions in the supply of iron ore, coal, limestone and other materials, or the transportation of those supplies, could cause a shutdown or slowdown of plant production. These suppliers and transporters were controlled by separate unions that rarely coordinated their strikes. A strike could be resolved with the iron miners or steel workers, for example, only to have the coal miners go on a separate strike. Putting the plant functions in standby mode was no small task either; furnaces could take weeks to cool down and to be reheated and many had to be kept hot or their linings would disintegrate.

In February 1948, the United Mine Workers union warned of an impending coal strike. The steel plant was running practically at full capacity and had only a week to ten days' supply of coal. If a strike were to ensue, the plant's Horse Canyon coal mine would most likely be shut down. On March 16, 1948, the United Mine Workers staged a nation-wide coal strike that lasted well over a month. Utah's 3,600 members of the United Mine Workers joined John L. Lewis' strike for miners' pensions and forced twenty-one mines to suspend operations, accounting for 97 percent of Utah's coal production.[29]

The Geneva plant was forced to curtail operations to a bare minimum, halting steel production and putting thousands of workers out of work. Companies all over the United States were shut down. General Motors Corporation, for example, was shut down and ran out of steel to produce cars. The following statement was made in the *Salt Lake Telegram* published on April 19, 1948:

Prolonged Coal Strike is National Calamity

The coal strike may be officially over but the nation will continue to pay the bill for the lost coal production for some time to come.

Effect of the strike on steel output is just now beginning to be felt by those industries which depend in large measure on steel for raw material. General Motors has announced that all of its automobile fabricating plants will be closed down by this week end, forcing men out of their jobs. G.M. said it was running out of pig iron and steel. Its stockpiles of those items were exhausted while the coal strike was on, and new supplies following resumption of coal mining are not yet available. In fact, General Motors anticipates it will be unable to resume operations at its fabricating plants before May 1.

Undoubtedly other industries will feel the effect of the loss of coal and steel production, with resulting unemployment. The situation in respect to steel production is not actually clearing up yet. Coal production has been resumed in spotty fashion around the country, with many mines supplying coal to steel companies still idle or operating at a low rate. For instance, Utah's own Geneva steel plant is still down because coal miners have not returned to work in Geneva's mines. For the United States Steel Corporation as a whole, only 20 of 31 mines were operating last Friday and those that were operating were doing so at 44 per cent of capacity.

Every day of lost coal production means lost steel production. Every day of lost steel production in the present tight steel situation means the slowing down of industry in America and delay in the rehabilitation of Western Europe.

It is disturbing to note the ripple-in-the-pond pond repercussions of a nation-wide coal strike. It means far more than idleness for a few hundred thousand coal miners. It means far more than lost profits for the coal operators. Any prolonged shutdown on coal production means idleness for hundreds of thousands of other workers, lost profits for industry, lost taxes for government, lost production and essential goods for the public. It quickly mushrooms into a national calamity.

The American people are getting a lesson on that right now. It should impel them to insist that some way be found to settle the differences between employers and employees in this vital industry without doing such harm to the nation as a whole. In this connection it should be noted that another coal strike is possible June 30, when the present UMW contract expires at which time the traditional coal miners' policy of "no contract, no work" might go into operation.[30]

A year later in March 1949, Geneva set several new production records.

> Open-hearth ingot production was 117,898 net tons. This is over 1,000 tons greater than the previous record month of December, 1948, when 116,804 net tons of ingots were produced. The record production of slabs and blooms for March was 105,226 net tons. The previous record month for these products was November, 1948, when 93,290 net tons were rolled.
>
> New monthly production records were also established for pig iron and furnace coke. 88,101 net tons of pig iron were produced in March. The previous high was 87,163 net tons in December, 1948. Furnace coke production was 79,766 net tons compared with the previous high of 79,585 net tons in December, 1948.[31]

In September 1949, the nation's coal miners went on another nation-wide strike, lasting about a month and then on October 1, the United Steelworkers went on a forty-two-day nation-wide strike, which shut down Geneva and Columbia's Southern Utah mines.

> Effects of the steel strike still are being felt in Utah and the nation and resulting losses were heavy.
>
> It is estimated that steel company employees over the country lost $178,000,000 in direct wages. Figures compiled by Steel magazine show that more than 8,500,000 net tons of ingots were lost from the 1949 production in the six weeks since the strike first started. The loss in steel ingots from the strike's beginning until operations return to the prestrike rate will amount to 10,500,000 tons.
>
> Operations are increasing at Geneva Steel Co. plant as well as those in other parts of the nation and officials said that by the end of the week the production rate should attain a "respectable level."[32]

In December 1949, Dr. Walther Mathesius, president of the Geneva Steel, spoke at the property tax school for 100 county commissioners and assessors, conducted by the Utah State Tax Commission. He said that manpower, resources and federal taxes were similar to other states; therefore, it was State and local taxes that caused an advantage or disadvantage to industries. He said that State taxes had gone from $11,700,000 in 1937 to $32,000,000 in 1948, and local taxes had jumped from $16,250,000 in 1948 to $33,700,000 in 1949. He said that U.S. Steel had conducted a survey of Utah taxes compared with taxes in other states where U.S. Steel operated and came to the conclusion that any increase in State or local taxes would place the Utah operations at a competitive disadvantage.[33]

In December 1950, Geneva announced its plan to expand.

> Geneva Steel Co. will spend $4,263,000 in the next year on expansions at its Provo facilities, Dr. Walther Mathesius, president, announced Thursday. Dr. Mathesius said the installations include one new open-hearth furnace, bringing the number of such steel making furnaces to 10 at the plant, two overhead traveling cranes; one two-hole soaking pit furnace, making 16 at the plant, and necessary building extensions and storage facilities. The United States Steel Corp. subsidiary will add 116,000 tons of steelmaking capacity to its Geneva plant by the expansion.

This increase from 1,400,000 to 1,560,000 net tons of steel a year is estimated at 11%. Some 75 additional employees will be needed. Dr. Mathesius said work would commence immediately on the new project which has received approval of the national security resources board.[34]

In January 1951, according to a company official, Geneva's records indicated that steel production at the Geneva plant during 1950 had "the highest rate of continuous operation ever reached." This was close to 1,500,000 tons annually or 50 percent above the 1949 total production and the production rate so far in January was well above even the 1950 rate. Steel supply was having a difficult time catching the demand, many customers were not able to get their orders filled and some shops were booked more than a year ahead.[35]

On April 8, 1952, once again Geneva was plagued by striking workers. It put the entire plant on standby mode with the exception of a few coke ovens and one open-hearth furnace in anticipation of a strike by the United Steelworkers. The strike would directly affect about 5,000 workers in the steel industry in Utah.[36] The strike lasted almost a month.[37] The steel union went out again in June for fifty-five days and the plant was idled once again.[38]

On July 1, 1956, the United Steelworkers union went on a nation-wide strike. Total workers at Ironton and Geneva were well under a thousand with an estimated 5000 laid off from both plants. The Consolidated Western Pipe Plant had approximately 100 men at work with 350 idle as a result of the strike. The strike was settled after thirty-nine days.[39]

In January 1958, Geneva and Ironton began to suffer a problem of a different kind. The supply of steel in the market, which was so far behind in the late 1940s and for most of the 1950s, finally caught up with and passed the demand. Both Geneva and Ironton were cutback as a result and between 900 and 1000 workers were put out of work at the two plants. Most of the employees were called back in November, bringing the total number of employees of the two operations to 5,200. The Consolidated Western Steel Division Pipe Plant, a subsidiary of U.S. Steel but not a part of Geneva Works, remained closed down; about 300 workers were laid off earlier in the year.[40]

On July 15, 1959, the United Steelworkers of America went out on a nation-wide strike. 4,800 steel workers were laid off at the Geneva and Ironton works. In Cedar City and Milford some 420 workers were either out on strike or had been laid off their jobs and approximately 800 Columbia and Geneva coal miners near Dragerton were laid off. The strike did not end until the federal government intervened and the Supreme Court upheld the Taft-Hartley injunction. The strike lasted almost four months (116 days) and was the longest in the history of U.S. Steel. It crippled both local and national economies and caused severe hardships to steel workers and their families along with many other businesses and employees. The strike was described by some observers as one of the worst steel labor disputes in history, coming at a time when the country's economy was booming after a recession. It was the sixth major steel strike since World War II.[41]

The Taft-Hartley Act of 1947 was sponsored by Senator Robert A. Taft and Representative Fred A. Hartley. Among a number of other provisions, the Act authorized the President to intervene in strikes or potential strikes that create a national emergency and obtain an injunction to stop the continuation of a strike.[42]

In February 1958, the Columbia-Geneva Steel Division announced that a new coal cleaning plant was to be constructed in Carbon County, near Wellington, Utah. The facility was designed to wash up to 600 tons of coal per hour. Standing thirteen stories high, the steel-clad structure dominated a 1,400-acre site on the Price River about two and a half miles southeast of Wellington.[43]

United States Steel Corporation completed its Wellington coal preparation plant in March 1958. The plant was located along the D&RGW mainline, one and a half miles south of Wellington. The plant blended the coal from U.S. Steel's Sunnyside, Utah, and Somerset, Colorado mines to produce a better quality of coal for coking at the Geneva steel plant, by washing the coal to reduce its ash and sulphur content.[44]

It is curious to see that some of the best steel-making coal available in Utah had to be washed before it was used to make coke and then to make pig iron. Undoubtedly, the move to invest in a wash plant demonstrated the company's need to more predictably produce a higher quality of coke and therefore a higher-quality iron.

The early pioneers of ironmaking in Southern Utah desperately wanted the coal that was available in the mountains near Cedar City to be suitable for use in their blast furnaces. They tried everything to make it work, but ultimately the only pig iron of reasonable quality manufactured in the area was made using charcoal from the local pinion and juniper trees.

Iron County coal was not used for much other than home heating and to fuel a small power plant at the mouth of Cedar Canyon. History proved that the coal had too much sulfur to be very useful and it lacked the necessary fixed-carbon levels to make good coke. The best of Utah's coal was considered to be of marginal quality for coking compared to coals found in other regions of the world and it needed to be washed to remove contaminants. However, it was used extensively for iron-making in Utah and California because nothing better was available.

Kaiser Plant

Kaiser purchased half of its supply of iron ore from Utah Construction Company from 1945 to 1948 and a decreasing amount on and off after that until 1958. It also purchased most of its coal from Carbon County, Utah. Like the Geneva plant, a portion of Kaiser's facilities in Fontana, California was financed and built for the government during World War II. Kaiser received a large loan from the federal government when it purchased the newly built blast furnace after the war.

When Geneva went to the Interstate Commerce Commission in 1947 to request relief from high railroad freight rates, especially from Northern Utah to the California, where much of its output was shipped, Kaiser spoke up. First of all, it did not want United States Steel, Geneva's owner and one of its direct competitors, to get a freight discount that put Kaiser at a disadvantage. Secondly, if U.S. Steel was going to get its freight rates lowered on the Utah-California haul, Kaiser wanted a similar reduction on its Utah-California haul and its hauls to other locations. Eventually the ICC worked out a solution that both parties accepted.[45]

In July 1954, an article concerning Kaiser's operation in Fontana was published in the *Iron and Steel Magazine* which gave a good description of the Fontana Plant.

Coke Plant and Blast Furnace Expansion at Fontana
by Clarence R. Lohrey, Asst. Gen. Supt., Kaiser Steel.

When production began in 1943 and for the first six years of operations at Kaiser, the steelmaking facilities consisted of six open-hearths rated at 185 tons each, one blast furnace with a 25 ft. 6 in. hearth to produce 1200 tons of hot metal per day, and two batteries, 45 ovens each, of coke ovens to supply the metallurgical coke requirements. The usual auxiliaries, such as sintering plant, material handling equipment, skullcracker, slag disposal equipment, etc., were all a part of the original plant.

In the beginning, blast furnace ore was obtained from the company-owned Vulcan mine located in the Mojave Desert about 200 miles from the plant. Coking coal was supplied from the Sunnyside mines, located in Carbon County, Utah, some 800 miles from Fontana.

The high sulphur content of the Vulcan ore, often times more than 1.5 per cent indicates that, as delivered, it was not a particularly desirable blast furnace material. It was found that by a crushing and screening treatment the -5/8 in. ore containing a high percentage of the sulphur could be sintered, thereby eliminating approximately 95 percent of this element. A mixture of the coarse ore (+5/8 in.) and the sintered fines made an acceptable economic burden for the blast furnace. As the Vulcan deposit became depleted it became expedient to crush and sinter all the Vulcan ore available, and to supplement the coarse +5/8 in. Vulcan ore with ore from the Utah Construction Co. mines in Utah. Various combinations of these materials made up the iron bearing burden for the blast furnaces until the company's ore deposits at Eagle Mountain were developed for mining in 1948.[46]

The Railroads

The dramatic growth in the steel industry during and after World War II was not lost on the railroads; they were part of virtually every facet of the steel business. They hauled iron ore, coal and limestone to the plants, along with other raw materials, equipment and supplies. They also hauled the products manufactured by the plants to their various destinations inside and outside of Utah. They were connected at the hip, so to speak, and therefore enjoyed the good times and were forced to endure the bad times with the business. The reverse was also true; the railroad industry had a huge effect on the steel industry. Freight rates could help the iron and steel industries to be profitable or cause financial ruin. If the railroad suffered a shortage, the steel industry would also suffer a shortage, if it had a shutdown due to a problem or a labor disruption, the steel industry would suffer right along with it.

The post-war era was a boom time for the railroads. In addition to the freight business, there was a substantial increase in passenger traffic. On a national level, the railroads aggressively advertised attractive destinations such as the National Parks and they helped build hotels and infrastructure to handle the tourists. They had to add people, track, locomotives and cars all over the country and especially in the State of Utah with the steel plants and the National Parks of Southern Utah. Many of the older, infrequently used rail lines, had to be beefed-up or rebuilt to handle the heavier traffic. In Southern Utah they constructed lodging facilities and operated a bus service to the National Parks.

In 1946, statements made by the president of the Union Pacific Railroad, on a tour of the Utah parks, were published in the following article:

Railroad Head Predicts Utah Era of Progress

Cedar City – "Utah, Idaho and western Wyoming are on the crest of an era of progress, the like of which has never been seen in any interior region of the nation."

George F. Ashby, president of Union Pacific railroad, predicted Tuesday during a three-day tour of Utah park facilities.

In addition to the Geneva steel plant at Provo, which Mr. Ashby describes as "the nucleus for one of the greatest industrial developments ever known in the intermountain region," he disclosed the possibility of a huge chemical development in fertilizers and allied lines which would mean development of additional natural resources on a tremendous scale.

Union Pacific already has placed orders for 1000 additional ore cars to handle the anticipated traffic, he said.

Traffic Increase

"The present volume of traffic on the railroad is considerably above expectations, and with farm crops at record production levels, and the expansion in prospect in connection with Geneva we are very optimistic over the future," Mr. Ashby said.

"We of the Union Pacific railroad have been aware of the possibilities and are prepared for their advent. Anything which helps Utah also helps Union Pacific," he added.

Mr. Ashby was accompanied by E. G. Plowman, vice president of United States Steel Corp., who was equally enthusiastic about possibilities.

Supply Problem

"The increasing load on the ore mines here will bring railroad car supply problems which we are attempting to estimate," he said. "When the ore mines are operating at capacity, probably a matter of weeks, it will require nearly a thousand ore cars on the road constantly."[47]

In 1947, the railroad was involved with Geneva and Kaiser's requests made to the Interstate Commerce Commission for freight rate reductions. The dispute was eventually resolved.

In 1949, when Columbia decided to reopen the Desert Mound area for mining, some two miles of track on the primary rail line running between Iron Springs and Iron Mountain had to be relocated. In the 1920s, when the railroad line was extended from Iron Springs to Desert Mound, the full extent of the Desert Mound deposit and the existence of nearby ore deposits that were hidden beneath the surface were unknown and the line had unknowingly been constructed over a portion of several of the ore bodies in the area. In addition, a spur was required to access the new Desert Mound loadout facilities and several sidetracks were needed to be able to store and switch both empty and loaded railcars.

In February 1949, the railroads had difficulty moving cars around on sidings and even on main lines due to heavy snows and prolonged subzero weather.[48]

In August 1950, the Union Pacific Railroad Company completely replaced twenty-four miles of track between Lund and Iron Mountain with heavier weight track (nine inches from top to bottom) to be able to support the increased traffic and heavier loads of ore from the iron mines. The track ran from Lund toward Cedar City and then branched off at Iron Springs and ran to Iron Mountain.[49]

In September 1950, the Utah Construction Company shipped a small quantity of iron ore to Gary Indiana to be used in open-hearth furnace feed. "Carrying of ore from Iron Springs to Gary is believed to be one of the longest hauls of such material by railroads in the history of steel making."[50]

In 1954, a railroad spur and extra siding track was built into the Comstock mining area to accommodate the mine that was opened there by the Utah Construction Company for Colorado Fuel & Iron. The spur linked into the line that ran between Iron Mountain and Desert Mound.

The railroad industry was also impacted by the disruptive coal and steel strikes in 1946, 1948, 1949, 1952, 1956 and 1959.

The Mines

As discussed previously, when World War II ended, the Geneva plant and the Ironton number two blast furnace were shut down or put on standby and it took several years to get them up and running again. Once all the details were finalized and the post-war economic boom started to become a reality, there was a growing market for the iron and steel produced by the plants. For the iron mines in Southern Utah, this was great news, but its magnitude was unpredicted and overwhelming. This was especially true for the Columbia Iron Mining Company that was required to supply all of the iron ore to the Geneva plant, the number one Ironton furnace and eventually the number two furnace at the Ironton plant.

Iron County was a busy place. Columbia had two pits operating and needed to open two more. Colorado Fuel & Iron, using Utah Construction Company as its contract miner, was shipping from two pits and needed to open another. Utah Construction Company was mining on its own behalf at Iron Springs and needed additional locations. This situation caused both Columbia and Utah Construction to scramble to buy equipment and to build new ore processing and loading facilities. When the short-term issues were resolved, the longer-term issue of where to mine next needed to be addressed.

Columbia owned a large number of claims and had more than adequate reserves locked up for many years into the future. However, the two operating pits at Iron Mountain were not huge; and Columbia would have to open new pits soon. A substantial portion of Columbia's reserves were deep and would require considerable up-front capital in the form of pre-stripping to bring them into production. Additionally, some of them had large quantities of low grade ore that could not be direct-shipped and would need to be stockpiled or require some sort of beneficiation. CF&I had no such problems. Its newly opened deposits at Iron Mountain were substantial and CF&I had a massive outcropping deposit just around the corner at the Comstock area, northeast of the Iron Mountain pits.

The Utah Construction Company, new to being a full-time miner in the area, had no reserves at all to start with and had to scramble to buy or lease claims.

The following article published in the *Iron County Record* on November 15, 1945, only three months after the Japanese surrender, discussed the mining situation in Iron and Beaver Counties. Iron was being shipped in the largest quantities but the lead-zinc, fluorspar, coal, gold and gypsum mines were also mentioned.

Mining Takes Place as Leading Industry of Iron County
Note: This is another in the series of articles dealing with the activities of the Iron County Post-war Planning Committee. It was prepared by the Mining committee, composed of Parley Dalley, Emil Roundy, Robert Fenton, Roice Knight, John Foster, Wilford Fife, Leslie Wa[ ], Arthur Jones and Clair Hulet.

Mining has become one of Iron County's leading industries. While the principle ore being mined and shipped is iron ore, yet substantial tonnages of other products such as lead-zinc ore and coal are also being produced.

All the iron ore smelted by the Columbia Steel and Geneva Steel smelters near Provo, comes from Iron County. The Colorado Iron and Fuel Company and the Kaiser smelters obtain much of their ore here. Bethlehem Steel has used a limited amount from the Three Peaks Deposit east of Iron Springs.

Three different government surveys of the Iron Springs Mining District have been carried on recently to determine the amount and nature of the ore deposits there. When reports on these surveys are published they should raise considerably, the previous estimate of forty million tons of available ore in the district.

Although much depends on the continued operation of the Geneva Steel Plant, yet, should this plant be closed, there must be continued production sufficient to satisfy the other interests.

The New Arrowhead Mine, about thirty miles north-west of Lund, has shipped approximately three thousand tons of lead-zinc ore during the past three years. This mine, formerly known as the "Uncle Bim," is owned and operated by Wilford, Otto, and Carl Fife and Wes McCune.

The output of several mines, just across the county line in Beaver County, is shipped from Lund, Utah. These mines are the Wah Wah, a lead-zinc property, and four fluorspar mines, the Cougar Spar, Hilt, Utah, and Spaats. Substantial amounts of ore have been shipped from all of these.

Production of fluorspar at the Cougar Spar Mine, a Tintic Standard Property, has stopped for the present, but development work [is] being carried on which promises not only an increase in production but a better quality of ore. A mill for concentrating the ore has been built at this mine at a cost in excess of one hundred thousand dollars.

Six coal mines are being operated in the vicinity of Cedar City, the Macfarlane and Webster mine in the main canyon, the Nelson and Tucker mines in Right Hand Fork, and the Williams and Graff mines on Kanarra mountains. Production from these mines, which has been limited during the war period, on account of labor shortage, should be able to meet all local needs as the labor situation improves.

Cedar City is the logical center for the development of the great cannel coal deposits of Western Kane County. The establishment of a processing and by-products plant using this coal is one of our future possibilities.

Leasing and operation of gold properties in western Iron County which has been discontinued during the war should be resumed in the near future.

Utilization of the vast quantity of high grade gypsum in the immediate vicinity of Cedar City should be promoted. No other locality offers a better setting for manufacture of plaster board and other gypsum products. Reopening of the plaster mill now standing idle should be encouraged.[51]

Dr. Walther Mathesius, President, Geneva Steel Company, made a presentation to the American Iron and Steel Institute in San Francisco, California on November 5, 1948, which basically set some guidelines for future mine planning. The presentation was particularly appropriate because the planning of some of pits that had been mined in Iron County up to that point was not focused on recovering the entire ore body but only the portion of the ore body that was easily and cheaply accessed. Even some of the pits designed later on had similar issues.

Mr. Mathesius told the institute that the future of the steel industry looked promising but "the days of 'high-grading' and of 'robber-mining' were gone." He said that in the past, some essential raw materials appeared to be inexhaustible, but were now becoming limiting factors. Because of this there was a need for careful planning and conservation of the natural resources and that everything possible should be done to get maximum yield from the raw materials on which the iron and steel industry must rely for its future production.

As an example, Mr. Mathesius mentioned that the Sunnyside coal district east of Price was the only area in the vast fields of Carbon and Emery counties from which coal with fair coking properties could be produced at reasonable costs. And even the Sunnyside coking coal was marginal to the point that it had to be blended with low volatile Oklahoma coal.[52]

Mr. Mathesius repeated his message in 1951, "The raw materials are adequate to provide for a sound and steady growth. They are not plentiful enough to permit careless or lavish exploitation or exuberant expansion of the production facilities dependent upon them."[53]

A number of the mining operations fell prey to this problem, some for mostly legitimate reasons such as technology or financial considerations. Nevertheless, there was a substantial amount of iron ore that was wasted over the years that could have been saved through conservative practices such as better pit planning or saving marginal grade ore by segregating it rather than discarding it over the waste dump.

Taxes

It seems that the State and the County were always on the lookout for new and innovative ways to collect more taxes from the mining operations so that they could reduce the taxes for everyone else in the County. Industry always was, and continues to be, a tempting tax target for governments, local, state and federal. The iron mines were no exception.

Early in 1948, the Utah State Tax Commission and Columbia had a disagreement over the net proceeds tax calculations for calendar year 1947. In August 1948, the State Tax Commission sustained its original mine occupation and net proceeds tax assessment against Columbia Iron Mining Co. based upon what the Commission "felt truly represented the actual value of ore mined" rather than price paid for the ore under a contract.[54] United States Steel Corporation was a vertically integrated company, with both Columbia Iron Mining and Geneva Steel as subsidiaries. Columbia and Geneva, if left to their own devices, could set the transfer price between them at almost any value depending on which company they wanted to appear to have the most profit.

The net proceeds tax assessment was usually based on the price per ton of iron ore but the Commission claimed that Columbia's transfer price was too low. The State therefore used the unit price that Kaiser paid for its ore from the Excelsior mine to calculate the tax rather than using the transfer price that Columbia had set. Since CF&I was in a similar situation in regard to its mines, the Commission also adjusted its transfer price.[55] Columbia registered a formal protest against the assessment to the Commission. In July 1949, Walter Mathesius, President of the Geneva Steel Company, visited Cedar

City and met with civic and municipal leaders to discuss the tax situation with regard to the assessment of Geneva Steel Company's holdings in Iron County.

The company representatives pointed out that a specific formula for assessing taxes against a mining company had been set up by law, but that in 1947 the State Tax Commission determined to assess the Company on an arbitrary value basis. This, the Company claimed, was in violation of the law, and therefore the taxes for the year were paid under protest, and the Company filed notice that it would sue for a refund of the difference. The Company was asking for a refund of $37,241.34 of the total taxes paid to Iron County in the year 1947. Similar suits were filed against the State and Iron County for refund of taxes paid. The State Tax Commission agreed and refunded the amount requested, however Iron County officials would not make the refund and prepared to fight the case in the courts.[56]

A hearing was held on the case in January 1950, and Fifth District Judge, Will L. Hoyt, upheld the State Tax Commission's contention that the Commission may set a value on ore for tax purposes where the ore is sold under contract between two subsidiaries of the same parent company. This decision was very important for Iron County because it affected not only the year 1947 but also the taxes to be collected in subsequent years.[57]

The following newspaper article, published in January, 1949, makes it clear that the goal of the Iron County attorney was to increase the taxes on the iron ore industry so taxes could be lowered on everyone else.

> County Attorney, Durham Morris, spent three days of last week in Salt Lake City drafting a Bill to give Iron County more taxes on iron ore being mined and shipped out of the County. Mr. Morris also conferred with various individuals and organizations to gain support for the Bill in the present session of the Utah State Legislature. Senator L. N. Marsden, and Representative E. Ray Lyman, with the aid of other Iron County officials, will endeavor to have the bill enacted into law by the Legislature, which convened Monday.
>
> If the bill, drafted by Mr. Morris, becomes a law, it will insure additional revenues for Iron County, from the mining operations which are increasing in the County. Mr. Morris states that in his opinion there is great need for reduction of taxes on homes, farms, and livestock, in Iron County, and if additional revenues are ensured through the enactment of the proposed bill, taxes on homes, farms, and livestock, could be reduced.[58]

In May 1951, the State Tax Commission arrived at a new method of setting iron ore values for taxation purposes that, if put into effect, would more than double the taxes on mining operations while other property values in the County would remain the same. The proposed method of arriving at the value of iron ore properties would use the value of pig iron produced from a ton of ore, less the cost of transportation and reduction. Protests against the new assessments were filed with the Tax Commission almost immediately by the Geneva Steel Company and the Colorado Fuel & Iron Company.[59]

In December 1956, the *Iron County Record* published an article concerning the taxes paid into Iron County coffers for 1957. The four largest taxpayers in the county were the Columbia Iron Mining Company with $591,799.26, the Colorado Fuel & Iron Company with $307,247.99, the Utah Construction Company with $187,605.00 and the Union Pacific Railroad Company with $110,965.57. All four of these companies were

Iron Mining & Manufacturing

directly connected to the iron mining industry. The total tax paid by these companies was almost $1.2 million, which accounted for 70 percent of Iron Counties' revenue for 1956.[60]

Organized labor disputes

On January 21, 1946, the United Steelworkers of America employed at the Columbia Iron mine went on strike and although there were only thirty-five members of the union, nearly seventy-five others were put out of work due to the strike, bringing the out-of-work total in the area to 110. The Ironton Plant was also shut down. The workers were off the job for about a month.[61]

From mid-March to mid-April, 1948, the United Mine Workers went on strike, the iron mines remained open and could have continued working but Geneva and Ironton were shut down so no iron ore was required from the mines.[62]

On October 1, 1949, the C.I.O. United Steelworkers went out on a nation-wide strike that lasted forty-two days. Geneva and Ironton plants were shut down for the duration.

Nation Steel Strike Idles 165 Workers at Local Columbia Iron Mines

Operations at the Columbia Iron Mines have been almost at a complete standstill this week with 165 workers out as a part of the nation-wide steel strike. According to Carroll Brown, Cedar City, President of the C.I.O. United Steelworkers Local, the local management and labor leaders are in complete agreement, following a joint meeting Monday evening. The two parties have gotten together and there will be no picket lines at the mines.

However, 34 salaried employees are still on the job. This is the result of a national policy adopted last spring which allows these workers to continue working during a strike. The workers went off the job Saturday, October 1, at 12:01 a.m.

Utah Construction Co. has not been affected by the steel strike since its employees are members of the American Federation of Labor. Shipments by the company have been curtailed, but mining operations are still continuing.

Biggest shutdown in shipments was the consignment to Colorado Fuel and Iron at Pueblo, Colorado.

Equipment which was being installed in the new Columbia Power Plant by Utah Construction was also stopped because of the strike.[63]

The losses to the country overall because of the forty-two-day strike were substantial.

Effects from Steel Strike Still Being Felt in Utah
By Clarence D. Williams

Effects of the steel strike still are being felt in Utah and the nation and resulting losses were heavy.

It is estimated that steel company employees over the country lost $178,000,000 in direct wages. Figures compiled by Steel magazine show that more than 8,500,000 net tons of ingots were lost from the 1949 production in the six weeks since the strike first started. The loss in steel ingots from the strike's beginning until operations return to the prestrike rate will amount to 10,500,000 tons.[64]

On April 8, 1952, the United Steelworkers of America went on strike. The Geneva and Ironton plants were shut down and didn't start back up until the end of July. The Columbia mines continued working, doing stripping and maintenance work, but were not able to ship any ore.[65]

On June 5, 1952, the local union decided to go on strike and approximately 220 iron mine workers employed at Iron Mountain and Desert Mound by the Columbia Iron Mining Company walked off the job. They decided to join the strike to ask for settlement on the same terms given other steel workers in the nation and to settle a local pay dispute of eighteen months. The dispute involved an 8-1/2 cent hourly pay raise, retroactive to December 1, 1950, under a job reclassification agreement, which they claimed, had never been paid. In addition to the 220 miners who were idled by strikes, nearly 150 other workers were put out of work.

By June 26, 1952, the effects of the strike were being felt on the local economy. About seventy employees of the Utah Construction Company, although not on strike, were given early vacations because they had completed the stripping operations they had been engaged in since the strike started. Utah Construction's ore shipments to CF&I in Pueblo and Kaiser in Fontana were stopped because those plants had also been shut down by the strike.[66] Geneva and Ironton workers returned to work the last week in July, when the nation-wide strike ended.[67] However, the miners at the Columbia waited a week longer to return to work. Finally, in the first week of August 1952, the striking workers, along with hundreds of others that were put out of work as a result of the strike, went back to work.

On August 31, 1952, the president of Local 2751 of the United Steelworkers of America reported that every hourly employee of the Columbia Iron Mining Company at Iron Mountain and Desert Mound had voluntarily become a member of Local 2751 and that each would be entitled to an 8-1/2 cent wage increase, retroactive to December 1, 1950.

On July 1, 1956, the United Steelworkers union went on a nation-wide strike. Approximately 241 members of the local union participated in the walkout. Other businesses were also affected, for instance, the Union Pacific Railroad Company made a reduction simultaneous with the strike. At Utah Construction the discontinuation of ore shipments to CF&I in Colorado forced the company to reduce its manpower to almost one-half of the workforce. Many men reportedly left the area in search of temporary work to tide them over until work at the mines could be resumed. The strike was settled after thirty-nine days.[68]

On July 15, 1959, the United Steelworkers of America union went out on a nation-wide strike. The strike shut down Geneva and Ironton, the Columbia iron mines in Cedar City and the Columbia and Geneva coal mines near Dragerton. Numerous others, in connected businesses, were also put out of work. Somewhat ironically, Utah Construction signed a contract with its workers the week before the strike but still had to reduce its workforce because there was no market for the ore being mined while the strike was on.

In February 1949, prolonged subzero weather, heavy snowfall and high winds caused large snow drifts and created blizzard conditions in much of Utah. The coal mines in Carbon and Emery Counties and the iron mines of Iron County were all shut down due to weather. The railroads were also at a virtual standstill because of similar problems. The supply of iron ore and coal to Geneva was cut off and the plant was left with only three or four days' supply available. The plant was on the verge of shutdown when the weather finally broke and deliveries resumed.[69]

Columbia Iron Mining Company

As mentioned above, the Columbia Iron Mining Company was particularly impacted by the Geneva plant coming on line, and that had not been anticipated in the daily production requirements and or in the long range plans that were made prior to the plant's construction. As the pits got deeper, it became increasingly difficult to supply the entire Geneva and Ironton ore requirement from the two pits at Iron Mountain. The Black Hawk Pit was starting to have problems even before the big increase in 1944 and the Pinto Pit was midway through its life. To make matters worse, as the pits became deeper the prevailing water table was encountered and water had to be pumped from the pits as a regular part of the mining operation. The water added complexity to the operation, hampered production and created safety issues.

The reality for both the short and long term was that additional pits needed to be opened up to supplement and eventually replace the two Iron Mountain pits that were getting deeper at an accelerated rate. The Geneva and Ironton plants needed a guaranteed supply of iron ore to be able to operate on a long-term basis.

> Representatives from the Geneva Steel Company and the Columbia Iron Mining Company met to thoroughly discuss and assess the mine operating problems, mineable ore reserves, and the urgent need existing that dictated new mining areas be made available as soon as possible. In the interests of conservation and complete utilization of the ore reserves it was agreed to mix the low-grade ore, some of less than 40 % iron content, with the higher grades as uniformly as possible. Mixing facilities had been built at Geneva to aid in this process.[70]

The opening of additional pits was a critical issue. As Chapter 7 outlined, Columbia owned five deposits at Iron Mountain and part of a sixth, two of which were already being mined at the time. Only one of the remaining deposits, the Burke ore body, outcropped on the surface. The other three, including the Rex, the Lime Cap and the A and B deposit, were covered by a considerable amount of overburden. Columbia had a number of other claims in the district, including ore deposits in the Comstock, Desert Mound and Iron Springs mining areas.

Opening up a third pit at Iron Mountain on the outcropping Burke ore body was an obvious choice. In fact, work had already begun on the Burke Pit by 1951. Another pit needed to be opened in addition to the Burke Pit, however, and that decision was more difficult. All of the large outcropping deposits were already being mined by Columbia or one of the other mining companies, the deeper ore bodies would require substantial lead time, planning and investment to open, and time was of the essence. Ultimately, Columbia decided to redesign and reopen the Desert Mound Pit where mining was suspended back in 1936.

Due to the fact that Columbia's men and equipment were already fully occupied, working to meet the demand of the furnaces at Ironton and Geneva, Columbia contracted the Utah Construction Company to pre-strip the overlying overburden from the Short Line and Desert Mound claims in the Desert Mound mining area starting in mid-1949 and from the Burke claim at Iron mountain starting in mid 1953.

In 1951, after a new processing facility had been constructed at Desert Mound and Utah Construction Co. had completed its pre-stripping work, Columbia commenced mining operations in the Desert Mound and Short Line pits. Production was split equally between Desert Mound and Iron Mountain. This relieved some of the pressure that the operating pits at Iron Mountain had been experiencing due to the hectic production schedules that had been imposed on the mine since the opening of the Geneva plant.

During 1947, an unexpected problem began plaguing the iron mines. There had been a dramatic increase in pump-well farming in the Newcastle, Beryl and Enterprise areas. The increased pump load, combined with the load of the large crushers and power shovels at the iron mines, was more than the local power company could supply. The frequent power outages and poor voltage control caused damage to mining equipment as well as loss in production. The power company came to the decision to notify the mining companies that they could not operate mining equipment during daylight hours. This rationing of power was the last straw for Columbia and it felt that its only recourse was to build its own power plant.[71]

On March 18, 1948, Columbia Iron Mining Company announced that it planned to construct a new power plant to provide for the electric power requirements of its operations near Cedar City, Utah at an estimated cost of $400,000. The plant was to be built at Iron Mountain and would contain three diesel-powered generators each with a capacity of 750 kilowatts. Power transmission lines were also to be run from the power plant to Desert Mound. All the power generated by the plant was to be used by Columbia. The first of the units began operation in early September with the installation of the other two units being completed in late October.

Mr. G. D. MacDonald of Columbia explained that company had installed the new power plant because the power purchased from the Southern Utah Power Company had become undependable and the company could not risk any down time at Ironton or Geneva caused by Columbia's inability to mine and ship ore from its operations in Southern Utah. Although the cost of the power provided by Southern Utah Power might have been less than that from the company generators, the cost of relining a blast furnace if ore became scarce, was so great that the saving at Ironton and Geneva would offset the cost of building the power plant.

Mr. MacDonald also stated that the Company felt that it had been accused unjustly by the pump farmers of using power to which the farmers were entitled. He stated that the mines had been using the same amount of power for the past six years, and it was the growth of Cedar City and the pump wells that has caused the tremendous load on the existing power system.[72]

Even though the Utah Public Service Commission was probably aware of Columbia Iron Mine's new power plant at Iron Mountain, they still needed to upgrade and strengthen the power grid in the vicinity of the iron mines and the New Castle-Beryl farmers and meet their public commitment to provide reliable power to their customers. They called a meeting in February of 1949 and invited sixteen community and industry leaders to discuss the acute shortages of electrical energy that had occurred the previous two summers and which were projected to occur the following summer. The dispute between the pump-well farmers and the iron ore miners was acknowledged and "immediate steps" were supposedly going to be "taken to insure an adequate supply" of power.[73]

The Commission's commitment to take "immediate steps" to ensure an adequate power supply did not result in action for another two years. On April 1, 1951, the power company began building a new 69,000-volt line from Cedar City to Iron Mountain. The new line had more than double the capacity of the old line and served the iron mines and irrigation areas of Enterprise and Escalante valleys.[74]

Columbia wasn't the only mining company to have power supply problems. Utah Construction Company at Iron Springs was encountering similar issues and was in the process of building a power plant at Iron Springs. It had gone so far as to start buying equipment before the situation abated.[75]

In January 1958, the Columbia Iron Mining Company completed a new office building located at 1552 West 200 North in Cedar City and an open house was held for the public on February 7. Previously, the local headquarters for the mining company had been located at Iron Mountain. People from both Iron Mountain and Desert Mound operations moved into the new office building. The reinforced concrete block structure had 8,204 sq. ft. of space on the ground floor with a full basement underneath. The basement housed an employees' lunch room, a main central chemical laboratory, heating and air conditioning plants and more office space. The new tan and blue building with exterior adjustable metal louvers, was "a demonstration of U.S. Steel's faith in the long-range future of this area."[76]

In June of 1958, G. D. MacDonald, Superintendent of the Columbia Iron Mining Company at Cedar City, was honored by the University of Utah for outstanding accomplishment in the field of mining engineering during graduation exercises and was awarded the highly-coveted professional degree of Engineer of Mines. At the time, the degree had been awarded only five times in the history of the University. MacDonald joined Columbia in 1940, and over the years had worked as mine engineer, general foreman, mine superintendent and General Superintendent.[77]

Columbia Iron Mining Company Handbook

The following extract is from the 1959 *Columbia Iron Mining Company Handbook*. Although lengthy, it gives extremely useful information and insights concerning the Iron Mountain and Desert Mound mining operations of the Columbia Iron Mining Company that could not be found elsewhere.

Exploration Methods

As mining operations have progressed, depleting the outcropping and readily accessible ore, the operating companies have organized exploration programs staffed with specialists to seek new ore bodies to maintain reserves well in advance of anticipated abnormal demands. Exploration usually requires reconnaissance mapping to determine relief, stratigraphy, and rock types. Recently the air-borne magnetometer has become a "must" in seeking regional magnetic anomalies. Investigation of favorable zones is then pursued by precise geological mapping supplemented by detailed ground magnetometer surveys. Should evaluation of all data indicate a possible ore body, the area is then tested by diamond drilling.

A confirmed ore body is then drilled systematically to ascertain position, shape, depth of cover, quality, and quantity of ore. Detailed geological maps, sections, and drill hole logs, are then prepared to guide the mining engineer in preparing a complete mining plan and schedule.

Mining Practice

Three mining companies are operating at five locations in the Iron County area producing in excess of 4,000,000 net tons of iron ore annually: The Columbia Iron Mining Company, Colorado Fuel & Iron Corporation, and Utah Construction Company. All mining is done by open pit methods and all are similar operations other than minor differences in equipment and final product requirements.

The Columbia Iron Mining Company is currently operating at two locations—the Iron Mountain Mine and the Desert Mound Mine which was re-opened in 1949. Since the iron ores vary so much in composition in relatively short distances and uniformity of final product requirements is so essential, several ore faces must be available at all times. This requires close pit planning and mining schedules. Depending upon the type of ore required, it may be necessary to blend ores from several locations within a mine or from two different mines. This may be accomplished in part by combining the ore before and through the crusher, or later by proper spacing of the railroad cars containing specific ore grades.

The current pits have been laid out in plan, from the summarized results of exploration, to permit maximum extraction of the ore body. Development and mining were planned on benches 35 feet in height with approximately a 63-degree wall slope on each bench. Two benches are finally consolidated to a 70-foot wall, and a safety berm, 35 feet in width, is left at the base resulting in an overall pit slope of 45 degrees. Adverse haulage roads in the pits are usually 50 to 60 feet in width, limited to a plus 8% grade, and constructed along the pit wall without deleting the safety berms effectiveness. Precise scheduling coordinated with good pit planning allows development to continue at lower levels as the ore mining progresses at higher levels. The development of later pits has required the removal of large quantities of overburden before reaching the ore. At present this has not exceeded the removal of two yards of waste for one ton of ore recovered, but this waste to ore ratio will increase until finally, underground methods of mining will be required.

Iron Mountain and Desert Mound Mining Operations

The Pinto, Blackhawk, and Burke ore bodies at Iron Mountain produced 26,610,000 N.T. of ore and 24,940,000 C.Y. of stripping from 1936 to 1959 at a strip ratio of 0.94 tons per cubic yard. The Short Line and Desert Mound ore bodies at Desert Mound and the Pioche ore body at Iron Springs produced 10,430,000 N.T. of ore and 27,950,000 C.Y. of stripping from 1951 to 1959 at a strip ratio of 2.68 tons per cubic yard.

Between the six pits Columbia had electric track-mounted rotary drills that use 9" and 7-3/8" tri-cone bits that drilled in ore at the rate of 25 ft./hr., and in waste at the rate of 20 ft./hr. For secondary drilling, they had two air-operated, tire-mounted drills that use 1-4/8" carbide bits and have a 40' boom and a 315 CFM (100 psi) air compressor.

For blasting, wet holes war surplus TNT is poured loose into the hole. In dry holes prilled ammonium nitrate is mixed with 10% fuel oil or 25% TNT and poured loose into the hole. Primacord and high-explosive primers are used for detonating and drill cuttings are used for tamping. The powder factor was 0.33 pounds per ton in ore and 0.5 pounds per cubic yard in waste. A half stick of dynamite and detacord is used for secondary blasting.

Columbia had five 4-1/2 cubic yard electric shovels and one 3-1/4 cubic yard electric shovels. In ore the shovels loaded haul trucks at a rate of 390 tons per hour, in waste they loaded at 180 cubic yards per hour.

They had sixteen 40-ton dump trucks with 600 h.p. engines, fifteen 25-ton dump trucks with 300 h.p. engines and one 32-ton dump truck with a 350 h.p. engine. The trucks hauled ore at 90 tons per hour and waste at 45 cubic yards per hour. The average haul distance was 3/4 of a mile and there was usually 4 trucks per shovel.

The operation was scheduled three shifts per day, five days per week with 160 hourly employees and 12 supervisors. All hourly employees were members of the United Steelworkers of America union.

Each ore level was drilled out ahead of the mining faces with holes on 25' centers. An ore sample was prepared from each hole and sent to the Lab. The lab analyzed each ore sample for iron, phosphorus and sulphur. This information was plotted on level maps and used for scheduling shovels.

Processing Plant at Iron Mountain

The trucks dump ore that was hauled from the mine into the hopper, where a 5' by 15' pan feeder operating at 400 tons per hour, carries the pit-run ore from the hopper to the 48" by 60' jaw crusher. A 42" by 180' conveyor belt then carries the ore to a 6' by 10' scalper screen where the minus 2-1/2" by 5" ore is scalped off and the remaining ore goes through the 18" by 5' gyratory crusher and is crushed to a minus 3-1/2" thickness. A 30" by 175' conveyor belt then carries the ore to the two 6' by 12' finishing screens where it is separated to minus 1/4" slot, a plus 1/4" minus 3" slot, or passes over the screens and drops directly into the loading bins. Seven men were required to operate the complete plant.

Processing Plant at Desert Mound

The ore is dumped into the hopper and drops onto a 5' by 17' pan feeder that feeds ore to the 48" by 60" jaw crusher at the rate of 400 tons per hour, where it is crushed to minus 8-1/2 inches. It is then carried by a 42" by 45' conveyor belt to a 6' by 12' scalper screen where the minus 1-1/2" by 5" ore is scalped off and the remaining ore goes through the 18" by 5' gyratory crusher and is crushed to a minus 3-1/2" thickness. A 42" by 350' conveyor belt carries the crushed ore to 42" by 400' conveyor which drops it into one of five 30,000-ton stockpiles.

A 5' by 17' pan feeder and two 48" by 15' belt feeders drop the ore from the stockpiles onto a 42" by 450' conveyor at belt a rate of 500 tons per hour. The conveyer takes the ore to two 6' by 16' finishing screens where it is separated to a minus 1/4" slot, a plus 1/4" minus 3" slot and a plus 3" slot. The ore drops into the loading bins after it passes through or over the screens. The ore is sampled mechanical sampling equipment as it drops into the loading bins. Ten men are required to operate the preparation plant.

Illustration 9.1. This picture shows one of what was, at the time, the world's largest haul trucks, posed at the Burke Pit. The Iron County Record *printed the photo with this caption: "Boyd Paulson, left, a superintendent at Utah Construction Company, and electrician Wesley "Shine" Thompson relax at the front wheel of the world's largest dump truck. This huge truck's size is further proven by comparison to the jeep in the rear of the picture, with A. F. Geiger at its side. Unloaded, this monster tips the scales at 52 tons and will carry a load in excess of 50 tons. The length of the huge dump truck is 36.5 feet with a width of 13.8 feet and a height of 13 feet. Bed dimensions alone are 22 by 12.5 by 4 feet. Four of these trucks were in use at the Utah Construction Company project sites."[84] (Photo from York Jones)*

Sampling and Loading

Each railroad car of ore loaded was automatically sampled and the sample was prepared and sent to the Lab. The Lab analyzed each car sample or car sample composite for iron, silica, alumina, lime, magnesium, phosphorus, sulphur, manganese, and moisture.

The smelter requirements were as follows

1. Geneva Blast Furnaces Lot requirements: 17,000 NT, plus 48% iron, minus 0.35% phosphorus, minus 0.100% sulphur, minus 1% iron variation between lots, and minus 30% fines.

2. Ironton #2 B.F. – Lot requirements: 1,200 NT daily, plus 48% iron, minus 0.17% phosphorus, minus 0.1% sulphur, minus 2% iron variation between lots, and 35 - 40% fines.

3. Ironton #1 B.F. – Lot requirements: 750 NT daily, plus 47% iron, minus 0.35% phosphorus, minus 0.1% sulphur, minus 3% iron variation between lots, and 35 - 50% fines.

4. Geneva O.H. Furnaces – Lot requirements: By individual cars, plus 52% iron, minus 0.40% phosphorus, and minus 0.05% sulphur.[78]

Iron Mountain Mining Area

A March 10, 1949 article in the *Iron County Record* discussed three new trucks bought by Columbia. The trucks were manufactured by LeTourneau and had an improved design compared to the old trucks.

Columbia Mines Receives Three of Country's Largest Ore Trucks

They say that good things are worth waiting for, and these days the people out at the Columbia Iron Mines are believing it.

Having been shipped on January 10 from Vicksburg, Mississippi where they are manufactured, three new 40-ton hauling units finally arrived here in Cedar City March 2, according to H. L. Macintosh of the J. K. Wheeler Machinery Company, who made the delivery. The Le Tourneau trucks are the largest in the country, weighing 20 tons, and can carry a pay load of approximately 40 tons or about twice their own weight.

The trucks, being so large and weighing so much, each needed a flat car for the long trip across the country to here. Because of their size, the railroad would only ship them by local freight and so the delay.

Gigantic is the word in describing everything about the new trucks. They stand 10 feet from the ground to the top of the cab. The tires are 6 feet four inches in diameter, costing about $1100 apiece. The truck itself costs around $40,000. They are the largest off-highway hauling unit in the country, and travel at 24 miles per hour.

All controls are electrical. The push button steering is so simple, say the manufacturers, that a child could operate one. A small toggle switch is flipped either right or left to turn. The braking system is also electrically operated from a button in the cab. A new feature is the elimination of the hydraulic lift. Steel cables run from the dumping gate in the rear forward underneath the curved body up to an electric hoist near the top of the cab. By electrically winding the cable, the body is lifted. Delays because of hydraulic failure are thereby eliminated.

The trucks are equipped with 300 horsepower supercharged diesel engines. Output of the generators is enough to light a fair-sized village.

The J. K. Wheeler Machinery Company of Salt Lake City made the delivery of the trucks to the Columbia Iron Mining company, a division of the Geneva steel company. The trucks are already in operation at the mine."[79]

The Burke Pit

In April 1953, a contract was signed between the Columbia Iron Mining Company and the Utah Construction Company for a large stripping program at Iron Mountain in the Burke Pit, owned by Columbia. Preliminary surveys were started soon after the signing and actual excavation began two weeks later. The program required between 100 to 125 additional employees to be hired to work for Utah Construction. The work done at Iron Mountain was very similar to the work done previously by Utah Construction at the Short Line and Desert Mound pits.

Illustration 9.2. The Pinto Pit around 1950. The pit was opened in the 1940s by Columbia to supplement production from the Blackhawk Pit. The Burke Pit was opened up later. By 1951, as can be seen in the photograph, the Pinto Pit, in the center, had a good start but the Burke Pit, in the upper left, was just getting started. All three pits were needed to meet the high demand of the Ironton and Geneva Plants. In 1953, Columbia made the decision to augment their mining capacity and contracted the Utah Construction Company to temporarily move on location and remove much of the remaining overburden covering the Burke ore body. (Photo from York Jones)

The new contract with the Columbia Iron Mining Company was separate and not related to Utah Construction's mining activities at Iron Springs and the additional work required new crews that had to be recruited. The project lasted throughout 1953 and into March of 1954. Once the pre-stripping was completed by Utah Construction, Columbia resumed their mining activities in the pit.[80]

The Burke ore body was located on the southwest side of Iron Mountain. The ore originally outcropped with an exposure of about 1,600 feet in length and 350 feet wide. The deposit was a typical metasomatic replacement of Homestake Limestone. Drilling operations by U.S. Steel and the U.S. Bureau of Mines showed that the deposit was composed of two ore bodies at depth, the Burke No. 2 and the Burke No.3. The Burke No. 2 ore body was larger, and the ore extended to a depth of about 1,000 feet. The ore was variable in thickness but averaged about 150 feet and consisted principally of hard, dense mixtures of magnetite and hematite estimated at sixteen million tons of ore.[81]

In May 1953, the Utah Construction Company received four new Euclid haul trucks to be used for stripping overburden at Iron Mountain.[82] In September 1953, a new electric shovel was purchased by Utah Construction Company. The shovel arrived at Iron Mountain to be used on the contract stripping project on the Burke Pit. When the stripping project was completed the new shovel was used at Iron Mountain to work at

Illustration 9.3. "The world's largest shovel on two crawlers is now operating at Utah Construction Co.'s Burke No. Two mine after approximately three weeks of assembly at the Utah Construction site. The shovel has an over-all height of 43 feet. The dipper capacity is 10 cubic yards and the shovel weighs 386 tons. Nine railroad cars were needed to ship the shovel to Cedar City. Controlled entirely by electricity, the manual operation is practically identical to smaller shovels now in use by the company. Manufactured by Marion Shovel Co. of Marion, Ohio, the 191-M was first put into operation Sunday evening, according to Boyd Paulson, mine superintendent. Also shown are two 50-ton capacity, twin engine Euclid trucks and a P&H 1600 electric shovel."[85] (Photo from York Jones.)

the Blowout and Duncan pits and later moved to the Comstock Pit around the mountain to the northeast.[83] In March 1954, when Utah Construction Company completed a portion of its stripping on the Burke Pit, forty of the temporary employees were laid off. The surge of layoffs caused concern and a number of rumors in Cedar City. The company responded to these rumors by pointing out that the previous April over a hundred men were hired by the company to work on the Burke Project. The project was a short-term stripping contract and when the operation and the contract were completed those men were released. The men were released according to the union seniority clauses, and those same men would be rehired on the same basis as opportunities arose.

The situation was exacerbated by the fact that in March CF&I also ceased taking ore for its Pueblo plant for a time and around twenty Utah Construction employees were temporarily laid off.[86] In early January 1955, Utah Construction completed the Burke stripping contract and another seventy men that had been working on the project were laid off.[87]

Illustration 9.4. A blast at the Burke Pit in 1953. This photo was one of a number taken with a high-speed camera in order to analyze the blast. Note the overburden drills at the right, which some might say were parked a bit too close to the blast. (Photo from York Jones.)

The Rex Deposit

In the late 1950s, U.S. Steel began to seriously evaluate its options for a future ore supply for Geneva and Ironton. It owned or had access to three properties that could potentially fit the bill. The first option was the A and B deposit located at Iron Mountain near the Blowout and Black Hawk pits. It had an estimated reserve of thirty to forty million tons. It was beneath 300 to 400 feet of cover but the bottom of the deposit extended over 2,000 feet into the earth.

The second option was the Section 9 ore body, sometimes referred to as the Desert ore body. It was located approximately half way between Iron Mountain and the Desert Mound mining area. It had an estimated reserve of forty million tons and was situated 700 to 900 feet below the surface. It was discovered by aerial magnetic surveys sponsored by U.S. Steel. An extensive drilling program was conducted on the Section 9 ore body during the 1958 to 1961 time period. The deposit had very high iron content but also a high sulfur content and the whole of the ore body was below the water table

The third option and the one that was selected, was the Rex ore body, located on the west flank of Iron Mountain, north of the Burke Pit. The deposit had some ore on the surface; however, the main body of ore was deeper. The estimated ore potential of the Rex ore body exceeded 100 million tons.

Illustration 9.5. Loaded ore cars at Iron Mountain, waiting to be shipped. If it looks confusing, it probably was. Utah Construction's facilities and loadout were on the left and Columbia's facilities and loadout were across the tracks on the right. There were at least seven sets of rails running through the area to accommodate all the cars that were coming and going. Some cars were loaded with open-hearth ore and others with blast furnace ore. The Columbia cars went to Geneva and Ironton, the Utah Construction cars went to Pueblo Colorado for CF&I. Many of the workers of the two companies were both friends and competitors. (Matheson Special Collections)

Once the decision was made to pursue the Rex deposit as the next target for U.S. Steel, Columbia conducted a massive exploration and drilling program to define the boundaries and depth of the deposit, to better understand the quality of the ore and to engineer an optimal pit configuration to access and mine the ore. The deposit was drilled primarily on 200-foot centers in both north-south and east-west directions with some 100-foot infill holes and some holes on 400-foot centers near the margins of the deposit.

A large open pit mine was designed which was simply named the "Rex." It was determined that of the 100 million tons of mineralization, about three fourths could be direct shipped, with the remainder requiring upgrading. Pit walls were designed with a layback angle of forty-five degrees. Pre-mine stripping was calculated to be about ninety-eight million cubic yards, with an additional 180 million cubic yards of stripping required during mining. Pre-mine stripping was expected to take four to six years and cost between 200 and 300 million dollars in current terms. A total stripping volume of about 280 million cubic yards, producing 100 million tons of ore, resulted in a strip ratio of 2.8 cubic yards per ton, compared to a historic value of about 2:1 for most of the other ore bodies. The plans included a beneficiation plant to upgrade the lower quality ore to be mined from the Rex. There were also nearly eight million tons of low-grade ore in the vicinity that would be a potential source of addition feed for the plant.[88]

U.S. Steel was pleased with the outcome and plans were put in place to start construction of the mine. Water rights were purchased in the New Castle Valley to be used in mining and processing.

When U.S. Steel began to move ahead to mine the Rex deposit, it immediately ran into property stalemates. The Rex was a large ore body with a large surface area, especially when the layback of the pit walls was considered and the large dump areas that would be required for the waste material were included. At twenty acres per claim, dozens of claims were involved, and given the notoriety of the deposit, there were a number of hold-outs by claim and property owners who demanded large sums of money for their holdings.

An example of this was the mining claim by the name of Sunbeam No. 8, Survey 7201, under the name of Arthur E. Moreton and his co-claimants. This claim was surveyed in 1946. Before U.S. Steel could mine the Burke Pit adjacent to the proposed Rex ore body, it paid Arthur E. Moreton $180,000 plus a royalty of twenty-five cents per ton on all extracted tonnage.

Another one of the claims associated with the Rex ore body was the Iron Sandstone, survey No. 7225, dated 1949, under the name of Arthur E. Moreton and L. F. Luke. Another claim associated in the same area was the Lime Cap, dated 1948, under the name of William C. Murie and Arthur E. Moreton. The procurement of many of the claims became very difficult and raised the question of whether or not mining plans could proceed. Another key claim that U.S. Steel needed but couldn't seem to negotiate at a reasonable price, was the Roger Claim dated 1949. This included the MS&L claim under the name of Marie Wood and Arthur E. Moreton.

In 1956, U.S. Steel finally purchased all of the outstanding claims that were needed to be able to mine the Rex deposit. The following article that was published in the *Iron County Record* in March, 1956 told about the negotiations with the final claim holders, most of whom belonged to the Murie family.

Negotiations Brought to Conclusion on Land Transfer Deal

Negotiations were completed last week by the Columbia Iron Mining Co. and several residents of this area for a parcel of land including 18 or 19 mining claims that are in the area of proposed development in the company's iron ore mining processes. It is estimated that terms of the purchase were nearly one million dollars.

Most of the land owners holding claims in the area known as the Rex Ore Body in the Iron Mountain area are residents of southern Utah, including Wm. C. Murie, Mr. and Mrs. Rex Murie. Mr. and Mrs. Melvin Murie and Ernest Murie, all of Cedar City. Also Included were Mr. and Mrs. Cleo Wood of Hurricane.[89]

Despite all of the time, effort and money spent on the Rex deposit by U.S. Steel to procure the mining claims, to buy the water rights, to drill hundreds of exploration holes and pay for thousands of hours on studies and plans, especially at the local level, the upper management of U.S. Steel had still not committed to mining the deposit. In 1958 planning on the Rex ground to a stop and Utah Construction Company was asked to supply 20 percent of the total Geneva ore requirement. It became obvious that something was in the works for the future other than developing the Rex.

There were a number of issues that affected the company's decision regarding the Rex, but the difficulty, expense and the lengthy amount of time it took to obtain the rights to mine the deposit, including ongoing royalties, had to be on the list. The increasing level of State and County taxation and the continual disruptions caused by organized labor also must have been a consideration. The huge amount of up-front stripping costs was certainly not encouraging.

The A and B, Section 9 and Rex deposits are still there, all 180 million tons of high grade iron ore, waiting, perhaps for another time.

The Rex ore body is situated on the west side of Iron Mountain, directly north of the Burke Pit. It was discovered in 1944–45 during the U.S. Bureau of Mines investigation of the district using a magnetometer. The deposit produced the strongest and most extensive anomaly observed in the Pinto-Iron Springs Mining District by the magnetic surveys conducted by the Bureau. It was initially called the "Milner Hill Anomaly."

The pear-shaped anomaly extended northward for about 3,000 feet and eastward for more than 3,000 feet.

> [However,] the only large outcrop of ore within the confines of the anomaly lies on top of Milner Hill and extends over an area of about 7,500 square feet. A large amount of ore float covered the slopes of the hill, and in particular the west slope, where large ore boulders commonly 3 and often 6 to 10 feet in diameter constitute a mantle that extends far west of the hill itself.[90]

It was determined that the pod of ore exposed on top of Milner Hill itself was not connected to the much deeper Rex ore body, which was unexposed.

A potential drill-hole site was located on the basis of the magnetometer study. It was actually several hundred feet southeast of the positive center of the Milner Hill anomaly, but it provided an excellent test of the anomaly. The hole was drilled using a diamond bit core drill. The drilling was stopped, in ore, at a depth of 1,374 feet to permit replacing the small drill rig with a large rig. Unfortunately, the project was terminated before the hole could be deepened, so the full depth of the ore in that location was not determined.

> The hole showed that the central part of the Milner Hill anomaly was underlain by (1) about 600 feet of sandstone containing little or no disseminated magnetite; (2) below this, about 700 feet of heavily mineralized sandstone and siltstone which has an average magnetite content of about 45 percent and which may be regarded as low-grade ore; (3) and finally, at least 70 feet, and possibly much more, of replacement, medium to high-grade, magnetite-hematite ore with a magnetite content of 50 percent or more, probably in Homestake Limestone.[91]

A substantial amount of further drilling was conducted by the Columbia Iron Mining Corporation in the following years to better define the ore body. The drilling operations confirmed what the magnetometer study and limited drilling by the Bureau of Mines had indicated, that the Rex deposit was the largest deposit in the Pinto-Iron Springs Mining District.

The following geologic conclusions were made: the main Rex ore body was found to be a metasomatic hydrothermal replacement of Homestake Limestone, but mineralization was also strong in overlying brecciated Entrada Sandstone and Iron Springs formations. A mineralized zone more than 750 feet thick exists in this deposit and the estimated ore potential of the ore body was found to exceed 100 million tons of ore.[92]

Between 1957 and 1960, all three of the Columbia Iron Mining Corporation's pits at Iron Mountain were depleted and abandoned. Over its lifetime, the Black Hawk Pit produced about twenty million tons of ore, the Pinto Pit produced about ten million tons of ore and the Burke Pit produced about sixteen million tons of ore. After the closure of the pits at Iron Mountain, Columbia focused all of its mining efforts on the operations at Desert Mound and Iron Springs.

Desert Mound Mining Area

After a series of evaluations and studies, Columbia decided to re-open operations at the Desert Mound mining area. The pits at Desert Mound were mined by the Utah Iron Ore Corporation from 1924 through 1936. The earlier mining activities focused most of their efforts on ore removal and less on pit development and overburden haulage. As a result, when the pits got deeper it became too difficult and expensive to continue so the pits were abandoned. This left a considerable portion of the ore body in the ground, unmined.

Because of tight finances and very limited technology, the early miners did not have the tools to determine the extent of the ore bodies they were mining prior to commencing operations. They had sunk hand-dug shafts and driven hand-dug drifts, but only near the surface and some of the ore bodies were wide and very deep. Many times, the length, breadth and depth of the deposits on which they were mining remained a mystery to them.

In the intervening time after mining had ceased in the Desert Mound area, other sizable ore bodies were discovered in the area as a result of airborne magnetometer work. One nearby ore body, called the Short Line, was completely covered by over 150 feet of alluvium. The extent of the old, partially mined Desert Mound ore body was also better defined. At the time of the earlier operations, since no one was aware of the existence of ore beneath the surface in the Short Line deposit and other deposits, some two miles of railroad had been built over parts of the ore deposits and had to be relocated along with some of the overburden that had been dumped too close to the new pit boundaries.

At the time, Columbia's men and equipment were fully occupied mining the Pinto and Black Hawk pits at Iron Mountain, so Utah Construction Company was contracted to pre-strip the overlying overburden from the Short Line and Desert Mound claims. To uncover the ore, a total of five million cubic yards of overburden material had to be removed over the two ore bodies. In addition, a system of haul roads was constructed so that ore could be hauled to the crushing plant and waste could be hauled to the various dumps.

While Utah Construction was stripping the overburden from the Short Line Pit, Columbia built its new ore processing plant and loading facilities at a nearby location. The plant was a completely new facility and was structured to provide for stockpiling and blending of different ores. In July 1951, when the plant construction was completed,

Illustration 9.6. A thirty-ton capacity Euclid truck being loaded by an 80-D Northwest shovel at Desert Mound, February 1, 1950. (Photo from York Jones.)

Columbia started its mining and stripping activities in the Short Line and Desert Mound pits.

The Desert Mound Mining Area did not come near the Iron Mountain Mining Area as far as total reserves. However, it did rank second in the District, and was Columbia's home base for many years after its Iron Mountain pits were depleted. Although there were numerous mining claims covering the area, there were only eleven ore bodies of consequence in the Desert Mound Mining Area, three of which were mined: the Desert Mound, Short Line and King ore bodies. Unfortunately, like Iron Mountain, the other eight ore bodies were never mined, primarily because of their depth.

The existence of these eight was not known at first. Their presence was revealed by either the U.S. Bureau of Mines during its geophysical surveys of the district in 1944-45 or by aerial magnetic surveys conducted by the U.S. Steel Corporation. The eight ore bodies were Section 2, Section 3, Section 4, Section 9 East, Section 9 West, State Section 2, Thompson and Little Jim. Six of these were named simply after the name of the survey section in which they were located.

Desert Mound ore body occurred in a low hilly area about one mile southwest of Granite Mountain. The Homestake Limestone member was on an east-west strike and dipped 20° to 30° south along the Desert Mound ridge. These sedimentary rocks formed the south slope and top of the ridge, and the underlying quartz monzonite porphyry formed the north slope. The ridge was cut by north-trending faults. This cross-faulting and shearing was regarded as pre-mineralization. The Desert Mound ore body was a typical replacement type ore body in the Homestake Limestone. The deposit dipped 20°

to 25° south, and the thickness of the overburden increased in that direction. The deposit was about 1,400 feet long, ranged from fifty to 250 feet thick and extended down-dip at least 1,000 feet. Ore was mainly hematite containing one-half to one percent pyrite in certain zones and had a relatively high phosphorous content.

Mining started in the surface outcrops in 1926 by the Milner Corporation on the Desert Mound and King No. 1 claims. Mining moved from the Desert Mound to the Contact claim in 1931. Mining continued on the Contact and King No. 1 claims at Desert Mound until 1936, when operations shifted to Iron Mountain. Mining was resumed on the Desert Mound ore body in 1949 by U.S. Steel Corporation and was more or less continuous after that. The Desert Mound ore body was owned by the CF&I and the Milner Corporation. The ore body contained about twenty million tons.[93]

Short Line ore body was situated near the Desert Mound ore body, at the southwest end of Granite Mountain. The deposit was originally concealed by more than 100 feet of alluvium and was discovered by a ground magnetometer survey. Initial drilling was conducted in 1930. A total of twenty-three churn drill holes were made during this period, mainly on the east half of the deposit. The U.S. Bureau of Mines completed six diamond drill holes on the deposit in 1942-45. Additional drilling was conducted by U.S. Steel and production began in November 1949. The Short Line ore body was a replacement of the Homestake Limestone. The deposit had a maximum east-west length of about 1,800 feet and an average width of 300 feet. In some sections ore replaced the full thickness of Homestake Limestone, from 150 to 300 feet. At depth, along the south margin, the ore became localized along a brecciated zone and extended to an undetermined depth. The ore was mainly hematite, a soft fine granular mixture with sporadic ribs of hard dense ore. The deposit averaged about 49 percent iron and 0.12 percent phosphorus. The property was owned by U.S. Steel and the Milner Corporation. The Short Line deposit produced about six million long tons of ore. The pit was later largely refilled by waste rock from the excavation of the Desert Mound ore body.[94]

King ore body was located a short distance northeast of the Desert Mound ore body on the southwest side of Granite Mountain. A magnetic anomaly outlined by the U.S. Bureau of Mines prompted the cutting of seven exploratory churn drill holes. Brecciated and mineralized porphyry rock was encountered in six holes; the seventh was cut in barren Homestake Limestone. The average iron content was 28.2 percent. The King claims were owned by the Milner Corporation. The ore body was considered noncommercial with an ore potential possibly of 100,000 tons of low-grade ore, however it appears to have been mined in conjunction with the adjacent Desert Mound ore body.[95]

Section 2 ore body is located southwest of Desert Mound. The deposit is non-outcropping and was discovered by aerial magnetic surveys by the U.S. Steel Corporation. The deposit is a nearly complete replacement body of the Homestake Limestone member and thins in each direction. The property was extensively drilled by U S. Steel. The deposit is owned by the Iron County Land Company. The top of the ore body lies from 900 to 1,300 feet below the desert surface. The Section 2 ore deposit has an estimated iron ore potential of more than twelve million tons.[96]

Section 3 ore body lies southwest of Desert Mound and Granite Mountain. Section 3 ore deposit is a small replacement type occurrence in Homestake Limestone. The top of the ore lies 600 to 800 feet below the surface and was discovered by aerial magnetic surveys by U.S. Steel Corporation. The property was drilled by U.S. Steel which leased

Iron Mining & Manufacturing

Illustration 9.7. Desert Mound Plant site and facilities, July 1951: hopper, processing plant, loadout, shops, warehouse, office, etc. (Photo from York Jones)

the property from the Milner Corporation. The ore potential of this deposit is about five million tons.[97]

Section 4 ore body is situated southwest of Desert Mound and Granite Mountain. This small deposit lies 900 feet below the surface and was discovered by aerial magnetic surveys by U.S. Steel; the deposit is a metasomatic replacement of Homestake limestone. The property, owned by Nicholas Savage and the Washington Hunter estate, has an estimated ore reserve of about one million tons.[98]

Section 9 ore body is located southwest of Desert Mound and Granite Mountain. This deposit lies 700 to 900 feet below the surface and was discovered by aerial magnetic surveys by U.S. Steel. An extensive drilling program was conducted during 1958–61.

The deposit, a metasomatic replacement of Homestake Limestone, was cut by five or six north-trending faults of varying magnitudes. The deposit shows considerable brecciation and may be separated into two ore bodies. The Section 9 West ore body has an ore potential of about fifteen million tons and the Section 9 East ore body has a potential of about twenty-five million tons. The East ore body is owned by Eugene McCahill of Minneapolis, Minnesota, and the West ore body is owned by Nicholas Savage and the Washington Hunter estate.[99]

State Section 2 ore body occurs on Utah State land, due south of the Desert Mound ore body and southeast of Granite Mountain. A magnetic anomaly was mapped over the deposit by the U.S. Bureau of Mines in a geophysical survey in 1944–45. The property was leased from the State by U.S. Steel, who drilled the property.

Illustration 9.8. Desert Mound revisited, July, 1951. The old Milner and CF&I pits abandoned in 1936 can be seen in the center of the photo. The mining activities of the 1930s only excavated a small portion of the Desert Mound ore body and none of the Short Line deposit. In 1949, pre-stripping began on the Short Line. When it was completed, the operation moved to the Desert Mound. The pre-stripping work was done by Utah Construction, under contract to Columbia. The beginnings of Short Line Pit can be seen at the bottom of the photo and the start of the "new" Desert Mound Pit can be seen in the right center. The Desert Mound ore body was a massive deposit that underlaid both of the old pits and would eventually swallow up both of the pits into one, much larger pit. The Short Line Pit, in the foreground, was later partially backfilled with overburden from the Desert Mound Pit. (Matheson Special Collections)

A small replacement type ore deposit was disclosed in Homestake Limestone, about 500 feet below the surface, averaging approximately 40 percent iron, and has an ore potential of one to two million tons.[100]

Thompson ore body lies due west of the Desert Mound ore body on the southwest end of Granite Mountain. This deposit is not exposed at the surface but lies beneath a low hill of Entrada sandstone and the Iron Springs Formation. It was discovered by the U.S. Bureau of Mines during its geophysical surveys of the district in 1944–45. Exposed sedimentary rocks strike east-west and dip about 20° south. The ore lies from less than 200 to more than 300 feet below the surface, is about 600 feet long and 300 feet wide, and ranges from eighty-five to 235 feet in thickness. The property is leased by the U.S. Steel Corp. The ore potential is about three million tons.[101]

Little Jim ore body is situated between the Desert Mound and Short Line ore bodies on the southwest end of Granite Mountain. A magnetic anomaly was disclosed by the U.S. Bureau of Mines investigation during 1944–45. The deposit appears to be similar to

Iron Mining & Manufacturing

Illustration 9.9. *Desert Mound.* By the time this photo was taken in 1956, the old Milner and CF&I pits had become part of the much larger Desert Mound Pit. The "mound" of Desert Mound was no longer a hill; it had become a big hole in the ground. The "Rattler Pit" that can be seen in the upper right hand of the photo was a small ore deposit excavated along the way. (Rights holder of photograph unknown)

the King ore body, consisting of mineralized and brecciated porphyry. The property is owned by the Milner Corporation and leased by the U.S. Steel Corporation. The ore potential is small and contains only low-grade ore.[102]

The Columbia Iron Mining Company issued Utah Construction a contract to pre-strip the overlying overburden from the Short Line claim in mid 1949. At the time Utah Construction was mining in the Iron Springs area and at the Duncan and Blowout pits at Iron Mountain. Work commenced the first week of August 1949 removing 3,000,000 cubic yards of overburden material from the Short Line deposit. The job was kept separate from the operations at Iron Springs and had its own offices. It employed approximately seventy-five to 100 men, used three large electric mining shovels and twenty-four Euclid trucks along with a few dozers and scrapers and was expected to last for at least nine months. Al Geiger was the superintendent and Rex Harris was the office manager.[103]

In May 1950, when the Short Line stripping operation was nearly completed and the major part of the ore had been exposed, Utah Construction signed another contract with Columbia and moved to the adjoining Desert Mound ore body where it continued its stripping operation to remove an additional 2,000,000 cubic yards of overburden. There was a short work stoppage before the new contract went into effect, so that the pit could be measured and the amount of excavation computed.[104]

Illustration 9.10. The Texas City, Texas disaster, April 16, 1947: (left) a parking lot 1/4 mile away from the explosion; (right) remains of a five-story rubber factory beside the dock. (Courtesy of Special Collections, University of Houston Libraries)

In July 1951, when Utah Construction completed its stripping contract and Columbia had finished erecting its ore processing plant, Columbia took over and began its own stripping and mining operations and started shipping ore to Geneva and Ironton.

Ammonium Nitrate as an Explosive

On April 16, 1947, the deadliest industrial accident in U.S. history occurred in the port of Texas City, Texas. The disaster occurred when a cargo ship, docked at the port and carrying 2,200 tons of ammonium nitrate fertilizer in its hold, first caught fire and then detonated when its cargo reached critical heat and pressure. The massive explosion ignited the ammonium nitrate in a second cargo ship, which exploded fifteen hours later. It set off explosions and fires in the nearby refineries and chemical tanks, leveled 1,000 buildings in the city, sheared the wings of two airplanes flying by, sent a fifteen-foot high mini-tsunami a hundred miles, killed 567 people and injured thousands of others.[105]

As a result of this calamity, the mining industry, along with the rest of the world, realized that a "new" explosive had been discovered. Nitroglycerine, dynamite, and black powder in various combinations had been used for many years as the explosives of choice by the mining industry and the manufacturing of these products was monopolized by the powder companies. After careful and extensive testing, it was found that low density, prilled ammonium nitrate fertilizer, mixed with the proper percentage of hydrocarbons and raised to a critical pressure, made a good explosive at about one fourth the cost of the commercial dynamite. This discovery revolutionized blasting in the mining industry. Bulk trucks were introduced that could load literally millions of pounds of explosives in a relatively short period of time. The following is from the Columbia Iron Mining Company Handbook regarding the use of ammonium nitrate (NH_4NO_3)

Blasting with Prilled Ammonium Nitrate at Desert Mound 1959

A. History

Blasting has always been a major operating problem at the Columbia Iron Mining Company because every ton of ore and stripping removed has to be broken out from the solid face. The stripping varies from the hard, fine grained sandstone, conglomerates and quartzite through medium hard limestone and monzonite to soft altered material. The ore is a mixture of magnetite and hematite with the hardness varying from medium hard to soft.

Illustration 9.11 The Blowout Pit in 1950. Most of the hill portion of the deposit is gone. (Photo from York Jones)

Since the start of operations in 1936, the Columbia Iron Mining Company tried a variety of explosives from a variety of manufacturers, trying to combine safety and efficiency in their blasting operations. As of March 1957, a mixture of grained ammonium nitrate (Nitrainite) and pelletized TNT (Pellatol) was being used in wet and dry blasting with fair results at a comparatively high cost.

During the spring of 1957, the Geneva Works started producing prilled ammonium nitrate as a fertilizer and on March 11, 1957, the Columbia Iron Mining Company detonated its first blast using prilled ammonium nitrate mixed with fuel oil (added for its carbon content to create an "oxygen balance" and high gas volumes) as a blasting agent. It was immediately apparent that there was considerably more work done, pound for pound, by this mixture than by the explosives used previously. Because of this and mainly because the cost of blasting agent dropped from 14¢/lb. to 4¢/lb., prilled ammonium nitrate mixed with fuel oil has since then been used in all dry blast holes.

Since that first blast in March 1957, there has been a continuous program at the Columbia Iron Mining Company of testing this mixture of prilled ammonium nitrate and fuel oil to determine: the best ratio of nitrate to fuel oil; the best method of mixing it; the best method of detonating it; the best type of prilled ammonium nitrate; the best type of oil; the minimum diameter of blast hole; and a possible method of using it in wet holes.

Since October 1958, a completely different concept has entered the blasting picture—that is the mixing of prilled ammonium nitrate with water, pelletized TNT, and other additives to form an explosive slurry. This type of mixture was discovered and developed recently by Dr. Melvin A. Cook and associates of Salt Lake City, Utah in an effort to develop a cheap, effective ammonium nitrate explosive that would be water compatible. Because it is such a fast, powerful explosive, it is also proving to be economically feasible in dry blast holes in hard and medium hard material.

On December 5, 1958, the Columbia Iron Mining Company detonated its first blast using prilled ammonium nitrate slurry as an explosive in wet holes in soft material, and on January 7, 1959, it made its first blast using this slurry in dry holes in hard material. The results in the wet holes were good and in the dry holes were outstanding.

B. *Prilled Ammonium Nitrate Mixed with Fuel Oil*

Ingredients: The prilled ammonium nitrate used is purchased from Geneva Works in 50-pound bags at 3.6¢/lb. with freight at 0.5¢/lb. It has a density of 48 lbs./cu. ft., has a 4% coating of diatomaceous earth, has 92% of prills between -8 and +14 mesh, and has 33.5% nitrogen. Test blasts were made with a high density (55 lb./cu. ft.), Allied Chemical Company, prilled ammonium nitrate made by the "short tower" process. The work done, pound for pound, seemed to be the same as Geneva prills, but the blasts often gave off a yellow smoke, indicating incomplete detonation.[106]

Iron Springs Mining Area

In the 1950s, the Columbia Iron Mining Company had opened up the Burke Pit at Iron Mountain and re-opened the Desert Mound Pit at the Desert Mound mining area. Its next endeavor was to open up the Rex deposit at Iron Mountain, but it became apparent that it was not going to be the next source of iron ore for Columbia to mine. This meant that Columbia still needed another location to supplement the Desert Mound and Short Line pits when the Iron Mountain pits were depleted. As it had with the Desert Mound deposit, Columbia looked around at what reserves were available and decided to reopen the old Pioche Pit at Iron Springs, which was the first ore body to be mined back in the 1920s.

The old tunnels and glory holes were still there but only a small portion of the reserve had been removed by the earlier operation. The property was redesigned and in 1959, Columbia began mining in the Pioche Pit, this time using modern open pit methods and equipment, enabling far more of the deposit to be recovered. A road was constructed around the north and west side of Granite Mountain for the ore to be hauled to the Desert Mound processing and loading facility, where the ore could be crushed, screened, loaded and shipped to Geneva. Some of the old tunnels could still be seen in the walls of the new open pit.

Pioche ore body lies at the north end of Granite Mountain. The Pioche and Vermillion deposits are often regarded as one deposit because of their proximity, but they are separated by a northeast trending fault with a 300-foot breccia zone. The Pioche ore body was a metasomatic replacement deposit in the Homestake Limestone. At the Pioche deposit the Homestake Limestone strikes essentially east-west and dips 30° to 45° north. The ore body was somewhat crescent-shaped and could be traced on the surface for more than 1,200 feet along the strike. The deposit dipped northward and was displaced by step-faulting. The ore body was of moderate size and contained about four million tons.[107]

Utah Construction Company

Utah Construction Company, which was new to being a full-time miner, and was the last player to enter the mining game, did not own any reserves at all in the beginning, unlike CF&I and Columbia. It worked hard to secure ore to supply its contracts. However, it was able to work with the Walker Brothers and others in the Iron Springs mining area to lease or buy enough reserves to justify building a processing plant and tipple and buy equipment to start a mining operation. The company was continually on the lookout for new reserves and bought or leased many claims, not only from third parties, but also from Columbia and CF&I, mining ore deposits that were too far from their plants or too small or too inconvenient for them to use. Utah Construction initiated extensive prospecting, claim locating and development programs that continued for many years and was able to buy and or lease the claims on one large ore body, the Lindsay Hill group, and a substantial number of smaller ones.

Over the years, Utah Construction Company opened and mined more pits than CF&I and U.S. Steel combined. It contract-mined for CF&I at Iron Mountain and Comstock, and for U.S. Steel at Iron Mountain and Desert Mound. It eventually built a beneficiation plant at Iron Springs and an Alluvium Plant at Comstock to better supply its customers with iron ore of consistent quality and a higher grade. This allowed it to mine and sell lower quality ores that otherwise would have been unsalable.

The Utah Construction Company mining complex was not a captive operation. This meant that it was not owned by the end users, the smelting companies. Utah Construction was therefore free to sell on the open market to anyone that needed iron ore. Its primary customer from 1944 to 1958 was Kaiser Steel in Fontana, California. The company also supplied the Ironton Number 2 blast furnace while the furnace was owned by Kaiser-Frazer Parts Co.

Iron Springs Mining Area

Beginning in July, 1948, Utah Construction Company contracted to deliver 40,000 tons of iron ore from the Lindsay Hill mine at Iron Springs to Boeki Cho, the Japanese board of trade. The ore was to be used in Japan to further the MacArthur recovery program which called for supplying the Japanese with raw material to rebuild their economy. The entire shipment, which took several months, was approximately 400,000 tons. On July 28th, the first shipload left from Long Beach, California, for Japan and was said to be the largest iron ore shipment in history. Despite what the article in the *Iron County Record* stated, the ore was mined at Iron Springs and not Iron Mountain. [114]

Utah Construction Company also had an ore contract with Carnegie-Illinois Steel Co. steel plants in South Chicago, Illinois and Gary, Indiana. The steel plants were using small quantities of high-grade lump ore, about 4 train car loads a day, for special uses in their open-hearth furnaces.[115]

In August 1951, Utah Construction moved its offices from Main Street in Cedar City to a new office building at Iron Springs. At the same time, the mining company's offices at Desert Mound and at Iron Mountain were also moved to Iron Springs to consolidate all of the office forces in one location. The new office and warehouse at Iron Springs

Illustration 9.12. Utah Construction Company, 1949. This image shows wagon drills working in the Blowout Pit at Iron Mountain. On the left is Mel Olds, in the center is Oliver Phillips and on the right is Bert Bonzo. Drilling was very slow as a result of the hard magnetite ore. The tungsten-carbide bit was just being developed. These drills were extremely noisy and the compressed air blew dust and rock particles out of the hole and into the air. At that time the workers wore no hardhats, safety glasses, hearing protection or dust masks. Luckily, the ore contained very little free silica and no silicosis was reported. (Photo from York Jones)

was of steel construction, lined on the inside and insulated and still stands at that location.[116] The following is from an account written by Jim Smith in 1960.

> Chet Robinson and LeGrande Robb both had been on the carpenter work of plant construction, Ed Price and Eddie Miller who had come from Iron Mountain operations were off due to steel strike until the middle of June, 1946, when shipments again resumed to Kaiser Company. Ore Shipments increased to about 50,000 tons per month. At about this time TKD-57 had a hydrotarder installed (a water tank on top of cab to help cool the transmission retarding system) and this meant a great deal as on this truck, loads per shift doubled.
>
> Utah Construction Company Engineer was Emery Willes. He evidently had some instruction from the Company regarding the Pioche Claim as he checked both the old tunnels and ore deposit and ran lines to [the] Iron Springs plant for a possible road. Ted Karr was master mechanic, with Bob Nelson, Max Barton and Bill Garner as mechanics.
>
> The production crew in the pit in late 1946 was Jim Stevenson, shovel operator, Clayton Lewis, shovel operator, Sadie Hunter, oiler, Alger Orton, trac-

Iron Mining & Manufacturing

Illustration 9.13. Iron Mountain facilities: Utah Construction busses, haul trucks and buildings on the near side of the track, Columbia's crushers, loadout and maintenance shop on the far side. (Photo from York Jones)

tor operator, Stan Bryan, tractor operator, J. Lamoreaux, A. Clark, Crandall, Bob Miller, Ted Miller, R. Wilcock, Wells Batt, Glen Grant, Ab Stevens and H. Nelson were Euclid operators.

Drill crew - Bill Heyborne was foreman, G. Heyborne compressor operator, and Deb Mortenson, C.A. Rollins, Vince Mullinder, Bert Bonzo, George Rhoades, Delmar Davis, Bob Muir, George Carpenter, and John Dalton in the drill and powder crew.

All drilling at this time was by wagon drill. Powder used in shooting, 60% bag powder with 2×8 stick used for primer. At this time the superintendent tried to have blasting of ore about 3/4 pound to a ton and 1/2 pound to a yard stripping. 1947 was not too bad a year but had some slow months of ore shipments.

The year 1948 started slow and late in the summer began to go pretty well. The "F" belt structure started up in 1948. The tunnel was completed in July, and the "F" belt structure started August, 1948 and was completed February 13, 1949. The riggers were J. Hamic, foreman, R. Boswell, L. G. Adams, E. McKee, and W.L. Hamic. Dell Lundmark was Utah Construction foreman on the project. Plant engineering design was by Glen Enke.

This new addition to the plant was to be a blending stockpile, with the tripper, having limit switches to regulate travel distance.

The reason for blending of ore was to be able to ship Kaiser Frazer Company at Ironton, ore blended to meet very rigid specs. Along about this time came our first export order and Iron Springs was a very busy place. Loading railroad cars

Illustration 9.14. Comstock Pit and ore processing facility, mid to late 1950s. (Photo from York Jones)

was a 24-hour operation, six days and sometimes seven days a week. The foreman on swing shift was Tracy Blood and on graveyard Howard Savage.

Haul crew hauled ore two shifts to keep loading operation going. Ore shipments were as high as 165 carloads ore per day. Our biggest month of shipping was 212,475 tons ore in one month at Iron Springs. Our production crew at Iron Springs reached 122 men and I believe this is the most men on production at Iron Springs.

About this time electric power was in strict supply in Cedar as the power company had only the diesel plant and a few small hydro plants. Pumping was at a very high rate and power was almost rationed. Finally, we had to work production crews swing and graveyard shifts to be able to get power. Then the steam plant was put in operation. Columbia built a power plant. Utah construction was in the process of building a power plant at Iron Springs and had gone so far toward it as to buy some equipment. A set of unit construction costs was also made out for a power plant.

In the winter of 1948 we really had a lot of snow and had great difficulty to get to town and back to Iron Springs. Snow depth at the mine was not bad, but out by the radio station strong winds drifted the snow to a depth of five to six feet on the roads. At this time, we had five D-8 cats trying to clear the roads as far in as the stockyards and almost to Woolsey's ranch and toward Iron Springs on the mine side of radio station.

I remember an incident earlier when we had to load ore for Kaiser on Sunday. The track men were Bob Nelson and Mondell Rasmussen, both master mechanics and Bill Heyborne, a general foreman. Hy Humpherys, who also was a general foreman, the cat operator, Jim Smith, timekeeper and weigh master.

It is a problem to think back and have dates in correct order.

I believe it was in 1947 that we got the four 7 LD trucks at Iron Springs and had hydrotarders installed for the braking system. At that time, they seemed to be wonderful trucks and very powerful. I've heard conversations between a cat operator and truck driver about which had the most power. The LD out did the D-8 cat.

Along late in 1949 our orders had dropped off. No ore shipments and Desert Mound was getting ready to open up. The 120-B shovel (SHE-22) was pulled from Iron Springs to Desert Mound with two 7 LD trucks and two D-8 cats.

The year 1949 started out to be a fairly busy year. Sample schedule below of loadings:

Kaiser Company, Fontana	10 cars per day – 2-1/2" minus
Kaiser Company, Fontana	2 cars per day – 2-1/2 to 10 lump
Carnegie Illinois, Steel	4 cars per day – 2-1/2 to 10 lump
Ideal Cement Company	3 cars per week - 5/8" minus
Anaconda Company	1 car every 2 weeks – 2-1/2 × 10"
U.C. Co. Export	30–50 cars per day to start on advice Ex-Import
Kaiser Frazer at Ironton	17–20 cars per day

Kaiser Frazer worked at Ironton (this furnace was the government furnace, not U.S. Steel; later however, it was bought by U.S. Steel) for a few months and then closed down. During the period we shipped to Kaiser Frazer at Ironton we also shipped to the Lone Star Steel Company, Lone Star Texas. This plant was also leased by Kaiser Frazer Company. The plant superintendent for Kaiser Frazer was a Mr. Marron.

The year 1950 picked up in production as in this year we shipped to Carnegie Illinois Steel and to both Kaiser and Geneva along with Export Ore. This was a pretty big year for Iron Springs. The Office at Iron Springs was completed in July, 1950. George D. Leigh and Jim Smith moved in the Office.

Our ore shipments were about 50,000 tons open-hearth ore per month. At this time, we shipped both 10" minus and open-hearth. Our Carnegie, Illinois, steel orders came in July and it was a problem to rustle cars as the ore had to be shipped in an Eastern Railroad car. The requests for cars they wanted were battleship hoppers and solid bottom gondolas. Finally, the participating railroads furnished cars to ship back east. We were notified by these railroads, the car number of the cars turned over to U.P. at either Omaha or Council Bluffs. Milwaukee Road and Great Northern also furnished jeeps for loading to go to Geneva and was a great help. When it got close to time for ore movements in Great Lakes area we would load the jeeps with open-hearth ore and ship them to either South Chicago or Gary, Indiana.

Production was a difficult problem too as the ore from the Lindsay Pit has never been too good for lump ore. It was also a problem to balance off the 2-1/2 inch minus with enough ore above 1/4 inch to meet specs.

Our Export ore finally was 2-1/2" minus, originally we shipped 10" minus. We had a lot of reports from Metropolitan Stevedoring Company in regards to the ore as sometimes the ore was in slabs as long as 29 inches. This caused a great deal of trouble with their covered conveyor. Pictures were even taken and sent

Illustration 9.15. The Lindsay Hill started out as several smaller pits, each named for the claim on which it was located, as is seen in the above photograph, taken sometime in the mid to late 1940s. As time progressed and the pit boundaries expanded, the pits merged into one large continuous pit and the sections of the pit retained the names of their original claims. (Matheson Special Collections)

to us about their trouble. Finally, Chris hired a couple of laborers here at the plant to try to break the largest chunks of ore with sledge hammers.

Geneva gave us a contract this year, 1950, for ore for 450,000 gross tons and we shipped at the rate of nearly 70,000 tons per month. Geneva used open-hearth from Iron Springs which was 2-1/2" to 5/8", about 19,000 tons per month, and at the beginning it was a tremendous tonnage. But when you load and ship up to 10,000 tons per day it takes a lot of ore from the plant.

This year, 1951, also was a good year, as in April, truck drivers numbered 35 drivers and two truck foremen, with nine cat operators, eight shovel operators, with three pit foremen working 24 hours, six days a week. Attached is a copy of men working at Iron Springs with about 122 men in production crew. Iron Springs office also had quite a few. J. K. Smith, G. D. Leigh, M. F. Halden, Jack Robb, Gary Jones, and Ralph Perkins.

Iron Springs had been either a feast or famine set up with lots of ore to go when working, down to nothing. But it has held up fairly well with Kaiser taking ore until February, 1958.

Our Superintendent was C. A. Mason until, I think, December 1, 1955, when Boyd Paulson became Superintendent, as Chris Mason retired. In the spring of

Iron Mining & Manufacturing

Illustration 9.16. The Lindsay Pit. On July 28, 1959, when this photo was taken, the Armstrong, Excelsior and Lindsay pits had become connected and a sizable waste dump had been built up to the east of the pit. The small mounds made by each truck dumping its load can be seen on the top of the dump in the lower center. (Photo from York Jones)

1956 E. C. DeMoss became Superintendent, as Boyd Paulson traveled to San Francisco. In the beginning, our office manager was C. J. Wasmuth, who along with Chris, came to Cedar City from Davis Dam.

Carl Wasmuth got sick in 1950 and O. S. Augason was sent to Cedar from Salt Lake to take charge of office, however he did not stay long as Rex Harris was put in charge of both Cedar and Desert Mound offices.

The original U.C. Company office was upstairs above First Security Bank and then to the Parry building next to Western Auto and then to Leigh Hotel Building and from there to Iron Springs.

Office personnel in Cedar that I can remember included Caddie Middlesworth, Noel Rollo, George Foster, Gadfrey Mueller, Elton Jones, Ronald D. Burns, Pierce, Opal McClure, up to coming to Iron Springs main office in 1950.

From the beginning, Iron Springs operation has worked smoothly and well. There have been very good personnel working. All the foremen, including master mechanics have climbed from working assignments to foremen jobs.[117]

On September 4, 1958, Geneva Steel issued a purchase order to the Utah Construction Company to supply 20 percent of Geneva Steel's total iron ore requirement. Utah Construction had made occasional shipments to Geneva over the years, but having a continuous contract was a major breakthrough for Utah Construction. As was seen in the previous account, Utah Construction shipped iron ore to several locations around the country and at times it was famine rather than feast. Geneva was a steady customer, right in the back yard, so to speak.

Unfortunately, the good news for Utah Construction was not so good news for the local Columbia Iron Mining employees. This move extended the Columbia ore reserves in the area but the underlying message was that U.S. Steel, the parent company of Columbia, was having second thoughts about investing further in new pit development using the Rex ore body or other reserves that it owned in Iron County.

Utah Construction Company for CF&I

During the 1950s, Utah Construction continued to operate the Duncan and Blowout pits at Iron Mountain for CF&I. In 1954, Utah Construction opened the Comstock Pit in the Comstock mining area and had a railroad spur and rail siding built as well as a crushing plant, load-out facility, shops and offices. The Comstock mining area was several miles to the northeast of the five pits that were operating at the time in the Iron Mountain mining area.

Comstock ore body, which was overlain by a number of claims, was one of the largest deposits in the district, second only to the Rex deposit in size. With three operating pits, CF&I was able to shift activities from one pit to the other to meet blast furnace specifications, to balance strip ratios, to respond to emergency pit conditions etc. Over time, for several reasons, the Comstock Pit became the location of choice and the Iron Mountain pits were operated less and less.

Colorado Fuel & Iron controlled the largest share of the Comstock deposit and Columbia Iron Mining Company owned a smaller portion under the Mountain Lion claim. As Utah Construction's operations progressed, most of the ore was shipped to CF&I in Pueblo but the portion from the Mountain Lion claim was shipped to the Geneva plant at Provo. Interestingly, one company used a conveyor-belt weightometer to weigh the ore, whereas the other firm insisted on using traditional truck scales.

CF&I had its own mining engineers on site who called most of the shots when it came to ore control and mining locations, unlike Utah Construction's operations at Iron Springs which had a separate engineering department to plan the mining. At times, this led to disagreements, but mostly things went smoothly.

In early March 1954, the Colorado Fuel & Iron Corporation's Pueblo Colorado plant temporarily ceased taking ore from its Utah mines because of high ore inventories at the plant due to the reduction of war contracts and the relaxation of emergency stockpiling. The public was concerned by layoffs but were reassured that when CF&I had consumed its excess inventory, orders would again appear at the iron mine and those who were laid off would be rehired and operations would resume at the affected mines. Company officials also stated that there had been a nationwide "leveling off" in the demand for steel due to the fact that government demands for war implements had been reduced.[108]

Indeed, shipments to the CF&I plant in Colorado resumed in late April 1954 when the plant's ore inventories had been reduced to the prescribed levels. The employees who had been laid off were put back to work.[109]

The Comstock Ore Body was located on the northeast side of Iron Mountain. The property was owned by CF&I Corporation. The ore body was a huge roof pendant replacement deposit in Homestake Limestone and was the largest roof pendant in the district. It measured about one mile long and about 2,000 feet wide. It was cut by several faults of small to large displacements producing a juxtaposition of sedimentary blocks.

The deposit was overlain by a number of claims including the Comstock, Copper Fraction, Dear, Sunbeam, Strip, Emma, and Mountain Lion group of claims, and was one of the largest known ore reserves in the district, with a total ore potential that exceeded sixty million tons. Production began in 1954. Mining operations were conducted under contract by Utah Construction & Mining Company.[110]

Mountain Lion ore body was located on the northeast side of Iron Mountain. This was a metasomatic replacement deposit associated with the largest roof pendant of the Homestake Limestone in Iron Springs district. It was a northward extension of the huge Comstock ore body. Surface exposures of the deposit were more than 2,000 feet in length. It was bounded and cut by faults of varying magnitudes and often showed brecciation. The property was owned by the U.S. Steel Corporation. The Mountain Lion ore potential was approximately fifteen million tons.[111]

Dear ore body joined the Copper fraction and Comstock lode claims on the south and was located on the northeast side of Iron Mountain. The deposit was a small replacement body mainly in Homestake Limestone at the south end of the huge Comstock ore body. Iron ore had replaced limestone, forming commercial ore, and occurred in brecciated porphyry. Huge brecciated masses of quartz monzonite porphyry were mineralized by fracture fillings and partial replacements of porphyry. Many brecciated blocks several feet in diameter were exposed in the Dear Pit. Several porphyry blocks were surrounded by forceful movements and by partial iron ore replacements. Brecciation was of major importance in the localization of the Dear and Comstock ore bodies. U.S. Steel Corporation was owner of the property which had an ore potential of 1 million tons or more.[112]

Queen of the West ore body was located on the east side of Iron Mountain. The ore body was a small roof pendant replacement deposit in Homestake Limestone and was completely surrounded by quartz monzonite porphyry. The ore outcrop originally measured about 600 feet along the strike and was 200 feet wide. Replacement of the roof pendant was not complete. The property was owned by CF&I Steel Corporation, which started mining the ore body in 1956; the deposit was depleted in 1967. The property produced about 500,000 tons of ore.[113]

Great Western Pit Helene E. Beatty 1937 to 1960 shipped high grade flux ore all over the United States from float ore and mined ore on and around the Great Western claim on the south flank of Three Peaks. Some of the local men hired to hand pick ore were Trenton Jones, Dee and Ross Woolsey, Jack Berry and sons, and Ellis and Aubra Lambeth. This pit generated about 234,000 tons of ore.[119]

Bethlehem Steel used a limited amount from the Three Peak Deposit east of Iron Springs.[120]

Wildcat Strike

A couple of months before the devastating 116-day United Steelworker's strike in July 15, 1959, the unions at Iron Springs staged a rare wildcat strike in support of a discharged worker.

Mine Employees Yield to Strike Call

Approximately 130 men went off the job at the Iron Springs operations of the Utah Construction Company Wednesday morning, when a wildcat strike was called as the result of the discharge of one of the employees at the mine. The firing of the man resulted from arguments developing from a misunderstanding over overtime work during the past week end.

Employees of the company left the job Wednesday morning in a sympathy gesture toward the discharged worker, although there was no official authorization for such a strike from Union channels.

As we go to press there is indication that the strike will come to an end sometime today, Thursday, and that the men will return to their jobs. It has been indicated that the controversy with the disgruntled employee could be resolved by noon and as soon as the striking employees accept this settlement, work should be resumed.[118]

General Interest

Iron Mt. Accident Seriously Hurts Cedar City Driver [1948]

James E. Lawrence, 37, Cedar City, is in serious condition at the county hospital from injuries suffered when his truck collided with a huge truck operated by the Utah Construction Company on the Iron Springs ore haul road between the mine and crusher about 11:15:00 p. m. Wednesday. Mr. Lawrence suffered a fracture of his left hip, and extensive cuts about the left leg, chin, upper lip and left hand.

The truck driven by Mr. Lawrence was deemed a total wreck by mechanics, while the company owned truck suffered no damages according to Carl Wasmuth of Utah Construction Company.[121]

Truck Driver Fatally Injured in Collision at Cedar City [1950]

CEDAR CITY March 1 – A collision of two ore trucks near here Tuesday fatally injured the driver of one and injured the other.

Leonard Dalton, 27, Parowan was killed.

In serious condition Wednesday at a local hospital was Pat Peterson, 21, Ogden.

The accident occurred when the two drivers maneuvered their vehicles in a pit being excavated being by Utah Construction Co. at Desert Mound, 10 miles west of here.

Crushed in Cab

Mr. Dalton was crushed in the cab of his truck as it crashed into the trailer of the Peterson vehicle while the two vehicles were changing sides of the road so Peterson's truck could pull up into loading position.

A steering wheel and side panel had to be cut away before rescuers could remove Mr. Dalton from the truck and take him to a Cedar City hospital where he died an hour and a half later of skull fracture, crushed chest and shoulder.

Mr. Peterson suffered a fractured pelvis, ruptured bladder and other internal injuries.[122]

Parowan Man Killed in Railroad Accident [1950]

Apparently stepping in front of a Union Pacific freight train, Karl Skougard, 36, Parowan, was killed Tuesday at 6 p.m., while working at Iron Springs mining area 11 miles west of Cedar City, according to Durham Morris county attorney.

The victim was walking around the end of a car on a loading track and stepped in front of the 20-car train which was approaching, according to Mr. Morris. Two eyewitnesses to the accident said the victim apparently did not hear the train which had left Cedar City earlier enroute to Lund.

Investigators were told by Keith Bauer of Cedar City that Skougard's body was pulled under the train but was not run over by any of the wheels. C. H. Husbands, fireman on the train was another witness. The train came to a stop within 200 yards after the accident, according to Mr. Morris.

Mr. Skougard was an employee of the Utah Construction Co. which is carrying on mining operations at Iron Springs. Investigating the accident were Mr. Morris, Chief of Police Tony Lambert and Iron county sheriff Arthur Nelson.

The Victim was born on Feb. 6, 1912, at Parowan, a son of Thomas C. and Etta Bentley Skougard. He is a graduate of the Parowan High School and married Eunice Barton of Paragonah. Survivors are his parents, his widow, both of Parowan; three sons, Roger 10, Douglas, 8, and Dwayne, 4, and a sister, Mrs. Howard Dehm of Huntington Park, Calif. Arrangements for the funeral services have not been made.[123]

Young Driver Dies in Wreck at Local Iron Mines [1951]

Richard Middleton, 21, died on Wednesday forenoon of injuries suffered when he was pinned beneath the steel cab of a huge ore truck at the iron mine at Iron Springs after the truck had raced out of control for a mile down a steep incline and turned over as it struck a bank. Middleton was injured at about 10 p.m. Monday while working at the Utah Construction mine west of Cedar City.

He was driver of one of the ore trucks hauling ore from the mine on the side of the hill to the crushing plant a mile and a half below. For some reason the truck, loaded with approximately 35 tons of ore, got out of control as Middleton started down the long 9 per cent grade toward the crusher. Unable to bring the speeding truck under control the driver managed to keep it on the road for more than a mile, passing another loaded truck driven by Dee Pritchard of Parowan, but the truck going at a terrific speed struck a bank at the side of the road and rolled over pinning the driver beneath the cab. A 30-ton railroad jack was required to raise the cab enough to remove the driver, workers reported.

Company officials report that they have been unable to determine what caused the truck to break out of control as it started down the grade.

The driver suffered a crushed chest, internal injuries, head injuries and a fractured right leg and right arm.

Mr. Middleton was born in Los Angeles on March 27, 1930, a son of William H. and Roxey Mackelprang Middleton, but spent most of his life in Cedar City and vicinity. He attended Cedar City school and graduated from the Cedar City High school. He served in the Navy for a short period during 1948. He married Madge Jones of Cedar City on Aug. 12, 1950, in Pioche, Nevada.

He is survived by his widow, two small sons, Billy and Mike, and his mother, all of Cedar City, and one brother, Jay Middleton, who is serving with the United States Air Force in Alaska. Also surviving are two grandmothers, Mrs. F. W. Middleton and Mrs. Peter Mackelprang, both of Cedar City.

Funeral arrangements have not been completed, pending word from his brother in Alaska.[124]

Marlo Topham Loses Three Fingers In Conveyor Belt [1953]

Marlo Topham is in the Iron County hospital suffering the loss of parts of three fingers and a fourth badly crushed as the result of an accident at Iron Springs last Friday. The accident happened when Topham was performing his job greasing the machinery on which he worked. His hand was caught in a conveyor belt which resulted in the loss of the fingers on his right hand.[125]

Battery Explosion Starts $200,000 Fire at Desert Mound Warehouse [1953]

Fire, apparently started by the explosion of a battery charger, completely destroyed a Utah Construction Company warehouse at the Desert Mound mining operations early Monday morning, and resulted in approximately $200,000 damage.

The 80-foot long building, a converted quonset hut structure covered with sheet metal, collapsed as the fire inside reached such intense heat that the metal was literally melted away.

It was a multiple purpose structure, housing three electrical air compressors, a large supply of heavy truck tires, truck batteries, and repair parts. In addition, it housed the workmen's locker room, and also office space, it was understood. Destruction of the tires and batteries and other supplies resulted in very heavy loss.

The crew of men working at the Desert Mound operation was laid off following the fire, but returned to work Wednesday, it is understood.

Workmen who were nearing the end of their shift, some of whom were on the ore dump some distance away, said they saw the explosion but before they could reach the building the interior was enveloped in flames and it was impossible to get any of the supplies out of the warehouse. Time of the explosion was set at about 6 a.m.

The Cedar City firefighting equipment was rushed to the scene of the fire, but lack of sufficient water pressure made it impossible to do much to combat the flames. Water stored in an elevated 2,000-gallon tank was used, but there was not enough pressure to keep a heavy flow pouring onto the flames.

Members of the Cedar City volunteer fire department report the fire to be perhaps the worst in Iron County history.

No one was in the building at the time of the explosion. Firemen report that had the explosion taken place while the men were changing shifts the fire could have been more disastrous.[126]

Enterprise Resident Dies from Industrial Mishap [1958]

Raynell Jennings, 31, of Enterprise died Tuesday at the St. Mark's Hospital in Salt Lake City from injuries received Sept. 15, in an electrical accident at Columbia Iron Mines, near Cedar City.

Mr. Jennings, an equipment operator at the mines was burned while moving a rotary drill from Iron Mountain mine to the Desert Mound mine. He had raised a telephone wire to allow the drill frame to pass beneath when an electric arc occurred from power line above the telephone wires, resulting in severe burns.

Mr. Jennings began his employment at Columbia Iron Mine March 16, 1951.

He is survived by his wife, Arvilla, and three daughters, Deborah 7, Allyson 6 and Jillynn, 2.[127]

Utah Construction Honored by American Legion [1953]

Chris Mason, Boyd Paulson, Rex Harris and Oliver D. Hole were the recipients for the Utah Construction Company of an award, presented by the national organization of the American Legion for the company's "Record in the employment of physically handicapped veterans," Friday, Nov. 20 at a banquet at Hotel El Escalante.

Representatives from the local, state and district offices of the American Legion were in attendance at the banquet and the presentation was made by Robert Shelby, western states employment officer for the American Legion. J. Floyd Wignal, state adjutant and a number of regional personnel were in attendance at the presentation.

According to Claude Edwards, local representation for the A. M., The award was given because of the company's policy of granting veterans re-employment rights and for the total number of veterans employed, which is estimated at approximately 200. The first and foremost reason, Mr. Edwards explained, however, is for the consideration for the employment of disabled veterans. Mr. Edwards gave figures indicating that at least four veterans with arm amputations, one veteran minus a leg, and an Indian with 100 per cent disability and one minus a hand, have been under employment at the Utah Construction site west of Cedar City. Further, Mr. Edwards continued, approximately 50 men with between 10 and 35 per cent disability have also been employed by the company.

Mr. Mason, general superintended for the company received the certificate of appreciation while Mr. Harris, office manager; Mr. Paulson, superintendent, and Mr. Hole, personnel manager, were in attendance as company represent-tatives.

The large certificate, presented at the banquet, which is signed by Arthur J. Connell, national commander, reads as follows:

"The national executive of the American Legion, upon the recommendation of the National Employment Committee of the organization, has conferred on Utah Construction Company, Cedar City, Utah, this certificate of appreciation in recognition of the sincere appreciation of the three million members."[128]

Baseball

The 1950s saw a great deal of interest in local baseball teams. Large crowds commonly gathered to witness the hometown rivalries. Of the six teams, Utah Construction fielded two teams. Even within the company there was a good deal of competition. The Desert Mound team was the stripping crew working at Desert Mound where Al Geiger was the Manager, and the Utah Construction crew consisted of men from Iron Mountain and Iron Springs, that operation being managed by Chris Mason. Added to this interest was the very competitive Columbia Iron Mining (U.S. Steel)'s competitive and longtime winning teams. In some instances, the local mine managers were accused of hiring a man who could play baseball first and work as an iron miner second. The following article gives some interesting details on one of the championship games:

Desert Mound Tips Columbia Miners to Take City Softball Championship
[1952]

Desert Mound came from behind in the second half of the Cedar City Softball league to capture first place and give that team the league championship after winning both the first and second half. In one of the toughest games of the season played Tuesday evening Desert Mound beat Columbia Iron Mines, which team was tied for the second half play, 5 to 4, in what could be called the league championship game.

Desert Mound ended the regular league season with a 15 win and 5 loss record. Its losses were suffered at the hand of Utah Parks, who tipped the champions twice, the Iron County Record, which won two from the miners, and Columbia who tipped the winners in their second encounter of the season.

League standings, with two make-up games to be played, both involving Bradshaw Chevrolet, are as follows:

Desert Mound	8	2	.800
Columbia	7	3	.700
Utah Parks	6	3	.555
Record	4	5	.444
Bradshaw	2	6	.250
Utah Construction	1	9	.100

In the game between Columbia and Desert Mound, Columbia out-hit the mounders 11 to 4, but could not push over the necessary runs. Desert Mound collected two hits with Columbia committing three errors and with two men hit by pitched balls in the fifth inning to score all five of its runs. Columbia's runs came two in the third and one each in the fifth and seventh.

Bradshaw Chevrolet scored the most surprising upset of the season when it threw Utah Parks 10 to 2. Bradshaw has make-up games remaining with Utah Parks and Iron County Record. In other games played in the league during the week Desert Mound trounced Iron County Record 9 to 0 in a lop-sided affair. Desert Mound also won an encounter against Bradshaw Chevrolet, and Columbia walked over Utah Construction.

Some outstanding ball has been played in the league this season with several extra-inning games played. The longest of the season was an encounter between Utah Parks and Columbia, which the Parks won 7 to 6 after 14 innings of play. With the first half ending in a three-way tie for first, Desert Mound played two games in one night, one a four extra-inning affair, to emerge winner of the first half, and thus set the team up for the league championship won on Tuesday evening. George Sturzenegger, chucker for the mounders, who pitched every game they played, has turned in an outstanding performance from the beginning to the end of the season.

Members of the Desert Mound squad are: D. Ned Sargent and E. A. "Rusty" McClure, co-managers, Sid Thompson, Harris Nelson, Sargent, McClure, O'dell Christensen, LaMar Clark, Roger Felt, Gordon Sargent, Don Ray Melling, Dix Cloward, Dono Webster, Alma Garrett, Dayle Perkins, Neil Christiansen, George Sturzenegger, Ballard Larson, Jack Childs, and Cal Gubler.[129]

CHAPTER TEN

A Slow Decline
1960–1980

THE DECADE AND a half following World War II was a boom time for the iron ore business, despite the disruptions caused by striking unions. The iron mines in Iron County provided a good living for hundreds of people both directly and indirectly and provided a high percentage of the Iron County's tax revenues for many years. However, the steel industry was continually plagued by crisis and turbulence, and issues in the steel industry almost always filtered down to the iron mines. As the 1950s drew to a close, a number of critical issues appeared on the horizon for the Iron County mines. Some had their roots in the 50s, but others were new to the post-war world.

Columbia desperately needed to prepare a new pit or pits for mining to replace the three pits at Iron Mountain that had been recently depleted. This turned out to be more problematic than anticipated, as it took considerable time and money to gain control of the dozens of claims that had been staked out over the top of the massive Rex ore body.

In the 1960s there started to be growing concern for the environment. The movement gained momentum until in 1970, the federal government formed the Environmental Protection Agency (EPA) which began operation on December 2, 1970. The EPA affected the iron mines to some degree but the greatest impact was on the smelters, eventually leading to huge investments in air and water pollution control.

Probably the most critical long-term concern was the onslaught of imported steel from foreign countries, the worst case being the issue of "dumping," where steel was sold into the country that was priced at or below the cost of production. The first concern was Japan on the west coast, but Korea and China also began to flood the U.S. steel market as did several others. The federal government gave lip service to the problem but was hesitant to develop or enforce strict laws for fear of becoming "protectionist." Administrations gave foreign aid to countries to help them build their steel industry only to have them turn around and compete with American producers. The military also bought large quantities of steel from foreign countries.

The United States Steel Corporation also had other objectives. The company had substantial taconite iron ore reserves in Minnesota and Canada and in an experimental sort of way, wanted to see if it could plan and build mining and beneficiating facilities at Atlantic City, Wyoming, that were capable of preparing a satisfactory blast furnace product from low-grade taconite ore. In 1960, the announcement by U.S. Steel that it was going to shut down a portion of its operations in Iron County in favor of building a new Wyoming mine, marked the beginning of a long, slow decline in U.S. Steel's presence in Iron County.

The Smelters
Ironton Plant

The Ironton plant, put into operation in 1924, was thirty-five years old in 1960. Even during the high-production years of the 1950s, it had a roller coaster ride. When steel demand slowed, the Ironton furnaces were the first to go down and the last to come back up. The old plant was the poor step-child of the Columbia-Geneva Division of U.S. Steel. Its situation only got worse in the 1960s.

The Ironton plant had two batteries of by-product coke ovens totaling fifty-six ovens. The first battery of thirty-three ovens was constructed in 1923, the same year that the plant was constructed. The second battery of twenty-three ovens went into operation in April 1928. By 1960, modernization and improvements in operating efficiency at the newer and much larger Geneva Plant coke plant in recent years removed the need for the older Ironton coking facilities.[1]

In July 1960, the Number 1 blast furnace was taken out of production for repairs and in October 1960 the Number 2 blast furnace, which ordinarily employed approximately 280 people, was placed on standby status due to a reduction in orders for steel. This action shut down the entire Ironton plant and put it on a standby basis. The Ironton Number 2 blast furnace came back on line in March or April of 1961.[2]

In August 1961, Ironton's fifty-six idle coke ovens were placed on "cold standby" using a new process successfully employed by mills in the East. Traditionally, idle coke ovens were kept hot to prevent damage from shrinkage; gas was burned between the refractory oven walls to maintain a temperature of about 1,800 degrees Fahrenheit. The new process called for slowly cooling the coke batteries over a period of about two months. As the oven brickwork shrunk with cooling, the steel framework for the batteries was tightened. After the temperature dropped to about 300 degrees Fahrenheit, requiring some six weeks, the batteries were topped with sand, then asphalt, to guard them against moisture damage and then were allowed to cool to ambient temperature.[3]

In February 1962, Ironton's Number 2 furnace was again taken out of production and placed on standby. In March, Columbia-Geneva closed the sintering operations and virtually all of the Ironton plant facilities were placed on a stand-by basis, ready for future service if needed. The fifty-six coke ovens were also put on a standby basis. About 100 employees were laid off with the closure. When running at full capacity the plant employed about 350 people.[4]

In January 1963, Columbia-Geneva Steel announced that the Ironton coke ovens would be permanently abandoned. The decision affected about sixty coke oven employees that were severed from the payroll. Although these employees hadn't been working since the plant shut down, they were still technically on the U.S. Steel payroll in layoff status. The balance of the Ironton employees, who did not work on the coke ovens, remained on the U.S. Steel payroll in layoff status. The Number 1 furnace and the coke ovens had not been in production since October 1960.

The Number 1 furnace was taken out of production for repairs in 1960 and was never fired up again. The Number 2 furnace was shut down and placed on standby in 1962 and never came back on line. At some point in time the furnace was taken off standby and its fires extinguished. In 1966, with no fanfare and very little public notice, United States Steel announced the permanent discontinuance of operations at Ironton.

In 1968, it announced the transfer of the Ironton plant to Brigham Young University for dismantling and conversion into an industrial park.⁵

The Ironton Plant operated for almost forty years, from in 1923 until 1962. It was the first smelter to use iron ore from Iron County in substantial commercial quantities on a financially sound basis. It was later overshadowed by the massive Geneva Plant built nearby, but it was the foundation of the iron and steel industry in Utah and the sole Western U.S. supplier of pig iron to California for a number of years.

Geneva Plant

In February 1960, Geneva's Number 2 blast furnace was idled for relining and major overhaul. The furnace was last relined in 1955. Nearly two million tons of molten iron were turned out by the 230-foot high furnace before it was taken off line. During the four-month overhaul, the unit's steel shell was jacked up an additional twelve feet, the diameter of the hearth was increased by eighteen inches, and the height of its three stoves was boosted by some forty feet. Work was also done to increase the iron making capacity of the twenty-story furnace from 1,300 tons per day to over 1,500. The furnace was brought back on line in July 1960.⁶

In mid-1960, the steel industry suffered a nation-wide slump in demand and over several months, close to 1,000 men were laid off at the three U.S. Steel facilities in the Utah Valley, Geneva, Ironton and Consolidated Western Pipe. Both of the Ironton blast furnaces and two of the Geneva open-hearth furnaces were shut down. Some of the downstream industries were also cut back.⁷

The slump continued until March of 1961, at which time the two open-hearth furnaces and the Ironton Number 2 blast furnace were brought back on line and about 350 men were put back to work. The addition of the two open-hearth furnaces brought Geneva's furnace production up to eight. About 115 employees returned to work with the beginning of operations in the plant's structural steel rolling mills. Despite the industry downturn, U.S. Steel projected that early in 1961, demand would pick up and made quite a few improvements to its steelmaking facilities in the West to be ready for the increased business.

Improvements included a continuous annealing line at Pittsburg Works in California, a new coal drying plant at Wellington, Utah, a new raw materials research laboratory at the Geneva Works near Pleasant Grove, rebuilding of Geneva's Number 2 blast furnace, a new iron mine in Wyoming, a fourth reheat furnace in the Geneva rolling mills, and a scheduled start on the installation of a temper mill for hot-rolled coils of steel, also at Geneva.

The amount of steel consumed in 1960 was among the highest in history even though a shift from inventory building to inventory reduction resulted in an over-all drop in steel production. It was noted, however, that producers of competing materials and foreign steel mills were a formidable threat and that the competitive struggle for customers undoubtedly would continue to intensify.⁸

The American steel industry had a challenging time in 1962 and the Geneva and Ironton plants were no exception. Part of the blame could be attributed to the Federal Government. The military was one of the largest consumers of steel and many of its steel orders were being filled by foreign steel producers. In addition, substantial foreign aid was being spent on building competing steel mills in foreign countries. In August 1962, Senator Wallace F. Bennett (R-Utah) made several telling statements about the situation.

I think it is shocking that the Administration would buy steel abroad when unemployment is so serious at home. It is known that there are nearly a thousand steel workers out of work at the Geneva mill, and the Ironton mill has been shut down completely. In addition, about half of Utah's steel workers are on a four-day week. Coal miners in Emery Counties and iron miners in Iron County have been laid off because the steel mill is operating at its lowest level in history, about 55 per cent of capacity.... I intend to press the Administration to reverse its present policies so that all steel purchased by our Federal Government agencies will be bought in America rather than abroad. I am deeply distressed that the Administration refused my request that it rescind a 3500-ton order for the Navy that went to Germany. The Columbia-Geneva Division of U.S. Steel was the low bidder on nearly half of this steel. This order would have given 300 Utah steel workers at least a month's work.[9]

Senator Bennett continued to protest what appeared to be the Administration's blatant disregard for the plight of the American steel industry and its workers. The following article was published in October in the *Springville Herald*:

Bennett Protests Aid to Build Steel Plants in Foreign Lands

Sen. Wallace F. Bennett (R-Utah) Monday sent President Kennedy a letter protesting the sending of $322.5 million to foreign countries for construction and modernization of steel plants, which, he said will compete with American steel companies.

In a strongly worded letter, Sen. Bennett referred to a speech President Kennedy made Sept. 26, pointing out that the steel industry in the United States is in serious trouble. "Your speech was entirely correct in pointing out the problem, but unfortunately nothing has been done to remedy this serious situation," he said.

Sen. Bennett said: "Since your Administration took office, government loans and gifts to foreign countries for building steel mills has totaled $322.5 million. Most of these mills compete directly or indirectly with American mills and contribute substantially to the shockingly high level of unemployment among our steelworkers, such as the ones at Utah's Geneva Plant. These workers are tired of being taxed by the Federal government to give away money to foreign countries to build steel mills that will cost them their jobs. I think they have a right to be angry, and I think your Administration should immediately reverse this policy of creating unemployment at home."

Sen. Bennett said that the allocation for $15 million to Communist Yugoslavia for a steel mill is particularly alarming to American steelworkers. "The giving of American funds to countries which have much lower rates of unemployment than we do also seems incredible," he said. "We are giving millions for steel mills to foreign countries which have less than 1 percent unemployment, while our own steel industry has an unemployment level of 10 to 20 percent."[10]

In August 1963, work began at U.S. Steel's Geneva Works to overhaul, modernize and enlarge the Number 1 blast furnace, the last of three such overhauls to be undertaken over the past three years. The four-month furnace rebuild boosted iron making capacity by adding twelve feet to the unit's height and eighteen inches to the hearth diameter. It was estimated that enough refractory bricks would go into relining furnace and stoves to reach end-to-end a distance of nearly 300 miles. The repair and enlargement were completed in March of 1964.[11]

In October 1965, the Geneva Steel works announced a cutback in production to a "more nearly normal level of operations following an extended period of peak production." The change in force reduced the number of operating open-hearth furnaces from eight to six, and blast furnace production was cut from three to two. The rolling mills and service units were also cutback. The reduction involved 300 to 400 persons. The plant had been running at about 5,200 persons for the previous seventeen months.[12]

In November, the number of operating open-hearth furnaces was reduced from six to five, but in late December there was a moderate increase in operations and the sixth furnace came back on line. The moderate increase in operations of the plant resulted in 100 to 200 workers being put back to work.[13]

In April 1967, Geneva's Number 2 blast furnace was shut down for a major overhaul. The furnace had operated 2,325 days since it was relined and enlarged in 1960. In that time, it produced a total of nearly 3.8 million tons of iron. This surpassed the record of 2.57 million tons set by the Number 1 furnace and set a new American steel industry record for a furnace having carbon bosh construction. The main combustion area, or bosh, was lined with carbon brick rather than the conventional ceramic brick. The task of overhauling and re-lining the furnace took three months and cost several million dollars.[14]

In 1967, Geneva Steel officials declared that their plant was "the cleanest integrated steel plant in America." U.S. Steel was a pioneer in the field of scientific research in preventing industrial air pollution and a leader in activity promoting clean-up efforts. With regard to the 1960s trend of concern for the environment, it appears that U.S. Steel was doing its best to keep ahead of the pack.[15]

A year later, Boyd C. Erickson, the senior pollution control engineer at Geneva Steel Co., made a presentation to the Utah County Women's Legislative Council which was published in the *Springville Herald*.

Air Pollution Control Devices Explained at March UCWLC Meet

U.S. Steel, in [the] last 15 years, has spent $200 million for air and water pollution control and Geneva had a share of this, he said. One dollar of every $25 spent goes for this purpose.

One hundred sixty-five cars of raw materials per day are processed at Geneva, but dust created in handling is kept to a minimum. Fifteen tons of coal produces 10 tons of coke, with five tons of volatile material removed. [The] by-product plant processes 70 million cubic feet of coke oven gas per day. It requires one ton of iron, two tons ore, 600 pounds of limestone and five tons of air to produce a ton of steel. One hundred million cubic feet of gas is discharged and one-quarter million pounds of dust caught per day.

One billion cubic feet of gas per day is cleaned at the plant. Steam use proved too costly and damaging to the equipment, but wet scrubbers proved efficient and maintenance is reduced with a minimum of discharge of pollutants. Eight electrostatic precipitators are now in operation, and there are test stations all over the valley, in the plant, and into Salt Lake valley.

There is still a significant problem in the coke area, and all the steel companies in America are attempting to solve this problem. Geneva Steel is one of the cleanest in the country, for an integrated plant. Its aim is to keep its pollution at a minimum and use technology as it becomes available.[16]

In January 1970, a tongue-in-cheek letter was written to the editor of the *Utah Daily Chronicle* by U.S. Steel concerning Geneva's air pollution.

Air Pollution

Editor: The past four or five months have witnessed many letters to the editors of Salt Lake daily newspapers by junior faculty members at the University of Utah who seem to suffer a great deal these days from the fear of pollution and go coughing from class to class.

A number of these have set forth views on this rather popular question at the expense of the fellow citizens who make steel in Utah.

For members of the academic community, including the Uinta Chapter of the Sierra Club and Wasatch Mountain Club, who wish to alloy their concern with facts, this is an open invitation to obtain information on air and water conservation at Geneva Works before filling the air with uninformed, if well intentioned, opinions on this subject. It may hold true, even on pollution, that it's never too late to learn. Kindly direct requests for information to the undersigned to take advantage of this opportunity.

Dave, Director of Public Relations United States Steel.[17]

As discussed previously, in the early 1960s, Senator Wallace F. Bennett attempted to curb the amount of money being spent on foreign steel. By 1970, the problem had not gone away. Worse, foreign steel, and especially Japanese steel, was being imported and sold on the West Coast. The following article was published in the *Pleasant Grove Review*.

Burton Calls for Foreign Steel Market Change, Help Economy

Rep. Laurence J. Burton, Republican candidate for U.S. Senate, today called again for marketing of foreign steel imports on a regional basis to lessen the economic impact on the domestic industry. In talks with employees during a plant tour of U.S. Steel's Geneva Works, Burton said concentration of Japanese steel imports in west coast markets poses "a serious threat" to Utah's steel operations.

While the voluntary quotas pledged by steel-producing nations seem to be working well in most areas, Burton said this is not true in the west coast markets, where the bulk of Japanese steel is marketed.

He noted that in 1969, Japanese imports exceeded by 21 per cent the quota negotiated in 1968. Steel market analysts have predicted, Burton added, that 1970 imports into the western market, most of it from Japan, will reach a new record of 3 million tons.

"If these figures are correct, that would represent an increase of 100,000 tons over the 1969 import figures," the Utah Congressman said. "For the steel industry in Utah, this would represent the loss of any potential for growth."

Burton said that in 1968 domestic producers supplied 7.7 million tons of the total western market. The 1970 market forecast is for a total of 9.5 million tons for the western market, of which imports will take roughly 3 million tons if voluntary quotas are not kept.

"Domestic producers would then be left with a 6.5-million-ton slice of the market pie, a smaller slice than the 7.7 million tons they had in 1968," he noted.

Burton said Geneva has traditionally supplied about 25 per cent of the western market for products manufactured at the Utah plant. But, he said, the growing Japanese imports have taken about 31 per cent of the market.[18]

In 1979, the environmental issues surrounding the Geneva Plant resurfaced, this time led by the powerful United States Environmental Protection Agency (EPA). Geneva needed to get a permit from the EPA to be able to continue operating. The EPA wanted to use the occasion to force United States Steel to spend $177 million on air pollution control equipment and facilities. U.S. Steel stated that it was willing and able to spend $50 million but the higher amount demanded by the EPA could make the plant economically unfeasible.[19]

The local citizens formed a group called the Citizen's Coalition to Save Geneva. The group held rallies, sent letters, involved the Governor, Senators and Congressmen and generated a dialog with the EPA. In a rally attended by Senator Orrin Hatch and Congressman Gunn McKay, Diet Stone, the chairman of the Citizen's Coalition said, "We are asking our congressmen to form a non-partisan coalition to present a united front in representing our interests to the EPA officials in Washington, D.C. and with President Carter's administration." "The situation is becoming critical; the time for playing games is over. We need a definite response from the EPA."

The previous week, the United States Steel Corporation had announced the closing of sixteen different steel facilities throughout the nation. These plants employed over 13 thousand people. In making this announcement, U.S Steel's chairman of the board, David M. Roderick, listed Geneva as a "troubled" facility and explained that its future depended upon the outcome of the EPA negotiations.[20]

The citizens and the politicians responded in overwhelming numbers. After all, a third of Utah Valley's work force at that time was employed either directly or indirectly by U.S. Steel. However, the battle did not end quickly; it raged on for another year. The EPA added water pollution to its list of complaints. Finally, the issue appeared to be settled on October 30, 1980, when U.S. Steel agreed to install new control facilities at an estimated cost of approximately $78 million to be completed by December 31, 1982. It also agreed to spend an estimated $16.5 million for additional treatment of water released by Geneva into Utah Lake to be completed by July 1984.[21]

Kaiser Plant

Kaiser faced continued opposition as it tried to expand in the postwar consumer economy. The company remained prosperous into the 1960s, but the 1970s it faced new competition from abroad. Japanese industry, using new steelmaking technology, sought markets for their cheaper steel. The Western steel industry, relying on technology a century old, was particularly vulnerable to the flood of low-cost steel from overseas. By the time Kaiser closed the Fontana steelworks in late 1983, the firm had grown to be the ninth-largest steelmaker in the nation. That position masked its reputation as one of the weakest companies in the industry.[23]

The Mines

The 1950s had been good for the iron mining industry in Iron County, but with the rumors concerning U.S. Steel's move to Wyoming beginning to grow, the local citizens were unsure about the future. The residents were reassured that the steel market looked strong and, if anything, increases were expected in Southern Utah ore production in 1960. The following article was published in the *Iron County Record*, quoted here in part, reassured the people about the future.

Mining Outlook Good

Considerable apprehension has been manifest by local residents since the announcement by U.S. Steel Columbia-Geneva Steel Division, that [it] plans for extensive development of the company's holdings at Lander, Wyoming. It is feared by many that this development may result in a reduction of operations at the mines west of Cedar City. We have been assured by company representatives that the development at Lander is designed to supplement the source of iron ore from the Cedar City mines, and that the program will not result in curtailment of operations here.... The increasing market for steel in the West, particularly on the west coast, would seem to indicate, that there should be no reduction in operations at the mines in the foreseeable future, and Columbia officials are confident that this will be the case.[24]

In August, barely two months later, company officials from both Columbia Iron Mining Company and Utah Construction Company had to explain to the public that there was a "general lag in the steel industry throughout the United States." A four-day a week work schedule had gone into effect at Columbia's mining operations in Iron County for an indefinite period of time. Colorado Fuel & Iron ordered Utah Construction to discontinue mining operations at the Comstock Pit, with no indication given as to when additional ore would be called for. CF&I did not shut down steel production from its plant at Pueblo but used ore from its inventories at the plant.[25]

By November, the situation had not improved. The two blast furnaces at Ironton were shut down in October, leaving only the Geneva furnaces operating. The reduced demand resulted in Columbia Iron Mining Company releasing nine men. With the curtailment of ore for Colorado Fuel & Iron at Pueblo, Colorado, all mining by Utah Construction at the Iron Mountain and Comstock locations was stopped and twenty-three men were laid off. Utah Construction's mining activities at Iron Springs and work on the beneficiation plant which was under construction at the time, were not cut back. The length of the curtailment was unknown at the time and the companies were told only that it would be governed by demands for steel from the Provo and Pueblo plants.[26]

Eventually, the slump in demand for steel ended, the operations resumed and the men that were laid off were called back to work. 1961 was a better year than 1960 for production of iron ore by the mines. In January 1962, an economic forecast was made for iron ore production from Iron County for the current year. The forecast was sponsored by the University of Utah, College of Southern Utah, Cedar City Chamber of Commerce and the *Salt Lake Tribune* and presented by Royden G. Derrick, president of Western Steel Co., of Salt Lake City.

Derrick estimated the iron ore output in Iron County in 1962 would be 3,900,000 tons, which would be an increase of 360,000 tons over the 1961 mining output. He indicated that improvements in Colorado Fuel & Iron Company's furnaces would more than compensate for any loss of production caused by the startup of the Wyoming taconite mine in the fourth quarter of 1962. He added that there would also be an over-all increase in steel production during the year which caused the forecast to be higher. This was not to be the case, and iron ore production in Iron County was significantly impacted by the operation of the Wyoming mine.[27]

Taxes

The mining industry in Iron County and the associated taxes that it generated were always of great interest to the county. A combination of the assessed valuation and the mill levies imposed were a controversial issue with the mining people. The county attempted to make the economics of mining appear better than the remainder of the county taxpayers. This move increased the mining taxes and reduced the tax burden on

IRON COUNTY ASSESSED VALUATION, 1958–1965

Year	By Utah State Tax Commission	By Iron County Assessor	Total valuation	Change over previous year
1958	41,793,511	8,608,759	50,402,279	
1959	40,472,958	8,798,407	49,271,365	- 1,130,905
1960	34,263,126	9,592,370	43,855,496	- 5,415,869
1961	31,266,812	9,563,977	40,830,789	- 3,024,707
1962	31,861,288	9,795,306	41,656,594	+ 825,805
1963	31,195,675	10,086,113	41,281,766	- 374,806
1964	25,992,119	10,348,404	36,340,523	- 4,941,265
1965	20,321,389	10,687,369	31,008,758	- 5,331,765

Total decrease in assessed valuation since 1958: $19,393,512[28]

Table 1. Iron County Assessed Valuation, 1958–1965.

other properties. The *Iron County Record* published an interesting article in that regard in August 1965.

IRON COUNTY'S ASSESSED VALUATION CONTINUES DOWN SINCE 1958 PEAK

Iron County's Valuation since the peak year of 1958 has taken a decided and steady drop downward principally owing to reduction of output from iron mining operations.

The study, which is indicated by the accompanying chart, reveals that although the assessed valuation as set by the state has dropped sharply owing to the mining situation, that other general property valuates have gone up as indicated by the assessment of the county assessor.

The assessed valuation of the county in 1958 was its peak at $50,402,279. The state tax commission assessment was listed at $41,793,511 while the County Assessor's assessment was listed at $8,608,759. The state assessment involves all utilities and mining operations and is, of course, the principal assessment made.

The state's assessment over the period indicated through 1965 has dropped 21½ million while the county's assessment has risen only 1½ million, leaving a total loss of assessed valuation of $19,393,512.

Iron County mill levy has, as of necessity, risen during the same period of time, to help compensate for the loss of revenue to the county by the reduction in the assessed valuation.

In 1958 the mill levy for a resident in Cedar City was 64 mills. In 1964 the mill levy was 82.9 and the levy for 1965 has not been set by the Iron County Commission.

The rise in mill levy has not, however, kept pace with the reduction in assessed valuation. In 1958 for instance a 100 percent collection of assessed valuation of the county would have brought back $3,225,740 revenue. In 1964 with a mill levy of 82.9 and a total assessed valuation of $36,340,523 the tax revenue based on 100 percent collections would be $3,012,620.

With a drop of assessed valuation of $5,331,765 in 1965 from 1964 and based on the same mill levy as 1964 the tax revenue, again based on 100 percent collections, would be reduced by $442,010.

A Slow Decline

Illustration 10.1. York F. Jones, Mine Operations Manager at Utah International, Inc. presents check to Francis C. Betenson of First Security Bank for property taxes in Iron County for 1975. Witnessing the transaction is Larry Huser, Office Manager. In background is a 10-cubic yard shovel and two new trucks at Comstock Pit, representing a nearly one-million-dollar investment by the mining company. (Photo from York Jones)

This trend has resulted in a tightening of the belt by County officials in order to keep the mill levy down and live within the amounts collected as a result of the reduced assessed valuation.

The picture, however, is not quite as bleak as it looks on the chart. It is interesting to note that although the assessed valuation has dropped because of the reduction of what has been the principal economic industry of the county, other assessed valuations are going up in personal property holdings being assessed by the county assessor.

Although not verified it would seem that once a decline of this type started in an area other valuations would also tend to reduce. That has not been the case in Iron County and it would indicate that possibly some other factors are moving in to take the place of the losses suffered by the decline of a major industry in the county.[29]

Although Iron County's iron ore production decreased when U.S. Steel began shipping iron ore to Geneva Works from Wyoming, the output was still sufficient to give Utah fourth place in the ranking of iron-producing states in 1967.[30]

In November 1975, York F. Jones, Cedar City Operations manager for Utah International, publicly presented to Iron County a $173,439 check covering Utah International's county property taxes for 1975. The mining industry, along with associated operations and services, accounted for nearly 37 percent of the total county taxes paid. The top six taxpayers in the county were the Union Pacific Railroad at $175,087.68, Utah International at $173,089.69, Mountain States Telephone Company at $146,266.04, U.S. Steel Corporation at $140,308.31, California Pacific Utilities Company at $130,237.96 and CF&I Corporation at $128,678.36.

Jones used the opportunity to announce that the company had purchased a new electric powered P&H 1900 mining shovel costing approximately one million dollars. The shovel was designed to handle 15 cubic yards of earth but was equipped with a 10-yard bucket at the mine, owing to the heavier iron ore. The unit weighed 402 tons and was put in service at the Comstock Mine. In addition to the new shovel, two new 75-ton capacity trucks and a new drilling rig were also purchased during the year.[31] Jones also stated that he believed "Mining to be Basic."[32] He concluded by noting that, a statement made in an *Iron County Record* article published in January 1930 was just as valid in 1975 as it had been at publication. The original 1930 article follows:

What Mining Does

Mining is unique among industries in that, instead of employing outside capital upon which to build prosperity, it creates new wealth. It takes ores from the ground, where they are useless, and changes them into taxes, dividends, wages and the necessities and luxuries of life for hundreds of thousands of people.

It is a major factor in the progress of related industries and every citizen in a metal producing state, whether farmer, laborer, teacher, or grocer, benefits directly from mining operations. Without mining, there would be no industries, no automobiles, telephones, stoves, surgical instruments, motion pictures, or any one of millions of services and commodities we now enjoy.

In short, mining is a great industry and an essential factor in the building of a civilization. If we, as a nation and as individuals, are to progress to the limit of our possibilities, mining must be encouraged.[33]

In December 1975, York Jones received a letter from Iron County treasurer LaMar Jensen comparing local taxes paid in 1953 to those paid in 1975, which appears as a summary in Table 2. Three years later, Jensen released the Iron County tax figures for the tax year with the following comment:

Iron Mining Continues Base for Iron County

The impact on Iron County by the mining industry was forcibly asserted when taxes for the 1978 year were paid.

Utah International, who contracts delivery of iron ore to CF&I Steel in Pueblo, Colo., and U.S. Steel, Geneva Works in Utah County, was the largest taxpayer for the year, according to records of LaMar Jensen, Iron County treasurer.

Utah International paid $233,622.88 in taxes for the year. They were followed by United States Steel with a tax bill of $204,115 and the Los Angeles-Salt Lake Railroad with a tax assessment of $143,206.23.

Somewhat down the line on total taxes was CPNational (formerly Cal-Pac) who paid out $71,199.52.

The implications of the mining industry is found in each of those figures as the mining industry is responsible for the greater part of railroad activity in the county and a single industry is the largest user of power supplied by CPNational.

York Jones, manager of the Cedar City Operations of Utah International, indicated that his company alone pays approximately $50,000 per month for electri-

Valuation	1953	1975	Change
By Iron County Assessor	8,229,371.00	17,710,720.00	+115%
State Tax Commission	31,390,366.00	13,446,605.00	-.57%
Total	39,619,737.00	31,157,325.00	-.21%
Total taxes levied	*1,326,014.00	*2,432,164.00	+.83%
Mil Levy			
State Schools	3.60	None	-100%
County Schools	19.15	49.75	+160%
County Purposes	7.05	19.35	+174%
Top Taxpayers			
Columbia Iron Mining Co.	485,603.09	140,308.00	
CF&I Steel Corp.	201, 381.69	128,678.00	
L.A. & S.L. Railroad	98, 795.00	175,087.00	
Excelsior Iron Mining Co.	68, 614.91	(Ut. Const. Paid)	
Southern Utah Power Co.	29, 169.70	130,237.00	
Utah Construction Co.	28, 677.19	173,089.00	
American Tel. & Tel.	10, 791.41	146,266.00	
Total	923, 032.99	893,665.00	
Percent of total taxes paid	*69. 6%	36.7%	

*(Estimated) [34]

Table 2. *Comparison of Tax Revenues*

city. During the year, freight for the shipment of iron ore from Iron County would have amounted to between $18 and $20 million, Jones estimated....

Currently Utah International is under contract to ship ore to Geneva Steel in Utah County. Contract negotiations are now underway for possible contract extensions Jones indicated. Efforts are being made to complete the negotiations before the expiration of the existing contract, he indicated.

Many steel projects marketed in the southern Utah area, are direct products of Iron County, Jones pointed out. Much of the fencing wire, bailing wire, nails, etc. marked CF&I were produced from ore supplied from this area he said.

The compounded effect of the mining industry continues to be a major contributor to the economic base for Iron County and is destined to play a part in the future, as it has in the past, Jones emphasized.[35]

Utah International Large Tax Payer

On November 30, Utah International paid its taxes to the County via First Security Bank, amounting to $380,470. This is an increase of about 63 percent over 1978, according to York Jones, manager.

The tax includes Property Tax as well as Net Proceeds Tax. This tax equates with an *ad valorem* tax, he said. Earlier in the year an additional $104,000 tax was paid to the State for Mine Occupation Tax, or Severance Tax, Jones reported.

Iron County derived its name from the iron deposits located within its borders, and the tax base is still very dependent on the active iron mining in the county, Jones points out. Utah International's taxes are only a part of the mine tax base. CF&I Steel Corporation, U.S. Steel Corporation, and Union Pacific Railroad, are among the major contributors.

The mining operation manager also pointed out that 80 percent of the county taxes are assigned to the School Tax Levy, which makes the schools very dependent on the mining industry. "With the advent of new schools to meet our population growth, and the uncertain economics of the steel industry, the prudent use of the tax funds becomes vital," he suggested.[36]

Environmental Regulation

While Iron County's mines remained generally healthy, it was becoming clear that factors beyond the county would affect local mining operations. The early 1970s saw the growth of a movement to minimize environmental damage and curb large-scale pollution, including byproducts of mining and smelting. York Jones commented on the environmental issues facing Geneva and the iron mines.

> Some concerns about the mining operations in Iron County have been expressed in recent reports, according to Mr. Jones. Among the concerns are the Environmental Protection Agency (EPA) Hearings on Air Quality that are scheduled to be held in Cedar City, today, Thursday, and in Orem as well.
>
> "As far as Utah International in its iron ore operations is concerned, there is no problem with air quality problems in the Iron County area," Jones indicates. "However, should Air Quality standards result in the loss of production in the Geneva Steel operations in Utah County it could directly affect our operation and economic base of Iron County," he pointed out.
>
> Approximately half of the ore produced by Utah International also is shipped to the Geneva plant. The balance is shipped to Pueblo, Colo. under contract with CF&I Steel.
>
> A reduction in the capacity of Geneva Steel would directly affect the ore mining operations in Iron County. "Not only would it affect Utah International's contractual obligations to Geneva but would also affect the amount of ore shipped directly by United States Steel from their mining operations in Iron County," he suggested.[37]

A week later in December, a hearing was held in Cedar City by the EPA to receive comments from the public. It became clear in the meeting that although the EPA regulations wouldn't affect the iron mines directly, they could have a huge impact on Geneva Steel. Officials from both Utah International and U.S. Steel operations reinforced the fact that they were among the largest employers in Iron County and its largest taxpayers.

EPA Standards Discussed at Public Hearing

Concern over the indirect effects to southern Utah of the Environmental Protection Agency's air quality standards were raised at a public hearing held last week in Cedar City. While none of the guidelines would affect Cedar City directly, the stringent requirements could have a disastrous effect on Geneva Steel which purchases most of the iron ore mined in Southern Utah.

Dennis Stansbury, engineer at Utah International, Inc. stated, "Our main concern is that if Geneva cannot comply, the direct effect it would have on Cedar City." Besides being a large employer in Iron County, Utah International is the county's largest taxpayer having paid $233,622.88 during the past year in county taxes, and $95,000 in state mine occupation taxes. The company also has contracts with CF&I Steel in Pueblo, Colorado but its operation would be greatly reduced if Geneva Steel were forced to close due to its inability to comply with the regulations and still operate at a profit.

Norman Heaton, superintendent of the Desert [Mound] Mine voiced many of the same objections raised by Stansbury and also questioned the effectiveness of the standards. He said, "Establishing these controls is not only expensive but also results in minimal impact on air pollutants." The Desert [Mound] Mines are affiliated with U.S. Steel Corporation and pay the second largest tax bill in Iron County of $204,115.

The Los Angeles-Salt Lake Railroad with an assessed tax of $143,206.23 going to Iron County would also be affected if Geneva shut down since much of its business involves shipping iron ore from the area to the Geneva Steel Works.

Simultaneous to the Cedar City hearing, Geneva Steel was protesting the air quality standards at a public hearing in Orem. Claiming that foreign steel in 1978 accounted for over 40 percent of the total steel market in the 13 western states, "a new record."

Geneva steel, in a published statement on its position on the air quality standards, feels that the government has been ineffective in encouraging U.S. produced steel. They state that a government plan to maintain steel import prices called the Trigger Price Mechanism has been a failure. Citing foreign competition and the great expense involved in refitting old facilities to meet stringent air standards, Geneva Steel questioned whether it can continue to make a reasonable profit.

While Geneva Steel expressed concern over controlling its air pollutants, they objected to specific standards which they felt to be excessive and to stringent time schedules for compliance. "When demands are made for retrofitting more controls on these older production facilities, the cost-benefit relationship is unfavorable because of the exorbitant cost to gain the last few percentage points of efficiency. We simply cannot afford to apply this cost—which produces little benefit—and remain competitive in the western market. The economic impact is magnified when stringent time schedules are imposed," stated U.S. Steel representatives at the public hearing in Orem.[38]

In August 1979, a Utah Air Conservation hearing was held in which similar concerns were voiced. York Jones, Manager at Utah International, testified. Jones was concerned that that if the requirements were made too stiff on Geneva, that the operation would be forced to close, which would directly affect Utah International and the area's economy.[39]

Continuing Labor Issues

County Valuation Dropped Five Million by Strike

The 1959 strike against the steel industry, which affected the operations of both Columbia Iron Mining Co. and Utah Construction Company in Iron County along with a changed base assessment of mining production, were instrumental in a reduction of five and one half million dollars in the assessed valuation of Iron County.

Valuation based on production was instrumental in reducing the public utilities portion of the county valuation from $40,472,958 in 1959, to $34,263,126 over six million dollars. An increase in the assessment of the county from $8,743,795 in 1959 to $9,503,264 took up some of the slack for an actual drop in valuation for Iron County of $5,450,363 according to County Assessor, Hillman Dalley.

The 1960 valuation of the county has been set at $43,766,390 compared to $49,216,753 in 1959.

Cedar City, on the other hand, has shown nearly one-half million dollar increase in valuation from $5,492,494 in 1959 to $5,966,394 for 1960. Dalley pointed out that this is an actual increase in valuation of $473,990. Following is a complete rundown on the valuation figures for 1959 and 1960:

IRON COUNTY	1959	1960
Assessed Valuation	$ 8,743,795	$ 9,503,264
Public Utilities	$40,472,958	$34,263,126
Total Valuation	$49,216,753	$43,766,390
CEDAR CITY		
Assessed Valuation	$4,565,426	$5,029,649
Public Utilities	$ 927,068	$ 936,745
Total Valuation	$5,492,494	$5,966,394[40]

The three-year contract signed in 1962 between the Utah Construction and Mining Company and the Operating Engineers, Laborers and Teamster unions at the mines called for the renegotiation of wages and insurance in 1963 and 1964. In May of 1963 the time was up, so in June negotiations were started on those items. On August 7, the company made an offer but the membership voted to not accept it. An attempt was made by a federal mediator to avert a strike but it proved unsuccessful and a strike was called and pickets appeared at the company's operations on August 12. Ralph Long, superintendent of the Cedar City operation, indicated that the strike was the first that had been made against the company in a wage dispute since operations began in Cedar City over twenty years earlier.[41]

The striking miners voted to accept a new offer made by the company on August 23 and returned to work on August 26. There were 114 members of locals of the three trade unions who led the strike, however the remainder of the workforce, not affiliated with the unions, did not attempt to cross the picket line and were also out of work for the duration.[42]

In April 1967, 134 workers at Utah Construction and Mining Company operations walked off the job over a disciplinary action that was taken against one of the employees who happened to be a union steward. The walkout included members of the Operating Engineers Local No. 3, Laborers Local No. 79, Teamsters Local 222 and non-union members employed by the company.

The union claimed that the contract with the union had been "abused" and that the individual member had been "discriminated against." The company said that the issue was, in fact, a working-hours dispute. The worker had not fulfilled his commitment on hours worked and was disciplined by being laid off for one week. The strike occurred on Monday and had not been resolved by Wednesday.

The Union was holding out for the reinstatement of the Operating Engineers' Steward. The company stated that the contract contained a specified process for resolving disputes and grievances through the proper and agreed upon channels and offered to negotiate the problem after the men were back on the job. It is unknown how long the strike lasted but it did not last long enough to appear in another newspaper report.[43]

A Slow Decline

Painful Steel Strike Averted; Workmen's Wages Increased

Good news came to some 5,000 steel workers in this area Tuesday night, with announcement there would be no steel strike; that the U.S. Steelworkers Union had approved a new billion-dollar 3-year labor contract— the largest in its 32-year history. Union President I. W. Abel placed the price of the new strike-averting pact in the range of 90 cents to a dollar. The strike had been called for Wednesday night and plans were being made at the local Geneva plant to bank the blast furnaces and to begin open-hearth banking in preparation for an orderly shutdown of the plant. Industry negotiators indicated the settlement was higher than they had hoped for but declined to comment on what might happen to steel prices.

The contract generally provides for: wage increase of 44 cents, 20 cents an hour immediately, and 12 cents each in the second and third years. Steelworkers now average $3.84 an hour, including overtime. A 30 percent increase in pension benefits, enabling a man with 30 years' service to retire with a minimum of $195 a month. Incentives, or bonus pay, amounting to an average of 10 cents an hour, the details to be worked out. Additional wage increases for top job classifications averaging out at seven cents.

Added Insurance. A $30 vacation bonus for each week of regular vacation. An additional $1,000 in life insurance, a new major medical plan, one additional holiday, a boost in unemployment benefits, increased night differential pay, pension benefits for widows, bereavement pay and jury witness duty pay.

The contract was approved after a stormy three-hour meeting of the 600-member Basic Steel Industry Conference. The best previous steel contract was the 47 and three-tenths cents an hour won in 1965, during the last negotiations. Before that, also in three-year pacts but backed up by strikes, the union gained 45 and seven-tenths cents in 1956 and 40 cents in 1959.[44]

On May 31, 1971, the labor contract between Utah Construction and Mining Company and the Operating Engineers, Teamsters and Laborers union expired. A contract offer was made by the company on June 1 but the parties failed to reach an agreement or make any progress. The employees worked on a day to day basis under the terms of the expired agreement until October 27, at which time they walked out on strike in an effort to bring negotiations to a head. 150 workers were involved in the strike.[45]

On November 21, 1971, discussions got underway between the company and the three union organizations that were on strike, with the aid of a federal mediator who had been called in to help with the negotiations. The mediator met with each side separately to understand their positions. A Union representative indicated that the differences on the contract were not only concerned with money, but also health and retirement.[46]

Steelworkers Approve Agreement Calling for Binding Arbitration

The United Steelworkers union and the Steel Companies have approved an experimental agreement which calls for binding arbitration to decide difficult contract issues. The agreement will put an end to nationwide strikes and help to stabilize the steel industry which is constantly under attack from foreign competition.

According to the agreement, a five-man arbitration board will convene with the union and the negotiators for the 10 big steel companies [when they] are unable to agree on contract items. The plan will allay customer strike fears and eliminate the need for the traditional stockpiling of steel at agreement time. The agreement establishes timetables for the 1974 basic steel contract negotiations and assures workers a three percent wage hike each year in 1974, 1975, and 1976 It also guarantees a $150 bonus for each worker.

By eliminating the strike threat, the steel companies believe they can pay each worker a bonus and still be ahead. Both the union and the industry have been seeking away to eliminate the large steel buildup during contract negotiations. Union leaders contend that more than 100,000 jobs have been eliminated in basic steel mills in recent years as the result of foreign steel coming into this country.[47]

On August 15, 1974, the contract between Utah International Inc. and the Operating Engineers Local No. 3, Laborers No. 295, and Teamsters Local No. 279 expired. Meetings were held between the parties starting on July 31 and the company put an offer on the table. However, the company's offer was rejected, the unions choose to go on strike and 177 employees walked off the job.

The Company's settlement agreement increased the shovel operator's wage from $5.14 per hour to $6.03 per hour and laborer's wage from $4.10 per hour to $4.51 per hour and comparative increases for other workers in between those rates. A cost of living clause was also added. Other changes offered were: one additional holiday, improvement to the vacation plans, additional money into the health and welfare plans, more money into the pension plans, and higher weekly indemnity payments. Three days funeral leave was added and various local issues settled in favor of the Union. The Union wanted wages increases from 28 to 63 cents per hour higher than what the company had offered.[48]

The parties met off and on during the following month with proposals and counter proposals being offered, however no accord was reached.[49] Finally, on September 27, all the outstanding issues were resolved and the striking workers voted to go back to work. All employees were back to work by October 2.[50]

Columbia Iron Mining Company

Wyoming, Desert Mound and Iron Springs Mining Areas

In early 1960, the U.S. Steel, Columbia-Geneva Steel Division, announced that it would be opening a new iron mine at Atlantic City, Wyoming. When the announcement was made, the residents of Cedar City voiced a number of legitimate concerns, but U.S. Steel told them that they had nothing to worry about, as captured in the following newspaper article, quoted in part.

Mining Outlook Good

We have been assured by company representatives that the development at Lander is designed to supplement the source of iron ore from the Cedar City mines, and that the program will not result in curtailment of operations here. They point out that the demand for steel in the west as a result of expanded industry of the area and a tremendous growth in population makes it necessary to supplement the supply of ore for Geneva.

Many local residents have feared that the development of the ore deposits in Wyoming in recent years would result in curtailment or abandonment of mining operations west of Cedar City, which of course would be a disastrous blow to Iron County. Closing of the mines here would create a most serious tax revenue problem, because of the large sums the mining companies pour into the tax coffers of Iron County, and the Iron County School District.[51]

In retrospect, the comments made by the U.S. Steel representatives back in June of 1960 were very disingenuous, misleading and just plain lies, given the substantial reduction in iron ore shipped from Southern Utah once the Wyoming mine began operating. Graham D. MacDonald who worked for Columbia for many years, in his publication titled "The Magnet," made the following observation about the statements that were made in 1960 and the subsequent news article: "This is a typical production from the U.S. Steel's Public Relations office in Salt Lake City, who knew that the Wyoming project had received Corporation approval June 1, 1960, and who also knew what it would do to the Southern Utah operations."[52] The new U.S. Steel mine was located at Atlantic City, Wyoming, in Fremont County, thirty miles southwest of Lander, at the south end of the Wind River Mountains. By rail, it was over 355 miles from the Geneva Plant.

Atlantic City started out in 1868 as a prosperous gold mining camp. It was named after a mineral rich quartz vein they called the Atlantic Ledge due to its location on the east side of the Continental Divide. At its peak, the town had a population of some 2000 people but the boom only lasted about a decade before the gold ore began to play out. It had several mini booms and busts throughout the years but it was a ghost town by the 1950s when U.S. Steel became interested in the large iron ore deposit three miles northwest of the town. Most of the mine employees lived in Lander but the mine took the name of Atlantic City.[53] Construction on the project began in June 1960.

> The ore was taconite, a fine-grained magnetite, deposited as alluvium with very fine-grained quartz sand, which had solidified over time into one of the hardest rocks that existed in the country. The ore assayed at about 30% iron with the balance being mostly silica. It was very similar to a so-called taconite ore that the Corporation owned a lot of in Minnesota, and more than a lot of the same they were looking at in Canada.[54]

To be able to use the ore in a smelter it had to be ground into fine powder and separated from the surrounding rock and then formed into pellets and heated to partially melt the particles back together. The end product was a small round pellet, usually less than three fourths of an inch in diameter, which contained plus 60% iron and plus 10% silica. The concentrate produced from the Wyoming mine was substantially more expensive than the raw ore from Southern Utah and because of the high silica, it was also more expensive for Geneva to process.

> It appeared that the Atlantic City Project was, in part, an elaborate and very expensive pilot plant operated as a test for potential future developments on the taconite deposits that U.S. Steel owned in Minnesota and Canada.[55]

Many Southern Utah employees were transferred to the Wyoming mine site to help with development drilling and long-range mine planning. Most left their homes in Southern Utah with substantial trepidation, and many returned later when they had a chance, however there were many advancement opportunities with the opening of a new mine and some found new work in a new location "fascinating." As the mine got closer to being operational, even more Iron County miners were transferred. Of the workforce that remained behind in Utah, some continued to be employed, some retired and others were laid off.

The construction contract was for over sixty million dollars and included three new dams, miles of railroad across the Continental Divide, six miles of new highway, new

Illustration 10.2. Aerial view of U. S. Steel's operation at Desert Mound on April 6, 1970, looking southeast. The Desert Mound Pit is located at the top center of the photograph, the crushing and stockpiling facilities are on the right and the old Short Line Pit that was mined out in the early 1960s is at the bottom center of the photograph. At this point, the waste from the Desert Mound Pit was being dumped into the Short Line Pit. It can be seen from the depth of the Desert Mound Pit that it was getting close to its final depth. (Matheson Special Collections)

plant roads and railroad, a concentrator plant, a pelletizing plant, crusher, mills, warehouses, office building, and mine structures.[56]

In August 1962, the move to the Wyoming operation was completed by Columbia Iron Mining Company and the mine began shipping 1.5 million tons annually of agglomerated taconite pellets to the Geneva plant which was about fifty percent of its iron ore requirement. U.S. Steel cut production from its mines in Southern Utah by more than three fourths. Ore receipts at Geneva were fifty-four percent from Wyoming, twenty-five percent from the Columbia Iron Mine at Desert Mound, and twenty-one percent from the Iron Springs operation of Utah Construction.[57] Despite the rosy predictions by Columbia officials and the Salt Lake forecasters, the total ore shipped from the iron mines in 1962 was 2.82 million tons, over a million tons less than the 3.9 million tons that was projected. From 1962 to 1968, ore production from the Iron Springs district averaged 2.02 million long tons. Production during 1968 was 1,763,511 long tons.[58]

On December 13, 1963, the Columbia Iron Mining Company was dissolved and became simply the United States Steel Corporation, ending a life of twenty-seven years.

On January 1, 1964, the Columbia-Geneva Steel Division was completely dismantled.[59] On December 31, 1964, the announcement was made that Graham D. MacDonald, long-time Southern Utah resident, was promoted to General Superintendent–Western Ore Operations for the U.S. Steel Corporation and transferred to Atlantic City, Wyoming, a move that he was not excited about. MacDonald was responsible for the Iron Mountain and Desert Mound iron mines near Cedar City, Utah; the Keigley Quarry, near Payson, Utah; and the Atlantic City Ore Operations, near Lander, Wyoming.[60]

In 1962, U.S. Steel cut production from its Southern Utah mines to less than a million tons per year to make room for the ore coming from Wyoming. The ore from Southern Utah came from two main sources: (1) the Desert Mound and Pioche pits that was mined, processed and shipped by U.S. Steel from its Desert Mound facility, and (2) the Mountain Lion Pit that was mined, processed and shipped by Utah Construction from its Comstock facility in conjunction with mining from the Comstock Pit for CF&I.

In 1967, United States Steel moved its offices in Cedar City back to Desert Mound, abandoned its building in town and gave it to College of Southern Utah.[61] Production from the Desert Mound and Pioche pits continued to decline during the 1970s. In 1972, about twenty men were laid off from their jobs at the Desert Mound operation.

The reasons given for the cutback were adjustments being made to the production schedules of the Western Ore operations division and the shutdown of a blast furnace at the Geneva plant.[62]

On July 20, 1975, the operations at Desert Mound Mine were suspended with a four-week vacation shutdown for most employees. Others were laid off but received supplemental unemployment benefits under the existing labor contract in addition to unemployment compensation from the State. A total of thirty-five employees were affected by the cutback. Officials attributed the cutback in ore production to the shutdown of a blast furnace at Geneva Works last spring, which followed a sharp decline in steel demand in the thirteen western states. The shutdown continued through the third quarter to the end of September.[63]

U S Steel Shuts down Operation—Iron Mines Close

U.S. Steel's Cedar City ore operations, which have been operating at reduced levels since July 20, will stop ore shipments at the end of this week, for the remainder of 1975, U.S. Steel officials said Monday. The shutdown is the result of continuing low volume steel demand at Geneva Works in Utah County. Some 45 employees are affected by the shutdown in ore mining operations, officials said. While on layoff they will receive supplemental unemployment benefits under the existing labor contract, plus unemployment compensation from the state, it was reported. Resumption of mine operations will be directly related to demands for steel in the western division of U.S. Steel, it was stated. The projected demand for 1975 has not materialized and the spokesman would not speculate on the future demands.[64]

On January 10, 1977, almost a year and a half later, about ten employees were called back to work to get the equipment in condition to start shipping ore to Geneva on January 19th. Officials stated that resumption of iron ore shipments reflected anticipated improvement in the Western steel markets.[65]

Illustration 10.3. In April of 1964, Utah Construction moved a 120-B shovel intact, on a railroad car, from Iron Mountain to the Smith Pit at Iron Springs, during a spring snowstorm. The shovel weighed 330,000 pounds and Utah was charged $587 by the railroad to move it. (Photo from York Jones.)

Utah Construction Company for CF&I

Iron Mountain (Blowout Mining and Iron Mountain Plant)

Mining and stripping in the Blowout Pit at Iron Mountain was intermittent during the year. The Industrial Commission, Carlyle F. Gronning, visited the project on November 3, 1966, and officially closed down this pit. The reasons given were public opinion and employee discontent. The small slide of October 3 produced a chain of events involving safety, employees refusing to work in the pit, and complaints to the Industrial Commission. Formal notification by letter was never received. Dewatering the pit and some maintenance work was the only activity in the pit until June 2, of this year.

Ore shipments from the stockpiles continued until January 9, at which time the blast furnace stockpile was depleted. The open-hearth stockpile contains approximately 35,000 gross tons of ore and we are still not shipping any of this type of ore.

Repairs on the Iron Mountain Plant, railroad scales, and the 120-B shovel continued during the spring months.

On January 23, CF&I personnel called and, anticipating the closing of the Blowout, expressed a desire for us to mine the Duncan Pit as soon as possible and to move the SHE-1 shovel there. Transformer installation and dewatering

Illustration 10.4. The Blowout Pit, October 1966. Equipment used in the pit was a 120-B Bucyrus Erie, a five-yard shovel, a Joy 58-BH rotary drill and Letourneau Westinghouse LW-32 haul trucks that carried about forty-five tons. The Iron Mountain plant can be seen in the distance. (Photo from York Jones.)

began. On February 6, we were told to delay plans for moving the shovel from the Blowout Pit.

On March 22, the UC&M Co. Safety Committee met concerning the Blowout Pit and its safety. On May 25, a joint meeting between CF&I, UC&M, and the State Industrial Commission, was held and mining was scheduled to begin May 31. Rain delayed the start-up until June 2. Considerable time was spent scaling the walls and cleaning the road in the Blowout Pit. At this time, with the starting of the Iron Mountain Plant, we had all of the men on the seniority lists, in all three crafts, on call-back.

The separation of ore and waste in the Blowout mine was slow and difficult. Selective drilling and blasting is almost impossible in the small confined working limits of this pit. The drilling of the ore is hard and the blasting requires the use of slurry powder because of water. Mr. Douglas Pack of Intermountain Research Company, met with us and discussed the use of a pumper truck for our blasting material. A test was conducted in connection with the blasting of the ore and waste using slurry powder from the pumper truck. DBA-10 aluminized slurry, delivered from the pumper truck to the holes, was used with good success, although the truck was too small and too slow. Mining continued on schedule

Iron Mining & Manufacturing

Illustration 10.5. The P&H 1900 electric shovel with a ten-cubic-yard bucket loading a seventy-five-ton capacity Euclid R-75 haul truck in the Comstock Pit, October 1976. (Photo from York Jones)

with good production during the summer months. We worked five 9-hour days per week. At this time, the shipping rate was at 22,000 n.t./month for the blast located in the plant area. The west tunnel, which is under the blast furnace stockpile has a deflection on one spad location of about six inches over a period of six years. The wood laminated tunnels appear safe, although time and deterioration are not on our side.

On August 5, fire destroyed a building which was being used as the compressor and warehouse building.

During the weekend of September 23, the rainfall was well over 5" at Iron Mountain. The mean for the month of September over a 35-year period of time is 0.65-in. The year's rainfall was 16.34 in. (October '66 through October '67 inc.). The average yearly rainfall for the years recorded is 10.66 in. a year. The 1959 total precipitation was 5.2 in.

On September 29, we moved out of the Blowout temporarily for two weeks because of the south pit wall showing movement. Apparently, the clay and entrada formation has taken on a lot of moisture and will not support its own weight. The banks were changed, and work was resumed on the 16th of October. At this time, shipments were reduced to 12,000 tons per month. At the close of the fiscal year the shovel was on the 6075 elevation and the plant and crusher stockpile inventory was 93,300 gross tons in the blast furnace stockpile and

Illustration 10.6. The Blowout Pit in 2017, the water has a striking blue color due to a small amount of copper present in the ore, leached out by the water over time. (Photo by Evan Jones)

35,000 gross tons in the open-hearth stockpile. Total shipments this year were 123,974 net tons. The mining costs were higher than our estimates due to the adverse conditions that were encountered.[66]

Blowout and Duncan Pit Depleted

The Blowout Pit was owned by CF&I Corporation and was mined under contract by the Utah Construction & Mining Company. The elevation of the top crest of the pit was 6,700 feet, and the last lift that was removed was on the 6,075 elevation, making the pit almost 700 feet deep. The haul road was constructed at an eight- to ten-percent grade, and in 1968 it made over two complete circles before reaching the bottom.

The shovel removed the last of the ore from the 6,075 elevation in 1968 and the pit was abandoned. Mining operations had been virtually continuous from 1947 through 1968. The pit produced 7,168,047 tons of ore during its lifetime. After the pit dewatering pumps stopped running, the water level rose several hundred feet. Considering the fact that in the beginning the ore was above the surrounding ground, the bottom of pit ended up 900 feet below where it started.

The Blowout Pit was not the largest deposit but was one of the most famous in the area. It was one of the earliest claims staked and was the first to be patented. Some of the longest claim battles were fought over its ownership. When mining was started on the deposit in 1943 by Utah Construction Company, the ore outcropped on the surface and was protruding out of the ground, by some accounts, as much as 150 to 200 feet, hence the name "the Blowout Pit." Mine planning was quite straightforward and proceeded very well for a number of years. Only limited overburden stripping was required since the ore was already on the surface. Special provisions for haul roads and ramps were minimal. The mine plan was simple: clean up the ore, then drill, blast and load it, then haul it to the crusher.

However, as time went on, when the outcropping ore was removed, the working elevation of the pit became lower than the ground around it. At this point, more complex mine planning was required, and it was absolutely critical to understand the extent of the ore body, the various costs of operation and the revenue that could be anticipated from selling the ore. The pit could no longer be mined *ad hoc*. An adequate amount of waste material had to be removed from around the perimeter of the ore body for haul ramps, benches and back slopes, or the pit walls would become very steep and dangerous and valuable ore would be left behind.

However, overburden stripping added substantially to the cost of mining, so it was expedient to avoid unnecessary work in the process. In the case of the Blowout, the deposit went very deep into the earth, possibly much deeper than the initial design engineers understood. They made their best estimates, using the economic parameters available at the time, and began mining below the surface of the ground. A single access ramp was designed in the waste material around the perimeter of the ore body.

The ramp was designed at a steep 8- to 10-percent grade; it wrapped around the inside of the pit like a corkscrew, making over two and a half turns before reaching the working face. There was continual pressure to make the ramp narrower and the pit walls steeper. It became increasingly difficult to maintain the ramp.

As if things weren't bad enough, when the mining operation reached a certain elevation, it passed the water table and pumping operations had to be initiated. The water continually flowing out of the sides and bottom of the pit negatively impacted the integrity and stability of the pit walls and ramp and added extra cost and complexity to the mining. Water-proof explosives had to be used. Rocks were continually dribbling down the sides of the pit, usually small, but occasionally large, causing distress and danger to the people who were working below. The workers complained about their safety and the unions wanted the pit to be shut down.

As time went on, it is a sure bet that the mining engineers at the time had thoughts of going back to the top of the pit and removing additional material along the pit boundary to uncover additional high-grade ore at the pit bottom. They most likely did enough planning to be able to make estimates of the additional yardage of waste that would need to be removed and the extra tonnage of ore that would be recovered. Using the prevailing economics of the time they would have calculated the resultant extra cost that would be incurred if such an operation was undertaken. Management would have reviewed the evaluation.

By that time in the life of the pit, the economics were stacked against them and no such operation would take place. Ultimately, the pit was abandoned for safety reasons with mostly solid, high-grade iron ore in the pit bottom, extending who knows how much further into the ground.

Comstock and Queen of the West – 1967 – Mining, Maintenance, and Plant

Mining and stripping in the Comstock area for CF&I was routine and as scheduled. The costs were in line with forecasts.

The CF&I policy of not allowing stockpiling in the plant, curtailed the efficiency of the entire operation. When ore is loaded, it depends on the mining, hauling, crushing, and loading to be one operational function.

The Queen of The West Pit, which is south and adjacent to the Comstock, supplied about 39% of the ore that was mined, and 13% of the waste that was removed. Development of the Queen of The West Mine progressed on schedule by using SHE-74, 6 cubic yard shovel. Mining began on February 8, 1967. The only major delay was on the shovel, for a two-week period in June, when part of the electrical motor-generator set was rewound.

Mining continued at a high rate during the winter and spring months. Some overtime was necessary in loading the ore in the cars in order to meet the railroad schedule and the required tonnage to CF&I.

An area clean-up crew removed and separated the scrap iron around the plant and shop area which improved the appearance of the area considerably.

In August, repairs on the deck of the truck scales necessitated the use of the stockpiles to maintain an even shipping rate of the ore. At this time repairs were also made on the jaw crusher.

Drilling and blasting in the Comstock area this year, had no outstanding problems. Some water was encountered which made it necessary to use slurry type powder. The material to date in the Comstock has been easy to drill and not difficult to blast, however, the presence of water appears to be becoming more prevalent.

The 1968 budget was outlined late in the year and does call for the replacement of some small equipment and two crawler tractors this next year.

The weather pattern over the entire operation was normal and only a few hours were lost due to snow storms. Some cold weather prevailed in the first part of January with a low of -17 degrees.[67]

In October 1972, an *Iron County Record* article told of the ten millionth ton of iron ore shipped from the Comstock Mine since February 1954.

10,000,000th ton of iron ore shipped to CF&I

On October 6, Union Pacific Railroad Car No. 88131, containing the 10,000,000th ton of ore shipped to Colorado Fuel and Iron Corporation in Pueblo, Colo. was shipped from the Comstock Mine. The story really began back during February 1954, when the first pound of ore was loaded and shipped by six people, who still work for Utah International, Inc., at the Comstock, Mine. Those men are Howard Savage, Scott Batt, Ray Simkins, Carl Stratton, Blaine Jones, and Joe Leeder. Savage actually records an even earlier responsibility with this ore being shipped, in that he worked on the construction of the Comstock Plant. After construction was completed he then joined the Utah International, Inc. staff as a mine foreman at the Comstock mine.

Jim Wark, resident engineer, and LaVoy Woolsey, mining engineer assistant, are the men who control the Comstock operations for the CF&I Steel Corporation. The present-day Utah International, Inc. operations have Bob Diederich as mine manager, York Jones as assistant mine manager, and Howard Savage as Comstock mine foreman. Also, under Diederich's and Jones's direction is the Iron Springs Mine, which ships ore primarily to U.S. Steel Corporation at Geneva. A total of 17,330,000 tons of ore have been shipped from the Iron Springs Operation to date. The Comstock Mine, located on Iron Mountain west of Cedar City, employs about 60 of the approximately 200 people who work for Utah International, Inc., at the Cedar City Operations. "UTAH," is one of the major employers in Iron County, a fact which is not commonly recognized.[68]

In November 1977, officials of CF&I at Pueblo, Colorado, ordered Utah International to suspend operations at the Comstock Mine and discontinue the shipment of ore to the Pueblo plant for the next two months. The reduction in deliveries resulted in about forty of Utah International's 200 employees being laid off. Officials at Pueblo stated the discontinuation was caused by the lack of sales from the Pueblo plant. No specific date was given by CF&I concerning when ore shipments were to resume but it was assumed by Utah that they would recommence sometime in January.[69]

After all the large near-surface ore bodies had been opened up in the district, the mining companies began to look at other surface deposits that were not quite so large and not quite so spectacular. U.S. Steel left Iron Mountain and moved to the Desert Mound and Pioche deposits, both of which had been partially mined in the 1920s. Utah Construction worked its way north and west from the large Lindsay Hill deposit around Granite Mountain to the Little Mormon, Vermillion, Eclipse and Twitchell ore bodies. The Vermillion deposit was partially mined in the 1920s in conjunction with the Pioche.

When U.S. Steel reopened the Pioche deposit, the ore was hauled west and south, past the Vermillion, Eclipse and Twitchell deposits to the Desert Mound facility for processing and shipping. When Utah Construction Company began mining the Vermillion, Eclipse and Twitchell deposits, the ore was hauled east and south past the Pioche deposit to the Iron Springs facility for processing and shipping.

Utah Construction also extended its operation north and east across Iron Springs Gap to the Three Peaks area and opened up the Smith, Jones, Zelma, McGarry, Irene and Blackbird deposits. It also revisited the old Great Western Deposit that had been partially mined previously. None of these deposits had large reserves but they each added up to help supply the smelters. Utah Construction even bought a diesel-powered drill and mining shovel that were used specifically for remote locations where the mine power line network was not available.

Utah Construction Company

There were only four ore bodies of consequence in the Iron Springs Mining area that were not mined, the Clive-Constitution, Georgia, Wall Street and Jeanette. Three ore bodies in the Three Peaks Mining Area were not mined, the April Fool, Ashton and State Section 16, but clearly mining was reaching a point of diminishing returns.

Little Mormon ore body was located immediately south of the Pioche ore body on the northeast side of Granite Mountain. This contact replacement of the Homestake Limestone was associated with four small faults that displaced the contact zone. The ore body was located where the largest fault crosses the contact. The deposit had a surface outcrop, 375 feet long with an apparent width of 110 feet. The Homestake Limestone struck northerly and dipped 30° to 35° east. The ore body replaced about 50 feet of the lower part of the limestone and also dipped toward the east. The property was owned by the U.S. Steel Company and had an estimated ore potential of about 1 million tons. The deposit was leased to Utah International.[70]

Vermillion ore body was located at the north end of Granite Mountain. The deposit was immediately west of the Pioche ore body, where a northeast-trending fault with a 300-foot breccia zone separated the two deposits. The Vermillion ore body had an east-west strike for about 600 feet and dipped gently north. It was a replacement of Homestake Limestone and averaged about fifty feet in thickness. The Homestake Limestone cropped out on the south side of the deposit and dipped about 30° north.

Overburden increased rapidly toward the north. Homestake Limestone was exposed throughout the Vermillion Pit, but a few hundred feet west it was faulted down by the Clive marginal thrust fault, bringing the Iron Springs Formation in fault contact with porphyry. The Vermillion ore body was much smaller in length, thickness and depth than the nearby Pioche ore body; it was owned by U.S. Steel and leased to Utah International, Inc. The ore potential of this deposit was about two million tons.[71]

Eclipse ore body was located west of the Vermillion property on the north end of Granite Mountain. The deposit occurred in a step-faulted block of Homestake Limestone as a small replacement body. Drilling operations exposed fourteen feet of ore in one hole and nineteen feet in another. A small magnetic anomaly extended for about 700 feet along strike. The west end of the anomaly swung southwest and conformed to the direction of the marginal Clive thrust fault. This ore body was owned by James Murphy of Chicago, Illinois, was leased to Utah International Inc. and had an ore reserve of at least 500,000 tons.[72]

Twitchell ore body was located between the Clive-Constitution and Eclipse ore bodies on the northwest side of Granite Mountain. The ore body was non-outcropping and occurred along the Clive fault which brought the Iron Springs Formation in fault contact with quartz monzonite porphyry. The fault had vertical to high-angle reverse dips and showed considerable brecciation. Iron ore occurred as breccia fillings and minor replacements of the Iron Springs Formation and has marked silicification. The ore potential was between half a million and one million tons.[73]

Smith ore body was located on the south end of Three Peaks. The ore deposit was a replacement of Homestake Limestone which occurred as a roof pendant in quartz monzonite porphyry. The ore was associated with a recumbent fold north of the Homestake Limestone, was bounded on both sides by the basal siltstone member of the Carmel Formation and had completely replaced up to 200 feet of limestone. Strike length of the east deposit was about 600 feet. This deposit produced about 1 million long tons of high-grade magnetite ore. The length of the west ore deposit was somewhat greater; it had an ore reserve of about 300,000 tons. The ore was good grade magnetite with some hematite and was mined intermittently for several years. The property was owned by Utah International.[74]

Jones ore body was located on the south end of Three Peaks, a short distance east of the Great Western fissure vein. The Jones ore body was a fissure vein in quartz monzonite porphyry. The strike length was about 300 feet and the average width was approximately three feet. The ore potential was perhaps only ten thousand tons of magnetite ore.[75]

Zelma ore body was located at the south end of Three Peaks, a short distance northwest of the Great Western ore body. The Zelma deposit was a fissure vein in quartz monzonite porphyry with a strike length of about 800 feet and a maximum width of ten feet. The property, owned by the Jones Brothers Company, had an ore potential of about 50,000 to 100,000 tons.[76]

McGarry ore body was located on the west side of Three Peaks. The deposit was either a small roof pendant replacement of in-folded Homestake Limestone or a down-faulted slice of limestone completely surrounded by porphyry. Basal Homestake Limestone was present. Ore was exposed at the surface in an area 380 feet long with a maximum width of sixty feet. The property was owned by James Murphy of Chicago and leased by Utah International. The ore reserve was only 150,000 tons averaging about 55.7 percent iron and 0.3 percent phosphorus.[77]

Irene ore body was located on the northwest side of Three Peaks and was a replacement type deposit in a small roof pendant of Homestake Limestone. It was steeply dipping, surrounded by quartz monzonite porphyry and was only partly replaced. The strike length of the deposit at the surface was about 300 feet and the maximum width was about fifty feet. The property was owned by Jones Brothers Company and leased by Utah International Inc. The property produced about two million tons of high-grade ore, low in silica, sulfur and phosphorus.[78]

Blackbird ore body occurred near the north end of Three Peaks. This ore body was a fissure vein deposit in quartz monzonite porphyry and consisted principally of magnetite. The fissure vein was lens-like in form and dipped about 80° east; at the surface the vein had a strike length of 740 feet and a maximum width of about thirty feet. Abundant apatite in the ore gave it a high phosphorous content. The property was owned by James Murphy of Chicago, Illinois and leased by Utah International Inc. Ore potential of the vein was about 300,000 tons.[79]

Great Western ore body was located near the south end of Three Peaks, a fissure vein in the selvage joint zone of quartz monzonite porphyry. The original fissure had an average strike of north 65° east with a dip of 75° northwest, a surface strike length of about 750 feet and a maximum width of twenty-five feet. The vein was the largest known in the Three Peaks area. The ore was composed of hard, dense magnetite with small amounts of hematite and limonite. The ore contained quartz, apatite and calcite. The average iron content was greater than sixty percent. Production from this property from 1937 to 1957 totaled about 80,000 tons. Utah International, Inc. owned the property in the 1960s.[80]

Clive-Constitution ore body lies on the northwest side of Granite Mountain. The northeast-trending Clive fault brought the Iron Springs Formation in fault contact with quartz monzonite porphyry. Drill holes revealed mineralized breccia along the Clive fault and replacement ore in Homestake Limestone. At least six drill holes passed through the full stratigraphic thickness of Homestake Limestone, encountering about fifty-five feet of ore near the base between 738 and 793 feet below the surface. Drilling also suggests that ore extends up the thrust fault for about 600 feet toward the surface with an average thickness of about thirty-three feet. A magnetic anomaly extends for about 1,200 feet along the strike. Ore cut by the drill holes ranges from fairly soft mixtures of magnetite and hematite to somewhat harder ore, largely magnetite. If ore extends 200 feet down-dip replacing limestone beds, the ore potential is at least one million tons. The property is owned by James D. Murphy and Mildred R. Quinn and leased by Utah International Inc.[81]

Georgia ore body lies on the west side of Granite Mountain and is associated with the northeast-trending Clive thrust fault. Drill holes show a replacement ore body in Homestake Limestone occurring as a wedge along the Clive fault. Ore also occurs as breccia fillings and replacements along the fault zone. The ore body was covered by about ninety feet of alluvium. The Georgia ore deposit was owned by J. M. Palmer of Cedar City and was leased by Utah International, Inc. The property has an ore reserve of about 250,000 tons.[82]

Wall Street ore body is located on the east side of Granite Mountain. The deposit is a fissure vein in quartz monzonite porphyry; the vein length is about 500 feet. The property is held by the Charlotte Mining Company. The ore potential is small, probably 35,000 tons.[83]

Jeanette ore body is located on the southeast side of Granite Mountain. The deposit is a fissure vein in quartz monzonite porphyry. The main vein, which averages about five feet in width, can be traced for more than 300 feet. It strikes to the northeast and is associated with smaller veins with a similar attitude. The ore potential is only a few thousand tons.[84]

April Fool ore body lies on the northwest side of Three Peaks. The property is covered by alluvium. It was discovered by a U.S. Bureau of Mines magnetometer investigation of the area in 1944–45 and is held by the Charlotte Mining Company. An anomalous area about 1,700 feet long was drilled. The ore body lies about 250 feet below the surface and averages about 113 feet thick. The April Fool ore body is a replacement of Homestake Limestone which occurs as a foundered slab or sliver of limestone completely surrounded by porphyry. The ore consists of soft granular material with ribs of hard ore. Blocks of unreplaced limestone are common. Magnetite is the main mineral but hematite is common in parts of the deposit. The ore potential of this deposit is probably between half a million and one million tons. The stripping ratio for open pitting this deposit would be high.[85]

Ashton ore body lies on the west side of Three Peaks. This deposit is a fissure vein about six feet wide and 300 feet long in quartz monzonite porphyry and lies slightly more than one mile north of the Great Western fissure vein deposit. A forty-seven-foot shaft appears to be the major development on this property which is held by Jones Brothers Co. of Cedar City. The property has a small ore potential, perhaps in the range of 50,000 to 100,000 tons.[86]

The State Section 16 ore body occurs on Utah State land on the southwest side of Three Peaks. A magnetic anomaly mapped by the U.S. Bureau of Mines in 1944–45 prompted exploration by diamond drilling. One hole, drilled by the Bureau in 1951, additional holes in 1962 and 1963 and subsequent holes drilled by the Utah Construction and Mining Company, reveal a metasomatic replacement type ore body in Homestake Limestone. The limestone formation and ore body dip about 60° south. Ore lies 800 to 1,000 feet below the surface and is principally magnetite. The ore potential of this deposit is approximately one million tons.[87]

Beneficiation Plant

There was a large amount of low grade iron ore in many of the mining areas, much of which had already been discarded and lost. Some of the ore was intrinsically lower grade as it was deposited as part of a larger ore body. Other ore started out as high grade but as part of the mining process became intermixed with waste material. This was particularly true when mining operations encountered a contact zone where the ore interfaced with waste; any mixed material went to the dump. Close inspection of the old waste dumps reveals many rocks and boulders of iron ore that, if separated, could have been sold as high-grade rather than be discarded.

In the late 1950s, Utah Construction decided that it would build a beneficiation plant that would economically separate iron ore from waste material thereby upgrading the low-grade ore to make it marketable. Most of the iron ore was magnetite and therefore was magnetic and the plant used that attribute to pull the ore from the non-magnetic waste with which it was intermingled. However, some of the ore was non-magnetic hematite so the plant also included a heavy-media circuit that separated the ore using specific gravity rather than magnetism. Magnetite has a specific gravity of about 5.0, compared the surrounding rock of around 2.5. The specific gravity of water is 1.0.

Even before the decision was made to build the beneficiation plant, Utah began building low-grade stockpiles all around the area. The low-grade was hauled out of the pit and stacked to allow the regular direct-ship ore to be mined. Later, when time allowed, the piles would be hauled to the plant and processed and upgraded. Some of the low-grade from U.S. Steel's operations was even purchased, hauled and run through the plant. In addition to saving the low-grade resource, the plant allowed Utah to ship a higher-grade product to the smelters with much less variability. As it turned out, the product was far superior to the direct-ship ore that had previously been sold by the mines. Many times, the other companies in the area with only direct-ship capability could have used such a resource when the ore available in their pits did not meet smelter specifications.

Utah Construction Invests in Future of County with Beneficiation Plant

A step to extend the life of the iron mining industry in Iron County has been taken by the Utah Construction and Mining Company.

In August 1960, work on construction of a one million three hundred-thousand-dollar beneficiation plant was undertaken for the purpose of up-grading non-shippable ores from properties within the Southern Utah mining district. This plant was completed on April 15, 1961, and after technical problems are eliminated, the plant will be capable of handling approximately 120 tons of lean ore per hour for up-grading to about 60% iron content. The ore is then ready for shipment to the steel mills throughout the Western United States.

According to Ralph Long, project manager of the company operations in Iron County, the beneficiation plant will be integrated into the present operation at Iron Springs but may also be used to process low grade ores from other properties in outlying areas.

Ore to be processed through the new plant will be sent through the original crushing system, then automatically taken through a secondary crusher and a gyro-cone crusher to a huge silo from which the ore will be sent through the plant by an intricate system of conveyor belts.

Upon leaving the beneficiation plant, the fine waste material is pumped to a tailings pond and the coarse waste material is carried on a conveyor belt to the waste dump. The concentrated iron ore is carried to stockpiles by conveyor belts where it is then, through an underground belt system, blended with other ores for shipment.

Utah Construction and Mining Company, in its Iron County operations, has stockpiled considerable amounts of low grade ore that will, after up-grading, be a marketable product. The plant will take ore as low as 20% iron content and this means that other ores, yet to be mined in the area, but with low iron content, can now be mined. This further lengthens the life of the very important iron mining industry in Iron County.

This was a company project and the design and metallurgical departments of the company designed the plant. Much of the steel used in the plant was fabricated at Provo. Some of the steel for another beneficiation plant, located in Peru, is being fabricated in Provo for an affiliate of Utah Construction and Mining Company.

In the beneficiation of iron ore, water plays a most important part. Water rights were obtained for a well near the plant site and water is piped to the plant for use

A Slow Decline

Illustration 10.7. Beneficiation Plant at Iron Springs. (Photo from York Jones)

there. A special "thickener" was installed at the plant to reclaim all the water possible and to conserve this very important resource.

Use of the thickener has greatly reduced the water needed from the well for plant operation.

Since the operation of a beneficiation plant is new in the mining industry of Southern Utah (it is one of three in the Western United States) the company obtained the services of Tom Erspamer of Hoyt Lake, Minn. as mill superintendent. Mr. Erspamer is well acquainted with iron ore beneficiation, having worked in several of the plants operating on the Minnesota Iron Range. Other personnel needed for plant operation were regular employees transferred from other duties at the mine.

Utah Construction and Mining Company has a forward attitude concerning the iron mining industry of Southern Utah. Expenditures of nearly one and one-half million dollars for construction of this plant is an indication of this outlook and will have an effect on the economy of this area. The new beneficiation plant and other plans now in process are designed to give longer life to the iron ore industry of this area, based on the extended period of recovery of raw materials in the Pinto and Iron Springs mining districts.[88]

Iron Springs Ore

The main production from the Iron Springs district is direct-shipping ore. Generally, the grade of direct-shipping ore ranges from 45 to 68 percent iron with an average iron content between 50 and 55 percent. This ore only requires crushing and screening prior to shipping. Ores with iron content from 20 to 45 percent are upgraded by Utah Construction and Mining Company's beneficiation plant at Iron Springs. This low-grade ore is being stockpiled by other companies for future processing. Open-hearth and blast furnace ores are shipped from the district. Open-hearth ore must be coarse, dense, high-grade and low in impurities, from minus 7 inches to plus 2-1/2 inches in diameter. The finer and lower-grade ores are used for blast furnace ore, all minus 2-1/2 inches in diameter. U.S. Steel's specifications for iron ores vary somewhat, but the following examples are general guidelines which iron producers are required to meet.

Iron ore specifications of U.S. Steel Corp. for their furnaces (percent)

	Open-Hearth Furnaces	Blast Furnaces
Fe	58.0 minimum	50.0 minimum
SiO_2	7.0 maximum	10.0 maximum
S	0.05	0.10
P	0.40	0.25
Cu	0.04	0.04
Ni	0.04	0.04
Pb	0.01	0.01
Zn	0.01	0.01
As	0.01	0.01[89]

Magnetic concentration of iron ores was introduced in the Iron Springs district by the Utah Construction and Mining Company. They began direct shipping of iron ores from the Iron Springs district in 1944. As its reserves of direct-shipping ore diminished and as the need for higher-grade furnace feed at the Geneva Works increased, beneficiation facilities were added to meet the specifications of the steel mills. Such a plant was installed at Iron Springs where it began operations in April 1961 (Erspamer, 1964). Grinding, scrubbing and wet magnetic separation facilities were capable of handling 2,500 tons per day of minus 1-1/4-inch ore.

Three years later a revised contract called for a higher-grade product, and the Utah Construction and Mining Company expanded its Iron Springs plant to handle 4,000 tons per day of minus 1-1/4-inch ore. Nearly all run-of-mine ore is processed at the plant by crushing, grinding, screening and open-hearth cobbing, wet beneficiation of blast furnace ore by scrubbing and wet magnetic separation and stockpiling, blending and loading of concentrates for shipment. In 1967 the Utah Construction and Mining Company mined 398,152 tons of ore in the district, of which 19,247 tons were direct-shipping ores. The remaining 355,014 tons, with an average iron content of 42.7 percent, were shipped to the beneficiation plant. During the same year this company shipped 248,205 long tons of concentrates from mined ore with an average iron content of 58 percent to the Geneva works.[90]

Alluvium Plant

As discussed previously, the iron ore deposits in the Pinto-Iron Springs Mining District occurred as replacements in the Homestake Limestone, as fillings and replacements in broken and faulted areas and in smaller veins in the surrounding rock. As weathering progressed, the magnetite and hematite debris moved down-slope and

Illustration 10.8. Alluvium Plant. The dragline that excavated the alluvial material can be seen on the right. It dug and dumped the rock and dirt onto the grizzly, on the front corner of the mobile plant. Oversized rock was screened off and slid back into the cut. However, the bulk of the material fell through the grizzly. After the ore was separated, it was transported by belt and dumped into a holding bin with the truck parked under it, which can be seen on the left side of the photo. The waste material was returned to the cut via a stacker conveyor belt suspended by cables as seen in the center of the photo. When there was enough ore to make a full load, the 100-ton-plus truck hauled it twelve miles to Iron Springs. The control room/office/lunch room was the small building on top of the structure. A contest was held to name the mobile plant. The name that was chosen was ALTIS, which stood for Added Life To Iron Springs. Although it seemed like the plant produced only a small stream of iron ore, once cleaned, it was very high-grade and made it possible to blend a larger portion of low-grade ore to make a marketable final product. (Photo from York Jones)

concentrated in the alluvium. Significant quantities of magnetic ore were contained in some of the alluvial deposits in the area; this was particularly true of the eastern slope of Iron Mountain, down-slope of the massive Comstock-Mountain Lion deposit.

In the late 1950s, Utah Construction Company decided to investigate these alluvial deposits to see if the ore intermixed in them could be economically recovered. In 1958, a laboratory test model of a high-speed drum magnetic separator was purchased and installed in the company's research laboratory at Palo Alto, California. A year later, trenches were dug in alluvium with a backhoe and the material sampled. A bucket drill was contracted and used to determine the depth of alluvium and to obtain additional samples. Laboratory and pilot plant test results justified a more detailed investigation.

In 1962, a full-scale model was set up at the Iron Springs pilot plant and large-scale tests were run. The results of the tests were favorable; the alluvial deposits ranged from 3 to 20 percent iron, averaging about 10 percent. It was also found that a sizable portion of the ore was magnetite in appropriate size ranges which was favorable for recovery using magnetic separation methods. The bucket drilling showed that the alluvium was up to 100 feet thick in places.

During the time that the testing was being conducted, a mobile plant was conceived and the design process began. In 1963, the final design and construction contract was awarded to Bodinson Manufacturing Company of San Francisco. The mobile magnetic iron ore concentrator went into operation in 1964 on the McCahill-Thompson property on the northeast side of Iron Mountain.

Absence of titanium in the ore, relatively high magnetite concentration, and large quantities of debris between twenty-eight mesh and twenty-four inches allowed an especially favorable operation. Three percent iron is roughly the inherent iron analysis of the intrusive rock. A cutoff as low as 6 percent iron was used in alluvial concentration. A typical structure of the crude alluvium follows:

Structure of Crude Alluvium

Size	Percent
+8"	2
-8" +4"	12
-4" +3/4"	15
-3/4" +1/4"	11
-1/4"+100 mesh	35
-100 mesh	25

Mining depths to 100 feet or more were contemplated and planned for. The process used in recovering iron ore from crude alluvium was essentially a size separation followed by magnetic separation of size fractions. Oversize was eventually used as open-hearth ore, the undersize in the blast furnaces.[91]

The mobile plant designed and built by Utah Construction was one of a kind. The best way to describe it was that it was like a "dry land dredge." The plant, weighing 550 tons, received alluvium material from a 151-M Marion Electric Shovel, converted to a dragline configuration, with a seven-cubic-yard bucket. The material was screened into a coarse fraction and a fine fraction; each stream then passed over a magnetic head pulley, or cobber, that separated the iron ore from the waste. The two products recovered by the plant were trucked to Iron Springs. The coarse, high-grade iron ore could be direct shipped and the low-grade fines were further processed by the Iron Springs Beneficiation Plant. The Alluvium Plant moved under its own power on tracks and followed the dragline down the cut as it was dug. Land reclamation took place after the mining was completed.[93]

In its lifetime the alluvium plant and its associated dragline covered a substantial amount of ground and in doing so, also operated on quite a number of mining claims. Most of the claims had no ore body or lode associated with them, only the ore that was within the alluvium. However, a few did, and when a lode was encountered, a pit was opened and the ore was mined conventionally. Some of the mining claims encountered were the Black Rock #1, Blue Jay, Yellow Jacket, Black Magnetic, Last Chance, Homestake, McCahill-Thompson and U.C. Placer.

Illustration 10.9. "Utah Construction and Mining Co. recently purchased this new Kenworth end-dump truck for its Cedar City operations. The new unit is currently being used to haul iron ore field concentrate from the mobile concentrator to Iron Springs, a distance of 12 miles. The truck is capable of hauling in excess of 100 tons. Overall length of the unit is 43 feet and it is 14 feet wide."[2] *The truck was nicknamed 'The Blue Goose,' because of its shape and color. This type truck was used because the tires on the regular mine trucks would overheat and separate on the 12-mile haul. Other tractor-trailer units were used later. (Photo from the article quoted and cited herein)*

Alluvium Mining Operation 1967

The alluvium operation functioned very well this year with operating costs well below the forecasts. The total field concentrate was 330,777 N.T. and 54.5 Fe.

For five months of the year the operation was on a 7-day week, Thursday's day shift being for repair work. This 7-day, 3-shift, 4-crew system continued from February 20, until August 7, and then returned to the 5-day, 3-shift operation.

Following approval from U.S.S. to mine the lode ore on the Yellow Jacket claim, steps were taken to haul the tails away by truck and expose the ore zone. The mining cuts in the alluvium are parallel to the strike of the ore zone. This removal of tails began late in October and was discontinued on March 20.

Most of the mining this past year has been on the Black Rock #1, Blue Jay, Yellow Jacket, and Homestake mining claims. Our mining plan for the alluvium operation was set up to avoid mining on the U.C. Placer No. 13 and 14.

During periods of high concentrate productivity from the alluvium plant ore was stockpiled at the plant site and later removed to Iron Springs.

The Kenworth end-dump truck was out of service for eight days for installation of standard forged 6" axles on the trailer which have worked much better.

In March we reduced the D-9 work shifts from 20 to 10 per week to accommodate more adequately the work load requirements. On April 10, it was agreed with the Union and the Company to maintain the D-9 shifts (one per shift) and work the men part time on the plant.

On April 18, a high wind swung the 150-foot tails stacker on the plant around and collapsed it. The control cable on the bull-wheel failed. The four crews were dispersed to swing shift, and men and equipment worked in the Comstock waste. Also casting off the waste from the future Yellow Jacket Pit with the SHE-67 dragline was undertaken at this time. On May 15, the operations were back on schedule.

On the 13th of June lightning hit the substation and caused the transformers and wiring in the dragline to malfunction. A two-day delay was encountered and some crews were on standby.

The depth of cut being removed by the dragline is still erratic, and in some locations 58 ft. to bedrock. A method of recovering the oversize from the dragline cut is still under study and needs refinement.

Late in October the dragline was shut down for major repairs. The hoist drum and some of the component parts were worn-out. This delay took 10 days.

A test was started in July to compare two makes of tires on the 100- ton Kenworth hauling unit. Eight of the tires are Michelin and the other eight are Firestone tires. This test is still underway.[94]

In 1967, Utah Construction and Mining Company produced 300,578 long tons of dry crude field concentrate with an average grade of 53.5 percent iron content. It shipped 227,711 long tons of alluvial concentrates with a minimum 60 percent iron content from the Iron Springs beneficiation plant.[95]

Yellow Jacket ore body was located on the northeast side of Iron Mountain. The deposit was immediately south of the Homestake ore body and was a contact metasomatic replacement in Homestake Limestone. Replacement was not complete as shown by the presence of chlorite, epidote and other silicates in the ore. Limestone strikes northwest and dips from 70° to 80° northeast. Original outcrops of ore were about 375 feet along strike, and the ore body dipped steeply parallel with Homestake Limestone beds. The property was owned by U.S. Steel. Since the ore was high in silicates and sulfur, it was treated at the Iron Springs beneficiation plant. The ore potential of this deposit was at least two million tons.[96]

Last Chance ore body was located on the east side of Iron Mountain, a small outcropping replacement type ore body a short distance east of the Comstock ore body. The property was owned by CF&I Steel Corporation. The deposit appears to have a potential of about one million tons.[97]

Iron Springs Mining and Maintenance 1967

Through the cooperative efforts of all of the departments, the ore sales to U.S.S. were fulfilled this past year, which entailed maintaining the proper chemical and mechanical balance of the ore.

Chemical blending and the production of open-hearth ore became more of a problem than has been normal, and for the most part, this condition controlled the schedule. However, the moving of equipment and men to accomplish the proper blending of ore did not present any major difficulties. For the major part of the year one day-shift mining crew was able to maintain the necessary ore and waste removal.

A new D-8 Cat was delivered in February for the Iron Springs plant. A considerable amount of time was spent during the year on cleaning the safety benches and pit back walls.

The State Industrial Commission requested a campaign to control the dust on the rotary drills on this job. Both of the 50-R Drills were converted to accommodate "wet" drilling. The 58-BH Drills will soon be converted to the same system.

In April, the last two of seven Michelin tires (size 2100×35) were removed from an LW-65 truck. The first five tires ran an average of 1,600 hours each, with no recaps, before sidewall separation occurred. The last two had 1416 hours each before they were recapped and had 2,221 hours on the recap before there was evidence of sidewall failure. These hours are well below normal.

This year we started an equipment inspection and schooling program on our Cat equipment, through Wheeler Machinery Company. This program will coincide with our intensified planned maintenance on all of the equipment.

On August 6, a D-8 and a D-9 were sent to a derailment on the main line of the Union Pacific Railroad, north of Milford, Utah, to assist in removing the wreck.

In October, a test-run was completed on the Mountain Lion low grade stockpile by hauling 4,400 tons of ore to the Iron Springs plant. This should determine the rate in which this ore can be used in conjunction with the Iron Springs ore.

The annual October "Deer Hunt" vacations, numbering forty, were scheduled with very little difficulty in connection with the planned shut-down of the mill on the 17th. After the vacations were completed, 13 men were put on reduction in force.

Drilling and blasting in the Iron Springs area had no outstanding problems this year. Powder factors for the job were about .39/N.T. in ore and about 0.77/C.Y. in waste. Last year the total powder used at the Cedar City operation was 1,076,460 pounds. The NH_4NO_3 was 876,950 lbs. of this total.

Iron Springs production costs were in line with forecasts. We moved equipment and men between the Iron Mountain, Comstock and the Iron Springs mining areas more this year than in the past. This does make more efficient use of the equipment and personnel, but somewhat complicates the day-to-day scheduling.

*In our planned maintenance program, we hope to achieve the optimum balance between maintenance expenses and production costs. With this in mind we changed most of our reporting system in the shops and centralized the bookkeeping. A good deal of time was spent in the planning of this planned maintenance program this past year.[98]

Eclipse Pit Mining

As the author, I can't help but add a bit of my personal experience at the Eclipse Pit as well. In the early 1970s, Utah Construction and Mining Company mined the Vermillion and Eclipse ore bodies using modern open pit technology. Remnants of the old glory holes, tunnels, raises, ventilation shafts, railroads etc. were still in existence from the 1920s. Encountering the old underground workings in an active open pit mine caused a number of challenging problems. Issues included, but were not limited to, difficulties in drilling and blasting, crushers and chutes getting plugged with railroad ties and debris, tearing of conveyor belts by tramp iron and rails, and the danger of equipment falling through the pit floor into hidden tunnels below. Old mine maps drawn in 1925 were obtained and the tunnel locations were plotted on mine plan maps as best as possible, given the different coordinate systems. Working in the engineering department, I was assigned the task.

One particularly memorable experience occurred when the mine had progressed to the level just above the location of the old West Drift that had been extended to the edge of the Eclipse deposit. One of the rows of blast holes was aligned right down the centerline of the drift. When the rotary blast-hole drill drilled the holes, many of the holes penetrated the tunnel below and bottomed in "open air." When the blasters came on site to load the holes with explosives, they could not load them correctly because the explosives kept emptying into the open space below. Bags and rocks were used in an attempt to plug the bottom of the blast holes to allow the explosive to rise high enough in the holes for proper breakage, with only limited success. In the end, the blasters did the best they could, and the loaded holes were ready to be detonated, realizing that hundreds of extra pounds of explosives were piled on the tunnel floor below and that most likely the amount of explosives in the actual drill-holes was insufficient for proper fragmentation.

In addition to the tunnel below, there was an old shaft just outside the perimeter of the pit that had been used for access and ventilation. It was square and about eight feet by eight feet. It was open on the top, reinforced with timber on the sides, had a ladder attached to one side and was partially caved in. It should also be noted that the ore in the Eclipse and Vermillion deposits had higher levels of hematite and was colored deep red and purple in places, hence the name "Vermillion." When the shot went off, much of the air blast vented into the old drift and it is possible that some of the extra explosives on the floor also detonated. As a result, a tremendous cloud of purplish red dust shot from the old air shaft into the sky like a cannon. Along with the thick dust were broken timbers, chunks of rock, pieces of wood and bats, lots of bats. It was quite a sight, especially since many of the men did not know beforehand that the old shaft even existed.

A few weeks later when mining progressed into the level that contained the old drift, all sorts of debris was encountered; railroad ties, rails and spikes, even remnants of an old rail car and other artifacts, all crushed by the blast and collapsing rock. The material had the potential of tearing the conveyor belts or plugging the crusher or one of the chutes, so workers were stationed along the beltway to pull off the trash when it was observed. I was able to salvage a small section of the lightweight rail that was used in the mine. In the 1960s, U.S. Steel mined the Pioche Pit by open pit methods and it had remnants of tunnels readily visible high up in its pit walls.

On November 14, 1974 the following announcement was made.

York F. Jones Assumes Management of Utah International Here

York F. Jones assumes responsibility as Mine Manager at the Cedar City, Utah operations for Utah International Inc. Jones, a native of Cedar City, began his career with Utah International in 1951, during the construction phase of the Cedar City Mine. Since then he has held positions as engineer, mine engineer, mine superintendent, and assistant mine manager. York, who has studied mine engineering at the University of Missouri, also attended and graduated in civil engineering at the

College of Southern Utah. He will replace Mr. Robert C. Diederich, who will manage a new operation in Craig, Colorado.[99]

In 1975, York Jones wrote the following description of the Utah International operation located at Iron Springs.

Iron Springs Operations 1975

The Iron Springs operation of Utah International Inc. is unique in the district in that not only is direct-shipping ore mined, but low-grade ore, too, is mined and concentrated. Also, it is the only non-captive mine in the district.

The ore shipped from Iron Springs must meet rigid structural and chemical specifications. Two products are shipped, open-hearth ore and blast furnace ore. Each of these products is defined structurally and must meet six chemical specifications. The open-hearth concentrate is structurally defined as an ore ranging in size from 1-1/4 in. to 4 in. and must meet more stringent chemical specifications than are required of blast furnace ore. The minus 1-1/4 in. concentrate is shipped as blast furnace ore.

Since the character of the ore varies from pit to pit, the above chemical specifications are determining factors in the mining program. An ore body may contain one deleterious element in excess of specifications while having insignificant quantities of another. In the case of some undesirable elements the content will always be close to the maximum specifications, while in others it may range from traces to several times the allowable maximum.

As a result, ore control and blending are major problems. In order to facilitate blending, five pits are being operated, which may expose many ore faces. In addition to these faces, there are ten to twelve low-grade stockpiles near the pits that may be reclaimed and beneficiated to produce a saleable product.

Pits are designed with walls at 63-1/2° slopes with a 25-ft. safety bench for each 100 ft. of depth. This results in an overall slope of 58°. The mine is operated on 25-ft. lifts. This has been chosen as the optimum bench height to permit selective mining while still maintaining adequate production rates.

Ore Control

The primary guide to mining is the mine control drilling. The ore on each 25-ft. lift is drilled at 20-ft. centers by a track drill, and the cuttings are collected for analysis. This drilling is kept as far in advance of the mining as possible. As soon as mining on one lift exposes ore on the next lift, drilling is begun. This is done in order to provide maximum information for mine planning. The assays from drilling are plotted on maps representing 25-ft. horizontal sections of the pit. In addition, face and blast-hole samples are used to supplement the mine-control drilling in areas where the character of the ore changes rapidly. From data provided by these sampling methods, the engineering department schedules the daily mining. Considerable emphasis is being placed on long-range mining forecasts. The primary purpose of these forecasts is to plan the mining so that a uniform product will be shipped throughout the life of the mine. These forecasts are based on data derived from mine control drilling and ore reserves.

The ore reserves are calculated from development drilling in the conventional manner using vertical sections. The ore reserve data is programmed for an IBM computer. There are two phases of this program. First, the crude ore reserves are calculated from the development. In order to utilize the most basic data available, each assay interval is assigned an area of influence and this is punched into a card with the corresponding assays. The crude ore reserves are then calculated from this data and accumulated on both vertical sections and horizontal sections through the ore bodies.

In the second phase of the program, these crude ore reserves are converted to concentrate reserves. Fifteen factors, or parameters, must be applied to each of the data cards in order to develop the tonnage, recovery, and grades of the concentrate which will be produced from the crude ore. These parameters are based on information obtained from milling experience. The ore reserves have been divided into twelve ore types, each of which requires its own set of parameters. The result is that 180 parameters must be applied to the ore reserves in order to calculate the concentrate reserves. The use of high speed data processing has made these calculations possible and economical.

Drilling & Blasting

Another facet of the operation which requires considerable attention is drilling and blasting. Careful control is exercised because it is desirable to maintain the structure of open-hearth ore. In essence, the ore is broken only to the point that it may be readily handled by the available equipment. To accomplish this, only single-row shots are drilled in ore. In some areas it is advantageous to drill inclined holes. These are empirical combinations and are varied to compensate for the change in character of the ore.

Blast holes are primed with a 1-pound non-dynamite booster and a primadet delay cap. The primary blasting agent is a mixture of fertilizer grade Ammonia Nitrate and Diesel Fuel. Drilling and blasting practices in waste are common to the mining industry. Multiple row shots are detonated with primadet delays, spacing and burden range between 15 and 24 ft. This powder factor is deliberately kept high in order to facilitate maximum shovel production.

A Bucyrus Erie 50-R and two Joy 58-BH's are used for primary drilling. The 50-R has been modified from the standard 12-in. bit to a 9-in. bit. Comparable bit life for the smaller, less-expensive bits, and increased penetration rates, have resulted in decreased drilling costs. This large drill has a distinct advantage over the smaller 58-BH in extremely hard drilling but is not readily transported. Therefore, this drill remains in one pit which has predominately hard drilling. The two Joy drills, which drill a 7-3/8 in. hole, perform the blast hole drilling in the other four pits. These drills are hauled between pits with a low-bed equipment trailer. Tungsten carbide insert bits are used on both drills when drilling extremely hard magnetite ore.

As a result of efforts to maintain structure, a high percentage of broken ore is too large to be fed to the primary crusher. In order to handle this large quantity of secondary drilling adequately, a mobile plug drill was built. The basic elements of this unit are a Pitman 50-HB aerial platform and a 315-cfm compressor mounted on a 2-ton truck. The articulated boom rotates 360 degrees, has a maximum horizontal working radius of 35 ft. At maximum radius the working height is reduced to 27 ft. A Gardner-Denver drifter is mounted on the man-platform at the end of the boom. The drifter rotates about a horizontal pivot and is positioned by a hydraulic cylinder. The orientation of the drill and location of the platform is controlled from the platform. The unit is capable of drilling a large number of boulders from one set-up and is able to travel rapidly between pits.

Mining

The ore is mined with three electric shovels and one diesel shovel. The electric shovels are 151-M Marions, equipped with 6-1/2 cu. yd. buckets, and the Bucyrus Erie 120-B with a 4-1/2 cu. yd. bucket. The diesel shovel is a 93-M Marion with a 2-1/2 cu. yd. bucket. The demand for a flexible mining operation requires this large compliment of mining equipment. The electric shovels are kept in the larger pits where the stripping and mining load is the heaviest. The diesel shovel, being smaller and hence more mobile, is best adapted to mining the smaller more remote pits and to recovering low-grade stockpiles. Like the Joy drills, this shovel is transported on the low-bed equipment trailer. 988 loaders are used for mining stockpiles.

The haulage fleet consists of eight 32-ton and three 65-ton Letourneau-Westinghouse Haulpak trucks. The 32-ton LW's are equipped with Cummins NT 380 turbocharged engines rated at 380hp, and the 65-ton LW's are powered by 700hp Cummins V-12 turbocharged engines. Both types of trucks are equipped with Allison powershift transmissions.

Haulage distances from mine to plant range from 1-1/2 miles to 12 miles. Adverse grades rarely exceed 8%. The haul roads from the pits to the plant are all favorable grade with maximum grades of 5%. Pit cleanup and dump maintenance is performed by one D-8 Caterpillar crawler tractor and an 824 Caterpillar rubber-tired dozer. A 666 Wabco motor patrol is used for road maintenance.

Ore Processing

The primary crusher consists of a 48 × 60 in. Traylor jaw crusher which reduces the ore to about 7". The crushed product is screened at 4" and the oversize is crushed through 4". The crushed ore is sized and passed over a magnetic separator. The reject and the undersize is re-crushed and sent to the mill feed pile. The product which is 4" × 1-1/4" is sent to the open-hearth stockpiles for shipment.

The mill feed is scrubbed and screened at 1/4". The coarse fraction, minus 1-1/4" × 1/4" is concentrated with belt magnetic cobbers. The fine fraction is pumped to drum-type, wet magnetic separators for concentration. The mill has permitted the use of low-grade material that was formerly stockpiled and has made possible the shipment of a superior product.

Manpower

The hourly employment for the entire project varies between 140 and 190 men. The salaried employment is about 40. There are three unions on the project. These are: (1) the Operating Engineers, Local Union No. 3, of the International Union of Operating Engineers; (2) the International Brotherhood of Teamsters, Chauffeurs, Warehousemen, and Helpers of America, Local Union No. 222; and (3) Laborers International Union of North America, Local Union No. 295.[100]

General Interest

Iron Mining Company Employees Injured [August 1960]

Two employees of the Utah Construction and Mining Co. were injured Monday evening in an accident at the Iron Springs pits of the company west of Cedar City. Hospitalized were James Stephenson, shovel operator, with fractures of the leg, hip and pelvis, and Bud Burns, shovel oiler, who sustained hip and back injuries.

Cause of the accident, according to company officials, was the partial failure of the brakes on an ore truck. When the brakes gave way on the truck it backed into the side of the shovel caving it in on the two men.

They were rushed to the Iron County Hospital in Cedar City for treatment.[101]

CHAPTER ELEVEN

The Closures
1980–1987

MANY OF THE issues of the 1960s and 1970s had not abated by the 1980s—in fact, some of them had grown worse. Disruptions and shutdowns of the smelters and mines due to strikes and labor unrest continued to occur on a regular basis. It had become apparent that smelters and their suppliers of iron ore and coal could be seriously curtailed by local and national labor strife. Wages and benefits for the employees had increased such that they were beginning to affect smelters' ability to compete, especially with the glut of foreign steel imports.

There were other financial factors that directly impacted the cost of doing business in Iron County and the State of Utah. Every time the mining industry turned around, the State and Local governments were devising a new tax or a new way of interpreting an old tax so that more dollars could be extracted from the mines and less from the residents and the other businesses of the county. By the end of 1970s, the mines and the associated industries such as the railroad and the power company were contributing over 70 percent of the county's budget.

During the 1970s, the EPA required massive and very expensive changes to be made to the old smelters in the United States, including Geneva. Most of the demands were met; however, the changes had an impact on the bottom line of the companies and the cost of the finished products that were being manufactured. The new equipment had large up-front capital costs, including the high cost of installation, and frequently the plant was shut down during much of the construction. Additionally, the new equipment generally brought with it higher operating costs.

Transportation costs were always a concern because the Geneva plant was located inland, far from the major markets and without access to lower-cost ocean freight rates. The most critical concern continued to be competition with imported steel from foreign countries, especially if "dumping" was involved. At the end of the 1970s, United States' steel makers were teetering on the edge of financial failure. The combination of the high cost of doing business in the States and the low-priced steel from foreign competitors had the entire steel market in a state of flux. Even minor changes in the price of steel would send shock waves throughout the market.

There are those who would argue that what protections that the steel industry did enjoy from foreign competitors, did as much harm as good. They blocked competition and allowed the industry to succeed without having to spend resources on innovation and improved practices. The companies did not adopt the latest technologies and labor productivity lagged behind other industries. Powerful labor unions ensured high labor costs and very limited labor competition. The industry as a whole was lulled into thinking that "all was well." Whatever the cause, the domestic steel industry did not fare well when pitted against the foreign steel suppliers.

The combination of these serious factors eventually led to the complete shutdown of the iron mines in Iron County and much of the steel industry in the United States. In the long run, issues surrounding the steel industry, the smelters and the companies that ran the smelters were the final straws that led to the closure of the Geneva, Pueblo and Fontana plants, the demise of the companies that ran them and the mines that supplied them.

The Smelters

Geneva Plant

The Citizen's Coalition to Save Geneva didn't disband after the fight with the EPA. They, along with the politicians, tried to take on the issues associated with the dumping of foreign steel in the United States. The following article in the *Pleasant Grove Review* expressed it well.

Hatch Voices Concern at Geneva

"I am aggravated with the administration, and I am aggravated with Congress that they haven't done anything about the problem of the dumping of foreign steel in this country," Senator Orrin Hatch told officials of U.S. Steel's Geneva Works here Friday.

Senator Hatch, meeting with Superintendent Robert W. Raybuck, said he believes "the State Department is one of the biggest problems we have because they allow the dumping of steel from foreign countries."

"The State Department has been a flaw in every administration for the past 20 years," he said, adding the State Department and the Commerce Department survive no matter what the administration. "Something has to be done and it is up to Congress to do it," Senator Hatch said.

"I think that Congressional action is the only way we can resolve it (the problem)," he said. The Senator said there is no short-term solution, but he feels all the steel industry is asking for is a "fair shake."

He complemented Supt. Raybuck and other steelmen for "hanging on" in the face of problems currently faced by the steel industry.

Supt. Raybuck said he feels the market has "bottomed out" but said he doesn't know when an upturn will take place. Geneva currently has 1700 of its 4500-5000 employees on layoff status, with others working on a reduced schedule.

"I am sick and tired of this game that is being played, and I want to see the laws enforced," Senator Hatch told the steelmaker.

Raybuck said over 80 percent of the products produced at Geneva go to the steel plant in Pittsburg, California where they are finished. "We are still up to 45 percent of our steel making capacities here," he said. "Our work force here is very quality competitive and we are a low-cost producer compared to many other places," the Steel Superintendent said.[1]

The 1980–83 time period was a terrible time for the steel industry. The world was in a deep recession and the steel industry was one of the hardest hit. During this time, U.S. Steel, Utah International and Colorado Fuel & Iron all closed down their mining operations in Iron County. U.S. Steel's Horse Canyon Mine in Carbon County was also shut down along with Kaiser Steel's operations in California.

The Closures

Steel industry bids 1982 good riddance

Pittsburgh – It was supposed to be the year the American steel industry revived. It turned into the worst 12 months since the Great Depression. Christmas 1982 was the grimmest in 50 years for the major steelmakers and some 160,000 laid-off workers. Conditions may improve in the New Year, but only from rock-bottom to mediocre. 'This has been a totally disastrous year,' said Charles Bradford, a steel analyst at Merrill Lynch, Pierce Fenner & Smith in New York. 'You've got to go back to the thirties to get something like this.'

But a year ago, Bradford and most other experts expected the industry to improve in 1982. They were counting on an economic recovery that still hasn't materialized, and they never guessed the bottom would fall out of the market as steel customers -- balking at high interest rates—decided to use up their inventories instead of placing new orders.

Now, the talk is of bankruptcies, or at least of a merger among the weaker steel companies. The industry is expected to lose $1.5 billion to $2 billion this year as it operates mills at one-third of capacity, the lowest level in 50 years. Most big companies have to use 60 percent to 70 percent of their factory capability just to break even.

Steel shipments this year are expected to sink to about 60 million tons, far below the 100.3 million-ton level in 1979, the last good year the industry had. The industry has laid off 50 percent of its workforce in the past three years. At least half those employees are gone for good, analysts say. At last count, almost 160,000 white- and blue-collar employees were on lay-off. About 70,000 others left the industry more than two years ago and aren't included in the statistics, the American Iron and Steel Institute says.

'This is getting to be doggone serious,' said Charles Grese, president of United Steelworkers union local 1557 at U.S. Steel Corp.'s Clairton works. Only 800 of the local's 4,000 members are still on the job. 'We never thought it would be this serious a problem,' Grese says. 'We thought it would be a temporary problem.[2]

The Geneva Steel plant was being assaulted from all sides: the high cost of labor, the threat of strikes, high transportation costs, high taxes, EPA costs, antiquated facilities and last but certainly not least unfair market competition from foreign steel makers. In retrospect, the big question of the day should have been, "which threat was going to be the one to deal the final blow?" As it turns out, the answer to the question was "none of the above" and "all of the above."

On December 16, 1985, United States Steel dropped a bomb, so to speak, and announced that it was unable to continue to fight the foreign competitors, so it was going to join them. Behind closed doors, U.S. Steel worked out a deal with Pohang Iron and Steel Co., Ltd., a South Korean steel company, which would phase out U.S. Steel's need for hot-rolled steel coils from the Geneva Plant by 1990. The move would eliminate two-thirds of Geneva Steel's market within four years.

The public's reaction was not good; neither was that of the press, the business leaders nor the politicians who had been working so hard for so long to keep the Geneva plant open. Comments like the following came streaming in:

> Last year about this time, this newspaper published an editorial taking issue with U.S. Steel's handling of Geneva and commenting on a study by BYU's Dr. Warner

Woodworth—a study which indicated that the company was operating the plant in a way that justified shutting it down.

Honesty is a major issue in U.S. Steel's treatment of its Geneva Plant over the past few years.

It isn't known how long negotiations have been going on between U.S. Steel and Pohang Iron and Steel - but it's a safe bet that the sacrifice of Geneva has been on the agenda for a long time.

It's ironic that the plant was used as a bargaining chip to make a deal with one of the foreign influences U.S. Steel has been complaining about over the past years.

It's also obvious that Geneva's parent company feels it has no commitment to keep the local plant in operation. Monday's announcement makes that clear.[3]

The following article captured a similar reaction to U.S. Steel's announcement from Utah Senator Jake Garn.

Garn reacts to Geneva report

United States Steel announced this week from Pittsburgh, Pa., a joint venture with Pohang Iron and Steel Co., Ltd. (POSCO) of South Korea. The announcement indicates within four years the likely closure of U.S. Steel's Geneva Plant in Orem in favor of modernizing a California operation.

"Utahns have fought for years to keep the old open-hearth furnaces working at Geneva. With guts, tenacity and outstanding productivity, Geneva workers have battled with more modern steel plants across the Pacific Ocean. They have never given up hoping for modernization from U.S. Steel and promised market protection from the federal government to provide time for plant improvements. Regrettably, U.S. Steel appears to have other plans and the administration has also reneged on its promise of 18.5 percent import limitations. (Imports have been as high as 27 percent nationally and are currently 65 percent in Geneva's West Coast market.)"

Garn said, "We will not give up the fight, no matter how dark the future looks. The one slim hope we have left is to control the continued dumping of steel on the American market. If the U.S. steel sales can be revived by 1990 perhaps there will be some work for Geneva to do. Unfortunately, the workers have squeezed about as much life out of that old, World War II vintage plant as they can."

"While I appreciate that Geneva employees will not be thrown out on the street next week, I am terribly disappointed in U.S. Steel's decision not to modernize the Utah plant. We have cooperated with U.S. Steel Corp. for years under the impression that Geneva would be made competitive on a long-term basis. This obviously is not the case."[4]

Congressman Howard Nielson (R-Utah) was also critical of U.S. Steel and scheduled a Congressional hearing to uncover details of U.S. Steel's deal with Pohang, examine the impact of imported steel on domestic steel and evaluate the troubled Trade Readjustment Act (TKA-TAA). Nielson praised members of the Coalition to Save Geneva, saying that without their efforts, the state would probably have lost Geneva some time ago. He also said that both the unions and the companies were to blame for allowing American steel to be priced out of the market.[5]

In June 1986, a "Save American Industry and Jobs Day" rally was held in Orem, Utah. Union leaders said the rally was being held simultaneously throughout the nation to protest the decline of America's steel and other basic industries which had resulted in the loss of over 11 million American jobs since 1979, and to discuss possible answers to turn the industrial decline around.

Panel members were Senators Jake Garn and Orrin Hatch, Representative Howard Nielson, congressional candidates Wayne Owens, Gunn McKay, and Dale Gardiner, Garth Mangum, Professor of Economics at the University of Utah and Warner Woodworth, BYU professor and author of a study on Geneva Steel. Ed Mayne, president of the Utah State AFL-CIO, served as panel moderator.

Everyone agreed that the United States was in a trade war where steel was concerned, and that symbolic gestures of voluntary restraint by other countries were not enough and did not work. There needed to be a new trade act passed so that fair trade could be assured.[6]

As part of its diversification plan, U.S. Steel acquired Marathon Oil on January 7, 1982, as well as Texas Oil and Gas several years later. Recognizing its new scope, it reorganized its holdings as USX Corporation in 1986, with U.S. Steel (renamed USS, Inc.) as a major subsidiary.[7]

Even though it was likely that USX had been working on the deal with POSCO for a long time, the announcement took everyone off guard, business leaders, politicians, suppliers and especially the workers. People were unsure how to proceed after the devastating announcement but in July 1986, when the United Steelworkers and USX could not agree on a new nation-wide contract and the union asked for a supporting vote from the local members to sanction a strike, it seemed like the right thing to do. On July 17, the three union locals working at Geneva voted on whether or not to authorize the international president to call a strike if he deemed it necessary. The vote was not even close; the local members overwhelmingly supported the union with a 935–0 vote.

Faced with the possibility of an August 1 strike, job orders for steel declined precipitously and USX started preparing to idle the plant. Even if the negotiations were successfully completed before the deadline, order cancellations would force a shutdown of at least two to three weeks. The company and the union met on and off for two weeks and resolved a number of issues, with both sides making concessions. However, the union was not completely satisfied, and 22,000 USX employees throughout the nation walked off the job on August 1.[8]

USX had given four years for "employees and communities to make any necessary adjustments to the economic impact of this development and to plan for the future." Apparently, the local union didn't want to wait for four years and have their negotiating advantage eroded away to nothing, but the union was in a poor position to bargain. The only thing that the strike accomplished was to cut the worker's "adjustment" time to find other work from four years to barely six months. The following article more completely explained the situation.

Strike or Lockout, Union Faces Tough Battle

Is it a strike or a lockout? That is the big question now facing the workers idled by the work stoppage at USX's Geneva Works. The answer is crucial for those workers.

Striking union members are not eligible for unemployment insurance benefits. If the state officials who make such decisions determine that Geneva workers are on strike, there will be no unemployment benefits.

If, on the other hand, those officials rule that USX has locked out employees who are willing to work if the company would let them, then the more than 2,000 steelworkers idled by the work stoppage will be eligible for unemployment aid. Although those benefits amount to a fraction of the actual income of Geneva workers, the funds would help the workers through what may be an extended period of no work.

The decision will be a complex one. The problem focuses attention on the plight of unions throughout the country. These once-strong bargaining groups used to be able to apply the leverage that strikes gave them to negotiate some of the most lucrative contracts and attractive benefits programs in the world.

Not any more—at least not in the steel industry.

The weakness of the union's position was apparent even before the work stoppage began, as USX management began preparing its steel plants for a strike. That was a natural move, since a few weeks ago steelworkers voted overwhelmingly to support a strike if union negotiators felt that step was necessary to force USX's management to come to an agreement.

With the plants on the way towards a shutdown, the steel company's management had no need to allow the steelworkers into the plant after the current contract had lapsed. To be sure, USX can negotiate from a much stronger position with the plants idling and union members cooling their heels.

Loss of income to the company is not a bargaining issue for the union, since USX is no longer making money in the steel business. In fact, the company reported a profit of $14 million this second quarter thanks to other business enterprises despite losing $42 million as a steelmaker.

To the contrary, that loss is one of the bargaining chips with which the company is trying to force the steelworkers to accept a cut in wages.

So, it should have come as no surprise when last Thursday night after negotiations had failed, Geneva locked its doors and refused to allow the local steelworkers into the plant without a current contract.

Union officials argue that because they were willing to work under the lapsed contract until a new accord can be hammered out, they were locked out of the plant.

USX's stand is that since steelworkers had voted to support a strike, and since union negotiators refused to accept the company's contract offer, the union is in effect on strike, and will be until a contract is agreed upon.

Just how state employment officials will rule has yet to be seen, but in this case, the company has the stronger bargaining position.

It is the union members who have nothing to gain, and everything to lose, by holding out.

Those members will be reduced to living at unemployment benefit levels or lower while USX goes on making money with its other enterprises. And Utah County's economy will suffer as well.

That's a battle the union will have a hard time winning—whether they are on strike or locked out.[9]

In February 1987, after the plant had been idled for 184 days, a press conference was called and it was announced that the union's contract with USX had been ratified.

Ratification results by union members nationwide were an overwhelming 19,621 in favor of accepting the contracts to 4,045 against. Local union members voted 93 percent in favor of accepting the contract which called for an approximate $2 an hour cut in wages and benefits.

The next Monday, about eighty workers took physicals at the plant in preparation to return to the maintenance operation at Geneva. While the long-range future of Geneva Steel looked bleak, it was hopeful that the plant would be in full operation by summer.[10]

However, one month later in April, USX squelched any hope that it might reopen the Geneva plant when it announced that it planned to close the plant on July 1.[11] USX permanently closed several other plants at this time, eliminating several thousand jobs.

Several days later, on April 10, the law firm Young and Kester of Springville, representing a group of about 300 former employees of USX's Geneva Works, filed a class action lawsuit in Fourth District Court in Provo. Allen K. Young of the law firm said that the employees that they represent, believe that the USX Corp. broke its announced agreement to keep Geneva open until 1989. They wanted USX to reopen and continue to operate the plant through 1989 like it said it would before the strike or pay the suing workers $520 million in punitive damages and $520 million for lost wages and benefits.

Young said "What we want is our jobs back, as they (USX) promised. If they won't, then all we want is a billion dollars of their money here in Utah, the pawn has got the king in check, and we intend to go forward." He also announced that "the suit represents only those workers who have retained him as their attorney in it. It does not represent the union. Anyone who would still like to join the suit can do so, however, by contacting his office in Springville."

George Gardner, president of Steelworkers Union Local 2701, when contacted, stated that he doubted the union would participate in the lawsuit, that it could hurt some people and help some people, depending on their status regarding pension and retirement. He said if the plant should reopen, employees who don't return to the plant might not be able to collect their benefits until 1989 when Geneva would close permanently.[12]

The lawsuit turned out to be just a lot of hot air: a grand bravado but a wasted effort.

CF&I and Kaiser Plants

The Minnequa Steel Works, operated by Colorado Fuel & Iron and located in Pueblo, Colorado operated several blast furnaces until 1982. The main blast furnace structures were torn down in 1989, but due to asbestos content many of the adjacent stoves and support buildings remain. The stoves and foundations for some of the furnaces can be easily seen from Interstate 25, which runs parallel to the plant's west boundary. On November 7, 1990, CF&I filed for protection under Chapter 11.[13]

Kaiser Steel was enduring its own winter of discontent.

The Long Winter of Kaiser Steel

The industrial empire it once anchored is gone, and the firm struggles to survive, beset by an internal battle for control and a hostile economy.

For the war-weary populace of Southern California, the dedication of Kaiser Steel's Fontana blast furnace, a few days after the Christmas of 1942 was a patriotic extravaganza, even making the front page of the *Los Angeles Times*. College students sang. A young radio reporter named Chet Huntley acted as master of ceremonies. And storied industrialist Henry J. Kaiser watched as his bountiful wife Bess, sporting a large orchid, threw the switch to fire up the blast furnace that Kaiser named after her in a sentimental moment.

With that, the first complete steel mill west of the Rockies roared to life. "It was a glorious event," recalled Martie Hubble Bernhart, a Burbank resident who attended the dedication with the Pomona College Glee Clubs. "Bess came in like a gunboat—with that big bosom and those huge flowers," she said. "And Henry J. with his big scowl, and he made a speech. With that big scowl, he looked so tycoonish."

Those were the glory days of Kaiser Steel, founded by Henry J. Kaiser to provide steel for his wartime shipbuilding efforts. Historian Mark S. Foster called Kaiser Steel the "linchpin" of the powerful Kaiser industrial empire that included businesses in aluminum, cement, electronics, automobile manufacturing and health care.

The empire is gone now, although many fragments survive. Henry J.'s massive Fontana steel mill was sold in 1984. And for Kaiser Steel itself, survival has seldom been easy, and in the past few years has become even tougher...

In the latest developments, cash-strapped Kaiser Steel announced last month that it can no longer afford the health benefits plans for 5,000 retirees, many of whom live in Southern California....

From the beginning, Kaiser Steel was plagued by limitations. When Henry J. wanted to build a West Coast steel mill in 1940, he was opposed by the Eastern steel giants and their supporters in Washington.

Authorization and government financing for the steel mill finally came, but not until three months after Pearl Harbor was attacked. And rather than allowing the steelworks to be built on the coast as Kaiser wished, Washington insisted that the plant be constructed 55 miles inland to protect it from Japanese attack. That resulted in higher transportations costs.

Japanese Competition

After the war, Kaiser faced continued opposition from established steel companies as it tried to expand to serve the postwar consumer economy. Still, the company prospered in the 1950s and '60s. But the 1970s was a rocky decade as Japanese steelmakers attacked. The Western steel industry was particularly vulnerable to the flood of low-cost steel from overseas.

By the time Kaiser closed its Fontana steelworks in late 1983, it had become the ninth-largest steelmaker in the nation but was widely considered to be one of the weakest companies in the shell-shocked industry. "There were a lot of mistakes made," said Elliot Schneider, director of perspective research for Gruntal & Co., a New York investment firm. "The unions wanted too much.... The management gave in too easily," said Schneider, who began following Kaiser Steel in the 1960s. "It was a question of being fat, dumb and happy."[14]

The Mines

Despite Geneva Steel's difficulties, it managed to operate until August 1986, was down for a little over a year, then fired up under new ownership and operated until the late 1990s. The mines in Southern Utah were not so fortunate and fared much worse.

Illustration 11.1. The Desert Mound Pit, 2018. (Photo by Evan Jones)

United States Steel Corporation

U.S. Steel's operation at Desert Mound had been on the ropes, so to speak, ever since the opening of the Atlantic City Mine in 1962 and the subsequent 75 percent reduction in output. The fact that Utah Construction was supplying part of the ore to Geneva and had a beneficiation plant which allowed it to consistently supply a higher ore grade didn't help matters.

Twenty to twenty-five men were laid off in October 1972 in order "to adjust to production schedules of the Western Ore operations division." In July 1975, the operation was shut partially down and was completely down by the end of September 1975. Production didn't resume until over fourteen months later in January 1977. Desert Mound operated another four years until February 10, 1980, when the operation was closed for good. The following news article gave the details.

Desert Mound Mine Operation to Close

Iron mining operations at U.S. Steel's Desert Mound Mine will be closed down for the foreseeable future effective the week of Feb. 10. This decision was confirmed on Tuesday by Kenneth L. Prothero, General Superintendent of Western Ore Operations.

The open pit mine supplies iron ore to steel making operations at Geneva Works near Provo. Most of the approximately 70 employees at the Desert Mound Mine will be affected by the action, Mr. Prothero said. A few employees will be required to serve as watchmen at the facility.

Mr. Prothero said that the shutdown of mining operations was necessary to balance ore supplies with iron production at the integrated steel plant. Most of the iron ore for steelmaking at Geneva comes from the Atlantic City Mine near Lander, Wyoming.

"Startup of the southern Utah mining operations will depend on steel demand in the western market," Mr. Prothero said. He added "This market has been the hardest hit in the nation by imports of foreign steel."[15]

This marked the end of mining operations at Desert Mound. The mine had operated on and off for fifty-six years since the Milners started mining at Desert Mound in 1924.

Utah International Inc.

The Comstock mine had suffered a few ups and downs over the years but nothing like the Desert Mound operation. It was a consistent supplier to CF&I's Pueblo Colorado plant. In March 1980, in an unprecedented move, CF&I, rather than keeping Utah International in the dark, as was their usual custom, sent a letter of intent to Utah's mine manager, stating it wanted to renew the mining contract and build a beneficiation plant at the Comstock location.

Mine contract assured for UI

Continuation of the mining operation and the development of an additional beneficiation plant were assured for Utah International, Inc. this week when they received a letter of intent to continue a contract with CF&I Steel.

York Jones, mine manager for the Utah International operations in Iron County, reported Tuesday that the letter of intent from CF&I Steel would ensure that Utah International would renew its contract to continue to mine ore for the Colorado based firm.

"We also anticipate that we will be given authorization to construct an additional beneficiation plant at the Comstock operation," Jones indicated. Currently Utah International has a beneficiation plant at Iron Springs.

"Within the year we are anticipating that the mill at Iron Springs will also be moved to Comstock," Jones indicated. The mine manager indicated that the available ore reserved at Iron Springs is nearly exhausted and that the continued mining efforts of Utah International in behalf of CF&I Steel will be concentrated at Comstock.[16]

This was exciting news for Utah International and its employees, especially considering the uncertainty the steel market had experienced over the past few years. With plans being made to build a beneficiation plant at Comstock, it appeared that that mining operations would continue many years into the future.

Unfortunately, the big plans discussed in March did not pan out. Out of the blue, apparently with no warning, nine months later in January of 1981, Utah International received notice from both of its customers, that the ore from the mines would no longer be needed.

This came as a shock, as barely one month previously Utah International had been in the newspapers as Iron County's largest taxpayer. Both the radio and the newspaper announced that Utah International would be closing its operations in Iron County. The following announcement was made over the radio.

Mine Shutting Down

Utah International announced today they are beginning a suspension of all mining operations in the Cedar City area indefinitely. Cedar City Manager, York

Illustration 11.2. The Comstock-Mountain Lion Pit, 2016. (Gilbert Development)

Jones, says he notified all salaried and hourly employees at a meeting this morning, of their termination or transfer. Jones says they have procedures to go through for the closure of the mine and those procedures should be completed in the next month.

Jones says Utah International has been mining iron ore for CF&I Steel Corp. in Pueblo, Colorado since 1943, and he says they have shipped to Pueblo for the same period, and they supply ore to Geneva Steel in Orem.

Jones says "We've just priced ourselves out of the market." He says the reasons for the economic problems are complicated and deal with all aspects of running the mine. Jones added praise for the work force at the mine and said his operation was one of the finest in the Company.

Utah International is the largest tax payer in Iron County; Jones says they paid 500 thousand dollars in taxes last year. Jones says the effect on Union Pacific, which serves the rail needs of the mine, will be marked as well. Iron County then loses its top three property tax payers in Utah International, U.S. Steel, which closed a mine at Desert Mound last year, and the Union Pacific Railroad. Jones says Utah International employed 250 employees a year ago and they've been scaling down since then.[17]

On February 16, 1981, Union Pacific operated the last train of iron ore from Iron Mountain to the Colorado Fuel & Iron plant in Pueblo, Colorado.[18]

Year	Tons	Year	Tons
1966	653,203	1974	879,752
1967	627,631	1975	951,044
1968	577,644	1976	945,066
1969	625,559	1977	814,952
1970	634,689	1978	717,234
1971	769,313	1979	651,894
1972	772,420	1980	632,493
1973	917,118	1981	72,405

Table 1. Ore Shipments from the Comstock Plant (Long tons)

In December 1980, Utah International Inc. was again Iron County's highest tax payer, paying 36 percent more than it did in 1979.

Mine top tax payer

Utah International Inc. recently paid county taxes amounting to $516,875 via First Security Bank. This is an increase of about 36 percent over 1979. The tax includes property tax as well as net proceeds tax. (This tax equates with an *ad valorem* tax.) Earlier in the year an additional $108,000 tax was paid to the state for mine occupation taxes (severance tax). According to company officials, Iron County derived its name from the iron deposits located within its borders, and the tax base is still very dependent on the active iron mining in the county. Utah International's taxes are only a part of the mine tax base. Information from LaMar Jensen, county treasurer, indicates the major tax contributors in the county and the amount they pay are Utah International, $517,000; U.S. Steel Corp., $455,000; CF&I Steel Corp., $20,000; Union Pacific Railroad, $139,000; C. P. National, $70,000; and AT&T, $235,000 Many of the above tax payers are associated with mining directly. A large percent of the county taxes are assigned to the school tax levy, which makes the schools very dependent on the mining. With the advent of new schools to meet our population growth, and the uncertain economics of the steel industry, the prudent use of the tax funds becomes vital, said the company.[19]

A month and a half later, in January 1981, a totally unexpected announcement was made by Utah International. It was quite a coincidence that the announcements from U.S. Steel and CF&I came at virtually the same time and makes one wonder what exactly precipitated the action. The following article was published in the *Iron County Record*.

Mine to close; workers laid off

The approximately 50 to 60 remaining employees of the Utah International Mine west of Cedar City were told Monday that the mine was closing down completely and that they should begin looking for new work. The laying off of the remaining workers completes a gradual phasing out that began at the mine about one year ago. At that time there were 250 employees. Salaried personnel were given one month's notice, said Manager York Jones, while hourly employees were given only a week. However, there is a chance those deadlines could be extended. He also commented that plans called for the complete closure of the mine. Some of the men will be offered transfers, but certainly not all of them. We're going to be shutting it right down, Jones continued. Just as soon as we can, we're going to be shutting it down to zero. Causes for the shut-down are basically financial, said Jones. He cited raises in railroad freight charges and increased taxes, among other items. It has become economically not competitive. Utah International has been one of the major employers and the largest taxpayer in the county. The mine has shipped ore primarily to two plants: Geneva Steel in Orem and CF&I in Pueblo, Colo.[20]

In January 1982, an unexpected announcement was made by Geneva. The Comstock-Mountain Lion Pit had been operated over the years by Utah International. The equipment, offices, shop and loadout facilities were owned by Utah and the opera-tion had been shut down since early 1980. The Ore body at the mining area consisted of a southern section, the Comstock claim, owned by CF&I and a northern section, the Mountain Lion claim, owned by U.S. Steel. While the pit was operating, Utah International mined ore from both sections, sending the ore to the appropriate owner.

Apparently, Geneva's need for ore was quite dire, because it planned to move equipment from Desert Mound or make arrangements with Utah International to use its equipment to mine from the Mountain Lion claim and truck it across the desert and crush and load at Desert Mound. The operation lasted for only a month or two and was shut down in May. It is unknown how much actual tonnage was shipped during that period.

U.S. Steel Mining Operations Set to Resume Soon in County [January 1982]
Cedar City – Partial mining operations at the U.S. Steel Mountain Lion mine west of here will be starting again in the near future. According to Jack Bollow, manager of public affairs for the Mountain States region, the operation will be employing about 45 men by the end of March. However, he also cautioned that all hiring of men would first include the call back of any of the 70 local workers who were laid off over a year ago when the mine ceased operations.

Lee Kleinman confirmed that saying that the company had "indicated that they were going to be calling a few men back, but they would call back those who had worked before first." This was in accordance with union regulations.

According to an official statement of the company read by Bollow for the Record, "Stripping operations will begin early next month on the Mountain Lion iron ore body near the Desert Mound Mine west of Cedar City. An estimated 30 to 35 employees will return to work over the next three or four weeks to carry out the removal of waste material or overburden in preparation for the mining of iron ore."

The statement continued further that once mining operations were in full swing, the total number of about 45 men and women would be hired and working.

"The resumption of mining operations is necessary to restore stockpiles of iron ore used to make sinter at Geneva Works near Provo, said Bollow. In this process, blended ore and coke fines are roasted into chunks or clinkers large enough for charging into the blast furnaces at the integrated steel plant."

He also said that because the operation was for stockpiling at Geneva, that there was no estimate of how long the operation would continue. That would depend on the economy and on the steel market, he said. As long as there is a demand for the ore, the operations could continue.

He also explained further that after iron mining resumes, ore from the Mountain Lion body will be crushed and screened at the Desert Mound operation, then shipped to the Utah County mill.

"Work is now underway to prepare Desert Mound processing facilities and mining equipment to return to operation," he said.

Mining operations of both U.S. Steel and Utah International were halted in western Iron County late in 1980, with over 70 local men being either laid off or transferred.

The closing of the mines has since been a concern not only for employment personnel, but for local government officials who have wondered how they would replace the large tax base provided by the mines.[21]

Ore Mining Operations Face Immediate Shutdown [May 1982]

Cedar City – Mining operations at the Mountain Lion ore body near Desert Mound Mine west of here will be suspended for the immediate future, beginning May 28.

The announcement of the shutdown came Tuesday morning from U.S. Steel officials. It will affect 20 employees. The mine has been providing iron ore for iron making at the firm's integrated steel plant Geneva Works, near Provo. However, operations at Geneva have been curtailed in recent months due to a severe decline in steel demand caused by the current recession.

Moreover, Geneva's ability to compete for those limited orders continues to be adversely affected by sharp increases of foreign steel, said the company. "Much of it, we believe, is being dumped in violation of the federal trade laws," said a company spokesman. As a result, some 1500 of Geneva's 4900 employees have been laid off.[22]

This marked the end of U.S. Steel's mining operations in Southern Utah.

Horse Canyon Coal Mine [October 1982]

East Carbon – The domino principle is in full effect in Utah as the slowdown at U.S. Steel's Geneva plant in Orem has prompted the closing of the company's Horse Canyon Mine near here.

U.S. Steel officials announced recently that the mine will cease operations, leaving 73 miners out of work. Company spokesman Jack Bollow said resumption of mining at the site would occur when economic conditions merit, "but there are no plans to resume operations for the foreseeable future."

The Horse Canyon shutdown is the latest in a number of reductions that have hit Carbon and Emery County mines.[23]

On October 1, 1983, operations at U.S. Steel's iron mine in Wyoming were suspended indefinitely and on April 1, 1984, the plant facilities were permanently shut down, dismantled and sold for scrap. Much of the ore reserve was left behind, un-mined. The large pit is now a good-sized lake about 300 feet deep and is said to be a fine fishing spot.[25]

In 1982, when all mining ceased in Iron County, the Comstock-Mountain Lion Pit was the only operating pit in the area that had appreciable un-mined ore reserves remaining. There were others with substantial reserves, but none had been developed and each would have required a large capital investment and lengthy work to uncover them and bring them into operation. The Comstock-Mountain Lion deposit had a good portion of its ore left and stripping had kept pace with the mining, with no obvious

The Closures

Illustration 11.3. An estimated 200 million tons of iron ore lies at the bottom of this lake in the former pit of the Atlantic City, Wyoming Mine.[24] (Photo by Ernie Over)

"high-grading" having taken place. In fact, a significant amount of exposed ore was available without requiring much stripping at all.

In 1985, U.S. Steel contracted Gilbert Construction Company out of Cedar City to begin mining on its Mountain Lion claim. At first Gilbert may have hauled the ore to U.S. Steel's Desert Mound facility to be processed and shipped, or they may have brought in their own crushing and screening setup from the beginning.[26]

On August 1, 1986, the United Steelworkers of America union went on a nationwide strike and the Geneva Plant was shut down.

General Interest

Smith dies in mine accident [May 1980]

An accident at the Iron Springs Mine resulted in the death of George Smith 31, of Parowan last Sat. May 10.

Smith reportedly was pushing ore from a stock pile to the conveyor belt using a bulldozer. He had gotten out of the vehicle to check the operation when the bank which he was standing on gave way and he fell 100 ft. being covered with the ore and dying from suffocation.

Iron County Sheriff Ira Schoppmann said that the accident occurred at approximately 9:40 p.m. at the mine of Utah International. Smith is survived by a wife and two children as well as other family members in the area.[27]

CHAPTER TWELVE

After the Closures
1987–2015

ON APRIL 2, 1987, USX announced that it planned to permanently close the Geneva plant. To the relief of the workers and the community, another hope surfaced. A company by the name of Basic Manufacturing and Technologies of Utah (BMT), a new Orem, Utah firm, started discussions with USX to purchase the plant and operate a scaled-down steelmaking operation. It also talked to the union. USX assured BMT that it would continue to spend the $3 million monthly cost to keep the steelmaking facilities at Geneva warm as long as negotiations continued or until July 1987.[1]

Geneva Plant

On April 24, 1987, a market report compiled by Wall Street steel analysts Peter F. Marcus and Donald F. Barnett (the Marcus report) was released by the Geneva Advisory Board. The 21-member board was formed the previous year when USX, then U.S. Steel, announced that the steel works would probably be closed in 1989. The advisory board retained Marcus, a vice president of Paine-Webber Inc., and Barnett to determine if potential markets for Geneva-made steel currently existed. The eighty-page report had been delivered to the Geneva Advisory board two weeks earlier and made public after sensitive business data had been removed.

> The summary report says the viability of the Geneva plant is very questionable and only when granting a series of best case and possibly even heroic assumptions does it appear that the plant is a viable entity—and even then, possibly only for a while.
>
> The best-case assumptions include paring operating costs by a further $50 a ton; labor productivity per ton of hot-rolled temper-rolled band rises from 3 to 3.05 man-hours per ton shipped, and for plate from 4.7 to 4.75 per ton despite a precipitous decline in volume.
>
> To achieve this, the hourly workforce would have to be reduced by 47 percent from 1,800 to 960 and the salaried workers by 52 percent from 343 to 165 people. No barriers to flexibility in work practices could exist.
>
> Employment costs per hour, including benefits, would have to be sharply cut from just about $25 prior to the USX (including significant overtime payments) to about $17; and sizable concessions would have to be received from suppliers of all services and materials, including coal, iron ore and electricity.

Moreover, the work force would have to be highly dedicated to the success of the plant; shipments to the 'trade' (customers other than USS-POSCO) boosted to about 680,000 tons per annum; and prices would have to hold at the level they were in June of 1986.

Many key Geneva managers would also have to remain at the plant.

Substantial loans would also have to be available from either the state or other sources which would greatly reduce the equity contribution of any new investor group.

The report estimates at least $40 million would be necessary to restart the plant, plus the price at which USX sells the facility.[2]

The analysts didn't give the plant much of a chance for a long life, even if restarted. They said that major problems included: remoteness of the markets, old equipment, sub-par product quality, below-average cost reduction opportunities after the initial decline, and the need to upgrade product mix. All in all, the report was very pessimistic. There would be very little margin for error at the plant and a large number of optimistic assumptions that would need to come about for profit levels to even be moderate.

BMT said that it was aware of the Marcus report but was doing its own feasibility and marketing study. It said that in spite of the pessimistic outlook of the survey, that it was continuing discussions with USX on the possibility of purchasing the steel plant.[3]

BMT continued to negotiate with USX and the union and was convinced that, under the proper management, the Geneva Works could turn a profit. USX had scheduled the facility to be permanently closed on July 1, 1987, but the date was extended at BMT's expense. The steelworkers approved a labor contract that reduced wages somewhat but included profit sharing in return. Negotiations began with potential lenders and BMT claimed to be optimistic that the new labor agreement and the level of customer interest that had been generated in reopening the plant would allow it to make a profit. Customer interest came not only from the traditional markets in the Mountain West and West Coast but also from the Midwest and even east of the Mississippi. Orrin Hatch announced that a long-awaited $200,000 federal allowance had been granted to study options for the plant.[4]

On July 29, 1987, an article appeared in the *Orem-Geneva Times* announcing that Basic Manufacturing Technologies, Inc. had successfully arranged the financing to buy the Geneva plant from USX and that the ownership of the plant would be transferred almost immediately. The plant was expected to begin production in the middle of August and provide jobs for approximately 800 workers. Details of the transaction were not given.[5]

Despite the announcement made in July, BMT's purchase did not make the July 31 deadline. One of BMT's unnamed financial backers opted out at the last moment, leaving BMT short. USX stated that it would extend the deadline for the third time until August 31. However, if the funds were not collected by the newly established deadline, USX was going to close the plant down.[6]

The purchase finally took place, as announced, on August 31. The transaction was met with cautious optimism. Over the years U.S. Steel had made many statements and promises that never quite came through and this pledge could be easily viewed as more of the same. There were valid concerns that BMT would not be successful in overcoming the numerous hurdles that surely would come their way. The following article more fully explained the situation.

BM&T Must Prove Its Ability to Turn Profit at Geneva

Workers started returning to the Geneva Steel Plant this week after Business Manufacturing and Technology bought the plant from USX Corporation late Monday.

It's been 13 months since work at the plant stopped—first when local steelworkers were locked out during a contract dispute and later when USX announced its intentions to mothball the plant after contract differences between the corporation and national union had been ironed out.

Within a month, over 1000 people are scheduled to be working again at Geneva, turning out plate steel, as well as hot-rolled and tempered band and sheet steel and steel pipe.

BM&T has orders to fill through the end of this quarter, and a contract for 40 percent of the plant's production over the next five years.

The sale of the idled plant came as time was running out for BM&T to secure financing to purchase the plant. Details of the sale will not be made public.

The plant's re-opening is good news for Utah Valley; the local economy has suffered with each layoff at Geneva. But pardon us if we take a wait-and-see attitude towards the "new" Geneva Steel of Utah.

After all, the old Geneva Steel did not operate in such a way as to inspire confidence, especially in recent years as the local work force was gradually cut back and then abruptly cut off—first with a hope of reopening and then with the threat of a final shutdown.

BM&T's rescue of Geneva Steel still leaves a lot of questions—questions which can only be answered with time.

The biggest question, of course, is can Geneva Steel make a profit? The company claims that by operating the plant without the contractual baggage that plagued the plant when it belonged to USX Corp., steelmaking can still be a profitable enterprise.

Competition is still tough, however. Foreign steelmakers are selling their product at prices which have closed plants all over the United States. It was USX's agreement with one of the foreign steelmakers that caused the corporation to stop making steel in Utah County in the first place.

Will BM&T be able to secure enough concessions from workers to make up the difference when that difference was great enough to convince USX to buy foreign steel rather than produce its own?

How many local steelworkers are willing to make those concessions?

Will the plant be modernized so it can continue to compete?

Another question is the cleanup of the environment surrounding the plant. Many see the sale of the plant as a means for USX to avoid having to pay the necessary millions to carry out that clean-up effort.

The residents of Utah Valley have learned through past experience to view many of the goings on at Geneva Steel with a jaundiced eye, and USX often operated the plant in a manner that warranted such skepticism.

As it takes over the plant, BM&T will have to earn the trust of local residents by demonstrating a desire to operate efficiently and at a profit, and by being honest and open with the local public.

In other words, avoid the mistakes and mystery behind which USX Corp. operated the Geneva Steel Works in recent years.[7]

True to their word, only six weeks after the purchase, the first blast furnace, two open-hearth furnaces, slag and rolling mills and enough coke ovens to support the blast furnace, were fired up. After being down for thirteen months, the plumes of smoke coming from the stacks were met with mixed reactions from the public.

Don't be alarmed, folks, worst is over at Geneva

The plume of dense black smoke that spiraled skyward Saturday was hailed by some as a signal of prosperity. Others accept it simply as an inconvenience that goes along with steelmaking at Geneva.

Both concepts are true. Saturday's exhibit was the first visible sign that Geneva is indeed back in business. As for the inconvenience of smoke in the atmosphere, Joe Cannon, the new owner, promises that was as bad as it gets. In fact, it was only a short-lived burst of excessive smoke in connection with the charging up of the first coke oven batteries.

"We've been going through two weeks of intensive patching and sealing," said Boyd Erickson, director of engineering and environmental compliance at the plant. "The coke ovens now require burning the coke to create carbon to make a tight seal between the bricks. The ovens are built without mortar and depend on the carbon to complete the seal. We'll see emissions at first but it will taper off rapidly," he said.

The No. 1 blast furnace was to start today with only minimal visual effect. Two open-hearth furnaces will be started Thursday and the slag and rolling mills also will be started on Thursday. A finished product will be out about the first of the month.

In a press conference Friday, Cannon assured that even with the intense smoke of the first charging up of the coke ovens, the plant is within the state environmental standards. Anxious to be a good neighbor in the community, Cannon said as long as the plant operates within those standards, we are not polluting. He said Orem is the headquarters of Geneva Steel now, not Pittsburgh, and he is a resident of the community himself and has an interest in not polluting.

He said the press conference was called because he wanted to let people know what was going on. Earlier the plant was swamped with calls relating to the haze that hung over the valley. Many people blamed Geneva. However, the haze was from forest fires throughout California and Idaho. While Geneva wasn't yet in operation, the calls made Cannon recognize people were concerned.

Monte Keller, representative of the State environmental agency, said the smoke generated during the startup will not be a health hazard. He said the state standards allow forced closure of the plant if that should ever happen, but it would be counter-productive, he said, because then it would have to be started up again with the increased smoke. He said the only time they might discourage operations would be during a bad inversion day.

Erickson also assured that officials at the plant do not expect any problems with the clean water act. He said the water system at Geneva drains to a single point and is completely treated before entering Utah Lake.

Cannon quipped; "it's cleaner than the water in the lake." He added that Geneva Steel of Utah, the new name, has a high commitment to run as clean as it can.

E. Billings "Bud" Patten, plant manager, said Basic Manufacturing Technologies (purchasing company) is trying to develop an esprit de corps to make the plant as safe and clean as possible. I've noticed a great change in attitude already, said Patten." It's more conservative, efficient and effective."

Keller applauded the concept, if the management is committed, we've got the problem licked, he said. He termed Geneva's pollution equipment as state of the art. But there's really no such thing as zero emissions.

Whatever residents will see in the future, they need to remember that Geneva will be operating at 50 percent capacity from former days. That means that there'll only be 50 percent of the smoke, said Cannon.[8]

On October 3, 1987, following a ribbon cutting ceremony, the first sixteen-car train load of steel coil, completely made under the new ownership, headed for Friedman Industries in Lone Star, Texas, amid the cheers and hand waving of about 100 happy onlookers. That meant that a check for payment would be sent back in about two weeks and a stream of revenue would finally be coming to the plant.

Applauding the achievement were Senators Jake Garn and Orrin Hatch of Utah, Lieutenant Governor Val Oveson, officials of BMT, county commissioners, mayors, union leaders, political leaders, Provo/Orem Chamber of Commerce members, and family members. Congressman Howard Nielsen was unable to be at Saturday's event.

BMT officials stated that the plant had already hired back 1200 former employees and about 300 new workers, substantially more than the 800-900 projected earlier. "Senator Hatch said it was a great event for the whole state. It will bring industry in and will generate funds for all of Utah. He said he believed the plant is here to stay but a lot will depend on its relationship with the union. He said contrary to popular belief, there is a great demand for steel all over the country."[9]

In mid-November, another milestone was reached; the second blast furnace was fired up. The furnace was called into service to produce pig iron using raw iron ore rather than the high-priced steel scrap metal that had been used up to that point. Additional coke ovens were also fired up at that time. The plant was doing even better than BMT officials believed when they purchased the plant and the strong market was expected to continue for some time.

One problem, however, was a shortage of railroad cars for shipping steel coils to customers. During the time when the plant had been shut down, Denver & Rio Grande Western and Union Pacific had moved most of their idle cars to other locations.[10]

Despite the millions of dollars spent on state-of-the-art air and water pollution control equipment, the complaints about the reactivated steel mill began to roll in. Times had changed from back in the 1950s when no one seemed to notice or care about the five blast furnaces, ten open-hearth furnaces and the dozens of coke ovens that were operating with little or no environmental control. More people had moved into the valley and were living closer to the plant. Other sources of pollution had certainly increased as well, but most of all, the expectations of the public had changed dramatically. The following article gave an idea of some of the issues.

Geneva smoke irks neighbors but officials claim compliance

State inspectors were observing processes at Geneva Steel of Utah yesterday and today. The plant is in the process of performing regularly scheduled tests of compliance to air quality standards, says Jack Bollow, director of public relations.

The inspection follows on the heels of numerous complaints that the plant is emitting more than its share of pollution in Utah Valley.

According to Bollow, there are several issues to be considered when you talk about pollution: air inversions, the tough dry winter, air circulation, and the approved method of cooling slag at the plant. Put them all together and there is a lot of confusion, said Bollow.

He said the clean air noticed Monday and Tuesday of this week are due to air circulation, snow and rainfall, and the inversion change.

He said the main area of disagreement about processes at the plant concern the method of cooling slag. This method was approved in 1985 when USX went to the state and gained approval, he said.

Bollow said a complaint recently resulted from a 20-minute period while one of the plant's open-hearth furnaces was under maintenance and repairs. The resulting plume of smoke reportedly produced 100 percent opacity, or the amount of sunlight obscured by the smoke, according to Mike Behling, health compliance scientist for the air quality bureau.

Bollow said the state agreed that everything else at the plant was in compliance and has provided special circumstances to cover the open-hearths while any are under repair.

According to Boyd Erickson, engineer and director of environmental control at the plant, the workers at the hearth were burning out a glob of metal that had spilled and solidified in the corner of the oven when Behling got his reading.

Erickson said the smoke was vented out a smokestack for safety reasons without going through pollution-control apparatus.

Bollow says the pollution control equipment at the plant is the best technology available for a steel plant that has to be retrofit. It's the best equipment we can get for this old plant, says Bollow. We still have to meet standards. We are doing it and we are capturing 97 percent of particulates. Officials at the plant confirm that the controls are in use 24 hours a day.

Lots of people don't agree. In a recent meeting at the Orem City Center, citizens for clean air met with officials of the Utah Bureau of Air Quality and the Utah Environmental Center. Although Calvin Bartholomew, a professor of environment at Brigham Young University, showed data confirming that much of the problem in the valley can be blamed on wood burning stoves and vehicle emissions, many of those at the meeting pointed the finger at the steel plant.

I don't want to stop driving my car, said one man. I just want that plant to stop polluting my air.

Another suggested that the only solution would be to band together and reimburse Basic Manufacturing and Technology for their expenses and buy the plant back (so it could be closed or converted to another purpose).

The plant was purchased from USX for $40 million last year after being closed a year.

One woman at the meeting, holding a small child, claimed that her asthmatic child had no attacks during the year the plant was closed but had several attacks this past year.

June Wickham of the Utah Environmental Center said that Salt Lake City is one of 35 cities in the nation that fail to meet clean air standards. She said controls of air quality will be difficult until there is more money and more manpower to monitor and enforce standards. She suggested that while fines for violations seem to be small penance for industries the same amount if funneled to the environmental control agencies would go a long way.

There seem to be no easy answers and none apparently that would please everyone, but plant officials say they are in compliance according to state standards. I helped set the national standards for the Environmental Protection Agency, said Joe Cannon, one of the new owners of the plant, I want clean air as much as anybody. I live here.[11]

Almost a year later, public opinion concerning Geneva's air pollution problem, had not got any better. In fact, anti-Geneva sentiment seemed to be growing every day. Geneva maintained that it was fully compliant with state and federal air pollution regulations and publicly stated that as soon as the regulations became stricter, Geneva would comply. However, the public wanted Geneva to go beyond the regulations to reduce its emissions and especially the particulates that they could see and knew that they were breathing. In February 1989, County Commissioner Brent Morris decided to take on Geneva Steel's failure to reduce air pollution. He called the company Utah County's sacred cow that had been totally supported by Senator Orrin Hatch and Governor Norman Bangerter. Morris asked Geneva to do more than simply comply with federal standards, and instead to take an active role in seeing that Utah Valley's air was cleaned up.

Geneva officials responded by telling Utah Valley residents that the plant was doing all that it could until the government told it what to do next. They stated that the air might look bad but wasn't hurting people and dismissed the poor visibility issue as a problem with Utah Valley air that had existed long before Geneva ever came along. The BMT officials were warned that if Geneva maintained "that we can't have Geneva without the pollution, it won't be long before popular opinion dictates that Utah Valley can do without both Geneva Steel and its pollution."[12]

It became obvious that Geneva was going to have to do something to address its environmental footprint in Utah Valley, regardless of whether or not it was technically compliant with state and federal air pollution regulations. With the problem being made worse by inversions that regularly trapped the smoke, the local citizenry was growing tired of the air pollution in their valley and were attributing most of the problem to Geneva.

In December 1989, Geneva took out a full-page ad which appeared in a number of local newspapers, detailing the investment that it was going to be making in environmental controls, long before it was mandated by the state or federal government.

It was going to replace the ten open-hearth furnaces with two Basic Oxygen Process furnaces or "Q-BOP," which would reduce particulate emissions by 92 percent. This was a state-of-the-art system in the steel industry. Instead of cleaning pollution after the fact, it prevented the creation of pollution in the first place. A coke-oven-gas catalytic sulfur removal process would be installed, cutting sulfur emissions by 95 percent and total plant particulate emissions by an additional 37 percent. A biological wastewater treatment plant was to be installed to significantly reduce particulate emissions from the slag cooling operations. These changes would move overall particulate emission control from 92 percent to 96 percent. The combined investments would cost the company $70 million.[13]

Almost two years later, on September 17, 1991, a ribbon-cutting ceremony was held for Geneva Steel's two new oxygen process furnaces, presided over by Utah's Governor, Norman H. Bangerter. Also attending were local legislators, county commissioners, city council members, engineering classes from local colleges, Geneva employees, retirees and their families.

Governor Bangerter praised the efforts that Geneva Steel management had made to modernize the steel plant. He applauded Geneva for the Outstanding Achievement Award that they had received from the Environmental Protection Agency for developing the nation's first State Implementation Plan to control fine particulate emissions.

Geneva Steel President, Robert J. Grow, spoke about the eight open-hearth furnaces that were being replaced by the new two new oxygen process furnaces. He said that Geneva's open-hearth steel-making furnaces were one of the last vestiges of America's industrial revolution of the late 1940s and were the last to be shut down in all of North America. He said that eight open-hearth furnaces produced 340 tons of steel every four hours and the new oxygen furnaces could produce 225 tons in forty-five minutes. The new furnaces were more productive, more efficient and, importantly, created much less air pollution. The cost of the new furnaces was $80 million, $10 million more than was projected in December 1989.[14]

Bankruptcy and Closure

The modernization efforts made by Geneva seemed to solve most of the complaints about pollution and the 1990s were relatively free of environmental problems. However, in 1997, the old issues of low-priced steel imports, increasing domestic capacity and a roller coaster steel market again began to raise their heads. Once again, Geneva was finding it difficult to compete in the steel market. Geneva Steel was the only integrated steel mill still operating west of the Mississippi River. Despite its heroic efforts to meet environmental expectations, reduce costs and remain competitive, Geneva was fighting a losing battle.

On March 24, 1997, Geneva announced that thirty-eight administrative and management employees and twenty-two contract employees would be immediately transferred or laid off. They said that budgets would be cut, along with sponsorships and contributions. Chairman and CEO, Joseph A. Cannon, stated that they were trying to systemically change the way they did business by making changes in customer service, employee relations and operations in order to remain competitive in the current steel marketplace.[15]

The company's operating results for fiscal 1998 and for the first fiscal quarter of 1999 were severely affected by a dramatic surge in steel imports beginning in the summer of 1998. As a result of record high levels of low-priced steel imports and the resultant deteriorating market conditions, the company's shipments and profit margin declined precipitously. Decreased liquidity made it impossible for the company to service its debt and fund ongoing operations. In January 1999, the company announced that it could not make a $9 million interest payment due on January 15 and filed for bankruptcy and sought Chapter 11 protection on February 1, 1999.

Joseph A. Cannon, chairman and chief executive officer made the following statement:

> The decision to seek Chapter 11 reorganization was made after a painstaking examination of the potential impact on all of Geneva's stakeholders. We at the Company believe that this action is truly in the best interests of the enterprise as a whole. Filing for Chapter 11 protection now eliminates months of uncertainty for all involved and allows us to continue to produce and ship steel without interruption to our customers. Although Chapter 11 is indeed strong medicine, we believe the result will be a much stronger and healthier Geneva Steel. Our goal is to emerge from Chapter 11 as a stronger, more financially viable company. We believe that our mill is capable of competing with anyone. With our balance sheet restructured, we expect that Geneva Steel will be producing steel for many years to come.[16]

Geneva continued its financial battles for two more years and emerged from the Chapter 11 bankruptcy filing in January 2001. In November 2001 the company said that lower-priced imported steel and weak demand had made it impossible to turn a profit. The September 11 terrorist attacks and languid economy had done nothing to increase demand for Geneva's products.

Geneva decided that it was going to shut down the plant temporarily, hoping to save money and wait out the weak market. Most of the company's 1,200 workers were laid off during the shutdown. Geneva officials said that full production would resume once steel prices increased but didn't say when that might happen. Geneva lost nearly $48 million during the first six months of 2001. The company said that it planned to meet with its creditors to discuss a repayment agreement. If it couldn't reach an agreement, Geneva officials said, they might have to file bankruptcy again.[17]

The temporary shutdown didn't help nearly enough, and Geneva filed for bankruptcy January 25, 2002. Ken Johnson, president and CEO, stated that "the combination of several significant adverse market developments, combined with the requirements of our secured lenders, have caused Geneva's current liquidity crisis and forced us to seek protection under the Bankruptcy Code." The Website for United Steelworkers of America stated that thirty companies had filed for bankruptcy since December 1997 and more than 100,000 retirees and their dependents would lose healthcare benefits following bankruptcies and liquidations.[18]

Ironically, amidst all of Geneva's market and financial problems, President George W. Bush proposed a thirty-percent tariff on imported steel in March 2002. The steel industry and the unions were pushing for a forty-percent tariff, but authorities said Bush's decision was a compromise between protecting the U.S. steel industry and while minimizing harm to foreign steel trade so that American manufacturers could still rely on cheap steel.[22]

Unfortunately for Geneva and many of the other American steel manufactures, the proverbial horse was already out of the barn. The following came from the October 24, 2002 issue of the *Salt Lake Tribune*:

> Idled workers from the Geneva Steel mill in Vineyard were reeling Wednesday after learning that their company's last likely hope—$250 million in financing from Deutsche Bank—has evaporated.

Geneva, which filed for Chapter 11 bankruptcy reorganization in January, was counting on the loan to fund its rebirth and restore jobs to many of the plant's 1,200 workers laid off since late last year.

Geneva wanted the Deutsche Bank loan to repay an existing $108 million debt and to finance the purchase of a new $80 million electric arc furnace, allowing the company to melt scrap steel instead of producing the metal from iron ore. Companies that operate electric arc furnaces, known as mini-mills, are among the most profitable in the steel industry.

The steel maker now faces the unsettling prospect of either finding a buyer for its Utah County plant or selling off its assets piecemeal, processes that already are under way. Geneva's current lenders—who have allowed the mill to use the money raised from selling its existing inventory to fund its limited operations while in bankruptcy—required the company to shop its assets as a condition for receiving the interim financing, Johnsen said.

Independent steel industry analyst Chuck Bradford in New York said Deutsche Bank's pullout did not come as a surprise.

"Geneva's electric arc furnace [plan] was an extraordinarily bad idea," Bradford said. "Utah does not have enough scrap to support even one mini-mill. Nucor Steel operates a mini-mill in Tremonton and they have to import steel scrap from the West Coast to operate."

And Deutsche Bank is not exactly known for its involvement and expertise in the metals industry, he said, "So what you had was Geneva going far afield to try and find financing."[20]

Geneva did not give up without a fight. Throughout 2002, it continued to try to obtain financing to be able to keep on operating the plant. In October, lenders granted Geneva a fifth and final extension since January 25 for cash to pay its expenses. More extensions would not be granted until the loan application was filed by the Deutsche Bank based in Germany. The deadline for obtaining financing from Deutsche was November 15.[21]

The loan was not granted by the deadline and the company started to lay off the remaining employees. Company officials maintained that there was still hope and that they were a long way from "shutting off the lights and liquidating the assets," however the plant was not reopened, and its assets were eventually sold off.[22]

Geneva Plant Sold and Dismantled and the Site Reclaimed

After the final and unsuccessful attempt was made to operate the plant, and there were no buyers who were willing to pay large amounts of money to step in and take over the plant, there was nothing left to do but sell it for scrap and try and get as much value from it as possible. The first items to go were any pieces of equipment that had value and willing buyers. A Chinese firm made an offer which was accepted, but it was, of course, for about 10 cents on the dollar.

Chinese Mill Negotiating for Geneva Assets

Geneva Steel LLC, a Vineyard, UT-based integrated steel producer has completed negotiations with Qingdao Iron & Steel Group Company Ltd., Shandong province, China, whereby Qingdao would buy most of Geneva's mill production equipment which it would transport overseas to its operations southeast of Beijing on the Yellow Sea.

Geneva's major lines included in the proposed sale include its 235-ton Q-BOP, or bottom-blown oxygen steelmaking furnace; its 126-in. slab caster; a 132-in. steel plate and strip mill; and the 132-in. plate finishing lines. The variable-width caster, which can also be used as a dual-cast, two-strand caster of up to 68.5 inches each, is considered Geneva's greatest asset.

Geneva Steel filed for bankruptcy in February 1999 after defaulting on a $9 million bond payment. In mid-2000, the Emergency Steel Loan Guarantee Board extended an offer of guarantee to Citicorp USA, Geneva's administrative agent, in connection with a proposed $110 million term loan to help finance the plan of reorganization the company had been developing. In November 2000, the U.S. Bankruptcy Court for the District of Utah confirmed Geneva's Plan of Reorganization. Geneva emerged from Chapter 11 in January 2001, only to file for Chapter 11 protection again on January 28, 2002.

Qingdao Steel produces long products and tubulars, including wire rod, deformed bar, round bar, seamless tube, cold-rolled ribbed steel, welded mesh, cold drawn pipe, strapping, welded pipe and nails. The company's annual capacity is 1.2 million metric tons of raw steel and 1.15 million metric tons of finished steel.[23]

Geneva Gets Chinese Offer

Less than 10 cents on the dollar. That's what a Chinese company is offering to pay for bankrupt Geneva Steel's equipment. According to court documents, Qingdao Iron and Steel Group Company said it is willing to buy the defunct company's assets for $35.3 million in cash—nearly $5 million less than what Joseph Cannon and a group of investors purchased the plant for from U.S. Steel in 1987. The offer is less than 10 percent of the more than $400 million the Vineyard-based company poured into a modernization campaign to upgrade its facilities during the 1990s. And the sale, if approved by the bankruptcy court, will cover about one-third of the roughly $108 million still owed to Geneva's secured creditors, namely the U.S. government and CitiCorp.[24]

The sale to the Chinese company was completed in February and March 2004 and dismantling began soon thereafter. In June 2005, it was time to take down some of the larger structures with the use of explosives. The following article from the Deseret Morning News told the story not only of the demolition, but also of some of the feelings about the old plant:

Razing of old mill signals 'end of era'

Vinyard – In a matter of seconds at daybreak Thursday, 5,000 pounds of explosives brought down decades of Utah history. More than 300 drill holes full of explosives riddled the two smokestacks, nine stoves and three blast furnaces that once forged iron at Geneva Steel. Piece by piece, the now-shuttered Utah County steel mill is being dismantled.

And for many who worked at Geneva, Thursday marked the most difficult day since the plant's closing. "Watching those furnaces go down, it's obviously the end of an era now," said plant manager Michael Curtis, a 25-year Geneva employee who is overseeing the dismantling. "The skyline will always permanently be changed now." But the skyline isn't quite as clear as planned: Four of the 170-foot-tall stoves refused to tumble Thursday.

Grant Mackay, owner of the Murray-based company contracted for the demolition, said the concrete of the stoves was harder than in other places. The snag in the demolition was nothing too serious, however, he said. Crews will clear the debris and rewire the stoves soon.

The furnaces, stoves and stacks stood for 61 years, built during World War II by the federal government for about $200 million. The mill's location was chosen because it was so far inland that it couldn't be bombed and raw materials to support the mill could be found nearby. Geneva operated under several owners from 1944 until its final shutdown in November 2001. There also was a temporary closure in 1987.

The plant employed about 1,400 people when it closed. Several former workers were among the crowd gathered at 6 a.m. to witness the implosion.

Jim McClure grew up in Pleasant Grove and started as a laborer at Geneva Steel in 1973. He worked 14 years at the plant, eventually working his way up to general foreman. McClure said watching the heart of the mill come down was difficult. "It's emotional," he said. "This was a good job for a lot of years for a lot of people. And this is an era that's coming to an end."

For Curtis, the task to oversee the mill's destruction also is emotional. "It's hard for me to see the plant go because it was a good mill and still is a perfectly good steel mill—but just the wrong time," he said. "But I guess . . . I was running the plant when we shut down, and I'd rather do it than turn it over to someone else."

Curtis said a lot of families supported by the steel mill had lingering hopes it would re-open, even after repeated bankruptcy filings. "It's been very difficult for a lot of families; there's some that were hanging on, hoping it would start up, but watching these come down, it is a little bit hard," he said, "because it's obviously over for a steel mill." Curtis said a Chinese company is currently dismantling machinery and sending it overseas. The lot should be empty by late next year. "By the end of 2006 we intend to have all of the above-ground structures leveled, scrapped, hauled off," he said.

Once the land has been cleared, the environmental cleanup phase of the project will begin and continue for a year. After the cleanup phase has been completed, new commercial and residential developments will eventually be built on the 1,750-acre parcel.

"I hope to see some development here... (I'd) like to see a park in here of some kind, for some open space, and then get some more people back to work," Curtis said. "Nothing's going to happen to this place as far as the steel. They need to develop it so that there are jobs for people in the valley."[25]

On December 23, 2005 Anderson Development, purchased Geneva Steel's 1,700-acre plant site for $46.8 million and assumed control of its demolition, cleanup and development. Geneva had already sold its core steelmaking equipment to Qingdao for $40 million and its water rights for $88.5 million to the Central Utah Water Conservancy District. The estate still is expected to sell its emission credits and could realize more revenues from outstanding litigation matters. The property came with 8,000-acre feet of water rights, more than enough to develop the site.

The demolition of existing structures was ongoing and expected to be completed in 18 months. Roughly 75 percent of the site's environmental remediation costs was to be paid by U.S. Steel, the former owner of the bankrupt steel mill. Anderson Development was to pay the remaining costs, amounting to about $10 million to $12 million. Total cleanup was estimated to cost approximately $40 million and was estimated to take four years to complete.[26]

Anderson Development spent the nine years between 2005 and 2014 cleaning the site. Hundreds of thousands of tons of concrete were broken up and removed. Much of was recycled and used for roads and fill material on the site, as was the slag from the steel mill. The location is expected to be filled with single-family homes, several high-density housing areas, a townhouse project, retail stores, office space and even an industrial area. A stop for the FrontRunner light-rail train is planned and work had just begun on an IMAX theater.[27]

In June, 2014, Utah Valley University officials announced the purchase of an additional 125 acres of land within the old Geneva land area, bringing its total at the Vineyard site to 225 acres, effectively doubling UVU's physical footprint in Utah County.[28]

The Mines

On January 26, 1981, the announcement was made that Colorado Fuel & Iron of Pueblo, Colorado would no longer be mining or shipping iron ore from its Comstock mine in Southern Utah. On February 16, 1981, Union Pacific hauled the last train load of iron ore from Iron Mountain to the Pueblo Plant. CF&I completely shut down operations at its Colorado plant in 1982 and went bankrupt in 1990. Utah International Inc. had mined under contract with CF&I from 1943 until the shutdown. During that time, as the pit expanded to the north, Utah International also began contract mining the Mountain Lion claim owned by U.S. Steel that was immediately adjacent to the Comstock claim and part of the same large ore body.

In January 1981, with the shutdown of the CF&I Comstock-Mountain Lion Pit and its own operations at Iron Mountain and Iron Springs, Utah International completely stopped shipping ore to U.S. Steel's Geneva plant.

U.S. Steel's Desert Mound operation had shut down a year previous in 1980 but in January of 1982, U.S. Steel announced that starting in April, the company planned to mine ore from the Mountain Lion Pit, haul it across the desert to Desert Mound to be crushed and processed and then ship it to the Geneva plant. They did this for only two months before shuttering the operation on May 28, 1982.

From 1981 until 1983 most of the ore for the Geneva plant was supplied by U.S. Steel's mine at Atlantic City, Wyoming, until it too shut down in October 1983.

Gilbert Development Corporation and Geneva

In 1985, United States Steel contracted Gilbert Construction Company of Cedar City to begin mining on its Mountain Lion claim. Gilbert built a new crushing and loading facility near the Mountain Lion Pit. It was possible but not probable that Gilbert hauled the ore across the desert to the Desert Mound facility to be processed and shipped.[29]

On August 1, 1986, the United Steelworkers of America union went on a nation-wide strike and the Geneva Plant was shut down. The Geneva Plant stayed down for thirteen months until September 1987 when Basic Manufacturing Technologies Inc., who bought the plant from U.S. Steel, put it back into production. As part of the deal, BMT became the owner of U.S. Steel's mining properties in Southern Utah. BMT continued to use Gilbert Development to mine its ore from the Mountain Lion deposit.

In 1988, BMT purchased the old Comstock ore processing and the loading facilities, shops, offices etc. at the Comstock mining area from BHP-Utah International along with any claims that were owned by BHP-Utah, including the Tip Top mining claim on the peak of Iron Mountain. In the same year they also purchased CF&I's mining properties which included the Comstock, Chesapeake and Excelsior claims. That gave BMT access to the rest of the Comstock Pit and the smaller CF&I ore bodies that were located on the southeast side of Iron Mountain. Good coking coal was purchased outside of Utah from several sources, one as far away as Kentucky.[30]

In August, 1988, announced that BMT would be divided into two divisions: Geneva Steel Division and Geneva Development Division. The division was said to simply be a formal acknowledgement of operations that already were in existence. Joseph A. Cannon will be president of the steel division and his. Brother Christopher B. Cannon will head the development division. Both will operate under the corporate umbrella of BMT[31]

In 1988, Geneva Steel Co.'s iron ore mines west of Cedar City produced an estimated 550,000 tons of iron ore. The rate for 1989 was expected to be slightly more than that.[32]

In a letter dated June 2, 1989, Geneva officials were notified by USX that their Minnesota operation would no longer produce the taconite pellets, and would replace them with significantly higher priced self-fluxing taconite pellets that contained lime and other products, different from those specified by Geneva's agreement with USX. Basic Manufacturing and Technologies, the operator of the Geneva plant, filed a federal lawsuit against USX Corporation August 1989, claiming a breach of contract by USX. The lawsuit originally filed this month in 4th District Court in Provo and then moved to U.S. District Court. Geneva contended that the self-fluxing pellets contained products that were available from its own facilities in Utah. "Without taconite pellets, Geneva Steel cannot produce steel and its operations must cease," the suit said[33]

Gilbert Development Corporation, under contract with Geneva Steel Company or its subsidiary Iron Ore Mines LLC, mined the Comstock-Mountain Lion Pit. Production was between 500,000 and 1,000,000 tons per year and averaged about 864,000 metric tons per year through 1991. High-grade ore was direct-shipped to the Geneva Steel plant and "lean ore" (39–42 percent Fe) was stockpiled. Geneva Steel stopped taking ore from Gilbert in 1995. Geneva Steel declared bankruptcy and was dissolved in 2002.[34] Using Gilbert as a contract miner, Geneva Steel mined the following tonnage from 1987 to 1995.

Year	Tons
1987	119,278
1988	547,926
1989	855,448
1990	816,519
1991	794,000
1992	430,920
1993	450,000
1994	180,000
1995	91,000
Total	4,285,091[35]

Iron Mining & Manufacturing

Illustration 12.1. Gilbert Development truck-loader operation in the Comstock-Mountain Lion Pit. (Photo courtesy of Gilbert Development)

The Comstock-Mountain Lion Pit lay dormant for the next ten years until Palladon Iron Company became interested in the area and acquired the property in 2005.

Gilbert Development Corporation and Palladon

On January 27, 2005, Colorado-based Palladon Ventures Ltd. and Western Utah Copper Co. agreed to buy the iron ore properties and interests of Iron Ore Mines LLC's in Iron County, Utah. The purchase price was $10 million.[36]

The property purchased by Palladon included 6,326 acres net mineral and surface acres, including 400 acres of irrigated farm land valuable principally for its water rights. Within this area is the all of the Comstock-Mountain Lion deposit containing an estimated 27,600,000 tons of ore assayed at 47.1 percent iron, most of the Rex deposit containing 98,200,000 tons at 39 percent iron, and several stockpiles containing around 13,800,000 tons at 40.9 percent iron, for a total of 139,600,000 tons at 40.9 percent iron.[37]

The following news release made a few days later provided further detail about Palladon Ventures Ltd.'s plans for Southern Utah.

Southern Utah steel mill proposed

Palladon Ventures Ltd. has never developed a major mining project, but that is not stopping the "junior mining" company from talking up its plans for southern Utah. Having secured a contract giving it the right to buy an idle iron ore mine near Cedar City for $10 million from the bankrupt Geneva Steel, the company whose shares trade for 32 cents on the Toronto Venture Exchange and its partner, Western Utah Copper Co., say they want to develop a steel mill that will cost as much as $1 billion adjacent to the mine.

Before the two companies can move forward on their billion-dollar steel mill plan, though, they must raise approximately $10 million by April 9 to complete the acquisition of the Cedar City area iron-ore property from Geneva subsidiary Iron Ore Mines LLC, which last operated the property in 1995.

Palladon, however, appears far from the strongest company financially. While its unaudited financial statement for the nine-month period ended Nov. 30 indicates the company is holding $2.1 million in cash, it also lost $1.4 million during that same nine-month period. The company concedes there is no market for iron ore from the property it intends to buy.

Illustration 12.2. Gilbert Development operation at the Comstock-Mountain Lion Pit. (Photo courtesy of Gilbert Development)

"For this reason," the company said in a statement, "Palladon and [Western Utah Copper] believe that the best use for the iron ore . . . may be to process the ore on-site to produce direct-reduced iron nuggets or 'hot metal' as feed for an adjoining steel plant, with the steel products to be sold into the growing markets of the southwestern United States."

Palladon President George Young, whose resume lists a stint as general counsel and acting general manager of the Intermountain Power Agency, understands the company's plans will be viewed with skepticism. "We've already met with a lot [of skepticism] but think we can do this," he said. "We've already got companies interested in joint venturing with us. Geneva was an old, antiquated mill with a lot of problems. We believe we can put a mill near the site and that with the close proximity of the iron ore deposits, operate a modern facility with significantly lower costs than the industry standard."[38]

On April 30, 2005, an article published in the *Park Record* of Park City, Utah, told of Palladon's plans and reflected some of the local resident's skepticism about the project. Building a mine in the area was not too difficult to believe, but building a full-blown steel mill was a big stretch.

Company outlines mining-venture plans

Cedar City, Utah (AP) A representative from a company considering mining iron ore west of Cedar City told city officials and residents the operation could bring hundreds of jobs to the area.

Russ Fotheringham. a Palladon Ventures Ltd. business developer, met Tuesday with Mayor Gerald Sherratt and residents. Foiheringham said the company estimates that about 400 jobs could be created as a direct result of the mining operation, and there would be about 1,200 indirect jobs. 'This deposit is a world-class deposit, known far outside Utah." he said. The company estimates there are enough iron ore assets to last at least 40 years. It's the largest deposit in the West, with the highest concentration of iron in the United States, he said.

The company, which has not yet done a feasibility study, envisions developing the project in three stages: The first would be to mine the ore and sell it to create a cash flow. The second phase would be to build a plant to process the ore. The third would be to manufacture steel products. The company hopes to get into the first phase by the end of the year after completing a feasibility study that is to start in about a month and be completed about October.

Resident York Jones, former mine manager for Utah International, said he believed a lot of the information was premature because the company had not completed a feasibility study. Fotheringham said the company's plant would run on coal and use a high-smelting process that is environmentally friendly and is being used in Australia. Jones said the only plant he knew of that used the proposed process was one in western Australia that failed.

Another resident said he is concerned because the company seems to have such little experience and lost $2 million on its last financial statement.[39]

A news release made by Palladon on July 14, 2005, stating that Palladon had selected Gilbert Development Corporation, a company with local operations, as a mining partner perhaps gave a little more credibility to the announcement, at least to the mining part.

Palladon Mobilizes Mining Contractor to Mine Comstock Iron Ore

Broomfield, Colo., July 14, 2005 – Palladon Ventures Ltd. is pleased to announce the selection of Gilbert Development Corp., of Cedar City, Utah, to conduct contract mining at the Comstock Iron Mine in Iron County, Utah. Gilbert will mobilize immediately to commence first phase mining activities. Palladon plans to produce iron ore concentrate for sale to domestic and international customers.

Gilbert has been a mining contractor for over 30 years and has extensive expertise in crushing and magnetic separation. In 1983 the firm began contract mining for USX Corp. and Geneva Steel on the Comstock Iron Mine. Between 1983 and 1997 Gilbert moved over 5 million tons of iron ore and waste from the mine site. Following mobilization, Gilbert will commence mining high-grade zones of the pit in order to build stockpiles for further processing and shipment.

Don Foot, VP of Palladon Iron Corp., said "Gilbert brings to Palladon intimate knowledge and experience in the Comstock Iron Project. Their extensive year-round experience in mining and loading at the site will provide great assistance in the resumption of mining activities and will enhance our ability to provide consistent product to the marketplace. Gilbert also holds the highest rating in safety from MSHA and OSHA, a point that is very important to Palladon.[40]

On August 26, 2006, Palladon Ventures Ltd. announced that Luxor Capital Partners, LP had acquired 35% of the Mountain Lion/Comstock Iron Project from Palladon's joint venture partner, Western Utah Copper Company, and 15 percent from Palladon, for a total of 50 percent, making Luxor an equal partner participant in the Iron Mountain Project. It was the intention of Palladon to use proceeds of the transaction advance the iron project. It intended to service its loan from Luxor through proceeds of iron ore sales from the recently signed agreement with a Chinese purchaser to sell 1 million metric tons of iron ore annually.[41]

The following excerpt from Utah Geological Survey's 2004 report gives more detail about the properties that were purchased.

Iron Springs-Pinto [*sic*] Mining District

Palladon (65% joint-venture ownership) and WUCC (35% joint-venture ownership) have entered into an agreement with Iron Ore Mines LLC to purchase its iron properties in the Iron Springs-Pinto mining district in southwestern Utah for $10 million. Iron Ore Mines' property contains two iron deposits, the Comstock/Mountain Lion and the Rex. The Iron Springs-Pinto district has been one of the most productive iron ore districts in the western U.S. The bulk of the district's production occurred between 1923 and 1995, with its most productive period between 1947 and 1965 while being operated by U.S. Steel.

The Iron Ore Mines' property contains approximately 2000 ha (4940 acres) of patented mining claims and other fee lands and an additional 400 ha (990 acres) of unpatented mining claims. The measured reserve remaining in the Comstock/Mountain Lion pits is 25 million mt [metric tons] (27.6 million st [short tons]) of ore averaging 47.1% Fe with a 0.3:1 stripping ratio. The Rex deposit, which has never been mined, contains a measured reserve of 80.9 million mt [metric tons] (89.2 million st) of ore averaging 39% iron, and could be amenable to open pit mining. Near the Comstock/Mountain Lion deposit are several low-grade stockpiles estimated to contain a total of 12.5 million mt (13.8 million st) of ore averaging 42% iron. Palladon and WUCC are proposing to reopen the mine and construct an on-site smelter with a capital cost of $1.1 billion.[42]

On August 28, 2006, Palladon Ventures announced its first sale of iron ore from its mine at Iron Mountain near Cedar City Utah. The following press release was made:

Palladon Announces First Iron Sale

The first order was a 500-ton shipment of crushed feed material to a cement industry customer, who trucked the material from the mine site. The material is from a stockpile holding approximately 100,000 tons of iron ore grading an average of 56% Fe. This material was mined, crushed, and stockpiled by Geneva Steel prior to the shutdown of their operations at Iron Mountain in 1996. Permitting has been approved for the removal of these materials under existing reclamation bond agreements.

Many cement plants in the southwestern United States use up to 5% iron content as flux material in cement processing. Pure magnetite can also be mixed with other mill scale products as feed, thus Iron Mountain potentially represents an excellent source of run-of-mine ore or stockpiled feed material for cement producers in the region. Palladon intends to sell the rest of the Geneva stockpile and evaluate other stockpiles for commercial viability for this new business channel. In addition, run-of-mine ore does not require additional processing once crushed and will initially be purchased at and shipped from the minesite.[43]

On September 14, 2006, the Federal Surface Transportation Board approved the lease and operation of the rail line known as the Comstock Subdivision in Iron County, Utah, by Palladon Iron Company (PIC Railroad LLC) from Union Pacific Railroad Company. The board further approved the Iron Bull Railroad Company LLC, to operate the line. The Iron Bull Railroad Company was controlled by the Albany & Eastern Railroad Company.[44]

On January 9, 2007, Palladon Ventures Ltd. announced that its former joint venture partner, Western Utah Copper Company, had purchased Palladon's interest in the Western Utah Copper Project for $3 million in cash, and $10 million payable as a one-percent Net Smelter Royalty from copper produced from current "reserve" properties, and a two-percent Net Smelter Royalty from copper produced from newly discovered ore bodies. Palladon announced that "Proceeds of the sale will be used to pay down principal on the outstanding term loan to Luxor Capital Partners on the debt outstanding for the Iron Mountain Project. The WUCC joint venture restructuring allows us to focus both our efforts and our cash resources more effectively on the development of the Iron Mountain Project."[45]

On May 22, 2007, Corriente Master Fund of Fort Worth, Texas, acquired beneficial ownership of ten million shares of Palladon Ventures Ltd. common stock and was warranted the purchase of up to five million additional common shares, giving them 13.2 percent ownership of Palladon, with the five million shares and potentially 19.8 percent if the additional shares are purchased.[46]

In June 2007, Palladon was successful in securing a long-term contract to supply iron ore to with Holcim Inc.'s plant in Utah.

June 21, 2007

Palladon Ventures announced that a five-year renewable contract had been executed with Holcim Inc., for the sale of iron ore materials used in the cement manufacturing process. Iron ore material was to be sold at the Comstock/Mountain Lion Mine at Iron Mountain, Utah, and shipped by truck by Holcim to their 800,000-ton capacity Devils Slide facility near Morgan, Utah. Holcim Ltd. is one of the leading global manufacturers and suppliers of cement, aggregates, and mineral components. Holcim Ltd. operates in over 70 countries around the world, employing over 90,000 people. In the United States, Holcim Inc. is one of the largest suppliers of Portland and blended cements, operating 14 manufacturing plants and over 70 distribution facilities, supplying more than 14 million metric tonnes of cement and related materials annually.[47]

On July 4, 2007, Palladon Iron Corporation, a direct subsidiary of Palladon Ventures, Ltd., officially changed its name to Iron Bull Mining and Milling.[48]

On April 1, 2008, Palladon Iron Corporation signed a five-year sales agreement with China Kingdom International Minerals & Metals Co., Ltd. for the sale of two million metric tons per year of run-of-mine iron ore. However, because of a general downturn in the world-wide economy, coupled with difficulties in arranging shipment from west-coast ports, Palladon's shipments of ore to China were substantially delayed. In addition, much of the track on the line between Iron Springs and the Comstock mining area had to be rehabilitated. There was not enough room at the mine to load a whole train. The Comstock Division, as it was called, was leased by Palladon Iron Company Railroad from Union Pacific. Iron Bull Railroad, another Palladon company, was to be the operator.[49]

By September 2008, Palladon was ready to mine iron ore as explained in the following news release.

Palladon Ventures Ltd.: Mining Begins Today at Iron Mountain

Salt Lake City, Utah (Marketwired - Sept. 11, 2008) – Palladon Ventures Ltd. through its subsidiary, Palladon Iron Corporation, resumed mining operations today at the Iron Bull Mining & Milling facility at Iron Mountain, Utah. The historic mine has produced over 80,000,000 tons of material since 1853 but has not been actively mined since 1996. Blasting and mining began today as the Iron Mountain site went into full operation. The first run-of-mine iron ore to be sent to China was mined from benches

Illustration 12.3. Utah Southern test train from Comstock to Iron Springs, 2008. (Photo courtesy of Robert Lehmuth, utahrails.net)

> 6350 and 6400 and moved to the crusher pad. Mining operations are currently at approximately 5,000 tons per day. This production will increase to approximately 6,000 tons per day as we reach full production in the next four weeks. This newly-mined material will be used to replenish the current stockpile, which will be maintained at 130,000 tons.[50]

In a letter dated September 30, 2008, Utah Southern Railroad Company (USRC) notified the Surface Transportation Board that, effective October 1, 2008, the name of Iron Bull Railroad Company (IBRC) was being changed to USRC. It was said that the Iron Bull name was changed to prevent confusion with a mining company of the same name.[51]

> Palladon began mining ore-grade material from the Comstock Pit on September 11, 2008, and since that time has mined and crushed, without magnetic upgrading, about 160,000 st [short tons] of high-grade, run-of-mine material averaging about 52.5% Fe and 0.2% P. Of the mined ore, 150,000 st has been placed in a stockpile and 10,000 st has been loaded into rail cars awaiting shipment. Separately, since August 2006, Palladon has sold from the small Geneva Steel-era high-grade stockpile at the Comstock mine moderate amounts of iron ore, averaging about 1500 lt [long tons]/month to Holcim Inc., which company trucks the iron ore to its Devil's Slide cement plant in northern Utah.[52]

As of February 4, 2009, Palladon Iron Corporation, a wholly-owned subsidiary of Palladon Ventures Ltd., faced substantial hurdles in initiating shipments of its ore from the Port of Long Beach. With its main customer in China, Palladon tried to route its ore through other

Iron Mining & Manufacturing

Illustration 12.4. An engine of the short-lived CML railroad line, December 29, 2011. (Photo by Robert Lehmuth, utahrails.net)

ports. "The Chinese buyers of iron ore reiterate their desire for immediate delivery of high-quality magnetite ore and Palladon is making every effort to make this happen quickly and economically," read one industry article.[53]

One month later, on March 31, 2009 Palladon sent out another news release in which it stated that both they, and their partners in China, had been working to ship run-of-mine ore to China, but they were unable to do it economically and were therefore suspending their efforts in the short term.[54]

The management and leadership of Palladon Iron Corporation was changed in January 2010 to reflect the management and leadership of Gilbert Development Corporation, which had been the extraction contractor for all products being mined at Iron Mountain since the mid-1980s, when first U.S. Steel and after 1987, Geneva Steel, were the principle customers.[55]

That was not the end. On March 22, 2010, Palladon Ventures Ltd., announced that due to its inability to make its loan payments when due, and in order to avoid enforcement or foreclosure, Luxor Capital Partners, LP agreed to accept a 78.3 percent interest in Palladon Iron Corporation capital stock, in full satisfaction of all amounts due under the loan agreements. After the settlement, Palladon Ventures Ltd. owned 21.7 percent of Palladon Iron Corporation.[56]

Palladon Reorganized as CML

Some time in March 2010, Palladon Iron Corporation was reorganized as CML Metals Corporation. The CML name came from the name of the ore body being actively mined, the Comstock-Mountain Lion ore body. CML was the operating company of the newly organized CML Holdings. CML Metals Corporation was 78 percent owned by Luxor Capital Group and 22 percent owned by Palladon Ventures, Ltd. Palladon Iron

Illustration 12.5 Ore processing facility. (Photo courtesy of Gilbert Development)

Corporation's CEO was Dale Gilbert who was also President and CEO of Gilbert Development Corporation, the project's mining contractor. Also, on Palladon's Board of Directors was Steve Gilbert, founder of Gilbert Development Corporation.[57]

On June 11, 2010, the newly formed CML Metals Corporation signed an agreement that helped advance the sales and shipping of iron ore from its Iron Mountain operations located west of Cedar City, Utah. The offtake agreement was with China Kingdom International (CKI) for the shipment of 600,000 dry metric tons annually of run-of-mine iron ore to be shipped through the port of Richmond, California. CML was actively pursuing the construction of an ore concentration facility which would enhance the price of the iron ore.[58]

An article published in the *Deseret News* on July 11, 2010 explained that the company had spent two years soliciting customers for iron ore but the economy soured and forced a halt to its operations in 2009. The company stated that it was going to start shipping ore later in July and that it had plans to build a concentrator to boost the grade of the iron ore to be able to increase its profitability. The concentrator would grind the iron ore into a flour-like consistency and then separate the ore from the waste using magnets.[59]

On November 4, 2011, the federal Surface Transportation Board approved to change in operators from Iron Bull Railroad Company (IBRC) to Utah Southern Railroad Company (USRC) on the Comstock Subdivision line between Iron Springs and Iron Mountain, Utah.[60]

Less than a month and a half later, on December 14, 2011, after several contract disputes, CML Metals evicted Utah Southern Railroad from the property and took over rail operations at the mine and on the line leased from the Union Pacific from Comstock to Iron Springs. One month later on January 11, 2012, the change was made official.

As of August 2013, CML Metals was shipping their ore to the Port of Long Beach, California, by way of Union Pacific's former Los Angeles & Salt Lake line, no longer shipping iron ore through either Stockton or Richmond, California. Shipments averaged three ninety-two-car trains weekly.[61]

On October 23, 2013, Palladon Ventures made a press release updating its progress at Iron Mountain.

Illustration 12.6 (left) Gilbert Development ore stockpile. (right) Gilbert loadout facility at the Comstock-Mountain Lion Pit. Compare the size of this setup to the loadouts of earlier days shown in illustration 9.13. (Photos courtesy of Gilbert Development)

Palladon Ventures-CML Update

Vancouver, British Columbia – Palladon Ventures Ltd. announces the following update for CML Holdings, Inc.

Based on conversations with CML management, Palladon is pleased to provide the following update for CML logistics, plant operations, hedging arrangements, liquidity, and resource development activities.

Logistics

Earlier this year, as previously reported, CML secured port access in Southern California at the Port of Long Beach, California and shipped its first fully-loaded Supramax on March 31, 2013. During the calendar quarter ended September 30, 2013, the Company successfully transitioned to using Panamax vessels, resulting in the largest iron ore shipments the Company has loaded to date. CML will retain the flexibility to use Supramax vessels. The Company successfully loaded and shipped three Panamax vessels during the months of August and September from the Port of Long Beach destined for China. These loads averaged approximately 70,000 metric tonnes with contained Fe averaging nearly 65%. The company completed loading and shipped its fourth Panamax from the Port of Long Beach during the first half of October.

As expected, the new port facility has increased CML's export capacity and helped to lower unit costs, as employing larger vessels reduces unit shipping costs. In addition, Long Beach is substantially closer to the mine than CML's prior ports, providing for some lower maintenance costs related to the CML rail cars.

CML is exploring, with the Port of Long Beach, the use of larger ocean vessels, such as Post Panamax vessels carrying in excess of 100,000 tonnes, which may assist CML in lowering their freight costs.

Plant Operation

As reported earlier in 2013, CML replaced both the original and temporary filter presses used to remove water from the tailings with centrifuge de-watering equipment. The centrifuges have worked as planned during this year and CML has now removed the original filter presses from the tailings drying circuit. CML is currently in the process of acquiring additional centrifuge equipment to support the anticipated increase in production upon installation of its hyperbaric disk filters.

Earlier in 2013, CML entered into an agreement to replace the filter presses used to remove water from their concentrated iron ore with hyperbaric disk filters. The Company is in the process of completing the structure to house the hyperbaric disk filters and is on schedule to receive component parts of the equipment over the next 30 days. The hyperbaric disk filters are expected to be installed and operating by the end of January 2014.

CML is producing at approximately 75% of capacity, which is a rate of operation that fills a Panamax vessel approximately every 2.5 weeks. Once the new hyperbaric disk filters are installed, CML expects production to increase to 100% of original design capacity of two million tons per year. This increase in production should result in a decrease to its unit costs, due to the relatively fixed plant, rail lease, and G&A costs being spread over more tons while also benefiting from specific cost savings anticipated by using the hyperbaric disk filters.

Hedging & Liquidity

As of September 30, 2013, CML had cash on the balance sheet and no debt. CML had 90,000 metric tons hedged at approximately $126 per ton for the rest of calendar 2013.

Resource Development

CML has completed the pre-feasibility study for the Rex deposit and is currently working on optimizing the mine plan and related economics. The completion of the optimization exercise is anticipated to allow CML to bring the analysis to economic reserve classification.

Corporate

CML is currently in litigation with both its insurance carriers and the manufacturer of its original filter presses. Because of the nature of litigation, no further comment is available on these cases.

John Cutler, CEO of Palladon, commented: "CML continues to make good progress in many aspects of its business. Importantly, CML appears to be only months away from producing high grade concentrate at a rate of two million tons per year."

About Palladon Ventures Ltd.

Palladon owns a significant minority interest in CML, which is focused on advancing the Iron Mountain project, an iron ore mine located west of Cedar City, Utah.[62]

By October 2014 CML Metals had solved most of the numerous problems and difficulties with which it had been confronted over the years. It had refurbished and was operating the Comstock rail line, constructed a concentrating plant to upgrade the ore, solved problems with dewatering the product, fought and won battles to get ore shipped through the California ports and was making regular shipments of iron ore to its customers. But despite all of the progress it had made, not unlike a number of its predecessors, the plummeting price of iron ore on the world market resulted in the shutdown and closure of CML's operations. The following article in the October 17, 2014 *Spectrum* detailed the story.

CML Mines suspend production, layoff more than 100 workers

Iron County – Officials from CML Metals Corp. announced Friday they would be suspending production at the Comstock Mountain Lion Mines for an indefinite period of time. The announcement comes with the layoff of the entire crew working at the mines located on an over 8,300-acre land west of Cedar City—it has been mined since the late 1800s. While company officials were not able to give out the exact number of employees, Dale Gilbert, president and CEO of CML Metals, said the layoffs will affect more than 100 people.

In March, Gilbert said there were 127 employees at the site. This round of layoffs marks the second in a year. Also, in March, CML Metals announced the layoff of 24 employees pointing to new and more efficient equipment as the reason.

This time, however, the decision came as a result of a downturn in the market that has sent iron ore prices plummeting in six months from $112 a metric ton to $82, Gilbert said. The mines annual production capacity was about 2 million metric tons of iron ore. Metric tons are how the iron ore is weighed in the world market. In U.S. standard, one metric ton is equal to about 2,000 pounds.

"Iron ore export prices have fallen significantly during the past year," Gilbert said. "And with the world market so up and down we just felt we couldn't keep going." Gilbert said he didn't know why the market had been so volatile recently but noted there have been many factors that have played into it.

With the company having paid nearly $750,000 in taxes in 2013, the mines have had a huge role in the area's economy, said Scott Jolley, president and CEO of the Cedar City Chamber of Commerce. "This decision will have an effect on the local economy," he said. "CML Metals tried to purchase as much as possible locally, all their bolts, screws, and parts came from local suppliers. The local fuel distributors who they purchased all their fuel from, they're going to feel a hit from this. They (suppliers) all are." Jolley said he believes the decision is temporary and that the mines will be back online at some point.

His opinion in part comes from a news release from CML Metals Friday that stated the company would continue to have a care and maintenance team responsible for the upkeep of the mining equipment.

Cedar City Economic Director, Danny Stewart was surprised to hear the announcement but said he believes the decision does not reflect the state of the local economy.

Shauna Clark, whose husband worked at the mines, said the announcement came as a shock to both of them. "It's affected us greatly because we had no notice, no time to prepare, no anything. Our insurance and dental is over by the 31st and it's like a 'what do we do now' situation," Clark said. Clark's husband does have some other prospects but it will mean relocating and taking lower pay, which is not something they're looking forward to. "In this industry, you have to go where the work is," she said. "It's also hard for them to go back to a $10 to $14 an hour job and start back from the bottom."

Gilbert has not had a chance to meet with the employees due to how fast the news of the layoffs spread but expressed his gratitude to everyone.63

Palladon/CML Metals mined and sold the following tonnages between 2008 and 2014 at which time operations were suspended.

Year	Tonnage
2008	201,122
2009	37,111
2010	234,489
2011	1,272,321
2012	1,583,400
2013	1,354,486
2014	1,100,000
Total	5,782,929[64]

Ironically, and as evidence of the how unexpected the shutdown was, two extensive articles written about CML Metals Corporation were published in national mining magazines near or after the time that the mine was shut down. One was published in the September 2014 issue of the *Engineering and Mining Journal* and the other in the January 2015 issue of the trade journal *Coal Age*.

Gilbert Development Corporation Buys CML

Six months after the shutdown, Palladon Ventures Ltd. made the announcement that it was basically exiting the iron ore business in Southern Utah and selling its assets to Gilbert Development. The following two press releases were made.

Palladon Ventures-Sale of CML Metals

Vancouver, British Columbia, April 6, 2015 (Marketwired) – Palladon Ventures Ltd. provides the following update. All amounts are in US dollars.

After conducting a lengthy sales process and considering all available alternatives, CML Holdings, Inc. has entered into an Asset Purchase Agreement (APA) with Gilbert Development Corporation (GDC) for the sale of virtually all the assets of wholly-owned CML Metals Corporation. The terms of the APA specify a cash payment of $4.5 million, the assumption of as much as $9.9 million of liabilities, and the sharing of any recoveries from specified litigation. The APA cash proceeds will be used to pay retained obligations and to establish a small cash reserve.

While circumstances could change, it is unlikely that Palladon will realize any value for its investment in CML Holdings...

Finally, Palladon's efforts to raise funds have been unsuccessful, so it is uncertain whether Palladon will be able to fund future operations. In an effort to conserve liquidity, Palladon officers and directors have not taken compensation for several months. As disclosed in the November 2014 interim financial statements, the Company borrowed a total of $150,000 from two directors and the CFO to fund operations.[65]

Palladon Ventures: Update

Vancouver, British Columbia, May 27, 2015 (Marketwired) – Palladon Ventures Ltd. provides the following update.

Due to a lack of financial resources, Palladon is unable to meet the compliance requirements necessary to remain a reporting issuer that is not in default of Canadian securities laws. This includes being unable to conduct an annual audit and produce audited financial statements for the year ended February 28, 2015.

As a result, Palladon anticipates that trading in its shares will be halted and that ultimately it will be delisted from the TSX Venture Exchange and cease traded by the applicable securities regulatory authorities. The specific timing for the foregoing events is currently unknown, but occurrence thereof will significantly impair or terminate the liquidity of the shares.

Palladon management will endeavor to keep Palladon in existence in its domicile of British Columbia, in the eventuality that there is a recovery from CML Holdings or CML International.

Unless there is a significant corporate development, Palladon does not expect to issue further news releases.[66]

One year after the CML operation was shutdown, Gilbert Development assembled a substantial presentation about its operation, presumably for to potential customers.[67]

The following information appears on their website. It appears that even now, CML and Gilbert Development are anxiously waiting for a time when once again they will be able to mine, process and sell iron ore from Iron County.

Background

Gilbert Development Corporation had been the contract miner for the two previous owners, USX (1985–1987) and Geneva Steel (1987–1995), as well as the current owner CML Metals Corporation (2007-present). Productions of 2 million metric tons of ore and 2 million metric tons of waste per year. Responsibilities have included: Mining of open pit existing mines, opening of new pits (including 'tip-top' sitting on the highest point on Iron Mountain that many said could never be mined), blasting, hauling, crushing, processing of iron ore, waste haulage, pit dewatering, reclaiming of low grade waste dumps, magnetic separation, wet concentrate processing, loading/scheduling with Union Pacific Railroad, and railroad expansion. Gilbert Development in association with Crusher Rental and Sales have designed/built/ maintained and operate all processing facilities including a train load-out rated at 6000 shtph [short tons per hour], tunnel reclamation system, and crushing facilities capable of producing more than 2000 shtph.

There is extensive ground water in our open pit mine operation that is dewatered 24 hours per day, 7 days a week.[68]

Deposits Mined by Gilbert Development Corporation

During the time that Gilbert was operating in the Comstock mining area, in addition to the Comstock and Mountain Lion deposits, they mined several small iron ore deposits, the Tip Top, Chesapeake, Excelsior and Duluth.[69]

After the Closures

Illustration 12.7 Gilbert Development ore processing and loadout facilities, railroad, and stockpiles at the Comstock mining area as they exist in 2018. (Photo by Evan Jones)

Comstock ore body is located on the northeast side of Iron Mountain. The property was owned by CF&I Steel Corporation. The Comstock ore body was a huge roof pendant replacement deposit in Homestake Limestone and was associated with the largest roof pendant in the Pinto-Iron Springs Mining District. The roof pendant measured about one mile long and about 2,000 feet wide. It was cut by several faults of small to large displacements, producing a juxtaposition of sedimentary blocks. Brecciation of porphyry and sedimentary rocks was important in localization of the iron mineralization. This deposit underlay Comstock, Copper Fraction, Dear, Sunbeam, Strip, Emma and the Mountain Lion group of claims, and was known to be one large continuous ore body. This deposit was one of the largest known ore reserves in the Pinto-Iron Springs Mining District, with a total ore potential of approximately sixty million tons. Production began in 1956 and mining operations were conducted under contract by Utah Construction and Mining Company. Much of the iron ore production of CF&I Steel Corporation came from the Comstock ore body. A total of 4,161,041 long tons of ore had been mined from the Comstock deposit through 1968.[70]

Mountain Lion ore body was located on the northeast side of Iron Mountain. This was a metasomatic replacement type of deposit, associated with the largest roof pendant of the Homestake Limestone in Pinto-Iron Springs Mining District. It was a northward extension of the huge Comstock ore body. Surface exposures of the deposit were more than 2,000 feet in length. It was bounded and cut by faults of varying magnitudes and often showed brecciation. The property was owned by U.S. Steel Corporation. Through 1968, a total of 3,281,332 long tons of ore were mined by CF&I from the Mountain Lion deposit on an ore exchange agreement. The ore body has been outlined by drilling operations. The Mountain Lion claim constituted an ore potential approximating fifteen million tons.[71]

Tip Top ore body was located near the peak of Iron Mountain. The deposit was a fissure vein in quartz monzonite porphyry and was about 800 feet long and two to thirty feet wide. The vein was located on the Tip Top patented lode claim and was owned by Utah International, Inc. The property had an ore potential of 100,000 to 200,000 tons.[73]

Chesapeake ore body was a fissure vein deposit in quartz monzonite porphyry on the east slope of Iron Mountain. The property was held by CF&I Steel Corporation. The main vein could be traced for nearly 2,100 feet. Two veins were present for more than half the strike distance and were cut by two northwest-trending faults. The veins varied from about two to ten feet in width, with an average thickness of about four feet. No development work had been done on this property before 1968. The ore potential is perhaps between 100,000 and 200,000 tons.[73]

Excelsior ore body was located on the Excelsior lode claim high on the east side of Iron Mountain. The ore body was a fissure vein about 1,000 feet long and from two to twenty feet wide. It was cut by three northeast-trending faults which offset the fissure vein. The iron ore mineral was high-grade magnetite. The property was owned by CF&I Steel Corporation. No development work had been performed on the property prior to 1968. The deposit had an ore potential in the range of 150,000 tons.[74]

Duluth ore body was located on the southeast side of Iron Mountain. The property contained five patented claims owned by U.S. Steel Corporation. Iron ore occurred mainly as fissure veins in quartz monzonite porphyry, and several small mineralized roof pendants of Homestake Limestone outcrop. Limited exploratory work and no development work had been done prior to 1968. The deposit had an ore potential of 500,000 tons.[75]

Pot Metal ore body lies on the east side of Iron Mountain, southeast of the Comstock-Mountain Lion deposit along the brecciated Calumet fault zone. The structural setting of this deposit is similar to that of the Blowout ore body. Downslope and east from the main brecciated zone, the Homestake Limestone has a nearly vertical dip, with several small replacement pods of ore. The deposit consists of several replacement pods and fissure veins in the breccia zone and porphyry. The ore is high in silica. The property, owned by CF&I Steel Corporation, has an ore potential of less than a million tons and has never been mined.[76]

General Interest

Cedar City man killed in mining accident

Cedar City, February 3, 2015 – A Cedar City man was killed in a mining accident over the weekend. Mark Rowley, 56, was working at the CML Metals mines, 2700 S. Comstock Road, west of Cedar City, when he got caught in a conveyor belt just before 6 p.m. Saturday. Rowley was working in an area by himself, said Iron County Sheriff's Sgt. Del Schlosser. He was believed to have been trapped between 15 to 60 minutes before he was found. Lifesaving measures were attempted but Rowley died at the scene. An autopsy was expected to shed more light on his exact cause of death. Schlosser said Rowley's body had very few signs of obvious trauma and nothing that would suggest a fatal injury. The accident was being investigated Monday by the Mine Safety and Health Administration.[77]

CHAPTER THIRTEEN

In the End

THE INITIAL ATTEMPTS at producing metallic iron from the abundant deposits of iron ore discovered by the pioneers in Iron County were largely met with frustration and disappointment, mostly through no fault of the hard-working settlers. Constructing an iron-manufacturing complex in the middle of a wilderness while building a community and trying to support one's self was a tall order. The colonists were not accustomed to the resources available in the area and many of the materials that they used were just not up to the task. The fire brick and stone wouldn't hold up under the heat of the furnace, the coal made terrible coke, the iron had impurities, the creek was undependable, and they had to deal with grasshoppers, drought, floods and potential Indian threats.

The next attempt was much more successful, as the settlers gained control of the quality of the materials. Using charcoal instead of coal and better sources of iron ore, they produced and sold hundreds of tons of good iron. The high cost of production and transportation took its toll, however, and the operation eventually had financial difficulties and shut down. Another attempt was made with the best of intentions, but it never even finished the erection of the first of several furnaces planned before internal and external forces brought it to an end. The external issues continued to keep the development of another iron-making facility on the back burner. The polygamy crisis and World War I took their toll.

It took almost seventy-five years from the first discovery of the iron deposits in 1849 until they were mined in commercial quantities in 1923. Sixty-four years were required from the date when the first mining claim was filed on the Blowout ore body in 1879 until mining started on it in 1943. It took nineteen years for the railroad to cross the thirty-seven miles from Milford to Lund and another twenty-four years to bridge the remaining thirty-three miles from Lund to Cedar City.

When all the pieces finally came together and the railroad finally came to Cedar City in 1923, it was cause for great celebration: The President of the United States, his wife and entourage were in attendance, making the already momentous occasion even more exciting for the locals. Having a rail line meant that mining could finally begin in earnest, as residents had long been hoping. Iron County did not get the smelter they sought, but at least they did get the iron mines.

The first mines had their share of technical problems, especially the first Columbia mine at Iron Springs. Modern mining machines were not available at the time and much of the work had to be accomplished using manual labor and horse-drawn equipment. The Milner mine at Desert Mound was a substantial improvement but still depended on a small in-pit railroad with a coal-fired, steam-powered locomotive and mining shovel. As the technical mining issues were addressed, productivity increased significantly. The enterprise was a success but it ultimately ran out of ore because it lacked the technical and financial ability to remove the additional overburden required to mine deeper.

By the time Columbia built its new mine at Iron Mountain, many of the improvements in mining technology had been made, but the equipment was relatively small and somewhat crude by today's standards. The ore was still hard, abrasive and heavy, and was tough on machinery but the demand for ore was good, costs were manageable, prices were sufficient, and the business was successful.

Construction of the massive Geneva plant during World War II was a major game-changer for the iron industry in Iron County and in Utah. The federal government added four huge blast furnaces in northern Utah, new pits were opened in all five mining areas of the District and production soared. Despite record-breaking output, the plant and mines were regularly shut down by the various labor unions of both the steel and coal industries, staging one or more strikes almost every year. Numerous parties were negatively impacted including the employees, mining and smelting companies, railroads, power companies, other suppliers, local and state governments, merchants, end users and residents. The steel and coal strikes had devastating effects on the national and local economies but in the long run, equally damaging was the reality that every strike, and most threatened strikes, increased the cost of producing iron and steel thus reducing the ability to compete in the world market. The strikes were successful in increasing the wages and benefits for the workers, but there were many who argued that the increases were not enough to cover the losses incurred during the strikes.

The unions were not the only ones wanting a bigger piece of the pie. County and State governments discovered innovative ways to extract taxes from the mining operations, reducing the burden for the rest of the county's tax payers. The tax commissions of the State and County were very proud that over time the mining industry paid over 70 percent of the tax revenue in Iron County. Other businesses were no better. The railroads were in a monopolistic position and were famous for charging just less than the maximum the market would bear.

In the late 1960s, another complication appeared, that of the Environmental Protection Agency. Many of the demands of the EPA were legitimate and necessary; however, from a practical point of view, sometimes huge amounts of money were required to achieve seemingly very small increases in environmental benefit, causing substantial financial hardship on operators. Additionally, the EPA was regularly pressured to adopt the not-so-hidden agendas of the political party in power, targeting certain industries in what appeared to be an attempt to force them out of business. The smelters were particularly vulnerable to the EPA.

At the mines, multiple pits were required to keep costs and production constant over time. The best mine plans paired higher cost pits with lower cost pits to create a balance. Deep pits with steep, long hauls, water issues and potentially higher strip ratios had higher costs. Newly opened pits, especially ones with outcropping ore bodies had lower operating costs. Pits in deeper ore bodies with no surface outcrop had higher initial development costs.

When mining began in the Pinto-Iron Springs Mining District, the best and most easily accessed ore deposits were chosen first. As time went on, these were mined out and replaced with deposits that had higher strip ratios, lower quality or were smaller in size. In the 1970s, both U.S. Steel and Utah International began searching to find the next suitable ore reserve to mine. Old pits were re-opened, deposits that had previously been passed over were re-evaluated and mined, beneficiation and alluvium plants were built, and low-grade stockpiles were processed. U.S. Steel was mining from the deepest part of the Desert Mound and Pioche pits. Utah International was in the deepest part of the Lindsay Pit and was mining every small ore body it could find. Local employees and residents were dealt a crippling blow when the massive Rex deposit was bypassed in favor of moving much of U.S. Steel's production to Wyoming. Several other large deposits were also bypassed despite being thoroughly explored.

The cumulative effect of the increasing cost of labor and taxes, including the costs and production disruption of the strikes, the deeper pits and the additional environmental costs, was to increase the overall cost of manufacturing steel and therefore the price of the products produced. Tragically, at the same time that the price of domestic iron and steel products was on the rise, the price of imported iron and steel products was falling. Many of the countries affected by the war rebuilt their industries, sometimes with the aid of the U.S. government, using the latest technologies which were more productive and more efficient than the smelters in the U.S. To make matters worse, many of the foreign companies had much lower labor and operating costs and some were accused of charging less than their cost of production, in other words, dumping. As a result, much of the imported iron and steel at the time was sold in the U.S. at prices lower than in their own country and dramatically lower than comparable products sold by the domestic producers. It seems that neither the federal government nor the steel companies fully understood the magnitude of the problem that was taking place and neither took appropriate action to remedy the situation.

As more and more foreign iron and steel was purchased and imported, the unit-cost of domestic iron and steel rose even further because of the fixed costs associated with its manufacture. Despite the desperate pleas made by the affected industries, communities and legislators, little was done to curb the dumping and market flooding practices of exporting countries. The domestic producers responded by reducing production and trying to cut costs, adding newer, higher-tech equipment, but frequently they entered a death spiral from which it was almost impossible to extricate themselves.

Not all the blame can be placed on foreign steel exporters, labor unions, and government entities. Many times, the steel companies themselves did not make sound decisions. They were lulled into a sense of wellbeing by the fat years. They were quick to enjoy the profits but slow to invest in and adopt needed improvements and cost cutting measures. What protection the companies did have from foreign competitors had the effect of reducing competition and allowing the industry to succeed without spending adequate resources on innovation and improved practices. Productivity in the steel industry lagged behind other industries.

As a result, the mining and smelting of iron ore and manufacturing of steel in the United States, was slowly but surely becoming uneconomic, socially unacceptable and unviable. One at a time iron mines and steel plants, many still in perfect operating condition, were forced to shut down. The current CML mine is able to produce ore but is unfeasible without a market. The decline of the iron and steel industry in the United States is sad indeed. It is not that iron and steel are not needed or used in society, steel continues to be needed and used in almost every application; however, the majority of it is not being manufactured in the United States. Other countries like Australia are mining the coal and iron ore and countries like China are manufacturing the finished or semi-finished products and selling them to the US.

The mine and smelter closures in the 1980s brought an end to many successful years of iron mining in Iron County. Iron ore was supplied from the Comstock mining area at a reduced level to Geneva from 1987 to 1995 and to small users and China from 2008 and 2014. However, once again these operations were shut down by the market. Over the 162 years of mining (1852–2014), somewhere between 100 and 125 million tons of iron ore were mined and sold from Iron County. Another 200 to 300 million tons of rock and dirt were dug and hauled out of the way to provide direct access to the ore.

Iron ore was shipped to locations all over the country, and even to Japan and China. Millions of dollars were paid to thousands of employees and millions were paid to local, county and state governments in taxes. Millions more were paid by the smelter operators, railroad companies, power companies and other suppliers to the employees and governments in Northern Utah. There is no question of the benefits that accrued from the iron mining industry to individuals and to the economy of the county and the state. As time passes, however, how many will remember the magnitude of the contribution that was made when they look to the west of Cedar City and see the remnants of an industry that Iron County may never see again?

Will the market for iron ore from the western United States ever return? Probably not. In our modern world, mines and smelters are generally distained and are hated by some. Governmental laws and regulations are almost impossible to repeal. We have only limited ability to influence foreign countries, and imports continue to dominate the American market. With no domestic smelters, ore could be lying on the surface and still be uneconomic if the market price is too low.

Despite our advances, the challenges facing today's mining and manufacturing industries may supersede even those faced by their predecessors in the nineteenth century. Given the current hurdles to jump, unless something quite exceptional occurs, the remaining iron ore in the District will likely stay in the ground, never to see the light of day.

Unmined and Untouched

Ironically, depending on the geologist's estimates, there are between two and four hundred million tons of iron ore still in place in the Iron Springs Mining District That is roughly three times the amount that was extracted over all the previous years of mining. The bulk of the reserve is contained in seven large ore bodies at Iron Mountain, Comstock and Desert Mound. The table below provides an overview of the scale of iron mining in the southwestern corner of Utah.

Estimated Mined and Unmined Pinto-Iron Springs Ore Reserves[1]

Mined		Unmined		
Ore Body	Tons	Ore Body	Est. Tons	Total
Comstock				
Comstock	15,000,000	Comstock	28,000,000	
Mountain Lion	5,000,000	Mountain Lion	10,000,000	
Chesapeake	150,000	Homestake	3,000,000	
Dear	200,000			
Duluth	500,000			
Excelsior	600,000			
Homestake	1,000,000			
Last Chance	1,000,000			
Queen of the West	500,000			
Tip Top	150,000			
Yellow Jacket	2,000,000			
Pot Metals	1,000,000		1,000,000	
Total	27,100,000		42,000,000	69,100,000

In the End

Desert Mound

Desert Mound	18,000,000	Section 2	12,000,000	
Short Line	6,000,000	Section 3	5,000,000	
		Section 4	1,000,000	
		Section 9 East	25,000,000	
		Section 9 West	15,000,000	
		State Section 2	1,500,000	
		Thompson	3,000,000	
Total	24,000,000		62,500,000	86,500,000

Iron Springs

Armstrong	300,000	Clive-Constitution	1,000,000	
Eclipse	500,000	Georgia	250,000	
Lindsay	16,000,000			
Little Allie	3,000,000			
Little Mormon	1,000,000			
Pioche	4,000,000			
Twitchell	500,000			
Vermillion	2,000,000			
Total	27,300,000		1,250,000	28,550,000

Iron Mountain

Black Hawk	13,000,000	A and B	35,000,000	
Blowout	7,000,000	Calumet	3,000,000	
Burke	10,000,000	Burke	5,000,000	
Duncan	3,000,000	Duncan	2,600,000	
Pinto	7,000,000	Lime Cap	5,000,000	
		McCahill	20,000,000	
		Rex	100,000,000	
Total	40,000,000		170,600,000	210,600,000

Three Peaks

Great Western	300,000	April Fool	1,000,000	
Irene	2,000,000	Ashton	100,000	
Jones	10,000	State Section 16	1,000,000	
McGarry	150,000			
Smith	300,000			
Zelma	75,000			
Total	2,835,000		2,100,000	4,935,000

District Total	121,235,000		278,450,000	399,685,000

What Remains

When industries permanently shut down, their factories, buildings, smokestacks and furnaces are torn down and the sites reclaimed for other uses. Railroads are now banished to the outskirts of our cities or converted into mass transit lines. The old tracks and yards have been torn up, beds converted into greenways, and once-vibrant depots converted into restaurants or other businesses or simply torn down.

Most of the facilities and buildings of the earliest iron mining and manufacturing sites in Iron County are gone. Nothing remains at the Cedar City iron works site. One reconstructed coke oven along with a few foundations and ruins have been preserved at the Iron City iron works site. There is nothing to indicate that the first Iron Springs or Desert Mound sites even existed. A few scattered buildings and foundations remain at the Iron Mountain and Comstock sites. Evidence of a few faint foundations still exists at Desert Mound. Several buildings are still standing at the Iron Springs site, including the shop and office, but gone is the processing plant. The old Columbia office building was just torn down in Cedar City in March 2019. There are a few vestiges of the old Cedar City railroad loop, including a few buildings and the depot which has been converted into restaurants and shops. Most of the tracks are gone and the trains travel only to the very west edge of town and the businesses that depended on them have been forced to relocate or shut down. The CML operation at Comstock is dormant but remains essentially intact.

Today, most surface coal mines and underground mines can be reclaimed to the point that it is difficult to determine that the mine ever existed. However, open-pit metal mines are generally too large and too voluminous to be reclaimed. Most of the local pits still exist in much the same condition as they did when they were vacated. Some of the benches and haulage ramps are filled in with rubble and debris where the pit walls have sloughed in over the years. Several of the deeper pits have been partially filled with water that has risen to the level of the prevailing aquifer. The Pioche, Short Line, King and Pinto pits were wholly or partially backfilled with overburden from nearby pits. The Lindsay Pit complex at Iron Springs is currently being filled with Iron County's municipal waste.

Although the pits are still there, gone are the sounds of the clanking shovel buckets, the rocks dropping into empty truck beds and the roaring of diesel engines powering loaded haul trucks up the steep grades. Gone are the blasts, the air horns of the trains and the sound of the rocks rolling down the side of the waste dump. The only sound now is the wind and the occasional caw of a crow echoing off the walls of an empty pit.

Memories of the sacrifices made by the early pioneer settlers have quietly slipped into the past. The hard work and dedication of the residents who stayed and of the thousands who worked in the industry is easily forgotten. Many residents of Iron County, especially the newcomers, are not connected to a time when mines were central to the Utah economy. Many have no idea of what a piece of iron ore looks like and some may not even know how or why Iron County got its name.

Appendices

1. Aerial views of the Pinto-Iron Springs Mining Areas

2. Mining and Smelting Companies

3. Analyses of Cedar City Iron Samples

Iron Mining & Manufacturing

Appendices

Appendix 1 Satellite Views of the Iron Springs Mining Areas

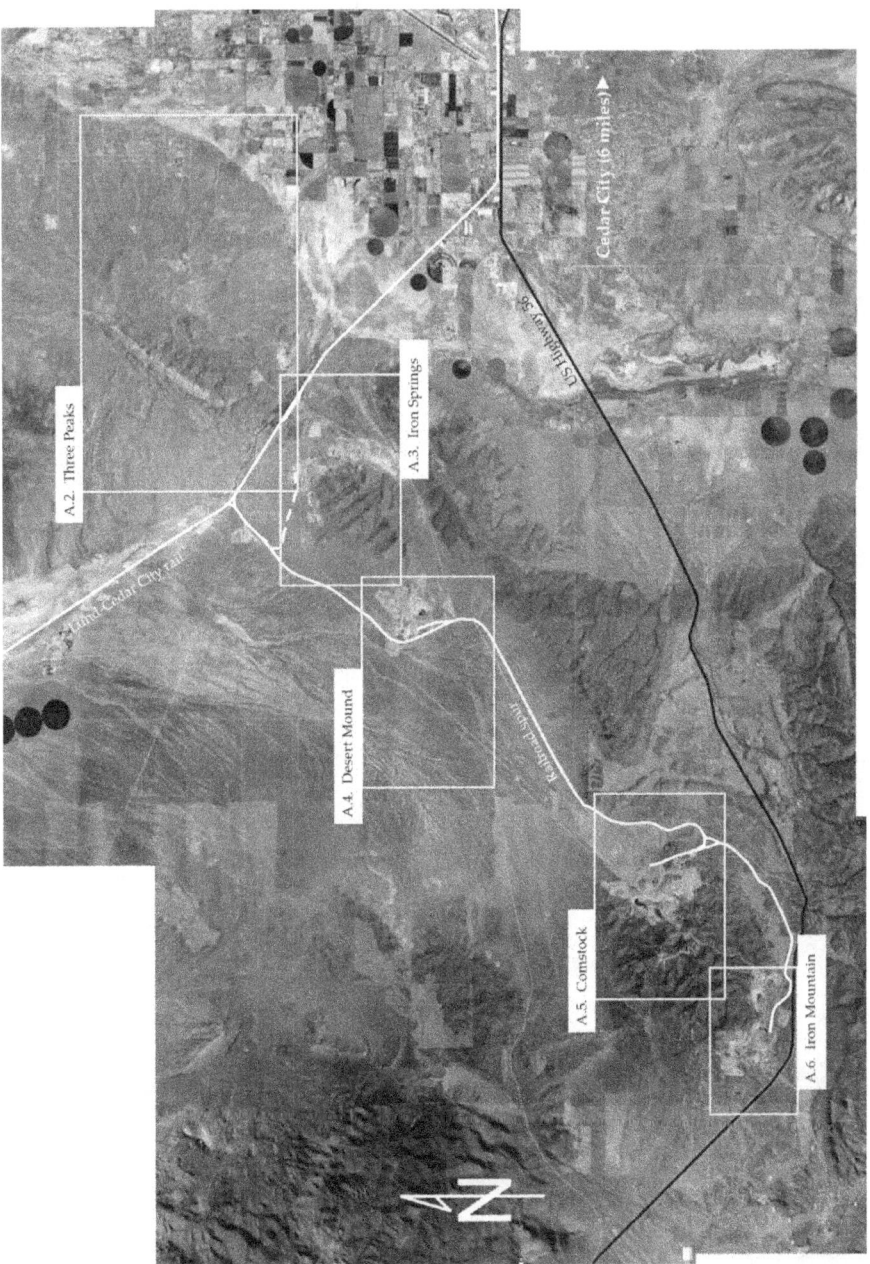

Illustration A.1. Index view of iron-mining areas in the Iron Springs Mining District (Satellite images extracted from Google Maps; overlays by Evan Jones and Richard Saunders. The names of unmined ore bodies are given in italics).

Illustration A.2. Three Peaks mining area.

Appendices

Illustration A.3. Iron Springs mining area.

Iron Mining & Manufacturing

Illustration A.4. Desert Mound mining area.

Appendices

Illustration A.5. Comstock mining area.

Iron Mining & Manufacturing

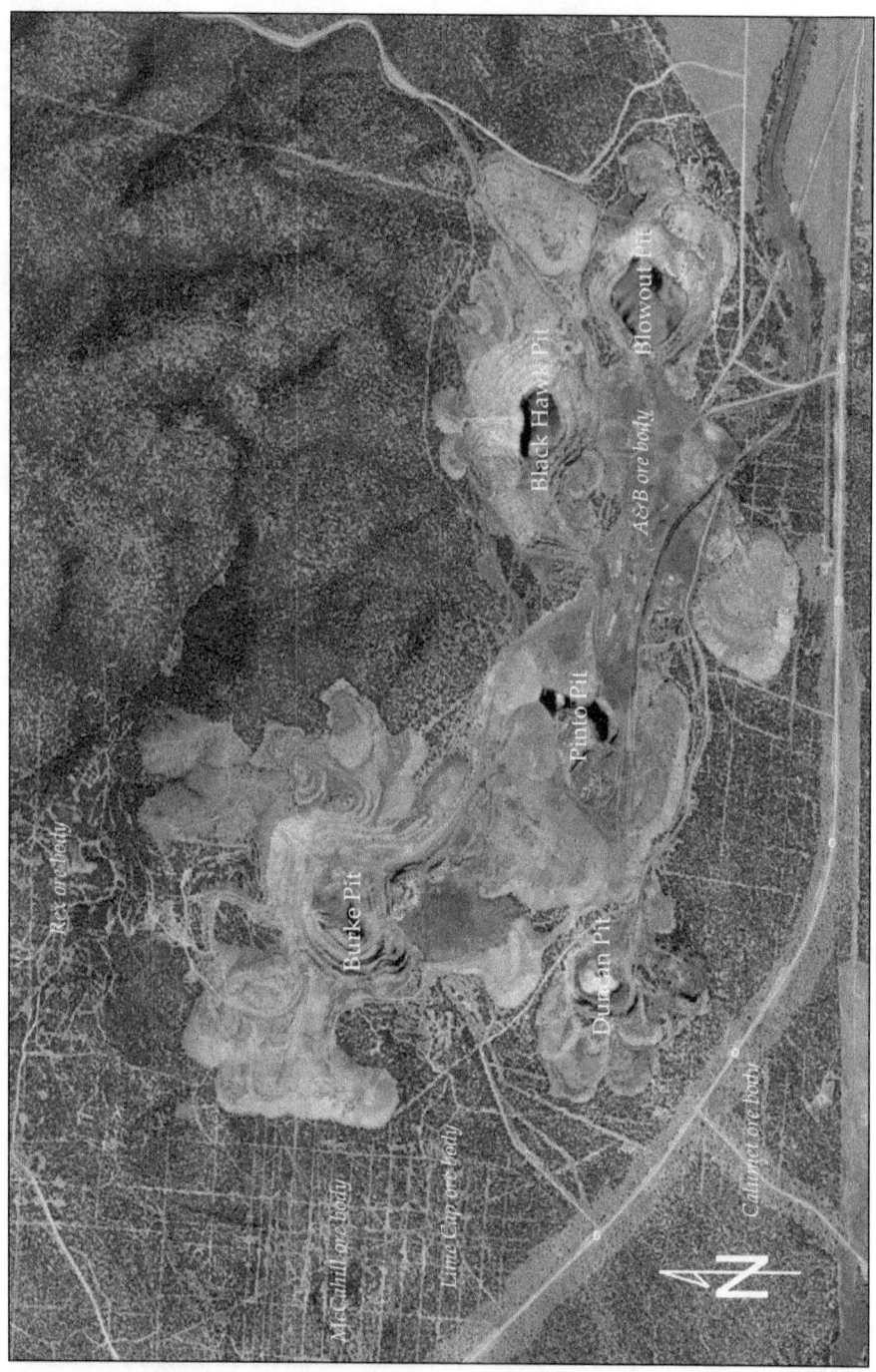

Illustration A.6. Iron Mountain mining area.

Appendices

Appendix 2: Mining and Smelting Companies which Operated in Utah

MINING COMPANIES

Columbia Steel Corporation
　Incorporated November 1922; operated the Iron Springs mine 1923–1926. Mined the Pioche, Vermillion and Eclipse deposits.

Columbia Iron Mining Company
　Incorporated July 1930 as a subsidiary of United States Steel Corporation; began mining at Iron Mountain in 1936; merged back into U.S. Steel December 13, 1963.

United States Steel Corporation
　Incorporated February 25, 1901; bought out Columbia Steel Corporation in 1930; became its own miner in 1963; ceased all mining in Iron County in 1982. Mined the Black Hawk, Pinto, Burke, Desert Mound, Short Line, Pioche and Vermillion pits.

Milner Corporation of Utah
　Incorporated 1910s?; staked and bought numerous mining claims 1915–1924; incorporated the Utah Iron Ore Corporation 1924.

Utah Iron Ore Corporation
　Incorporated 1924 as a subsidiary of Milner Corporation; operated Desert Mound 1924–1936.

Utah Construction Company
　Incorporated 1900; began operating its own mines in 1944, shipping to Kaiser same year; became Utah Construction and Mining Company in 1950s; reincorporated as Utah International in 1971; sold to General Electric in 1976; ceased all mining in Iron County in 1981; became Part of BHP in 1984; presently BHP Billiton. Contract mined the Blowout, Duncan and Comstock pits for CF&I 1943–1981, contract mined Mountain Lion Pit for U.S. Steel 1949–1981; pre-stripped Short Line, Desert Mound and Burke pits for U.S. Steel. Mined the Lindsay, Little Mormon, Eclipse, Twitchell, Smith, Great Western, McGarry, Irene, Blackbird, Jones and Zelma, Black Rock #1, Blue Jay, Yellow Jacket, Black Magnetic, Last Chance, and Homestake ore bodies.

Gilbert Development Corporation
　Incorporated 1975; contract mined for U.S. Steel 1985–1986, for BMT 1987–1995, for CML 2007–2014; bought out CML in 2014. Mined the Comstock, Mountain Lion, Tip Top, Chesapeake, Excelsior and Duluth.

Iron Mining & Manufacturing

Smelting Companies

Columbia Steel Corporation
> Incorporated November 1922; operated Ironton smelter 1923–1930; became a subsidiary of U.S. Steel 1930, operated Ironton 1930–1946 for U.S. Steel; dissolved and became part of Geneva Steel 1946.

Geneva Steel Company
> Incorporated August 1943, subsidiary of the United States Steel Corporation until 1986; operated Ironton smelter 1946–1960, Geneva 1946–1986.

United States Steel Corporation
> Incorporated February 25, 1901; set up the Columbia Steel Corporation in 1930; built and operated the Geneva Plant in 1943–1945, incorporated Geneva Steel Company 1946; absorbed into USX Corporation 1986.

Colorado Fuel & Iron Company (also Colorado Coal and Iron Company)
> Incorporated 1872; built the Pueblo Steel Works 1881, plant modernized 1899, renamed Minnequa Works 1901. Began smelting Iron County ore 1943. Closed 1982, bankruptcy 1990.

Kaiser Steel Corporation
> Incorporated in 1914; built the Kaiser Steel plant in Fontana, California 1942. Began using Iron County ore, 1944. Bought and operated the No. 2 Ironton blast furnace 1947; shut down 1983; Fontana Steel Mill sold 1984.

Basic Manufacturing Technologies, Inc.
> Incorporated 1985; purchased Geneva plant and changed its name to Geneva Steel of Utah 1987; operated Geneva plant 1987–2002; dissolved after the Geneva plant closed.

Appendices

Appendix 3: Analyses of Cedar City Iron Samples

THREE IRON SAMPLES from the Cedar City Iron Works site were collected by York F. Jones around 1976. A chemical analysis of each was made by Jack Mervis and Keith Hanks. Images are reproduced with Standard Nital Etch & 100X Magnification.

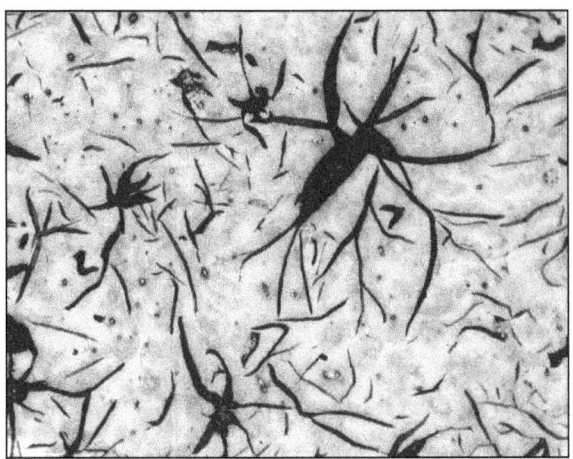

Illustration A.7. Sample 193. Graphite flakes in a fine pearlite matrix.

Sample 193: CORNER OF INGOT, CAST IRON. Low silicon with relatively normal sulfur and phosphorus, but low silicon for what we would presently call low-phosphorus pig iron. Manganese in all samples is very low. Apparently, none added. Grey iron micro structure with superimposed graphitic flakes presently described as class C in a matrix of mainly pearlite with both ferrite and scattered carbide colonies and grain boundary envelopes. This is a type of cast iron (structure) which has very poor properties and is of very little commercial value in this condition. It tends to be both soft and brittle at the same time. There might also be some of the phosphorus eutectic, steadite, present which really doesn't help much. This would be classified as a mottled structure with a poor graphite dispersal as noted above.

The early fore-runners of the present blast furnaces were of two general types; viz., hearth-type using natural drafts and equivalent shaft-type furnaces which could be compared to small blast furnaces using ore mixed with charcoal for fuel, reducing, and oxide shielding (all three). The blast furnace process was recognized as starting in about 1300 BC.

In Utah, the Deseret Iron Company operated a shaft-type (blast) furnace in Cedar City commencing operations in 1852. Typical products: Fry pans, wagon parts, pots, kettles, plows, tillers.

Corner of Ingot: Si 0.80, S 0.058, P 0.48, Mn 0.02, Cu 0.01, Ni 0.05, C 3.73
Foundry Low-Phosphorus Pig Iron, 1977

(Nominal Analysis) Si 1.50, S 0.05 X, P 0.31/0.50, Mn 0.50/0.75, C 3.50

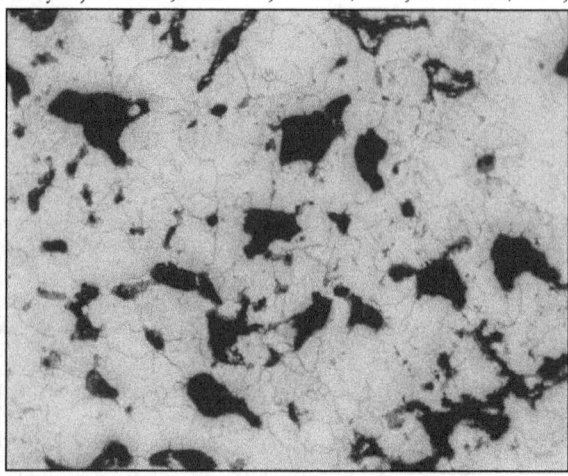

Illustration A.8. Sample 194. Photomicrograph at 100X showing typical structure of wrought iron. White areas are the highly-refined iron matrix. Dark areas are cross sections of iron-silicate slag filaments.

Sample 194: WROUGHT IRON (Sand Mold). Wrought Iron with high phosphorus and silicon, and somewhat higher than expected carbon. Chemical check could have included some highly segregated areas such as internal slag pockets, and not be representative of the actual metal composition.

Apparently, a direct process wrought iron generally known as sponge iron, which is still produced today for special processing. This particular ingot reportedly poured into a sand mold was probably produced in a shallow hearth furnace or pack using charcoal as both the fuel and the reducing agent. Such direct reduction from the ore by a smelting process results in a spongy mass of relatively pure low carbon iron mixed with much slag. This mass is generally hammered into useful articles while still hot, and this refining squeezes out the slag to some degree and refines the structure in general. The sand mold could account for the high silicon content, and the carbon could be somewhat higher than expected as it is hard to get a true sample of the metal because of the slag and other impurities trapped within the piece.

Wrought sponge iron of this type was the main source of iron and steel for many centuries before the blast furnace process was developed. Such material can be produced from pig or cast iron by using (generally) either the charcoal hearth or puddling process in conjunction with a cupola or crucible-type melting unit, both of which could have been used at Cedar City.

The structure shown in the photomicrographs are typical of transverse sections of wrought iron. Typical products: Axles, straps, bands for barrels, and wheels, braces.

Sand Mold: Si 0.92, S 0.027, P 0.20, Mn 0.04, Cu 0.02, Ni 0.04, C 0.12

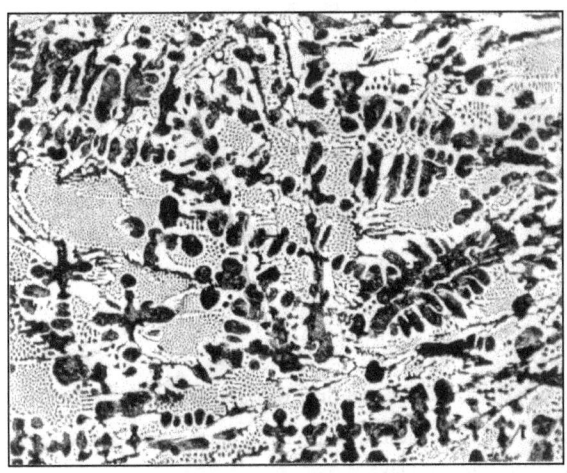

Illustration A.9. Sample 195. Ledeburite and graphite flakes in a fine pearlite matrix. White constituent is cementite.

Sample 195: CHILL CASTING. White iron dendritic pattern micro structure with rosette-type graphitic colonies in a matrix of phosphide eutectic (sleadite) and iron carbide (FeSO) resulting in relatively hard but brittle cast iron, rapidly cooled.

The general description of the process, original Cedar City operation and typical products, are the same as that shown under No. 193. Neither this nor the type of casting (cast iron) shown in 193 or 195 would have too great properties, but they are not bad efforts for the 19th century.

Portion of First Pour: Si 0.40, S 0.10, P 0.24, Mn 0.01, Cu 0.03, Ni 0.04, C 3.60

Glossary

adit A horizontal or near-horizontal drift or passage from the surface into a mine.

adobe, dobies A building material made from earth, mud or clay, including un-fired bricks made from mud or clay.

air furnace A furnace which pre-heats the combustion air entering a blast furnace.

air cylinder A large piston type mechanism that pumps air into the blast furnace.

alloy A combination of metals or other elements with a metal to enhance the properties of the final product.

alluvium plant A plant built to separate iron ore from other non-iron material using magnetic separation.

andirons, dog irons, fire dogs A pair of metal stands, usually made of iron, for holding logs above the floor in a fireplace.

basal siltstone Part of the Carmel Formation. It is the weak siltstone layer above the Navajo Sandstone below which the magma intrusions entered. The layer has an average thickness of 50 feet.

basic oxygen process A method of steelmaking in which oxygen instead of air is blown through carbon-rich molten pig iron.

batholith A large mass of intrusive igneous rock, larger than 40 mi^2 in area, that is formed from cooled magma deep in the Earth's crust.

bear *see* salamander

beneficiation plant A plant constructed to upgrade iron ore using magnetic or heavy media separation processes.

Bessemer process A process for making steel by blowing air through molten pig iron.

blacksmithing Creating objects from wrought iron or steel by forging the metal, using tools to hammer, bend, and cut.

blast The hot or cold combustion air that is blown into the blast furnace at above atmospheric pressure.

Glossary

blast furnace A furnace used to smelt iron ore to produce pig iron, using coke as a fuel and limestone as a flux.

blasting The controlled use of explosives to break rock for excavation.

blower A device that pumps or blows air into a blast furnace.

bog ore, clay ore, lean ore Low grade, impure, hydrated iron ore (FeO(OH)), deposited in wet environments.

bogus Another word for slag. The blast furnace by-product left over after a desired metal has been separated from the gangue.

bosh The hottest section of the blast furnace, just above the hearth, below the barrel and stack, also where the tuyeres are located.

breccia A rock composed of broken fragments of minerals or rock, cemented together by a fine-grained matrix.

calcination, roasting A process where ore is heated to remove moisture, CO_2, sulfur and other impurities.

casting house The building where castings are made, basically part of a foundry.

cast iron An iron-carbon alloy with a carbon content greater than 2% with a relatively low melting temperature.

charcoal A lightweight hydrocarbon created by heating wood in the absence of oxygen to remove water and other volatiles.

charge The collective group of materials fed into the blast furnace consisting of iron ore, limestone and fuel (usually coke).

cinder, cynder Another word used for slag. The blast furnace by-product left over after a desired metal has been separated from the gangue.

Claron Formation A sandstone-limestone-conglomerate formation above the Iron Springs Formation, displayed at Cedar Breaks and Bryce Canyon. Its thickness ranges between 1,000 and 1,500 feet.

coal A sedimentary rock-fossil fuel formed from compressed ancient plant matter and is primarily carbon.

coal washing: A process in which coal is washed with water to remove extraneous material such as dirt, clay and sulfur.

coke A high carbon material made by heating coal in the absence of oxygen, to drive off moisture, volatiles and impurities.

coke oven An oven used to heat coal to produce coke.

cupola, cubelo, cubalo A small, cylindrical shaped furnace to heat iron or iron ore, sometimes used like a foundry other times like a blast furnace.

dolomite A mineral composed of calcium magnesium carbonate, sometimes used instead of or in combination with limestone as a flux in a furnace.

dragline A large excavating machine that digs, hoists, swings and dumps material, using a bucket pulled and suspended by wire ropes.

drift A near-horizontal passageway or tunnel in an underground mine used for access, haulage, ventilation, exploration, etc.

Edmunds Act A federal statute signed into law on March 23, 1882, declaring polygamy a felony.

electric arc furnace A furnace that heats its charge by means of an electric arc which passes through the charge material.

electric induction furnace An electrical furnace in which the heat is generated by electromagnetic induction of the metal.

Entrada Sandstone The maroon colored formation directly above the Homestake Limestone and below the Iron Springs formation with a thickness of up to 250 feet.

fire brick Bricks made of ceramic material, built to withstand high temperatures, used to line furnaces, kilns, smokestacks, etc.

fire clay Clay that is resistant to high temperatures, suitable for lining furnaces. Also used in utensils such as crucibles and retorts.

fire rock, fire stone Native rock that can withstand high temperatures, usually somewhat porous with tiny holes to release heat without spalling or cracking.

flux A material used to benefit melting and remove impurities such as silica, alumina, and sulfur from molten iron by forming slag.

forge A hearth used to heat metals, to then be worked and shaped by beating, hammering, pressing, etc.

foundry A factory, including a furnace, designed to melt and sometimes refine metallic iron and produce various shaped castings.

gangue The commercially worthless impurities that surround, or are closely mixed with, a wanted mineral in an ore deposit.

glory hole A vertical mine shaft with an enlarged top like a funnel, into which ore is pushed or dropped to be hauled out of the mine from below.

granite An igneous rock that contains between 20% and 60% quartz, formed by magma that cools deep within the earth.

hearth The bottom part of a fireplace or furnace. In a blast furnace, the location where the molten iron collects.

hematite One of several iron oxide minerals, (Fe_2O_3), ranging in color from black to red with a rust-red streak.

Homestake Limestone Part of the Carmel Formation and the host strata for most of Iron County's iron ore when it came out of solution and replaced the limestone. Its thickness averages 250 feet.

ingot A block of relatively pure metal, typically oblong, and suitable for further processing.

Iron Springs Formation The strata above the Marshall Creek Breccia and below the Claron Formation, in places exceeding 3,000 feet in thickness.

Glossary

kiln A thermally insulated oven, that produces temperatures sufficient to complete some process, such as converting coal to coke.

laccolith A mass of igneous rock, typically lens-shaped, that has intruded between rock strata causing uplift in the shape of a dome.

limestone A sedimentary rock composed mainly of calcium carbonate ($CaCO_3$), comprised mainly of skeletal fragments of ancient marine organisms.

lode claim A mining claim designed to cover a lode, defined as a mineral deposit occurring in solid rock, usually as a vein or an ore body.

magma intrusion A body of molten igneous rock beneath the surface of the Earth that forces itself between the rock layers and then slowly cools.

magnetite One of several iron oxide minerals, (Fe_3O_4), ranging in color from black to brownish black with a black streak. It is attracted to a magnet and can be magnetized. It is the most magnetic of all the naturally-occurring minerals on Earth.

Markagunt Plateau An 800-square-mile plateau located in southwestern Utah between Interstate 15 and U.S. Route 89. encompassing Cedar Breaks National Monument and part of the Cedar Mountain District of Dixie National Forest.

mineral streak test An easy way to determine the color of a mineral in powdered form. It is done by scraping a specimen of the mineral across an unglazed piece of porcelain known as a streak plate.

mining shovel A bucket-equipped machine with wire ropes, usually electrically powered, used for digging and loading fragmented rock, usually into trucks for mineral extraction.

Mohs hardness scale A qualitative ordinal scale characterizing scratch resistance of various minerals through the ability of harder material to scratch softer material, talc having a hardness of 1, and diamond 10.

Navajo Sandstone The formation just below the Carmel Formation which contains the bulk of the iron ore deposits. It was formed by wind-blown sand, is up to 2,300 feet thick and is prominently visible in Zion National Park.

open-hearth process A steelmaking process in which the charge is heated directly by burning fuel as well as by the furnace walls on a shallow hearth. Excess carbon and other impurities are burnt out of pig iron to produce steel.

patented claim A mining claim for which the federal government has issued a patent (deed). The owner must prove the claim contains locatable minerals that can be extracted at a profit. Currently there is a moratorium on granting new patents.

pig iron The product of a blast furnace with a very high carbon content, typically 3.8–4.7%, along with silica and other constituents of dross, which makes it very brittle and not very useful directly as a material.

puddling furnace A furnace constructed to pull heat over iron without the furnace fuel coming into direct contact with the iron, thus keeping the impurities of the fuel separated from the charge. It is used to create wrought iron or steel from the pig iron.

portal The entrance to an underground mine, the mouth of an adit or tunnel.

quartz monzonite porphyry An intrusive igneous rock that is formed when magma slowly cools deep beneath the earth's surface. It has visible large-grained crystals and contains between five and twenty percent quartz. Granite contains more than twenty percent quartz.

raise A vertical or near-vertical opening or shaft, driven upward from a lower level to connect with an upper level or in some cases the surface, such as a glory hole.

salamander The solidified mass of incompletely smelted iron and rock remaining in a furnace after being shut down or cooled unexpectedly; alternately, a *bear*

sand mold A hollow container made from a mixture of sand and clay used to give shape to molten metal when it is poured in, cools and hardens.

sandstone A sedimentary rock consisting of sand or quartz grains cemented together, typically red, yellow, or brown in color.

shaft A vertical or inclined opening that starts on the surface and goes into the mine.

slag The blast furnace by-product left over after a desired metal has been separated from the gangue.

sponge iron Iron produced from the direct reduction of iron ore into iron by a reducing gas or elemental carbon produced from natural gas or coal. It has iron content very similar to pig iron.

steel An alloy of iron and carbon and other elements. The quantity of these other non-iron elements combined with various physical treatments determine qualities such as hardness, tensile strength, ductility, brittleness and resistance to corrosion.

stock An igneous intrusion that has a surface area of less than forty square miles, differing from batholiths only in being smaller. The term usually refers to smaller, relatively isolated and individual intrusions, less than about twelve miles in diameter.

stone coal A term usually meaning anthracite coal, but was commonly used by the pioneers referring to any type of hard coal as opposed to either soft coal or charcoal.

timp The crown or arch of the opening in front of the hearth of a blast furnace.

tunnel head The upper portion or top of the blast furnace, surrounded by a gallery where there are openings through which the charge is fed.

tuyere, tweer A tube, nozzle or pipe located in the bosh area of a smelter, through which combustion air is blown into the furnace.

wrought iron Iron heated and mechanically worked (wrought) with tools such as hammers, rollers, shapers etc. Before the development of effective methods of steelmaking, wrought iron was the most common form of malleable iron.

Notes

Chapter 1
1. Kenneth C. Bullock, *Iron Deposits of Utah*, vol. 88 (Salt Lake City: Utah Geological and Mineralogical Survey, 1970), 27–41, 63, 82.
2. Vélez de Escalante, Silvestre, *The Dominguez and Escalante Journal: Their Expedition through Colorado, Utah, Arizona, and New Mexico in 1776*, ed.. Ted J. Warner (Salt Lake City: University of Utah Press, 1995).
3. Herbert E. Bolton, "Pageant in the Wilderness: The Story of the Escalante Expedition to the Interior Basin, 1776," *Utah Historical Quarterly* 18 (1950): 194–203.
4. LeRoy R. Hafen and Ann Hafen, *The Old Spanish Trail: Santa Fé to Los Angeles* (Lincoln Nebraska: University of Nebraska Press, 1954), 109–129; "The Old Spanish National Historic Trail," Oldspanishtrail.org.
5. Pauline Udall Smith, *Captain Jefferson Hunt of the Mormon Battalion* (Salt Lake City: Nicholas G. Morgan, Sr., Foundation, 1958); LeRoy R. Hafen and Ann W. Hafen, *Journals of the Forty-Niners: Salt Lake to Los Angeles* (Lincoln: University of Nebraska Press, 1954); Addison Pratt, *The Journals of Addison Pratt*, ed., S. George Ellsworth (Salt Lake City: University of Utah Press, 1990), 385.
6. Isaac C. Haight journal, December 28, 1849, in *Journal History of the Church of Jesus Christ of Latter-day Saints*, vol. 27 (July–December 1849), Church History Library, Church of Jesus Christ of Latter-day Saints, Salt Lake City, Utah. Hereafter cited as *Journal History*. This is a vast series of chronological scrapbooks of historical source material, compiled in the early twentieth century by staff of the predecessor to the Church History Library (CHL).
7. John Brown journal, January 8, 1850, *Journal History*, vol. 28 (1850).
8. John D. Lee, "Journal of the Iron County Mission, John D. Lee, Clerk," ed., Gustive O. Larson, *Utah Historical Quarterly* 20, n. 1 (January 1952): 109–112.

Chapter 2
1. Brigham Young, "Dependence on the Lord, coal and iron works, family excursions," May 27, 1855, in *Journal of Discourses*, 27 vol. (Liverpool and London: F. D. Richards and Daniel H. Wells, 1852–1886), 2:282. Hereafter *Discourses*.
2. "Little Salt Lake," *Deseret News*, July 27, 1850.
3. Lee, "Journal of the Iron County Mission," *UHQ* (1952), 110–112.
4. "Volunteers," *Deseret News*, November 16, 1850.
5. Brigham Young, "Letter to Dr. J. M. Bernhisel," November 20, 1850, *Journal History*, vol. 28 (1850).
6. Brigham Young, "Governor's message," *Deseret News*, January 11, 1851.
7. "An ordinance to provide for the organization of Iron County," *UHQ* (1940), 195.
8. Lee, "Journal of the Iron County Mission," *UHQ* (1952), 116–117.
9. George A. Smith journal, January 15, 1851, CHL.

10. Lee, "Journal of the Iron County Mission," *UHQ*, 275–276; George A. Smith journal, January 16, 1851, CHL.

11. Leonard J. Arrington, "Planning an Iron Industry for Utah, 1851–1858." *Huntington Library Quarterly* 21, no.3 (May 1958): 237–260.

12. George O. Zabriskie and Dorothy Louise Robinson, "U.S. Census for Utah, 1851," *Utah Genealogical and Historical Magazine* 29 (April, July 1938): 65–72, 130–142.

13. John W. Van Cott, *Utah Place Names* (Salt Lake City: University of Utah Press, 1990), 437.

14. George A. Smith, "General Conference talk," *Frontier Guardian*, October 31, 1851, in *Journal History* vol.29 (1851).

15. John Urie, *Early History of Cedar City and Vicinity* (Cedar City, Utah: Privately Published, n.d.). Copy at Cedar City Library, Cedar City, Utah.

16. George A. Smith, "General items," *Deseret News*, November 29, 1851.

17. Henry Lunt diary, November 10, 1851, typescript, L. Tom Perry Special Collections, Brigham Young University.

18. William R. Palmer, "Pioneer fortifications," *Improvement Era*, March 1951, 148–50, 183–87.

19. William R. Palmer, *First Forts at Cedar City, as Told by David Bulloch* (Cedar City, Utah: Privately Published, n.d.), William R. Palmer Collection, Barbara and Col. A. L. Matheson Special Collections, Southern Utah University.

20. *The Making, Shaping and Treating of Steel*, 7th ed. (Pittsburg, Pa.: United States Steel Corporation, 1957).

21. Mathew Carruthers, "Local correspondence," *Deseret News*, February 21, 1852.

22. Henry Lunt diary, May 10, 1852, BYU.

23. John M. Bourne, *The Iron Mission and the Deseret Iron Works, 1851–1858* (Salt Lake City: Utah State Historical Society, 1972), 5.

24. Minute Book of Deseret Iron Works, May 11, 1852, CHL.

25. "Manufacture of Iron in Utah," *Millennial Star* 17, n. 1 (January 6, 1855): 1–2.

26. Henry Lunt diary, May 27, June 7, 8, 22, 1852, BYU.

27. Henry Lunt, "Local correspondence–interesting from Iron County," *Deseret News*, July 24, 1852.

28. Henry Lunt diary, June 26, 29, July 14, 1852, BYU.

29. Chemical analysis of various samples of iron ore, iron and limestone excavated near the site of the old Iron Works and near the Red Hill in Cedar City was arranged by York F. Jones in 1976. A copy of the full report is in the York F. Jones papers, Matheson Special Collections; a summary appears in Appendix 3.

30. Henry Lunt diary, July 16, 17, 20, 30, August 13, September 7, 8, 22, 1852, BYU.

31. Morris A. Shirts and Kathryn H Shirts, *A Trial Furnace: Southern Utah's Iron Mission* (Provo, Utah: Brigham Young University Press, 2001), 250.

32. William R. Palmer, "Graphic story of pioneer Iron Works of Cedar," *Iron County Record*, September 7, 1933.

33. Henry Lunt diary, October 1, 1852, BYU.

34. Henry Lunt, "Local correspondence," *Deseret News*, November 6, 1852.

35. Brigham Young, Heber C. Kimball and Willard Richards, "Eighth general epistle," *Deseret News*, October 16, 1852.

36. George A. Smith, "Minutes of the General Conference," *Deseret News*, October 16, 1852.

37. E. Crane Watson, "History of iron manufacturing in early days of Cedar," *Iron County Record*, December 19, 1924.

38. George A. Smith, "Local correspondence – GSL City Dec. 8, 1852," *Deseret News,* December 11, 1852.
39. Henry Lunt diary, December 10, 17, 30, 1852, BYU.
40. Brigham Young, Heber C. Kimball and Willard Richards, "Sixth general epistle," *Deseret News,* November 15, 1851.
41. "Manufacture of Iron in Utah," *Millennial Star* 17 (1855): 2.
42. "Manufacture of Iron in Utah," *Millennial Star* 17 (1855): 2–3.
43. Bourne, *Iron Mission,* 12.
44. Erastus Snow, "To my friend 'The News,'" *Deseret News,* December 25, 1852.
45. "Utah Territorial Legislature," *Deseret News,* January 22, 1853, 2.
46. Minute Book of Deseret Iron Works, November 18, 1853, CHL.
47. Minute Book of Deseret Iron Works, November 7, 1853, CHL.
48. Henry Lunt, "Local correspondence," *Deseret News,* March 19, 1853.
49. Minute Book of Deseret Iron Works, February–April, 1853, CHL; Richard Harrison diary, February–April 1853, typescript, L. Tom Perry Special Collections, Brigham Young University; Henry Lunt diary, April 1, 1853, BYU
50. Henry Lunt diary, April 4, 1853, BYU.
51. "History of Parowan Stake, 1851–1980," CHL.
52. Minute Book of Deseret Iron Works, April 2, 1853, CHL.
53. "Manufacture of iron in Utah," *Millennial Star* 17 (1855): 5.
54. Henry Lunt diary, May 19, July 18, 1853, BYU.
55. "Indian difficulties," *Deseret News,* July 30, 1853.
56. "Indian difficulties," *Deseret News,* July 30, 1853.
57. Shirts and Shirts, *Trial Furnace,* 319–23.
58. Brigham Young, "To the Saints," *Deseret News,* July 30, 1853.
59. Brigham Young, "Proclamation by the Governor," *Deseret News,* October 1, 1853.
60. Ryan Elwood Wimmer, *The Walker War Reconsidered* (Provo: Brigham Young University Press, 2010), *passim.*
61. Brigham Young, May 27, 1855, *Discourses,* 2:283.
62. Henry Lunt, "Items from Iron County," *Deseret News,* October 15, 1853.
63. Erastus Snow and Franklin D. Richards, "General items," *Deseret News,* December 15, 1853.
64. "Manufacture of Iron in Utah," *Millennial Star* 17 (1855): 3–5.
65. Shirts and Shirts, *Trial Furnace,* 285–294.
66. Arrington, "Planning an Iron Industry for Utah," 251–252.
67. Minute Book of Deseret Iron Works, January–September 1854, CHL.
68. "Manufacture of Iron in Utah," *Millennial Star* 17 (1855): 6.
69. Lucius N. Scovil, "Trip to Parowan, Iron County," *Deseret News,* January 4, 1855.
70. Thomas Bladen to John Taylor, July 1856, Minute Book of Deseret Iron Works, CHL.
71. George A. Smith, "Iron County Iron Works," *Deseret News,* December 21, 1854.
72. Bourne, *Iron Mission,* 14.
73. E. J. Steptoe, "Military road," *Deseret News,* December 14, 1854.
74. Minute Book of Deseret Iron Works, January 7, 1855, CHL.
75. York F. Jones, "Summary of furnace charges made between January 2 and January 8, 1855," York Jones papers.
76. Minute Book of Deseret Iron Works, January 1855, CHL.

77. "Chemical analysis of various samples of iron ore, iron and limestone excavated near the site of the old Iron Works and near the Red Hill in Cedar City arranged by York F. Jones in 1976," York Jones papers.

78. *Methodology and Specifications Guide: Metallurgical Coal* (S&P Global Platts, June 2018), 9, http://www.platts.com/IM.Platts.Content/MethodologyReferences/MethodologySpecs/metcoalmethod.pdf (accessed July 24, 2018).

79. A simple explanation can be found in Marshall Brain and Robert Lamb, "How Iron and Steel Work: Creating Iron," howstuffworks.com, accessed July 24, 2018,

80. J. C. L Smith, "Home correspondence," *Deseret News,* May 2, 1855.

81. Arrington, "Planning an Iron Industry for Utah," 254.

82. L. O. Littlefield, "Incidents of travel," *Deseret News,* May 13, 1863.

83. L. O. Littlefield, "Incidents of travel," *Deseret News,* May 20, 1863.

84. George A. Smith, "Home correspondence," *Deseret News,* May 30, 1855.

85. Brigham Young, May 27, 1855, *Discourses,* 2:281–283.

86. "Grasshoppers, &c.," *Deseret News,* June 27, 1855.

87. Minute Book of Deseret Iron Works, February 1856, CHL.

88. Leonard J. Arrington, *Great Basin Kingdom: An Economic History of the Latter-day Saints, 1830–1900* (1959; Urbana: University of Illinois Press, 2004), 127–129.

89. Bourne, *Iron Mission,* 16–17; Isaac C. Haight to Heber C Kimball, August 20, 1856, quoted in *Journal of Discourses, 2*:282.

90. Minute Book of Deseret Iron Works, July 12, 1856, CHL.

91. Shirts and Shirts, *Trial Furnace,* 379.

92. Isaac C. Haight journal, August 4, 1856, typescript, Matheson Special Collections, Southern Utah University.

93. Isaac C. Haight journal, March 1857, SUU.

94. Bourne, *Iron Mission,* 17.

95. Isaac C. Haight journal, April 6–September 30, 1857, SUU.

96. Isaac C. Haight journal, September 1857, SUU.

97. Arrington, "Planning an Iron Industry for Utah," 257.

98. Minute Book of Deseret Iron Works, November 16, 1857, CHL.

99. Isaac C. Haight journal, March 10, 12, 14, 1858, SUU.

100. Minute Book of Deseret Iron Works, March 30–October 15, 1858, CHL.

101. Brigham Young to Isaac C. Haight, October 4, 1858, Letterbook 4, p. 432–433, Office Files, Copybooks, Brigham Young papers, CHL.

102. Minute Book of Deseret Iron Works, November 1, 1858, CHL.

103. Arrington, "Planning an Iron Industry for Utah," 259.

104. Janet Burton Seegmiller, *A History of Iron County* (Salt Lake City: Utah State Historical Society, 1998), 326.

105. Isaac C. Haight journal, April 29, 1859, SUU.

106. Minute Book of Deseret Iron Works, November 7, 1859, CHL.

107. Henry Lunt, "Correspondence – Cedar City, Iron County," *Deseret News,* August 27, 1862.

108. Shirts and Shirts, *Trial Furnace,* 398.

109. Minute Book of Deseret Iron Works, May 16, 1867, CHL; Seegmiller, *History of Iron County,* 326.

110. Arrington, "Planning an Iron Industry for Utah," 258–259.

111. "Correspondence," *Deseret News,* October 12, 1865.

112. Shirts and Shirts, *Trial Furnace,* 409, 410.

113. Arrington, "Planning an Iron Industry for Utah," 258–259.

Notes

Chapter 3
1. "Items," *Deseret News*, August 5, 1868.
2. "Correspondence," *Deseret News*, April 7, 1869.
3. "Items," *Deseret News*, August 12, 1868.
4. "Legislative," *Deseret News*, February 17, 1869.
5. "Resolution exempting certain iron works from taxation," Minutes of the Utah Legislature, February 17, 1869, Chapter XXVII, in *Journal History* vol. 74 (January–March 1869), 9.
6. Seth M. Blair, "Correspondence," *Deseret News*, May 18, 1870.
7. "Utah Iron Mining Company," August 16, 1870, Articles of Incorporation Record Books, Utah State Archives & Utah State History, Salt Lake City, Utah.
8. "Southern Iron Works," *Salt Lake Herald*, September 8, 1870.
9. Erastus Snow, "Local and other matters," *Deseret News*, March 8, 1871.
10. Richard S. Robinson, "Correspondence," *Deseret News*, May 10, 1871.
11. "Local and other matters," *Deseret News*, August 30, 1871.
12. Census report for Iron County, 1872, York Jones papers, SUU.
13. "To Capitalists," *Salt Lake Herald*, June 22, 1872.
14. "Iron County," *Deseret News*, October 8, 1873.
15. "Iron County," *Deseret News*, October 8, 1873.
16. "Local and other matters," *Deseret News*, November 5, 1873.
17. "Great Western Iron Company," *Salt Lake Herald*, November 11, 1873.
18. J. Morgan, "Correspondence," *Deseret News*, October 13, 1875.
19. "Great Western Iron Company," September 4, 1874, Articles of Incorporation Record Books, Utah State Archives.
20. "Fired up," *Salt Lake Herald*, October 9, 1874.
21. Henry Lunt, "Territorial dispatches," *Deseret News*, October 21, 1874.
22. "Local and other matters – Utah iron," *Deseret News*, November 4, 1874.
23. "The iron company," *Salt Lake Herald*, January 28, 1875.
24. "Great Western Iron Co.," *Salt Lake Herald*, April 13, 1875.
25. J. Morgan, "Correspondence," *Deseret News*, October 13, 1875.
26. "Local News–Great Western Iron Company," *Salt Lake Herald*, November 28, 1875.
27. Seegmiller, *Iron County*, 328; "The St. George Utah Temple–history," p.5, http://wchsutah.org/documents/st-george-temple-history-1.pdf (accessed July 11, 2018).
28. "Chemical analysis of two samples of iron ore from Old Iron Town arranged for by York F. Jones in May 1978," York Jones papers.
29. "News from the iron region," *Salt Lake Herald*, January 9, 1876.
30. "The iron interest," *Salt Lake Herald*, February 1, 1876.
31. "The Great Western Iron Company," *Salt Lake Herald*, April 25, 1876.
32. "The first," *Salt Lake Herald*, June 22, 1876.
33. "Iron stock for sale," *Salt Lake Herald*, August 11, 1876.
34. "Notice," *Deseret Evening News*, August 28, 1876.
35. "Notice," *Deseret Evening News*, November 13, 1876.
36. "Auction sale," *Salt Lake Herald*, May 11, 1877.
37. "Editorials–Iron and justice gain the victory," *Deseret News*, February 2, 1881.
38. Charles S. Wilkinson, "Utah's great iron deposits," *Salt Lake Tribune*, December 31, 1899.
39. "Editorials–Iron and justice gain the victory," *Deseret News*, February 2, 1881.
40. "Important suit settled," *Ogden Herald*, August 03, 1881.

41. "Local and other matters–Iron suits," *Deseret News,* October 11, 1882; "Chips," *Salt Lake Herald,* December 30, 1882; "Iron mine cases," *Salt Lake Herald,* January 05, 1883; "Local and other matters–An unexpected decision," *Deseret News,* April 18, 1883.

42. "The iron interest," *Ogden Junction,* March 17, 1880.

43. "Zion's Central Board of Trade," *Tullidge's Quarterly Magazine* 1 (1881): 420.

44. *Articles of Association of Zion's Central Board of Trade* (Salt Lake City: Publisher Unknown, 1879), https://archive.org/details/articlesofassoci00zion.

45. "Newberry on Utah's minerals," *Salt Lake Herald,* November 20, 1880.

46. "Iron," *Deseret News,* January 26, 1881.

47. "Board of Trade," *Salt Lake Herald,* April 21, 1881.

48. "Practical measures for Zion's progress," *Deseret News,* April 27, 1881.

49. "Zion's Central Board of Trade," *Deseret News,* June 1, 1881.

50. Thomas Taylor, "Editorials–More about iron," *Deseret News,* August 24, 1881.

51. Andrew Jenson, *The Latter-day Saint Biographical Encyclopedia,* 4 vol. (Salt Lake City: Andrew Jenson History Company, 1914), 2: 500–505.

52. "Iron–A company organized for the manufacture of iron," *Salt Lake Herald,* August 26, 1881.

53. "Local and other matters–Utah Iron Manufacturing Company," *Deseret News,* August 31, 1881.

54. "The Edmunds Bill," *Salt Lake Herald,* February 16, 1882.

55. A. H. Cannon," A circus scourge-Grand concert-Iron manufacture," *Journal History,* 27 July 1883, p.6. The source is a *Millennial Star* article, but the date inked on the clipping is incorrect.

56. Leonard J. Arrington, "Iron Manufacturing in Southern Utah in the Early 1880's: The Iron Manufacturing Company of Utah," *Bulletin of the Business Historical Society* 25, no. 3 (September 1951): 157–158; "The Iron Manufacturing Company of Utah," *Deseret Evening News,* August 4, 1883.

57. "Manufacture of iron," *Deseret News,* August 8, 1883.

58. "Iron works," *Southern Utonian,* August 24, 1883.

59. "Utah news," *Millennial Star* 45, n. 39 (September 24, 1883): 623, *Journal History,* vol. 170 (September 1883).

60. "Local and other matters–Fine prospect," *Deseret News,* September 5, 1883.

61. "Southern interests," *Salt Lake Herald,* October 3, 1883.

62. "The iron interest," *Salt Lake Herald,* October 16, 1883.

63. "Zion's Central Board of Trade," *Deseret News,* October 17, 1883.

64. "Local and other matters–The iron industry," *Deseret News,* October 24, 1883.

65. "The Iron Manufacturing Company of Utah," *Southern Utonian,* October 26, 1883.

66. "Local and other matters–The iron industry," *Deseret News,* November 7, 1883.

67. "Iron manufacture," *Salt Lake Herald,* January 17, 1884.

68. "The iron district," *Salt Lake Herald,* October 6, 1886.

69. "Sold," *Southern Utonian,* December 28, 1883.

70. "Iron, iron, iron," *Southern Utonian,* February 1, 1884.

71. Arrington, "Iron Manufacturing," 161.

72. "Geo. Q's Swindle," *Salt Lake Tribune,* September 26, 1885.

73. "Rustlings," *Southern Utonian,* August 17, 1888.

74. Arrington, "Iron Manufacturing," 161.

75. "The conference," *Salt Lake Herald,* April 6, 1884.

76. "Fifty fourth annual conference–Apostle Erastus Snow, President Taylor," *Deseret News,* April 9, 1884.

77. "The Board of Trade," *Salt Lake Herald*, April 9, 1884.
78. "From Wednesday's daily–Going south," *Deseret News*, April 23, 1884.
79. "Utah news," *Millennial Star* 46, n. 21 (May 26, 1884): 326, *Journal History* vol. 179 (May 16–31, 1884).
80. "The iron mines," *Salt Lake Herald*, April 26, 1884; "The iron mines," *Salt Lake Herald*, May 4, 1884.
81. Arrington, "Iron Manufacturing," 163.
82. [---] Wallace, "Iron County," *Salt Lake Herald*, April 18, 1884.
83. Thomas Taylor, "Iron manufacture," *Salt Lake Herald*, October 26, 1884.
84. "Stockholders' meeting," *Deseret Evening News*, March 21, 1885.
85. "Notice," *Deseret News*, April 22, 1885.
86. "Notice," *Deseret Evening News*, September 23, 1885.
87. "The iron district," *Salt Lake Herald*, October 6, 1886.
88. Arrington, "Iron Manufacturing," 164.
89. "Local and other matters–The iron industry," *Deseret News*, November 7, 1883.

Chapter 4

1. "Our iron and coal," *Salt Lake Tribune*, August 13, 1881.
2. "Utah's metallic wealth," *Utah Enquirer*, February 10, 1888.
3. Thomas Taylor, "Iron ore deposits," *Salt Lake Herald*, December 25, 1889.
4. "City and Neighborhood," *Salt Lake Tribune*, December 4, 1890.
5. Thomas Taylor, "Wrong impressions," *Iron County News*, December 6, 1890.
6. E. G. Jr., "Neglected wealth," *Salt Lake Herald*, October 18, 1891.
7. G. D. MacDonald III, *The Magnet: Iron Ore in Iron County, Utah* (Cedar City, Utah: Privately published, 1990), 14–15.
8. H. Lee Scamehorn, *Mill and Mine: The CF&I in the Twentieth Century* (Lincoln: University of Nebraska Press, 1992), 7–10.
9. "Big deal for iron claims," *Salt Lake Herald*, August 27, 1903.
10. "Pueblo a city that promises much for the future," *Leadville Democrat*, February 5, 1881.
11. "Iron County's iron mines to be worked," *Iron County Record*, November 14, 1913.
12. "Iron County's iron mines to be worked," *Iron County Record*, November 14, 1913.
13. "F.U. Nelson gives opinion," *Iron County Record*, November 28, 1913.
14. "Present status of iron smelter," *Iron County Record*, December 25, 1914.
15. MacDonald, *Magnet*, 14.
16. "The completion of the pacific railroad," *Deseret News*, May 19, 1869.
17. "City jottings," *Salt Lake Tribune*, May 9, 1880.
18. "Chips," *Salt Lake Herald*, June 13, 1880.
19. "The Horn Silver output," *Salt Lake Tribune*, May 20, 1891.
20. "Our iron and coal," *Salt Lake Tribune*, August 13, 1881.
21. "Extension to stateline," *Salt Lake Tribune*, February 19, 1898.
22. "Cedar City junction," *Salt Lake Tribune*, January 25, 1899; "Southern Utah gives glad welcome to nation's chief executive," *Iron County Record*, June 29, 1923.
23. Van Cott, *Utah Place Names*, 237.
24. "Cedar City junction," *Salt Lake Tribune*, January 25, 1899.
25. "Utah State news," *Iron County Record*, May 12, 1905.
26. William H. Sontag, *National Park Service: The First 75 Years. Biographical Vignettes*, n.13 (Philadelphia: Eastern National Park & Monument Association, 1990).
27. "Our mining heritage," http://marysvale.org/history.htm (accessed July 11, 2018).

28. "D&RGW Marysvale branch history," December 3, 2014, http://drgw.net/info/MarysvaleBranch (accessed July 11, 2018).
29. "A push for Utah iron," *Salt Lake Tribune*, November 28, 1899.
30. "Marysvale extension," *Iron County Record*, July 3, 1903.
31. "Local news," *Iron County Record*, August 13, 1904.
32. "Cedar City happenings," *Iron County Record*, May 26, 1916.
33. "Good prospects for a railroad," *Iron County Record*, October 15, 1915.
34. "Local news," *Iron County Record*, December 3, 1915.
35. "Hundred million iron plant looms," *Iron County Record*, June 14, 1918.
36. "Origin of our mining laws," *Mining & Scientific Press*, September 23, 1905, 203; Curtis H. Lindley, *A Treatise on the American Law Relating to Mines and Mineral Lands* (San Francisco: Bancroft-Whitney, 1914), 50–63; "Mineral Lands and Regulations in General, 30 USCA ch. 2; *Mining Claims and Sites on Federal Land*, P-048 (Washington: US Bureau of Land Management, 2011), 3–7.
37. MacDonald, *Magnet*, 11–13.
38. "Pinto Iron Mining District," Utah Division of Archives and Records Service, https://archives.utah.gov/research/inventories/23961.html (accessed July 11, 2018).
39. United States General Land Office Mining district by-laws, 1872–1909, Series 3651, box 1, folder 26 (reel 1), Iron Springs Mining District, Utah Division of Archives and Records Service.
40. MacDonald, *Magnet*, 11–13.
41. "A push for Utah iron," *Salt Lake Tribune*, November 28, 1899.
42. "Marvelous promise of Utah's iron fields," *Salt Lake Herald*, December 28, 1902.
43. "Utah's great iron deposits," *Salt Lake Tribune*, December 31, 1899.
44. "The Iron Manufacturing Company of Utah," *Deseret Evening News*, September 4, 1883.
45. "Utah iron mines attract notice," *Deseret Evening News*, May 6, 1901.
46. "May get iron mines of Utah," *Salt Lake Herald*, December 19, 1901.
47. "Great purchase of iron lands," *Salt Lake Tribune*, April 19, 1902.
48. "Iron claims are bought," *Salt Lake Herald*, April 19, 1902.
49. "Payment of iron claims," *Salt Lake Herald*, July 20, 1902.
50. "Iron County's iron deposits," *Deseret Evening News*, September 26, 1902; "Taylor iron lands," *Deseret Evening News*, April 7, 1903.
51. "Taylor iron lands," *Deseret Evening News*, April 7, 1903.
52. "Mining notes," *Salt Lake Herald*, April 15, 1903.
53. "Calls off deal for Utah iron," *Salt Lake Herald*, June 16, 1903.
54. "Big deal for iron claims," *Salt Lake Herald*, August 27, 1903.
55. "Taylor estate sells iron lands," *Deseret Evening News*, August 26, 1903; "Big deal for iron claims," *Salt Lake Herald*, August 27, 1903.
56. "Big deal for iron claims," *Salt Lake Herald*, August 27, 1903.
57. "Big iron mine deal is closed," *Salt Lake Herald*, February 14, 1908.
58. "Coal and iron claims sold," *Iron County Record*, September 30, 1921.
59. "Activity in iron district," *Salt Lake Tribune*, October 4, 1902.
60. "From the iron fields," *Deseret Evening News*, January 30, 1903.
61. "An immense concern," *Salt Lake Tribune*, November 27, 1902.
62. "Big deal for iron claims," *Salt Lake Herald*, August 27, 1903.
63. "Homestake and Comstock," *Iron County Record*, September 4, 1903.
64. "Utah iron for pueblo plant," *Iron County Record*, November 21, 1903.
65. "Utah iron for pueblo plant," *Iron County Record*, November 21, 1903.

Notes

66 "Local news," *Iron County Record*, August 13, 1904.
67. "Utah iron mines enormously rich," *Deseret Evening News*, December 6, 1904.
68. "Colorado Fuel & Iron in suit with Walker brothers over claims," *Salt Lake Herald*, August 5, 1903.
69. "Iron decision mixed," *Salt Lake Herald*, June 7, 1904.
70. "That Walker iron deal," *Salt Lake Herald*, February 18, 1906.
71. "Kaiser plant contracts for million tons local iron ore," *Iron County Record*, November 2, 1944.
72. "Walker bros. agree to dispose of claims," *Washington County News*, August 11, 1921.
73. "Another steel plant in Utah seems likely," *Salt Lake Telegram*, July 1, 1923.
74. "Utah's great iron deposits," *Salt Lake Tribune*, December 31, 1899.
75. "Iron County iron exhibit," *Iron County Record*, February 27, 1904.
76. "Developing new coal supply," *Iron County Record*. November 28, 1913.

Chapter 5

1. "To develop Utah steel resources," *Iron County Record*, November 18, 1921, 7.
2. "Pacific Steel Corporation prepares to utilize Utah Milner deposits for pig iron plant costing $7,500,000," *Salt Lake Telegram*, September 7, 1922, 9.
3. "New Utah steel companies are scheduled to form merger," *Salt Lake Mining Review*, November 30, 1922, 21.
4. "Flood of good news," *Iron County Record*, March 9, 1923, 1.
5. "Ironton chosen official title of steel town," *Salt Lake Telegram*, March 28, 1923, 2.
6. "150 men work on steel mill," *Salt Lake Telegram*, May 9, 1923, 2.
7. "Making rapid progress at steel plant," *Salt Lake Mining Review*, October 15, 1923, 16.
8. "Columbia Steel plants at Ironton are rapidly nearing completion," *Salt Lake Mining Review*, January 30, 1924, 17.
9. "Utah's iron industry begins with the flowing of pig iron at Ironton plant Wednesday," *Springville Herald*, May 2, 1924, 1.
10. "Big steel day celebration," *Iron County Record*, June 13, 1924, 5.
11. "Second unit of steel plant," *Iron County Record*, June 6, 1924, 5.
12. "To develop Utah steel resources," *Iron County Record*, November 18, 1921, 7; "Steel from Utah iron ore," *Iron County Record*, December 23, 1921, 1.
13. "California is prime market for steel production in Utah," *Salt Lake Telegram*, February 22, 1926, 2
14. "Utah iron mines and Columbia Steel activities start things," *Salt Lake Mining Review*, May 30, 1926, 9.
15. "New Utah steel companies are scheduled to form merger," *Salt Lake Mining Review*, November 30, 1922, 21.
16. "To develop Utah steel resources," *Iron County Record*, November 18, 1921, 7; "Steel from Utah iron ore," *Iron County Record*, December 23, 1921, 1.
17. "Flood of good news," *Iron County Record*, March 9, 1923, 1.
18. "New bridge over coal creek now completed," *Salt Lake Telegram*, October 5, 1923, 17.
19. "Traffic flows over new highway bridge over coal creek on north main street," *Iron County Record*, October 16, 1952, 1.
20. "Railroad's new branch line from Lund to Cedar City, Utah," *Union Pacific Railroad internal correspondence to all traffic representatives and local agents*, March 15, 1923, File No. C–5101–3905–2. U.P.R.R. Omaha, Nebraska. York Jones papers.

21. "R.R. work progressing," *Iron County Record,* April 13, 1923, 1.

22. "Concerning the Lund–Cedar City, Utah, branch," *Union Pacific Railroad internal correspondence to all traffic representatives and local agents,* June 15, 1923.

23. "Southern Utah gives glad welcome to nation's chief executive," *Iron County Record,* June 29, 1923, 1.

24. "Southern Utah gives glad welcome to nation's chief executive," *Iron County Record,* June 29, 1923, 1; "Mrs. Harding game, but she balks at riding Zion horse," *Ogden Standard–Examiner,* June 28, 1923, 1.

25. "Southern Utah gives glad welcome to nation's chief executive," *Iron County Record,* June 29, 1923, 1; "Mrs. Harding game, but she balks at riding Zion horse," *Ogden Standard–Examiner,* June 28, 1923, 1.

26. "Mrs. Harding game, but she balks at riding Zion horse," *Ogden Standard–Examiner,* June 28, 1923, 1.

27. "Southern Utah gives glad welcome to nation's chief executive," *Iron County Record,* June 29, 1923, 1.

28. "Southern Utah gives glad welcome to nation's chief executive," *Iron County Record,* June 29, 1923, 1; "Mrs. Harding game, but she balks at riding Zion horse," *Ogden Standard–Examiner,* June 28, 1923, 1; "President visits Southern Utah," *Beaver County News,* June 29, 1923, 1; David Dary, *The Oregon Trail: An American Saga* (Alfred A. Knopf, 2004), 322–323; John W. Dean, *Warren Harding* (Holt, 2004), 147–149: Robert K. Murray, *The Harding Era, 1921–1923: Warren G. Harding and his Administration* (Minneapolis: University of Minnesota Press, 1969), 438–450.

29. "Pressure exerted building road," *Iron County Record,* July 13, 1923, 8.

30. "Union Pacific spending thousands of dollars in local improvements," *Iron County Record,* March 30, 1929, 1.

31. "Local news," *Iron County Record,* July 6, 1923, 8.

32. "Another steel plant in Utah seems likely," *Salt Lake Telegram,* July 1, 1923, 1.

33. "Golden rail laying, Cedar City, Utah," *The Union Pacific Magazine,* October 1923, York Jones papers.

34. "Cedar City's celebration the biggest ever staged in Southern Utah," *Iron County Record,* September 14, 1923, 1.

35. Lafayette Hanchett, "Two prayers," *Manti Messenger,* August 3, 1923, 1.

36. "Flood of good news," *Iron County Record,* March 9, 1923, 1.

37. "First iron ore shipped," *Iron County Record,* October 12, 1923, 1.

38. "Railroad's new branch line from Lund to Cedar City, Utah," *Union Pacific Railroad internal correspondence to all traffic representatives and local agents,* March 15, 1923, File No. C-5101-3905-2.

39. "Hotel Escalante sale completed," *Iron County Record,* July 2, 1970, 1; "General business conditions of Cedar City," *Iron County Record,* August 24, 1923, 17.

40. Wayne K. Hinton, "The Development of Zion National Park," historytogo.utah.gov/utah_chapters/from_war_to_war/thedevelopmentofzionnationalpark.html; Bryce Canyon (accessed December 1, 2018); "National Park Service," https://www.nps.gov/brca/learn/historyculture/index.htm (accessed December 1, 2018); "Cedar Breaks National Monument: History," http://www.zionnational-park.com/cbhistory.htm (accessed December 1, 2018).

41. "Tourist hotel promised," *Salt Lake Herald,* August 19, 1919, 10.

42. "Cedar City will care for tourists to Zion Park," *Salt Lake Tribune,* November 27 1919, 11.

43. "Cedar's new hotel," *Iron County Record,* January 16, 1920, 4.

Notes

44. "Terminal fund for Cedar City raised," *Salt Lake Telegram,* February 3, 1923, 2.
45. "New Union Pacific hotel at Cedar City to open tomorrow," *Salt Lake Telegram,* March 28, 1924, 2.
46. "General business conditions of Cedar City," *Iron County Record,* August 24, 1923, 17.
47. "News notes from all parts of Utah," *Iron County Record,* April 11, 1924, 3.
48. Thomas E. Byrnes, "Resembles corridors of the Leviathan," *Iron County Record,* March 21, 1924, 1; Kenneth C. Bullock, *Iron Deposits of Utah,* 48, 51, 54.
49. "Flood of good news," *Iron County Record,* March 9, 1923, 1.
50. "First iron ore shipped" *Iron County Record,* October 12, 1923, 1.
51. "Much activity at Iron Springs," *Iron County Record,* May 25, 1923, 1; "Much activity at the iron mines," *Iron County Record,* July 20, 1923, 1.
52. Thomas E. Byrnes, "Resembles corridors of the Leviathan," *Iron County Record,* March 21, 1924, 1.
53. James F. Younger, "Letter from our Iron Springs Correspondent," *Iron County Record,* July 14, 1922, 4; "Iron Springs notes," *Iron County Record,* August 8, 1924, 2.
54. Thomas E. Byrnes, "Resembles corridors of the Leviathan," *Iron County Record,* March 21, 1924, 1.
55. "First iron ore shipped," *Iron County Record,* October 12, 1923, 1; Thomas E. Byrnes, "Resembles corridors of the Leviathan," *Iron County Record,* March 21, 1924, 1; "Much activity at the iron mines," *Iron County Record,* July 20, 1923, 1.
56. "First iron ore shipped," *Iron County Record,* October 12, 1923, 1.
57. "Columbia Steel items," *Iron County Record,* February 22, 1924, 1.
58. "First iron ore shipped," *Iron County Record,* October 12, 1923, 1.
59. Thomas E. Byrnes, "Resembles corridors of the Leviathan," *Iron County Record,* March 21, 1924, 1.
60. "Much activity at the iron mines," *Iron County Record,* July 20, 1923, 1.
61. Thomas E. Byrnes, "Resembles corridors of the Leviathan," *Iron County Record,* March 21, 1924, 1
62. Thomas E. Byrnes, "Resembles corridors of the Leviathan," *Iron County Record,* March 21, 1924, 1
63. "Miner killed at Iron Springs," *Iron County Record,* April 11, 1924, 1.
64. Thomas E. Byrnes, "Resembles corridors of the Leviathan," *Iron County Record,* March 21, 1924, 1.
65. Thomas E. Byrnes, "Resembles corridors of the Leviathan," *Iron County Record,* March 21, 1924, 1.
66. Thomas E. Byrnes, "Resembles corridors of the Leviathan," *Iron County Record,* March 21, 1924, 1.
67. Thomas E. Byrnes, "Resembles corridors of the Leviathan," *Iron County Record,* March 21, 1924, 1.
68. Colleen Whitley and Janet Seegmiller, *From the Ground Up: The History of Mining in Utah* (Logan, Utah: Utah State University Press, 2006), 205.
69. "Miner killed at Iron Springs," *Iron County Record,* April 11, 1924, 1.
70. "Columbia Steel items," *Iron County Record,* February 22, 1924, 1.
71. "Will diamond drill iron ore," *Iron County Record,* April 3, 1925, 8.
72. "Iron King starts after ore deposit," *Salt Lake Telegram,* February 22, 1926, 11; "Weekly shipment of ore about normal," *Salt Lake Telegram,* April 24, 1926, 6.
73. "Unknown Title," *Salt Lake Tribune.* December 13, 1926; "Jas. F. Younger passes out," *Parowan Times,* June 30, 1926, 14.

74. *Annual Iron Ore Production: The Iron Springs District, 1849–2014* (Salt Lake City: Utah Geological Survey, 2015). The table is an internal document maintained by UGS, received from Ken Krahulec in 2018.

75. Janet Burton Seegmiller, *A History of Iron County* (Salt Lake City: Utah State Historical Society, 1998), 329; G. D. MacDonald III, *The Magnet* (Cedar City, Utah: Privately Published, 1990), 19.

76. "Columbia Geneva Steel Division History," *United States Steel Corporation Handbook* (United States Steel Corporation, 1959).

77. "One man killed one injured," *Iron County Record,* August 17, 1923, 1.

78. "Columbia Steel items," *Iron County Record,* February 22, 1924, 1.

79. "Miner killed at Iron Springs," *Iron County Record,* April 11, 1924, 1.

80. "County hospital notes," *Iron County Record,* July 17, 1925, 1.

81. "Hospital notes," *Iron County Record,* June 18, 1926, 1.

82. "Buried at Iron Springs," *Iron County Record,* July 9, 1926, 1.

83. "Jas. F. Younger passes out," *Parowan Times,* June 30, 1926, 14.

84. "Iron Springs has fire," *Iron County Record,* February 25, 1927, 1.

Chapter 6

1. "Another road to tap iron ore," *Iron County Record,* January 18, 1924, 1.

2. "Unknown Title," *Salt Lake Tribune,* December 13, 1926.

3. "Columbia Steel operates large plant in Utah," *Salt Lake Telegram,* December 25, 1927, 61.

4. Alex Rollo, "Does Southern Utah appreciate the Columbia Steel Corporation?" *Iron County Record,* July 10, 1929, 5.

5. "Columbia Steel sells to Unites States Corp," *Iron County Record,* November 2, 1929, 1.

6. "Hints at large expansion plan," *Iron County Record,* April 26, 1930, 4.

7. "Las Vegas gives warning," *Iron County Record,* July 2, 1930, 1.

8. "Blast furnace being relined," *Iron County Record,* August 29, 1931, 1.

9. "Steel contract may stimulate Desert Mound activities," *Iron County Record,* March 9, 1933, 1.

10. MacDonald, *Magnet,* 58.

11. "Another road to tap iron ore," *Iron County Record,* January 18, 1924, 1.

12. "Milner ore bodies tapped," *Iron County Record,* July 18, 1924, 1.

13. "Iron ore production by Utah Iron Ore Corporation," *Salt Lake Mining Review,* July 30, 1926, 7.

14. "Another road to tap iron ore," *Iron County Record,* January 18, 1924, 1.

15. "Taylor iron lands," *Deseret Evening News,* April 7, 1903, 6.

16. "Taylor estate sells iron lands," *Deseret Evening News,* August 26, 1903, 1.

17. Bullock, *Iron Deposits of Utah,* 39–55.

18. Bullock, *Iron Deposits of Utah,* 39–55.

19. "Local news," *Iron County Record,* July 18, 1924, 5.

20. "Milner ore bodies tapped," *Iron County Record,* July 18, 1924, 1.

21. "Utah Iron Ore Corporation resumes iron ore production," *Salt Lake Mining Review,* December 30, 1924, 13.

22. "Desert Mound activities," *Iron County Record,* April 3, 1925, 1.

23. "Big development at Desert Mound," *Iron County Record,* September 4, 1925, 6.

24. "Unknown Title," *Salt Lake Tribune,* December 13, 1926.

25. "To erect crusher at Desert Mound," *Iron County Record,* January 8, 1926, 1.

Notes

26. "Mammoth iron ore crushing plant at Cedar City goes into action," *Salt Lake Mining Review*, May 30, 1926, 17.
27. "Iron ore production by Utah Iron Ore Corporation," *Salt Lake Mining Review*, July 30, 1926, 7.
28. "Iron Springs has fire," *Iron County Record*, February 25, 1927, 1.
29. "Short time strike at Desert Mound," *Iron County Record*, March 6, 1929, 1.
30. "Ore shipments from Desert Mound doubled," *Parowan Times*, March 23, 1934, 1.
31. "Iron mining group files first papers," *Iron County Record*, July 9, 1930, 1.
32. "Milner Corporation asks County for tax reduction," *Iron County Record*, February 16, 1933, 1.
33. "Ore shipments from Desert Mound doubled," *Parowan Times*, March 23, 1934, 1.
34. "Commissioners attend to considerable important business," *Iron County Record*, August 23, 1934, 4.
35. "Local news," *Iron County Record*, October 4, 1934, 1.
36. "I.C.C. grants permit to build Utah spur," *Salt Lake Telegram*, November 16, 1934, 21.
37. "Iron Mountain rails are laid," *Salt Lake Telegram*, August 15, 1935, 20.
38. "Leslie Morris died Wednesday," *Iron County Record*, April 15, 1927, 1.
39. "Sustains serious injury," *Iron County Record*, June 10, 1927, 1.
40. "Loses life when crushed between two freight cars," *Milford News*, December 7, 1928, 1.
41. "Contacts with electric wire, instantly killed," *Iron County Record*, March 1, 1930, 1.
42. "Hands badly scalded by escaping steam," *Iron County Record*, May 31, 1930, 1.
43. "Impressive rites held for Wm. Stephens," *Iron County Record*, June 21, 1934, 1.
44. "Iron ore succumbs to agriculture," *Iron County Record*, April 30, 1930, 1.
45. "Stacey scores home run," *Iron County Record*, May 27, 1931, 1.
46. "Local news," *Iron County Record*, May 30, 1931, 1.
47. "Geology, chemistry classes' survey," *Iron County Record*, May 13, 1927, 3.
48. "More investigation," *Iron County Record*, January 7, 1927, 1.
49. "Iron mine production may be increased in the near future," *Iron County Record*, December 22, 1928, 1.
50. "Corporation reaps Utah's wealth," *Iron County Record*, September 27, 1930, 1.

Chapter 7

1. "Commissioners attend to considerable important business," *Iron County Record*, August 23, 1934, 4.
2. "Utah plants will invest half million," *Salt Lake Telegram*, March 20, 1935, 1.
3. "Power company constructs line to Iron Mountain," *Iron County Record*, April 4, 1935, 1; "Ore shipments to start," *Iron County Record*, March 19, 1936, 1.
4. "A payroll builder," *Parowan Times*, September 9, 1938, 5.
5. "Expands operation," *Mt. Pleasant Pyramid*, September 16, 1938.
6. "Notice," *Iron County Record*, October 4, 1934, 4; "Power company constructs line to Iron Mountain," *Iron County Record*, April 4, 1935, 1.
7. "Work to commence at once on Iron Mountain R. R.," *Iron County Record*, April 18, 1935, 1.
8. "Which route? Desert Mound or Woolsey canyon," *Iron County Record*, April 18, 1935, 1.
9. "Iron Mountain rails are laid," *Iron County Record*, August 15, 1935, 20; "Ore shipments from Iron Mountain soon to start," *Iron County Record*, January 30, 1936, 1.

10. "Will diamond drill iron ore," *Iron County Record,* April 3, 1925, 8.

11. "Columbia takes option on Iron County deposit," *Iron County Record,* May 25, 1925, 1; "Columbia Steel do prospecting," *Iron County Record,* May 29, 1925, 1.

12. "Columbia Steel acquires Milner iron properties," *Salt Lake Telegram,* September 19, 1925, 2; "Columbia Steel secures more iron," *Iron County Record,* September 25, 1925, 6.

13. "Steel firm gets iron ore option," *Iron County Record,* July 6, 1928, 2.

14. Bullock, *Iron Deposits of Utah,* 49.

15. Bullock, *Iron Deposits of Utah,* 53.

16. Bullock, *Iron Deposits of Utah,* 41.

17. Bullock, *Iron Deposits of Utah,* 44.

18. Bullock, *Iron Deposits of Utah* 51.

19. "Power company constructs line to Iron Mountain," *Iron County Record,* April 4, 1935, 1.

20. "Which route? Desert Mound or Woolsey canyon," *Iron County Record,* April 18, 1935, 1.

21. Bullock, *Iron Deposits of Utah,* 41.

22. "[ ] operations at Iron Mountain will be under way soon," *Iron County Record,* August 1, 1935, 1.

23. "Iron Mountain rails are laid," *Salt Lake Telegram,* August 15, 1935, 20.

24. "Ore shipments from Iron Mountain soon to start," *Iron County Record,* January 30, 1936, 1.

25. "Ore shipments to start," *Iron County Record,* March 19, 1936, 1.

26. "Local news," *Iron County Record,* September 3, 1936, 1.

27. E. S. O'Connor, "[Iron Mountain]," *Salt Lake Tribune,* December 13, 1936.

28. E. S. O'Connor, "Iron pays Utah bills," *Iron County Record,* July 22, 1937, 4.

29. Alex H. Rollo, "Columbia Mining Co. operations second largest in nation," *Iron County Record,* September 30, 1937, 4.

30. MacDonald, *Magnet,* 22–25.

31. "Karl Heyborne has miraculous escape from death," *Iron County Record,* March 28, 1940, 10.

32. "Mine worker loses life in drill accident," *Iron County Record,* June 17, 1943, 1.

Chapter 8

1. Alan Axelrod, *Encyclopedia of World War II,* 2 vol., ed. Jack A. Kingston (New York: Infobase Publishing, 2007), 1:659.

2. "Defense Plant Corporation (DPC)," https://what-when-how.com/the-american-economy/defense-plant-corporation-dpc (accessed July 11, 2018).

3. "White House parley studies plans for iron plant at Mt. Pleasant," *Salt Lake Telegram,* April 22, 1941, 1.

4. "Cedar accorded chance for new pig iron plant," *Iron County Record,* May 15, 1941, 1.

5. "Ironton plant to receive blast furnace addition," *Springville Herald,* March 19, 1942, 1.

6. "Ironton plans shipment hike," *Salt Lake Telegram,* April 1, 1942, 24.

7. "500 beehive coke ovens wait construction in Carbon area," *Salt Lake Telegram,* May 20, 1942, 6.

8. "New pig iron plant ready for operation," *Pleasant Grove Review,* May 14, 1943, 1.

9. "Columbia Steel Corporation, Ironton, Utah-Timeline," September 9, 2015, http://utahrails.net/industries/columbia-steel.php (accessed July 11, 2018).

Notes

10. "Columbia coal mine," April 15, 2016, http://utahrails.net/utahcoal/utahcoal-columbia-geneva.php (July 11, 2018).
11. "Vineyard landowners receive checks for iron plant land," *Salt Lake Telegram,* March 9, 1942, 13.
12. "Geneva Steel Plant has 9000 workers on job, with peak of 11,000 seen by August," *Salt Lake Telegram,* May 28, 1943, 9.
13. "Completion of Geneva works predicted by end of year," *Salt Lake Telegram,* June 2, 1943, 6.
14. "Geneva Steel Co. to operate plant during war," *Pleasant Grove Review,* August 20, 1943, 1.
15. "Production of pig iron begun Monday," *Springville Herald,* January 6, 1944, 1.
16. "World War II ends," *Topaz Times,* August 15, 1945, 1.
17. "Geneva will run until sale okeh," *Salt Lake Telegram,* October 8, 1945, 1.
18. "Geneva to cease steel production," *Salt Lake Telegram,* October 10, 1945, 1.
19. "Geneva to quit producing steel," *Salt Lake Telegram,* October 11, 1945, 6.
20. "RFC asks for sealed bids on sale, lease of Geneva," *Salt Lake Telegram,* December 14, 1945, 1.
21. "Truman says U.S. may run Geneva," *Salt Lake Telegram,* January 24, 1946, 1.
22. "Huge ore supply included in Geneva contract," *Salt Lake Telegram,* February 2, 1946, 1.
23. "Geneva bidding extended another 30 days," *Salt Lake Telegram,* March 1, 1946, 1.
24. "7 firms submit bids on Geneva," *Salt Lake Telegram,* May 1, 1946, 1.
25. "Geneva sale to U.S. Steel wins approval of WWA," *Salt Lake Telegram,* May 23, 1946, 1.
26. "Utah leaders open fire on CF&I plan," *Salt Lake Telegram,* May 23, 1946, 1.
27. "House debates sale of Geneva plant," *Salt Lake Telegram,* May 27, 1946, 1.
28. "Sale of Geneva plant to U.S. Steel okehed," *Salt Lake Telegram,* June 18, 1946, 1.
29. "Geneva prepares for production," *Salt Lake Telegram,* June 21, 1946, 1.
30. "Geneva sets operation of 2 blast furnaces," *Salt Lake Telegram,* June 28, 1946, 1.
31. *International Directory of Company Histories,* vol. 7, s.v. "Geneva Steel" (Chicago: St. James Press, 1993), 193–195. The sixty-percent claim is widely reported but no reliable source documenting the figure has been located.
32. Leaone Foutz Carson, "Geneva, then and now," *Mountain West Magazine,* November 1976.
33. "California Furnaces," http://www.steel-photo.org/tag/kaiser-steel (accessed July 11, 2018).
34. "'Pig farm to pig iron in 8 months' tells story of Kaiser mill," *Salt Lake Telegram,* December 30, 1942, 2.
35. "Kaiser plant contracts for million tons local iron ore," *Iron County Record,* November 2, 1944, 1.
36. "Development at iron mines expected to start in near future," *Iron County Record,* September 10, 1942, 1.
37. "Ore shipments to Kaiser plant to start in near future," *Iron County Record,* November 23, 1944, 1.
38. "Local iron mine development expected soon," *Iron County Record,* July 23, 1942, 2.
39. "Development at iron mines expected to start in near future," *Iron County Record,* September 10, 1942, 1.
40. W. E. Young, *Iron Deposits, Iron County, Utah* (Washington, D.C.: U.S. Dept. of Interior, Bureau of Mines, 1947).

41. Kenneth L. Cook, *Magnetic Surveys in the Iron Springs District, Iron County, Utah,* (Washington, D.C.: U.S. Dept. of Interior, Bureau of Mines, 1950).

42. "Engineer figures iron ore reserve," *Salt Lake Telegram,* December 20, 1946, 20.

43. "Iron County to benefit by Provo plant expansion," *Iron County Record,* October 23, 1941, 1.

44. "Local iron mine development expected soon," *Iron County Record,* July 23, 1942, 2.

45. "Geneva plant ready to blow in blast furnace, advancing date of Utah's first steel production," *Salt Lake Telegram,* January 3, 1944, 11.

46. MacDonald, *Magnet,* 27, 29.

47. Bullock, *Iron Deposits of Utah,* 51.

48. "Huge ore supply included in Geneva contract," *Salt Lake Telegram,* February 2, 1946, 1.

49. "Engineer figures iron ore reserve," *Salt Lake Telegram,* December 20, 1946, 20.

50. "Sale of Geneva Steel mill assures continued activity at County mines," *Iron County Record,* June 20, 1946, 1.

51. Bullock, *Iron Deposits of Utah,* 45.

52. H. L. Humphries, *Recollections of H. L. Humphries* (Cedar City, Utah: Privately Published, 1960?).

53. Bullock, *Iron Deposits of Utah,* 36.

54. Bullock, *Iron Deposits of Utah,* 44.

56. "Kaiser plant contracts for million tons local iron ore," *Iron County Record,* November 2, 1944, 1; "Ore shipments to Kaiser plant to start in near future," *Iron County Record,* November 23, 1944, 1.

57. Jim Smith, *Recollections of Iron Springs* (Cedar City, Utah: Privately published, 1960), 1944–45.

58. Bullock, *Iron Deposits of Utah,* 49; J. H. Mackin, *Geology and Iron Ore Deposits of the Granite Mountain Area, Iron County, Utah,* Miscellaneous Field Studies Map MF-14 (U.S. Geological Survey, 1954).

59. Bullock, *Iron Deposits of Utah,* 49.

60. Bullock, *Iron Deposits of Utah,* 41.

61. W. E. Young, *Iron Deposits, Iron County, Utah*

62. "Iron County scrap salvage reaches 1,286,000 lbs.," *Iron County Record,* October 15, 1942, 1.

63. "Fire destroys buildings on Iron Mountain," *Iron County Record,* June 29, 1944, 1.

Chapter 9

1. MacDonald, *Magnet,* 35.

2. "Steel strike affects 100 local workers," *Iron County Record,* January 24, 1946, 1; "Picket lines withdrawn at Ironton plant," *Sunday Herald,* February 17, 1946, 1.

3. "Kaiser to produce pig iron in Utah," *Salt Lake Telegram,* December 18, 1947, 1.

4. "Kaiser-Frazer blast furnace at Ironton begins operations," *Springville Herald,* May 20, 1948, 1.

5. "Kaiser to produce pig iron in Utah," *Salt Lake Telegram,* December 18, 1947, 1; "Kaiser–Frazer blast furnace at Ironton begins operations," *Springville Herald,* May 20, 1948, 1.

6. "Magazine reports Utah ore is going to Japan," *Springville Herald,* September 2, 1948, 8.

7. "Kaiser-Frazer to spend $350,000 on improvements," *Springville Herald,* July 29, 1948, 1.

Notes

8. "Furnace closing will idle 300," *Salt Lake Telegram*, May 19, 1949, 19; "Parts firm closes Ironton furnace," *Salt Lake Telegram*, May 25, 1949, 8.

9. Robert W. Bernick, "U.S. Corp. leases Ironton plant," *Salt Lake Telegram*, May 9, 1951, 1.

10. "Geneva operating Ironton ovens," *Salt Lake Telegram*, October 30, 1951, 22.

11. "Geneva operating Ironton ovens," *Salt Lake Telegram*, October 30, 1951, 22.

12. "Geneva plant to close at midnight," *Salt Lake Telegram*, April 8, 1952, 1; "1500 workers go back to Geneva jobs," *Salt Lake Telegram*, May 5, 1952, 15.

13. "Geneva's furnaces back in operation," *Salt Lake Telegram*, July 28, 1952, 13.

14. "Ironton plant to close January 4," *Springville Herald*, December 31, 1953, 1.

15. "Ironton plant to close January 4," *Springville Herald*, December 31, 1953, 1.

16. "No. one blast furnace at Ironton plant to resume operation," *American Fork Citizen*, October 7, 1954, 6.

17. "Blast furnace goes into operation after relining," *American Fork Citizen*, March 24, 1955, 3.

18. "Ironton number one to receive deserved overhaul," *Iron County Record*, June 6, 1957, 12.

19. "Steel plant call-back December 1 means merrier Christmas for many," *Springville Herald*, November 20, 1958, 1.

20. "Geneva hits war time operation pace," *Springville Herald*, February 27, 1947, 7.

21. "A 'warm' welcome for industry?" *Salt Lake Telegram*, February 15, 1947, 4.

22. "Utah Supreme Court upsets unwise attempt to tax–gouge an industry," *Salt Lake Telegram*, August 3, 1949, 10.

23. "Slap in the face for the West," *Salt Lake Telegram*, February 28, 1947, 6.

24. "Fontana 'ruin' seen in cut for Geneva," *Salt Lake Telegram*, March 12, 1947, 5.

25. "Reduced rates from Geneva may begin April 1," *Springville Herald*, March 20, 1947, 1.

26. "Dragerton, Utah, purchased by Geneva Steel for $1,553,000 from War Assets Board," *Iron County Record*, March 6, 1947, 4.

27. "Secretary of State sees doubled Utah output," *Salt Lake Telegram*, October 16, 1947, 17.

28. "Geneva employees number over 6000," *Springville Herald*, September 23, 1948, 9.

29. "3600 miners join Utah coal walkout," *Salt Lake Telegram*, March 16, 1948, 1.

30. "Prolonged coal strike is national calamity," *Salt Lake Telegram*, April 19, 1948, 12.

31. "Production record established at Geneva in March," *Springville Herald*, April 14, 1949, 4.

32. Clarence D. Williams, "Effects from steel strike still being felt in Utah," *Salt Lake Telegram*, November 18, 1949, 32.

33. "Speaker says jump in Utah taxes will hurt industry," *Salt Lake Telegram*, December 13, 1949, 17.

34. "Geneva announces expansion plans," *Salt Lake Telegram*, December 28, 1950, 1.

35. "Geneva output continues at peak rate," *Salt Lake Telegram*, January 19, 1951, 28.

36. "Geneva plant to close at midnight," *Salt Lake Telegram*, April 8, 1952, 1.

37. "1500 workers go back to Geneva jobs," *Salt Lake Telegram*, May 5, 1952, 15.

38. "Geneva's furnaces back in operation," *Salt Lake Telegram*, July 28, 1952, 13.

39. "Steel strike 'depression' is noted in most businesses," *Springville Herald*, July 5, 1956, 1; "Steel strike tension felt on local scene," *Iron County Record*, July 5, 1956, 1; "Steel workers return to jobs in local operations," *Iron County Record*, August 9, 1956, 1.

40. "Steel plant call-back December 1 means merrier Christmas for many," *Springville Herald*, November 20, 1958, 1.

41. "Steel strike hits business, many family incomes here," *Springville Herald*, July 16, 1959, 1; "Steel strike, lay-offs puts 420 in unemployed ranks in Cedar and Milford," *Iron County Record*, July 16, 1959, 1; "Steel strike ends," *Springville Herald*, November 12, 1959, 1; "Workers return to jobs in Cedar City area," *Iron County Record*, November 12, 1959, 1; "Smoking stacks signal return of steel workers," *Orem-Geneva Times*, November 12, 1959, 1.

42. *Encyclopedia Britannica Online*, s.v. "Taft-Hartley Act," https://www.britannica.com (Accessed December 1, 2018).

43. "Coal cleaning plant sets starting date," *Springville Herald*, February 20, 1958, 5.

44. "Geneva Steel-Columbia-Geneva Steel Company," April 6, 2018, http://utahrails.net/industries/geneva–steel.php (accessed July 11, 2018).

45. "Fontana 'ruin' seen in cut for Geneva," *Salt Lake Telegram*, March 12, 1947, 5.

46. Clarence R. Lohrey, "Coke plant and blast furnace expansion at Fontana," *Iron and Steel Engineer*, July 1, 1954.

47. "Railroad head predicts Utah era of progress," *Salt Lake Telegram*, August 20, 1946, 18.

48. "Cold weather closes Southern Utah mines," *Salt Lake Telegram*, February 15, 1949, 24.

49. "UP lays new track to iron mine area," *Iron County Record*, August 31, 1950, 3.

50. "Utah iron ores shipped east," *Salt Lake Telegram*, September 19, 1950, 24.

51. "Mining takes place as leading industry of Iron County," *Iron County Record*, November 15, 1945, 1.

52. Robert W. W Bernick, "Ore lack may limit West's steel output," *Salt Lake Telegram*, November 5, 1948, 36.

53. MacDonald, *Magnet*, 32.

54. "Commission OK's Columbia iron mine levy," *Iron County Record*, August 19, 1948, 7.

55. "Commission OK's Columbia iron mine levy," *Iron County Record*, August 19, 1948, 7.

56. "Columbia Iron, city in joint meeting to discuss tax problem," *Iron County Record*, July 7, 1949, 1.

57. "Iron County wins tax case brought by Columbia Mining Co. for $37,000," *Iron County Record*, January 26, 1950, 1.

58. "Mine tax bill drafted by County Attorney," *Iron County Record*, January 13, 1949, 6.

59. "Tax Commission changes iron ore tax valuation," *Iron County Record*, May 17, 1951, 1.

60. "Columbia Iron Mines contribute over one-half million in taxes," *Iron County Record*, December 6, 1956, 1.

61. "Steel strike affects 100 local workers," *Iron County Record*, January 24, 1946, 1; "Picket lines withdrawn at Ironton plant," *Sunday Herald*, February 17, 1946, 1.

62. "3600 miners join Utah coal walkout," *Salt Lake Telegram*, March 16, 1948, 1; "Prolonged coal strike is national calamity," *Salt Lake Telegram*, April 19, 1948, 12.

63. "Nation steel strike idles 165 workers at local iron mines; no pickets will be posted at plant here," *Iron County Record*, November 6, 1949, 1; "Columbia resumes operations as strike ends," *Iron County Record*, November 17, 1949, 1.

64. Clarence D. Williams, "Effects from steel strike still being felt in Utah," *Salt Lake Telegram*, November 18, 1949, 32.

Notes

65. "Geneva plant to close at midnight," *Salt Lake Telegram,* April 8, 1952, 1; "Geneva's furnaces back in operation," *Salt Lake Telegram,* July 28, 1952, 13.
66. "Steel strike felt in Cedar; Utah Construction idled," *Iron County Record,* June 26, 1952, 2.
67. "Geneva's furnaces back in operation," *Salt Lake Telegram,* July 28, 1952, 13.
68. "Steel strike tension felt on local scene," *Iron County Record,* July 5, 1956, 1; "Steel workers return to jobs in local operations," *Iron County Record,* August 9, 1956, 1.
69. "Cold weather closes Southern Utah mines," *Salt Lake Telegram,* February 15, 1949, 24.
70. MacDonald, *Magnet,* 32.
71. MacDonald, *Magnet,* 33.
72. "Geneva Steel Co. to build $400,000 power plant," *Iron County Record,* March 18, 1948, 1; "First iron mine power unit begins operation," *Iron County Record,* September 2, 1948, 6.
73. "Southern Utah eyes spring power dearth," *Salt Lake Telegram,* February 7, 1949, 13.
74. "Power company gets official okeh on $2,000,000 expansion program for Cedar and nearby area," *Iron County Record,* February 15, 1951, 1.
75. Smith, *Recollections of Iron Springs, 1946–50.*
76. "Construction to begin on Columbia mine office building," *Iron County Record,* March 7, 1957, 1; "Columbia Iron Mining Company schedules new office open house," *Iron County Record,* January 30, 1958, 1.
77. "G. D. MacDonald to receive U mining award," *Iron County Record,* May 22, 1958, 10.
78. "Operating Department: Iron Mountain & Desert Mound Mines," *Columbia Iron Mining Company Handbook* (USA: Columbia Iron Mining Company, 1959).
79. "Columbia Mines receives three of Country's largest ore trucks," *Iron County Record,* March 10, 1949, 1.
80. "Stripping contract signed by Utah Construction Co.," *Iron County Record,* April 16, 1953, 1.
81. Bullock, *Iron Deposits of Utah,* 44.
82. "Relaxing at the wheel," *Iron County Record,* May 21, 1953, 13.
83. "Now in operation at Utah Construction mine," *Iron County Record,* September 3, 1953, 1.
84. "Relaxing at the wheel," *Iron County Record,* May 21, 1953, 13.
85. "Now in operation at Utah Construction mine," *Iron County Record,* September 3, 1953, 1.
86. "Local mining operation cutback explained, true figures revealed," *Iron County Record,* March 4, 1954, 1.
87. "Utah Construction to lay off 70 man force," *Iron County Record,* December 30, 1954, 1.
88. *Mineral Potential Report for the Cedar City Planning Area, CCPA Final Report* (Salt Lake City, Utah: Utah Geological Survey, June 2012), 65, 66.
89. "Negotiations brought to conclusion on land transfer deal," *Iron County Record,* March 22, 1956, 2.
90. Kenneth L. Cook, *Magnetic Surveys in the Iron Springs District, Iron County, Utah, 4586,* (Washington D.C.: Bureau of Mines Report of Investigations, 1950), 45.
91. Cook, *Magnetic Surveys in the Iron Springs District,* 46.
92. Cook, *Magnetic Surveys in the Iron Springs District,* 45; Bullock, *Iron Deposits of Utah,* 53.
93. Bullock, *Iron Deposits of Utah,* 45, 59.

94. Bullock, *Iron Deposits of Utah*, 53.
95. Bullock, *Iron Deposits of Utah*, 49.
96. Bullock, *Iron Deposits of Utah*, 53.
97. Bullock, *Iron Deposits of Utah*, 53.
98. Bullock, *Iron Deposits of Utah*, 53.
99. Bullock, *Iron Deposits of Utah*, 53.
100. Bullock, *Iron Deposits of Utah*, 54.
101. Bullock, *Iron Deposits of Utah*, 54.
102. Bullock, *Iron Deposits of Utah*, 49.
103. "Utah Construction opens new Desert Mound work," *Iron County Record*, September 1, 1949, 2.
104. "Utah Construction awarded new Geneva contract," *Iron County Record*, May 4, 1950, 11.
105. Hugh W. Stephens, *The Texas City Disaster, 1947* (Austin: University of Texas Press, 1997), 100.
106. "Blasting with prilled ammonium nitrate at Desert Mound," *Columbia Iron Mining Company Handbook*.
107. Bullock, *Iron Deposits of Utah*, 51.
108. "Local mining operation cutback explained, true figures revealed," *Iron County Record*, March 4, 1954, 1.
109. "Utah Construction Co. to resume CF&I ore shipments," *Iron County Record*, April 22, 1954, 1.
110. Bullock, *Iron Deposits of Utah*, 45, 59.
111. Bullock, *Iron Deposits of Utah*, 51.
112. Bullock, *Iron Deposits of Utah*, 45, 59.
113. Bullock, *Iron Deposits of Utah*, 51.
114. "Japan gets ore shipments from Iron Mountain," *Iron County Record*, July 29, 1948, 5; "Magazine reports Utah ore is going to Japan," *Springville Herald*, September 2, 1948, 8.
115. "Utah iron ores shipped east," *Salt Lake Telegram*, September 19, 1950, 24.
116. "Utah Construction to move office out to Iron Springs," *Iron County Record*, August 9, 1951, 14.
117. Smith, *Recollections of Iron Springs*, 1944–45.
118. "Mine employees yield to strike call," *Iron County Record*, April 2, 1959, 1.
119. MacDonald, *Magnet*, 58.
120. "Mining takes place as leading industry of Iron County," *Iron County Record*, November 15, 1945, 1.
121. "Iron Mt. accident seriously hurts Cedar City driver," *Iron County Record*, August 5, 1948, 12.
122. "Truck driver fatally injured in collision at Cedar City," *Salt Lake Telegram*, March 1, 1950, 11.
123. "Parowan man killed in railroad accident," *Iron County Record*, September 14, 1950, 1.
124. "Young driver dies in wreck at local iron mines," *Iron County Record*, November 8, 1951, 1.
125. "Marlo Topham loses three fingers in conveyor belt," *Iron County Record*, February 7, 1952, 11.
126. "Battery explosion starts $200,000 fire at Desert Mound warehouse," *Iron County Record*, October 9, 1953, 1.
127. "Enterprise resident dies from industrial mishap," *Iron County Record*, November 30, 1958, 9.

Notes

128. "Utah Construction honored by American Legion," *Iron County Record*, November 26, 1953, 1.

129. "Desert Mound tips Columbia miners to take city softball championship," *Iron County Record*, August 21, 1952, 6.

Chapter 10

1. "U.S. Steel abandons coke ovens at Ironton plant," *Springville Herald*, January 3, 1963, 1.

2. "Ironton steel plant on stand-by basis," *Springville Herald*, October 20, 1960, 1; "Improving business conditions noted in newsletter," *Iron County Record*, April 13, 1961, 2.

3. "Ironton coke ovens placed on new stand-by process," *Springville Herald*, August 3, 1961, 1.

4. "Ironton closes; Lay-off [ ] 100 men," *Springville Herald*, March 22, 1962, 1.

5. "History of Ironton plant recalled as property transfer to BYU accomplished last week," *Pleasant Grove Review*, September 26, 1968, 7.

6. "Geneva Steel's No. 2 furnace begins operating," *Pleasant Grove Review*, July 21, 1960, 3.

7. "Prospective order sparks hopes for more work at steel plants," *Springville Herald*, August 25, 1960, 1.

8. "Market decline results in mining layoffs," *Iron County Record*, November 24, 1960, 1; "Increased orders for Western steel mills expected in 1961 says Columbia-Geneva head," *Pleasant Grove Review*, December 29, 1960, 1; "Geneva Steel to start two more furnaces in production," *Pleasant Grove Review*, March 2, 1961, 1.

9. Steel contract let through efforts of Senator," *Iron County Record*, August 2, 1962, 8.

10. "Bennett protests aid to build steel plants in foreign lands," *Springville Herald*, October 11, 1962, 3.

11. "Work begins on overhaul of Geneva furnace," *Springville Herald*, August 1, 1963, 1; "Blast furnace back on duty at Geneva mill," *Springville Herald*, March 19, 1964, 1, 2.

12. "Geneva Steel calls for cutback," *Pleasant Grove Review*, October 14, 1965, 1.

13. "Geneva Steel announces plans to call back 100–200 workers," *Springville Herald*, December 23, 1965, 1.

14. "Blast furnace down for repair," *Springville Herald*, March 2, 1967, 1.

15. "Geneva Works cleanest integrated steel plant in country, says report," *Springville Herald*, February 9, 1967, 1.

16. "Air pollution control devices explained at March UCWLC meet," *Springville Herald*, March 14, 1968, 4.

17. Dave [---], "Air pollution," *Utah Daily Chronicle*, January 6, 1970, 2.

18. "Burton calls for foreign steel market change, help economy," *Pleasant Grove Review*, October 29, 1970, 1.

19. "EPA should give go-ahead to Geneva clean air plan," *Iron County Record*, September 27, 1979, 2.

20. "Hatch, McKay to testify Friday at Geneva hearing," *Pleasant Grove Review*, December 6, 1979, 1.

21. "Rumors of steel plant closure unfounded so far," *Orem-Geneva Times*, July 10, 1980, 1; "Senator Orrin Hatch among speakers at Geneva job rally," *Springville Herald*, August 7, 1980, 10; "Geneva, EPA reach agreement on water, air pollution issues," *Springville Herald*, October 30, 1980, 9.

23. Nancy Rivera Brooks, "The long winter of Kaiser Steel," *Los Angeles Times*, February 9, 1987.

Iron Mining & Manufacturing

24. "Mining outlook good," *Iron County Record*, June 9, 1960, 2.
25. "Mine operations curtailed by industry lag," *Iron County Record*, August 25, 1960, 1.
26. "Market decline results in mining layoffs," *Iron County Record*, November 24, 1960, 1.
27. "Economic view emphasizes iron ore output," *Iron County Record*, January 18, 1962, 1.
28. "Iron County's assessed valuation," *Iron County Record*, August 5, 1965, 9.
29. "Iron County's assessed valuation continues down since 1958 peak," *Iron County Record*, August 5, 1965, 9.
30. "Utah's iron ore industry: Overview," February 20, 2016, http://utahrails.net/mining/iron-mountain.php (accessed July 11, 2018).
31. "Mining-railroads-utilities share major tax burden of Iron County," *Iron County Record*, November 27, 1975, 1.
32. "Mining-railroads-utilities share major tax burden of Iron County," *Iron County Record*, November 27, 1975, 1.
33. "Mining-railroads-utilities share major tax burden of Iron County," *Iron County Record*, November 27, 1975, 1.
34. LaMar G. Jensen (Iron County Treasurer) to York F. Jones, December 23, 1975, York Jones papers.
35. "Iron mining continues base for Iron County," *Iron County Record*, December 7, 1978, 1.
36. "Utah International large tax payer," *Iron County Record*, December 6, 1979, 13.
37. "Iron mining continues base for Iron County," *Iron County Record*, December 7, 1978, 1.
38. "EPA standards discussed at public hearing," *Iron County Record*, December 14, 1978, 21.
39. "Jones testifies at air hearing," *Iron County Record*, September 13, 1979, 1.
40. "County valuation dropped five million by strike," *Iron County Record*, July 21, 1960, 1.
41. "Open pit miners vote to strike," *Iron County Record*, August 15, 1963, 1.
42. "Striking unions accept negotiations offer," *Iron County Record*, August 29, 1963, 1.
43. "Labor walkout Monday idles Utah Construction in county," *Iron County Record*, April 6, 1967, 1.
44. "Painful steel strike averted; workmen's wages increased," *Springville Herald*, August 1, 1968, 1.
45. "150 workers at Utah Construction go out on strike," *Iron County Record*, October 14, 1971, 1.
46. "U.S. mediator hears both sides in 30-day old strike," *Iron County Record*, November 25, 1971, 1.
47. "Steelworkers approve agreement calling for binding arbitration," *Orem-Geneva Times*, April 12, 1973, 1.
48. "Strike deadlock halts activities at Utah International," *Iron County Record*, August 22, 1974, 1.
49. "Negotiations stymied in 28 day strike Cedar City mine," *Iron County Record*, September 12, 1974, 1.
50. "Iron miners return to work approve three year contract," *Iron County Record*, October 3, 1974, 1.
51. "Mining outlook good," *Iron County Record*, June 9, 1960, 2.
52. MacDonald, *Magnet*, 48.

53. "Atlantic City, Wyoming," https://www.legendsofamerica.com/wy-atlanticcity.html (accessed July 11, 2018).
54. MacDonald, *Magnet*, 43.
55. MacDonald, *Magnet*, 43.
56. "Mine transferees find construction exciting," *Iron County Record*, September 15, 1960, 9.
57. MacDonald, *Magnet*, 48.
58. Bullock, *Iron Deposits of Utah*, 57.
59. "Columbia Iron Mining Co. merges with U.S. Steel," *Iron County Record*, December 12, 1963, 1.
60. "G. D. MacDonald to head USS Western Ore Operations," *Iron County Record*, December 31, 1964, 1.
61. "United States Steel Gives Cedar City Office Building to College," *Iron County Record*, March 23, 1967, 1.
62. "U.S. Steel cuts back force at Cedar mine," *Iron County Record*, October 5, 1972, 1.
63. "U.S. Steel cuts back operation at Desert Mound," *Iron County Record*, August 21, 1975, 1.
64. "U.S. Steel shuts down operation: iron mines close," *Iron County Record*, September 25, 1975, 1.
65. "Iron mines resume operation," *Iron County Record*, January 6, 1977, 1.
66. Utah Construction and Mining Company, "Iron Mountain (Blowout Mining and Iron Mountain Plant)," *Annual Report, Cedar City Operations* (Cedar City, Utah: Utah Construction and Mining Company, 1967).
67. Utah Construction and Mining Company, "Comstock and Queen of the West," *Annual Report* (1967).
68. "10,000,000th ton of iron ore shipped to CF&I," *Iron County Record*, October 12, 1972, 1.
69. "Iron mines cutback workers," *Iron County Record*, November 3, 1977, 1.
70. Bullock, *Iron Deposits of Utah*, 49.
71. Bullock, *Iron Deposits of Utah*, 54.
72. Bullock, *Iron Deposits of Utah*, 48.
73. Bullock, *Iron Deposits of Utah*, 54.
74. Bullock, *Iron Deposits of Utah*, 54.
75. Bullock, *Iron Deposits of Utah*, 48.
76. Bullock, *Iron Deposits of Utah*, 55.
77. Bullock, *Iron Deposits of Utah*, 51.
78. Bullock, *Iron Deposits of Utah*, 48.
79. Bullock, *Iron Deposits of Utah*, 44.
80. Bullock, *Iron Deposits of Utah*, 48.
81. Bullock, *Iron Deposits of Utah*, 45.
82. Bullock, *Iron Deposits of Utah*, 48.
83. Bullock, *Iron Deposits of Utah*, 54.
84. Bullock, *Iron Deposits of Utah*, 48.
85. Bullock, *Iron Deposits of Utah*, 41.
86. Bullock, *Iron Deposits of Utah*, 41.
87. Bullock, *Iron Deposits of Utah*, 54.
88. "Utah Construction invests in future of County with beneficiation plant," *Iron County Record*, May 11, 1961, 9.
89. Bullock, *Iron Deposits of Utah*, 57.

90. Bullock, *Iron Deposits of Utah*, 55.
91. Bullock, *Iron Deposits of Utah*, 55.
92. "New equipment," *Iron County Record*, February 24, 1966, 14.
93. York F. Jones, "Alluvium Plant," *Iron Mining in Southern Utah* (Cedar City, Utah: Privately published, 1974).
94. Utah Construction and Mining Company, "Alluvium Operation," *Annual Report* (1967).
95. Bullock, *Iron Deposits of Utah*, 57.
96. Bullock, *Iron Deposits of Utah*, 48.
97. Bullock, *Iron Deposits of Utah*, 49.
98. Utah Construction and Mining Company, "Iron Springs Operation," *Annual Report* (1967).
99. "York F. Jones assumes management of Utah International here," *Iron County Record*, November 14, 1974, 1.
100. York F. Jones, "Iron Springs Operation," *Iron Mining in Southern Utah*.
101. "Iron mining company employees injured," *Iron County Record*, August 25, 1960, 2.

Chapter 11
1. "Hatch voices concern at Geneva," *Pleasant Grove Review*, September 9, 1982, 10.
2. Cynthia Piechowiak, "Steel industry bids 1982 good riddance," United Press International archives, January 1, 1983, https://upi.com/3966571.
3. "US Steel drops a bomb on Geneva," *Pleasant Grove Review*, December 18, 1985, 2.
4. "Garn reacts to Geneva report," *Pleasant Grove Review*, December 24, 1985, 3.
5. "Congressional hearing to be held concerning Geneva Steel," *Pleasant Grove Review*, January 22, 1986, 14.
6. "Rally spotlights local steel workers' plight," *Pleasant Grove Review*, June 25, 1986, 1.
7. John Leopard, *Duluth, Missabe & Iron Range Railway* (St. Paul, Minn.: MBI, 2005), 105. US Steel merged the railroads in 1937 and the book discusses in depth the company's challenges.
8. "Steelworkers await word as Geneva begins shutdown," *Orem-Geneva Times*, July 30, 1986, 1.
9. "Strike or lockout, union faces tough battle," *Pleasant Grove Review*, August 6, 1986, 2.
10. "Geneva Steelworkers hopeful but confused about work future," *Orem-Geneva Times*, February 4, 1987, 1.
11. "USX squelches hope for Geneva," *Orem-Geneva Times*, April 8, 1987, 1.
12. "Steel workers hope suit will force plant reopening," *Pleasant Grove Review*, April 15, 1987, 1.
13. Scamehorn, *Mill and Mine*, 186–189.
14. Nancy Rivera Brooks, "The long winter of Kaiser Steel," *Los Angeles Times*, February 9, 1987.
15. "Desert Mound mine operation to close," *Iron County Record*, February 7, 1980, 1.
16. "Mine contract assured for UI," *Iron County Record*, March 13, 1980, 1.
17. York F. Jones, "Mine shutting down," transcript of January 26, 1981 radio announcement, York Jones papers, SUU.
18. "Utah's iron ore industry: UP's Iron Mountain branch," February 20, 2016, http://utahrails.net/mining/iron–mountain.php (accessed July 11, 2018).
19. "Mine top tax payer," *Iron County Record*, December 11, 1980, 15.
20. "Mine to close; workers laid off," *Iron County Record*, January 29, 1981, 4.

21. "U.S. Steel mining operations set to resume soon in county," *Iron County Record,* January 28, 1982, 1.

22. "Ore mining operations face immediate shutdown," *Iron County Record,* May 20, 1982, 1.

23. "Plant shuts down," *Iron County Record,* October 21, 1982, 19.

24. Ernie Over, "Remaining iron ore deposits at former Atlantic City mine site getting second look, Commissioners told," *County 10* (blog), June 26, 2012, http://4dc.b85.mwp.accessdomain.com/2012/06/26/remaining-iron-ore-deposits-former-atlantic-city-mine-site-getting-second-look-commissioners-told (accessed November 28, 2018).

25. J. David Ingles, "Arrivals & Departures," *Trains,* January 1984, 13; Peter H. Kuck, "Iron Ore," *Minerals Yearbook 1985* (Washington: United States Geological Survey, 1985), 521.

26. "Comstock Iron Mine," http://www.gilbertdevelopment.com/projects-3 (accessed July 11, 2018).

27. "Smith dies in mine accident," *Iron County Record,* May 15, 1980, 1.

Chapter 12

1. "USX squelches hope for Geneva," *Orem-Geneva Times,* April 8, 1987, 1.

2. "Report pessimistic about chances for Geneva opening," *Pleasant Grove Review,* April 29, 1987, 1.

3. "Report pessimistic about chances for Geneva opening," *Pleasant Grove Review,* April 29, 1987, 1.

4. Cathe Owens, "BMT deal brews high hopes for slumbering steel giant," *Orem-Geneva Times,* July 1, 1987, 1.

5. "The Geneva Steel Plant," *Orem-Geneva Times,* July 29, 1987, 4.

6. Cathe Owens, "BMT receives one last chance to negotiate Geneva purchase," *Orem-Geneva Times,* August 12, 1987, 5.

7. "BM&T must prove its ability to turn profit at Geneva," *Pleasant Grove Review,* September 2, 1987, 2.

8. Jeanne Thayne, "Don't be alarmed, folks, worst is over at Geneva," *Orem-Geneva Times,* September 16, 1987, 1.

9. Jeanne Thayne, "Geneva celebrates as first load of steel leaves plant," *Orem-Geneva Times,* October 7, 1987, 1.

10. "Second furnace opens," *Orem-Geneva Times,* November 18, 1987, 1.

11. "Geneva smoke irks neighbors but officials claim compliance," *Orem-Geneva Times,* March 9, 1988, 1.

12. "Challenge shows growing discontent with Geneva," *Pleasant Grove Review,* February 1, 1989, 2.

13. "Joe Cannon comes clean," *Orem-Geneva Times,* December 13, 1989, 3.

14. Clyde E. Weeks, "Geneva cuts ribbon on two new Q-BOP furnaces," *Orem-Geneva Times,* September 18, 1991, 1, 14.

15. "Layoffs announced at Geneva Steel," *Orem-Geneva Times,* March 6, 1997, 11.

16. "Geneva Steel seeks chapter 11 protection," *Orem-Geneva Times,* February 3, 1999, 1.

17. "After months of losses, steel maker shuts down," *Park Record,* November 17, 2001, 25.

18. Scarlett M. Barger, "Geneva attempts to regroup," *Orem-Geneva Times,* February 6, 2002, 1, 3.

19. Scarlett M. Barger, "Bush passes tariff on imported steel; steelworkers to examine," *Orem-Geneva Times*, March 6, 2002, 1.
20. "Knockout punch for Geneva?," *Salt Lake Tribune*, October 24, 2002, 1.
21. Scarlett M. Barger, "Geneva fighting to the end," *Orem-Geneva Times*, October 10, 2002, 1.
22. "More employees laid off after Geneva denied lender," *Orem-Geneva Times*, November 27, 2002, 3.
23. "Chinese mill negotiating for Geneva assets," *Skillings Mining Review*, December 31, 2003.
24. Dave Anderton, "Geneva gets Chinese offer," *Deseret Morning News*, December 31, 2003.
25. Marin Decker, "Razing of old mill signals 'end of era'," *Deseret Morning News*, July 1, 2005.
26. Dave Anderton, "Sandy-based firm closes on Geneva property," *Deseret Morning News*, December 24, 2005.
27. "Development Taking Shape on Old Geneva Steel Site," *KSL.com*, May 5, 2014, https://www.ksl.com/article/30081911/development-taking-shape-on-old-geneva-steel-site (November 24, 2018)
28. Benjamin Wood, "UVU acquires 125 acres in Vineyard to expand campus," *Deseret News*, June 19, 2014.
29. "Comstock Iron Mine," in "Three Cedar Solar Projects," Gilbert Development, date unknown, http://www.gilbertdevelopment.com/projects-3 (accessed July 11, 2018).
30. G. D. MacDonald III, *The Magnet* (Cedar City, Utah: Privately Published, 1990), 56; "Geneva leases two iron ore mines in Utah," *Springville Herald*, October 5, 1988.
31. "Geneva divisions announced," *Orem-Geneva Times*, August 31, 1988/
32. "Utah Mining Industry may strike it rich in '89," *Deseret News*, January 29, 1989.
33. "Utah firm's suit says USX broke pact to sell iron ore," *Deseret News*, August 17, 1989.
34. William B. Wray, and Alysen D. Pedersen, *Iron Resources and Geology of the Property of Palladon Ventures Ltd.* (Salt Lake City: Utah Geological Association, 2009), 154–155.
35. *Annual Iron Ore Production: The Iron Springs District, 1849–2014* (Salt Lake City: Utah Geological Survey, 2015). The table is an internal document maintained by UGS, received from Ken Krahulec in 2018.
36. "Companies will buy iron ore properties," *Deseret News*, January 28, 2005.
37. "Palladon Ventures Ltd. Announces Agreement to Purchase Utah Iron Ore Property," January 27, 2005, http://www.marketwired.com/press-release/palladon-ventures-ltd-announces-agreement-to-purchase-utah-iron-ore-property-529491.htm (accessed November 24, 2018).
38. Steven Oberbeck, "S. Utah steel mill proposed," *Salt Lake Tribune*, February 9, 2005.
39. "Company outlines mining-venture plans," *Park Record*, April 30, 2005.
40. "Palladon mobilizes mining contractor to mine Comstock iron ore," July 14, 2005, https://www.thefreelibrary.com/Palladon+Mobilizes+Mining+Contractor+to+Mine+Comstock+Iron+Ore.-a0134032813 (accessed November 24, 2018).
40. "Palladon Mobilizes Mining Contractor to Mine Comstock Iron Ore," July 14, 2005, https://www.thefreelibrary.com/Palladon+Mobilizes+Mining+Contractor+to+Mine+Comstock+Iron+Ore.-a0134032813 (accessed November 24, 2018).
41. "Palladon Ventures Ltd. Announces Restructured Financing and Iron Project Transactions," August 26, 2005,

Notes

https://investorshub.advfn.com/boards/read_msg.aspx?message_id=7518129 (accessed November 23, 2018).

42. "Iron Springs-Pinto District," *2004 Summary of Mineral Activity in Utah* (Salt Lake City, Utah: Utah Geological Survey, 2004), 14.

43. "Palladon Announces First Iron Sale," August 28, 2006, http://www.marketwired.com/press-release/palladon-ventures-ltd-tsx-venture-pll-609668.htm (accessed November 23, 2018).

44. US Dept. of Transportation, Surface Transportation Board, "Michael R. Root and Albany & Eastern Railroad Company-Continuance in Control Exemption-Iron Bull Railroad Company LLC," September 14, 2006, 71 Fed.Reg. 54337, STB Finance Docket n. 34898, document E6-15239.

45. "Palladon Sells Interest in Western Utah Copper Project," January 9, 2007, http://www.marketwired.com/press-release/palladon-ventures-ltd-tsx-venture-pll-630009.htm (accessed November 23, 2018).

46. "Corriente Master Fund, L.P. announces acquisition of common shares and warrants of Palladon Ventures Ltd.," May 22, 2007, https://www.newswire.ca/news-releases/corriente-master-fund-lp-announces-acquisition-of-common-shares-and-warrants-of-palladon-ventures-ltd-533785471.html (accessed November 23, 2018).

47. "Utah's iron ore industry-Palladon Iron Company," http://utahrails.net/mining/iron-mountain.php (accessed July 11, 2018).

48. "Palladon Unveils Iron Bull Mining and Milling to the Iron County Community, July 4, 2007," July 4, 2007, http://www.marketwired.com/press-release/Palladon-Unveils-Iron-Bull-Mining-and-Milling-to-the-Iron-County-Community-TSX-VENTURE-PLL-748296.htm (accessed November 23, 2018).

49. Wray and Pedersen, *Iron Resources and Geology of the Property of Palladon Ventures Ltd.*, 155; "Palladon Iron Company," January 27, 2005, http://utahrails.net/mining/iron-mountain.php (accessed July 11, 2018); "Utah Southern Railroad (of 2006)," February 19, 2016, http://utahrails.net/utahrails/us-rr-2006.php (accessed July 11, 2018).

50. "Palladon Ventures Ltd.: Mining Begins Today at Iron Mountain," September 11, 2008, http://www.marketwired.com/press-release/palladon-ventures-ltd-tsx-venture-pll-899140.htm (accessed November 24, 2018).

51. "Utah Southern Railroad Company, LLC-Change in Operators Exemption-Iron Bull Railroad Company, LLC," document 2011-28642, 76 Fed.Reg. 68523.

52. Wray and Pedersen, *Iron Resources and Geology of the Property of Palladon Ventures Ltd.*, 155.

53. "Palladon Ventures Provides Corporate Update," February 4, 2009, http://www.24hgold.com/english/news-company-gold-silver-provides-corporate-update.aspx?articleid=372672 (accessed November 24, 2018).

54. "Clarification of the March 27, 2009 Press Release," March 31, 2009, http://www.marketwired.com/press-release/Clarification-March-27-2009-Press-Release-Entitled-Palladon-Iron-Corporation-Completes-TSX-VENTURE-PLL-968779.htm (accessed November 24, 2018).

55. "CML Metals Corporation," February 20, 2016, http://utahrails.net/mining/iron-mountain.php (accessed July 11, 2018).

56. "Palladon Ventures Ltd.: Luxor Capital Partners, LP, Realizes on Debt and Takes Majority Ownership Interest in Palladon Iron Corp.," March 16, 2010, http://www.marketwired.com/press-release/Palladon-Ventures-Ltd-Luxor-Capital-Partners-LP-Realizes-on-Debt-Takes-Majority-Ownership-TSX-VENTURE-PLL-1132762.htm.

57. "CML Metals Corporation," March 16, 2010, http://utahrails.net/mining/iron-mountain.php (accessed November 25, 2018).

58. "Palladon shareholder update regarding CML offtake agreement," June 11, 1010, http://www.marketwired.com/press-release/Palladon-Shareholder-Update-Regarding-CML-Offtake-Agreement-TSX-VENTURE-PLL-1275013.htm (accessed November 23, 2018).

59. "Utah Company Reopening Iron Mine Near Cedar City," *Deseret News*, July 11, 2010.

60. "Utah Southern Railroad Company, LLC-Change in Operators Exemption-Iron Bull Railroad Company, LLC," 76 Fed.Reg. 68523, document 2011-28642.

61. "Utah Southern Railroad," February 19, 2016, http://utahrails.net/utahrails/us-rr-2006.php (accessed July 11, 2018); "CML Railroad," September 6, 2015, http://utahrails.net/utahrails/cmlr.php (accessed July 11, 2018).

62. "Palladon Ventures-CML update," October 23, 2013, https://finance.yahoo.com/news/palladon-ventures-cml-113411877.html (accessed July 11, 2018).

63. "CML Mines suspend production, layoff more than 100 workers," *Spectrum (Cedar City, Utah)*, October 17, 2014.

64. *Annual Iron Ore Production,* table.

65. "Palladon Ventures-Sale of CML Metals," April 6, 2015, https://www.marketwatch.com/press-release/palladon-ventures-sale-of-cml-metals-2015-04-06-13173213 (accessed November 23, 2018).

66. "Palladon Ventures: Update," *Yahoo*, May 27, 2015, https://finance.yahoo.com/news/palladon-ventures-204359959.html (accessed July 11, 2018).

67. "CML Presentation, 12 October 2015," https://prezi.com/wcjbl7npjomj/cml-presentation/ (accessed November 24, 2018).

68. "Comstock Iron Mine," in "Three Cedar Solar Projects," posting date unknown, http://www.gilbertdevelopment.com/projects-3 (accessed July 11, 2018).

69. "Comstock Mining Area," July 11, 2018, https://www.google.com/maps/@37.6443339,-113.3606947,3706m/data=!3m1!1e3.

70. Bullock, *Iron Deposits of Utah*, 45.

71. Bullock, *Iron Deposits of Utah*, 51.

72. Bullock, *Iron Deposits of Utah*, 54.

73. Bullock, *Iron Deposits of Utah*, 44.

74. Bullock, *Iron Deposits of Utah*, 48.

75. Bullock, *Iron Deposits of Utah*, 45.

76. Bullock, *Iron Deposits of Utah*, 51.

77. Pat Reavy, "Cedar City man killed in mining accident," *Deseret News*, February 3, 2014.

Chapter 13

1. Data reported in the table is drawn from *Annual Iron Ore Production: The Iron Springs District, 1849–2014* (Salt Lake City: Utah Geological and Mineralogical Survey, 2015); Kenneth C. Bullock, *Iron Deposits of Utah*, vol. 88 (Salt Lake City: Utah Geological and Mineralogical Survey, 1970), 39–55.

Works Cited

Newspapers

(Utah newspapers dating as early as 1850 and as late as 2018 are publicly available in digital form on the Utah Digital Newspapers site, https://digitalnewspapers.org.)

American Fork Citizen (American Fork Utah)
Beaver County News (Beaver, Utah)
County 10 (blog; Riverton, Wyoming)
Deseret Evening News (Salt Lake City, Utah)
Deseret Morning News (Salt Lake City, Utah)
Deseret News (Salt Lake City, Utah)
Frontier Guardian (Council Bluffs, Iowa)
Iron County News (Cedar City, Utah)
Iron County Record (Cedar City, Utah)
Leadville Democrat (Leadville, Colorado)
Los Angeles Times (Los Angeles, California)
Manti Messenger (Manti, Utah)
Milford News (Milford, Utah)
Millennial Star (Liverpool, England)
Mt. Pleasant Pyramid (Mt. Pleasant, Utah)
Ogden Herald (Ogden, Utah)
Ogden Junction (Ogden, Utah)
Ogden Standard-Examiner (Ogden, Utah)
Orem-Geneva Times (Orem-Geneva, Utah)
Park Record (Park City, Utah)
Parowan Times (Parowan, Utah)
Pleasant Grove Review (Pleasant Grove, Utah)
Salt Lake Herald
Salt Lake Mining Review
Salt Lake Telegram
Salt Lake Tribune
Skillings Mining Review
Southern Utonian (Beaver, Utah)
Spectrum (St. George, Utah)
Springville Herald (Springville, Utah)
Sunday Herald (Provo, Utah)
Topaz Times (Topaz, Utah)
Utah Daily Chronicle (University of Utah)
Utah Enquirer (Provo, Utah)
Washington County News (St. George, Utah)

Books, articles, and reports

Annual Iron Ore Production: The Iron Springs District, 1849–2014. Salt Lake City: Utah Geological and Survey, 2015. [This table is an internal document maintained by UGS, received directly from the office.]

Arrington, Leonard J. *Great Basin Kingdom: An Economic History of the Latter-day Saints, 1830–1900*. 1959; Urbana: University of Illinois Press, 2004.

_____. "Planning an Iron Industry for Utah, 1851–1858." *Huntington Library Quarterly* 21, no.3 (May 1958): 237–260.

_____. "Iron Manufacturing in Southern Utah in the Early 1880's: The Iron Manufacturing Company of Utah." *Bulletin of the Business Historical Society* 25, no.3 (September 1951): 149–168.

Articles of Association of Zion's Central Board of Trade. Salt Lake City: Publisher unknown, 1879 (https://archive.org/details/articlesofassoci00zion).

Axelrod, Alan. *Encyclopedia of World War II*. 2 vol. Ed. Jack A. Kingston. New York: Infobase Publishing, 2007.

Bolton, Herbert E. "Pageant in the Wilderness: The Story of the Escalante Expedition to the Interior Basin, 1776." *Utah Historical Quarterly* 18 (1950).

Bourne, John M. *The Iron Mission and the Deseret Iron Works, 1851–1858*. Salt Lake City: Utah State Historical Society, 1972.

Bullock, Kenneth C. *Iron Deposits of Utah*, vol. 88. Salt Lake City, Utah: Utah Geological and Mineralogical Survey, 1970.

Butler, B. S., G. F. Loughlin, V. C. Heikes, et al. *The Ore Deposits of Utah*. USGS Professional paper 111. Washington: Government Printing Office, 1920.

Columbia Iron Mining Company Handbook (USA: Columbia Iron Mining Company, 1959).

Cook, Kenneth L. *Magnetic Surveys in the Iron Springs District, Iron County, Utah*. Washington D.C.: U.S. Dept. of Interior, Bureau of Mines, 1950.

Dary, David. *The Oregon Trail: An American Saga* (New York: Alfred A. Knopf, 2004).

Dean, John W. *Warren Harding* (New York: Henry Holt & Co., 2004).

Encyclopedia Britannica Online. https://www.britannica.com.

Hafen, LeRoy R., and Ann W. *Journals of the Forty-Niners-Salt Lake to Los Angeles*. Lincoln: University of Nebraska Press, 1954.

_____. *The Old Spanish Trail: Santa Fé to Los Angeles*. Lincoln Nebraska: University of Nebraska Press, 1954.

Ingles, J. David. "Arrivals & Departures," *Trains*, January 1984.

Jenson, Andrew. *The Latter-day Saint Biographical Encyclopedia*. 4 vol. Salt Lake City, Utah: Andrew Jenson History Company, 1901–1936.

Jones, York F. *Iron Mining in Southern Utah*. Cedar City, Utah: Privately published, 1974.

Journal of Discourses. 27 vol. Liverpool and London: F.D. Richards and Daniel H. Wells, 1852–1886.

Minerals Yearbook 1985. Washington: United States Geological Survey, 1985.

Lee, John D. "Journal of the Iron County Mission, John D. Lee, Clerk." Ed., Gustive O. Larson. *Utah Historical Quarterly* 20, n. 1 (January 1952): 109–112.

Leith, C. K., and E. C. Harder. *The Iron Ores of the Iron Springs District, Southern Utah*. USGS Bulletin 338. Washington: Government Printing Office, 1908.

Leopard, John. *Duluth, Missabe & Iron Range Railway*. St. Paul, Minn.: MBI, 2005.

Lindley, Curtis H. *A Treatise on the American Law Relating to Mines and Mineral Lands*. San Francisco: Bancroft-Whitney, 1914.

MacDonald, G. D., III. *The Magnet: Iron Ore in Iron County, Utah*. Cedar City, Utah: Privately published, 1990.

Works Cited

Mackin, J. H. *Geology and Iron Ore Deposits of the Granite Mountain Area, Iron County, Utah*. Miscellaneous Field Studies Map MF-14. U.S. Geological Survey, 1954.

———. "Some Structural Features of the Intrusions in the Iron Springs District," in *Geology of the Utah-Colorado Salt Dome Region, with an Emphasis on Gypsum Valley, Colorado*. Ed., William L. Stokes. Salt Lake City: Utah Geological Society, 1948.

The Making, Shaping and Treating of Steel. 7 ed. Pittsburg: United States Steel Corporation, 1957.

"Mineral Lands and Regulations in General, 30 USCA Ch. 2.

Mineral Potential Report for the Cedar City Planning Area-CCPA Final Report. Salt Lake City: Utah Geological Survey, June 2012.

Mining Claims and Sites on Federal Land. P-048. Washington: US Bureau of Land Management, 2011.

Murray, Robert K. *The Harding Era, 1921–1923: Warren G. Harding and His Administration* (Minneapolis: University of Minnesota Press, 1969.

"Origin of our mining laws." *Mining & Scientific Press*. September 23, 1905.

Pratt, Addison. *The Journals of Addison Pratt*. Ed. S. George Ellsworth. Salt Lake City: University of Utah Press, 1990.

Scamehorn, H. Lee. *Mill and Mine: The CF&I in the Twentieth Century*. Lincoln: University of Nebraska Press, 1992.

Seegmiller, Janet Burton. *A History of Iron County*. Salt Lake City: Utah State Historical Society, 1998.

Shirts, Morris A., and Kathryn A. Shirts. *A Trial Furnace: Southern Utah's Iron Mission*. Provo, Utah: Brigham Young University Press, 2001.

Smith, Pauline Udall. *Captain Jefferson Hunt of the Mormon Battalion*. Salt Lake City: Nicholas G. Morgan, Sr., Foundation, 1958.

Sontag, William H. *The National Park Service: The First 75 Years*. Philadelphia: Eastern National Park & Monument Association, 1990.

"The State of Deseret." *Utah State Historical Quarterly* 8, n.2–4 (1940).

Stephens, Hugh W. *The Texas City Disaster, 1947* (Austin, Texas: University of Texas Press, 1997).

U.S. Dept. of Transportation. Surface Transportation Board. "Michael R. Root and Albany & Eastern Railroad Company-Continuance in Control Exemption-Iron Bull Railroad Company LLC." September 14, 2006. 71 Fed.Reg. 54337, STB Finance Docket n. 34898, document E6-15239.

———. "Utah Southern Railroad Company, LLC-Change in Operators Exemption-Iron Bull Railroad Company, LLC." 76 Fed.Reg. 68523, document 2011-28642.

Urie, John. *Early History of Cedar City and Vicinity*. Cedar City, Utah: Privately published, 1959.

Utah Construction and Mining Company. *Annual Report, Cedar City Operations*. Cedar City, Utah: Utah Construction and Mining Co., 1967.

Van Cott, John W. *Utah Place Names*. Salt Lake City: University of Utah Press, 1990.

Vélez de Escalante, Silvestre. *The Dominguez and Escalante Journal: Their Expedition through Colorado, Utah, Arizona, and New Mexico in 1776*, Ed.. Ted J. Warner. Salt Lake City: University of Utah Press, 1995.

Whitley, Colleen, and Janet Burton Seegmiller. *From the Ground Up: The History of Mining in Utah*. Logan: Utah State University Press, 2006.

Wimmer, Ryan Elwood. *The Walker War Reconsidered*. Provo, Utah: Brigham Young University Press, 2010.

2004 Summary of Mineral Activity in Utah. Salt Lake City, Utah: Utah Geological Survey, 2004.

Wray, William B., and Alysen D. Pedersen. *Iron Resources and Geology of the Property of Palladon Ventures Ltd.* Salt Lake City: Utah Geological Association, 2009.

Young, W. E. *Iron Deposits, Iron County, Utah.* U.S. Dept. of Interior, Bureau of Mines, 1947.

Zabriskie, George O., and Dorothy Louise Robinson. "U.S. Census for Utah, 1851." *Utah Genealogical and Historical Magazine* 29 (April, July 1938).

"Zion's Central Board of Trade." *Tullidge's Quarterly Magazine* 1 (1881): 420.

York F. Jones papers. Box 4. Matheson Special Collections, Southern Utah Univ.

Census report for Iron County, 1872.

Columbia Iron Mining Company Handbook. USA: Columbia Iron Mining Company, 1959.

"Columbia Geneva Steel Division History." *United States Steel Corporation Handbook.* USA: United States Steel Corporation, 1959.

"Golden rail laying, Cedar City, Utah," *The Union Pacific Magazine,* October 1923.

Humphries, H. L. *Recollections of H. L. Humphries.* Cedar City, Utah: Privately Published, 1960?

Jones, York F. *Iron Mining in Southern Utah.* Cedar City, Utah: Privately Published, 1974.

Smith, Jim. *Recollections of Iron Springs.* Cedar City, Utah: Privately Published, 1960.

Union Pacific Railroad. *Internal correspondence to all traffic representatives and local agents* (1923).

Utah Construction and Mining Company. *Annual Report, Cedar City Operations.* Cedar City, Utah: Utah Construction and Mining Company, 1967.

"Chemical analysis of various samples of iron ore, iron and limestone excavated near the site of the old Iron Works and near the Red Hill in Cedar City arranged by York F. Jones in 1976."

"Chemical analysis of two samples of iron ore from Old Iron Town arranged for by York F. Jones in May 1978."

Chemistry & photomicrographs of Cedar City iron samples. The samples were collected by York F. Jones and the analysis made by Jack Mervis and Keith Hanks, presumably in 1976.

LaMar G. Jensen to York F. Jones, December 23, 1975.

"Railroad's new branch line from Lund to Cedar City, Utah," *Union Pacific Railroad internal correspondence to all traffic representatives and local agents*, March 15, 1923, File No. C-5101-3905-2.

"Summary of furnace charges made between January 2 and January 8, 1855."

"Mine shutting down," Transcript of radio announcement made January 26, 1981 with quotes from York F. Jones.

Unpublished material

Articles of Incorporation Record Books, Utah State Archives. Incorporation papers were filed with the county clerks until 1962. Those records are now accessible through the Research Center of the Utah Division of State History, Salt Lake City, Utah.

Bourne, John M. "The Iron Mission and the Deseret Iron Works, 1851–1858." Utah Division of State History.

Brown, John. Journal. Church History Library (the journal is duplicated in the *Journal History of the Church*, vol. 28 (1850)).

Harrison, Richard. Diary, typescript. L. Tom Perry Special Collections, Brigham Young University.

"History of Parowan Stake 1851–1980." Church History Library.

Haight, Isaac C. Journal (typescript). Matheson Special Collections, Southern Utah University.

Journal History of the Church of Jesus Christ of Latter-day Saints, 1830–2008. Church History Library.
Letterbook. 4 (1858). Brigham Young papers. Church History Library.
Lunt, Henry. Diary (typescript). L. Tom Perry Special Collections, Brigham Young University.
Minute Book of Deseret Iron Works. Church History Library.
Palmer, William R. "First Forts at Cedar City, as told by David Bulloch." William R. Palmer collection. Matheson Special Collections, Southern Utah University.
George A. Smith Journal. Church History Library.
United States. General Land Office. Mining district by-laws, 1872–1909 (Series 3651, box 1, folder 26 (reel 1)). Iron Springs Mining District. Utah Division of Archives and Records Service.

Internet Sources

Discrete digital resources in the form of links, subpages, citations, and HTML transcripts are cited individually by URL in the respective notes and are not listed separately in the bibliography.

Index

A and B deposit, 234, 264, 294, 302, 306, 421
Abel, I. W., 345
Aberdeen (townsite), 186
Adams and Smith, 81, 83, 84, 112
Adams Claim, 119, 150, 152, 274
Adams, David B., 23, 32, 35, 44, 51, 52, 76; G. W., 245; Harry M., 180, 181; L. G., 318; R. David, 51, 114, 183; Robert, 27
adit, 141, 186, 189, 196, 205
adobe, 26, 40, 114, 116
Adshead, William, 35
Ahlstrom, Charles, 73; Charles, II, 73; David, 73; Magnus, 151; Sarah, 73
air furnace, 32, 34, 37, 73, 78, 95, 100, 102
Alexander, Anna, 72
Alexander, Gennmith, 72
alluvium plant, 316, 362, 363, 364, 365, 418
Ammon (Ute Indian), 37
Anderson Development, 399, 400
Andrews, Jens, 72
Andrus, James, 125
April Fool deposit, 264, 356, 359, 422
Armenta, Gilbert, 72
Armijo, Antonio, 8
Armstrong deposit, 150, 152, 273, 274, 322, 421
army troops, 55, 60, 61, 64, 67, 136, 143, 176, 261
Arrapin (Arapeen, Ute Indian), 37
Arthur, Christopher, 39, 56, 60
Arthur, Christopher Jones, 60
Arthur, Joshua, 55
Ash Creek, 7, 10
Ashby, George F., 286
Ashton deposit, 356, 359, 421
Ashworth, John, 35
Atlantic City Mine (Wyo.), 330, 332, 337, 346, 347, 349, 387, 400
Augason, O. S., 321
Backman, Gus P., 256, 258
Baker, Simon, 15
Bangerter, Norman H., 394, 395
Banks, Sister, 23
Barber, E. N., 249
Barlocker, Ernest, 189
Barnett, Donald F., 388
Barnson, C. Q., 222
Bartholomew, Calvin, 393
Barton, Eunice, 326
Barton, Max, 317
basal siltstone, 1–3, 251, 357

Basic Manufacturing and Technologies of Utah, 15, 388, 389, 392, 393, 401
Basinger, W. S., 172
Bateman, Father, 24
Batt, Scott, 355
Batt, Wells, 317
Bauer, Keith, 325
Bayer, Charles P., 181
Beaver (Utah), 7, 9, 13, 50, 52, 60, 76, 86, 88, 100, 104, 108, 123, 124, 125, 130, 131, 148, 224, 288, 289
Beddo, William, 35
Behling, Mike, 393
bell, 46–48, 163
beneficiation, 288, 305, 316, 337, 359, 360, 361, 362, 366, 381, 382, 418
Bennett, Wallace F., 332, 333, 335
Benson, Arch, 325
Benson, Eugene, 73
Benson, Ezra T., 13, 28
Bentley, Richard, 81
Bergstrom, J. W. Dr., 222
Bernhart, Martie Hubble, 380
Bernhisel, J.M., 12
Berry, Jack, 324
Betenson, Francis C., 339
Black Hawk deposit, 228, 232–244, 264, 265, 294, 302, 307, 421
Black Magnetic deposit, 95, 147, 148, 364
Black Rock #1 claim, 178, 364–365
Black, L. F., 279
Blackbird deposit, 356, 358
Bladen, Thomas, 23, 27, 35, 50, 51, 52
Blair, George E., 71; Jedediah, 71; Lenora, 71; Martha, 71; Preston A., 73; Sarah, 71; Seth M., 23, 68–71, 73–76; Texana, 71; Vilate, 71; Wilmirth, 71
Blake, of New Haven, 120
blast furnace, 18–21, 24–27, 29, 31, 33, 42–81, 93, 95, 99, 100, 102–104, 108–120, 126, 141, 144, 147, 154, 158–162, 165–167, 171, 183, 195, 200, 201, 203, 213, 226–239, 243–244, 248–255, 259–262, 264–265, 269, 276–280, 285–288, 295, 298, 304, 316, 323, 330–334, 337, 345, 349–352, 362, 364, 369, 379–380, 385, 391–392, 398
blasting, 141, 192, 195, 207, 238, 240, 241, 243, 297, 313, 314, 317, 351, 355, 367, 370, 407, 414, 418
Blood, Tracy, 318

Index

blower, 42, 52, 63, 68, 73, 74, 85, 99, 116
Blowout deposit, 82, 93, 95, 99, 118–120, 124, 138, 139, 146–152, 155, 226, 232, 234, 239, 241, 262, 266–268, 285, 301, 302, 311, 314, 317, 323, 349–354, 416, 417, 421
Blue Jay, 364, 365
Boden, Roscoe, 258
Bog ore, 34, 41, 45, 46, 62, 63
Bogus, 53–55
Bollow, Jack, 385, 386, 393
Bonzo, Bert, 317
Bosh, 20, 40, 41, 44, 53, 54, 57, 100, 116, 334
Bosnell, James, 35
Boswell, R., 318
Botchford, D. H., 162
Bowman, George, 269
Boyns, Karl, 269
Brabant, M. de, 180
Bradford, Charles, 375
Branard, J. F., 15
Brannan, Samuel, 8
breccia, 234, 268, 272, 273, 306, 309–311, 315, 324, 356–358
Brigham Young University, 227, 331, 375, 377, 393
Brown, Carroll, 292
Brown, Thomas D., 44, 45
Bryan, Stan, 317
Buhl, F. W., 143–145
Bulloch, David, 172, 181
Bullock, James, 36
Bullock, Thomas, 11
Burke deposit, 148, 232–235, 265, 294, 297, 299–303, 305–307, 315, 421
Burns, Bud, 372
Burns, Ronald D., 322
Burton, Laurence J., 335
Burton, R. T., 106
Bush, George W., 396
California Road, 8
Call, Anson, 14
Calumet deposit, 234, 264, 268, 416, 421
Campbell, Allen G., 86, 87, 98, 141, 143, 145, 146, 148, 233; Allen G. [Jr.], 148; Byron C., 148; Caroline Neil, 148; Robert L., 76
Cane, Albert, 212
cannon balls, 61, 67
Cannon, Abraham H., 98, 106–107
Cannon, George Q., 67, 98, 102, 105, 106
Cannon, Joseph A., 394, 395, 397–399, 401, 404
Carpenter, Dell, 223
Carpenter, George, 317
Carruthers, Matthew, 22, 25, 32, 37
Carter, Jimmie, 336
Cartwright, Thomas, 27, 35
cast iron, 22, 34, 61, 69, 74, 76, 126, 200, 213, 243
Center Creek (Parowan, Utah), 10, 14, 15, 64

Cervi, Eugene, 258
CF&I Pit, 204, 208, 220, 311, 312
Chamberlain, Lawrence, 72
Chandler, Harry, 180
Chapman, Robert, 35
charcoal, 10, 19, 21–23, 32, 34, 36, 38, 41, 43–45, 48, 53, 55–59, 62, 63, 69, 80, 85, 94, 104, 109, 112, 116, 120, 288, 420
Chatterley, Joseph, 32, 35, 56
Chatterly, Catherine, 56
Cheeseman, Walker, 154
Chesapeake deposit, 147, 148, 401, 414, 416, 420
Childs, Jack, 329
Christensen, C. L., 81; Cliff, 220; Hal, 185, 187, 188, 190, 191, 208, 212, 214, 215, 218, 219, 223; O'dell, 329;
Christiansen, Neil, 329
Christine, Oliver, 198
Church of Jesus Christ of Latter-day Saints, 9, 10, 30, 33, 65, 67, 68, 69, 74, 81, 87, 93, 97, 105, 113, 135, 157, 176, 2768
Citizen's Coalition to Save Geneva, 336, 374
Clark, A., 317; LaMar, 329; Shauna, 412; Tom C., 259
Claron Formation, 2, 3, 224
Clews, Joseph, 35
Clive-Constitution deposit, 264, 356, 357, 358, 421
Clothier, Roy, 217, 219
Cloward, Dix, 329
CML, 408–416
CML Railroad, 408
Coal, 1, 10, 16, 17, 19–29, 31–34, 36–39, 41, 43–53, 55–59, 62–64, 68, 69, 73–75, 78, 80, 83, 85, 86, 88–90, 92, 94, 96, 98, 99, 102–113, 116, 118, 120, 124, 126, 127, 131, 134, 135, 141, 143–146, 148–150, 156–160, 162, 163, 167, 200–202, 208, 215, 224–227, 229, 238–240, 249, 250, 251, 253–256, 259, 260, 261, 276, 277, 278, 281–286, 288–290, 293, 332–334, 336, 373, 386, 388, 401, 404, 413, 417–419, 422
Coal Creek, 16, 17, 23, 24, 28, 31–34, 38, 39, 47, 51, 52, 63, 64, 68, 167, 225
coal washing, 110
coke, 19, 22, 23, 27, 31, 32, 40, 41, 42, 44, 45, 46, 51, 53–59, 62, 75, 85, 89–93, 95–97, 103, 104, 107, 108, 110, 112, 113, 120, 124, 144, 158–162, 199–201, 229, 238, 249, 251, 253–256, 259, 261, 276–280, 283–285, 331, 334, 385, 391, 392, 394, 417
Colorado Fuel and Iron Company, 117, 126, 132, 133, 138, 142, 145, 148, 149, 151, 152, 156, 239, 255, 256, 257, 258, 260, 277, 288, 291, 292, 296, 323, 337, 355, 374, 379, 383, 400

Index

Colorado River, 7, 8, 79, 80, 118, 130, 169, 181
Colton, Don B., 180
Columbia Iron Mining Company, 216, 221, 228, 231, 233, 235, 236, 238,243 244, 245, 250, 254, 264–266, 276, 277, 288, 290–297, 300, 305–307, 311, 313–315, 322, 323, 328, 337, 340, 343, 348
Columbia Steel Corporation, 159–167, 171, 182–185, 188, 193, 198–202, 226, 230, 232, 236–239, 242–244, 249, 252, 259
Columbia (Utah), 160, 162, 213, 249, 250
Comstock deposit, 126, 138, 150, 151, 235, 266, 285, 288, 294, 301, 319, 323, 324, 337, 339, 349, 352, 362, 366, 383, 385–387, 400–403, 406, 407, 409–412, 414–416, 420
Comstock mining area, 232, 287, 323, 367, 401, 406, 414, 415, 419
Comstock, W. H., 181
Connell, Arthur J., 328
Consolidated Western Pipe Plant, 284, 332
Contact claim, 204, 309
Cook, David, 35, 37; Henry S., 56; Kenneth L., 263; Melvin A., 314;
Cora deposit, 152, 274
Coray, George, 56, 60
Cousins, William, 35
Cradlebaugh, John, 60
Creed, Wigginton E., 164, 165
Croton, Fred, 156
Cullen, Matthew, 86, 141, 143, 145, 146, 233, 239
Cullen, Nellie T., 148
cupola, 21, 22, 29, 34
Curtis, Erastus, 35
Cutler, John, 411
Cutler, John C., 98, 99, 102, 110, 146, 147
Daken, William, 36
Dalley, Hillman, 344
Dalley, Parley, 181, 288
Dalton, John, 317
Dalton, Leonard, 325
Dame, William H., 14, 16, 17, 29, 56, 108
Davies, Howe & Co., 85
Davies, William, 35
Davis Dam, 266, 267, 321
Davis, Delmar, 317
Dear deposit, 232, 323, 324, 415, 420
Decker, Zacariah B., 15
Dee claim, 269, 271, 274
Dehm, Howard, Mrs., 326
DeMoss, E. C., 321
Denny, C. M., 234
Denver & Rio Grande Railroad, 108, 118, 127, 130, 131, 133, 159, 200, 392
Depression, 202, 203, 216, 217, 219, 220, 246, 375
Derrick, Royden G., 337
Deseret (State), 11, 13

Deseret Iron Company, 30–33, 35, 38, 39, 48, 55, 57, 60, 61, 65, 239
Deseret Iron Works, 40, 43, 51, 52
Desert Mound deposit, 7, 126–128, 138, 144–147, 150, 156, 202
Desert Mound mining area, 138, 144, 202, 204–221, 244, 287–288, 296–299, 307–321, 348–349, 356, 381–382, 385–386, 400, 417
Desert Mound Pit, 148, 199–227, 294, 418, 422
Diederich, Robert C., 355, 368
dolomite, 20, 254, 261, 279
Domínguez, Atanasio , 6, 8
Dragerton (Utah), 281, 284, 293
dragline, 363, 364, 366
drift, 137, 141, 142, 150, 151, 158, 189–192, 194, 197, 205, 307, 368
drill, 73, 133, 141, 142, 150, 151, 191, 192, 207, 216, 218, 232, 233, 240, 241, 242, 245, 264, 267, 268, 269, 297, 303, 305, 306, 309, 317, 327, 351, 353–356, 358, 363, 367–371, 398
Duffin, Donald, 245
Duluth deposit, 414, 416, 420
Duncan deposit, 68, 73, 82, 99, 141, 146, 147, 148, 150, 234, 262, 266, 285, 301, 311, 323, 350, 421
Duncan, Asenath, 72; Chapman, 68, 70, 71, 74, 76, 82; Don D., 72; Emma, 72; Homer, 70, 72–75, 78, 81; John, 72; John C., 72; Mary, 72; Rosanna, 71; Rosetta, 71; Taylor C., 71
Dusenberry, Warren N., 81, 86
Easton, Alex, 24
Easton, John, 35
Eccles, David, 130
Eclipse deposit, 184, 190, 194, 274, 356, 357, 367, 368, 421
Edmunds Act, 97, 113
Edwards, Claude, 185, 217; Claude, 328; David V., 71; Elizabeth A., 71; Elizabeth G., 71; Evan, 71; Josiah E., 71; Lawson H., 71; Ralph, 269
Eldredge, H. S., 96, 97
El Escalante Hotel, 183, 184, 198, 328
Ellsworth, Edmund, Jr., 73
Emerson, P. H., 86
Enke, Glen, 318
Enterprise (Utah), 6, 197, 198, 223, 295, 327
Entrada Sandstone formation, 1, 2, 268, 272, 306, 310, 352
Environmental Protection Agency, 330, 335, 342, 394, 395, 418
Erickson, Boyd C., 334, 391, 393
Erepamer, Tom, 361, 362
Escalante, Silvestre Vélez de, 6–8
Evans, William, 35
Excelsior deposit (Comstock), 146–147, 341, 401, 415–416, 431

477

Index

Excelsior deposit (Iron Springs), 151–152, 268–269, 290, 322
Excelsior Iron Mining Co., 269, 341
exploration, 8–10, 13
Eyck, George Ten, 223
Eyre, John, 79
Fairless, Benjamin, 66
Fairy Queen, 181
Farnsworth, Mary, 181
Felt, Roger, 329
Fenton, Robert, 288
Fife, Alice, 72; Carl, 289; Jane, 72; Jeanette, 72; Joseph M., 72; Mary H., 72; Otto, 289; Peter B., 72; Peter M., 72; Wilford, 288, 289
fire brick, 24, 37, 41, 63, 73, 76, 102, 203, 279, 417
fire clay, 21, 26, 28, 36, 44, 53, 73, 95, 99, 120
fire rock (or fire stone), 21, 73, 95, 99, 120
Flannigan, Wallace, 197
floods, 39, 47, 62, 417
Foot, Don, 404
forts, 37, 38, 40, 64
Fossdill, R. E., 149
Foster, George, 322
Foster, John, 288
Foster, Mark S., 380
foundries, 31, 32, 61, 67, 69, 91, 92, 110, 111, 117, 120, 121, 126, 166, 203
Frémont, John C., 8
Frisco (Utah), 86, 87, 117, 122, 123, 129
Frost, Burr, 23
frue, 204
gangue, 6, 20
Gardiner, Dale, 377
Gardner, George, 379
Garn, Jake, 376, 377, 392
Garner, Bill, 317
Garrett, Alma, 329
Gates, John W., 146
Geiger, Al F., 269, 299, 312, 328
Geiser, Rev., 198
General Mining Law of 1872, 136, 139, 140
Geneva Steel Company, 253, 254, 255, 259, 278, 289, 290, 291, 294, 300, 401; plant, 250, 255, 257, 258, 259, 265, 278, 279, 280, 282, 285, 287, 289, 375, 390, 401
geology, 1, 112, 224, 227, 263
Georgia deposit, 356, 358, 421
Gilbert Development Corporation, 383, 401–404, 408–410, 413–415
Gilbert, Armenta, 72
Gilbert, Dale, 409, 412
Gilbert, James, 72
Gilbert, Steve, 409
glory hole, 187, 188, 190–197, 205, 208, 232, 233, 239, 315, 367
Good, James W., 181
Grader, 90, 132, 169, 177, 266
Graff Coal Mine, 289

Granger, Representative, 259
Granite Mountain, 5–6, 139, 149, 184, 264, 268, 270, 272–274, 308–311, 315, 356–358
Grant, Glen, 317
Grant, Heber J., 165, 176, 181, 182
Grant, Ulysses S., 136
grasshoppers, 50, 62, 75, 417
Gray, C. R., 180
Great Western deposit, 148, 156, 184, 274, 324, 356–358, 421
Great Western Iron Company, 78, 79, 81–85, 98, 101, 103, 105, 111
Great Western Iron Mining and Manufacturing Company, 77
Green E. F., 156
Greenwood, William, 35
Gregorson, 125
Gregory, John, 35
Grese, Charles, 375
Griffiths, John, 35
Groesbeck, Nicholas, 78, 81
Gronning, Carlyle F., 349
Groosby, Nicholas, 85
Groves, Elisha H., 14, 17, 23
Groves, John, 35
Groves, Sister, 23
Grow, Robert J., 395
Gubler, Cal, 329
Haight, Isaac C., 39–42, 45, 46, 50, 52, 53, 55, 56, 59–61, 65
Halden, M. F., 321
Hale, Matthew, 181
Hall, Charles, 15
Hamic, J., 318
Hamic, W. L., 318
Hamilton, Anna, 73; James, 72; John, 72; John C., 72; John J., 72; Mary, 72; Mary S.J., 72; Robert, 72; Samuel, 72; Sarah E., 73; William, 72
Hamilton's Fort (Utah), 76, 139, 173
Hanchett, Lafayette, 176, 181
Hanks, Almira A., 72; Ebenezer, 68, 70, 71, 73–76, 78, 79, 94, 239; Ebenezer II, 72; Jane A., 72; Nancy L., 72; Sarah, 72
Harding, Florence., 173–175, 179–181
Harding, Warren G., 172–176, 179–182
Harriman, E. H., 179
Harris, Rex, 312, 321, 328
Harrison, Richard, 23, 25, 26, 27, 35, 56, 74
Hatch, Orrin, 336, 374, 377, 389, 392, 394
Hauck, W. A., 247, 256
Hayes, Murray O., 226
Heaton, Norman, 343
hematite, 3, 6, 18, 19, 89, 95, 99, 119, 120, 124, 155–157, 200, 224, 226, 234, 235, 265, 301, 306, 308, 309, 313, 357–359, 362, 368
Hewett, William, 35

Index

Heyborne, Bill, 219, 317, 319; Charles, 215; G., 317; Karl, 244; Sam, 185, 245
Hills, L. S., 96, 97
Hinckley, Ira N., 81
Hoffman, Ray, 197
Holden, L. E., 120
Hole, Oliver D., 328
Holyoak, William, 79
home industry, 67, 87–89, 105, 107, 111, 239
Homestake deposit, 150, 151, 266, 268, 364–366, 420
Homestake limestone, 1–3, 185, 189, 234, 235, 265, 266, 268, 272, 273, 301, 306, 308–310, 315, 323, 324, 356–359, 362, 366, 415, 416
Hooper, W. H., 92, 96, 97
Horn Silver Mine, 129
Horn, Joseph, 14
Howard, E. O., 154
Howe, Amos, 89, 96, 97
Hoyt, Will L., 291
Hulet, Clair, 288
Hulse, Benjamin, 35
Humpherys, H. L., 266, 319
Hunt, Jefferson, 8, 9, 14
Hunter, Dell, 217; George, 35; Joseph, 35; Sadie, 317; Washington, 310
Huntley, Chet, 379
Hurricane (Utah), 7, 171, 173, 261, 305
Husbands, C. H., 325
Husbands, Sam H., 255
Huser, Larry, 339
Hyde, Orson, 47
igneous deposition, 2
Irene deposit, 356, 357, 421
Iron City (Utah), 67–71, 73, 75, 77–85, 93–95, 99–104, 107–109, 111–114, 116–119, 121, 122, 124, 129, 130, 149, 158, 228, 242, 266
Iron Manufacturing Company of Utah, 98–101, 103, 104, 109, 110, 112, 115, 116, 119, 146
Iron Mission, 11, 16, 23, 45, 46, 65, 87
Iron Mountain and Utah Valley Railroad, 78
Iron Mountain mining area, 219, 231–233, 244, 265, 299, 307, 323
Iron Springs Formation, 1, 2, 273, 306, 310, 356–358
Iron Springs mining area, 184, 274, 294, 315, 316, 325, 356, 367
Iron Springs Mining District, 6, 93, 95, 126, 138–141, 148, 150, 159, 184, 199, 204, 234, 244, 263, 264, 289, 306, 361, 362, 415, 418, 420
Ironton plant, 161–164, 166, 182, 185, 187, 193, 199, 201–203, 209, 212, 228–231, 233, 238, 244, 248–250, 264, 277, 278, 288, 292, 294, 331, 332
James, James, 29, 32, 35, 37
Jeanette deposit, 72, 356, 358

Jennings Raynell, 327
Jennings, Allyson, 327
Jennings, Arvilla, 327
Jennings, Deborah, 327
Jennings, Jillynn, 327
Jennings, William, 92, 95–97, 106–108
Jensen, LaMar, 340, 341, 384
Johnson, Ken, 396
Jolley, Scott, 412
Jones Brothers, 357–359
Jones deposit, 140, 274, 356, 357, 421
Jones, Arthur, 288; Blaine, 355; Burt, 219; Elton, 322; Eva, 179; Evan, 2, 21, 94, 115, 140, 353, 381, 415; Gary, 321; John P., 61; John T., 143; Madge, 326; Randall L., 181, 183; Thomas, 35; Trenton, 324; Uriah T., 133, 134; Witcher, 145; York F., 45, 82, 217, 267, 270, 299, 301–303, 308, 310, 314, 317–319, 322, 339–343, 350–352, 355, 361, 363, 368, 369, 382–385, 404
Judd, Thomas, 125
Kaiser Steel plant, 153, 247, 249, 255, 256, 260–262, 264, 269, 270, 276–278, 285, 289, 290, 293, 316, 318–321, 336, 374, 379, 380
Kaiser, Bess, 261, 380
Kaiser, Henry J., 247, 255, 256, 261, 278, 281, 285, 287, 379, 380
Kanarraville (Utah), 7, 47
Karr, Ted, 317
Kay, John, 35
Keele, Alexander, 37
Keeley, Thomas F., 148
Keigley Quarry, 254, 349
Keir, Alexander, 35
Keller, Monte, 391
Kershaw, Robert, 35
Kershaw, Samuel, 35
kiln, 19, 56, 57, 94, 116
Kimball, Heber C., 47, 50
Kimberly, P. L., 143–145, 147, 149
King deposit, 204, 264, 308, 309, 311, 422
Kleinman, Lee, 385
Knight, Roice, 245, 288
Knoll, 17, 18
Ladd, W. E, 142, 149
Lambert, Tony, 326
Lambeth, Aubra, 324
Lambeth, Ellis, 324
Lamoreaux, J., 317
Larson, Ballard, 329
Last Chance deposit, 364, 366, 420
LaVerkin (Utah), 171, 173
Lawrence, James E., 325
Lee claims, 152, 269, 274
Lee, John D., 14, 15, 35
Lee, Samuel, 35
Leeder, Joe, 355
Leigh, George D., 320, 321
Leigh, Howard H., 245

479

Index

Lerch, Mr., 143
Lessing, Roy, 215
Letham, Robert, 35
Lewis, A. B., 148; Clayton S., 269, 317; Fischer, 72; James, 15, 43; John L., 282; Philip E., 15; Tarlton, 14; Walter, 154; William, 35
Leyson Coal Mine, 45
Liberty Pole, 17, 18
Lime Cap deposit, 233, 234, 294, 305, 421
limestone, 1–3, 19–20, 34, 45–46, 53–59, 99, 109, 157–162, 199, 210, 215, 224, 234–235, 243, 254, 261, 265, 279, 334, 439
Lindsay deposit, 148, 152, 270–273, 274, 320, 322, 418, 421
Lindsay Hill, 153, 179, 184, 269–272, 316, 321, 356
Lindsay, J. R., 87, 139
Linford, Coach, 223
Listen, Commodore Perry, 60
Little Allie deposit, 152, 273, 274, 421
Little Jim deposit, 204, 264, 308, 311
Little Mormon deposit, 148, 184, 274, 356, 421
Little Muddy (Cedar City, Utah), 14–16
Little Salt Lake, 9–13, 15, 16
Little, Feramorz, 96, 97
Little, James A., 14, 16, 17, 36
Littlefield, Lyman O., 47
loader, 193, 371, 402
locomotive, 174, 187, 188, 204, 205, 209, 211, 214, 215, 286, 418
lode claim, 136, 137, 139, 146, 147, 150, 152, 153, 239, 274, 324, 416
Lohrey, Clarence R., 285
Long, Ralph, 344, 360
Lund, Robert C., 130
Lund (Utah), 126, 130–132, 135, 145, 149–151, 154, 155, 159, 160, 167, 169, 170–172, 176–179, 182, 183, 188, 199, 203, 217, 262, 268, 287, 289, 325, 417
Lundmark, Dell, 318
Lunt, H. W., 181
Lunt, Henry, 15–17, 23, 24, 26–29, 33, 34, 36, 38, 46, 56, 60, 79, 92, 93, 101
Lunt, William, 179
Lyman, E. Ray, 291
Lyman, F. M., 160, 107
Mabey, Charles R., 163, 181
MacDonald, G. D., 242, 295, 296, 347, 349
Macfarlane Coal Mine, 289
MacFarlane, Will, 212
Machen, Thomas, 35
Macintosh, H. L., 300
Mackelprang, Mrs. Peter, 326
Mackin, J. Hoover, 273
magma intrusions, 2, 3, 5, 272
magnetite, 3, 6, 18, 19, 62, 81, 95, 119, 155–157, 224, 226, 234, 235, 243, 263, 265,
268, 273, 301, 306, 313, 317, 347, 357–359, 362–364, 370, 405, 408, 416
Maguire, Don, 155
Manderfield, J. H., 134
Mangum, Garth, 177
Marcus, Peter F., 388
Marron, Mr., 320
Marsden, L. N., 291
Marshall, John A., 153
Marysvale (Utah), 117, 123, 130–133, 147, 150, 152
Mason, Chris A., 269, 321, 328
Mason, Robert Wiley, 35
Mather, Stephen, 180
Mathesius, Walther, 255, 278, 283, 284, 289, 290
Matheson, Gordon, 212
Maw, Herbert B., 248, 256
Mayne, Ed, 377
McAllister, Prof., 174
McCahill deposit, 234, 264, 421
McCahill, Eugene, 141, 310
McCahill–Thompson deposit, 364
McCarty, Con, 197
McClure E. A. (Rusty), 329
McClure, Opal, 322
McCune, Wes, 289
McDonald, L. G., 245
McGarry deposit, 148, 156, 356, 357, 421
McGarry, Ernest C., 148
McGarry, James C., 145, 148
McGurrin, Edward, 148
McKay, Gunn, 336, 377
McKay, Thomas E., 163
McKee, E., 318
McMillian, Gordon, 209
Meeks, Priddy., 23
Melling, Don Ray, 329
Middlesworth, Caddie, 322
Middleton, Amy D., 72; Anna E., 72; Billy, 326; George, 72; Jane, 72; Jay, 326; John, 72; Mike, 326; F. W., Mrs., 326; Richard, 326; Roxey Mackelprang, 326; William H., 326
Milford (Utah), 7, 104, 107, 118, 122–125, 129–131, 178, 182, 222, 284, 367, 417
Miller, Bob, 317
Miller, Eddie, 316
Miller, George, 72
Miller, Ted, 317
Milner Corporation, 159, 199, 203, 204, 210, 217, 220, 232–234, 308, 309, 311
Milner Hill Anomaly, 306
Milner Pit, 204, 209, 214, 215, 217, 220
Milner, A. T., 159; Archibald C., 138, 199; Clarence E., 199, 205, 208; Jay S., 199; Stanley B. (Colonel), 145, 147, 148, 151, 199
mine cars, 186–188, 190, 206, 209, 214, 232
mineralogy, 6

480

Index

Minersville, 7, 123
Mitchell, James, 35
Mitchell, William C., 35
Monson, E. E., 258
Moreton, Arthur E., 305
Morgan, Bud, 185
Mormon Battalion, 8
Morris, Brent, 394; Durham, 245, 291, 325, 356; Elias, 35, 40, 41, 60, 106, 107; Leslie Adams, 221
Morrison-Knudson Construction Company, 231, 236, 250
Morse, W. A., 23
Mortenson, Deb, 317
Mosdell, Tom, 214
Mountain Lion deposit, 323, 324, 349, 362, 367, 383, 385–387, 400–406, 409, 410, 412, 414–416, 420
Mountain Meadows, 10, 55, 64
Mueller, Gadfrey, 322
Muir, Bob, 317
Muir, J., 35
Muir, Thomas, 35
Mullinder, Vince, 317
Murdock, John R., 107
Murdock, Abe, 247
Murie, Ernest, 305; Melvin, 305; Melvin, Mrs., 305; Rex, 305; Rex, Mrs., 305; William C., 305
Murphy, James D., 357, 358
Navajo Sandstone Formation, 1–3
Nelson Coal Mine, 289
Nelson, Arthur, 326; Bob, 319; F. U., 127, 128; H., 317; Harris, 329; John, 35
Neslen, C. C., 165, 181
Newberry, John S., 89, 90, 119, 120, 124
Nielson, Howard, 376, 377
Noble Furnace, 40, 44, 56, 63
Nostija, Wayne, 219
Nuttall, L. J., 107
O'Conner, E. S., 212, 219, 228, 238, 239
Old Iron Town, 19, 20, 68, 82, 181, 239, 242
Olds, Mel, 317
Olson, Antone, 195
Olson, Glen, 195
O'Mara, Tom, 269
Orton, Alger, 317
Oveson, Val, 392
Owens, Wayne, 377
Pace, W. B., 79
Pacheco, Bernardo de Miera, 6
Pacific States Cast Iron Pipe Co., 166, 199, 200, 203, 230, 243
Pack, Douglas, 351
Page, Deseret, 80
Page, Daniel, 145; Robert, 145
Palladon Ventures Ltd., 402–406, 408–411, 413, 414
Palmer, J. M., 358
Palmer, William R., 26, 105

Parks, Arthur, 35
patented mining claim, 86, 137–139, 141, 145–148, 150, 152, 199, 204, 226, 227, 239, 353, 405
Paterson, Andrew, 35
Patten, E. Billings (Bud), 392
Paulson, Boyd, 299, 302, 321, 328
Perkins, B. A., 156
Perkins, Dayle, 329
Perkins, Ralph, 321
Perry, George, 35
Peteetneet (Timpanogos Indian), 14, 37
Peterson, Pat, 325
Petit, Leon T., 213
Phibbs, W. R., 163, 237
Phillips, Oliver, 317
phosphorus, 20, 22, 25, 45, 62, 63, 210, 298, 299, 309, 357, 358
Pierce, 322
Pierpont, Thomas, 85, 89
pig iron, 8, 20–22, 28, 29, 34, 45, 49, 60, 62, 67, 69, 70, 79, 81, 85, 93, 95, 99, 100, 102–104, 111, 112, 120, 121, 126, 132, 141, 147, 158–162, 165–167, 183, 199–203, 229, 230, 243, 247–249, 253–255, 259, 260, 261, 277–279, 282, 283, 291, 332, 392
pilot train, 174, 178
Pinney, Archibald, 72; Charles, 71; Mariana, 72; Matilda, 72; Susan, 71
Pinto deposit, 232, 233, 235, 265, 294, 297, 301, 307, 421
Pinto Mining District, 6, 89, 93, 120, 138, 140, 141, 148, 149, 217, 263, 405
Pinto (Utah), 8, 47, 74, 77, 224
Pintura (Utah), 7
Pioche and Bullionville Railroad, 103, 104, 113
Pioche deposit, 148, 183, 184, 194–196, 269, 274, 297, 315, 316, 349, 356, 357, 368, 418, 421
Pioche (Nevada), 70, 80, 83, 85, 103, 104, 111, 117, 122, 326
Pirate Prince, 266
Plowman, E. G, 287
Pollock, James A., 152
Pollock, Sam, 151
polygamy, 97, 113, 417
portal, 185, 186, 188, 189
Pot Metal deposit, 147, 148, 268, 416, 420
Pratt, Addison, 9
Pratt, Parley P., 9–13, 16
Preston, William B., 73, 92, 106
Pretsch, Henry, 156
Price, Ed, 316
Price (Utah), 261, 290
Pritchard, Dee, 326
Prothero, Edward, 35
Prothero, Kenneth L., 381, 382
Pucill, William, 198

Index

Pugmire, Jonathan, 35, 39, 42, 56
Pyper, Justice, 84
Qingdao Iron & Steel Group, 397, 398
quartz monzonite porphyry, 268, 271–273, 308, 324, 357–359, 416
Queen of the West deposit, 324, 354, 420
Quinn, Mildred R., 358
Railroad depot (Cedar City Utah), 131, 134, 169, 172–174, 176–178, 184, 186, 273, 275, 422
railroads *see* individual railroad names
Rains, L. F., 160–162, 165
raise, 190–192, 194, 195, 198, 205
Rasmussen, Mondell, 319
Rattler Pit, 312
Raybuck, Robert W., 374
Red Cloud claim, 148
Red Creek (Paragonah, Utah), 9, 14, 123
Reese, Dave, 214
Rencher, Umpstead, 78, 81, 85
Rex deposit, 233, 234, 264, 294, 303–306, 315, 323, 330, 402, 405, 411, 421
Rhoades, George, 317
Rich, Charles C., 9
Richards, Franklin D., 30–32, 36, 38, 39, 41, 60
Richie, Anna, 71; Elisabeth, 71; Rachel, 71; Robert, 71; Robert, 71; Sarah A, 71
Riddle, A. M., 258
Rivera, Juan Maria de, 8
Robb, Jack, 321
Robb, LeGrande, 316
Robertson, Richard S., 100, 103, 108
Robinson, Chet, 316;
Robinson, F. W., 172;
Robinson, Richard S., 74, 75
Roderick, David M., 336
Rodman, Admiral, 176
Rollins, C. A., 317
Rollo, Alex H., 201, 239, 241, 245
Rollo, Noel, 322
Roosevelt, Franklin D., 247
Roots Blower and Engine, 73, 74, 99
Ross, Bro., 26
Roundy, Emil, 288
Rowland, Job, 35
Rowland, Thomas, 35
Rutledge, R. H., 181
Ryan, Dennis, 233
salamander (bear), 20, 21, 43, 45
Sargent, Gordon, 329
Sargent, Ned, 329
Savage, Howard, 318, 355
Savage, Nicholas, 310
Schelp, S. V., 146
Scheuner, T. L., 70, 71
Schneider, Elliot, 380
Schoppmann, Ira, 387
Schwab, Charles M., 144
Scrapers (Fresnos), 191, 192, 195, 208, 312

Section 2, 3, 4 deposits, 204, 264, 308, 309, 421
Section 9 deposit, 204, 264, 302–303, 306, 308, 310, 421
sedimentary deposition, 7, 8
Seegmiller, Senator, 181
shaft, 137, 140–142, 150, 151, 188–192, 194, 205, 206, 210, 211, 243, 307, 359, 367, 368
Sharp, John, 92, 95–97, 107
Shearing corral, 183, 186
Shelby, Robert, 328
Shelton, William, 35
Shirts, Elsie, 71; Matilda, 71; Peter, 29, 35, 36, 68, 70, 71; Peter II, 71; Thomas, 71
Short Line deposit, 204, 220, 294, 297, 300, 307–309, 311, 312, 315, 348, 421, 422
Shovels: electric, 210, 212, 214, 216, 235–238, 240, 242–244, 267, 269, 270, 295, 297, 298, 301, 302, 308, 312, 339, 340, 350–355, 364, 371, 372; steam (Thew), 144, 178, 205–210, 214, 219, 232, 236, 242, 417
Shurtleff, Vincent, 39
Silver Reef (Utah), 117, 124, 125
Silver, William J., 85
Simkins, Charles, 61
Simkins, Ray, 355
Skougard, Douglas, 326; Dwayne, 326; Etta Bentley, 326; Karl, 325, 326; Roger, 326; Thomas C., 326
slag, 20, 22, 44, 45, 63, 261, 278, 279, 286, 391, 393, 395, 400
Smith deposit, 184, 274, 350, 356, 357, 421
Smith, Charles P., 36; Elias. A., 110; George, 387; George A., 11–14, 16, 22, 23, 28, 29, 32, 41–43, 46, 47, 56, 65, 68, 69, 74; J. K., 321; Jesse N., 76, 77; Jim, 269, 316, 319, 320; John C. L., 26, 31, 32, 37, 46; John L., 23, 24; O. K., 9; Philip K., 27, 35, 36; Thomas S., 14, 15
Smoot, Abraham O., 92
Smoot, Reed, 147, 180
Snow, Erastus, 30–32, 36, 38, 39, 60, 61, 74, 105–107
Snow, Lorenzo, 40, 47
Southern Utah Development Company, 135
Southern Utah Power Company, 228, 235, 236, 295, 340
Southern Utah University (College of Southern Utah), 337, 349, 368
Spanish Trail, 7, 8, 16
Spencer, D. S., 181
Spencer, Forman, 197
Spencer, Lee, 269
Spiers, John, 35
St. George (Utah), 7, 16, 47, 61, 70, 81, 88, 107, 122, 125, 130, 132, 133, 171, 174, 221
St. George Temple, 81

482

Index

Stacey, Jim, 223
Stack, William, 35
Stansbury, Dennis, 342, 343
Stapley, Blaine, 245
State Section 2 deposit, 204, 264, 308, 310
State Section 16 deposit, 264, 360, 421
steam engine, 20, 40, 52, 61, 64, 68, 74, 85, 94, 99, 116, 121, 194, 215
Stephens, William, 221–223,
Stephenson, James, 372
Stevens, Ab, 317
Stevenson, Jim, 317
Stewart, Danny, 412
Stoddard, David, 35
Stoddard, John, 35
Stoddard, Nat, 139
Stone, Diet, 336
Stones, William, 35
Stratton, Carl, 355
Strong, Superintendent, 178
Stubbs, Chester, 219
Sturzenegger, George, 329
sulfur (sulphur), 20, 22, 26, 44–46, 55, 56, 62, 108–110, 120, 123, 210, 234, 266, 285, 286, 298, 299, 303, 358, 366, 394
Sullivan, Evan, 195
Sullivan, J. D., 258
Sullivan, Leland, 195
Sutherland, George, 86
Taft–Hartley Act, 284
Tarantula Pit, 150, 204
taxes, 24, 65, 68, 69, 150, 240, 276, 277, 280, 282, 283, 290, 291, 337, 339–343, 373, 375, 383–385, 412, 418–420
Taylor, A. Bruce, 86
Taylor, John, 51, 88, 92, 96–98, 105–107, 113
Taylor, Thomas E., 84–87, 92, 93, 95, 98, 100–105, 108–110, 113, 119, 121, 122, 142, 145–147, 153, 155, 204, 266
Taylor, William, 155
Tennant, Thomas, 32, 39, 56
Texas City, Texas, 312, 313
Thatcher, Moses, 106–108, 112
Thompson deposit, 204, 308, 310, 420
Thompson, Sid, 329
Thompson, Wesley "Shine", 299
Thornbird, Thora, 165
Thorp, James, 35
Three Peaks mining area, 6, 62, 140, 268, 274, 289, 324, 356–358, 421
timp, 53–55, 58
Tip Top deposit, 148, 241, 401, 414, 416, 420
Topham, Marlo, 326
Toquerville (Utah), 7, 171, 173
truck, 134, 194, 203, 205, 207, 215, 238, 240, 242, 244, 264, 266, 267, 270, 275, 297–302, 308, 312, 313, 316, 318, 319, 322, 323, 325–327, 339, 340, 351, 352, 355, 363, 365, 367, 370–372, 385, 402, 406, 422

Truman, Harry S., 254, 255
Tucker Coal Mine, 289
Tullis, Otto, 197
tunnel, 40, 41, 51, 58, 80, 140, 141, 151, 156, 185–189, 191, 193–198, 205, 210, 226, 232, 239, 315, 317, 318, 351, 352, 367, 368, 414
tuyere (tweer), 20, 34, 50, 53, 54, 57–59, 73
Twitchell deposit, 184, 274, 356, 357, 421
U.C. Placer, 364, 365
Underwood, Gilbert Stanley, 131
Union Iron Company, 68, 69, 73
Union Pacific Railroad, 107, 108, 122–124, 128–132, 154, 166, 167, 170–172, 174, 177–184, 200, 203, 210, 217, 220, 228, 231, 236, 237, 239, 262, 268, 277, 286, 287, 291, 293, 325, 340, 341, 355, 367, 383, 384, 392, 400, 405, 406, 409, 414
United Mine Workers, 276, 277, 282, 292
United Steelworkers of America, 277, 278, 283, 284, 292, 293, 298, 345, 375, 377, 387, 396, 400
University of Utah, 296, 335, 337, 377
Urie, John, 16
Urkhart, Ken, 185
Utah Construction Company, 148, 152, 167, 221, 234, 250, 262, 266, 268, 269, 275, 277, 278, 285, 287, 288, 291, 293–296, 299–301, 305, 307, 315–317, 322, 324, 325, 327, 328, 337, 343, 349, 353, 356, 363
Utah International Inc., 273, 339–343, 346, 355–358, 368, 369, 374, 382–387, 400, 401, 404, 416, 418
Utah Iron Manufacturing Company, 95–103, 109, 110, 112, 113, 115, 116, 119, 146
Utah Iron Mining Company, 73–78
Utah Southern Railroad, 76, 78, 107, 129, 407, 409
Ute claims, 152, 274
Varley, Richard, 35
Vermillion deposit, 148, 184, 190, 194, 195, 196, 274, 315, 356, 357, 367, 368, 421
Vivian, John, 258
Volp, Paul, 269
vug, 268, 273
Waggoner, C. L., 259
Wagon–Box Camp, 17
Walkara (Wakara, Walker; Ute Indian), 34, 36–37
Walker Brothers, 87, 143, 145, 150, 152, 153, 154, 179, 315
Walker War, 36, 38, 40, 64
Walker, C. A., 154; D. F., 154; J. R., 146, 147, 154; James, 56; Jonathan, 61; Joseph, 35, 60; M. H., 146; Senter F., 154, 269; W. R., 154
Wall Street deposit, 356, 358, 388
Wanderer deposit, 148, 152, 274
Wark, Jim, 355

483

Index

Warren, Granville, 219
Warshaw, Judson S., 256
Wasmuth, Carl J., 269, 321, 325
Wassell, E. D., 89, 120
waterwheel, 16, 20, 25, 34, 40, 41, 50–52, 63, 64, 68, 73
Watson, J. D., 161
Webber, T. G., 92, 101
Webster Coal Mine, 46, 289
Webster, Dono, 329
West, Joseph, 130
Wheeler, J. K., 300, 367
Whipple, Edson, 14
White, John, 35
Whittaker, James, 26, 35, 56
Wickham, June, 394
Wignal, J. Floyd, 328
Wilcock, R., 317
Willes, Emery, 316
Williams Coal Mine, 289
Williams, Clarence D., 292; Pat, 245; Superintendent, 177
Williamson, James, 25, 35, 85
Wilson, Leroy A., 226, 227
Winder, John R., 95–97, 106, 107
Wood, Cleo, 305; George, 27, 28, 35, 42, 60; Marie, 305; Cleo, Mrs., 305

Woodhouse, John, 36
Woodruff, Wilford, 23, 70, 75
Woodworth, Warner, 375–377
Woolsey Ranch, 235, 319
Woolsey, Danah, 71; Dee, 324; Elizabeth A., 71; George W., 71; James A., 71; LaVoy, 355; Ross, 324; William A., 71
wrought iron, 22, 44, 61, 69, 70, 75, 76, 121
Yardley, John, 35
Yates, Thomas J., 226
Yellow Jacket deposit, 364–366, 420
Young, Allen K., 379
Young, Brigham, 9, 11, 12, 16, 23, 26, 27, 28, 36, 37, 38, 40, 46, 47, 48, 56, 59, 60, 64, 68, 75, 88, 163, 174, 266, 331, 393
Young, George, 403
Young, John W., 81, 85
Young, W. E., 263, 272
Younger (Utah; townsite), 185, 186
Younger, James F., 184, 186, 198
Zelma deposit, 274, 356, 357, 421
Zion National Park, 169, 171, 172, 175, 179, 181
Zion's Central Board of Trade, 88, 90, 92, 93, 95, 97, 101, 106, 107

About the Authors

Evan Y. Jones worked as an Engineer, Chief Engineer, Mine Superintendent, Mine Manager, Project Manager and Vice President. His career began with the Utah Construction and Mining Company at the Cedar City Operation in 1967. In 1973, he and his family moved to Farmington, New Mexico where he worked at the Utah International coal mines located there. He worked at the Navajo, San Juan and LaPlata mines and in the company's New Mexico office, followed by a year and a half in Australia. He also worked four years for the ARCO Coal Company at the Black Thunder and Coal Creek mines in Gillette, Wyoming. He graduated from Utah State University with degree in civil engineering and from Colorado State University with an MBA.

York F. Jones started working for Utah Construction Company in 1951 as an engineer and worked his way up the ranks as a Chief Engineer, Mine Superintendent, Assistant Mine Manager, and Mine Manager. He studied engineering at the University of Missouri and College of Southern Utah and got his degree in civil engineering. York was Mine Manager when the operations closed in 1981, retired in 1983, and worked 12 more years a mining consultant, closing down the mines and disposing of company assets. York was an active local historian of Cedar City. He and his wife, Evelyn, published several books related to the history of Southern Utah.

www.ingramcontent.com/pod-product-compliance
Lightning Source LLC
Chambersburg PA
CBHW050847160426
43194CB00011B/2057